LIBERALIZATION IN AVIATION

Liberalization in Aviation
Competition, Cooperation and Public Policy

EDITED BY

PETER FORSYTH
Monash University, Australia

DAVID GILLEN
University of British Columbia, Canada

KAI HÜSCHELRATH
ZEW Centre for European Economic Research and
WHU Otto Beisheim School of Management, Germany

HANS-MARTIN NIEMEIER
Bremen University of Applied Sciences, Germany

HARTMUT WOLF
Flensburg University of Applied Sciences, Germany

ASHGATE

Published by
Ashgate Publishing Limited
Wey Court East
Union Road
Farnham
Surrey, GU9 7PT
England

Ashgate Publishing Company
110 Cherry Street
Suite 3-1
Burlington, VT 05401-3818
USA

www.ashgate.com

British Library Cataloguing in Publication Data
Liberalization in aviation : competition, cooperation and
   public policy.
   1. Airlines--Deregulation.
   I. Forsyth, P. (Peter)
   387.7'1-dc23

   ISBN: 978-1-4094-5090-0 (hbk)
   ISBN: 978-1-4094-5091-7 (ebk – PDF)
   ISBN: 978-1-4724-0128-1 (ebk – ePUB)

The Library of Congress has cataloged the printed edition as follows:
Liberalization in aviation : competition, cooperation and public policy / by Peter Forsyth ... [et al.]
   p. cm.
   Includes bibliographical references and index.
   ISBN 978-1-4094-5090-0 (alk. paper) -- ISBN 978-1-4094-5091-7 (ebook) -- ISBN 978-1-4724-0128-1
   (epub)
   1. Airlines--Deregulation. I. Forsyth, P. (Peter)
   HE9780L53 2012
   387.7--dc23

                                                                                            2012043458

Printed in the United Kingdom by Henry Ling Limited,
at the Dorset Press, Dorchester, DT1 1HD

Contents

List of Figures

List of Tables

Acknowledgements

We would like to thank all contributors to this edition for carefully reviewing other chapters and providing helpful comments and suggestions. We are especially indebted to Oliver Wojahn and Frank Fichert for their exceptional review activity. We would like to thank Lorra Ward and Nathalie C. McCaughey for providing suggestions to improve the English language writing style and expressions. Furthermore, we are indebted to Fenja Fahle for preparing the index and to Adel Nemeth, Eric Njoya and Karsten Fröhlich for editorial assistance. We thank the Amsterdam School of Technology and the ZEW for hosting the GARS workshops.

Editors and Contributors

Paolo Beria is an Assistant Professor in Transport Economics at DiAP, Politecnico di Milano University. He obtained a Masters in Civil Engineering in 2003, specializing in transport, and a Ph.D. in urban projects and policies. He is engaged in research at Politecnico di Milano, and his fields of interest are economics, regulation and the assessment of transport projects and policies. He is a professor of Infrastructure Planning at Milan Politecnico and a lecturer at IULM University. Paolo is the co-author of two books written in Italian and he has numerous international papers published in journals and conference proceedings.

Peter Berster has been a member of the scientific staff at the Air Transport Research Division of the German Aerospace Center (DLR) since 1992. He holds a Ph.D. in transport geography from the Technical University of Bochum, Germany. He has developed particular expertise in the analysis of air transport supply and demand, the modal usage of business travellers using regional air transport services, constraints at international airports, and developments with low-cost carriers.

Volodymyr Bilotkach is a Senior Lecturer in Strategic Management and International Business at the Newcastle Business School, Northumbria University, and an Academic Fellow with Airneth, the worldwide scientific network for aviation research and policy. He received his Ph.D. in economics from the University of Arizona in 2005, and previously taught at the University of California, Irvine. Volodymyr's research focuses on various issues in the aviation sector, including airline partnerships and antitrust immunity; the effects of deregulation and airline mergers; airline network development; yield management; determinants of airport charges; and the role of political factors in airport infrastructure investment.

Guillaume Burghouwt is head of the aviation economics section of SEO Economic Research. He has extensive expertise in the measurement and modelling of connectivity of airports and airline networks. In addition, he is the Director of Airneth, the worldwide scientific network for aviation research and policy.

Kenneth Button is a Professor at George Mason University's School of Public Policy. He has published over 80 books and 400 academic papers in the field of transport economics, environmental analysis and industrial organization. He was an advisor to the Secretary General of the Organization for Economic Cooperation and Development where he was head of OECD work on international aviation and he has previously held visiting academic posts at the University of British Columbia, the University of California at Berkeley, the University of Bologna, and the University of Porto. He is editor of *Transportation Research D: Transport and the Environment*, and of the *Journal of Air Transport Management*.

Martin Dresner has served on the faculty of the R.H. Smith School of Business at the University of Maryland since 1988, where he is currently Professor of Logistics and Transportation. He received his Ph.D. in policy analysis from the University of British Columbia. Dresner's research focuses on two broad areas, air transport policy and logistics management. He has published over 60 papers in leading journals. Martin Dresner is the editor of *Research in Transportation Economics* and Vice President of the Air Transport Research Society.

Xavier Fageda is an Associate Professor at the Department of Economic Policy (University of Barcelona). He holds an MSc in Economics from the University of Warwick and received his Ph.D. from the University of Barcelona. He has been a visiting researcher at Cornell University and has published several papers on airline competition in international scientific journals.

Frank Fichert is a Professor of Economics and Transportation at the University of Applied Sciences Worms. He received his Ph.D. in economics at Mainz University and worked for several years as the managing director of the Research Institute for Economic Policy at Mainz University. His main research interests are competition policy in the transport sector, and the environmental aspects of transportation.

Peter Forsyth has been Professor of Economics at Monash University since 1997. His research has been on applied microeconomics, with particular reference to the economics of air transport, tourism economics and of regulation. He recently published a jointly edited book on *Airport Competition the European Experience* (Ashgate, 2010). He has, since 2000, been a frequent speaker at the Hamburg Aviation Conference, and in 2005 delivered the Martin Kunz Memorial Lecture. Recent work has involved using computable general equilibrium models to assess the economic impacts of tourism, including events, and in analysing tourism and aviation policy issues.

Karsten Fröhlich holds degrees in Economics from Bremen University of Applied Sciences and the University of Hertfordshire, and is currently employed as a research assistant in Bremen. In cooperation with Dresden Technical University he is working on his Ph.D. thesis. His main field of interest is industrial organization and in particular the vertical coordination between airlines and airports, product differentiation in the aviation industry and the economic regulation of airports. Karsten is also engaged in projects dealing with airline performance, and supply chain management in the aviation industry.

David Gillen is the YVR Professor of Transportation Policy at the Sauder School of Business and the Director of the Centre for Transportation Studies, University of British Columbia. In addition, he is a Research Economist at the Institute of Transportation Studies at the University of California, Berkeley. David has published more than 100 books, technical reports, journal papers, conference presentations and other articles in various areas of transportation economics, including airline competition and industry structure, airport economics and noise externalities, and transportation policy in Canada and the United States.

Wolfgang Grimme is a Research Associate at the Institute of Air Transport and Airport Research at the German Aerospace Center (DLR). Wolfgang holds a degree in business administration from the University of Giessen and joined DLR in 2005. His research topics focus on regulatory policy issues, environmental economics and intra- and intermodal competition. He is also a lecturer for airline and airport management at the International School of Management in Dortmund.

Tim Hazledine, a New Zealander, is a Professor in the Economics Dept of the University of Auckland. Previously, he taught at the University of British Columbia, Queen's University

Ontario, Balliol College Oxford, and Warwick, from which university he received his Ph.D. In recent years his research has focussed on pricing and competition in airline markets. His current interests include agglomeration economies and related urban transport issues.

Julia Hellmers studied in Hertfordshire and Bremen, and graduated with a Masters degree in Economics (Dipl.-Vw. (FH)). Her core subjects were International Economics and Logistics. In her thesis she investigated mergers and alliances in the European airline industry. After working as a research assistant at the University of Applied Sciences Bremen, focusing on supply chain management in air transportation, she currently works as a logistics planner in the automotive supplier industry.

Martin Holtz holds a Diploma in Economics from the University of Hamburg with research interests in industrial economics, game theory and transport economics. His diploma thesis was on mergers versus alliances in the aviation industry with respect to the AF-KLM merger. After five years of practical work in the aviation and logistics industry he now holds a position as a production planner in the biotechnology sector.

Kai Hüschelrath is head of the research group "Competition and Regulation" at the ZEW Centre for European Economic Research in Mannheim, Germany and coordinator of the Leibniz-ScienceCampus "Mannheim Centre for Competition and Innovation (MaCCI)". Since April 2009 he has also been Assistant Professor of Industrial Organization and Competitive Strategy at WHU Otto Beisheim School of Management in Vallendar. Kai studied economics and management at the University of Würzburg and holds a doctoral degree from WHU. From 2005 to 2006 he worked as an economist in the London office of Frontier Economics. His research focuses on competition policy and competitive strategy.

Kostas Iatrou is the Managing Director of AirTransportNews. He holds a Ph.D. in air transport management from Cranfield and is the author of the book *Airline Choices for the Future* (Ashgate Publishing, 2007). Kostas has participated, both as a moderator and as a speaker, in numerous air transport conferences. He is a Visiting Lecturer at Cranfield University, was an Assistant Visiting Professor at Daniel Webster Aviation College, is an Associate Editor of the *Journal of Air Transport Studies* and a member of the Networking Committee of ATRS.

Jakub Tomasz Kapturski is a graduate of the Department of Business Administration, University of the Aegean, Greece with specialization in tourism and air transport. He is also the holder of a Private Pilot Licence (PPL).

Ian Kincaid is the Vice President, Economic Analysis, with the InterVISTAS Consulting Group. Mr. Kincaid has over 15 years' experience in transport economics and policy, demand modelling and forecasting, and economic impact analysis. Prior to joining InterVISTAS, he was employed as a senior consultant at a London-based transport consultancy. Over his consulting career, he has worked for clients in Europe, North and South America, Africa, Asia and Australia. He holds a degree in economics from the University of Leicester and a Masters in Operational Research from the London School of Economics.

John King is a consultant who specializes in aviation policy and strategy. He has provided advice to a wide range of institutions, governments and corporations who have interests in aviation. Initially studying law and politics at University of Melbourne and The Australian National University, he later took a Master's degree in Transport Management from the University of Sydney. He is a course author at Swinburne University of Technology and a member of the Board of Advice at the Institute of Transport and Logistics Studies at the University of Sydney. He is also a Fellow of the Royal Geographic Society and a member of ATRS and GARS.

Richard Klophaus is a Professor of Business Management, Transportation and Logistics at the Worms University of Applied Sciences, Germany. He is also the Executive Director of the Centre for Aviation Law and Business, serving as a consultant for both government and the aviation industry. Current projects include airport planning studies. His career began at Lufthansa in the fields of network management, pricing and revenue management. Richard holds a Ph.D. in economics from the University of Mannheim.

Zheng Lei is a lecturer in the Department of Air Transport at Cranfield University. His research interests include air transport and tourism management, regional competitiveness and quantitative methods.

Rogier Lieshout is an aviation consultant at the aviation section of SEO Economic Research. His main areas of expertise are welfare impacts of aviation, demand forecasting and cost–benefit analysis. Furthermore, he has been involved with the development of several aviation models, such as discrete choice models, connectivity models and emissions models.

Lida Mantzavinou holds an MBA from IE Business School in Spain and Singapore, an MSc in Air Transport Management from Cranfield University in the UK and a BSc in Economics from the Athens University of Economics and Business. She has been researching the aviation industry throughout her academic career, and through her role as the assistant editor of *AirTransportNews*. She has conducted numerous studies related to the aviation industry, specializing on air transport liberalization, airline alliances and mergers, and open skies agreements. She is currently the Managing Director and Editor of *Aeronoticias*.

Keith Mason is the Head of the Air Transport Management Group, Department of Air Transport, at Cranfield University. He has 20 years' experience in developing and undertaking research for airlines, airports, governments, civil aviation directorates and air transport industry organizations. He lectures in air transport economics and marketing to graduate students. His research focuses on the business travel market, and airline business models. Keith is a Fellow of the Royal Aeronautical Society, a member of the Networking Committee of the Air Transport Research Society, and he is on the Editorial Boards of *Transportation Studies* and the *Journal of Air Transport Studies*.

William (Bill) Morrison is an Associate Professor of Economics, and the Director of the Laurier Centre for Economic Research and Policy Analysis (LCERPA) at Wilfrid Laurier University. He is a Research Fellow with the Centre for Transportation Studies at the University of British Columbia, and he has been a visiting professor at the Moore School of Business, South Carolina and the École Supériéure de Commerce – Toulouse. Dr Morrison's recent research in transportation focuses on airline competition and many aspects of airport operations and policy. He holds an undergraduate degree from Stirling University and graduate degrees from Carleton University and Simon Fraser University.

Kathrin Müller is a former researcher in the research group 'Competition and Regulation' at the ZEW Centre for European Economic Research in Mannheim, Germany. She studied economics at the Johannes Gutenberg-University Mainz, Germany, and at Jönköping International Business School, Sweden. Kathrin holds a doctoral degree in economics from the University of Tübingen. She has experience in applying econometric tools for research in industrial organization, policy analysis and consultancy. Recent research focuses on empirical studies in firm and industry dynamics.

Adél Németh received her Master in Economics at the University of Veszprém in Hungary. She has worked as a research and teaching assistant, especially for microeconomics and industrial organization. By participating in numerous seminars, workshops and conferences, she has deepened her knowledge in competition policy and air transportation. She worked for two years as a research assistant on aviation related topics at the University of Applied Sciences in Bremen. She is currently working on her Ph.D. thesis, 'Airline Mergers in Europe – Implications for Competition Policy' at Jacobs University Bremen, Germany.

Hans-Martin Niemeier is the Director of the Institute for Transport and Development at Bremen University of Applied Sciences. Previously he worked for the State-Ministry of Economic Affairs in the Hamburg Senate, on the privatization and regulation of the Hamburg Airport. He is Chairman of the German Aviation Research Society and lead partner of the research projects 'German Airport Performance' and 'German Aviation Benchmarking'. He has conducted studies on market power and the regulation of airports for the Netherlands Competition Authority. His primary research focuses on airport regulation and privatization, peak and congestion pricing, and benchmarking of air transport infrastructure.

Romano Pagliari obtained a Master's degree in transport and a Ph.D. in airport slot allocation from the Cranfield University School of Management. He presently lectures on airport economics and business issues in addition to organizing various airport management short course/CPD programmes. His research interests include airport economics and business development, and air transport issues that affect more remote regions. Romano Pagliari is currently the Director of the MSc in Airport Planning and Management programme, a member of the Scientific Committee of the International Centre for Competitiveness Studies in Aviation, and a member of the editorial board of the *Journal of Airport Management*.

Andreas Papatheodorou is an Associate Professor in Industrial and Spatial Economics with Emphasis on Tourism at the School of Business Administration, University of the Aegean, Greece. He is also the Director of the Laboratory for Tourism Research and Studies at the University of the Aegean. He has also served as an external examiner for Cranfield University. He gained an M.Phil in economics and a D.Phil in geography at the University of Oxford and commenced his academic career at the University of Surrey, UK. He is a Fellow of the UK Tourism Society and a Board Member of the Hellenic Aviation Society. He is also a Director at DATTEA Ltd, Cyprus and the Editor-in-Chief of the *Journal of Air Transport Studies*.

Konstantinos Polychroniadis is a partner at the Air Consulting Group. He participates in projects studying the petroleum industry and its relationship to aviation. He is also the founder of Chilloud Ltd, a performance measurement organization that specializes in total quality control and management through the use of mystery shopping techniques in the airline and airport industry.

Ian Stockman is a senior research officer at Cranfield University. He is currently working on consultancy projects and has previously worked for the International Civil Aviation Organization in Africa.

Cornelia Templin is working for Fraport, the operator of Frankfurt Airport. She studied Business Administration in Giessen and Los Angeles and started her career as a trainee in aviation management at Frankfurt Airport. She worked in the ground handling field for nine years and obtained her Ph.D. in 2007 on the deregulation of ground handling services in Europe. She completed her research on ground handling services while she was a visiting scholar at the University of British Columbia, Vancouver, at the Centre for Transportation Studies of the Sauder School of Business.

Mike Tretheway is the Executive Vice President and Chief Economist with the InterVISTAS Consulting Group, headquartered in Vancouver, Canada. He is an Adjunct Professor at the Sauder School of Business, at the University of British Columbia, where he taught from 1983 to 1996. He has a Ph.D. in Economics/Econometrics from the University of Wisconsin.

Dieter Wilken has been a member of the scientific staff at the Institute of Air Transport and Airport Research at the German Aerospace Center (DLR) since 1976. He holds degrees from the Technical University of Munich, Germany, and the University of California, Berkeley, USA in transport engineering. His primary research has been studies on analysing and forecasting air transport demand and supply in Germany, Europe and worldwide. Before joining DLR he worked in the United States, in Germany and in Paris with the OECD on developing a European model for forecasting passenger transport in Europe within the COST Action 33: 'The Future of European Passenger Transport'.

Hartmut Wolf is a Professor of Trade, Logistics and Maritime Economics at the Flensburg University of Applied Sciences. In addition, he is an economist at the Kiel Institute for the World Economy. His research focuses on international transport markets and the institutional aspects of the provision of infrastructure services and institutional economics.

Chapter 1
Introduction and Overview

Peter Forsyth, David Gillen, Kai Hüschelrath,
Hans-Martin Niemeier and Hartmut Wolf

In the last few decades, we have witnessed substantial liberalization trends in various industries, and in many countries around the world. Starting with the deregulation of the US airline industry in 1978, regulatory restructuring took place in many network industries such as telecommunications, electricity and railways. Most of the liberalization movements were initially triggered by the poor performance of existing regulatory frameworks: however, increases in competition, and the corresponding improvements in allocative and productive efficiency, are more typically associated with liberalization efforts.

From an academic perspective, the transition from regulated industries to liberalized industries has attracted a substantial amount of research, evidenced by the many books and research articles published on the subject. Although numerous ways to investigate regulation and deregulation processes are available, Perl's methodology (1997) condenses them in to three main questions:

1. What are the forces that have given rise to regulatory reform?
2. What is the structure of the regulatory change that has occurred to date, and what is likely to occur in the immediate future?
3. What have the effects been on industry efficiency, prices and profits, of the reforms that have occurred to date?

This book addresses all three questions. The largely completed liberalization process of national aviation markets leads to a focus on the assessment of the effects on variables such as efficiency, prices, or profits. On the other hand, the partially regulated nature of international markets demands an assessment of both the forces that have given rise to regulatory reform, and the state and future development of future liberalization efforts.

Although this book provides insights on a broad range of topics related to aviation liberalization in various parts of the world, it is beyond the scope to cover all relevant areas in detail. Previous German Aviation Research Society books provide detailed coverage of specific topics such as the economic regulation of airports, competition and predation in aviation markets, airport slots and airport competition.[1] Readers who are particularly interested in these topics will find our previous books useful complements to this one.

The contributions in this book are subdivided into five sections.

Part A, Liberalization and Airline Competition, is comprised of articles on various aspects of competition in liberalized airline markets, including the patterns and effects of entry, product differentiation strategies, competition in connecting markets and on thin (former) monopolized routes, failure of a national carrier, and the implications of competition on airline safety.

Part B, Liberalization and Low-cost Airline Competition, specifically focuses on the emergence and growth of low-cost carriers as one of the most important developments in the post-liberalization

---

1   See Forsyth et al. 2004, 2005 and 2010 and Czerny et al. 2007.

era in many countries around the world. The articles focus on the evolution of low-cost carriers in general, and their competitive (pricing) strategies in particular.

Although the liberalization of airline markets is aimed at increasing competition, cooperation among competitors is not necessarily bad. Cooperation might very well have the potential to improve performance and/or consumer welfare. Cooperation among airlines could take place in various areas and take various forms, and the focus of the articles in *Part C* of the book, Liberalization and Airline Cooperation, is horizontal mergers and alliances.

Access to infrastructure is a key precondition for workable competition in airline markets. If infrastructure capacities cannot meet the increase in demand following liberalization, and if existing infrastructure capacities are allocated by inefficient mechanisms, the benefits of competition are substantially reduced. *Part D*, Liberalization and Infrastructure, concentrates on selected infrastructure topics such as airport financial performance, ground handling and air navigation systems.

Although most national aviation markets have been liberalized in the last few decades, international aviation remains (at least partially) a regulated area. *Part E*, Liberalization and Public Policy, offers economic assessments of liberalization efforts to date, and also proposes ways that future liberalization can proceed.

Part A: Liberalization and Airline Cooperation

The deregulation of airline markets is generally aimed at encouraging competition, thereby realizing lower fares and improved services. The contributions in Part A study the many aspects of competition in various liberalized airline markets including patterns of entry and their effects, product differentiation strategies, competition in connecting markets and on thin (former) monopolized routes, the failure of a national carrier, and the implications of liberalization and competition on airline safety.

Chapter 2: Hüschelrath and Müller used T-100 traffic data and DB1B fare data from the US Department of Transportation to identify recent trends in the evolution of the domestic US airline industry. They also identified the patterns of entry and the effects of entry by network carriers, and low-cost carriers in particular. For the sample period from 1995 to 2009 they found that competition by low-cost carriers had a significant, competition-enhancing impact on the various characteristics of market structure and market performance. In particular, the entry activity of low-cost carriers also led to substantial fare reductions of, on average, 25 per cent for entries into monopoly markets. As route entries by network carriers do not show comparable effects, the existence and expansion of low-cost carriers must be considered as the main driver of competition in the domestic US airline industry.

Chapter 3: Fröhlich and Niemeier investigate the applicability of the economic theory of product differentiation to the airline industry. They seek to explore the product choices, the competitive strategies and the dynamic evolution of competition among airlines through the lens of models of product differentiation. While the chapter's aim is not to look for the model of product differentiation, it points out what the models can be used for and under what circumstances they are applicable. The authors conclude that the extent to which airlines differentiate vertically is limited to the extent of available airport capacity and the particularities of the market. Although the chapter provides examples from European markets, the models of product differentiation might also shed some light on the dynamic developments in other markets.

Chapter 4: Lieshout and Burghouwt analyse airline competition in connecting markets. They build on the insight that the rise of hub-and-spoke networks has changed the way in which airlines and airports compete. Competition not only takes place in a direct way, but also in an indirect way. Therefore indirect connections should be taken into account when calculating competition levels. In particular, the authors describe a methodology to measure competition, taking into account both direct and indirect connections. The methodology is then applied to estimate the competition levels on connecting routes via the 13 largest European hubs. It is shown, for example, that connecting flights via Lisbon and Madrid experience the least competition, in particular with respect to connections to and from Latin America. For a large part, this has to do with the geographical location of these hubs as well as the socio-economic and socio-political relationships between Spain/Portugal and various Latin American countries. The carriers of the Star alliance at the Lisbon airport, and the oneworld alliance at the Madrid airport are expected to achieve high yields in these connecting markets. On the contrary, the connecting flights via Zurich and Heathrow, on average, experience relatively fierce competition. As Zurich and Heathrow airports mainly serve the larger European destinations, competition on most of the connecting routes is high and yields are expected to be low.

Chapter 5: Fageda is specifically interested in the effects of airline competition on thin routes. Using data for Spanish airline routes for the period 2001–2008, he finds a decrease in the proportion of routes that are monopoly routes, and a reduction in the traffic levels that would be needed to break up monopolies. An estimation of pricing and frequency equations for those routes that were monopolies in 2001 shows that the increase in competition has implied lower prices and higher frequencies. The magnitude of the effect is significant both from an economic and statistical point of view.

Chapter 6: Beria, Niemeier and Fröhlich analyse the case of Alitalia, Italy's former flag carrier, as a case in point of a state-managed carrier failing due to the state's behaviour. The chapter starts with a historical overview of the most important events in recent Alitalia history. Thereafter, the main causes of the airline's weak competitive position relative to other European carriers are analysed. The authors argue that the underlying cause of the decline of Alitalia was the continuous political protection, the lack of a strategic vision in favour of short-term objectives and, in some cases in the past, poor managerial decisions.

Chapter 7: Papatheodrou, Polychroniadis and Kapturski investigate the relationship between airline market deregulation and safety, from both a theoretical and an empirical perspective. Their end result is rather inconclusive as the theoretical arguments take different directions: parts of the literature seem to support the view that liberalization had adverse effects on safety, while other authors believe that the implications for safety have been largely positive. Likewise, the empirical analysis is not conclusive on the existence of a systematic statistical pattern. Whether this is the result of relying on data that does not reveal the full complexity of the issue or is just the ultimate truth is not known. To complicate things even further, a lack of systematic behaviour may just be the result of countervailing powers (i.e. positive and negative implications) acting with the same intensity.

Part B: Liberalization and Low-cost Airline Competition

The emergence and growth of low-cost carriers (LCCs) must be considered as one of the most important developments in the post-liberalization era of aviation. In order to acknowledge this key role, the second part of the book is devoted to studies that focus on the evolution of low-cost carriers in general, and their competitive (pricing) strategies in particular.

Chapter 8: Mason, Morrison and Stockman examine airline entry and exit from the LCC sector for the period 1995–2011, and find that the real jump in growth began in 2002, continuing until 2006, with the number of exits also increasing significantly in 2003. Thus, while liberalization was a necessary condition for the growth of LCCs in Europe, the growth of LCCs was not closely correlated with key events in the liberalization process. In terms of the evolution of business strategies following liberalization, their analysis shows that LCCs are not simply one variety. Rather there are at least two definable stylized business models – the 'truly low-cost' (TLC) model and the 'full-service airline competitor' (FSAC) model – both of which seem to be successful strategies. Ryanair and Easyjet have sustained dominance in the LCC sector, both implementing business models that closely follow the TLC and FSAC models. To secure a larger slice of network carriers' markets, the FSAC model seems to be evolving slowly towards the full-service carrier model.

Chapter 9: Wilken and Berster provide an overview of the characteristics of low-cost carriers, their development in Europe, with a special emphasis on Germany – in terms of supply features such as networks, routes, flights and seats offered, and, to a lesser degree, of passenger demand, passengers carried, and on demand generation. They find, for example, that low-cost carriers entered the European market in the late 1990s and achieved a market share of about 34 per cent in 2008, while Full Service Network Carriers (FSNCs) provided 58 per cent of seats available at European airports in 2008, and charter and regional carriers had a share of almost 5 per cent and 3 per cent respectively. For the autumn of 2010, the authors analysed prices offered by the most important LCCs serving the German market. Average prices were calculated by considering all of the routes and time spans between booking and flying day. While average net prices vary from €22 to €70 between airlines, total prices, including taxes, levies and other surcharges, vary from €35 and €144. The difference between net and total prices varies thus between €7 and €27 on average, and in specific situations the difference may be much greater.

Chapter 10: Klophaus argues that airline liberalization effects are not limited to lower air fares. The impact of liberalization also led to the extinction of simple fare structures. Many airlines adopted a strategy to unbundle their services in order to create additional revenue. This chapter focuses on the practice of à la carte pricing among European airlines that are categorized as LCCs, using the example of Ryanair. It examines the economic rationale for charging a separate fee for checked baggage. Results indicate that revenue gains reported by airlines practicing à la carte pricing may not be the result of unbundling services, but of higher prices. Hence, for consumers, the benefit of unbundling to pay only for services required could be negated by price increases that are not transparent to them. This requires regulatory efforts to ensure clarity on LCCs websites and other advertising to allow consumers to compare total air fares.

Part C: Liberalization and Airline Cooperation

The liberalization of airline markets is aimed at increasing competition, however, cooperation among competitors is not necessarily bad and might very well have the potential to improve overall welfare and/or consumer welfare. Although cooperation among airlines might take place in various areas and take various forms, the focus of the chapters in Part C is on horizontal mergers and alliances.

Chapter 11: Holtz, Hellmers, Fröhlich, Grimme, Németh and Niemeier present an assessment of the synergies and the success of cross-border airline mergers and acquisitions in Europe. While alliances provide a number of advantages in accessing international markets, some of the disadvantages of alliances, like instability and intra-alliance competition, can only be overcome with mergers or acquisitions. However, airlines have great difficulties in reaping these potential synergies and improving their competitive position. Therefore financial markets are, in general, neutral to this strategy.

Chapter 12: Hazledine reviews recent Air New Zealand antitrust cases to assess the question whether open skies policies and antitrust policies are substitutes or complements. He argues that appropriate regulatory decisions were finally made in all three merger or cartel cases covering the trans-Tasman passenger air travel market over the 2002–2010 period. Allowing the large incumbent legacy carriers Air New Zealand and Qantas to cartelize their operations would most likely have had a seriously detrimental effect on competition, as mainstream analysis would predict. Allowing Air New Zealand to combine forces with the LCC Virgin is perhaps less clearly justifiable, but at least so far, problems in the market have not manifested themselves. He concludes that antitrust policies and open skies policies must be considered as complements, at least under the present regulatory regime. 'Openness' simply is not sufficient to safeguard competition.

Chapter 13: Iatrou and Mantzavinou argue that global airline alliances have developed in response to the economic demand of global markets and to the opportunities provided by deregulation and liberalization initiatives. These cooperative agreements initially took the form of simple code-share agreements; but as deregulation started to take effect in the European Union and a Single Internal European Aviation Market was created, and as the US authorities pursued more 'open' and less restrictive bilateral air services with other countries, the horizontal links between carriers took the form of deeper and more complex cooperation. With a worsening financial environment and with restrictive bilateral agreements being gradually replaced by multilateral agreements between groups of countries, usually on a regional level, airlines are reassessing their priorities and are considering whether mergers and consolidations are the only way to secure a sustainable future and a viable and competitive airline system. The authors expect some merger activity within the next five years on an intraregional level, and more probably within the EU, but the early stage of consolidation does not allow predictions on what the future aviation markets will look like.

Chapter 14: Bilotkach and Hüschelrath start off with the observation that over the last ten to fifteen years we have witnessed a substantial increase in the size and depth of airline alliances in international air transportation. From a size perspective, more and more individual airlines have decided to join one of the three remaining global airline alliances, Star, SkyTeam or oneworld. From a depth perspective the granting of antitrust immunity by the responsible authorities provided members of these alliances with increasingly more freedom to coordinate various aspects of joint operations, including scheduling and pricing decisions as well as the right to form revenue-sharing joint ventures in international markets. This chapter aims to develop and illustrate an understanding of the economic effects triggered by granting antitrust immunity to airline alliances. Differentiating between a competitive effects assessment and an efficiencies assessment, the author's approach not only identifies the key economic factors but also provides guidance on how to measure the respective sizes of the cost and benefit components in antitrust investigations.

Chapter 15: Bilotkach argues that frequent flier programme (FFP) partnerships on the US market appear more parallel than complementary. Such partnerships have a potential to make partners' products closer substitutes, leading to fiercer price competition. One response of partners to such a threat to profits may entail lowering costs. The author finds that an airline competing with a partner offers a 10–30 per cent lower frequency of service as compared to otherwise similar markets where the airline does not have any partnership with its competitors. At the same time, the author's research fails to find a substantial effect of these partnerships on the total frequency of service at the market level, indicating more limited effects on competition and consumer welfare than expected.

Part D: Liberalization and Infrastructure

Access to infrastructure is a key precondition for workable competition in airline markets. If infrastructure capacities cannot meet the increase in demand following liberalization and if existing infrastructure capacities are allocated by inefficient mechanisms, the benefits of competition are substantially reduced. The importance of infrastructure, and competition among infrastructures, is already reflected upon in three previous books edited by members of the German Aviation Research Society. Part D concentrates on selected specific topics such as airport financial performance, ground handling and air navigation systems.

Chapter 16: Lie and Pagliari investigate airport traffic growth and airport financial performance. They found that airports that embraced LCCs all experienced a dramatic increase in traffic. In particular, a cross-sectional correlation analysis revealed that there was a positive and strong relationship between passenger traffic and airport financial performance. In general, airports with more passenger throughput tended to have higher operating profits. This was especially the case at the start of the observation period in the financial year 1996/97. However, the strength of the correlation weakened in 2007/08 when LCCs became dominant players at many airports. By looking into the average annual growth rate, the authors also found a positive and strong correlation between passenger traffic and airport operating profit after removing the influence of the outliers. Higher operating profit growth was generally associated with higher passenger traffic growth. Nevertheless, airports dominated by LCCs experienced below average growth in operating profit, though there were several exceptional cases, notably Stansted and Liverpool airports.

Chapter 17: Templin concentrates on the deregulation of ground handling services, consisting of services such as passenger check-in, handling of cargo, transportation of luggage and also airline catering, fuelling, fresh water and toilet services. Ground handling markets in Europe were regulated to a great extent when the liberalization of the airline industry took place. However, pressure from airlines ultimately led to a deregulation of ground handling services and the implementation of Council Directive 96/67/EC on access to the ground handling market at European Community airports. This chapter focuses on the deregulation of airside handling services at European airport hubs. A brief introduction of the handling industry is followed by the reasons for the opening of ground handling markets and a description of the contents of Council Directive 96/67/EC. The effects of the deregulation of ground handling services at six major European hubs are analysed. The chapter concludes with an outlook of potential future developments in the industry.

Chapter 18: Button investigates the comparative inefficiencies of various air navigation systems. He does not seek to provide a ranking of the economic inefficiency of national air navigation system providers, or indeed the various generic forms that they may take, but rather considers how the different models of air navigation systems have performed over the recent past. He provides valuable guidance as to the elements of relative efficiency of navigation systems. However, he also indicates that the question of absolute levels of efficiency of navigation systems has to remain open due to the unavailability of suitable counterfactuals.

Part E: Liberalization and Public Policy

Although most national aviation markets have been liberalized in the last few decades, international aviation remains (at least partially) a regulated area. Part E of this book offers economic assessments of the liberalization steps to date, and also suggests the direction of future liberalization steps.

Chapter 19: Kincaid and Tretheway review the economic impact of international aviation liberalization. In particular, the chapter provides a summary of the pertinent research on the liberalization of the international air market. In line with much of the previous research, the analysis suggests that liberalization of market access (bilaterals) and ownership and control could bring about significant increases in traffic, substantial fare reductions for passengers, and economic and employment gains for the wider economy. These benefits were found for a diverse mix of countries, although the scale of the impact differed depending on the economic structure and development of the country, its geographic situation and the degree of liberalization it had already undertaken. The impact of liberalization on the home carrier is less clear-cut, although it is not necessarily the case that liberalization is harmful to those carriers. In any case, the potential harm to select carriers has to be weighed against the wider benefits that may accrue to passengers, to tourism and to the general economy.

Chapter 20: King's contribution traces the development of Australia's aviation relationship with European countries including showing how new European carriers, over time, have entered and exited the market. Traffic rights and the emergence of the code-share as a substitute for own aircraft operations is demonstrated together with the 2008 and 2009 negotiations concerning the establishment of a horizontal agreement with the European Union (EU). Future negotiations are discussed and obstacles identified. A brief review of the agreements and the physical operations between the Association of Southeast Asian Nations (ASEAN) and Europe is undertaken, as well as a similar review for New Zealand. While there are several aviation relationships between ASEAN States and EU States, and indeed, burgeoning relationships with the EU as an entity, ASEAN as an institution has little current capability to negotiate a comprehensive agreement with the EU. New Zealand, on the other hand, which has a very small operating relationship, has entered into an EU horizontal agreement.

Chapter 21: Forsyth discusses the economic evaluation of air services liberalization, and how it is changing in the light of a changing environment, affecting such issues as airline ownership and regional negotiations. Until about 20 years ago, air services negotiations were conducted on a basically mercantilist framework. Economists were very critical of this approach, and developed an alternative approach based on identifying a country's economic interests. This approach can be called the 'cost– benefit' approach, as it is based on measuring the costs and the benefits of the proposal. While this approach has not superseded the traditional mercantilist approach, it is increasingly being used. The cost–benefit approach pays particular attention to the main sources of cost and benefit – passenger benefits and airline profits. However, over time, airline markets have been changing, and this is having an impact on the balance of costs and benefits. In this article, the various factors that are changing are analysed. For example, with foreign ownership, only a small proportion of the home airline's profits may accrue to the country. Other factors include the existence of benefits from tourism, negotiation on a regional basis, and the forecasted growth of climate change policies on air transport. The chapter further reviews and assesses the impact of changes in the airline market that will have the effect of changing a country's willingness to pursue liberalization.

Chapter 22: Fichert studies multilateral interlining in deregulated air transport markets. He finds that, in principle, the multilateral interline system, organized by the International Air

Transport Association (IATA) for more than 50 years, makes flying more convenient and therefore provides benefits to consumers. Nevertheless, the extent of these benefits is declining due to an overall growth in air transport markets, which is increasing flexibility within one airlines' network. The extension of strategic airline alliances, providing seamless travel for most connecting passengers, is also contributing to the decline in benefits from the IATA interline system. It cannot be forgotten that the IATA tariff conferences simplified information-sharing and even collusion among competing airlines. However, competition authorities' general 'unease' with the traditional interline system was justified and this finally forced IATA to react, leading to the introduction of the Flex Fares and e-Tariffs system. The Australian Competition and Consumer Commission (ACCC) has granted its authorization for the new interline system only for a limited period of time, maintaining the opportunity to review whether the Flex Fares system has an influence on carrier specific fares. Therefore, in its redesigned form, the IATA multilateral interline system will remain in the focus of competition authorities' attention and will also leave some room for controversial debates among aviation economists.

Chapter 23: Dresner assesses US Bilateral Air Transport Policy. He argues that the United States has taken a reasonably consistent open-market approach to its air transport bilateral policies since the 1940s. Although there have been illiberal lapses, most notably Bermuda II, the US has been the leader in support of market-based bilateral agreements ever since Chicago and Bermuda I. In particular, no other country with a major origin/destination market has consistently supported an open-market approach to bilateral negotiations over a balance-of-benefits approach. However, the US policy also has been pragmatic, favouring competitive outcomes that support its interests (e.g., opening access to Heathrow; multiple designation of carriers), and opposing those that face domestic opposition (e.g., the removal of cabotage and ownership restrictions). Given the political reality of the US system, this open-market, but pragmatic approach, is likely to continue into the future.

Chapter 24: Gillen focuses on policy and the challenges of Canadian International Aviation. He finds that the Blue Sky policy has not been very successful in achieving 'open skies' type of agreements. The number of open skies policies is small and they are with countries that have relatively inconsequential passenger and trade markets. Canada still continues to negotiate air services agreements (ASAs) that are not in keeping with the Blue Sky policy. There is a lack of consistency in ASA content and focus. Where open sky agreements have been signed, they have been incremental to previous agreements, or held so secret that one could hardly judge the contents. The statistical analysis, albeit meagre due to the lack of full information, points to the success of liberal policies, and illustrates that open skies policies generate a four times larger impact. As for the Blue Skies analysis, the results are not statistically significant.

The Way Ahead

Reflecting on the various contributions of the book, the future challenges might best be described by '*maintaining the achieved benefits and realizing the additional potential benefits of liberalization*'. On the one hand, most national markets are liberalized, but for the benefits to be realized fully, this requires first and foremost an efficient and proactive competition policy. On the other hand, most international markets are only partially liberalized. In some regions, such as South America and Africa, regulation is the norm, and Asia presents a mixed picture. Many countries still impose capacity controls. Furthermore, some aspects of liberalization have not been pursued vigorously anywhere in the world, and an important aspect, which is not covered except briefly, is that of the ownership of airlines. Although there is little doubt that further liberalization will lead to further benefits to the consumers, it is important to develop a detailed understanding of the institutional backgrounds, and to constantly evaluate the effects of further liberalization of international airline markets.

References

Czerny, A.I., Forsyth, P., Gillen, D.W. and Niemeier, H.-M. (2007) *Airport Slots – International Experiences and Options for Reform.* Burlington, VT: Ashgate.

Forsyth, P., Gillen, D.W., Knorr, A., Mayer, O.G., Niemeier, H.-M. and Starkie, D. (2004) *The Economic Regulation of Airports – Recent Developments in Australasia, North America and Europe.* Burlington, VT: Ashgate.

Forsyth, P., Gillen, D.W., Mayer, O.G. and Niemeier, H.-M. (2005) *Competition versus Predation in Aviation Markets – A Survey of Experience in North America, Europe and Australia.* Burlington, VT: Ashgate.

Forsyth, P., Gillen, D.W., Müller, J. and Niemeier, H.-M. (2010) *Airport Competition – The European Experience.* Burlington, VT: Ashgate.

Perl, L. (1997) Regulatory restructuring in the United States. *Utilities Policy*, 6, 21–34.

PART A
Liberalization and Airline Competition

Chapter 2

Market Entry and the Evolution of the US Airline Industry 1995–2009

Kai Hüschelrath and Kathrin Müller[1]

1. Introduction

The importance of market entry for competition and innovation is largely undisputed in the field of industrial organization for two reasons. On the one hand, entry plays a crucial role as an equilibrium force in that it competes away excess profits to an equilibrium level. Such imitative entry occurs when the entrant can reap profits by copying the established firms product or method of production. On the other hand, entry also plays a creative role in markets, serving as a vehicle for the introduction and diffusion of innovations. Such innovative entry occurs when the entrant either finds new ways to saturate a certain customer's need or is able to produce a given product with less input. Innovative entry is seen as a disequilibrium force which propels the industry from one equilibrium state to another (see Geroski, 1991, 1995).

The US airline industry can act as a prime example for the relevance of both types of entry. On the one hand, since the deregulation of the industry in 1978, imitative entry into many routes significantly increased competitive pressures and forced the airlines to increase their productive efficiency, leading to lower fares and better service on many routes. On the other hand, deregulation allowed the appearance and growth of low-cost airlines which challenge the traditional network carriers with various forms of innovative entry. This unique combination of regulation and deregulation together with the presence of imitative and innovative entry makes the US airline industry a prime candidate for a closer examination of the role of market entry in the broader context of competitive interaction. This general interest is increased further by a lack of studies that take significant recent market developments into account such as both severe external shocks – like the attacks on 11 September 2001 or the recent economic recession – and severe internal shocks – like the mergers of American Airlines and Trans World Airlines in 2001 or Delta Airlines and Northwest Airlines in 2008.

Against this background and guided by a primer on the economics of entry in airline markets, this chapter uses T-100 traffic data and DB1B fare data from the US Department of Transportation to identify recent trends in the evolution of the domestic US airline industry in general and patterns and effects of entry by network carriers and low-cost carriers (LCCs) in particular. For the sample period from 1995 to 2009 we generally find that competition by LCCs had a significant and competition-enhancing impact on various characteristics of market structure and market performance. In particular, the entry activity of LCCs did not only experience significant absolute increases in the sample period but also led to substantial fare reductions of on average 25 per cent for entries into monopoly markets. An estimation of the welfare effects of three particular market entry events of the LCC JetBlue Airways revealed significant consumer savings of about $8

---

1   We are indebted to Volodymyr Bilotkach for his advice during the construction of the data set. Parts of this chapter make use of earlier research of both authors published in Hüschelrath (2009), Hüschelrath and Müller (2012) and Hüschelrath and Müller (2013).

million for the short- and medium-haul markets and nearly $29 million for the long-haul market in only the first year after entry. As route entries by network carriers do not show comparable effects, the existence and expansion of LCCs must be considered as the main driver of competition in the domestic US airline industry.

The remainder of this chapter is structured as follows. The subsequent second section provides a primer on the economics of entry in airline markets. The analysis is separated into a theoretical treatment of market entry and a more applied approach of market entry focusing on the eras of regulation and deregulation in the US airline industry. Subsequently, the third section gives an overview of recent market developments in the US airline industry between 1995 and 2009. Along the lines of the so-called structure–conduct–performance paradigm, the section sheds light on market size and major players, market concentration, fare levels, service levels, cost levels and profit levels. In the fourth section, an empirical analysis of market entry between 1995 and 2009 is conducted by differentiating between general patterns of market entry and selected effects of market entry on average fares and number of departures. Section five concludes the chapter.

2. A Primer on the Economics of Entry in Airline Markets

An important precondition for studying entry in airline markets is the development of an analytical framework. Such a framework will not only help to understand the general economics behind observed patterns of entry but will also allow an assessment of the (consumer) welfare effects of entry. Against this background, section 2.1 presents a theoretical approach to entry in airline markets. Given the identified divergence of model predictions and empirical observations, the theoretical discussion is complemented by a more applied approach in section 2.2, which focuses on the role of market entry in the eras of regulation and deregulation of the US airline industry.

2.1 A Theoretical Approach to Entry in Airline Markets

Free entry and exit is an essential assumption in the model of perfect competition. If the price of a good lies above average cost, the firm(s) in the market will realize supracompetitive profits. These supracompetitive profits are the central incentive for other firms wanting 'to join the party' (Saloner et al., 2001: 215). Over time, market entry will increase supply and will depress prices sufficiently for firms to return to normal economic profits. As 'abnormal' profits are competed away, entry will cease and the market will reach its long-run equilibrium. This point coincides with the minima of the firms' average cost curves, the points where the firms use their resources in the most efficient manner.

Although the model of perfect competition certainly is a useful benchmark, its fit with real markets is often limited. Oligopoly models basically aim at reaching a better fit with real competitive interaction by especially taking account of conditions surrounding entry such as the level of fixed cost, market size, cost differences between firms or heterogeneity of products. On a more technical level, strategic interaction in oligopolistic markets complicates competition analyses and makes market outcomes dependent on factors such as players, actions, timing, information and repetition (see Saloner et al., 2001: 187ff.). Although it is beyond the scope of this chapter to discuss all these factors in different oligopoly models, the following two subsections will discuss entry in two standard oligopoly models: a homogeneous Cournot model with symmetric and asymmetric costs.

2.1.1 Entry in a homogeneous Cournot model with symmetric costs Any judgement on the effects of entry requires the determination of a competitive benchmark in the first place. The standard Cournot model is 'the usual suspect' to fit into this role, basically due to its mathematical tractability but also due to significant econometric and experimental research which shows that Cournot models can be a good predictor of actual market behaviour and market results in an industry (characterized by capacity constraints).

In order to study the welfare effects of competition and entry in such a basic Cournot model, suppose that market demand is given by $P(Q) = a - bQ$, *where* $Q = \sum q_i$. There are n firms in the market, all with the same cost function $C_i = cq_i$. In the equilibrium, each firm's profit-maximizing output equates marginal revenue to marginal cost. The marginal revenue for firm i is given by

$$MR_i\left(q_i, \sum_{j \neq i} q_j\right) = \left(a - b \sum_{j \neq i} q_j\right) - 2bq_i \tag{1}$$

Setting this equal to marginal cost, the best-response function for every firm is given by

$$a - b \sum_{j \neq i} q_j - 2bq_i = c \tag{2}$$

Given the symmetry of the example, the best-response function for one firm is given by

$$a - b(n-1)q^c - 2bq^c = c \tag{3}$$

Solving the above for q^c gives the equilibrium output for each firm

$$q^c = \frac{a - c}{(n+1)b} \tag{4}$$

Industry output can be derived as

$$Q^C = nq^c = \frac{n(a - c)}{(n+1)b} \tag{5}$$

and the market price can be found by substituting Q^c into the demand function as

$$P^c = \frac{a + nc}{n+1} \tag{6}$$

The profits of each firm are then given by

$$\pi^C = \left(\frac{a - c}{n+1}\right)^2 \left(\frac{1}{b}\right) \tag{7}$$

while producer surplus (= industry profits) can be calculated to

$$PS = \left(\frac{a-c}{n+1}\right)^2 \left(\frac{n}{b}\right) \tag{8}$$

The consumer surplus is given by

$$CS = \left(a - \left(\frac{a+nc}{n+1}\right)\right)\left(\frac{(a-c)n}{(n+1)b}\right)\left(\frac{1}{2}\right) \tag{9}$$

leading to an expression for total welfare of

$$TW = \left(a - \left(\frac{a+nc}{n+1}\right)\right)\left(\frac{(a-c)n}{(n+1)b}\right)\left(\frac{1}{2}\right) + \left(\frac{a-c}{n+1}\right)^2 \left(\frac{n}{b}\right) \tag{10}$$

As $\partial CS/\partial n > 0$, the consumer surplus steadily increases with n. As $\partial PS/\partial n < 0$, the producer surplus is decreasing with n.

In order to allow a graphical interpretation of the effects of entry in a Cournot model, the general results above are applied to a certain market specification.[2] It is assumed that market demand is given by $Q = 1,000-1,000p$ (which is equivalent to an inverse demand function of $p = 1-0.001Q$) and marginal cost is given by $c = 0.28$. Inserting these values into the general expressions (8) and (9) leads to the following applied expressions for the producer surplus and the consumer surplus:

$$PS = \Pi = \frac{518.4n}{(n+1)^2} \tag{11}$$

and

$$CS = \frac{259.2n^2}{(n+1)^2} \tag{12}$$

Given these expressions, the producer surplus, the consumer surplus and the overall welfare can be computed for different numbers of firms in the market. Figure 2 shows the results for $n = [1,10]$.

Figure 2.1 shows that producer surplus is steadily decreasing in n (with decreasing increments), while consumer surplus is steadily increasing (with decreasing increments). Overall welfare is steadily increasing with n, also with decreasing increments. All three curves converge to the perfect competition outcomes.

One important caveat against the significance of the analysis so far is the absence of fixed costs which – although not directly influencing the pricing decision – certainly affect the profits of the firms in the market, firm decisions to enter a market as well as the socially optimal number of firms in the market. Figure 2.2 shows the results for the same market specification as above

---

2   The market specification is taken from Carlton and Perloff (2000: 161).

but adds a fixed cost of 10 for every firm in the market. It can be seen that consumer surplus is still steadily increasing (as it is independent of fixed costs) while producer surplus decreases with an increased slope. As a consequence, the overall welfare is not steadily increasing any more but reaches a maximum when three firms are in the market. This is basically because the society has to cover the fixed costs of every additional firm and a fourth firm would simply lead to a smaller increase in overall welfare than the additional fixed costs it creates. However, Figure 1.2 shows further that there is room for six firms in the market, as the entry of the seventh firm would cause a negative producer surplus. Therefore, under the chosen market specification, a socially inefficient high number of firms would join the market.

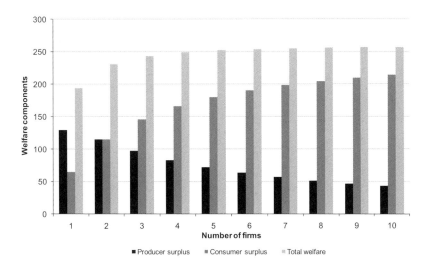

Figure 2.1   Welfare components in a linear *n*-firm Cournot model

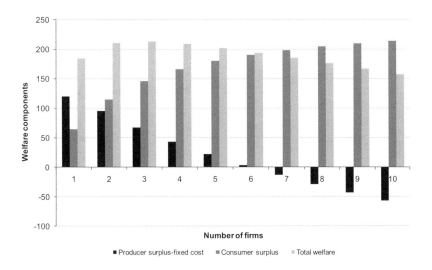

Figure 2.2   Welfare components in a linear *n*-firm Cournot model with fixed cost

Furthermore, if fixed costs of 50 are assumed, it is possible to show for the same market specification that it is socially optimal to have only one firm in the market, although a second firm would be able to make a positive profit. It is disputed in literature whether this constellation already constitutes a natural monopoly; however, it clearly shows that a policy which aims at maximizing the number of firms in the market can hardly be the optimal choice from an overall welfare perspective.

Based on these results, it is important for an assessment of market entry to ask whether entry into a monopoly market is somewhat 'more important' for the consumers (as well as overall welfare) than entry into markets with $n>1$ (non-colluding) firms, simply because the gains in consumer welfare are highest in such a constellation. Although it is obvious that the absolute gains depends on overall market size,[3] it can be exemplified for the market specification above that the *relative* gains in consumer welfare are indeed highest in a 'monopoly to duopoly transition'. For example, it can be shown that the consumer surplus increases by almost 80 per cent when an equally efficient firm enters the monopoly market. The producer surplus drops by about 11 per cent, leading to an overall welfare increase of nearly 20 per cent compared to the monopoly state. If a third firm enters the duopoly market, consumer surplus still raises by about 25 per cent, while producer surplus drops by about 15 per cent. Overall welfare rises by about 5 per cent.[4]

In a nutshell, analysing entry in a homogeneous Cournot model shows (for the assumed market specification) that entry into a monopoly market increases consumer welfare as well as overall welfare by the largest relative amount. If two or more (non-colluding) firms are already in the market, the 'delta' is significantly reduced. Second, it has been exemplified that the fixed costs level is an important feature in every analysis of competition in a market. Although the finding that entry into a monopoly market brings the largest delta is likely to hold for most markets, it has to be kept in mind that this does not automatically allow the conclusion that entry as such is socially desirable.

2.1.2 Entry in a homogeneous Cournot model with asymmetric costs   A critical assumption in the basic homogenous Cournot model is that the incumbent and the entrant face the same marginal cost function. For many industries such as the airline industry it is, however, reasonable to assume that marginal cost of the firms in (or entering) the market differs. The effects of this asymmetry on market performance are studied in the following by assuming a quantity setting duopoly consisting of an incumbent (former monopoly) firm I (a network carrier) and an entrant E (a low-cost carrier). The inverse demand function is assumed to be linear p = a–b(qI+qE) with a, b>0. Firms produce at constant marginal costs of cI, cE and fixed costs of FCI, FCE. Based on this basic set-up, two different market states have to be characterized in terms of its welfare effects: monopoly and duopoly.

In the *monopoly situation*, the profit function of the monopolist is given by

$$\Pi_I = (a - bQ)Q - c_I Q - FC_I \tag{13}$$

3   This means that entry into a small monopoly market can lead to a smaller absolute increase in consumer welfare than the entry of a third or fourth firm into a larger oligopoly market. However, the relative increase might still be higher in the monopoly market.
4   The exact percentages are as follows (absolute values in parentheses) –1 to 2: PS = –11.11% (–14.4), CS = 77.78% (50.4), TW = 18.52% (36.0); 2 to 3: PS = –15.63% (–18.0), CS = 26.56% (30.6), TW = 5.47% (12.6); 3 to 4: PS = –14.67% (–14.26), CS = 13.78% (20.09), TW = 2.40% (5.83).

The incumbent's profit is maximized by setting the marginal revenue equal to marginal cost which leads to the following quantity provided by the monopolist

$$Q^m = \frac{a - c_I}{2b} \tag{14}$$

Substituting the quantity expression into the demand curve leads to the monopoly price

$$p^m = \frac{a + c}{2} \tag{15}$$

Substituting the quantity expression and the price expression into the monopolist's profit function leads to the monopoly profit

$$\Pi^m = PS^m = \frac{(a - c)^2}{4b} \tag{16}$$

Finally, the consumer surplus can be derived as

$$CS^m = \frac{(a - p^m)Q^m}{2} = \frac{(a - c_i)^2}{8b} \tag{17}$$

In the *duopoly situation*, the profit functions of the incumbent and the entrant are given by

$$\Pi_I = \left(a - b(q_I + q_E) - c_I\right)q_I - FC_I \tag{18}$$

$$\Pi_E = \left(a - b(q_I + q_E) - c_E\right)q_E - FC_E \tag{19}$$

Both firms maximize their profit functions by choosing their quantity q under the assumption that the quantity of the rival is fixed. The non-cooperative Cournot equilibrium is determined by the interaction point of the two reaction functions in which the equilibrium quantities for I and E are given by

$$q_I^C = \frac{a - 2c_I + c_E}{3b} \tag{20}$$

$$q_E^C = \frac{a - 2c_E + c_I}{3b} \tag{21}$$

leading to an equilibrium price of

$$p^C = \frac{a + c_I + c_E}{3} \tag{22}$$

Firm profits in the equilibrium are

$$\Pi_I^C = \frac{(a-2c_I+c_E)^2}{9b} - FC_I \qquad (23)$$

$$\Pi_E^C = \frac{(a-2c_E+c_I)^2}{9b} - FC_E \qquad (24)$$

and the consumer surplus realized in the duopoly state can be calculated to

$$CS^C = \left(a-\left(\frac{a+c_I+c_E}{3}\right)\right)\left[\left(\frac{a-2c_I+c_E}{3b}\right)+\left(\frac{a-2c_E+c_I}{3b}\right)\right]\left(\frac{1}{2}\right) \qquad (25)$$

In order to allow a graphical interpretation of especially the effects of entry in a Cournot model, the general results above are applied to a certain market specification. It is again assumed that market demand is given by $Q = 1.000-1.000p$ (which is equivalent to an inverse demand function of $p = 1-0.001(q_1+q_2)$). The marginal costs of the incumbent are fixed to $c_I = 0.28$. However, the entrant's marginal costs are subject to change. In *scenario 1*, the entrant is equally efficient and therefore has constant marginal costs of $c_E = 0.28$. In *scenario 2*, the entrant has marginal costs of $c_E = 0.21$ and therefore a moderate cost advantage over the incumbent. In *scenario 3*, the entrant has a large cost advantage leading to constant marginal costs of $c_E = 0.14$. With respect to fixed cost, $FC_I = FC_E = 10$ is assumed in all three scenarios.

Given the market and scenario specifications, it is first possible to calculate consumer surplus, producer surplus and overall welfare of the two possible market states: monopoly and duopoly. Figure 2.3 shows the results for the three scenarios.

In scenario 1, the monopolistic producer realizes a relatively high profit while the consumers get a relatively small consumer surplus. The equilibrium market price is 0.64. In the duopoly situation, the consumer surplus increases significantly while overall producer surplus drops and is

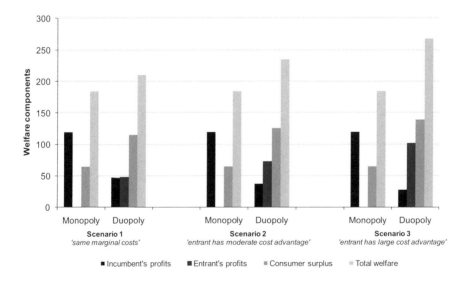

Figure 2.3   Welfare components for the three entrant scenarios

equally shared between the incumbent and the entrant. The equilibrium market price drops from 0.64 to 0.52. In scenario 2, the monopoly situation remains unchanged compared to scenario 1. In the duopoly situation, the cost advantage of the entrant leads to a higher duopoly total welfare, slightly higher consumer surplus as well as producer surplus. As the entrant has an efficiency advantage over the incumbent, it now gets a larger share of the producer surplus. The equilibrium market price drops further from 0.52 to 0.50. In scenario 3, the monopolist situation again remains unchanged. The effects in the duopoly situation are the same as described in scenario 2, however the effects are more distinctive due to the larger efficiency advantage of the entrant. Overall welfare in the duopoly situation increases moderately. The equilibrium market price in scenario 3 is 0.47.

In a nutshell, the discussion of the two basic Cournot models shows that the significance of free entry and entry incentives for competition intensity and market performance is not restricted to the model of perfect competition. Similarly, in standard Cournot oligopoly models, current abnormal profits are a central incentive for market entry. With a growing number of firms in the market, prices decline and per-firm output and profit ought to decrease. With an infinite number of firms in the market, Cournot competition leads to perfectly competitive outcomes. Incumbents facing entry have incentives to react with an increase in output, thereby triggering a downward trend on the equilibrium price. The introduction of fixed costs in the basic Cournot world has implications on the desirability of entry from a welfare perspective. Depending on factors such as market size, number of incumbent firms already in the market and the amount of fixed costs needed to start production, additional firms in the market may reduce the sum of producer and consumer surplus and are therefore socially undesirable. Finally, introducing asymmetric marginal costs leads to asymmetric market shares as the more efficient firm produces more (and realizes higher profits) than the less efficient firm. Consumers benefit through a drop in the equilibrium price compared to the case of a symmetric cost structure. In other words, low-cost entry typically is desirable in a homogeneous Cournot world.

2.2 Market Entry in the US Airline Industry

Complementary to the theoretical approach of market entry in the preceding section, another important part of a primer on the economics of entry in airline markets is an overview of the more applied role of market entry in general and market entry regulation in particular. Given the evolution of the US airline industry from the 1930s until today, the discussion differentiates between market entry in the era of regulation (1938–1978) and market entry in the era of deregulation (since 1978).

2.2.1 Market entry in the era of regulation   The beginning of commercial air transportation in the United States reaches back to the years after the First World War when an air postal service was implemented by the US Government. In the following years, the service network grew quickly and was extended to passenger air transportation. The world economic crisis triggered by the collapse of the New York Stock Exchange in October 1929 together with increasing difficulties for the government in managing the air transport business led to increasing demands to regulate the industry. It was believed that the airline industry was an 'infant industry' in which 'destructive competition' would foreclose the benefits of the 'public good' air transportation (see generally Vietor, 1990). As a consequence, in June 1938 Congress passed the Civil Aeronautics Act (CAA) which specified a detailed regulatory framework for the entire airline industry. This regulation basically remained effective until the deregulation of the airline industry in 1978.

The regulatory framework of the CAA and its interpretation by the installed regulatory authority, the Civil Aeronautics Board (CAB), can be subdivided into four areas: market entry and exit regulation, price regulation, cross subsidies and regulation of mergers and other forms of cooperation. Solely focusing on the regulation of entry and exit for the time being, the CAB restricted both entry into the industry as such and entry into specific routes by existing airlines (see Bailey et al., 1983). With respect to the former, the CAB received 79 applications between 1950 and 1974 to instal a company for interstate air transportation services, however, it rejected all 79 applications. For example, in 1941, the CAB argued in the case of Dixie Airlines that:

> the number of air carriers now operating appears sufficient to insure against monopoly in respect to the average new route case, and we believe that the present domestic air transportation system can by proper supervision be integrated and expanded in the manner that will in general afford the competition necessary for the development of that system in the manner contemplated by the Act. In the absence of peculiar circumstances presenting an affirmative reason for a new carrier there appears to be no inherent desirability of increasing the present number of carriers merely for the purpose of numerically enlarging the industry. (Phillips, 1969: 413)

Given the factual impossibility of market entry on a company level, the academic literature largely concentrates on the study of market entry into particular routes. In this respect, the CAB demanded application for a license before starting operations on a particular route. The granting of such a license was dependent on both subjective criteria ('fit, willing and able') and objective criteria ('public convenience and necessity'). While the large carriers usually passed the subjective criteria, the objective criteria were often particularly challenging to meet. This was particularly true for city pairs on which another carrier already operated as this incumbent carrier only needed to show that additional market entry would reduce its demand and would lead to financial losses in order to reach the rejection of the application by the CAB. In such an environment, it does not come as a surprise that between 1965 and 1978, less than 10 per cent of the applications were approved by the CAB (see Slovin et al., 1991). Exceptions of this rule of route monopolies were only observed on dense city pairs on which it was difficult for one particular carrier to meet the entire demand for air transportation (see generally O'Connor, 2001).

The main justification for the restrictive licensing activity of the CAB was the belief that a sustainable development of the industry can only be reached by avoiding destructive competition and by securing the financial stability of the industry. In this respect, the CAB used the allocation of lucrative route licenses as part of its more general levelling policy that aimed at avoiding bankruptcy of operating airlines. Furthermore, the licensing instrument was used to support the cross-subsidization policy of the CAB in the sense that operating a few smaller unprofitable city pairs was compensated by the allocation of a license for a larger profitable route.

With respect to market exit regulation, the CAB again had to approve all applications. The respective airlines were committed to show that the closure of the respective route would not cause any disadvantage for both cities involved. In most cases, the airlines were not able to provide such evidence and were forced to continue serving the respective route. In the case of bankrupt airlines, the CAB initiated mergers with healthier airlines in order to avoid market exits of entire airlines. This procedure ensured that both large and small markets were served independent of the destiny of a particular carrier.

2.2.2 Market entry in the era of deregulation   Although there were good reasons in the 1930s to regulate airline markets, increasingly these disappeared in the decades after the Second World War. For example, the technological developments in the aviation sector together with the significant growth of airline travel increased the complexity of regulation. In particular, towards the end of the 1960s, it became apparent that the regulatory inefficiencies such as quality competition between airlines, inefficient point-to-point route networks or the very expensive system of cross-subsidization were so severe that substantial reforms were inevitable. Due to the existence of a couple of political entrepreneurs led by Alfred Kahn and several airlines that voted for a complete deregulation, the planned regulatory reform developed to the deregulation of the airline industry by the Airline Deregulation Act in 1978.

Although deregulation triggered substantial changes in many dimensions of competition, one key accomplishment must be seen in the new freedom of airlines to decide on market entry and exit. In the years and decades after deregulation, this freedom was, on the one hand, used by the incumbent airlines to reorganize their route networks from inefficient point-to-point services to efficient hub-and-spoke networks. By connecting a smaller 'spoke' city to a large hub, the demand for travelling from the spoke city to any other location in the network is bundled into one airplane. As a consequence, it is possible to operate profitably even on smaller markets without any subsidy from the government.

On the other hand, due to the new possibilities to enter the airline industry as a new carrier in the deregulation era, market entry and competition by LCCs became possible. Led by the early (and still ongoing) success of Southwest Airlines, a former intra-state airline from Texas, the significance of low-cost airlines significantly began to rise in the late 1980s. In 1997, the US DOT identified a 'Low-cost Airline Service Revolution' due to the increasing number of passengers travelling with LCCs. As will be shown in Sections 3 and 4, this revolution has continued in the last 15 years and contributed significantly to the overall success of the deregulation of the US airline industry.

Although market entry was eased by the deregulation of the US airline industry, it would be superficial to automatically view the industry as 'perfectly contestable' in the sense of the theory of Baumol, Panzar and Willig (1982). In addition to the official certification processes[5] that still have to be passed before entering the industry, the following (hypothetical) analysis of the decision of an individual airline to enter a particular route identifies further obstacles of market entry in a deregulated environment.

Given the insights gained by the theoretical treatment of entry in the preceding section, it is to be expected that current profitability of a particular market typically is a key determinant in the decision of a potential entrant to enter the market. In general, it is reasonable to assume that a profit-maximizing, risk-neutral firm will enter a market if the net present value of expected post-entry profits is greater than the sunk costs of entry.[6] As post-entry profits depend on post-entry competition, the entry decision is connected to the expectations of the entrant about the conduct and performance of the firms after entry. Furthermore, the level of sunk costs incurred is a critical determinant of the entry decision (see Besanko et al., 1996: 396ff.). The higher the necessary sunk costs to enter an industry are, the higher is the risk of entry and the lower are the expected profits. Additionally, the entry condition above clarifies that profits immediately after entry are not necessary for a rational entry decision. It is sufficient that for example market growth expectations should promise sufficient profits in the future. With respect to airline markets, this

---

5   As described in more detail by Gudmundsson and van Kranenburg (2002), new airlines need two separate authorizations from the US Department of Transportation before commencing operations. The Office of the Secretary of Transportation (OST) assesses the applicant's management competence, ability to comply with regulation and financial resources to operate the airline, the Federal Aviation Administration (FAA) investigates whether the applicant's personnel, facilities, aircraft and manuals meet federal safety standards.

6   Furthermore, as investment capital is scarce, the entry decision for a special market depends on the existence and the profit expectations of other investment alternatives.

condition means that an entry decision must not be guided by the isolated profit expectations on the route actually entered but typically has to take account of the revenue and profit contribution of the respective passengers over the entire hub-and-spoke network of the respective airline. This reasoning suggests that the 'profitability of entry' assessments differ substantially between network carriers operating a large hub-and-spoke network and LCCs focusing more on the direct demand for travelling between two cities.

Although the expected profitability certainly is a key determinant of entry, empirical studies have regularly found evidence that abnormal profits are not competed away by entry but remain persistent for longer time periods (see generally Geroski, 1995, and Joskow et al., 1994, for empirical evidence from the US airline industry). This finding suggests that an entrant does not only have to answer the question 'Is entry profitable?' but also 'Is entry possible?'[7] In general, the latter question implies that a positive net present value (which at least outweighs sunk costs) is a necessary but not sufficient condition for entry as so-called 'barriers to entry' can reduce or even eliminate entry incentives. The term 'barriers to entry' is defined by Bain (1956: 3) as 'an advantage of established sellers in an industry over potential entrant sellers, which is reflected in the extent to which established sellers can persistently raise their price above competitive levels without attracting new firms to enter the industry'.[8] The sources of such barriers to entry are diverse. Besides legal entry barriers (such as entry regulation by the state), the literature focuses on the so-called private entry barriers which can be subdivided further into structural and strategic barriers to entry. While the former type is related to structural or technical characteristics of an industry (such as economies of scale, absolute cost advantages, e.g. favourable access to raw materials or a favourable geographic location, capital cost requirements or product differentiation advantages), the latter type is largely based on the notion of strategic entry deterrence, realizing that existing firms may deliberately behave in ways that decrease the probability of entry by other firms.[9]

With respect to the US airline industry, commentators leave no doubt that several potentially significant barriers to entry have developed after deregulation. For example, in the report *Aviation Competition – Challenges in Enhancing Competition in Dominated Markets*, the US General Accounting Office (2001) identified the following operating and marketing barriers which might constrain new entry into airline markets:

---

7   It should be mentioned that entry decisions are much more complex – in practice as well as in its examination by the economic profession – than described here. Montaguti et al. (2002: 23) for example distinguish between strategies of penetration, compatibility, pre-announcing and external routes to market. The choice of a certain kind of entry strategy largely depends on factors such as technology characteristics (such as network externalities or appropriability), the competitive environment (such as industry concentration or level of incumbency) and firm-specific factors (such as reputation, multi-market contact or the order of entry).

8   Stigler (1968) prefers a narrower definition. He proposes to think of a barrier to entry as 'a cost of producing (at some or every rate of output) ... which must be borne by a firm which seeks to enter an industry but is not borne by firms already in the industry'. Fisher (1979: 23), however, bases his proposal on social welfare when he argues that "[a] barrier to entry exists when entry would be socially beneficial but is somehow prevented ... The social benefit-cost calculation is not correctly reflected in the private benefit-cost calculation of the potential entrant". See McAfee and Mialon (2004) for a discussion of these and other definitions of barriers to entry.

9   The precise ways to reach this aim are diverse. Simply speaking, one option for the incumbent is to raise the structural entry barriers with the aim of making entry impossible or at least unprofitable. However, as such a strategy might not be sufficient or too expensive, the incumbent might consider strategic moves to complicate or even deter entry. The choice of a particular strategy again depends on its profitability and its possibility to succeed. For an overview of such strategies, see Hüschelrath (2005).

- access to airport facilities, such as gates, ticket counters, baggage handling and storage as well as take-off and landing slots;
- frequent flyer programmes;
- corporate incentive agreements;
- travel agent commission overrides;
- flight frequency; and
- network size and breadth.

Without wanting to provide a detailed discussion of all these potential barriers to entry, the example of airport gates can be used to explain the potential relevance of structural and strategic entry barriers. On the one hand, it is imaginable that an airport faces a binding constraint in the number of available gates in certain periods of the day. If such capacity problems foreclose the possibilities of an entrant to enter a certain route, gates must be classified as structural entry barrier. On the other hand, it is also imaginable that a certain airline owns a number of gates at a particular airport. If such an airline has free gates available and refuses to rent them to a potential entrant (at a reasonable price), gates must be classified as a strategic entry barrier.

In a nutshell, it can be said that although deregulation provided airlines with the freedom to enter routes on the basis of individual assessments of benefits and costs, structural and strategic entry barriers might impede market entry in a deregulated environment. The existence of such possibilities suggests that the respective competition authority is well advised to closely monitor the industry and to intervene in cases of anti-competitive behaviour that solely aims at securing market power of incumbent airlines at the costs of a reduced level of competition (and consumer welfare) in the respective markets.

3. The Evolution of the US Airline Industry – Recent Market Developments from 1995 to 2009

An important precondition for a detailed analysis of market entry is the provision of an overview of recent market developments in the US airline industry. Along the lines of the so-called structure–conduct–performance paradigm, the following subsections shed light on market size and major players, market concentration, fare levels, service levels, cost levels and profit levels. Given the increasing significance of LCCs in US domestic airline markets, the analysis differentiates between network carriers (NWCs) and LCCs.

3.1 Size and Players

A natural starting point for a characterization of recent developments of the US airline industry is the presentation of some basic data with respect to market size and major players. On average, in the sample period from 1995 to 2009, the US airline industry experienced a very significant growth in demand reflected in major measures of output such as number of passengers, available seat miles or revenue passenger miles. For example, the number of passengers increased from about 502 million in 1995 to 621 million in 2009.[10] As revealed by Table 2.1, a large and persistent fraction of about 95 per cent of these passengers was carried by the ten largest airlines in the market.

---

10   For comparative purposes, Eurostat reported about 751 million passengers for the 27 member states of the European Union in 2009. Data source: Eurostat, *Passenger air transport – 2009 and 2010 monthly data,*

Table 2.1   Ten largest airlines in the US domestic airline industry (1995 and 2009)

	1995				2009		
	Carrier	Passengers (millions)	Share (%)		Carrier	Passengers (millions)	Share (%)
1	Delta	86.8	17.3	1	Southwest (LCC)	109.5	17.6
2	American	70.2	14.0	2	Delta	102.5	16.5
3	United	69.6	13.9	3	American	84.1	13.6
4	US Airways	61.0	12.2	4	United	72.3	11.7
5	Southwest (LCC)	57.3	11.4	5	US Airways	72.1	11.6
6	Northwest	42.4	8.4	6	Continental	48.0	7.7
7	Continental	37.8	7.5	7	Northwest	32.4	5.2
8	Trans World	21.8	4.3	8	AirTran (LCC)	23.9	3.9
9	America West	17.7	3.5	9	JetBlue (LCC)	20.4	3.3
10	Alaska	13.8	2.8	10	Alaska	19.5	3.1
	Sum	**478.5**	**95.4**		**Sum**	**584.8**	**94.2**

Note: LCC = Low-cost carrier; Data source: US DOT, T-100 Domestic Segment Data.

As shown in Table 2.1, although the passenger share distribution largely remained constant, the players as such as well as their relative positions significantly changed in the sample period. While two large players – Trans World (2001) and America West (2005)[11] – ceased to exist, the very significant growth of Southwest boosted the airline from the fifth position in 1995 to the top position in 2009. Although recent merger activities between Delta and Northwest (2008) and United and Continental (2010) will significantly reshuffle the ranking in the coming years, the success of the LCC concept is not only reflected in the growth of Southwest but also in the appearance of two other LCCs in the 2009 ranking: AirTran[12] and JetBlue. These recent developments are reflected in an overall increase in the passenger share of LCCs in the group of the ten largest airlines from 11.4 per cent in 1995 to 24.8 per cent in 2009.[13]

In addition to the general significance of LCC traffic in the United States, the distinctive business concepts and strategies of LCCs in comparison to network carriers[14] justify a separation

Data in Focus, 48/2010, available at http://epp.eurostat.ec.europa.eu/cache/ITY_OFFPUB/KS-QA-10-048/EN/KS-QA-10-048-EN.PDF, accessed on 22 December 2010).

11   Interestingly, both acquiring companies – American in the case of Trans World and US Airways in the case of America West – experienced reductions in their passenger share in the period from 1995 to 2009 (despite their external growth through acquisitions).

12   Although AirTran was acquired by Southwest in September 2010, JetBlue remains an independent LCC with further growth potential.

13   Focusing on the entire group of US domestic passengers, the LCCs' passenger share increased from 12.7 per cent in 1995 to 29.8 per cent in 2009. Further low cost carriers are Allegiant Air, Frontier Airlines, Spirit Airlines, Sun Country Airlines and Virgin America. All other (non-regional) airlines in the T-100 Domestic Segment Database were classified as NWCs.

14   The group of majors is supported by a larger group of regional airlines. Most of those smaller airlines operate in small feeder traffic markets and often assist one particular network carrier in the operation of its

of the two groups. The additional insights that can be gained by such a split of the data set are shown in Figure 2.4 which plots the number of passengers carried by NWCs and LCCs between 1995 and 2009.

As shown in Figure 2.4, the demand of NWCs is much more volatile than the demand of LCCs. While both of the very significant external shocks in sample period – the 9/11 attacks in 2001 and the economic recession in 2008/09 – appear to have a significant impact on the number of passengers travelling with NWCs, LCCs' demand only shows reduced (but still positive) growth rates. One possible explanation for this observation is that especially a reduction in (national and international[15]) business traveller's demand puts the network carriers under pressure in turbulent economic times. In addition to an overall reduction in business flights, the effect might be aggravated by the possibilities of firms reducing travel expenses by switching from network carriers to LCCs. An alternative explanation for the observed differences could be seen in different positions of the NWC and LCC business models in their respective life cycles. While the NWC business model might have a clear focus on keeping the existing business rather than additional growth, the LCC business model might not have reached maturity yet and has therefore better possibilities to expand its business, even during the experienced economic downturns of the US economy.

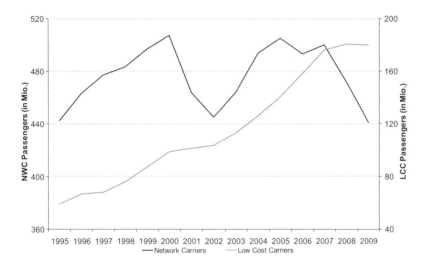

Figure 2.4   Passengers of NWCs and LCCs (1995–2009)

Source: US Department of Transportation (DOT), T-100 Domestic Segment Data.

---

hub-and-spoke network. Although most of these regional carriers are legally independent, their economic existence is often tied to a large network carrier. For example, in most instances, regional carriers do not issue their own tickets but refer to the network carrier for all flight bookings. In the empirical analysis of entry patterns and effects of entry below, regional airlines are excluded from the analysis. For all other analyses, regional carriers are merged to the respective major carrier for which they operate on a specific route.

15   Although the focus of this chapter is on US domestic rather than international traffic, the latter certainly has implications for the former. For example, a passenger travelling from Frankfurt via New York (JFK) to San Francisco (SFO) is counted as US domestic passenger on the route from JFK to SFO. As a consequence, fluctuations or even breaks in international demand can have substantial knock-on effects on the level of domestic demand of NWCs (while it leaves the demand situation of LCCs largely unaffected).

3.2 Market Concentration

Market concentration is viewed as one key determinant of competition intensity. For example, ceteris paribus, competition in a market with five airlines can be expected to be tougher than competition in a market with only two airlines. As a consequence, the average market price in the latter market typically lies above the market price in the former market.

Given this potentially important role of market concentration, an initial overview of the number of non-stop airport pairs together with the respective number of firms in the market provides first key insights. Table 2.2 presents such an overview.

As shown in Table 2.2, the overall number of airport pairs with scheduled airline services increased from 1962 routes in 1995 to 2658 routes in 2009, i.e. the airline network has become denser in the last 15 years. However, Table 2.2 also reveals that almost 76 per cent of all routes in 2009 were operated by a single airline. Although such a monopoly situation might look worrying at first glance, a closer look in the data reveals that, on the one hand, the large majority of these monopoly routes are actually very small (partly with only a few passengers per quarter) and hence, market entry by a second airline would simply be unprofitable. On the other hand, focusing on the more dense domestic routes shows that, for example in 2009, 81.6 per cent of all domestic passengers travelled in the largest 1000 routes. As shown in Figure 2.5, the share of monopoly routes is reduced significantly on those denser routes.

Table 2.2   Number of non-stop airport pairs and firms in the US domestic airline industry

Year	Number of firms in the airport pair									Total
	1	**2**	**3**	**4**	**5**	**6**	**7**	**8**	**9**	
1995	1445	398	95	12	6	2	2	1	1	1962
2009	2020	478	134	20	5	1				2658

Source: US DOT, T-100 Domestic Segment Data.

As shown in Figure 2.5, between 1995 and 2009 the share of monopoly markets decreased on average while the share of duopoly and other markets increased accordingly. Comparing the two groups of NWCs and LCCs, it becomes apparent that the latter group gained significance in all three subgroups. In relative terms, the shares in duopolies and other markets rose substantially between 1995 and 2009 resulting in an increased route overlap between NWCs and LCCs. In 1995, only 104 of the top 1000 routes showed such an overlap, but the number steadily increased to 305 routes in 2009.[16]

---

16   Although the finding of an increased overlap between NWCs and LCCs as such is robust, remember that the focus of the analysis in this chapter is on airport pairs rather than city pairs. Therefore, a flight between two primary airports (such as Chicago O'Hare and Houston Bush) is considered a separate market from a flight between two secondary airports of the respective cities (such as Chicago Midway and Houston Hobby). Given the LCCs focus on secondary airports, it can be expected that the degree of overlap has increased even further if city pairs were the focus of the investigation. For a general discussion of the delineation of airline markets and the differentiation in airport pairs and city pairs, see Brueckner et al. (2010).

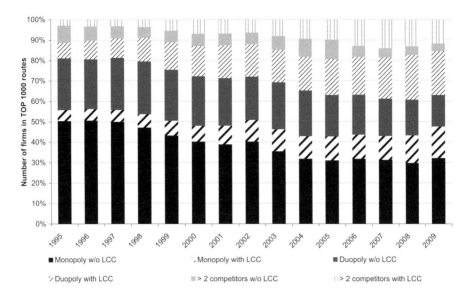

Figure 2.5   Number of NWCs and LCCs in the top 1000 markets (1995–2009)

Source: US DOT, T-100 Domestic Segment Data.

If the analysis is narrowed down even more to the largest 100 markets (representing about 23.4 per cent of all domestic passengers in 2009), the share of monopoly routes is reduced even further to 12 per cent, while 35 per cent of the markets are duopolies and the remaining 53 per cent are operated by more than two airlines. With respect to route overlap, the analysis shows that the number of routes in which NWCs and LCCs directly compete increased from 18 in 1995 to 45 in 2009.

In sum, it can be said that although the large majority of airport pairs is operated on a monopoly basis, the majority of domestic airline passengers travel on routes with more than one operating airline. In recent years, the route overlap between NWCs and LCCs increased substantially thereby increasing competitive pressures (and expecting a downward trend in fares).

3.3 Fare Level

A key accomplishment of the first two decades after deregulation was a significant downward trend in the average fare level which was basically continued for the sample period from 1995 to 2009. Although in nominal terms, the annual US domestic average itinerary fare[17] increased from $292 to $309, in real (1995$) terms, the average fare decreased from $292 in 1995 to $235 in 2009.

Although the downward trend of the average fare level is an important insight, individual average fares depend on various factors. For example, earlier studies on fare level developments

---

17   'Fares based on domestic itinerary fares, round-trip or one-way for which no return is purchased. Fares are based on the total ticket value which consists of the price charged by the airlines plus any additional taxes and fees levied by an outside entity at the time of purchase. Fares include only the price paid at the time of the ticket purchase and do not include other fees paid at the airport or onboard the aircraft. Averages do not include frequent-flyer or "zero fares" or a few abnormally high reported fares.' (Data) Source: Bureau of Transportation Statistics (BTS).

identified a so-called fare premium, i.e. large (often slot- or gate-constrained) hub airports charge higher average fares than smaller or non-hub airports. Although recent evidence suggests that this premium still exists, its size has recently been shrinking. For example, for the airports in the Greater New York region, the average domestic fare in 1996 lay about 26.6 per cent above the domestic average. In 2009, this difference was reduced to about 7.6 per cent. Although actual numbers differ, the trend of a decrease in the fare premium can also be observed for other cities/ regions such as Chicago or Dallas.[18]

Investigating the determinants of average fare levels further, the preceding section introduced the general argument that an increase in the number of (effective) competitors in a particular airport pair market should expect a decrease in the average fare level. In order to test this hypothesis, Figure 2.6 shows the market yield (defined as passenger revenues divided by revenue passenger miles) for NWCs and LCCs in monopoly, duopoly and other market structures for the top 1000 markets between 1995 and 2009.

As shown in Figure 2.6, monopoly markets show a higher market yield than airport pairs with more than one operating airline. Although this finding in basically true for both NWCs and LCCs, the yield level of NWCs is significantly above the yield level of LCCs. Furthermore, while the monopoly yield level of the NWCs shows a clear downward trend, the values for the LCCs largely remain constant. The same conclusion is basically true for a comparison of the duopoly and other

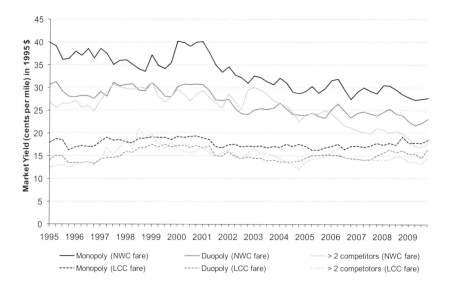

Figure 2.6   Market yield for NWCs and LCCs in monopoly, duopoly and other markets (top 1000, 1995–2009)

Source: US DOT, Airline Origin and Destination Survey (DB1B).

---

18   Data Source: Bureau of Transportation Statistics (BTS) at http://www.bts.gov/xml/atpi/src/ indextop100.xml (accessed on 22 December 2010). Despite the recent trend of a shrinking fare premium, BTS data reveals that the majority of the nearly 100 reported airports show higher average fares if the entire sample period from 1995 to 2009 is taken into account. Such an analysis finds, e.g., for Cincinnati an average fare premium of about 45.2 per cent, for Charlotte an average fare premium of about 34.9 per cent and for Newark an average fare premium of about 27.0 per cent.

markets. Ceteris paribus, this development suggests that the NWCs face an increase in competitive pressure, at least partly triggered by the increasing market presence of LCCs. This finding is in line with the significant increase in route overlap between NWCs and LCCs identified in the preceding section.

3.4 Service Level

Measuring the level of service in airline markets certainly is a multidimensional problem. While some studies focus on rather quantitative service indicators such as the number of departures or available seats from a particular city or region in a certain time frame, others develop an interest for rather qualitative indicators such as the type of connection (non-stop vs. one-stop) or the type of aircraft (jet flights vs. prop flights).

The existence and relevance of various indicators for service quality suggests the construction of a rating system that combines the respective criteria to an overall score. In this respect, Wichita State University (now in cooperation with Purdue University) derives a so-called Airline Quality Rating (AQR). The AQR is characterized as an objective method of comparing airline quality on combined multiple performance criteria. AQR scores for the calendar year are based on 15 elements in 4 major categories of airline performance: on-time performance (OT), denied boardings (DB), mishandled baggage (MB) and customer complaints (CC).[19] The AQR Scores reported for the sample period from 1995 to 2009 are presented in Figure 2.7.[20]

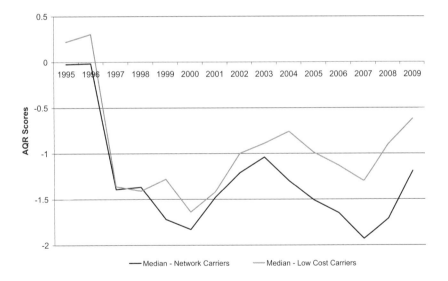

Figure 2.7   Airline Quality Rating Scores (AQR) for NWCs and LCCs (1995–2009)

Sources: Various AQR reports.

19   The category 'customer complaints' comprises the following 12 subcategories: flight problems; oversales; reservations, ticketing, and boarding; fares; refunds; baggage; customer service; disability; advertising; discrimination; animals; other.

20   The formula for calculating the AQR score is AQR $= [(18.63 \times OT) + (-8.03 \times DB) + (-7.92 \times MB) + (-7.17 \times CC)] / [8.63 + 8.03 + 7.92 + 7.17]$. For detailed information, see http://www.aqr.aero/ (accessed on 22 December 2010).

As shown in Figure 2.7, the AQR scores change significantly over the sample period. Following the significant drop in 1997 – caused by a change in the rating methodology – airline quality increased significantly between 2001 and 2004. After a steep decline in the years from 2005 to 2007, the last few years saw again increasing AQR scores. According to various AQR reports, the reasons for increases and declines in the AQR are typically multifaceted, i.e. they are the result of a better or worse performance in most or all of the four major areas of airline performance covered by the AQR.

Comparing the two major groups of airlines, Figure 2.7 shows on the one hand that the scores for both groups basically follow the same trend, suggesting that a set of external factors influence airline service performance. On the other hand, the figure shows that the group of LCCs outperforms the group of NWCs in almost every year in the sample period. Interestingly, while the difference between both groups was rather modest until 2003, it increased and remained persistent in the years from 2004 onwards. Given these findings, it can be concluded that – in a sense – the group of LCCs does not only provide (on average) cheaper flights but also offers (on average) a higher-quality product to its customers.

3.5 Cost Level

The lack of possibilities and incentives to operate efficiently in the era of regulation was reflected in an elevated cost level of all major airlines. In the 20 years following deregulation, the network carriers manage to reorganize their operations in general and their route network in particular. As a consequence, the average cost level decreased significantly. With the appearance and success of the LCC concept, the importance of the cost side of operations reached a new level. By strictly optimizing their operations, LCCs manage to operate at costs per available seat mile (excluding fuel) which are significantly below the average of the network carriers. Figure 2.8 compares the average cost levels (ex fuel) for NWCs and LCCs for the years 1995 and 2009.

As shown in Figure 2.8, NWCs have a substantially higher average cost level than LCCs. While the costs per available seat mile for the NWCs increased from 8.17 to 10.96 cents per available seat mile between 1995 and 2009, the group of LCCs experienced an increase from 6.01 to 7.06 cents per available seat mile. In the group of NWCs, the elevated cost level of US Airways is noticeable while the relatively high cost level of Southwest is peculiar in the group of LCCs. Figure 2.8 excludes the costs of fuel as they can hardly be influenced by the airlines. As reported by the IATA, the percentage share of fuel out of the overall airline operating costs increased from 13.4 per cent in 2001 to 34.2 per cent in North America in 2008. In the same time frame, the second-largest cost component, labour costs, experienced a percentage share reduction from 36.2 per cent to 21.5 per cent.[21]

3.6 Profit Level

After addressing revenues and costs in the preceding sections, the consequential final step is to cast an eye on the profitability of the US airline industry. Generally, post-deregulation developments showed both periods of operating profits (1984–1989 and 1994–2000) and periods of operating losses (1980–1983 and 1990–1993). The more recent developments plotted in Figure 2.9 reveal a similar pattern for the group of NWCs for the time frame from 2000 to 2009.

---

21   Data source: IATA Economic Briefing, Airline Fuel and Labor Cost Share, February 2010, available at http://www.iata.org/whatwedo/Documents/economics/Airline_Labour_Cost_Share_Feb2010.pdf (accessed on 22 December 2010).

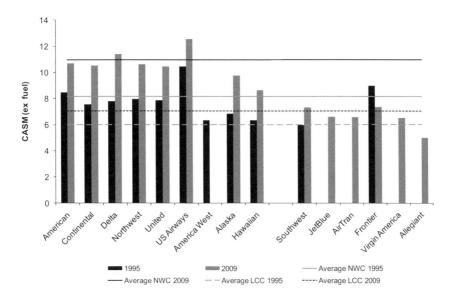

Figure 2.8   System total expense (excluding fuel) of NWCs and LCCs in cents per available seat mile (1995 and 2009)

Source: US DOT, Form 41 via BTS, Schedule T2, P6 and P52.

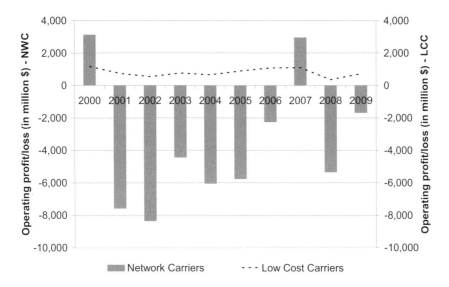

Figure 2.9   Operating profit (loss) of NWCs and LCCs (2000–2009)

Source: US Bureau of Transportation Statistics F41 Schedule P12 data; authors' calculations.

As shown in Figure 2.9, the profitability situation of the NWCs experienced significant variation from a historic operating loss of $8,358 million in 2002 to a significant operating profit of $3,127 million in 2000. In sum, the group of NWCs lost $35,418 million in the period from 2000 of 2009. Furthermore, it is interesting to note that all major NWCs experienced significant operating losses in the sample period with Continental (operating loss of $1,575 million) and American (operating loss of $10,666 million) delineating the spectrum. As a consequence, all major NWCs (with the exception of American Airlines until 2011) at some point needed the temporary protection of Chapter 11 bankruptcy regulation to be able to continue operations.

In the same time frame, the group of LCCs performed significantly better. Although several carriers experienced operating losses in several years, the entire group always realized a significant operating profit from at least $361 million in 2008 up to $1,168 million in 2000. In sum, the group of LCCs earned $8,038 million in the period from 2000 of 2009, with Southwest contributing by far the largest share of $5.570 million. In fact, Southwest is the only major carrier in the US that managed to report an operating profit in every year since deregulation. However, on aggregate, all LCCs in the sample realized an operating profit from at least $36 million in the case of Frontier up to $889 million in the case of JetBlue.

4. The Evolution of the US Airline Industry – Patterns and Effects of Market Entry from 1995 to 2009

Following the general theoretical and applied characterization of market entry in the first section and the overview of recent market developments in the US airline industry in the preceding section, this section provides a comprehensive characterization and discussion of empirical evidence of market entry events in the US airline industry from 1995 to 2009.[22] The analysis differentiates between patterns of market entry in Section 4.1 and selected economic effects of market entry on average fares and departures in Section 4.2.

4.1 Entry Patterns in the US Airline Industry from 1995 to 2009

In this section, entry patterns in the domestic US airline industry between 1995 and 2009 are investigated. In addition to the study of entry events in all non-stop airport pair markets, the section also analyses splits of entry data with respect to market size, type of market and length of haul.

4.1.1 Entry into non-stop airport pair markets   A natural starting point of the study of entry patterns is a general analysis of all entry events on the non-stop airport pair level. In this respect, Section 3.2 has already reported that the overall number of routes operated by commercial airlines increased from 1962 routes in 1995 to 2658 routes in 2009. These numbers alone suggest a

22   If not stated otherwise, the raw data in this section stems from the US DOT T-100 Domestic Segment database. We constructed a data-set of non-directional non-stop route (airport pair) markets. We dropped airline-route observations with less than 12 quarterly departures and airline-route observations which were only served one quarter between 1995 and 2010. An entry is determined by the quarter when we first observe an airline providing non-stop scheduled services. Since our data begins in 1995, all airlines enter by definition in 1995. Thus, we have to concentrate our entry analysis on the time frame from 1996 to 2009. Fare data is retrieved from the Origin and Destination Survey DB1B Market database. In calculating average fares, zero fares and abnormally high fares are excluded as well as fares which required the passenger to change the airplane more than twice.

significant entry activity in the sample period. This early finding is confirmed by Figure 2.10 which plots the number of route entries by NWCs and LCCs.

As shown in Figure 2.10, there are substantial differences in both the absolute number of entry events per year and the shares of entry events between NWCs and LCCs. On an absolute level, there have been on average 167 market entries per year with the years 2007 (244 entries) and 2003 (105 entries) delineating the value spectrum for the sample period. Focusing on the separation between NWCs and LCCs, the former group has launched entry into 1205 markets between 1996 and 2009, while the entry activities of the latter group add up to 1137 entry events. While the NWCs show significant entry activity between 1996 and 2000, the number of entries dropped significantly from 2003 onwards. Interestingly, since 2004 the group of LCCs has entered more markets per year than the group of NWCs. In the recession years 2008 and 2009, the difference in terms of entry events was particularly distinctive, confirming the stylized fact from Section 3.1 that the network carrier's business is more dependent on the general state of the economy than the low-cost carrier's business.

Although the focus of this chapter is on the role of market entry, there is no doubt that market exit can be a closely related phenomenon. For example, entry into one market can demand exit in another market as, e.g., a particular airplane can be operated more efficiently on the new route. Furthermore, any reorganization of the flight network typically triggers several entry and exit attempts. For example, airline mergers often lead to market exits either through the elimination of overlapping parts of both networks or by the decommissioning of entire hubs of one of the merging airlines.[23]

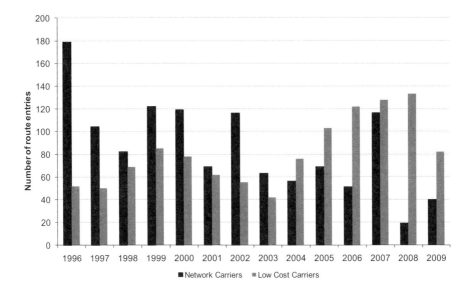

Figure 2.10   Number of route entries by NWCs and LCCs (all markets, 1996–2009)
Source: US DOT, T-100 Domestic Segment Data.

---

23   An example for such a merger is American/Trans World in April 2001. Due to the proximity of American's own hub at Chicago O'Hare to the Trans World hub in St. Louis, the latter was basically decommissioned after the merger and replaced by regional jet service. As a consequence, airline operations in St. Louis were reduced from over 800 operations a day to just over 200.

In order to take account of the interdependencies between market entry and market exit, Figure 2.11 shows the number of route exits[24] by NWCs and LCCs in all markets between 1996 and 2009.

As shown in Figure 2.11, there is significant variation in the number of route exits. On an absolute level, there have been on average 188 market exits per year with the years 2009 (359 exits) and 1999 (94 exits) delineating the value spectrum for the sample period. Focusing on the separation between NWCs and LCCs, the former group has experienced exit in 2247 markets between 1996 and 2009, while the exit activities of the latter group add up to 391.[25]

Although such an analysis of exit events already provides valuable insights on entry and exit dynamics, it does not allow a direct conclusion on how successful the respective entries in the sample period have been. Due to the unavailability of detailed route-specific profitability data, the success of the respective entry events has to be approximated by calculating survival rates. In the airline industry, survival rates basically reflect the relationship between the number of route entries that are still operated after a certain time period (for which it is assumed that unprofitable entry decisions have been reversed) and all route entries in the respective time period. Although the identification of survival rates is not straightforward Figure 2.12 shows the respective survival rates for NWCs and LCCs. An entry into a particular route is counted as 'survived' if it was still operated by the respective carrier at least two years after entry.

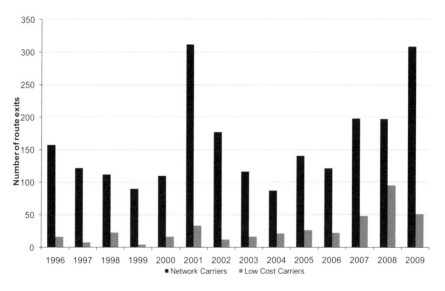

Figure 2.11   Number of route exits by NWCs and LCCs (all markets, 1996–2009)

Source: US DOT, T-100 Domestic Segment Data.

24   An exit is defined to have taken place in the quarter when we last observed an airline serving a non-stop airport pair between 1995 and 2010.

25   Note that the number of exits reported here refer to exits of particular airlines from particular routes. In most of the cases, the exited route remains to be operated by at least one other airline. As a consequence, it is not feasible to compare the exit rates derived here with the development in the number of non-stop airport pairs reported in Table 2.2.

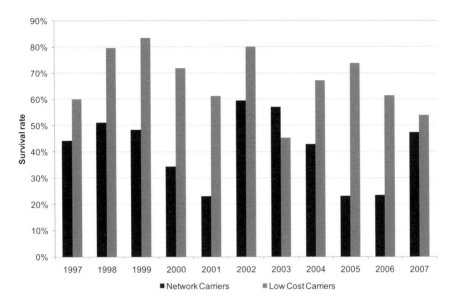

Figure 2.12 Survival rates of market entries by NWCs and LCCs (all markets, 1997–2007)
Source: US DOT, T-100 Domestic Segment Data.

As shown in Figure 2.12, although the survival rates of both groups largely follow the same (macroeconomic) trends, the group of NWCs has significantly lower survival rates than the group of LCCs. For example, while about 61 per cent of all LCC entries in 2001 were still operated by the respective airline two years later; the corresponding survival rate for the group of NWCs lies at about 23 per cent. Over the entire sample period, NWCs show an average survival rate of about 41 per cent while the LCCs value lies at about 67 per cent. Although these results allow the conclusion that LCCs entries are on average more successful then NWC entries, it has to be reminded that both groups of airlines follow rather distinct business concepts and are at different stages in their life cycles. These differences may explain a significant part of the variation in the survival rates.

4.1.2 Entry into the largest 1000 non-stop airport pair markets   In addition to the characterization of the general entry patterns in all markets, an analysis of the sub-sample of the largest 1000 markets[26] can add value. For example, if entry largely took place in smaller markets, its economic impact must be expected to be substantially smaller than in the case of significant entry activity in larger markets in which a large percentage of the overall US domestic passengers travel. In order to be able to investigate this issue further, Figure 2.13 plots the number of airport pair entries by NWCs and LCCs in the top 1000 markets between 1996 and 2009.

As shown in Figure 2.13, there are again substantial differences in both the absolute number of entry events per year and the shares of entry events between NWCs and LCCs. On an absolute level, there have been on average 71 market entries per year with the years 1997 (40 entries) and 2007 (123 entries), delineating the value spectrum for the sample period. Focusing on the separation between NWCs and LCCs, the former group has launched entries in 507 markets between 1996 and 2009, while the entry activities of the latter group add up to 491 entry events. While the NWCs

---

26   By definition, entry into the top 1000 markets is entry into mature markets.

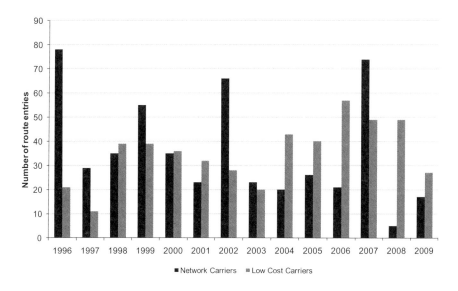

Figure 2.13   Number of route entries by NWCs and LCCs (top 1000 markets, 1996–2009)
Source: US DOT, T-100 Domestic Segment Data.

show significant entry activity between 1996 and 1999, the average number of entries dropped significantly from 2000 onwards. Again, since 2004 the group of LCCs has entered more markets per year than the group of NWCs (with the exception of 2007).

Comparing the absolute number of entries in Figures 2.12 (all markets) and 2.13 (Top 1000 markets) reveals that on average only 42 per cent of the entry activity in the entire sample period took place in the top 1000 markets with the lowest share of 26 per cent in 1997 and the largest share of 55 per cent in 2002. Differentiating between NWCs and LCCs, the analysis reveals that on average only 40 per cent of all NWC entries took place in the top 1000 markets, with the lowest share in 2008 with 26 per cent and the highest share in 2007 with 64 per cent. For the group of LCCs, an average share of 44 per cent can be calculated with 22 per cent in 1997 as the lowest share and 57 per cent in 2004 as the highest share. Given these results, it can be concluded that although an analysis of the top 1000 markets covered about 81.6 per cent of all domestic passengers in 2009, a restriction of the entry analysis to these dense markets covers on average less than half of all entry events. A large fraction of entry events apparently took place in smaller markets.

4.1.3 Entry into new non-stop airport pair markets   Providing airlines with the freedom to decide on market entry and exit was one of the key accomplishments of the liberalization of the US airline industry. Since then, airlines made frequent use of the gained possibilities to optimize their route networks and to provide efficient air services to their customers. Complementary to bringing competition to existing routes, an important part of an individual airlines' market success is the identification and realization of additional profit opportunities through the entry into new routes. Although the entry decision of the airline is typically profit driven, such 'innovative entry' clearly has positive impacts on consumers who are able to travel on the newly established airport-pair. In order to investigate the role of innovative entry, Figure 2.14 shows the percentages of entries by NWCs and LCCs in new markets between 1996 and 2009.

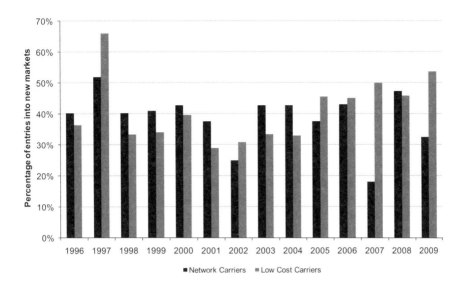

Figure 2.14   Percentage of entries by NWCs and LCCs into new markets (1996–2009)
Source: US DOT, T-100 Domestic Segment Data.

As shown in Figure 2.14, the percentage of entries in new markets is relatively high and constant. In sum, 937 of the 2342 entry events in the sample period where 'first mover' entries in airport pairs that have not been served before in the sample period by any other airline: 457 of these 'first mover entries' where conducted by NWCs while the remaining 480 first mover entries were undertaken by members of the group of LCCs. On average, the group of NWCs entered 33 new markets per year with 1996 (72 entries) and 2008 (9 entries) delineating the value spectrum. For the group of LCCs, 34 new markets entries were reported per year on average with the highest value of 64 entries in 2007 and the lowest value of 14 entries in 2003. As is expected the more dense routes are rather mature markets, it is likely that the first mover routes are relatively small and need time to develop a sufficient level of demand.

4.1.4 Entry into short-, medium- and long-haul non-stop airport pair markets   In its 1997 report *The Low Cost Airline Service Revolution* the US DOT expected a coexistence of NWCs and LCCs with the latter providing local passengers the benefit of additional service and lower prices on short- and medium-haul markets, while the former, by continuing to link the spoke city with its network, 'provide local passengers who prefer to use the network carrier's service and connecting passengers who wish to travel beyond the hub city in other city-pair markets additional, competitive alternatives' (US Department of Transport, 1997: 17).

In order to investigate the actual relevance of such a coexistence of NWCs and LCCs, Figure 2.15 provides an overview of the market entries of LCCs in all markets split into short-haul markets (< 750 miles), medium-haul markets (751–1500 miles) and long-haul markets (> 1500 miles).

Liberalization in Aviation

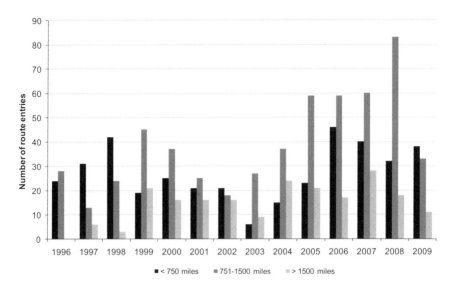

Figure 2.15   Number of LCC route entries in short-, medium- and long-haul markets (1996–2009)

Source: US DOT, T-100 Domestic Segment Data.

   As shown in Figure 2.15, there is significant variation in the entry behaviour across short-, medium- and long-haul markets. In sum, between 1996 and 2009, LCCs entered 1137 airport pair markets: 383 entry events (about 34 per cent) took place in short-haul markets, 548 entry events (about 48 per cent) in medium-haul markets and the remaining 206 entry events (about 18 per cent) in long-haul markets. While short-haul entry played the by far largest role in 1997 and 1998 with percentage shares above 60 per cent, its relative significance was reduced substantially since then reaching a low of 14 per cent in 2003. Medium-haul entry activity is relatively strong across the entire sample period with the lowest share in 1997 (26 per cent) and the highest share in 2003 (64 per cent). This recent switch from short-haul to medium-haul entry could be explained by reducing possibilities for profitable short-haul entry forcing LCCs to look for business opportunities in the medium-haul segment. Finally, with respect to long-haul entry activity, Figure 2.15 generally shows significant entry activity since 1997 with the lowest share of 4 per cent in 1998 and the highest share of 32 per cent of all LCC entry events in 2004. Therefore, it can be concluded that although the key business focus of LCCs remains on short- and medium-haul markets, even long-haul markets can be entered and operated on a permanent basis. This conclusion is supported by casting an eye on the respective exit rates. In the sample period, the long-haul segment experienced 59 market exits (equal to about 29 per cent of all exits), compared to 159 (about 30 per cent) in the medium-haul segment and 156 (about 41 per cent) in the short-haul segment.

4.2 Effects of Entry in the US Airline Industry from 1995 to 2009

Following the characterization of recent market entry patterns in the domestic US airline industry, the logical next step is to investigate the economic effects of entry. In this respect, the theoretical discussion in Section 2 generally revealed that market entry can be expected to lead to price reductions thereby benefiting consumers. Furthermore, (strategic) (re)actions by incumbent firms can also be expected before or after entry in an attempt to defend their market position.

In general, the effects of entry in US airline markets have been the focus of several empirical studies. For example, Joskow et al. (1994) examine quarterly data on major, non-stop city pairs in the US between 1985 and 1987 and find that entry generally is not induced by price levels substantially above the norm; entry reduces fares and increases output; exit increases fares and reduces output; incumbents cut prices and maintain output in response to entry; and survivors increase both prices and output in response to exit. In another study, Lin et al. (2002) conducted an investigation of factors contributing to competitive reactions to entry by incumbent airlines in the short and longer runs. Using data on 889 incumbent reactions to entry between 1991 and 1997, the authors found several factors that have a significant impact on the level of incumbent price cuts in response to entry. They include the size of the entrant's price cut, the number of passengers carried by the new entrant on the route, and the costs, size and number of complaints of the entrant. Interestingly, Lin et al. found no evidence that incumbents respond more aggressively to small, low-cost carriers than to other carriers. Incumbents reserve their largest price cuts for larger new entrants with higher costs. The longer-run results of this study indicate that even if the entrant is forced to withdraw from a route, prices do not rise to pre-entry levels.

Given this brief sketch of examples for existing research, the remainder of this section aims to analyse the effects of route entry on two different levels. First, all entry events in the top 500 routes between 1996 and 2009 are aggregated to investigate the overall effects of entry on average fares and the number of departures. Second, the particular effects of route entry by a low-cost carrier in a short-, medium-, and long-haul market are analysed by focusing on the effects of entry on average fares and the number of passengers. Furthermore, the analysis on the route-level allows an estimation of the welfare effects of entry.

4.2.1 General effects of route entry on average fares and departures   For an initial investigation of the general effects of market entry, all non-stop route entry events which took place in the top 500 markets between 1996 and 2009 were identified. In sum, the sample consists of 197 route entries of LCCs and 237 route entries of NWCs. For the group of LCCs, Figure 2.16 plots the average market yields and the average number of departures eight quarters before and after the respective entry event.

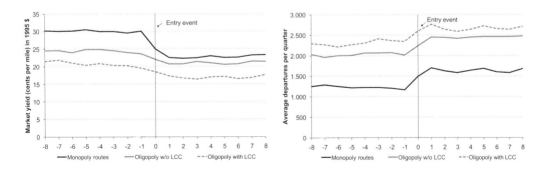

Figure 2.16   **Average yield and average departures for entry events in the top 500 markets two years before and after LCC entry events**

Sources: US DOT, T-100 Domestic Segment Data and Airline Origin and Destination Survey (DB1B).

As shown on the left side of Figure 2.16, entry on average leads to a significant decrease in market yield. As expected from the theoretical analysis in Section 2 above, the largest effects can be observed for entries of LCCs in monopoly routes. After an LCC has entered a former monopoly route, the average market yield drops by about 5 cents per mile (about 17 per cent) in the quarter of the entry event and a further 2 cents per mile in the quarter following entry leading to an average drop in yield of about 25 per cent. This effect is less pronounced for former oligopoly markets. Irrespective of the presence of a LCC in the market before entry, the average market yield drops by about 1 cent per mile in the quarter of entry and 1 additional cent per mile in the quarter following entry.

Turning from the left side of Figure 2.16 to the right side, the focus turns from the effects of entry on price to the corresponding effects of entry on quantity. In particular, the average number of departures per quarter is used to quantify the effect of LCC entries on the quantity provided by all airlines in the respective market. The analysis reveals that after a LCC has entered one of the top 500 routes, the average frequency of flights offered increased substantially in all types of markets. In the quarter in which LCC entry occurs, the frequency of departures increased on average by about 330 quarterly departures in former monopoly routes and additional 210 quarterly departures in the quarter following entry. The total increase of average frequency from the quarter before entry to the quarter after entry is about 440 quarterly departures in oligopoly markets in which no LCC was active before and about 410 quarterly departures in oligopoly markets in which at least one other LCC was already operating.

Turning from the effect of entry by a LCC to the corresponding effects of entry by a NWC, Figure 2.17 shows the results of the corresponding analysis for these types of entry.

As revealed by Figure 2.17, entries by NWCs have less pronounced effects on average market yields than LCC entries. For the cases of entry into oligopoly markets, no considerable effects on market yields can be observed. In case of former monopoly markets, the overall drop in average market yield amounts to about 2 cents (about 5 per cent). However, although the price effects are rather small, post-entry quantity shows comparable increases as in the case of LCCs. The average frequency of flights increased by about 380 quarterly departures in former monopolies, by about 280 departures per quarter in oligopolies without any LCC and by about 120 departures per quarter in oligopoly markets in which at least one other LCC is operating.

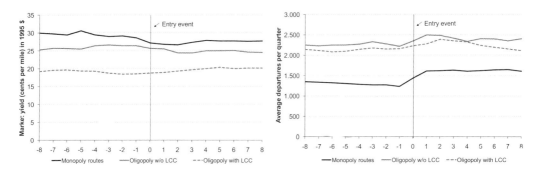

Figure 2.17   Average yield and average departures for entry events in the top 500 markets two years before and after NWC entry events

Sources: US DOT, T-100 Domestic Segment Data and Airline Origin and Destination Survey (DB1B).

Additionally, it is important to note that not only the supply (i.e. the number of departures) but also the demand (i.e. the number of passengers) increased following entry of a LCC or a NWC in one of the top 500 non-stop routes. For LCCs, the number of passengers carried per quarter increased from t_{-1} to t_{+1} by on average about 45 per cent for LCC entries in monopolies, about 25 per cent for LCC entries in oligopolies without LCC presence, and about 20 per cent for LCC entries in oligopolies with LCC presence. In case of NWC entries, the effects are significantly lower. The average number of passengers carried per quarter increases by about 23 per cent in former monopoly routes, by about 16 per cent in oligopolies without LCC presence and by only about 4 per cent in oligopolies with LCC presence. Interestingly, as our analysis does not find any effects of LCC or NWC entries on load factors, the entry-induced increase in supply is largely matched by increases in demand. Due to the increase in departures, travellers do not only profit from lower prices but also experience a higher service quality in terms of flight frequency.

Although these results should only be considered as rather rough estimates of the price and quantity effects of entry by LCCs and NWCs in the top 500 non-stop airport pair markets, the results clearly suggest substantial increases in consumer welfare when a carrier, especially a LCC, decides to enter a certain (concentrated) non-stop airport pair. These empirical findings confirm the results of the simple Cournot models discussed in Section 2 which suggested that low-cost entry (into a monopoly market) leads to larger price decreases than entry of an equally efficient firm.

4.2.2 Specific effects of route entries by a low-cost carrier   Following the study of general effects of route entry on route average fares and demand in the top 500 markets, this section analyses specific effects of entry by a LCC in a short-, medium- and long-haul route. Although the focus in this chapter is on entry into airport pairs rather than entry into the domestic US airline industry generally, the appearance and growth of JetBlue Airways allows the coverage of both categories.

4.2.2.1 A brief characterization of JetBlue Airways
JetBlue was founded by David Neeleman in February 1999 under the name 'NewAir'. Neeleman as well as several of JetBlue's key executives were former Southwest employees. In September 1999 the airline was awarded 75 take-off and landing slots at New York's JFK airport, followed by the granting of formal US authorization in February 2000. JetBlue started operations on 11 February 2000 with services from New York JFK to Buffalo and Fort Lauderdale and rapidly extended its route network in the following years. In December 2009, the network included 60 destinations in 21 US states complemented by destinations in 11 countries in the Caribbean and Latin America. JetBlue operates a base at New York's JFK airport and has developed focus city operations[27] in Boston, Orlando, Fort Lauderdale, Long Beach and San Juan (Puerto Rico). In 2005, JetBlue transported about 14.5 million passengers on US domestic flights. This number increased to about 20.4 million passengers in 2009 – a share of about 3.3 per cent of all domestic passengers – making JetBlue the ninth-largest airline in the United States. Despite the rapid growth of JetBlue in partly difficult periods of the US economy, the airline realized an overall net income of $201 million (after subtracting the net losses experienced in four of the ten business years).[28]

Although JetBlue is usually classified as a low-cost carrier, its business strategy has certain specific characteristics. First, the airline provides high-quality service in several important service

---

27   A focus city is typically defined as a location that is not a hub, but from which the airline has non-stop flights to several destinations other than its hubs.

28   The net losses were realized in 2000 ($21 million), 2005 ($20 million), 2006 ($1 million) and 2008 ($76 million). For the raw data, see http://www.transtats.bts.gov/Data_Elements.aspx?Data=6 (accessed on 22 December 2010).

dimensions such as in-flight entertainment and pre-assigned leather seats with more legroom. Second, JetBlue does not only concentrate – like most other LCCs – on short- and medium-haul markets but also enters long-haul markets typically only offered by the network carriers. Third, although considered a LCC, JetBlue has recently started to enter alliance agreements with foreign and domestic network carriers such as Aer Lingus and Lufthansa (code-share agreements) or American (interline agreement).[29] JetBlue is regarded as a future member of one of the three large global airlines alliances: Star, SkyTeam and oneworld.[30]

Despite this rather unconventional business strategy for a LCC, a quick look at the cost side of JetBlue reveals that it actually is a 'low-cost' airline. While the network carriers show average costs of 10.96 cents per available seat mile (ex fuel), the average number for the LCC group drops to 7.06 cents. In 2009, JetBlue had average costs of 6.62 and therefore clearly below even the average cost level in the group of LCCs.[31] Complementary to the low-cost–low fare approach, JetBlue offers a high-quality product. According to the AQR Scores described in Section 3.4 above, JetBlue always had a top rank in both the entire group of major airlines and the subgroup of low-cost airlines since its first appearance in the rating in 2003.

Given the availability of cost-level data and service-level data, the position of JetBlue in relation to the other major US airlines can be visualized by a so-called strategic map which plots the average costs per available seat mile against the AQR score. Figure 2.18 shows the strategic map for the year 2009.

As shown in Figure 2.18, the competition landscape of the US airline industry can be broadly delineated into two strategic groups: a group of LCCs that can be characterized by offering a

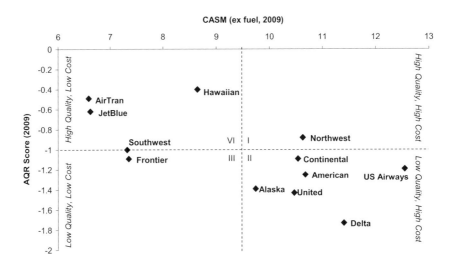

Figure 2.18   Strategic map of the US airline industry

Sources: 2010 AQR Report and US DOT, Form 41 via BTS, Schedule T2, P6 and P52.

---

29   See http://www.jetblue.com/about/ourcompany/lufthansa/ for a detailed characterization of the agreement with Lufthansa (accessed on 22 December 2010).

30   Since Lufthansa acquired a 19 per cent stake in JetBlue in December 2007, Star Alliance is the most likely choice.

31   Data source: US DOT Form 41 via BTS, Schedule T2, P6 and P52.

high-quality product for a low price and a group of NWCs with basically inverted characteristics. Although this result is partly driven by the definition of service quality which does not take particular advantages of the NWCs such as a large (domestic and international) travel network into account, the basic message of Figure 2.18 would likely hold if these factors are taken into account. With respect to JetBlue, Figure 2.18 confirms that the airline has a very favourable position, with the second rank in the cost dimension and the third rank in the quality dimension. These characteristics make JetBlue a particularly interesting object for the study of the effects of entry into short-, medium- and long-haul routes.

4.2.2.2 Effects of JetBlue entry into short-, medium- and long-haul routes
Given the characterization of JetBlue as a low-cost airline and the study of general effects of entry into the top 500 markets, an investigation of the market dynamics and effects of entry by JetBlue into particular markets is the final step in a comprehensive analysis of market entry events. As a starting point for such a detailed assessment, Figure 2.19 provides an overview of the overall number of entries and exits of JetBlue between 2000 and 2009.

As shown in Figure 2.19, after moderate entry activity in the first years of the company, the number of route entries on average increased significantly between 2004 and 2008 with a peak of 34 route entries in 2006. The first exits were observed in 2004 with a peak in 2008, probably at least partly triggered by the economic recession. In sum, from the beginning of its operations in 2000 until the end of 2009, JetBlue entered 142 airport pairs and exited 24: 63 of the entered routes have not been served by any other airline before in the sample period from 1995 to 2009.

Given this initial description of the patterns of entry and exit of JetBlue, the remainder of this section concentrates on the effects of JetBlue entry into particular airport pair markets. Having in mind the business concept of LCCs generally and JetBlue in particular, the subsequent analysis is separated into a short-haul route (New York JFK–Rochester), a medium-haul route (New York JFK–Fort Lauderdale) and a long-haul route (New York JFK–Seattle).

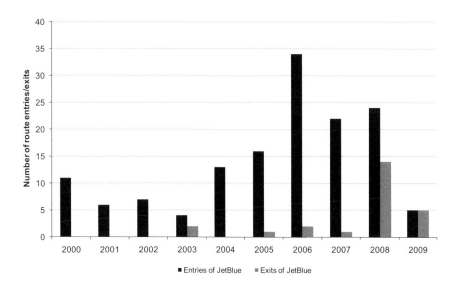

Figure 2.19   Number of entries and exits of JetBlue (2000–2009)
Source: US DOT, T-100 Domestic Segment Data.

4.2.2.2.1 JetBlue entry into a short-haul route: *New York JFK–Rochester*

The first entry event studied in the following is JetBlue's entry into the short-haul route between New York JFK and Rochester. The distance between both airports is 264 miles. The market dynamics as reported in T-100 Domestic Segment Data are displayed in the following Table 2.3.

As shown in Table 2.3, in the beginning of the sample period the route was operated by Delta only. Following a period in which the route was not operated at all, American Airlines and later Trans World entered the market. In the third quarter of 2000, JetBlue entered the market. Following the exit of American six quarters later, JetBlue was the only airline operating the route between the first quarter of 2002 and the second quarter of 2006. Since then, the route is operated by JetBlue and Delta.

Based on this characterization of the market dynamics for the sample period, Figure 2.20 shows the average market fare and passengers on the New York JFK–Rochester route between 1995 and 2009.

Table 2.3   Market dynamics on the New York JFK–Rochester route (264 miles)

Year/Quarter	Operating airlines
1995/1–1996/1	Delta Air Lines
1996/2–1997/4	No airline in the market according to T-100 data
1998/1–1998/3	American Airlines
1998/4–2000/2	American Airlines and Trans World Airways
2000/3–2001/4	American Airlines and JetBlue (LCC entry)
2002/1–2006/2	JetBlue (LCC)
2006/3–2009/4	JetBlue (LCC) and Delta Air Lines

Data source: US DOT, T-100 Domestic Segment Data.

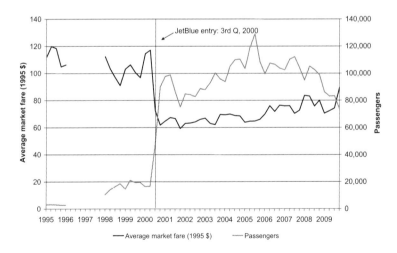

Figure 2.20   Average market fare and passengers on the New York JFK–Rochester route (1995–2009)

Sources: US DOT, T-100 Domestic Segment Data and Airline Origin and Destination Survey (DB1B).

As shown in Figure 2.20, the entry of JetBlue was followed by a large increase in the number of passengers travelling on the route. In particular, the number of passengers increased from on average about 71,950 passengers in the year before entry to about 333,600 passengers in the year after entry. Since its entry in the third quarter of 2000, the average passenger market share of JetBlue lay at about 93.7 per cent (within a value spectrum of 80.4 per cent and 100 per cent). Although the entry of Delta Airlines in the third quarter of 2006 led to market share losses of up to 19.6 per cent per quarter, the average market share of Delta lied at 9.2 per cent.

With respect to the average market price, the entry of JetBlue had a very significant impact, leading to a drop in the average price from \$106.4 to \$65.9 (about 61 per cent) in the first year after entry. Interestingly, the entry of Delta in the third quarter of 2006 on the one hand was followed by a one-time increase in demand. On the other hand, however, the entry of Delta appears to have no apparent effect on the average fare level. This finding for the New York JFK–Rochester route is a nice confirmation of the more general trend identified in the preceding section: while the entry of LCCs typically causes a significant drop in average market price, this effect often cannot be found in case of entries by network carriers. One explanation for this observation is that even the monopoly price of a LCC cannot be met by a NWC and the reason for entry into the particular market might not be to compete fiercely in order to realize a profit on that particular market but simply to collect passengers for further flights in the route network of the respective NWC.

4.2.2.2.2 JetBlue entry into a medium-haul route: *New York JFK–Fort Lauderdale*
The second entry event studied in the following is JetBlue's entry into the medium-haul route between New York JFK and Fort Lauderdale. The distance between both airports is 1069 miles. The market dynamics as reported in T-100 Domestic Segment Data are displayed in Table 2.4.

As shown in Table 2.4, in the beginning of the sample period, the route was operated by Delta only. Following the entry of Trans World in the fourth quarter of 1997, Tower Air decided to enter the market in the third quarter of 1998. The entry of JetBlue in the first quarter of 2000 was immediately followed by the exit of Tower Air (2000/2) and Trans World (2001/1).[32] Since then, the route is operated by JetBlue and Delta.

Based on this characterization of the market dynamics for the sample period, Figure 2.21 shows the average market fare and passengers on the New York JFK–Fort Lauderdale route between 1995 and 2009.

Table 2.4   Market dynamics on the New York JFK–Fort Lauderdale route (1069 miles)

Year/quarter	Operating airlines
1995/1–1997/3	Delta Air Lines
1997/4–1998/2	Delta Air Lines and Trans World
1998/3–1999/4	Delta Air Lines, Trans World and Tower Air
2000/1	Delta Air Lines, Trans World, Tower Air and JetBlue (LCC entry)
2000/2–2000/4	Delta Air Lines, Trans World and JetBlue (LCC)
2001/1–2009/4	Delta Air Lines and JetBlue (LCC)

Data source: US DOT, T-100 Domestic Segment Data.

32   Tower Air ceased operations in May 2000 and Trans World was acquired by American in April 2001.

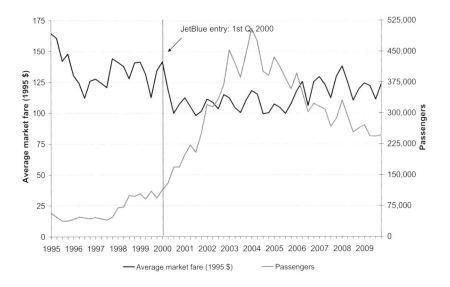

Figure 2.21   Average market fare and passengers on the New York JFK–Fort Lauderdale route (1995–2009)

Sources: US DOT, T-100 Domestic Segment Data and Airline Origin and Destination Survey (DB1B).

As shown in Figure 2.21, the entry of JetBlue again appears to have caused a clear increase in average passengers from on average about 399,500 passengers in the year before entry to 582,850 passengers in the year after entry. Since its entry in the first quarter of 2000, the average passenger market share of JetBlue lay at about 69.5 per cent (within a value spectrum from 64.6 per cent to 79.4 per cent), leaving the rest of the market for the only remaining direct competitor, Delta.

With respect to the average market price, the entry of JetBlue had a moderate impact leading to a drop in the average price from $128.1 to $110.6 (about 16 per cent) in the first year after entry. Interestingly, the average market price remained largely stable, although the last couple of years saw a very significant decrease in passenger numbers. While a record number of about 505,200 passengers travelled the route in the fourth quarter of 2003, the fourth quarter of 2009 only registered about 246,100 passengers on the same route. This decrease in passengers is almost certainly related to the inauguration of two additional JetBlue non-stop services to Fort Lauderdale from New York's La Guardia (LGA) airport in September 2004 and from Newark International Airport (EWR) in October 2005.

Investigating the potential interrelationships between market entry in the second and third airport in the Greater New York region in general and the potential competition between the three airports in particular a little closer, Figure 2.22 shows the average market fare and number of passengers for the New York LGA and EWR–Fort Lauderdale routes (1995–2009).

As shown in the left graph of Figure 2.22, JetBlue's entry into the LGA–FLL market (with a travel distance of 1076 miles) did not have a significant impact on the average market fare. One key reason for this observation can be seen in the fact that (in addition to an alternating number of NWCs) another LCC, Spirit Airlines, already entered the route in the first quarter of 1999 (the dotted line in Figure 2.22) and caused significant reductions in the average market fare. With respect to the number of passengers, JetBlue's entry was followed by a very significant but only

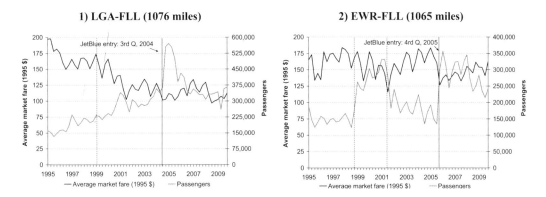

Figure 2.22   Average market fare and passengers on the New York LGA and EWR–Fort Lauderdale routes (1995–2009)

Sources: US DOT, T-100 Domestic Segment Data and Airline Origin and Destination Survey (DB1B).

temporary increase in demand. In the following years, demand settled down at about the pre-entry level. By the end of 2009, the route was operated by Delta, Spirit and JetBlue.

Turning from the LGA–FLL route to the EWR–FLL route (with a travel distance of 1065 miles), the right graph in Figure 2.22 shows that JetBlue's entry had a significant impact on the average market price from on average $172.0 in the year before entry to $134.8 in the first year after entry (a price reduction of about 27.6 per cent). Interestingly, the route was (in addition to an alternating number of NWCs) also served by Spirit Airlines between the fourth quarter of 1998 and the third quarter of 2001 (delineated by the dotted lines in Figure 2.22). As shown in Figure 2.22, the entry of Spirit led to a moderate downward trend in fares, but a very pronounced increase in passengers. Following the exit of Spirit, the number of passengers declined (and the average market price increased accordingly) until JetBlue decided to enter the route in the fourth quarter of 2005. This entry boosted the number of passengers from about 647,700 passengers in the year before entry to about 1,213,200 passengers in the year after entry. Since the fourth quarter of 2005, the route is operated by Continental and JetBlue with the former having a market share of about 63 per cent (by the end of 2009), leaving about 37 per cent for JetBlue.

After analysing the entry activity of JetBlue at all three large airports in the Greater New York region, the question of the reasons for such a large-scale entry remains open. One possible explanation could be that JetBlue would like to reduce the likelihood of market entry by other LCCs in the New York City–FLL market. Another explanation could be that customers do not view JFK, LGA and EWR as completely interchangeable. For example, as LGA is located closest to Downtown Manhattan, a group of customers may prefer to use this airport although prices at the alternative airports may be lower. Furthermore, the entry by JetBlue into EWR might be motivated by the significant role of the airport as (inter)national hub. In fact, plotting the relative average market prices for EWR and JFK/LGA against the volume shares of JFK/LGA for non-stop flights to FLL (shown in Figure 2.23) suggests that competition between EWR and JFK is stronger than between EWR and LGA.

As shown in Figure 2.23, the relative average market price of EWR flights compared to JFK and LGA flights increased from 2001 to 2005, reflecting the exit of Spirit and the absence of a LCC before the entry of JetBlue in the fourth quarter of 2005. Given the relative price increase for EWR flights, economic theory would on the one hand expect a drop in the volume share of EWR. This

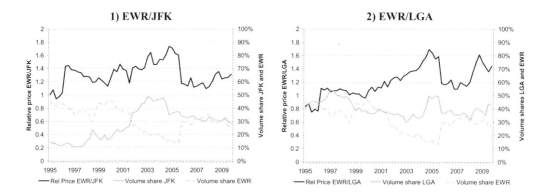

**Figure 2.23   Relative market prices and volume shares for EWR and JFK/LGA for non-stop
flights to Fort Lauderdale (1995–2009)**

Sources: US DOT, T-100 Domestic Segment Data and Airline Origin and Destination Survey (DB1B).

effect is clearly shown in Figure 2.23. On the other hand, an increase in the relative price for EWR
flights would create an expectation of a corresponding increase in the volume share of airports
considered as substitutes. In this respect, Figure 2.23 reveals that the relative price increase for
EWR flights at both alternative airports only led to a corresponding increase in the volume share
of JFK while the LGA volume share follows a different trend. This impression from the study of
Figure 2.22 is actually confirmed by the correlation coefficients: while the correlation coefficient
between the relative EWR/JFK price and the volume share of JFK can be calculated to 0.509, the
correlation coefficient between the EWR/LGA price and the volume share of LGA is found to be
–0.138. This finding can be taken as piece of evidence for direct competition between EWR and
JFK – potentially as a gateway for international flights (connecting to/from Florida)[33] – while
no indication for direct competition between EWR and LGA can be found. As a consequence,
JetBlue's entry into the EWR–FLL route might have been a more general move to secure and
expand its role in international and long-haul domestic traffic in the Greater New York region.[34]

4.2.2.2.3 JetBlue entry into a long-haul route: New York JFK–Seattle

The third entry event studied in the following is JetBlue's entry into the long-haul route between
New York JFK and Seattle. The distance between both airports is 2421 miles. The market dynamics
as reported in T-100 Domestic Segment Data are displayed in Table 2.5.

As shown in Table 2.5, in the beginning of the sample period, the route was operated by Trans
World and United. In the following years, American entered the route for the second and third
quarter and exited for the fourth and first quarter. Furthermore, since the fourth quarter of 1997,
United took over the role of Trans World in the sense that it operated the route for the entire year.
In the second quarter of 2001, JetBlue entered the market and since the second quarter of 2003
competes with American and Delta over the entire year.

---

33   LGA is a perimeter-controlled airport that can only be used for flights with a length of not more than
1,500 miles. This regulation rules out La Guardia as potential (inter)national hub as the perimeter rule applies
for both international flights and (long-haul) domestic US flights.

34   In addition to FLL, JetBlue has started non-stop services from EWR to Orlando, Tampa, Fort Myers
and West Palm Beach.

Table 2.5   Market dynamics on the New York JFK–Seattle route (2421 miles)

Year/Quarter	Operating airlines
1995/1	Trans World and United Airlines
1995/2–1995/3	Trans World, United Airlines and American Airlines
1995/4–1996/1	Trans World and United Airlines
1996/2–1996/3	Trans World, United Airlines and American Airlines
1996/4–1997/1	Trans World and United Airlines
1997/2–1997/3	Trans World, United Airlines, American Airlines and Delta Air Lines
1997/4	United Airlines, American Airlines and Delta Air Lines
1998/1	United Airlines and Delta Air Lines
1998/2–1998/3	United Airlines, American Airlines and Delta Air Lines
1998/4–1999/1	United Airlines and Delta Air Lines
1999/2–1999/4	United Airlines, American Airlines and Delta Air Lines
2000/1	United Airlines and Delta Air Lines
2000/2–2000/4	United Airlines, American Airlines and Delta Air Lines
2001/2–2001/3	United Airlines, American Airlines, Delta Air Lines and JetBlue (LCC entry)
2001/4–2002/1	United Airlines, Delta Air Lines and JetBlue (LCC)
2002/2–2003/1	United Airlines, American Airlines, Delta Air Lines and JetBlue (LCC)
2003/2–2009/4	American Airlines, Delta Air Lines and JetBlue (LCC)

Source: US DOT, T-100 Domestic Segment Data.

Based on this characterization of the market dynamics for the sample period, Figure 2.24 shows the average market fare and passengers on the New York JFK–Seattle route between 1995 and 2009.

As shown in Figure 2.24, the entry of JetBlue had a very significant impact on the average market price, leading to a drop from $380.5 to $267.1 (about 42 per cent) in the first year after entry. This effect is particularly remarkable because the market was already operated by two network carriers in the winter and three network carriers in the summer before the entry of JetBlue. Without being able to provide further evidence, it seems unlikely that the New York JFK–Seattle market experienced fierce (price) competition prior to the entry of JetBlue. As a consequence, the example suggests that even entry into an already oligopolistic market can cause significant positive effects on average fares and demand in cases in which competition intensity between the incumbent airlines appears to be low.

With respect to the number of passengers travelling between New York JFK and Seattle, Figure 2.25 shows large seasonal effects. This seasonality is also reflected in the market dynamics above by the reoccurring entry/exit of American Airlines in the summer/winter months. The entry of JetBlue appears to have caused a clear increase in average passengers from on average about 221,500 passengers in the year before entry to about 285,150 passengers in the year after entry, however, without affecting the seasonality of demand. Furthermore, although JetBlue's entry into the market was apparently successful and led to the expected average fare reductions following LCC entry, Figure 2.25 shows that JetBlue's passenger market shares are significantly lower than in the short- and medium-haul markets analysed.

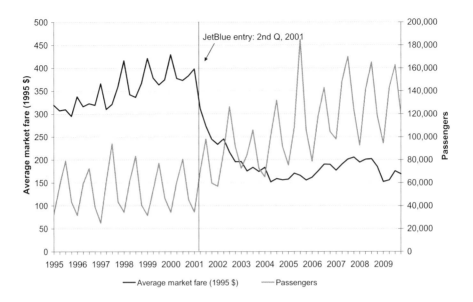

Figure 2.24   Average market fare and passengers on the New York JFK–Seattle route (1995–2009)

Source: US DOT, T-100 Domestic Segment Data and Airline Origin and Destination Survey (DB1B).

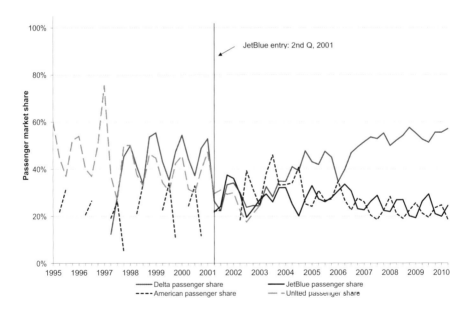

Figure 2.25   Passenger market shares for the New York JFK–Seattle route (1995–2009)

Source: US DOT, T-100 Domestic Segment Data.

As shown in Figure 2.25, although JetBlue managed to gain a passenger market share of up to 37.4 per cent in the first four quarters after entry, its average market share for the entire period of its market presence lies at about 26.4 per cent. Interestingly, since 2004, Delta has managed to increase its passenger market share from on average 29.1 per cent to 49.2 per cent, leaving both American and JetBlue with market share losses. As a consequence, it can be concluded from the example of the New York JFK–Seattle route that LCC entry does not guarantee a sweeping victory over the respective NWCs. In fact, the example has shown that NWCs are not only able to defend their market share but even have opportunities to extend it despite the presence of a LCC.

4.2.2.3 Estimation of the welfare effects of selected market entry events
Given the availability of detailed demand and fares data for the particular short-, medium- and long-haul routes studied above, this section aims at estimating the consumer welfare effects of these selected market entry events. In general, such an estimation needs to differentiate between two separate effects. On the one hand, a decrease in the average market price increases the consumer surplus for existing customers. If Q^M is the monopoly quantity, Q^D the duopoly quantity (with $Q^M < Q^D$), P^M the monopoly price and P^D the duopoly price (with $P^M > P^D$), the size of this *savings effect S* can be approximated by the following expression

$$S = Q^M*(P^M - P^D) \qquad (26)$$

On the other hand, a decrease in the average market price induces new customers to buy the product, thereby creating an additional consumer surplus. Assuming a linear demand function, the size of this *expansion effect E* can be approximated by the following expression

$$E = 0.5\,[(Q^D - Q^M)*(P^M - P^D)] \qquad (27)$$

Technically, the latter effect reduces the deadweight loss which is generally created by prices above marginal costs. The *consumer welfare effect of market entry CWE* (for a fixed time period) is then given by the sum of the savings effect S and the expansion effect E:

$$CWE = S+E = Q^M*(P^M - P^D) + 0.5\,[(Q^D - Q^M)*(P^M - P^D)] \qquad (28)$$

It is important to note that although equation (28) focuses on the transition from a monopoly state to a duopoly state, the general mechanics of the approach remain unchanged for other types of entry events, such as entry into a duopoly or triopoly market.

Given this basic theoretical framework, Table 2.6 presents the market data and the estimates of the consumer welfare effects for the three market entries of JetBlue discussed in the preceding sections.

As shown in Table 2.6, all three market entries led to significant increases in consumer welfare. While entry and competition in the short- and medium-haul markets allowed consumer savings of about $8 million in the year after entry, the estimation for the long-haul market suggest consumer welfare gains of nearly $29 million. The larger effect is basically driven by the larger travel distance and the correspondingly higher prices. Comparing the short- and medium-haul markets, the results also reveal that the absolute increase in consumer welfare is a function of both the price differential and the change in demand. While the price drop following entry was much more significant on the short-haul market, entry into the medium-haul market – with a lower impact on fares – in sum led to comparable total increases in consumer welfare.

Table 2.6   Consumer welfare effects of selected market entries of JetBlue

	New York JFK–Rochester	New York JFK–Fort Lauderdale	New York JFK–Seattle
Market data			
Average market fare in the year before entry	$106.4	$128.1	$380.5
Average market fare in the year after entry	$65.9	$110.6	$267.1
Number of passengers in the year before entry	71,949	399,496	221,498
Number of passengers in the year after entry	333,603	582,848	285,163
Consumer welfare effects			
Consumer welfare increase for existing demand	$2,919,215	$6,999,171	$25,112,012
Consumer welfare increase for additional demand	$5,308,095	$1,606,164	$3,608,963
Total increase in consumer welfare in the year after entry	$8,227,311	$8,605,335	$28,720,975

Source (market data only): US DOT, Airline Origin and Destination Survey (DB1B).

Although the estimation of the welfare effects of selected market entries of JetBlue come to important and relevant results, it should be mentioned at this point that these results should be understood as ballpark figures rather than a sophisticated econometric estimation (that would allow controlling for the impact of other factors). This is particularly true because the average price per airport pair used for the estimations on the one hand masks the prices charged by the different airlines and on the other hand ignores the frequently used possibilities of both groups of airlines to price discriminate. Furthermore, with respect to the size of the effect, it should be remembered that the derived figures only refer to the consumer welfare effects of entry of one particular low-cost airline in three particular markets for the 12 months following entry. This suggests that the overall effects of the market appearance of LCCs such as JetBlue and most prominently Southwest are so significant that it appears justified to speak of the 'low-cost carrier service revolution'.

5. Conclusion

Providing airlines with the freedom to decide on market entry was one of the key accomplishments of the deregulation of the US airline industry in 1978. Since then, airlines made frequent use of the gained possibilities to optimize their route networks and to provide efficient air services to their customers. Although market entry in deregulated US airline markets has been the focus of prior research, significant recent market developments such as severe external and internal shocks or the continuing growth of LCCs demands a revisit of this important topic. Against this background and guided by a primer on the economics of entry in airline markets, the chapter uses T-100 traffic data and DB1B fare data from the US Department of Transportation to identify recent trends in the evolution of the domestic US airline industry in general and patterns and effects of entry by network carriers and LCCs in particular.

Summarizing the key insights of the three main sections of the chapter, the primer on the *economics of entry in airline markets* showed in its theoretical part that market entry generally can be expected to lead to a drop in price and a corresponding increase in consumer surplus. However, in the case of positive fixed costs, the desirability of (additional) entry depends on factors such as market size, number of incumbent firms already in the market and the amount of fixed costs needed to start production. Furthermore, it was shown (for a certain market specification) that the relative gains in consumer welfare are highest in the case of entry into a monopoly market, simply because the benefits of competition are brought to the respective market. Additionally, it was shown that the introduction of asymmetric marginal costs leads to asymmetric market shares as the more efficient firm produces more (and realizes higher profits) than the less efficient firm. Consumers benefit through a drop in the equilibrium price compared to the case of a symmetric cost structure. Complementary to these theoretical insights, the applied part of the primer on entry in airline markets showed that although deregulation of the US airline industry provided the airlines with the freedom to enter routes on the basis of individual assessments of benefits and costs, structural and strategic entry barriers might impede market entry in a deregulated environment.

The section on *recent market developments in the US airline industry* revealed that the industry on average experienced a substantial growth in the sample period from 1995 to 2009. However, although the network carriers still carry the majority of domestic passengers, low-cost airlines were able to increase their overall passenger share from 13.3 per cent in 1995 to 29.8 per cent in 2009. This trend is also reflected in the development of market concentration, which showed a decreasing share of monopoly markets and increasing shares of markets in which NWCs and LCCs directly compete ('route overlap'). With respect to fares, the annual US domestic average itinerary fare (in real terms) experienced a significant downward trend in the sample period. A separation of the market yield with respect to the number of competitors per route showed that only the network carriers experienced a significant downward trend in both monopoly and oligopoly markets in the sample period. In the service level category, airline performance fluctuates significantly; however, the group of LCCs typically offers a higher-quality product than the group of NWCs. This competitive disadvantage of the network carriers is also identified in the cost level category which showed that the average cost level of the group of NWCs lies about 4 cents per mile (equal to about 55 per cent) above the average cost level of the group of LCCs. These quality and cost disadvantages of the group of NWCs are also reflected in the profit situation. While the group of NWCs in sum lost $35,418 million in the period from 2000 of 2009, the group of LCCs earned $8,038 million.

Finally, the section on *patterns and effects of market entry* in the US airline industry found significant entry activity for both NWCs and LCCs throughout the sample period between 1995 and 2009. However, while the network carriers show significant entry activity between 1996 and 2000, the average number of entries dropped significantly from 2003 onwards. Since 2004, the group of low-cost carriers has entered more markets per year than the group of network carriers. In addition, the analysis revealed that on average more than half of the entries of both groups took place in relatively small markets and about 40 per cent in new markets that have not been served before in the sample period by any other airline. Furthermore, it was found that LCCs recently started to enter long-haul markets with a travel distance of more than 1,500 miles.

Turning from the patterns of entry to the effects of entry, an aggregated analysis of all entry events in the top 500 routes between 1995 and 2009 showed that entry by a LCC on average led to a significant decrease in market yield. The largest effect – a reduction of market yield by about 5 cents per mile (about 17 per cent) in the quarter of the entry event and further 2 cents per mile in the quarter following entry (in sum about 25 per cent) – was observed for entries of LCCs in monopoly routes, followed by entry into oligopoly markets. By contrast, entry events by NWCs generally have less pronounced effects on average market yields. For the cases of entry into oligopoly markets, no considerable effects on market yields were observed. In case of former monopoly markets, the overall reduction in average market yield amounts to about 2 cents per mile.

The analysis of the specific effects of market entry by the LCC JetBlue Airways in short-, medium- and long-haul routes basically confirmed the trends of the aggregate analysis. Entry by JetBlue in the respective markets led to price reductions between on average 16 and 61 per cent in the year after entry. The number of passengers increased accordingly. An estimation of the welfare effects of three particular market entry events of JetBlue revealed significant increases in consumer welfare. While entry and competition in the short- and medium-haul markets allowed consumer savings of about $8 million in the year after entry, the estimation for the long-haul market suggest consumer welfare gains of nearly $29 million again only in the year after entry.

Given this recapitulation of the key result of the chapter, it can be concluded that the appearance and growth of LCCs surely is one of the most important developments in the deregulation era of the US airline industry. Given the substantial effects of low-cost carrier entry on market price and therefore consumer welfare, the responsible competition authorities are well advised to closely monitor the industry and to intervene in cases of welfare-reducing strategic behaviour of incumbents that only aim at deterring market entry of potential competitors. Such a proactive competition policy is an important cornerstone in an overall strategy to keep the US airline industry competitive and to continue harvesting the sweet fruits of deregulation.

References

Bailey, E., Kaplan, D. and Sibley, D. (1983) On the contestability of airline markets: some further evidence. In J. Finsinger (ed.), *Economic Analysis of Regulated Markets*. London: Macmillan, 48–64.

Bain, J. (1956) *Barriers to New Competition*. Cambridge, MA: Harvard University Press.

Baumol, W., Panzar, J. and Willig, R. (1982) *Contestable Markets and the Theory of Industry Structure*. San Diego, CA: Saunders College Publishing/Harcourt Brace.

Besanko, D., Dranove, D. and M. Shanley, M. (1996) *The Economics of Strategy*. New York: John Wiley & Sons.

Brueckner, J., Lee, D. and Singer, E. (2010) *City-Pairs vs. Airport-Pairs: A Market-Definition Methodology for the Airline Industry*. Working Paper, University of California, Irvine.

Carlton, D. and Perloff, J. (2000) *Modern Industrial Organization*. Reading, MA: Pearson.

Fisher, F. (1979) Diagnosing monopoly. *Quarterly Review of Economics and Business*, 19, 7–33.

Geroski, P. (1995) What do we know about entry? *International Journal of Industrial Organization* 13, 421–440.

Geroski, P. (1991) *Market Dynamics and Entry*. Oxford: John Wiley & Sons.

Gudmundsson, S. and van Kranenburg, H. (2002) New airline entry rates in deregulated air transport markets. *Transportation Research Part E*, 38, 205–219.

Hüschelrath, K. (2005) Strategic behaviour of incumbents – rationality, welfare and antitrust policy. In P. Forsyth, D. Gillen, O. Mayer and H.-M. Niemeier (eds), *Competition versus Predation in Aviation Markets*. Aldershot: Ashgate, 3–36.

Hüschelrath, K. (2009) *Competition Policy Analysis – An Integrated Approach*. Heidelberg: Physica.

Hüschelrath, K.and Müller, K. (2012) Low Cost Carriers and the Evolution of the Domestic U.S. Airline Industry. *Competition and Regulation in Network Industries*, 13(2), 133–159.

Hüschelrath, K. and Müller, K. (2013) Patterns and Effects of Entry in U.S. Airline Markets. *Journal of Industry, Competition and Trade*, forthcoming.

Joskow, A., Werden, G. and Johnson, R. (1994) Entry, exit, and performance in airline markets. *International Journal of Industrial Organization*, 12, 457–471.

Lin, J.-S., Dresner, M. and Windle, R. (2002) Determinants of price reactions to entry in the U.S. airline industry. *Transportation Journal*, 41, 5–22.

McAfee, P. and Mialon, H. (2004) *Barriers to Entry in Antitrust Analysis*. Pasadena, CA: Working Paper, California Institute of Technology.

Montaguti, E., Kuester, S. and Robertson, T. (2002) Entry strategy for radical product innovations: a conceptual model and propositional inventory. *International Journal of Research in Marketing*, 19, 21–42.

O'Connor, W. (2001) *An Introduction to Airline Economics*. Westport, CT: Praeger.

Phillips, C. (1969) *The Economics of Regulation*. Homewood, IL: Irwin.

Saloner, G., Shepard, A. and Podolny, J. (2001) *Strategic Management*. New York: John Wiley & Sons.

Slovin, M., Sushka, M. and Hudson, C. (1991) Deregulation, contestability, and airline acquisitions. *Journal of Financial Economics*, 30, 231–251.

Stigler, G. (1968) *The Organization of Industry*. Homewood, IL: Irwin.

US Department of Transportation (1997) *The Low Cost Airline Service Revolution*. Washington, DC: US Department of Transportation.

US General Accounting Office (2001) *Aviation Competition – Challenges in Enhancing Competition in Dominated Markets*. GAO/01-518T, Washington, DC: US General Accounting Office.

Vietor, R. (1990) Contrived competition: airline regulation and deregulation, 1925–1988. *Business History Review*, 64, 61–108.

Chapter 3

Competition among European Airlines – on the Role of Product Differentiation

Karsten Fröhlich and Hans-Martin Niemeier

> It is evident that virtually all products are differentiated, at least slightly, and that over a wide range of economic activity differentiation is of considerable importance.
>
> Chamberlin (1933: 57)

1. Introduction

For a long time in its history the airline business was a highly regulated and nationalized industry. Almost every country in Europe had its respective flag carrier,[1] markets were sealed off, competition was limited and effectively non-existent. International flights were regulated through restrictive cabotage rights (some of which are still in place) and restrictions of trade in air services. Each legacy carrier enjoyed a high degree of market power within its market. In the 1990s the European aviation market was liberalized, somewhat later than the liberalization process in the US, which took place in the 1980s. This induced to a lesser degree competition among legacy carriers, yet it sparked the introduction of a new business model; that of Low-cost Carriers (LCCs).[2]

Since the rise of LCCs, the airline industry has undergone profound changes. The issue of the correct business model has become increasingly important. The legacy carriers especially had to adapt their way of doing business and needed to cut costs. At the same time it can also be seen that not all LCCs are the same. Some have departed from the models of LCCs of the first days, like Ryanair and Southwest, and adopted a different approach. There is an increasing and ongoing debate over what a LCC really is. The recent move of Air Berlin, a former charter and LCC to join the oneworld alliance reflects the carrier's evolution.[3] Ryanair announced some time ago that they had plans for opening long-haul routes. The competitive responses of airlines following liberalization were and are in terms of product differentiation rather than direct price competition with the same product.

It is therefore surprising that the issue of product differentiation received so little attention in the air transport literature, although it is a well-researched field of industrial economics[4] and offers a variety of models to understand and explain the product choices and competitive strategies of airlines. Only in Shaw (2004, Chapter 5) and Klaas and Klein (2005) the issue is dealt with, but these authors used a marketing and business orientated approach based on the tools from strategic management. Borenstein and Netz (1999) and Salvanes et al. (2005) do in fact apply models of

---

1   In fact, flag carriers were typical in Europe, yet not in the USA, which never had a flag carrier. Hence the notation of legacy carriers is more precise in a global context.

2   Availability of secondary airports facilitated their development.

3   Albeit it could also be a sign of deeper rooted problems with the carrier's business model.

4   A review on the economic theory of product differentiation can be found in Eaton and Lipsey (1989) and in the book by Beath and Katsoulacos (1991).

product differentiation to the aviation industry; however they focus on the distribution of departure times.

This chapter will explore the dynamic evolution of competition in the aviation industry through the lens of product differentiation models. It starts with the situation prior to liberalization and explains how airlines chose their level of quality during that time. It then proceeds chronologically and applies different models of product differentiation to the changing business environment airlines faced. Thereby, the chapter will explain the necessary parts of the economic theory as it goes along. The chapter then proceeds to the emergence of LCCs and altering business models. The subsequent sections look at some extensions and the implications the product choices have on airline business models. The final section provides a summary of our discussion and a conclusion.

Before going on with the actual discussion, it is important to clarify definitions of product and product differentiation. Lipczynski et al. (2005), for example, describe product differentiation as the ability of producers to create distinctions, either physical or psychological in nature, between goods that are close substitutes to each other. It is also necessary to distinguish price discrimination from product differentiation. Varian (1989: 598) says that the 'conventional definition ... that price discrimination is present when the same commodity is sold at different prices to different consumers' is unsatisfactory. Instead he quotes Stigler (1987) who says that 'price discrimination is present when two or more similar goods are sold at prices that are in different ratios to marginal costs'. In the economic theory of product differentiation it is also necessary to clarify and distinguish differentiated products from different products. At the very beginning of their article Eaton and Lipsey (1989) state that, 'any set of commodities, closely related in consumption and/ or production, may be regarded as differentiated products'. It may be hard to draw a clear line between different and differentiated products as it is unclear what is precisely meant by 'closely related'. In reality a physical product is always some sort of bundle of attributes, or a combination of services (like retail services, signalling through image and branding, after sales services and support, etc.) and physical products. This leads to the discussion of how consumers rank and value the elements of each bundle, which leads to the distinction between horizontal and vertical product differentiation. In the terminology of Lancaster (1979), two main types of product differentiation can be distinguished: vertical and horizontal. The former refers to a situation in which one product differs in overall quality from all other products in the market (i.e. individuals have a clear ranking over which products to choose if the price were the same for all products). The latter, horizontal differentiation, refers to a situation where the products in the market are of same or similar overall quality, but suppliers offer slightly different attributes embodied in their products.

2. Regulated Airline Markets: Quality Choice under Monopoly

In the times prior to deregulation and liberalization, airlines chose a certain level of quality. In Europe, each state-owned flag carrier had a certain degree of market power and operated in a market tightly regulated by restrictive bilateral air service agreements. Airlines were designated and air fares were largely cost-based regulated. There was only limited price competition between the Full-Service Airlines (FSA) and some charter carriers (see Doganis, 2002; Arndt, 2004). First we look at how a monopolist chooses its level of quality, then the effects of regulation are analysed.

To examine how a monopolist sets quality, a model by Spence (1975) can be employed. It is assumed that the firm can only supply one quality (ϕ_i) at constant marginal costs. A higher quality will shift the demand curve outwards, but it also increases marginal costs. Figure 3.1 depicts such a situation. The left graph shows the low-quality product (ϕ_1) with demand of D_1 at price p_1 and quantity of q_1. The right graph shows a high-quality product (ϕ_2) with demand of D_2 ($D_2 > D_1$), price p_2 ($p_2 > p_1$) and quantity q_2 ($q_2 > q_1$). It can also be seen that the costs of the high-quality product are higher than that of the low-quality product ($c_2 > c_1$).

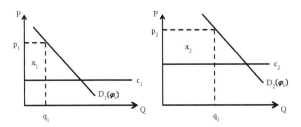

Figure 3.1   Quality choice under monopoly

If monopoly profits are greater for the high-quality product ($\pi_2 > \pi_1$), the monopolist would maximize profits by producing the high-quality product. However, this is based on the assumption that supplying a higher quality results in a higher demand. Usually, in models of (vertical) product differentiation, there is a willingness to pay for quality, which is assumed to be evenly distributed along the characteristics space. In the case of monopoly the producer will increase quality up to the point where the marginal willingness to pay equals the marginal costs of the higher quality, i.e. it will increase quality until the costs of the increase in quality are outweighed by the increase in demand. Theoretically it is not possible to say a priori whether the quality under monopoly will be high or low, as this depends upon the specific cost structures with respect to quality and on consumer preferences for quality.

In the case of airlines, viewed from a historical point, there seemed to be a tendency towards high-quality products. This is also indicated by the declining load factors in US domestic markets prior to deregulation depicted in Figure 3.2. The falling load factors are an indication that airlines offered an excess of daily flights on their routes to increase consumer satisfaction. The same can be seen in Figure 3.3 for the European market, where domestic passenger load factors were low before deregulation and increasing thereafter. However, it is not possible to tell whether the quality provided was actually desirable from a welfare economic point of view.[5] Moreover, the legacy carriers also differentiated the product inside the aircraft by providing cabins for up to four different classes (first, business, economy plus and economy class). It would seem that the quality provided was actually too high: legacy carriers cut some frills after deregulation and the entry of LCCs. Now, there are usually only two classes in most FSA aircraft and the first-class cabin is largely abandoned in Europe (Doganis, 2002, Chapter 9). The main message of this section is the statement that because of the historical conditions in the airlines industry, FSAs have an incumbent position on the upper end of quality range in the airline business.

---

5   Research that focused on the welfare effects of product differentiation (Lancaster, 1975; Spence, 1976; Dixit and Stiglitz, 1977; Carlton and Perloff, 2005) yield very mixed results. Product differentiation can either lead to excess differentiation or too less differentiation. An optimum is achieved only by coincidence.

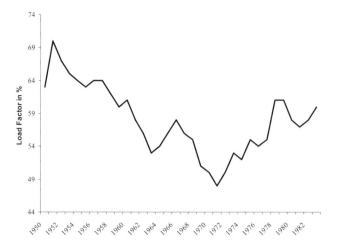

Figure 3.2   US domestic load factors 1950–1983

Source: Bailey et al. (1985), their Figure 1.1.

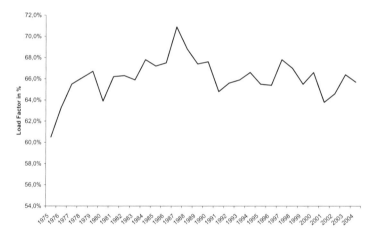

Figure 3.3   Domestic load factors of AEA airlines 1975–2004

Source: AEA.

3. The Emergence of Low-cost Carriers

Following deregulation in the USA and Europe, air passenger transport saw the rise of LCCs. Particularly of interest is the emergence of the LCCs that were established first, Southwest Airlines in the USA and Ryanair in Europe. These carriers positioned themselves on the lower end of the quality range. They offer a simple product, no frills, low frequencies, etc. (for an extensive analysis see Lawton 2001).

This feature of competition can be explained by the theory of product differentiation. Reisinger (2005), for example, developed such a model of vertical product differentiation with application to the airline industry.[6] In such models quality is the only parameter for differentiation and consumers have a strict preference for higher quality. Consumers are however differentiated in terms of income,[7] so that not all consumers can afford to buy high-quality products. In the basic model there are two firms producing one product each. Tastes and incomes are evenly distributed and each consumer buys only one product. Equilibrium is achieved once the two firms are differentiated as strongly as possible, whereby one positions at the top end of the quality range and the other at the lowest end. However, for such an outcome to be an equilibrium position the consumer incomes must be sufficiently heterogeneous, since otherwise no two firms could survive in such a market.

Reisinger (2005), who constructed a game theoretic model of sequential entry[8] in application to the airline industry, developed a three-stage game, where firm 1 first chooses quality, then firm 2 chooses quality and in stage three both firms compete on price. Furthermore, he considered entry of the LCC into the same route markets as the FSA, since otherwise the issue of product differentiation would not arise in the first place. Reisinger (2005) also used quality in a very general manner and described quality as all the factors that make up the flight quality (e.g. high frequency of flights, a large number of destinations, a high level of airport services, a high level on-board service, high seating comfort, availability of last minute check-in, punctuality,[9] no limits to weight and number of baggage to check-in for free, cleanliness of the cabin, friendliness of staff, etc.). The result is that the first mover chooses the high-quality product and the entrant the low-quality product.

The reason for LCCs to establish their products on the lower end of the quality range is to avoid price competition with the incumbent airline. Moreover, consumers in the market need to be sufficiently heterogeneous in terms of their willingness to pay for quality or income. The theory (and also Reisinger's model) predicts that the producer of the high-quality product makes higher profits than the producer of the low-quality product. However, this prediction can certainly not be observed in the airline business. Some LCCs have been more profitable than FSAs and they were less vulnerable to cyclical fluctuations. There is no generally valid conclusion for the airline business that FSAs are making higher profits than LCCs, which is contradictory to what theory would suggest. However, the prediction that FSAs would make higher profits is largely due to the fact that in the theoretical model of vertical product differentiation (at least in the basic ones) production costs are ignored, which would explain the mixed results on profitability. Another explanation for the profitability of LCCs comes from the restrictive assumption of evenly distributed consumers along the characteristics space. This must not be true in reality, and consumer distributions can change considerably in different markets.

The model of pure vertical product differentiation provides reasoning for the entry of LCCs in the market and also for establishing their product quality at the lower end. A question that remains is whether the airline industry could be an example of a natural oligopoly.[10] Information

---

6   The first theoretical models were developed by Gabszewicz and Thisse (1979) and Shaked and Sutton (1982, 1983). A textbook description can be found in Tirole (1989: 296–298).

7   The role of income in vertically differentiated markets was first analysed in the paper by Gabszewicz and Thisse (1979). Income is used synonymous with willingness to pay for quality and is henceforth used in this manner throughout the text.

8   General discussions of models of entry into vertically differentiated markets can also be found in Gabszewicz and Thisse (1980), Donnenfeld and Weber (1992) and Lutz (1997).

9   Although very often FSAs have worse punctuality records than LCCs, which is partly because LCCs fly from less congested airports and have no transfer passengers.

10   The proposition of natural oligopolies was made by Shaked and Sutton (1983). They show that in vertically differentiated markets, an upper bound in the number of firms, which they call the 'finiteness property', is persistent through the interplay of willingness to pay for quality and change in average variable

on quality-dependent costs was necessary to verify such results. A lot of quality features are fixed in the short run, especially those which are related to cabin design and layout, schedules and airport location. Only a few features are actually variable and escapable in the short run, such as free meals and on-board entertainment. Yet it is unknown how costs might actually increase with quality. Moreover, the natural oligopoly hypothesis is based on the assumption that there is only vertical differentiation, which is a very restrictive assumption for real-world applications.

4. The Emergence of Hybrid Carriers

The previous sections had a rather static view on the business model of LCCs. It has however become increasingly obvious that there is no single LCC business model. LCCs have differentiated their products compared to the generic LCC business model. Carriers have changed their business model not just with respect to their organizational design of their business models, but also with respect to the product they offer. More and more airlines are departing from the original LCC business model and offer some comfort features, higher frequencies and operate from more conveniently located airports (Baker, 2006). Thus economic models that incorporate only two distinct qualities must be expanded and take account for the fact that airline business models are changing. The question is how this can be explained through the economic theory of product differentiation.

This question will be examined by looking at a case study. Table 3.1 shows evidence from the German route market between Hamburg airport (HAM) and Munich airport (MUC) for the year 2006. The two airports are located in big agglomerations, which are important centres of economic activity, with a high level of income. Furthermore, MUC is the second hub for Lufthansa after Frankfurt airport. Both airports handle mostly FSA traffic and levy relatively high charges (compared to some other German airport, see Figure 3.4), yet they do have some LCC traffic. Neither HAM nor MUC are heavily congested or slot constrained. This makes them an ideal route on which FSAs and LCCs can compete for passengers. Although the Hamburg region has a remote airport (Hamburg-Lübeck), Munich does not. There would be potential for a route from Hamburg-Lübeck airport to MUC, though it has not been established so far.[11] There are three airlines which operate the HAM–MUC route: Lufthansa, Air Berlin,[12] and Germanwings. The latter is partly owned by Lufthansa, which makes this a route where the Lufthansa acts like a multi-product firm that competes against Air Berlin. The linear distance between Hamburg and Munich is approximately 611 kilometres. Alternative modes of transport are by train and car. The fastest train journey takes about 5.5 hours and costs 119 Euros.[13] The journey by car takes about 6.5 hours and costs about 410 Euros.[14]

---

quality-dependent costs. These costs may only rise disproportionately with quality. Under these conditions, even as the market size increases without bound or fixed set-up costs decline, there still exists an upper bound to the number of firms.

11   TUIfly established a route from HAM to Memmingen airport, which is roughly 110 kilometres away from Munich.

12   The route was formerly operated by DBA, which was taken over by Air Berlin and completely integrated into Air Berlin.

13   Source: Deutsche Bahn. Standard one-way fare (Normalpreis).

14   Source: ADAC. Based on one person in a middle-range car with an average of 15.000 kilometres p.a. and total costs of 53 cents per kilometre (journey distance by car is about 774 kilometres).

Table 3.1   Basic product features in the HAM–MUC market

	Average price in Euros	Daily frequency[‡]	Flexible tickets	Frequent flier programme	Free of charge amenities[§]
Lufthansa	253.34*	Up to 15	Yes	Yes	Yes
Air Berlin	73.99*	Up to 9	Yes	Yes	Yes
Germanwings	46.59[†]	Up to 3	Yes	Yes	No

* calculated from annual reports; [†] DLR, 2006; [‡] frequencies are usually lower at weekends; [§] e.g. newspapers, snacks and drinks, on-board entertainment etc.

Source: own compilations.

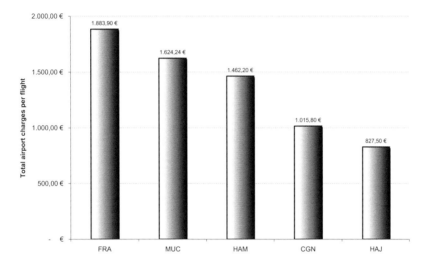

Figure 3.4   Total airport charges at selected German airports, 2006

Source: GAP database.

Notes: Charges include landing and passenger related charges and are calculated based on a 737-300 with an average seat load factor of 75 per cent and airports' reported traffic mix, excluding ground handling charges and taxes.

As can be seen, the airlines differ mainly in terms of prices and frequencies. All airlines offer flexible tickets (although at quite different prices) and frequent flier programmes, which is not typical for LCCs. The average price of Lufthansa is an average of business and economy, which means that the average for the economy class might actually be lower than stated. Additionally, the variance of the ticket prices of Air Berlin and Germanwings is likely to be higher than for Lufthansa's prices. The airlines differ quite significantly in terms of frequency. While Lufthansa and Air Berlin offer free of charge drinks and snacks, newspapers and on-board entertainment, Germanwings offers no such amenities, although drinks and snacks can be bought on board the aircraft. Thus there is evidence that on this route there are three distinct qualities offered by the three airlines.

There are two possible approaches that explain the emergence of these three qualities: first, the three airlines can be viewed as three firms, each offering one product quality. Second, the three airlines can be viewed as two firms, where Lufthansa offers the high- and low-quality product and Air Berlin offers an intermediate quality. However, the conclusions and implications of both approaches are similar.

When the three airlines are viewed as three firms, the model of pure vertical product differentiation is applicable. In section 3 it was established that if two firms were to co-exist in the market, consumers' incomes must be heterogeneous enough. If there are to be three distinct qualities, incomes would have to be even more heterogeneous than with the case of two qualities. If both, the demand (consumer heterogeneity) and the supply side (slope of the quality dependent cost function) conditions hold, the theory of vertical product differentiation would say that the market will become more fragmented, i.e. more than two different qualities will be on offer in that market.

For the second case, the multi-product firm model by Canoy and Peitz (1997)[15] seems to fit best. According to this model Air Berlin could not have entered this route with a pure LCC strategy because Lufthansa was the first mover on that route and it chose to produce the product line, i.e. the high and the low quality. Instead, Air Berlin offers also a high-quality product. Although the model would suggest that Air Berlin enters with the same quality as Lufthansa and differentiates horizontally, in this case Air Berlin's quality might be regarded as lower than that of Lufthansa, which makes Air Berlin more of a hybrid carrier rather than a LCC or FSA. However, quality is valued differently among consumers and some might actually see no big difference between them, for example if they do not need up to 15 flights per day. According to the Canoy and Peitz (1997) model there is no preference for variety in the low-quality segment, whereas in the high-quality segment there is. This could explain a diverging quality composition of Air Berlin. Furthermore, MUC is a secondary hub for Lufthansa which partially explains the high frequency.

In any case, the emergence of a third carrier that offers a differentiated product to that of the incumbent carriers can be explained through the theory of product differentiation. The implication is that the situation with three different qualities seems to be stable. What makes this situation possible and stable is the fact that both HAM and MUC have ample capacity. Moreover, the route connects two important economic centres of Germany and hence there is a large number of business travellers. Furthermore, the catchment areas of HAM and MUC are very large in terms of the population living in the regions,[16] and thus there is also a potential of leisure travellers as both cities are major tourist attractions for short-term city tourists. In other words, there is sufficient consumer heterogeneity on both ends of the route. It can therefore be concluded that the degree of vertical product differentiation in a given market is limited to the availability of airport capacity in and the socio-economic idiosyncrasies of that market. This means that there will only be several different qualities on a route if there is available airport capacity and the degree of consumer heterogeneity is sufficiently large, which will likely be the case in big urban regions.

There are of course other carriers that have evolved in recent years. EasyJet, for example, has increasingly moved to primary airports and is actively targeting the business traveller segment. In the US JetBlue Airways has achieved a reputation of being a carrier with quality superior to that of

---

15   This model is among a class of models that treat the issue of multi-product firms in relation to two-dimensional product-differentiation models. Other such models have been developed by Katz (1984) and Gilbert and Matutes (1993). For an excellent discussion of these models see Mañez and Waterson (2001: 26f.).

16   The region of Hamburg has approximately 4.3 million inhabitants; the agglomeration of Munich has about 4.6 million inhabitants.

other LCCs in the market. Worldwide there are more and more carriers that have departed from the original LCC model and have increased quality.

So far airline business models have been analysed without considering the implications of product differentiation on their organization and their strategy. FSAs have typically provided two (or more) classes in their cabins. The emergence of LCCs has put this bundling under pressure. Airlines must scrutinize their business models to sustain the future business environment.

5. Implications for Airline Strategy

Figure 3.5 shows a stylized airline business model. The main two determinants of total costs are product and organizational design. The product design falls into network choice (which determines the level of unavoidable costs) and choice of the overall quality level (where some features such as frequency may also relate to unavoidable costs). The organizational design falls into vertical design (of ground handling and maintenance, for example), ticket distribution and fleet composition.

From this it should be clear that LCCs can achieve a much lower cost base by operating a point-to-point network with a low quality level, an unbundled vertical structure, a simple distribution and a homogenous fleet. What is less clear is what influence the choice of the quality level has on the other factors.[17] For international destinations, for example, very high frequencies, a broad geographical coverage and a hub-and-spoke network seem indispensable. This would imply that in order to achieve a high quality there needs to be a heterogeneous fleet and, because of the

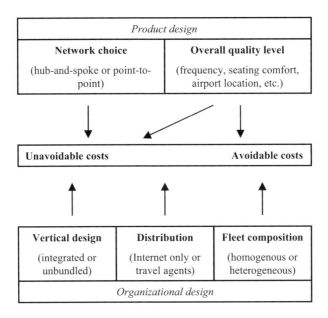

Figure 3.5   A stylized airline business model

Source: adapted from Morrison (2006).

---

17   It can also be argued that the choice of the business model determines the level of quality, but that would not change the following discussion.

increased business complexity, a vertically integrated structure. Thus, at very high levels of quality there is some influence on the other factors and with increasing quality there also comes the need for increasingly complex business models. For more intermediate levels of quality this might not be the case, or only to some extent. There is a large debate over whether the FSA business model can sustain in the light of intensifying LCC competition (Tretheway, 2004; Franke, 2004; Gillen, 2006). The general view is that the FSAs will sustain, yet there need to be adaptations.

In section 4 it we saw that some carriers tend to have hybrid business models. These carriers have much of the organizational design of LCCs, and much of the product design of FSAs. This was explained through the theory of product differentiation. The question is whether the emergence of hybrid carriers (HCs) is the end of the line or just a foot in the door. The airline industry has been changed by innovative LCCs like Southwest and Ryanair, which were followed by a wave of imitators. The rapid development of LCCs has led to manifold responses by the FSAs. Some have tried to set up LCC subsidiaries which, however, have often failed (see Morrell, 2005). FSAs have also increased their efficiency, for example by increasing their aircraft utilization. Dennis (2007) also points out that FSAs have managed to reduce labour costs. They have cut some frills (for example by offering less extravagant food and handing out only non-alcoholic beverages for free) and they have reduced distribution costs with little or no impact on the product design. They also had to adapt their pricing schemes. For example, they largely had to abandon minimum stay requirements for reduced fares. While Dennis (2007) sees some reasons why FSAs should not abandon their business class product, the survey results of Mason and Alamdari (2007) suggest that as business passengers 'downgrade', the business class product will disappear in short-haul markets.

As we pointed out in section 4, the important factors are the preferences of the consumers and the question whether there are enough consumers in a segment, and whether, given the size of the segment, a particular service can be offered to that segment, given the cost of producing that service.

6. Conclusions

This chapter demonstrates the relevance of the economic theory of product differentiation for the evolution of the airline industry. The theory provides a coherent framework to explain in particular the rise of LCCs and the growing trend of hybrid forms of airline business models. Economic models of product differentiation provide an understanding of the product choices and the competitive strategies of airlines.

The analysis of the quality choice must take account of the fact that legacy carriers had a high degree of market power in the past and is best explained through the model of quality choice under monopoly (see section 2). The emergence of the LCCs can be explained through the model of vertical differentiation (section 3). If markets are 'thick' enough (in terms of size, consumer heterogeneity and a high willingness to pay), there is the possibility that they become more vertically fragmented and there might be more than two distinct qualities in one market (section 4).

The chapter argued that the vertical segmentation among airlines could be of considerable importance and that many airlines differ in overall quality. Yet the extent to which this is actually happening depends on consumers' valuations of quality. One of the major conclusions from the discussion in this chapter is that the vertical product differentiation in a route market will be limited to the availability of airport capacity and the socio-economic characteristics of that route market. It is hard to draw definite conclusions from the discussion of the economic theory of product differentiation in relation to the business models of airlines. There are some indications that the business models are becoming blurred in short-haul markets. While FSAs have adopted some elements of the organizational design of LCCs, such as rethinking the distribution channels and abandoning travel agent sales channels, their overall product design remained largely unchanged. Whether or not they will have to change their product design in the future depends largely on the particularities of the markets.

An implication for economic policy is that deregulation brings not just direct price competition but also product innovation and product differentiation. Implications for airline management are that they need to carefully analyse the markets they operate or wish to operate. The parameters that were identified in this chapter will largely influence the product choice of airlines in different markets. For example: should they operate two distinct airlines (one FSA one LCC), should they offer economy only or economy and business class (or even business class only) or should they operate the market at all? The economic theory of product differentiation can help in answering such questions and in understanding and predicting the behavior of airline management's product choices.

This chapter provided examples from European markets, yet the models of product differentiation might also shed some light on the dynamic developments in other global markets. The Brazilian market, for example, has already seen the rise of an LCC that is now dominating that market (see Oliveira, 2003 and Evangelho et al., 2005). The Asian airline market is currently also experiencing a fast growth of LCCs (see Goh, 2005 for an overview and O'Connell and Williams, 2005 for a study involving two Asian airlines). It may be worth studying these markets in order to verify the results from the European experience.

References

Arndt, A. (2004) *Die Liberalisierung des grenzüberschreitenden Luftverkehrs in der EU* (Liberalisation of International Air Transportation in Europe). Frankfurt a.M.: Lang.

Bailey, E.E., Graham, D.R. and Kaplan D.P. (1985) *Deregulating the Airlines*. Cambridge, MA: MIT Press.

Baker, C. (2006) Blurring the model: low cost airlines and regional carriers swap tactics. *Airline Business*, May, http://www.flightglobal.com/articles/2006/04/28/206205/blurring-the-model-low-cost-airlines-and-regional-carriers-swap.html.

Beath, J., & Katsoulacos, Y. (1991). *The Economic Theory of Product Differentiation*. New York: Cambridge University Press.

Borenstein, S. and Netz, J. (1999) Why do all flights leave at 8am? Competition and departure-time differentiation in airline markets. *International Journal of Industrial Organization*, 17, 5, 611–640.

Canoy, M. and Peitz, M. (1997) The differentiation triangle. *The Journal of Industrial Economics*, 45, 3, 305–328.

Carlton, D.W. and Perloff, J.M. (2005) *Modern Industrial Organization*, 4th edn. Reading, MA: Addison-Wesley.

Chamberlin, E. (1933) *The Theory of Monopolistic Competition*. Cambridge, MA: Harvard University Press.

Dennis, N. (2007) End of the free lunch? The responses of traditional European airlines to the low-cost carrier threat. *Journal of Air Transport Management*, 15, 5, 311–321.

Dixit, A.K. and Stiglitz, J.E. (1977) Monopolistic competition and optimum product diversity. *The American Economic Review*, 67, 3, 297–308.

DLR (2006) *Low Cost Monitor 2/2006 – Eine Gemeinsame Untersuchung von DLR und ADV* (Low Cost Monitor 2/2006 – A Joint Investigation by DLR and ADV). Statistics on the German LCC market published by the German Aerospace Centre (DRL) www.dlr.de/fw.

Doganis, R. (2002) *Flying off Course – The Economics of International Airlines*, 3rd edn. London: Routledge.

Donnenfeld, S. and Weber, S. (1992) Vertical product differentiation with entry. *International Journal of Industrial Organization*, 10, 3, 449–472.

Eaton, B.C. and Lipsey, R.G. (1989) Product differentiation. In R. Schmalensee and R.D. Willig (eds), *Handbook of Industrial Organization, vol. 1*. Amsterdam: North-Holland, pp. 723–763.

Evangelhoa, F., Huseb, C. and Linhares, A. (2005) Market entry of a low cost airline and impacts on the Brazilian business travelers. *Journal of Air Transport Management*, 11, 2, 99–105.

Franke, M. (2004) Competition between network carriers and low-cost carriers – retreat, battle or breakthrough to a new level of efficiency? *Journal of Air Transport Management*, 10, 1, 15–21.

Gabszewicz, J. J.; Thisse, J.-F. (1979), Price competition, quality and income disparities, *Journal of Economic Theory*, 20, 3, 340–359

Gilbert, R.J. and Matutes, C. (1993) Product line rivalry with brand differentiation. *Journal of Industrial Economics*, 41, 3, 223–240.

Gillen, D. (2006) Airline business models and networks: regulation, competition and evolution in aviation markets. *Review of Network Economics*, 5, 4, 366–385.

Goh, M. (2005) Low cost carriers in Southeast Asia: a preliminary analysis. In W. Delfmann, H. Baum, S. Auerbach and S. Albers (eds), *Strategic Management in the Aviation Industry*. Aldershot: Ashgate, pp. 143–163.

Katz, M. (1984) Firm-specific differentiation and competition among multiproduct firms. *The Journal of Business*, 57, 1 (Part 2), 149–166.

Klaas, T. and Klein, J. (2005) Strategic airline positioning in the German low cost carrier (LCC) market. In W. Delfmann, H. Baum, S. Auerbach and S. Albers (eds), *Strategic Management in the Aviation Industry*. Aldershot: Ashgate, pp. 119–142.

Lancaster, K. (1975) Socially optimal product differentiation. *The American Economic Review*, 65, 4, 567–585.

Lancaster, K. (1979) *Variety, Equity, and Efficiency*. New York: Columbia University Press.

Launhardt, W. (1885) *Mathematische Begründung der Volkswirtschaftslehre* (The Mathematic Foundations of Economics). Leipzig: Engelmann.

Lawton, T.C. (2001) *Cleared for Take-Off: Structure and Strategy in the Low Fare Airline Business*. Aldershot: Ashgate.

Lipczynski, J., Wilson, J. and Goddard, J. (2005) *Industrial Organization: Competition, Strategy, Policy*, 2nd edn. Harlow: Pearson Education.

Lutz, S. (1997) Vertical product differentiation and entry deterrence. *Journal of Economics*, 65, 1, 79–102.

Mañez, J. and Waterson, M. (2001) *Multiproduct Firms and Product Differentiation: a Survey*. Warwick Economic Research Papers, No. 594, The University of Warwick.

Mason, K.J. and Alamdari, F. (2007) EU network carriers, low cost carriers and consumer behaviour: a Delphi study of future trends. *Journal of Air Transport Management*, 15, 5, 299–310.

Morrell, P. (2005) Airlines within airlines: an analysis of US network airline responses to low cost carriers. *Journal of Air Transport Management*, 11, 5, 303–312.

Morrison, W. (2006) *Evolving Airline Business Models and Strategies in Europe: So what Exactly is a Low-cost Carrier?* Presentation at the GARS-Workshop Benchmarking of Airports and EU-Liberalization – Two Challenges in One Workshop, 22 February, Hamburg Airport.

O'Connell, J.F. and Williams, G. (2005) Passengers' perceptions of low cost airlines and full service carriers: a case study involving Ryanair, Aer Lingus, Air Asia and Malaysia Airlines. *Journal of Air Transport Management*, 11, 4, 259–272.

Oliveira, A.V.M. (2003) *The Impacts of Liberalisation on a Brazilian Air Shuttle Market*. Warwick Economic Research Papers, No. 676, University of Warwick.

Reisinger, M. (2005) Why do low cost carriers arise and how can they survive the competitive responses of established airlines: a theoretical explanation. In P. Forsyth, D. Gillen, O.G. Mayer and H.-M. Niemeier (eds), *Competition versus Predation in Aviation Markets – A Survey of Experience in North America, Europe and Australia*. Aldershot: Ashgate, pp. 269–287.

Salvanes, K.G., Steen, F. and Sorgard, L. (2005) Hotelling in the air? Flight departures in Norway. *Regional Science and Urban Economics*, 35, 2, 193–213.

Shaked, A. and Sutton, J. (1982) Relaxing price competition through product differentiation. *The Review of Economic Studies*, 49, 1, 3–13.

Shaked, A. and Sutton, J. (1983) Natural oligopolies. *Econometrica*, 51, 5, 1469–1484.

Shaw, S. (2004) "Airline Marketing and Management", 5th edition, Ashgate, Aldershot

Spence, M. A. (1976) Product selection, fixed costs, and monopolistic competition. *Review of Economic Studies*, 43, 2, 217–235.

Stigler, G. (1987) *Theory of Price*. New York: Macmillan.

Tirole, J. (1989) *The Theory of Industrial Organization*, 2nd edn. Cambridge, MA: MIT Press.

Tretheway, M. (2004) Distortions of airline revenues: why the network airline business model is broken. *Journal of Air Transport Management*, 10, 1, 3–14.

Varian, H.R. (1989) Price discrimination. In R. Schmalensee and R.D. Willig (eds), *Handbook of Industrial Organization, vol. 1*. Amsterdam: North-Holland, pp. 597–654.

Chapter 4

Airline Competition in Connecting Markets

Rogier Lieshout and Guillaume Burghouwt

1. Introduction

Hub-and-spoke networks have been an essential feature of the operations of air carriers since the deregulation of the domestic US air transport market in 1978. They allow the hub airline to maximize the number of connected city pairs given a certain number of flights. Due to the consolidation of different origin–destination combinations on a limited number of routes, the hub airline may benefit from higher load factors, higher frequencies and the use of larger aircraft with lower unit costs (Dennis, 1994a, 1994b).

The competitive position of airlines and airports is usually expressed in terms of market shares in total passenger enplanements, number of aircraft movements or tonnes of freight. Although such indicators are valuable in themselves, they only focus on direct connections. The growth of hub-and-spoke operations has changed the way airlines compete in a structural way. On the one hand, airlines compete directly (from X to Y). On the other hand, they compete indirectly with a transfer at a hub (from X to Y via H). Focusing only on direct connections therefore leads to an incomplete picture.

Competition in direct markets has been addressed in a large number of studies, mostly for the United States and the European Union (Borenstein, 1992; Uittenbogaart, 1997; Gowrisankaran, 2002; Frenken et al., 2003; Fisher and Mamerschen, 2003) and recently Dobruzkes (2009). In addition, competition between airports and airlines sharing the same catchment areas has been subject of many studies, most of them using disaggregated airport–airline choice models (Pels et al., 2000; Ashford and Bencheman, 1987; Cohas, et al. 1995; Dresner and Windle, 1995; Pels, et al. 2003; Hess et al., 2007; Wilken, et al. 2007).

Competition in indirect markets has been less frequently addressed empirically. Hansen (1990) modelled airline hub competition in the US domestic market based on non-cooperative game theory, based on 1985 data. Brueckner and Spiller (1991) examine the effect of competition in hub-and-spoke networks and conclude that competition in a single market usually creates negative network externalities, causing a reduction of traffic throughout the network. Borenstein (1992) finds that competition levels in the US domestic aviation market increased as a result of intensified indirect services through hub airports, but decreased with respect to direct trips only. Burghouwt and Veldhuis (2006) analysed the development of market concentration levels and alliance market shares in the transatlantic market, taking into account both direct and indirect connections. The competition European hub airports face in their connecting markets has not been addressed empirically. In this chapter we analyse the competition between airlines in connecting markets with transfers at the 13 largest European hub airports.

The chapter is outlined as follows. First, we describe the methodology for analysing simultaneously direct and indirect competition. In Section 3 we consider the competition levels of the 13 largest European hubs in their connecting markets. Closely related is the share of competitive connecting markets per hub. In this section we will also identify the most important competitors for each hub. Conclusions and recommendations for further research are outlined in the final section.

2. Methodology

Against the background of hub-and-spoke networks, this article distinguishes two types of connections:

1. Direct connections: flights between airports X and Y without a hub transfer.
2. Indirect or hub connections: flights between airports A to B with a transfer at hub H.

The concept of hub connectivity is particularly important for measuring the competitive position of airline hubs in a certain market (e.g., how does Amsterdam Schiphol perform as a hub in the market between Hamburg and Los Angeles?).

The total cost of a trip by air consist of the costs of the price of the ticket and the time involved in making the trip. Passengers travelling indirectly experience additional costs over passengers travelling direct. This is because of the longer travel times, consisting of detour time and transfer time of an indirect connection.[1] However, the higher time costs for indirect travel are usually (partly) offset by lower ticket prices. As these lower ticket prices usually do not completely make up for the extra travel time, indirect connections are considered less attractive or of lower quality than direct alternatives, resulting in lower market shares.

For an indirect connection to be attractive, several things should be borne in mind. First the ticket price should be set right. When an indirect connection competes with direct alternatives, the price should be set under the price of direct alternatives to compensate for the longer travel time (all other aspects of the flight, such as service level, being equal). Second, the quality loss should be limited, meaning that the detour and transfer time remain acceptable for the passenger. Therefore, the geographical location of the hub in relation to airports X and Y is of importance. The closer hub H is located on the route between X and Y, the shorter the detour time will be. If a carrier is able to coordinate its incoming and outgoing flights effectively so that all incoming flights connect to all outgoing flights, the connecting time can be kept to a minimum.

In this section we present a consistent framework to determine the quality of direct and indirect connections. Second we will show how to calculate competition levels from these quality indicators. Third a description of the data requirements is given. We conclude with an example of how to calculate competition levels in connecting markets.

2.1 The Netscan Model

The Netscan model quantifies the quality of direct as well as indirect connections. In this section we discuss the methodology of the model in general terms. For a detailed discussion, see Veldhuis (1997), IATA (2000) and Matsumoto et al. (2008).

Netscan assigns a quality index to each connection, ranging between zero and one. A direct, non-stop flight is given the maximum quality index of one. The quality index of an indirect connection will always be lower than one since travel time is added due to transfer time and detour time. The same holds true for a direct multi-stop connection: passengers face a lower network quality because of an en-route stop compared to a non-stop direct connection.

If the perceived travel time of an indirect connection exceeds a certain threshold, the connection becomes unviable and the quality index equals zero. The maximum allowable perceived travel

---

1   The transfer time equals at least the minimum connecting time, the minimum time needed to transfer between two flights at hub H.

time depends on the travel time of a theoretical direct connection between these two airports. The travel time of a theoretical direct connection is determined by the geographical coordinates of origin and destination airport and assumptions on flight speed and time needed for take-off and landing. The further apart two airports are, the longer the maximum perceived travel time will be. For example, when the direct flight time between two airports is one hour, the maximum allowable perceived travel time will be about three hours, whereas this will be 24 hours for airports which are 12 hours apart by direct flight. By taking the product of the quality index and the frequency of the connection per time unit (day, week, and year), the total number of connections or connectivity units (CNUs) can be derived. In formulas the model takes the following form:

$$t_{xy}^{perceived,\ max} = (3 - 0.075 * t_{xy}^{flight,\ non-stop}) * t_{xy}^{flight,\ non-stop} \tag{1}$$

$$t_{x(h)y}^{perceived,\ actual} = \begin{cases} t_{xy}^{flight,\ actual} & \text{for direct flights} \\ (t_{xh}^{flight,\ actual} + t_{hy}^{flight,\ actual}) + & \\ (3 - 0.075 * t_{xy}^{flight,\ non-stop}) * t_{h}^{transfer} & \text{for indirect flights} \end{cases} \tag{2}$$

$$q_{x(h)y} = \begin{cases} 1 & \text{if } t_{x(h)y}^{perceived,\ actual} <= t_{xy}^{flight,\ non-stop} \\ 1 - \dfrac{t_{x(h)y}^{perceived,\ actual} - t_{xy}^{flight,\ non-stop}}{t_{xy}^{perceived,\ max} - t_{xy}^{flight,\ non-stop}} & \text{if } t_{xy}^{flight,\ non-stop} < t_{x(h)y}^{perceived,\ actual} < t_{xy}^{perceived,\ max} \\ 0 & \text{if } t_{x(h)y}^{perceived,\ actual} => t_{xy}^{perceived,\ max} \end{cases} \tag{3}$$

$$CNU_{x(h)ya} = q_{x(h)ya} \tag{4}$$

The maximum allowable perceived travel time $t_{x(h)y}^{perceived,\ max}$ between airports X and Y depends upon the non-stop flight time between both airports $t_{xy}^{flight,\ non-stop}$ multiplied by a factor which decreases with distance. The non-stop flight time is based on the flight time of an average jet aircraft. The actual perceived travel time between airports X and Y $t_{x(h)y}^{perceived,\ actual}$ equals the actual flight time $t_{xy}^{flight,\ actual}$ for direct flights. For indirect flights the perceived travel time equals the flight times on both flight legs and the transfer time at hub H $t_{h}^{transfer}$. As transfer time is considered more uncomfortable than flight time, the transfer time is penalized by a factor which decreases with distance.

If the actual flight time is smaller than or equal to the average non-stop flight time, then the quality index of the flight $q_{x(h)ya}$ equals one. In practice, this is only the case on direct flights operated by aircraft that are faster than the average jet aircraft on which the non-stop flight time is based. When the perceived travel time becomes larger than the maximum allowable perceived travel time, then the quality of the flight is zero and the connection will be considered unviable. In any other case, the perceived travel time lies between the non-stop flight time and the maximum allowable perceived flight time. In these cases, the quality of the flight depends on the relative difference between the perceived and maximum allowable travel time. When the perceived travel time is relatively small compared to the maximum allowable travel time, the quality of the flight will be high and vice versa. The connectivity $CNU_{x(h)ya}$ of an individual direct or indirect flight equals its quality $q_{x(h)ya}$.

The average share of hub H in total hub connectivity on a certain route can be calculated by dividing the hub connectivity of hub H by the total connectivity on the route. The share in the hub connectivity of all routes via H is calculated by adding up the connectivity of all routes via H and dividing this by the connectivity sum of all these routes.

2.2 Measuring Competition

In connecting markets, alliances/airlines compete in three different ways:

- *Using different hubs.* Usually carriers compete for connecting markets using different airports as hubs.
- *Using the same hub.* Occasionally two carriers compete for connecting markets using the same airport as a hub.
- *Direct flights bypassing the hubs.* Often carriers competing for a connecting market also face competition from direct flights. When available these direct flights are usually more expensive than connecting alternatives. The higher ticket price reflects the greater convenience of the direct flight in terms of travel time compared to a connecting flight.

The market share each alternative can obtain depends on the frequencies and ticket prices offered as well as the detour and transfer time of a connecting flight.

Competition is usually measured in terms of market concentration. Various concentration indexes or measures have been suggested in the field of industrial economics. The most frequently used are:

- *Concentration Ratio (Cn).* This is a summing up of the market shares of the n largest firms in a given market.
- *Herfindahl–Hirschman Index (HHI).* This is a summing up of the squared market shares. Small HHI means contestability, while an index equal to 1 means a market is absolutely monopolistic.

There are other measures of concentration, such as the Lorenz curve, Gini coefficient, inverse index and entropy. These are not as frequently employed in industrial economics and competition policy analysis as the concentration ratio and the Herfindahl–Hirschmann Index. A thorough review of these measures is outside the scope of this chapter. For further information see Singer (1965).

All concentration measures require data on competitor's market shares. For air traffic markets, one would ideally use actual passenger shares on competing direct and indirect flights: However such figures are difficult to obtain for the European air traffic markets. Therefore we shall estimate market shares using supply-side figures. These do not necessarily match with demand figures, as many more factors determine market share than just the supply (frequency) offered. Factors that are also relevant are price, total travel time, frequent flyer programmes etc. However, offered supply in terms of frequency should be a reasonable indicator for market share when competing airlines operate aircraft of similar size and with similar load factors. Using supply-side figures also has one important benefit; one can calculate how a proposed change in supply affects competition levels.

We chose the Herfindahl–Hirschman Index (HHI) to measure competition. For air traffic markets the HHI is calculated by summing the squared market shares of competing direct and indirect flights. The HHI is widely used to measure concentration in economic markets, including air traffic markets (Reynolds-Feighan, 1998) and it is easily interpretable.

However, it also has two important shortcomings. First, it is sensitive to the incorrect measurement of market shares. Since it involves squared market shares, any measurement error will also be squared. A correct measurement of the market shares depends to a large extent on a correct definition of relevant markets (Lijesen, 2004). A customer willing to travel from Amsterdam to Bangkok is not interested in the average concentration in the market between The Netherlands and Thailand, but in the concentration in the city pair market between Amsterdam and Bangkok. We overcome the first shortcoming by defining markets as airport pairs.

The second shortcoming of the HHI is its failure to account for close substitutes (Lijesen, 2004). Usually market shares of a specific city pair are calculated using frequencies. This implies however that direct flights are treated in the same way as connecting flights. As we mentioned before, connecting flights are of lower quality than direct flights. This quality aspect should be taken into account when calculating the concentration level at a certain city pair. Therefore, we calculate the concentration index using the connectivity shares of competing direct and indirect flights at specific airport pairs. Aggregating the squares of the connectivity shares of each of the competing alliances/airlines results in the Hirschman–Herfindahl concentration index of the market between X and Y:

$$HHI_{xy} = \sum_a \left(\frac{\sum_h CNU_{x(h)ya}}{\sum_a \sum_h CNU_{x(h)ya}} \right)^2 \tag{5}$$

Besides calculating competition levels on specific airport pairs, it is also possible to calculate the levels in specific markets or (hub) airports. For example, the average competition level on the connecting markets via a hub can be calculated by taking the competition levels of all connecting routes via the hub and weighing them with their respective seat capacities.

2.3 Data and Sample

The Netscan model uses timetable data from the Official Airlines Guide (OAG) on direct flights as input. Indirect flights are created within the model by connecting two direct flights taking into account minimum and maximum connecting times and a limit on the routing factor. The authors used the OAG flight schedules for the third week of June 2008. The CNU has been calculated for each individual direct and indirect flight. This means that when a flight is offered with a daily frequency, the CNUs for each of these seven flights as well as for each possible connection have been calculated. The reason for distinguishing between individual flights is twofold. First, the flights might be carried out by different airplane types during the week leading to different flight times and therefore differing CNUs. Second, the same flight might connect to different flights on for example a Monday than on a Friday.

Although the model allows for interline connections, only online connections are considered here. In other words, a transfer can only take place between flights of the same airline or global airline alliance. We distinguish three global airline alliances: SkyTeam, STAR and OneWorld. Appendix A contains the members of each of the three alliances.

The analysis considers hub connectivity and competition levels for the 13 largest European hubs. These airports have been listed in Table 4.1 and categorized by alliance. However, to be able to calculate shares in hub connectivity and competition levels for each of these airports, it is necessary to take into account all competing routes via all alternative hubs.

We will distinguish several geographical markets (Table 4.2).

Table 4.1   Hub airports by the alliance which uses the hub

SkyTeam	STAR	OneWorld
Paris Charles de Gaulle (CDG)	London Heathrow (LHR)	London Heathrow (LHR)
Amsterdam (AMS)	Frankfurt (FRA)	Madrid (MAD)
Rome Fiumicino (FCO)	Munich (MUC)	
Milan Malpensa (MXP)	Copenhagen (CPH)	
Prague (PRG)	Vienna (VIE)	
	Zurich (ZRH)	
	Lisbon (LIS)	

Table 4.2   Breakdown of geographical submarkets

Markets
Europe–Europe
Europe–North America
Europe–Latin America
Europe–Asia & Pacific
Europe–Middle East
Europe–Africa

2.4 Example

We illustrate the methodology with an example. On the airport pair Copenhagen–Singapore, STAR member Singapore Airlines is the only airline offering direct flights. The STAR alliance also offers indirect flights via Bangkok, Frankfurt, London (Heathrow), Munich, Tokyo (Narita) and Zurich. These direct and indirect flights compete with the indirect flights offered by the SkyTeam (via Amsterdam and Paris Charles de Gaulle) and OneWorld alliances (via London Heathrow). In this particular market, no non-allied carriers offer direct or indirect services.

Table 4.3 shows that Frankfurt has the highest connectivity-share on the airport-pair Copenhagen–Singapore. Not only is the indirect frequency via Frankfurt very high, Frankfurt is also well situated between Copenhagen and Singapore. This leads to relatively limited detour time compared to the flights via the other hubs. The SkyTeam and OneWorld alliances play a modest role on this route. From these CNU's we can now derive that the competition level (HHI) is 0.73.[2]

---

2 $HHI_{EWR-OSL} = \left[\left(\frac{98.3}{116.2}\right)^2 + \left(\frac{5.2}{116.2}\right)^2 + \left(\frac{12.7}{116.2}\right)^2\right] = 0.73$

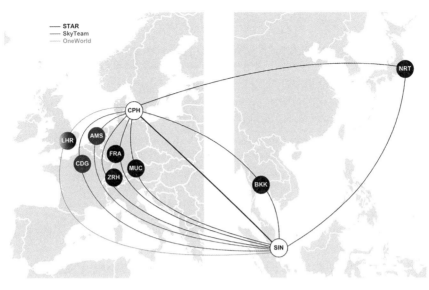

Figure 4.1   Competing hub airports in the Copenhagen (CPH)–Singapore (SIN) market

Table 4.3   Connectivity on the route Copenhagen–Singapore

Origin	Hub	Destination	Alliance	Frequency	CNU
CPH	Direct	SIN	STAR	3	3.0
CPH	BKK	SIN	STAR	58	24.9
CPH	FRA	SIN	STAR	77	32.0
CPH	LHR	SIN	STAR	39	17.4
CPH	MUC	SIN	STAR	15	6.0
CPH	NRT	SIN	STAR	14	3.9
CPH	ZRH	SIN	STAR	26	11.1
Subtotal				**232**	**98.3**
CPH	AMS	SIN	SkyTeam	7	3.1
CPH	CDG	SIN	SkyTeam	7	2.1
Subtotal				**14**	**5.2**
CPH	LHR	SIN	OneWorld	45	12.7
Subtotal				**45**	**12.7**
Total				**291.0**	**116.2**

Source: Netscan.

3. Empirical Results

3.1 Competition Levels

3.1.1 Competition level per hub   Figure 4.2 shows the HHIs on the connecting markets of each of the 13 selected European hubs. The STAR hub in Lisbon has the highest weighted average HHI, implying a high concentration level on its connecting routes. In other words, only a limited number of competing airlines/alliances offer direct or indirect services that compete with the connections offered by STAR via Lisbon, resulting in a low competition level. A relatively large number of connecting markets turn out to be served exclusively via Lisbon. Opposed to the other hubs in the sample, the airport is well connected to airports in the former Portuguese colonies Brazil and Cape Verde and to airports in the Azores, an autonomous region of Portugal. On most routes between Europe and these airports, the STAR flights via Lisbon have a monopoly, explaining the low competition level. The airlines of the STAR alliances can be expected to achieve high yields on these markets.

On the other end of the spectrum, we find Zurich. The concentration level on the connecting markets it serves is low; the airlines using Zurich as a hub experience competition on most of their connecting routes and therefore the average competition level for the airport is high. The same holds true for London Heathrow. A first explanation for this is that this airport is used as a hub by both the STAR and the OneWorld alliance. A second explanation has to do with the fact that Heathrow has a large origin-destination market. Most European hubs are dependent upon feeder traffic from smaller European airports to keep load factors on intercontinental routes at a reasonable level. The feeder routes from these smaller European airports often experience little competition, leading to relatively low average competition levels. Because of the large origin-destination market in London, the carriers operating from Heathrow are less dependent upon feeder

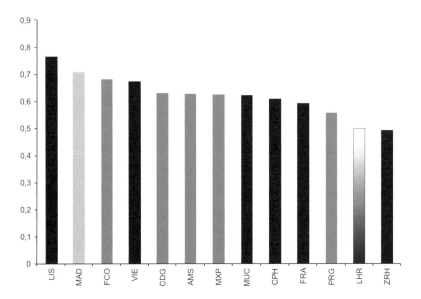

Figure 4.2   HHIs (weighted averages) on connecting markets per alliance hub

Source: Netscan.

traffic. These carriers therefore do not serve these smaller airports in the same way the other hubs do, and their share of monopolized connecting routes is relatively low, leading to a higher average competition level.

Another way of looking at the general competition levels is to consider the share of each hub in the total connectivity offered between Europe and the rest of the world (see Table 4.4). Not surprisingly, most of the connecting traffic is channelled through European hubs: Frankfurt, Paris CDG, Heathrow and Amsterdam together account for 23 per cent of all connectivity from Europe to the rest of the world. The most important other hubs are located in the United States: Atlanta (4.1 per cent), Chicago (3.2 per cent) and New York Newark (2.6 per cent). Yet direct connections between Europe and the rest of the world still account for the majority of connectivity (37.9 per cent).

Table 4.4   Connectivity shares of (in)direct flights in the markets between Europe and the rest of the world

Direct flights		37.9%
Indirect via		62.1%
FRA	Frankfurt Germany	7.3%
CDG	Paris (Charles De Gaulle) France	6.8%
LHR	London (Heathrow) England	4.7%
AMS	Amsterdam Netherlands	4.4%
ATL	Atlanta (Intl) GA USA	4.1%
MUC	Munich (Intl) Germany	3.2%
ORD	Chicago (O'Hare) IL USA	3.2%
MAD	Madrid Spain	2.9%
EWR	Newark/New York (Liberty) NJ USA	2.6%
PHL	Philadelphia (Intl) PA USA	1.5%
ZRH	Zurich Switzerland	1.4%
VIE	Vienna Austria	1.2%
FCO	Rome (Fiumicino) Italy	1.2%
IAD	Washington (Dulles Intl) DC USA	1.1%
IAH	Houston (G. Bush Intl) TX USA	1.1%
JFK	New York (Kennedy) NY USA	1.0%
DTW	Detroit (Metro Wayne) MI USA	0.9%
YYZ	Toronto (Pearson Intl) ON Canada	0.8%
SVO	Moscow (Sheremetyevo) Russian Fed.	0.8%
IST	Istanbul (Ataturk) Turkey	0.7%
CPH	Copenhagen (Intl) Denmark	0.6%
DFW	Dallas/Ft. Worth (Intl) TX USA	0.6%
HEL	Helsinki Finland	0.6%
LIS	Lisbon Portugal	0.5%
DXB	Dubai U.A. Emirates	0.5%
Other hubs		8.4%

Source: Netscan.

3.1.2 Competition level per hub and geographical submarket   In the previous paragraph we presented the average competition levels on connecting routes for the largest European hubs. Next, we will break down these figures by geographical market to find out the extent to which these markets are dominated by the hubs.

In Table 4.5, the average competition levels at each hub are broken down by geographical market. The weighted average HHI of the routes from North America via Frankfurt to anywhere else in the world, for example, is 0.59.[3] The competition levels via Frankfurt differ relatively little between the geographical submarkets. One should note that the airlines (in this case the STAR alliance operating via Frankfurt and all of its competitors on the routes the STAR alliance offers via Frankfurt) ultimately determine the level of competition.

With respect to Paris Charles de Gaulle, the connecting SkyTeam flights to and from Africa face little competition. In addition, the airport has a relatively strong focus on this geographical market: the hub is connected to a large number of African airports and many of them are served by only one airline. Examples of Air France routes via Paris with little or no competition are the routes originating/terminating in Abidjan (Cote d'Ivoire), Antananarivo (Madagascar), Rabat (Morocco) and N'Djamena (Chad). People from elsewhere in Europe wishing to travel to these former French colonies therefore need to travel via Paris Charles de Gaulle. Airlines can be expected to achieve high yields here.

Via Amsterdam the SkyTeam alliance experiences less competition on the connecting routes originating and terminating in Latin America. Most direct routes between Amsterdam and Latin America experience no competition from other hubs. This is especially true for the former Dutch colonies like Aruba, The Antilles (Curacao, Bonaire, St Martin) and Paramaribo (Suriname). People wishing to travel from Latin America to Europe and vice versa therefore often need to travel via Amsterdam. However, these connecting markets are often small in size and are mainly origin-destination markets with little transfer.

The STAR flights via Munich experience little competition on connecting routes to and from the Middle East. The airport has a strong focus on the routes to Ankara and Izmir in Turkey. European travellers can often only travel via Munich.

The OneWorld connections via Madrid encounter relatively little competition levels in all the geographical markets. This is especially true for the connecting routes from Latin America and Asia (Bangkok) via Madrid to the rest of the world and vice versa. Many unique connections between Europe and Latin America are channelled through Madrid, especially those to the former Spanish colonies: Quito (Ecuador), San Jose (Costa Rica), Guatemala City (Guatemala), San Juan (Puerto Rico) and Montevideo (Uruguay).

As we saw before, the (STAR) flights via Lisbon experience the least competition in its connecting markets. Competition is especially limited in markets originating and terminating in Europe, Africa and the Middle East. However, we should remark that overall service levels to intercontinental destinations are generally low. Lisbon for example is not connected to Asia or Australia by direct flights, therefore there are no connections possible to these continents via Lisbon.

The competition levels on the connecting routes via London Heathrow, Zurich, Copenhagen, Prague, Vienna and Rome Fiumicino do not differ much between the various geographical submarkets. The competition levels on the connecting routes via Milan Malpensa on the contrary differ relatively much by geographical region, but service levels to intercontinental destinations are low.

---

3   These are weighted averages of flights going in both directions. The competition levels of individual airport pairs are weighed with their respective seat capacities.

Table 4.5   HHIs per hub airport and geographical submarket

VVia	To/from						
	Europe	**North America**	**Latin America**	**Africa**	**Middle East**	**Asia & Pacific**	**Average**
FRA	0.60	0.59	0.56	0.60	0.58	0.57	**0.59**
CDG	0.62	0.63	0.64	0.76	0.59	0.54	**0.63**
LHR	0.49	0.49	0.57	0.53	0.51	0.49	**0.50**
AMS	0.62	0.64	0.81	0.68	0.56	0.56	**0.63**
MUC	0.63	0.60	0.50	0.53	0.74	0.56	**0.62**
MAD	0.70	0.63	0.75	0.67	0.67	0.77	**0.71**
ZRH	0.50	0.47	0.46	0.49	0.51	0.47	**0.49**
VIE	0.70	0.61	–	0.62	0.66	0.59	**0.67**
FCO	0.70	0.69	0.63	0.69	0.58	0.66	**0.68**
CPH	0.63	0.55	–	–	0.58	0.53	**0.61**
LIS	0.78	0.62	0.75	0.78	0.83	–	**0.77**
PRG	0.56	0.55	–	0.51	0.48	0.58	**0.56**
MXP	0.64	0.62	0.47	0.61	0.50	0.52	**0.62**

Note: When a hub airport has no direct flights to a certain geographical submarket, no connections via the hub to this submarket are possible. These are indicated by a dash –.

Source: Netscan.

3.2 Share of Monopolized Markets

In the previous section there appeared to be a strong relationship between the competition level in a certain market and the number of monopolized routes in that market. This seems obvious, but theoretically need not be the case. Competition levels in a connecting market can just as well be low on routes that are not monopolized, for example when a single alliance/airline is dominating all of its competitors in the market. In this section we will focus on the relationship between the number of monopolized markets and the competition level.

3.2.1 Share of competitive markets per hub   In Figure 4.3 we have plotted the average competition levels (HHI) at each hub against their shares of connecting routes with competition. The figure shows that 90 per cent of the connecting routes via Zurich experience competition (HHI < 1), whereas this is only the case for 40 per cent of the routes via Lisbon. The figure confirms the expected linear relationship between competition level and the share of routes that experience competition. The higher the percentage of connecting routes experiencing competition, the higher the average competition level in the connecting markets is.

3.2.2 Share of competitive markets per hub and geographical market   We have also broken down the share of competitive routes at each hub by geographical market. The results are depicted in Table 4.6. When this table is compared to Table 4.5, the relationship between competitiveness and the share of competing routes again becomes clear.

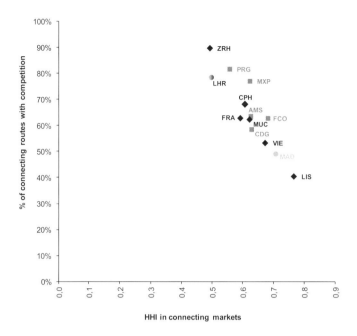

Figure 4.3   Competition levels and the share of competing hub routes

Source: Netscan.

Table 4.6   Share of connecting routes with competition per hub and geographical market

Via	Average competition levels on connecting flights between Europe and						
	Europe (%)	North America (%)	Latin America (%)	Africa (%)	Middle East (%)	Asia & Pacific (%)	Weighted average (%)
FRA	61	67	70	62	63	64	**63**
CDG	60	65	54	36	73	74	**58**
LHR	80	79	70	77	74	77	**78**
AMS	64	69	29	59	75	70	**63**
MUC	60	70	76	78	49	66	**62**
MAD	47	66	46	57	54	47	**49**
ZRH	88	93	93	86	89	93	**90**
VIE	51	67		55	54	62	**53**
FCO	60	66	71	59	72	67	**63**
CPH	64	75			83	84	**68**
LIS	40	78	37	36	38		**40**
PRG	81	86		86	83	81	**82**
MXP	74	79	86	77	92	80	**77**

Source: Netscan.

Note that some of the markets in Table 4.6 are rather small. Table 4.7 shows the relative size of the connecting markets for each hub in the sample. The connecting markets to and from Europe are largest for each hub. Vienna, Copenhagen and Prague have a stronger focus on Europe than the other hubs. Madrid and Lisbon have a strong focus on Latin America and focus less on connecting markets to North America and Asia and the Pacific than the other hubs.

3.3 Identification of Most Important Competitors

In this section, we identify the main competitors for each hub in the connecting markets they serve. We first identify all the connecting markets accommodated by the hub. Second, we calculate the shares in hub connectivity of all the hubs accommodating these routes. The hubs with the highest connectivity shares are considered to be the main competitors of the hub under investigation.

3.3.1 Most important competitors per hub   Table 4.8 shows the most important competitors in the connecting markets they accommodate for each of the hubs. In brackets the connectivity shares of each hub and its main competitors are given.

For example, in all connecting markets offered via Frankfurt, the airport has a share of 21 per cent of all connections, be it direct or indirect. The most important competitor in the markets served by the STAR alliance via Frankfurt is Paris Charles de Gaulle with a market share of 12 per cent. There is also competition from direct flights, which have a share of 12 per cent.

The four largest hubs have the highest shares in hub connectivity in the connecting markets. This is not the case for the smaller hubs. The connecting flights via the smaller hubs generally

Table 4.7   Relative size of the connecting markets for each hub in the sample

Via	Relative size of connecting markets to/from						
	Europe (%)	North America (%)	Latin America (%)	Africa (%)	Middle East (%)	Asia & Pacific (%)	Total (%)
FRA	54	17	2	7	8	13	100
CDG	49	15	7	16	4	9	100
LHR	45	21	4	9	8	13	100
AMS	52	16	7	8	6	11	100
MUC	68	14	1	1	4	11	100
MAD	64	7	19	6	3	0	100
ZRH	57	15	3	7	7	9	100
VIE	75	6	0	3	7	8	100
FCO	56	20	5	7	7	4	100
CPH	76	12	0	0	1	11	100
LIS	61	4	20	14	1	0	100
PRG	77	8	0	2	7	5	100
MXP	59	19	7	6	2	6	100

Source: Netscan.

Table 4.8   Most important competitors for each hub on its connecting markets

Hub	Five most important competitors (%)				
FRA (21)	CDG (12)	Direct (12)	LHR (11)	AMS (7)	MUC (6)
CDG (24)	FRA (13)	LHR (10)	Direct (9)	AMS (7)	MUC (5)
LHR (22)	FRA (14)	CDG (10)	Direct (8)	AMS (7)	MUC (5)
AMS (17)	FRA (13)	LHR (13)	CDG (12)	Direct (9)	MUC (5)
MUC (13)	FRA (16)	Direct (14)	LHR (11)	CDG (11)	AMS (6)
MAD (25)	Direct (13)	CDG (13)	FRA (10)	LHR (9)	AMS (4)
ZRH (9)	Direct (15)	LHR (14)	FRA (13)	CDG (11)	MUC (6)
VIE (11)	Direct (19)	FRA (15)	LHR (10)	MUC (8)	CDG (7)
FCO (13)	CDG (14)	Direct (14)	FRA (11)	LHR (9)	AMS (5)
CPH (8)	Direct (17)	FRA (14)	LHR (14)	CDG (8)	AMS (7)
LIS (19)	CDG (14)	Direct (14)	FRA (10)	LHR (8)	MAD (8)
PRG (6)	Direct (25)	FRA (10)	CDG (9)	LHR (8)	AMS (6)
MXP (4)	CDG (18)	Direct (16)	LHR (9)	FRA (9)	FCO (7)

Note: In some connecting markets hubs face competition from direct flights. The connectivity shares of these direct flights are denoted as 'Direct' in the table.

Source: Netscan.

encounter fierce competition from direct travel opportunities and to a lesser extent from indirect flights accommodated by the larger hubs.

Connecting flights via the largest hubs encounter most competition in their connecting markets from other large hubs. This is because of the sheer size of the networks of these hubs (see also Table 4.4). The hubs and their five most important competitors usually have a combined market share of 65–75 per cent in total hub connectivity.

3.3.2 Most important competitors per hub and geographical market   With the available data it is also possible to analyse the most important competitors for each hub in a specific geographical market. Although a full analysis for each of these markets is outside the scope of this chapter, we have listed the most important competitors for each hub in the North American market in Table 4.9.

On the connecting routes to North America, the largest European hubs again have a high market share, but as Table 4.9 shows, the hubs in the United States – mainly Chicago O'Hare (ORD) and Newark (EWR) – also play a part.

Table 4.7 showed that the relative size of the connecting markets via Zurich and Milan Malpensa to North America is rather large. However, the market share of these hubs in the total connectivity to North America is limited. The four large European hubs simply offer more connections on identical markets to/from North America.

Table 4.9   Most important competitors for each hub on connecting markets to/from North America

Hub	Five most important competitors (%)				
FRA (20)	LHR (14)	CDG (12)	AMS (7)	MUC (5)	Direct (5)
CDG (20)	FRA (13)	LHR (12)	AMS (7)	Direct (5)	EWR (5)
LHR (22)	FRA (14)	CDG (9)	AMS (6)	Direct (5)	ORD (4)
AMS (15)	LHR (14)	FRA (12)	CDG (12)	Direct (5)	ORD (5)
MUC (11)	FRA (19)	LHR (14)	CDG (11)	Direct (6)	AMS (5)
MAD (10)	LHR (17)	FRA (13)	CDG (12)	Direct (8)	MUC (4)
ZRH (6)	LHR (17)	FRA (14)	CDG (12)	Direct (7)	AMS (5)
VIE (5)	FRA (20)	LHR (18)	CDG (9)	Direct (8)	MUC (7)
FCO (11)	CDG (14)	LHR (12)	FRA (11)	Direct (7)	AMS (6)
CPH (6)	LHR (17)	FRA (15)	CDG (9)	Direct (8)	AMS (7)
LIS (4)	CDG (13)	FRA (12)	Direct (11)	LHR (11)	AMS (8)
PRG (3)	LHR (15)	CDG (12)	FRA (11)	Direct (10)	AMS (8)
MXP (5)	CDG (19)	LHR (11)	Direct (9)	FCO (9)	FRA (8)

Source: Netscan.

4. Conclusions

The rise of hub-and-spoke networks has changed the way in which airlines and airports compete. Competition not only takes place directly but also indirectly. Therefore indirect connections should be taken into account when calculating competition levels. This chapter described a methodology to measure competition, taking into account both direct and indirect connections.

The methodology was used to estimate the competition levels on connecting routes via the 13 largest European hubs. Connecting flights via Lisbon and Madrid experience the least competition, in particular with respect to connections to and from Latin America. For a large part, this has to do with the geographical location of these hubs as well as the socio-economic and sociopolitical relationships between Spain/Portugal and various Latin American countries. The carriers of the STAR alliance at Lisbon and the OneWorld alliance at Madrid are expected to achieve high yields in these connecting markets.

On the contrary, the connecting flights via Zurich and Heathrow on average experience relatively fierce competition. As these airports mainly serve the larger European destinations, competition on most of the connecting routes is high and yields are expected to be low.

The SkyTeam alliance face average competition levels on their connecting flights via Paris CDG and Amsterdam. Only on the connecting market to and from (former) colonies and overseas territories are competition levels low.

Not surprisingly there appears to be a strong linear relationship between the number of connecting routes via a hub experiencing competition and the average competition level on the connecting routes via the hub. For example, 90 per cent of the connecting routes via Zurich experience competition, whereas the routes via Lisbon experience competition only 40 per cent of the time.

The main hubs (Frankfurt, Paris Charles de Gaulle, London Heathrow and Amsterdam Schiphol) have the largest market share in the connecting routes they offer. These hubs especially compete with each other. The smaller hubs mainly face competition from direct connections, followed by competition from the main hubs.

We have demonstrated that the Netscan methodology can be used as a tool to analyse competition in connecting markets. As such, the approach outlined in this paper may help airports, airlines and governments to identify the most important competitors in the transfer market and calculate competition levels.

5. Further Research

As demand-side figures are hard to obtain for European airports, the methodology proposed here uses supply-side figures. To validate our methodology and compare its performance to other measures and methodologies, demand-side figures are necessary. Such an exercise could be performed for the US market using the DB1B dataset.

In this chapter competition was considered on an airport pair level, whereas airlines merely compete on a city pair level. Flights between London Heathrow and New York JFK not only compete with other flights between these two airports, but also with flights offered from airports nearby, such as flights between London Heathrow and Newark. This can be accounted for in future research by analysing competition on the city pair or multi-airport system level. Another topic for future research is the determinants behind competition in connecting markets. To what extent do hub airport characteristics for example impact connectivity shares?

References

Ashford, N. and Bencheman, M. (1987) Passenger's choice of airport: an application of the multinomial logit model. *Transportation Research Record*, 1147, 1–5.

Borenstein, S. (1992) The evolution of U.S. Airline Competition. *Journal of Economic Perspectives*, 6, 2, 45–73.

Brueckner, J.K. and Spiller, P.T. (1994) Economies of traffic density in the deregulated airline industry. *Journal of Law and Economics*, 37, 379–415.

Burghouwt, G. and Veldhuis, J. (2006) The competitive position of hub airports in the transatlantic market. *Journal of Air Transportation*, 11, 1, 106–130.

Cohas, F.J., Belobaba, P.P. and Simpson, R.W. (1995) Competitive fare and frequency effects in airport market share modelling. *Journal of Air Traffic Management*, 2, 1, 33–45.

Dennis, N.P. (1994a) Scheduling strategies for airline hub operations. *Journal of Air Transport Management*, 1, 2, 31–144.

Dennis, N.P. (1994b) Airline hub operations in Europe. *Journal of Transport Geography*, 2, 4, 219–233.

Dobruszkes, F. (2009) Does liberalization of air transport imply increasing competition? Lessons from the European case. *Transport Policy*, 16, 1, 29–39.

Dresner, M.E. and Windle, R.J. (1995) Alliances and code-sharing in the international airline industry. *Built Environment*, 22, 3, 201–211.

Fisher, T. and Mamerschen, D.R. (2003) Measuring competition in the U.S. airline industry using the Rosse-Panzar test and cross-sectional regression analyses. *Journal of Applied Economics*, VI, 1, 73–93.

Frenken, K., Van Terwisga, S., Verburg, T., Burghouwt, G. (2003) Airline competition at European airports. *Tijdschrift voor economische en sociale geografie*, 95, 2, 233–242.

Gowrisankaran, G. (2002) Competition and regulation in the airline industry. *Federal Reserve Bank of San Francisco Economic Letter 2002–01*, 1–3.

Hansen (1990) Airline competition in a hub-dominated environment: an application of noncooperative game theory. *Transportation Research*, 24B, 1, 24–43.

Hess, S., Adler, T. and Polak, J.W. (2007) Modelling airport and airline choice behaviour with the use of stated preference survey data. *Transportation Research Part E*, 43, 221–233.

IATA (2000) *Global Airport Connectivity Monitor*. IATA/ Hague Consulting Group.

Lijesen, M.G. (2004) Adjusting the Herfindahl index for close substitutes: an application to pricing in civil aviation. *Transportation Research Part E*, 40, 123–134.

Matsumoto, H., Veldhuis, J., De Wit, J., Burghouwt, G. (2008) *Network Performance, Hub Connectivity Potential, and Competitive Position of Primary Airports in Asia/Pacific Region.* 12th ATRS World Conference, Athens.

Pels, E. (2001) A note on airline alliances. *Journal of Air Transport Management*, 7, 3–7.

Pels, E., Nijkamp, P. and Rietveld, P. (2003) Access to and competition between airports: a case study for the San Francisco Bay Area. *Transportation Research*, 37A, 1, 71–83.

Pels, E., Nijkamp, P. and Rietveld, P. (2000) Airport and airline competition for passengers departing from a large metropolitan area. *Journal of Urban Economics*, 48, 29–45.

Reynolds-Feighan, A.J. (1998) The impact of US airline deregulation on airport traffic patterns. *Geographical Analysis*, 30, 234–225.

Singer, E.M. (1965) The structure of industrial concentration indexes. *Antitrust Bulletin*, X, January–April, 75–104.

Uittenbogaart, P. (1997) Airline competition on the route between Amsterdam and London. *Journal of Air Transport Management*, 3, 4, 217–225.

Veldhuis, J. (1997) The competitive position of airline networks. *Journal of AirTransport Management*, 3, 4, 181–188.

Wilken, D., Berster, P. and Gelhausen, M. Ch. (2007) Airport choice in Germany – new empirical evidence of the German Air Traveller Survey 2003. *Journal of Airport Management*, 1, 2, 165–179.

Appendix A

Table 4.10   Alliance members, 2008

SkyTeam	STAR	OneWorld
Aeroméxico	Air Canada	American Airlines
Air France	Air New Zealand	British Airways
Delta Air Lines	All Nippon Airways	Cathay Pacific
Korean Air	Austrian Airlines	Qantas Airways
CSA Czech Airlines	BMI	Iberia
Alitalia	Lufthansa	Finnair
Continental Airlines	SAS	LAN Airlines
Northwest Airlines	Singapore Airlines	Japan Airlines
KLM	Thai Airways International	Royal Jordanian
Aeroflot	United Airlines	Malev
China Southern Airlines	Spanair	
	Asiana Airlines	
	LOT Polish Airlines	
	US Airways	
	TAP Portugal	
	SWISS International Airlines	
	South African Airways	
	Air China	
	Shanghai Airlines	
	Turkish Airlines	
	Egyptair	

Chapter 5

Airline Competition in Liberalized Markets: Effects on Thin Routes

Xavier Fageda

1. Introduction

There has been a general increase in competition in European airline markets since 2001, including competition on both direct and indirect connections. The success of several low-cost carriers on many short-haul routes, and the expansion of capacity at many large airports are a result of this increase in competition. In fact, many European airlines are having financial difficulties and many analysts suggest that a consolidation process is needed because there may be too many airlines playing an active role in European markets.

In any case, there is general agreement that competition may help travellers to reduce costs and enjoy a higher number of alternatives to choose from when flying on a particular route. Indeed, extensive empirical literature analyses the influence of market structure variables on airline prices (Borenstein, 1989; Evans and Kessides, 1993; Marín, 1995; Berry et al., 1996; Dresner et al., 1996; Morrison, 2001; Carlsson, 2004 and others). Controlling for cost shifters, a typical result in these studies is that route concentration (along with airport concentration) substantially influences the prices charged by airlines to travellers. Other related papers quantify conduct parameters in airline markets (Brander and Zhang, 1990, 1993; Oum et al., 1993; Brueckner and Spiller, 1994; Fisher and Kamerschen, 2003; Fageda, 2006). Within this context, it is commonly found that, on average, airlines compete à la Cournot and that an airline's behaviour becomes more competitive when there is a decrease in route concentration.

It is also of interest to examine which routes benefit from an increase in competition. In the post-liberalization period, thick routes are, of course, enjoying lower prices and higher frequencies. Less clear is whether routes than cannot generate high traffic levels can also take advantage of a more competitive scenario in airline markets.

In this regard, the empirical literature on airline competition tends to focus attention on large markets, while the losers of the liberalization process may have been travellers that fly on thin routes. Density economies in the airline industry are widely recognized in the literature (Caves et al., 1984; Brueckner and Spiller, 1994). Thus, competition on thin routes may be difficult because cost minimization requires that a very few number of airlines offer services on those routes.

To our knowledge, only Starkie and Starrs (1984) for Australia, and Bitzan and Junkwood for the US (2006) empirically analyse the factors that determine prices in airline markets focusing the attention on thin routes. Starkie and Starrs (1984) do not find substantial differences in prices between monopoly and oligopoly routes, but they find that liberalization has been positive in terms of higher frequencies and more routes served. Bitzan and Junkwood (2006) find that fares are higher for those routes serving smaller communities but those higher prices are equally explained both by market power and higher costs.[1]

---

1   Concerning the US market, note that a concentration of traffic in a smaller number of large airports following deregulation was found (Reynolds-Feighan, 2000, 2001). Similarly, Goetz and Sutton (1997) found

Here we examine the dynamics of competition in the Spanish airline market, focusing attention on thin routes. We want to analyse whether thin routes are still monopoly routes in the post-liberalization period. Furthermore, we want to examine the effects on prices and frequencies if there is an increase in competition on thin routes. To this aim, we take advantage of data for 62 routes in the Spanish domestic market for the period 2001–2008. Using this data, we analyse the evolution of market concentration and estimate pricing and frequency equations.[2]

Our data shows a clear decrease in the proportion of routes that are currently monopoly routes and also a decrease in the concentration indicators. This is particularly true after the capacity expansions at the largest airports in Spain. Concerning the two largest airports, competition seems to be tougher in Barcelona-El Prat than in Madrid-Barajas. This may be explained by a higher presence of low-cost carriers in the former and the control of the latter by the largest Spanish airline, Iberia. Finally, our estimates find evidence that the increase in competition on thin routes has resulted in lower prices and higher frequencies for travellers. Thus routes of different traffic levels (including thin routes) seem to benefit from a more competitive scenario in the post-liberalization period.

The rest of the chapter is organized as follows. In Section 2, we mention some relevant aspects of the Spanish airline market and explore data in terms of market concentration. Then we estimate pricing and frequency equations, taking as explanatory variables the intensity of competition, route distance, demand and other market characteristics. Section 4 indicates which type of airline has entered the thin routes market. Finally, last section is devoted to the concluding remarks.

2. The Spanish Market

The Spanish market is the third-largest air transport market in the European Union of 27 countries. As Table 5.1 shows, the UK is the largest market (combined domestic and international traffic) with more than 200 million passengers, and Germany and Spain each moved about 165 million passengers in 2007. Concerning the domestic market, Spain is clearly the largest market in the EU27 with about 45 million passengers. The second-largest domestic market is Italy with 28 million passengers.

Here we focus our attention on the Spanish domestic market, a very important market in the context of the European Union. Our analysis is based on data for 62 non-stop pair links for the period that goes from 2001 to the winter season of 2008–2009, where the origin is the city with the largest airport. Our data set excludes multi-segment markets so that the empirical analysis is made for routes matching city pair markets. The frequency of the data is semi-annual so that we differentiate between the summer and winter season.

Note that Madrid-Barajas airport is the origin on 26 routes, Barcelona-El Prat airport on 24 and other airports (Palma de Majorca, Valencia, Bilbao and Seville) on 18 routes. In 2007, Madrid-Barajas was the fourth-largest airport in Europe in terms of total traffic of passengers, Barcelona-El Prat was the eighth and Palma de Majorca was the fourteenth. Both Madrid and Barcelona airports were subject to strong capacity constraints in 2001. A new runway has been operating at Barcelona

---

that the largest hubs enjoyed the highest increase in traffic in the period 1978–1993.

2   Note that we only consider directly served markets while it could be that thin routes are served indirectly by airlines. However, the focus of our analysis is on short-haul routes where the attractiveness of indirect flights is low.

Table 5.1   Passenger transport in the ten largest air markets in EU-27 2007

Country	Total air transport (000)	Total national transport (000)
United Kingdom	217,288	26,106
Germany	163,844	24,378
Spain	163,523	44,171
France	120,034	27,192
Italy	106,294	28,703
Netherlands	50,501	56
Greece	34,786	6,685
Ireland	29,840	888
Sweden	26,967	6,893
Portugal	24,324	2,953

Source: Eurostat.

airport since October 2004, and a new terminal building and two new runways have been operating at Madrid airport since February 2006.

We found several types of airlines operating in the Spanish domestic market. The two with the largest market share, Iberia and Spanair, are network carriers that belong to oneworld and Star alliance respectively. The third largest carrier, Air Europe, is owned by a tourist operator and has code-share agreements with several airlines of the SkyTeam alliance. There are other regional airlines that operate on a small number of routes, such as Lagun air or Binter Canarias. The Iberia group includes a large regional airline, Air Nostrum.

Additionally, several low-cost carriers have an increasing presence in the Spanish market. Since 2004, Vueling and Air Berlin are important players in this market. Clickair, a low-cost carrier in which Iberia is a relevant participant, has expanded operations in Barcelona airport since 2006. In the summer of 2009, Clickair and Vueling made effective a merger approved by the European Commission. Finally, Ryanair and easyJet are increasingly active in the Spanish market although they are present only on a very few domestic links.

Table 5.2 shows the distribution of routes by number of competitors in each of the periods for which we have data available. It makes sense to assume that the number of competitors at the route level will be strongly correlated with traffic density. Hence, our analyses below will focus on routes that were monopoly routes during either the summer season of 2001 or the winter season of 2001–2002.

About half of the routes in our sample were monopoly routes in 2001, while any routes had more than three airlines offering services in that period. Until the winter season of 2004, the proportion of monopoly routes was increasing. However, some thick routes took benefit from more than three airlines offering services. Hence it seems that competition in the Spanish market may have been focused on the thickest routes in the period 2001–2004.

Since the winter season of 2004 until the summer season of 2008, there has been a continuous decrease in the proportion of routes that were monopoly routes, and an increase in the proportion of routes with more than three competitors. Less than one-third of routes were monopoly routes during the summer season of 2008, and almost 20 per cent of routes had more than three airlines

Table 5.2   Distribution of routes by number of competitors

Period	Monopoly routes (%)	Routes with two competitors (%)	Routes with three competitors (%)	Routes with more than three competitors (%)	Total routes
Summer 2001	47	13	40	0	62
Winter 2001–02	53	18	29	0	62
Summer 2002	52	21	26	0	61
Winter 2002–03	62	22	17	0	60
Summer 2003	57	16	21	5	61
Winter 2003–04	55	22	19	3	58
Summer 2004	53	18	20	8	60
Winter 2004–05	48	27	17	8	60
Summer 2005	43	26	20	11	61
Winter 2005–06	39	34	18	8	61
Summer 2006	36	25	18	21	61
Winter 2006–07	33	26	26	15	61
Summer 2007	26	33	28	13	61
Winter 2007–08	23	34	28	15	61
Summer 2008	27	32	23	18	60
Winter 2008–09	31	30	30	10	61

Source: Own elaboration from OAG data.

offering services. Thus competition may have been generalized to routes with different traffic levels in 2005–2008.

In the last period with data available, the winter season of 2008–2009, there seems to be a general decrease in the number of competitors at the route level. This may be explained by the global economic crisis, which has resulted in a substantial reduction in the number of passengers moved on most routes.

Note that the total number of routes with at least one airline offering services remains quite stable in the considered period. Hence, we do not find a reduction in the number of routes served (at least when looking at our sample of routes). In fact, public service obligations in Spain have been imposed on routes that link the islands of Canary and Balearics. Most intra-Canarian and intra-Balearic routes move a high number of passengers per season.

Table 5.3 depicts the evolution of the mean Hirshman–Herfindahl index for all routes and distinguishes between routes with different origin airports. Overall, the concentration index is quite high, moving from 0.72 in the summer season of 2001 to 0.64 in the winter season of 2008–2009. There is even an increase in the concentration levels in the period 2001–2004 when considering all routes, while a decrease in these concentration levels can be observed since the winter season of 2004–2005.

Note that the increase in competition (in terms of the reduction of the Hirshman–Herfindahl index) is notable at Madrid airport since the winter season of 2006–2007, and at Barcelona airport since the winter season of 2004–2005. Recall that capacity expansions have been made at Barcelona airport in October of 2004 and at Madrid airport in February of 2006. In this regard, Fageda (2006) shows that capacity constraints at both airports have been an important entry barrier for new carriers in the Spanish market

Furthermore, concentration levels are similar at Barcelona and Madrid airports while higher at other airports. This aggregate measure of competition may hide some relevant differences in the current scenario at Madrid and Barcelona airports, as we will see below. Indeed, low-cost carriers have a strong position at Barcelona airport while Madrid airport remains controlled by the largest Spanish airline, Iberia. In Palma de Majorca, Air Berlin has become a very important player while the dominance of Iberia at the other airports (Valencia, Bilbao, Seville) is still generally strong. The dominance of Iberia at these three airports explains why we obtain such high concentration indexes for routes originating at airports that are not Madrid or Barcelona.

It is interesting to examine the implications of the increase in the number of competitors at the route level. Table 5.4 shows the mean comparison tests of traffic, frequency and price levels for monopoly and oligopoly routes for all the periods in which data are available. As expected, route traffic density is much higher for oligopoly than for monopoly routes. The mean number of passengers is always above 300,000 passengers per season for oligopoly routes, while it lies between 50,000 and 90,000 passengers for monopoly routes. Note that traffic levels for monopoly routes have been generally increasing since 2001. An interpretation of this tendency is that the route traffic levels that make it possible for more than one airline to offer services have been getting

Table 5.3   Evolution of the concentration index (HHI) by origin airport

Period	Mean HHI (all routes)	Mean HHI (Madrid origin)	Mean HHI (Barcelona origin)	Mean HHI (other origin)
Summer 2001	0.72	0.63	0.78	0.82
Winter 2001–02	0.76	0.66	0.83	0.82
Summer 2002	0.77	0.70	0.81	0.85
Winter 2002–03	0.82	0.76	0.86	0.90
Summer 2003	0.79	0.72	0.82	0.87
Winter 2003–04	0.78	0.72	0.80	0.89
Summer 2004	0.76	0.71	0.78	0.83
Winter 2004–05	0.72	0.69	0.72	0.80
Summer 2005	0.70	0.67	0.68	0.78
Winter 2005–06	0.69	0.65	0.65	0.84
Summer 2006	0.67	0.66	0.64	0.76
Winter 2006–07	0.64	0.58	0.59	0.84
Summer 2007	0.61	0.58	0.55	0.83
Winter 2007–08	0.60	0.57	0.56	0.75
Summer 2008	0.62	0.63	0.56	0.70
Winter 2008–09	0.64	0.64	0.57	0.77

Source: Own elaboration from OAG data.

Table 5.4   Mean comparison tests (monopoly and oligopoly routes)

Period	Mean number of passengers			Mean weekly frequency			Mean price		
	Monopoly routes	Oligopoly routes	Difference	Monopoly routes	Oligopoly routes	Difference	Monopoly routes	Oligopoly routes	Difference
Summer 2001	51,864	361,571	4.64*	18	76	4.67*	222	228	0.21
Winter 2001–02	49,589	320,092	4.19*	20	75	3.91*	192	168	–1.47
Summer 2002	64,309	359,321	4.34*	18	75	4.10*	246	236	–0.38
Winter 2002–03	65,419	386,514	4.55*	21	73	4.10*	212	192	–1.41
Summer 2003	61,819	423,910	5.34*	20	82	5.18*	209	195	–0.57
Winter 2003–04	65,262	390,545	4.36*	22	76	3.78*	191	136	–2.51†
Summer 2004	75,650	427,451	4.91*	21	78	5.19*	254	248	–0.17
Winter 2004–05	70,447	348,582	3.67*	27	76	3.06*	170	148	–1.06
Summer 2005	65,254	407,526	4.39*	24	75	3.43*	260	182	–2.48†
Winter 2005–06	61,290	339,017	3.67*	28	68	2.89*	126	135	0.49
Summer 2006	62,529	392,217	4.01*	19	68	4.17*	200	223	0.79
Winter 2006–07	57,206	350,598	3.21*	21	76	2.81†	188	136	–3.15
Summer 2007	65,517	389,254	3.26*	26	71	2.41†	212	176	–1
Winter 2007–08	50,693	331,851	2.75*	16	66	2.57†	236	129	–4.23*
Summer 2008	77,387	341,013	3.44*	19	62	3.23*	252	225	–0.6593
Winter 2008–09	90,148	347,473	2.78*	24	59	2.55*	172	143	–1.6

Source: Own elaboration from data from OAG, AENA and websites of airlines. . Significance at the * 1%, † 5%

lower. Along with the decrease in the proportion of monopoly routes that we observe in Table 5.2, this may imply that thin routes have benefitted from an increase in competition in the Spanish airline market.

In addition to this, the number of flights per week is much higher on oligopoly than on monopoly routes, so that airline competition may improve service quality for passengers. In contrast, prices are usually (not always) lower on oligopoly than on monopoly routes but differences are not statistically significant in many periods. Table 5.5, which shows the mean comparison tests for the whole period but distinguishing by the origin airport, provides a possible explanation of this fact. Indeed, price levels are quite similar for monopoly and oligopoly routes when considering routes which originate at Madrid airport, while they are much lower for oligopoly routes when considering routes which originate at Barcelona airport or other airports. Likely, the price behaviour of airlines at Madrid airport may condition the comparison tests of price levels between monopoly and oligopoly routes for the whole sample of routes. In this regard, Fageda and Fernández-Villadangos (2009) show that the airlines' conduct is much more competitive at Barcelona airport (near to the Cournot solution) than at Madrid airport (near to a joint profit maximization setting) after airport capacity expansions.

In any case, the analysis of the implications of an increase in the number of route competitors in terms of prices and frequencies requires considering other aspects that may influence those prices and frequencies. The next section undertakes an estimation of pricing and frequency equations that include as explanatory variables the intensity of competition and other variables related to cost and demand shifters.

3. The Empirical Analysis

We make some regressions here to examine the influence of an increase in competition in prices and frequencies, focusing our attention on 33 routes from our sample that were monopoly routes either in the summer season of 2001 and/or the winter season of 2001–2002. Of these 33 routes, 6 had Madrid as origin airport, 14 have Barcelona as origin airport and the rest had other airports as origin airport.

Our main interest is to assess whether thin routes have taken advantage of the increase in competition in the Spanish airline market. Since it is difficult to use a precise definition of what is

Table 5.5   Mean comparison tests (monopoly and oligopoly routes by origin airport)

Routes	Mean number of passengers			Mean weekly frequency			Mean price		
	Monopoly routes	Oligopoly routes	Difference	Monopoly routes	Oligopoly routes	Difference	Monopoly routes	Oligopoly routes	Difference
Madrid origin	97,613	503,840	10.15*	27.33	92.23	8.65*	181.41	181.82	0.03
Barcelona origin	54,736	274,804	13.50*	19.12	53.55	11.25*	220.36	186.88	−3.13*
Other airports (origin)	33,508	146,329	21.05*	17.03	45.87	12.59*	228.96	151.70	−6.22*

Source: Own elaboration from data from OAG, AENA and airline websites. Significance at the * 1%.

effectively a thin route, we restrict our analysis to those routes that were monopoly routes at the beginning of the period for which data are available. Most of these routes may be considered thin routes and certainly their traffic levels at 2001 were substantially lower in comparison with other routes. The mean number of passengers of the sub-sample considered was 50,653 passengers in 2001, while that mean number was 342,169 passengers when considering the rest of the routes.

We estimate the following pricing equation for the route k during period t:

$$p_{kt} = b_0 + b_1 Q_{kt} + b_2 dist_{kt} + b_3 HHI_{kt} + b_4 D^{summer} + b_5 D^{island} + e_{kt,} \tag{1}$$

Unfortunately, data of prices that European airlines charge to passengers is not generally available, so researchers must follow specific procedures to collect these data. This makes it very difficult, if not impossible, to have information on the average fares charged by airlines on the route.

In this regard, the dependent variable of equation (1), p_{kt}, is the lowest mean round-trip price charged by airlines offering services weighted by their corresponding market share. Information has been obtained manually from airlines' websites for a sample week of each of the summer and winter seasons since 2001. Hence, this study is drawn on (at least for Europe) a unique database of historical prices (2001–2008).

We follow these homogeneous rules in the data collection of prices. Price data refer to the city pair link that has as its origin the city with the largest airport. Additionally, the data was collected one month before travel, the price refers to the first trip of the week, and the return is on a Sunday. Following this procedure, we can exploit the variability of data across routes because we obtain data in homogeneous conditions for all of the routes in our sample.

We include the following explanatory variables in the pricing equation:

1. Demand (Q): total number of passengers carried by airlines on the route, including direct and connecting traffic. Information has been obtained from the websites of Spanish Airports and the Air Navigation (AENA) agency. The expected sign of the coefficient of this variable is ambiguous. More route traffic density may imply a better exploitation of density economics but higher demand levels may also lead airlines to charge higher mark-ups over costs.
2. Distance (*Dist*): number of kilometres that are needed to be flown between the origin and destination airport of the route. Data has been collected from the WebFlyer website. Obviously, distance is a major determinant of the costs that an airline must afford when providing services on a route, so that the sign of the coefficient of this variable should be positive.
3. Route concentration (*HHI*): index of Herfindahl–Hirschman at the route level. The concentration index is calculated in terms of airlines' departures.[3] Data on departures for each airline on each route have been obtained from the Official Airlines Guide (OAG) website. This variable will allow us to measure the influence of the intensity of competition of prices charged by airlines. In the case that competition reduces prices charged by airlines, the sign of the coefficient associated to this variable should be positive.
4. D^{island}: dummy variable that takes value 1 for routes with islands as endpoint. This variable may capture the absence of competition from other transportation modes like trains or cars,

---

3   Unfortunately, we do not have available data on the aircraft size used by airlines on the route. Hence we are not able to calculate the concentration index in terms of the number of annual seats offered by airlines.

so that we could expect a positive sign for the coefficient associated with this variable.[4] However, the proportion of price-sensitive travellers may be very high in the case of islands, so that it is not clear which should be the sign expected for the coefficient of this variable.

5. D^{summer}: dummy variable that takes value 1 for the summer season that goes from April to October. This variable accounts for differences across seasons.

6. We estimate the pricing equation using the Two-Stage Least Square estimator (2SLS-IV) since two explanatory variables, demand and route concentration, may be endogenous. Indeed, a simultaneous determination of prices and demand may be taken place and entry patterns on a route will also be influenced by prices charged on that route.

We use the following instruments for the demand variable: (1) Population (*pop*): total mean population in a route's origin and destination provinces (NUTS3). Data has been obtained from the National Statistics Institute (INE). (2) Gross domestic product per capita (*GDPc*): mean gross domestic product per capita in a route's origin and destination regions (NUTS2). Data, which is not available at the province level for the recent years of the considered period, have been obtained from the National Statistics Institute (INE). (3) Tourism (*tour*): number of tourists per capita in the destination region (NUTS2). Data has been obtained from the Institute of Tourist Studies (IET).

We use as an additional instrument for concentration at the route level, the concentration at the airport level ($HHI_{airport}$). The airport concentration index is calculated in terms of airlines' national departures both in the origin and destination airports for the route. Data on the percentage of departures for each airline on origin and destination facilities have been obtained from Spanish Airports and the Air Navigation (AENA) agency. Decisions at the airport level involve several routes so that we expect any endogeneity related to market concentration will be reduced by using airport concentration as an instrument for route concentration.

Our estimation procedure does not take into account the panel data nature of the sample. The use of a fixed-effects model is not appropriate in our context since this technique drops anything that is time-invariant from the model, such as route distance. Since the individual effects, the routes, are likely correlated with the error term (as indicated by Hausman test) the random-effects model is not appropriate either. Finally, the Hausman–Taylor estimator assumes that all explanatory variables are exogenous.

Tables 5.6 and 5.7 show the results of the pricing equation estimate. The variable for demand is negative and statistically significant so that density economies seem to be relevant even when just considering thin routes in the sample of routes. As expected, distance is positive and statistically significant but with an elasticity lower than one. Hence we find evidence of distance economies; prices per kilometre are reduced when increasing the distance of the route. In addition to this, prices seem to be higher for the summer season and we do not find substantial differences for routes with islands as end points.

Importantly, prices are substantially higher with an increase in market concentration. The variable for route concentration is statistically significant and the elasticities evaluated at the sample mean indicates that the magnitude of the effect is important. Indeed, a 10 per cent increase in route concentration implies about a 6 per cent increase in prices. Thus we find evidence that an increase in competition on thin routes has implied lower prices for travellers.

---

4   We are not able to consider a variable for high-speed train services in our analysis. The only route of our sample where high-speed train services were in place in all the considered periods was the route Madrid–Seville.

Table 5.6   Pricing equation estimates (IV regression)

Explanatory variables	Dependent variable: PR
Demand (Q)	−0.00045 (0.00022)[†]
Distance (*dist*)	0.10 (0.02)[‡]
HHI	134.43 (54.01)[†]
D^{Summer}	51.83 (7.75)[‡]
D^{island}	−3.84 (17.36)
Intercept	31.92 (71.25)
N	504
R^2	0.24
χ^2 (joint sig.)	28.55*

Instruments for demand and HHI: population, tourism, GDP per capita, airport concentration. Standard errors in parentheses. Significance at the * 1%, [†] 5%, [‡] 10%.

Table 5.7   Elasticities from estimates (evaluated at sample means)

Explanatory variables	Dependent variable: PR
Demand (Q)	−0.16[†]
Distance (*dist*)	0.29[‡]
HHI	0.58[†]
D^{Summer}	0.13[‡]
D^{island}	−0.002

Significance at the * 1%, [†] 5%, [‡] 10%.

Along with the effects on prices of an increase in competition, it is also of interest to examine the implications of more airlines offering services on a route and compare with total frequencies. This is generally considered to be a key indicator of the quality of service offered by airlines on a route. Hence we estimate the following frequency equation at route k in period t:

$$FQ_{kt} = c_0 + c_1 pop_{kt} + c_2 GDPc_{kt} + c_3 Tour + c_4 dist_{kt} + c_5 HHI_{kt} + c_6 D^{summer} + c_7 D^{island} + e_{kt} \quad (2)$$

where the dependent variable is the weekly total frequency offered by airlines on each route, FQ_{kt}. As explanatory variables, we use different variables that account for demand shifters; mean population of the endpoints of the route (pop_{kt}), GDP per capita of those endpoints ($GDPc_{kt}$) and tourism intensity at the destination region ($Tour_{kt}$). The simultaneous determination of frequencies and demand may be particularly high, so that we prefer to use the instruments of demand as explanatory variables instead of assuming the endogeneity of the variable of demand as we did in the implementation of the pricing equation. We expect a positive sign of the coefficient of all of these variables.

As in the pricing equation, we also take into account the route distance, differences across seasons and the fact that some routes have islands as end points. Concerning the variable of route concentration that measures the effects of the intensity of competition on frequencies, we make use of the airport concentration as instrument, as in the pricing equation, to consider the possible simultaneous determination of frequencies and concentration levels. In the case where competition increases frequency, the sign of the coefficient of this variable should be negative.

Tables 5.8 and 5.9 show the results of the estimates of the frequency equation. Concerning demand variables, population seems to be the variable more strongly correlated with frequencies. In addition to this, frequency decreases with an increase in distance. This could likely be explained by the fact that competition from other transport modes like trains or cars is reduced when distance increases. The influence of intermodal competition on frequencies seems to be better captured by the variable of distance than that for the variable for island, which is negative but not statistically significant. Note also that frequencies seem to be lower in the summer season.

Finally, it is important to stress that frequency decreases in a statistically significant way with an increase in route concentration. The elasticities evaluated at sample means indicate that the magnitude of the effect is quite high. Indeed, a 10 per cent increase in market concentration implies about a 7 per cent decrease in flight frequency. This means that airlines strongly compete in frequencies. The flight frequency that an airline offers on a route is a basic determinant of the quality of its services. A higher frequency implies a reduction of the schedule delay cost that is the difference between the desired and real time of departure for the traveller. In this regard, the negative relationship between frequencies and concentration is consistent with the S-curve effect of service frequency on airline's demand (Wei and Hansen (2005). Indeed, demand increases can be even more than proportional to frequency increases because of the quality effect.

Table 5.8   Frequency equation estimates (IV regression)

Explanatory variables	Dependent variable: FQ
Population	4.00e–06 (6.83e–07)*
GDP per capita	0.00006 (0.00025)
Tourism	0.16 (1.02)
Distance (*dist*)	–0.01 (0.003)*
HHI	–18.18 (5.56)*
D^{Summer}	–2.17 (1.04)†
D^{island}	–3.23 (8.71)
Intercept	34.16 (10.81)*
N	507
R²	0.31
χ² (joint sig.)	29.71*

Instruments for HHI: airport concentration. Standard errors in parentheses. Significance at the * 1%, † 5%

Table 5.9   Elasticities from estimates (evaluated at sample means)

Explanatory variables	Dependent variable: FQ
Population	0.49*
GDP per capita	0.05
Tourism	0.01
Distance (*dist*)	–0.29*
HHI	–0.71*
D^{Summer}	–0.05†
D^{island}	–0.01

Significance at the * 1%, † 5%,

To sum up, we find that travellers enjoy lower prices and higher frequencies due to the increase in competition when considering those Spanish routes in our sample that were monopoly routes in 2001. We obtain this result after controlling for variables for demand, costs and other market characteristics. As many of the monopoly routes in 2001 were thin routes, we can conclude that competition benefits have not been restricted to the densest routes.

4. New Entrants on Thin Routes

We have found some evidence that thin routes have benefitted from an increase in competition in the Spanish airline market. In this regard, it is of interest to examine which airlines have promoted competition on thin routes. Note that price rivalry may be tougher when the new entrants are low-cost carriers. However, some previous studies have found that those carriers may prefer to operate on high-density routes, particularly in the first years of operation (Bogulaski et al., 2004; Gil-Moltó and Piga, 2005).

Table 5.10 indicates the evolution of the market share of airlines that operate in the Spanish market concerning the sub-sample of routes that were monopoly routes in 2001. We differentiate between routes with different origin airports by showing the mean market share of different types of airlines for each group of routes. We focus the attention on the main Spanish airline (Iberia), low-cost carriers (Vueling, Clickair, Air Berlin, Ryanair and easyJet) and other carriers that include a network carrier (Spanair), a regional carrier (Lagun Air) and Air Europa. The latter airline cannot be included in any category since it has elements of a network carrier (code-share agreements with airlines of SkyTeam, connecting traffic) and other low-cost carriers (a single fare-class on most of its routes, a unique type of plane, a high focus on short-haul – and tourist – routes, etc.).

Iberia maintains a very high market share when looking at routes originating at Madrid airport. Currently, this airline has a mean market share of about 90 per cent in this group of routes. Our data show that Iberia lost market share in 2006–2007 just after the increase in capacity at Madrid-Barajas. However, Iberia has strengthened its position at this airport since 2008.

Although both Ryanair and easyJet have established Madrid airport as one of their operating bases, low-cost carriers have a very modest presence on domestic links from Madrid. The main competitor of Iberia on routes originating at Madrid airport, is Spanair, when it achieved an important increase in its market share in 2006–2007. However, the financial difficulties of the owner of Spanair, SAS, until 2009, has obliged this airline to reduce its operations. Now Spanair has been sold to a group of investors from Catalonia including the regional and local government. While SAS maintains its role as industrial partner of Spanair, the new owners of Spanair will likely concentrate their operations at Barcelona airport.

The scenario is quite different at Barcelona airport, where the market share of Iberia has been reduced to half of total flights in the considered period. In fact, Iberia only operates on the Madrid–Barcelona route while its regional partner, Air Nostrum, offers most of the connections from Barcelona airport. In contrast, low-cost carriers like Vueling or Clickair have a market share of about 25 per cent of total flights. Other carriers, particularly Spanair, also have a significant market share with about 25 per cent of total flights. However, note that Iberia had a participation in 20 per cent of shares for Clickair (with a call option of all shares). Recently, the European Commission authorized the merging of Vueling and Clickair effective from the summer season of 2009. Iberia will keep the control of 45 per cent of this new low-cost airline, which will use the brand name of Vueling. Although Vueling will in practice be an airline controlled by Iberia, it is not going to be a member of oneworld.

Table 5.10   Market share of different types of airlines by origin airport (monopoly routes in 2001)

Period	Routes with origin in Madrid			Routes with origin in Barcelona			Routes with origin in other airports		
	Iberia	Low-cost carriers	Other carriers	Iberia	Low-cost carriers	Other carriers	Iberia	Low-cost carriers	Other carriers
Summer 2004	1	0	0	1	0	1	0.95	0	0.05
Winter 2004–05	0.94	0	0.06	0.94	0	0.06	0.93	0.02	0.05
Summer 2005	0.95	0	0.05	0.89	0	0.11	0.88	0.06	0.06
Winter 2005–06	0.95	0	0.05	0.86	0	0.14	0.95	0.02	0.03
Summer 2006	0.93	0	0.07	0.84	0.04	0.12	0.91	0.03	0.06
Winter 2006–07	0.81	0.01	0.18	0.77	0.05	0.18	0.98	0.02	0
Summer 2007	0.77	0.02	0.21	0.58	0.2	0.22	0.94	0.03	0.04
Winter 2007–08	0.81	0.01	0.18	0.51	0.26	0.23	0.88	0.04	0.08
Summer 2008	0.9	0.02	0.08	0.56	0.24	0.2	0.85	0.1	0.05
Winter 2008–09	0.93	0	0.07	0.51	0.25	0.24	0.86	0.12	0.02

Source: Own elaboration from OAG data.

Figure 5.1 illustrates the different developments at Madrid and Barcelona airports by showing the market share of Iberia and low-cost carriers in terms of national departures from both airports. The market share of Iberia at Madrid airport moved from 62 to 58 per cent in the period 2001–2008, while low-cost carriers offer less than 10 per cent of total flights. In contrast, the market share of Iberia and low-cost carriers is very similar in 2008 at Barcelona airport, while Iberia controlled 66 per cent of total flights here in 2001. The much stronger position of low-cost carriers in Barcelona than at Madrid airport may explain our previous result when using mean comparison tests of prices in monopoly and oligopoly routes; prices are substantially different in oligopoly routes in comparison to monopoly routes for those routes with origin at Barcelona airport, while those differences are not statistically significant for those routes originating at Madrid airport.

The different situation at Madrid and Barcelona airports is mainly a consequence of the route network strategy of Iberia. Like other network airlines in Europe, Iberia is increasingly focusing its business on long-haul flights. Hence Iberia is concentrating operations at its hub, Madrid-Barajas, and domestic links are used to feed traffic to intercontinental destinations, particularly destinations in Latin America. This strategy could be threatened if other large network airlines develop a hub strategy at a nearby large airport like Barcelona. Iberia does not find it profitable to have two close large hubs but it has built a pre-emption strategy at Barcelona airport by consolidating a large low-cost carrier there. Indeed, Vueling may become an important entry barrier for network carriers wanting to develop a hub strategy at Barcelona airport because the feeding traffic will suffer from the tough competition. This complicates the opportunities for the development of a hubbing strategy by Spanair at Barcelona airport.

Regarding routes originating in other airports, Iberia maintains a high market share with low-cost carriers being its main competitors. Note here that the competition scenario may be different when considering Palma de Majorca and the other airports. Palma de Majorca is one of the main operation bases of Air Berlin: this airline has the largest market share at this airport and offers

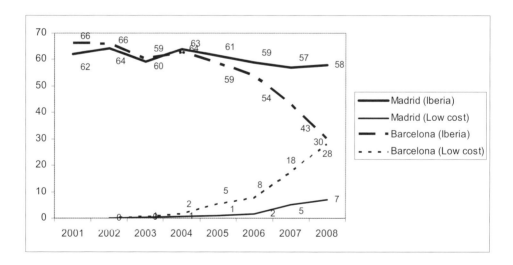

Figure 5.1   Evolution of airlines market share at Madrid and Barcelona airports

Note: The market share of airlines and low-cost carriers (Vueling, Clickair, Air Berlin, Ryanair, Easyjet) is in terms of national departures at both airports.

Source: AENA

a high number of flights to domestic links with origin in Palma. Iberia and its regional partner, Air Nostrum, has a very high market share of domestic links from the other considered airports (Bilbao, Seville, Valencia).

In short, we previously found that thin routes benefit from an increase in competition in the Spanish airline market when considering routes that were monopoly routes in 2001. However, this is particularly true in those routes originating at Barcelona and Palma de Majorca airports. Iberia maintains a very strong position on routes originating at Madrid and other smaller Spanish airports.

5. Concluding Remarks

In this chapter, we have shown an increase in competition on Spanish domestic routes that can be considered thin routes. By looking at the data of 62 Spanish routes for the period 2001–2008, we have found a general decrease in the proportion of routes that are monopoly routes and a decrease in concentration levels. Furthermore, our data reveal that traffic levels for monopoly routes have been generally increasing since 2001 so that it seems that route traffic levels that make it possible for more than one airline to offer services have been lowering in the period 2001–2008.

In addition to this, we have undertaken an estimation of pricing and frequency equations to analyse the implications of the increase in competition on thin routes. Since it is difficult to have a precise definition of what is a thin route, the empirical analysis has focused on 33 routes of our sample that were monopoly routes either in the summer season of 2001 and/or the winter season of 2001–2002. The mean number of passengers of the sub-sample considered was about 50,000 passengers in 2001, while that mean number was about 340,000 passengers when considering the rest of the routes.

After controlling for variables for demand, costs and other market characteristics, we find that a 10 per cent increase in route concentration implies approximately a 6 per cent increase in prices. We also find that a 10 per cent increase in market concentration implies approximately a 7 per cent decrease in flight frequency. Thus airline competition on thin routes has led to lower prices and higher frequencies and the magnitude of the effect seems to be relevant both from an economic and a statistical point of view.

The increase in airline competition on thin routes seems to be particularly remarkable for those routes originating at Barcelona airport in comparison to Madrid. The highest presence of low-cost carriers at the former airport may explain the different competition scenario at both airports.

From our analysis, we can infer that many routes with different traffic levels have benefited from the increase in competition in the post-liberalization period. However, that increase in competition is more modest on thin routes that originate either at large hubs or at small airports.

References

Berry, S., Carnall, M. and Spiller, P.T. (1996) *Airline Hubs: Costs, Markups and the Implications of Customer Heterogeneity*, NBER Working Paper, 5561, 1–38.

Bitzan, J. and Junkwood, C. (2006) Higher airfares to small and medium-sized communities – costly service or market power? *Journal of Transport Economics and Policy*, 40, 473–501.

Bogulaski, C., Ito, H. and Lee, D. (2004) Entry patterns in the Southwest Airlines route system. *Review of Industrial Organization*, 25, 317–350.

Borenstein, S. (1989) Hubs and high fares: dominance and market power in the U.S airline industry. *Rand Journal of Economics*, 20, 344–365.

Brander, J.A. and Zhang, A. (1993) Dynamic oligopoly behavior in the airline industry. *International Journal of Industrial Organization*, 11, 407–433.

Brander, J.A. and Zhang, A. (1990) A market conduct in the airline industry: an empirical investigation. *Rand Journal of Economics*, 21, 567–583.

Brueckner, J.K. and Spiller, P.T. (1994) Economies of traffic density in the deregulated airline industry. *Journal of Law and Economics*, 37, 379–415.

Carlsson, F. (2004) Prices and departures in European domestic aviation markets. *Review of Industrial Organization*, 24, 37–49.

Caves, D.W., Christensen, L.R. and Tretheway, M.W. (1984) Economies of density versus economies of scale: why trunk and locals service airline costs differ. *Rand Journal of Economics*, 15, 471–489.

Dresner, M., Lin, J.S.C. and Windle, R. (1996) The impact of low-cost carriers on airport and route competition. *Journal of Transport Economics and Policy*, 30, 309–329.

Evans, W.N. and Kessides, I.N. (1993) Localized market power in the U.S. airline industry. *The Review of Economics and Statistics*, 75, 66–75.

Fageda, X. (2006) Measuring conduct and cost parameters in the Spanish airline market. *Review of Industrial Organization*, 28, 379–399.

Fageda, X. and Fernàndez-Villadangos, L. (2009) Triggering competition in the Spanish airline market: the role of airport capacity and low cost carriers. *Journal of Air Transport Management*, 15, 36–40.

Fisher, T. and Kamerschen, D.R. (2003) Price–cost margins in the U.S airline industry using a conjectural variation approach. *Journal of Transport Economics and Policy*, 37, 227–259.

Goetz, A.R. and Sutton, C.J. (1997) The geography of deregulation in the US airline industry. *Annals of the Association of American Geographers*, 87, 238–263.

Gil-Moltó, M. and Piga, C. (2005) *Entry and Exit in a Liberalised Market*, WP.2005/10, Discussion Paper Series, Loughborough University.

Marín, P.L. (1995) Competition in European aviation: pricing policy and market structure. *Journal of Industrial Economics*, 16, 141–159.

Morrison, S.A (2001) Actual, adjacent and potential competition: estimating the full effect of Southwest airlines. *Journal of Transport Economics and Policy*, 35, 239–256.

Oum, T.H., Zhang, A. and Zhang, Y. (1993) Interfirm rivalry and firm-specific price elasticities in deregulated airline markets. *Journal of Transports Economic and Policy*, 27, 171–192.

Reynolds-Feighan, A. (2001) Traffic distribution in low-cost and full-service carrier networks in the US air transportation market. *Journal of Air Transport Management*, 7, 265–275.

Reynolds-Feighan, A. (2000) The US airport hierarchy and implications for small communities. *Urban Studies*, 37, 557–577.

Starkie, D. and Starrs, M. (1984) Contestability and sustainability in regional airline markets. *Economic Record*, 60, 274–283.

Wei, W. and Hansen, M. (2005) Impact of aircraft size and seat availability on airline's demand and market share in duopoly markets. *Transportation Research-E*, 41, 315–327.

Chapter 6

How Liberalization Can Go Wrong: The Case of Alitalia

Paolo Beria, Hans-Martin Niemeier and Karsten Fröhlich

1. Introduction

Liberalization of air transport has increased economic welfare in the United States of America and in Europe. These effects have been well studied and documented (for the US see Morrison and Winston, 1995; for Europe see Arndt, 2004; a good overview is given by Oum et al., 2009). While in the US private firms were forced to compete and adapt, in Europe state owned firms *had time to* adapt over the three stages of European aviation deregulation. Some of these former national airlines have been transformed into successful private airlines, while others found it difficult to adapt and some failed. This aspect of the liberalization of air transport has not been well studied.[1]

This chapter analyses one of the airlines, Alitalia (AZ), that has hitherto failed to adapt to competition. The expectation in the 1990s was that European flag carriers would consolidate because Europe had too many independent airlines. This consolidation process is still taking place, and some analysts expect that only three or four mega airlines and some niche carriers will survive (Doganis, 2001). In principle, as a major carrier AZ could have played an important role in this process. For instance, in the late 1990s the carrier was thought likely to form a strong alliance with KLM and become one of the major European global players. However, a few years later the Alitalia share price had collapsed due to heavy losses without any signs of recovery since. The question that needs to be asked is: why was AZ unable to evolve into a competitive airline as others European carriers seem to have done? The strong influence of trade unions in Italy is one of the popular answers. However, as we will show, this is just one aspect of the problems the carrier faced.

First, this chapter analyses the failure of AZ by providing some stylized facts. Then the performance of AZ with other European airlines is compared to provide some quantification of its poor performance. Third, the chapter will explain the major weaknesses in AZ's managerial strategy. While such weaknesses have also occurred at private airlines such as Pan Am and led to market exit, this chapter argues that the weak management performance is essentially caused by the political influence at AZ. The concluding section summarizes the main findings.

2. The (Sad) Tale of Alitalia – a Historical Overview

Alitalia started operations in 1947. As the Italian flag carrier it was a monopolist until the end of the last century, when liberalization in Europe began. In the following, the main historical events that appear to have driven AZ into its demise are outlined.

---

1 Doganis (2001) and Backx et al. (2002) are the exceptions.

Alitalia timeline 1990–2005

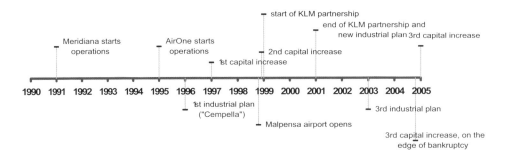

Figure 6.1   Main facts of Alitalia's history – period 1990 to 2005

2.1 Liberalization Starts

The first milestone in recent history is 1991, when Meridiana enters the Italian market. However, until the end of the 1990s Meridiana was more of an ally than a competitor. In fact the Italian antitrust authority enforced code-share agreements between the two companies (Spagnuolo, 2000). In November 1995 AirOne began operations in the domestic market. Despite its non-aggression policy AirOne was the only significant competitor for AZ for more than a decade (Spagnuolo, 2000).

Nevertheless, the Italian market remained substantially under monopoly conditions. AZ, which was 100 per cent owned by the Italian Treasury, never issued an industrial plan and remained without allies in the international marketplace throughout the 1990s. The carrier remained firmly in the hands of politicians, who defined the strategies and continued to generate a financial crisis lasting a further decade.

In 1996 the Cempella plan, named after AZ's CEO, Domenico Cempella, was implemented in a first attempt at solving some of the airline's problems. The plan consisted largely of cutting costs and raising investor capital in the stock market. These resources were used to strengthen the fleet. For the first time Milan Malpensa is mentioned as a key airport for the company relaunch, together with an alliance agreement with KLM. However, AZ's market share began declining from more than 90 per cent to less than 80 per cent in 1996. Apart from Meridiana and AirOne, other companies such as Alpi Eagles, Volare Airlines, Air Dolomiti, Gandalf and Air Europe started offering domestic and European flights.

2.2 Subsidies and Capital Injection

Since 1997 several capital increases were accorded to the airline. The first one amounted to 1,400m Euros in the period 1996 to 2000 (*Fisconelmondo*, 2008). This capital increase was immediately scrutinized by the European Commission (with the decision n.97/789), declaring it compatible with the EU norms as long as certain conditions are fulfilled by AZ to prevent anticompetitive behaviour. These conditions were partially met and in 2002 the Commission agreed to the full recapitalization without strings attached (C (2002) 2157; Giraudi, 2008; Crocioni and Newton, 2007). Despite being explicitly requested by the Commission, the pervasive political influence on AZ did not cease.

2.3 Malpensa and KLM

The new 'Malpensa 2000' airport (MXP) opened in October 1998 in Milan, allowing AZ to switch hub operations away from Rome Fiumicino to Milan (Beria and Scholz, 2010). At the same time, all flights from the existing Milan Linate airport, including those of the competing carriers, were transferred to MXP. Only few routes were kept to and from Linate. Local administrators in Rome began voicing complaints about the downgrading of their airport.

The announced merger/alliance between AZ and KLM was signed in January 1999 and scheduled for completion at the end of 2000. The new hub was a key element of this alliance. However, in September 1999, due to strong opposition to the shift of hub operations to MXP, the Italian authorities suspended the relocation programme. In particular, the contextual closure of Linate was defined by an EU sentence as anticompetitive and the airport remains operative (see below).

At the same time AZ was found guilty by the Italian Antitrust Authority of anticompetitive behaviour on domestic routes. The domestic market was characterized by high concentration, few competitors and 'significant barriers to entry'.[2]

2.4 2001, the Beginning of the End

The merger and the joint operations between AZ and KLM ended in August 2001, as decided one-sidedly by the Dutch carrier. The official line taken was that the partnership ceased due to the insufficient development of MXP and AZ's incomplete privatization. However, it appears that political opposition in Italy to changing AZ into an international carrier also played a key role. (This observation will be further discussed in section 4.1.2.) Thereafter, AZ decided by itself to start a peculiar double-hub scheme, moving back a significant part of connecting traffic to Rome Fiumicino.

2.5 2002–2005, Under the Axe of Competition

Without a strong partner from 2002 to 2003, AZ began facing increasing competition, including from Low-cost carriers (LCCs) eroding AZ's dominant position. This led to a general glut of flight services and subsequently significant decreases in air fares (CERTeT, 2003). AZ experienced a decline in load factors, leading to a marked worsening of the yield, a reduction of air services and finally a fall in revenues. In 2003 AZ's flights made up less than 50 per cent of the total domestic market.

The aviation crisis after 9/11 amplified firm-specific problems. In October 2003 the new CEO, Francesco Mengozzi, issued a new plan in order to resolve the situation. On the financial side, the plan foresaw a new capital increase and a decrease of the State ownership from 62 per cent to less than 50 per cent. However, this privatization was not accepted by labour unions and failed. Among the approved industrial measures was a 41 per cent cut of intercontinental flights, including some profitable routes. The company decided to focus on short- and medium-haul connections. This strategy revealed itself as unwise and did nothing to win the competition with the aggressive LCCs

---

2   Italian Antitrust Authority (AGCM) decree No. 12185, 10/07/2003. In 2001 the main four Italian carriers had a market share of 95 per cent of total passengers. AZ, with approximately 50 routes, controlled 60–70 per cent of the domestic market (CERTeT, 2003).

due to AZ's higher cost base. Despite the cuts in the network, AZ continued its politically driven 'duplication of routes strategy' focusing on MXP, Linate and Rome Fiumicino (see section 4.1.1).

In May 2004 Giancarlo Cimoli was nominated AZ's new CEO. At the same time the airline's losses reached a staggering one million euros per day. After a decade of heavy debt the airline was on the edge of bankruptcy (Boitani, 2008a). In October 2004, the Italian Government made a loan of €400 million, aptly termed a '*bridge loan*' because it had to be paid back within one year. The EC considered this loan as public help and applied the rule 'one time, last time', together with additional compulsory conditions.[3]

In December 2005 the airline, still in financial difficulty, issued a capital increase of €1 billion, almost half of it paid by the Italian State, thereby lowering its share to below 50 per cent. A few days later AZ repaid the €400 million loan of October 2004.

In hindsight, this privatization attempt appears trivial, as it was irrelevant with respect to who controls the firm (Scarpa, 2004). The only logical reason for it was to guarantee the survival of the carrier until the government elections of 2006. Once more political game play prevailed over industrial aspects (Ponti, 2007).

March 2006 is a new milestone in the Italian aviation market: Ryanair starts its route between Milano Bergamo and Rome Ciampino. It is the first time that a foreign carrier begins operations on a domestic route in Italy. Soon, many Italian domestic routes are routinely flown by foreign carriers, mainly Ryanair and easyJet[4] and more recently by a Lufthansa subsidiary.

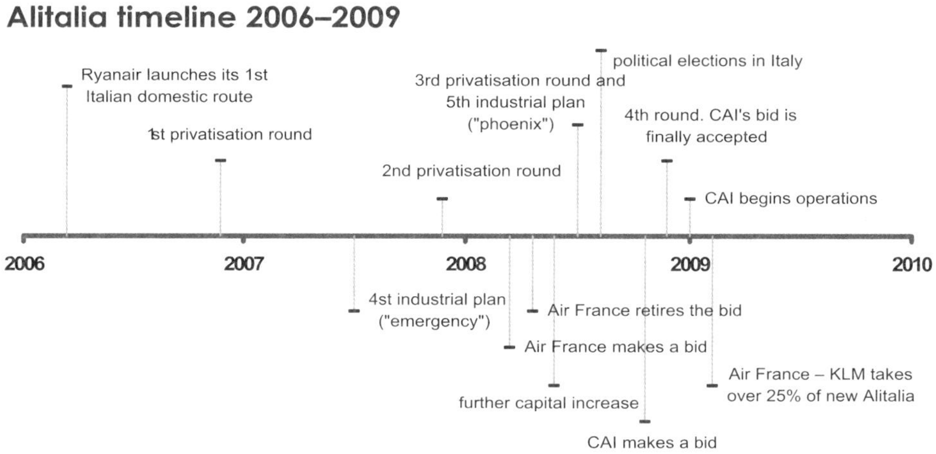

Alitalia timeline 2006–2009

Figure 6.2   Main facts of Alitalia's history – period 2006 to 2009

---

3   Conditions are: until 2014 Alitalia will not be allowed anymore to benefit of public money, the transfer is subject to the presentation of a realistic plan to restructure the company, the loan cannot be used to expand its competitive capacity for some years (for example by buying new aircraft) and the State must decrease its ownership to below 50 per cent (Ponti and Boitani, 2004).

4   Some examples: Milan Bergamo airport domestic passengers, the majority of which are served by Ryanair, passed from 280,000 passengers (2003) to 408,000 (2004) (CLAS, 2005). In 2007 the Ryanair route BGY–CIA alone moved 166,000 (ENAC, 2008). Ryanair operates ten Italian routes (2012) from Bergamo, ranging from daily to 3–4 times a day frequencies. Similarly, easyJet connects from MXP ten domestic relations. Both the Milan–Rome and Milan–Naples routes are served (2012) up to 5 times per day. More domestic low-cost connections exist, especially Sardinia–mainland and north–south.

2.6 The Never-ending Privatization

In 2006 AZ losses increased to around €2 million per day (Scarpa, 2007). In December the left-wing government embarked on the privatization path to sell its remaining 39.9 per cent of shares. The declared aim was to start a new 'transparent and non-discriminatory process'. Several applicants qualified for the share offer, including AirOne, AZ's main competitor. However, AZ appeared to be a rather unattractive buy: its fleet was obsolete and too diverse, with a low productivity, an almost worthless brand name and in a more than dire financial situation. Also, managerial know-how was insignificant, due to rapid politically driven management staff turnover. AZ's only two attractions are its slots on some congested airports and the quasi-monopoly it enjoyed due to political protection. However, these 'true' assets were not 'for tender' this time and eventually all potential buyers retired from the auction (Ponti, 2007).

In order to stop additional financial losses, AZ's management issued a further plan in August 2007 termed 'Emergency Plan 2008–2010'. One key issue was to abandon MXP as a hub in order to concentrate flight activities in Rome.

A second round of privatization took place in December 2007, with different rules: among a shortlist of interested participants, AZ would choose one single partner to start negotiations. AZ, as was later confirmed by the Italian Government, chose Air France-KLM and in the meantime, it sold three pairs of slots in London Heathrow for €92 million in order to obtain cash to continue operations.

In March 2008 AF-KLM made a bid to buy 100 per cent of AZ (including a 100 per cent share exchange[5]) and to recapitalize the firm with around €1 billion. In total, the offer is €1.7 billion and the Italian government would be issued with 1.4 per cent of AF-KLM's shares. However, the validity of the offer was bound to the following conditions: the full agreement of labour unions, a written commitment of the government to guarantee a full set of traffic rights (slots, etc.), agreements with Rome airport society (AdR) and maintenance firm (Fintecna) to support the plan, and the withdrawal of the Milan airport society's (SEA) request for reimbursement.[6] In return AZ is guaranteed to remain autonomous and Italian flagged and job losses were limited to 2100. The fleet was proposed to be shrunk to 149 airplanes, before the start of a renewal and expansion plan after 2010. AZ's hub would be Rome Fiumicino, which led to a new wave of complaints by Lombard politicians.

The political discussion surrounding the AF-KLM proposal was heated and amplified by the fact that political elections were close. The opposition leader, Berlusconi, and some left-wing political leaders termed the deal a '*clearance sale*' and called for its refusal. Consequently, AF-KLM retired its offer in April. However, AF-KLM's decision to withdraw might have been partially driven by the surge in oil prices and crisis in the air travel sector.[7] A day later the government approved a short-term loan of €300 million to AZ, to be repaid before 31 December 2008. The EC informally declared this loan a state aid and announced the rejection. In May, the loan is changed into a non-repayable capital increase.

In May 2008 the bank group Intesa Sanpaolo is put in charge as an advisor for AZ's new privatization process by the Ministry of Economic Affairs. At the same time, the laws governing

---

5   The exchange foresees one AF-KL share for each 160 AZ shares. In 1999, at the highest point, share value was €18.21. Now share value is down near to zero: AF-KL offer €0.099 each.

6   Requested in mid-2007 by the Milan airport concessionaire against AZ's retirement from the northern hub and amounting to €1.25 billion.

7   *Sole 24 Ore*, 'Alitalia: per AF 'ragioni industriali' dietro a ritiro', 22 April 2008.

the declaration of bankruptcy are suspended '*to face this extraordinary situation*', as stated by the Minister of Economy, Mr Tremonti.[8]

The advisor issued a restructuring plan, termed '*Piano Fenice*' (Phoenix plan), whose main points are:

- declaration of receivership, together with modifications of the law regulating this legal institution (*legge Marzano*);
- merger with AirOne into a new company free of the of debts and with less workers; and
- the application of a redundancy fund for more than 3,000 workers.

In September 2008 the administrator of AZ receives a bid for the purchase from CAI (*Compagnia Aerea Italiana*). CAI was a newly founded society on 26 August by BancaIntesa, AZ's advisor for the privatization process, and 15 other Italian shareholders. The purchase by this group had been strongly supported by the political power in order to 'guarantee' an Italian flag carrier and 'to avoid speculations' and a transfer to a foreign competitor.

CAI began a long bargaining process with the Italian labour unions, whose acceptance of all contractual aspects was a prerequisite of the bid itself. In September 2008 CAI retracted its bid after failing to reach agreement with one of the national labour unions (CGIL) and the unions representing pilots and cabin crew. The political debate and media attention climaxed when all parties involved accused each other of wrongdoing.

However, CAI did not fully retire from the takeover project and just a week later, signed the needed agreement with the labour unions. CAI's bid was renewed and finally accepted on 22 September 2008. CAI becomes the new owner of AZ and AirOne in November under the following additional conditions:

- CAI will pay €1,052,000,000 partially in cash and partially by taking off AZ's debt;
- CAI will operate for at least two years following the *Piano Fenice*;
- The CAI shareholders must keep the ownership of Alitalia for five years ("lock up"). Only after October 2013 they are allowed to sell their participation and leave the company;
- new contractual conditions for both pilots and cabin crew; and
- AZ's debt and any redundant workers are to be left in a bad company.

The agreement with the pilots was only signed after the direct intervention of a representative of Italy's Prime Minister Berlusconi.

Finally the 'new' AZ began operations in January 2009. All its debts had been transferred and the excess labour made redundant. The redundant workers were given generous redundancy conditions. One half of the flights operated previously by the former AZ and AirOne were cut. Flights to MXP were decreased by almost 89 per cent from 1,348 per week to 153 (*Corriere della Sera*, 2009a) and the increase of flights to Fiumicino did not compensate for this reduction. Moreover, flights became heavily concentrated on the Milan–Rome route (Boitani, 2009).

2.7 2009–2012, the End of the Story?

The privatization process did not end with the transfer of ownership to CAI. In January 2009, AF-KLM obtained the relative majority of AZ by buying a 25 per cent share of the new AZ for €320

---

8   *La Repubblica*, 30 May 2008.

million. The Italian investors obtained a speculative profit of approximately 14 per cent in one month (they paid 1,05 Billion for 100 per cent).

After an initial promise of returning to invest in MXP (*Corriere della Sera*, 2009b) the position of AZ towards both Milan airports changed again (*La Repubblica*, 2009b). Recently a definitive return to the conveniently located Linate and a near dismissal of MXP took place. The reasons for this are simple: at Linate AZ owns the majority of slots, enjoys market power on many routes,[9] and can focus on business travellers. Some degree of competition is present only at the Milan–Rome pair where the new high speed train 'Frecciarossa' already enjoys a 50 per cent share (*La Repubblica*, 2009a). Ryanair, easyJet and others continued to challenge AZ by offering new routes and services, but only from peripheral airports. Only in 2012 the liberalization of the route Milan Linate – Fiumicino started, when the Antitrust authority (AGCM) declared that the High Speed services does not guarantee the absence of a monopoly situation (in particular in the early morning and late evening). Consequently, Authority decided for a forced tender for a group of slots that were assigned, in number of seven, to easyJet.

In the meantime, the situation of the new Alitalia worsened again, in terms of network, passengers and financial performance. The initial capital is, after less than 5 years, nearly totally depleted (€ 851 millions lost), some services have been outsourced, routes reduced. Further redundancies are expected. In this context, the lock up period is terminating (October 2013) and the discussions about the future ownership of the carrier are at stake. It is likely that the current owners will sell the shares as soon as possible. The natural purchaser should be AirFrance, but rumors foresee also other players. It is however sure that the whole operation, whose aims were to save the carrier and its Italian flag is doomed to fail: Alitalia is now a fraction of the past airline, a lot of public money has been spent and also the "patriotic" aims will soon crash.

In conclusion, it must be emphasized that after the liberalization of the European aviation market, the successful merger with KLM, together with the launch of the new hub in MXP could have been the foundation for AZ to become a successful airline. The end of the AZ-KLM partnership, followed by a withdrawal from market-driven strategies to a politically dominated approach, ultimately doomed AZ to its decline. Its market share decreased in all markets in favour of both new entrants and old rivals. Furthermore, AZ failed with respect to cost control. Also the "private" experience showed that the airline is too weak to survive as it is.

3. Quantifying the Performance of Alitalia

This section provides some quantified insights into the financial and operational performance of AZ to determine the extent of the carrier's failure. The main emphasis is less on explaining AZ's bad performance than giving an idea of its scope. First, AZ is compared with other European mid-sized and regional airlines using a number of key performance indicators. The data used was taken from the *Airline Performance Indicators* consultancy report by Jacobs Consultancy (2008). Their publications reach back to 2001, cover a range of global airlines up to 2007 and report a number of annual key performance indicators for the airline industry. All financial data are converted into euros and reported in nominal terms. The carriers with which AZ's performance is compared with

---

9   This problem is especially evident in the Linate–Fiumicino route, where the only remaining competitor, Meridiana, dropped the 3 times a day route in March 2009. In fact, despite the low fare policy applied (€41), the available slots were too few to face competition with AZ, offering more than 40 couples of flights per day. Other Linate domestic routes 100 per cent dominated by Alitalia are Alghero, Reggio Calabria, Lamezia Terme, Brindisi and Bari. Napoli is more than 80 per cent dominated.

are the following: Iberia (IB), SAS (SK), Austrian Airways (OS), Finnair (AY), Cyprus (CY) and Turkish Airways (TK). These airlines were selected because they are European and appear to have a similar market dimension and/or airline structure. Furthermore, they are all legacy carriers and we have identified these carriers as regional hub-and-spoke carriers. CY, AY, OS and TK are chosen because they are more niche carriers and might serve as a reference point for AZ. SK and IB were chosen because they are of comparable size to AZ. The larger European carriers, such as AF-KLM, British Airways and Lufthansa were excluded because of their global reach and larger fleet. First, the literature on AZ's performance measurement is briefly reviewed, followed by information on profits, operational performance and revenues and costs of the chosen European regional hub-and-spoke carriers.

Bergamini et al. (2010) investigated the business model of AZ and measured the carrier's performance using Total Factor Productivity (TFP) methods. They found that productivity declined from 1998 to about 2002 and then rebounded until about 2006. In their view AZ suffered from high costs coupled with losses in market share. Barros and Peypoch (2009) use Data Envelopment Analysis (DEA) to evaluate the performance of European carriers. For AZ they had contradicting results depending on the DEA model applied. Some efficiency scores were low, while others were high. In their view the time trend and the demographic conditions of a carrier's home country are the major determinants of airline efficiency. Barbot et al. (2008) employed DEA and TFP to analyse the efficiency of airlines across the globe. Their results for AZ also indicate very low performance levels. Their findings lead them to conclude that low-cost carriers are generally more efficient than traditional ones and airlines of the same region have usually similar efficiency results, indicating a regional component as an explanatory variable. Overall the literature seems to confirm that AZ is generally performing poorly. However, an answer to why exactly this might be the case cannot be found in these studies. Figure 6.3 shows demand and supply, measured in passenger kilometres (RPK) and available seat kilometres (ASK), of AZ and its main competitor AirOne.

The following section provides a number of measures for AZ's performance. First, the decline of AZ's share price since going public in 1998 is shown. Economic theory predicts that in a competitive market the share value of a firm is a good indicator of its competitiveness. Figure 6.3 shows AZ's share price between 1998 and 2008. Initially the proposed merger with KLM and the creation of the MXP led to an increase in the share price because shareholders expected a successful partnership between the two carriers. Once this partnership ended the share price experienced a fall. Over time it crystallized that AZ was not and could not be made profitable. Within a decade it had lost 95 per cent of its original share value (see Figure 6.4).

The choice of an appropriate measure of airline profits is a difficult task. Earnings before interest, taxes and depreciation (EBITDA) appear most appropriate, but it excludes a potentially high degree of capital costs if airlines buy their aircraft. Furthermore, airlines might face large write-offs, different fuel price hedges or exceptional items in their profit accounts which all related to financial management, but have little to do with operational performance or strategic decisions concerning the business model. Earnings before taxes (EBT) on the other hand include the capital costs but also financial management's fortunes or misfortunes. For a more complete picture both EBITDA and EBT were used in our analysis as depicted in Figure 6.5.

As can be seen AZ, AY and CY, the only considerably smaller airline in the sample, have negative EBITDA. In terms of EBT, OS also shows negative values. Furthermore, when measured in terms of EBT, AZ shows losses throughout the entire period although the decade between 1998

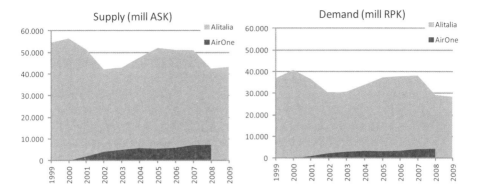

Figure 6.3   Demand and Supply for AZ and Air One

Source: Association of European Airlines database, year 2008

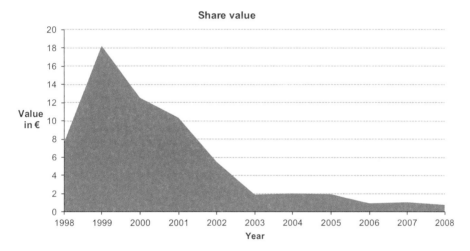

Figure 6.4   Alitalia shares value 1998–2008

Source: Borsa Italiana

and 2008 was a time of economic growth in Europe and generally positive returns in the European airline industry. In terms of overall profits AZ is clearly performing badly, even once measured in terms of profit margin. However, when performance is measured relative to the carriers' size, in terms of revenues, AZ's performance improves a little, although it remains the carrier with the highest losses. Figure 6.6 shows the costs per ASK for the seven airlines. It can be seen that low costs do not necessarily ensure a profitable airline, since SK has the highest costs per ASK but is not facing any substantial losses. As shown later in this section, SK has a clear focus on short-haul routes and covers its costs by achieving high yields on these routes. AZ on the other hand fails on all these accounts.

AZ has comparatively high costs (see Figure 6.6) and fails to achieve yields high enough to cover its shortcomings (see Figures 6.8 and 6.9). AZ's odd route structure will be discussed in sections 4.1.1 and 4.1.4, in Figure 6.7 high block hours per flight are shown for illustrative reasons.

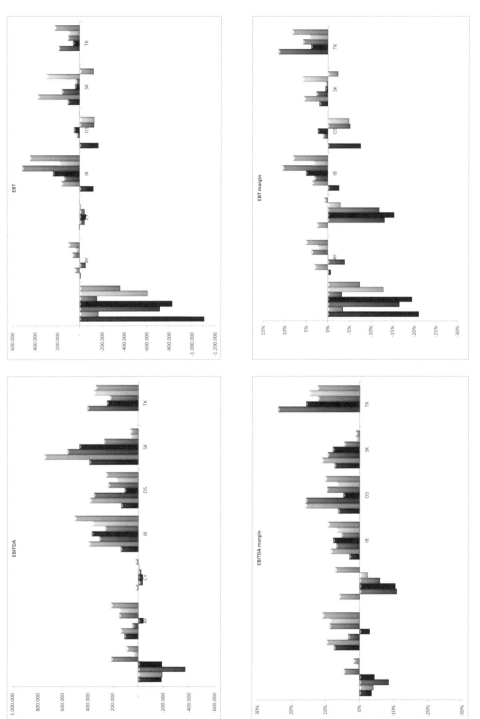

Figure 6.5   Airline profits (values in 1000s Euros and per cent respectively)
Source: Jacobs Consultancy, 2008

It is not unusual for a carrier that their overall costs are not covered by ticket sales, especially where a carrier maintains large cargo operations. However, once cargo and ancillary revenues are taken into account a carrier should break even. Once more AZ fails on this further account, as shown in Figure 6.10.

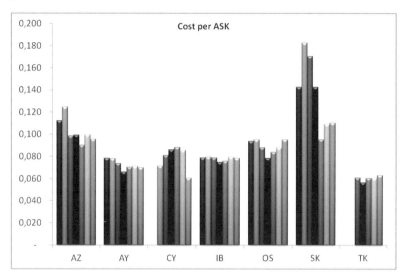

Figure 6.6   Costs per ASK in Euros

Source: Jacobs Consultancy, 2008

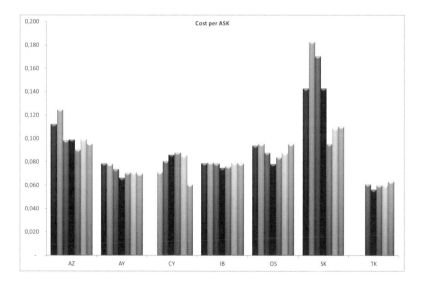

Figure 6.7   Average hours flown per flight

Source: Jacobs Consultancy, 2008

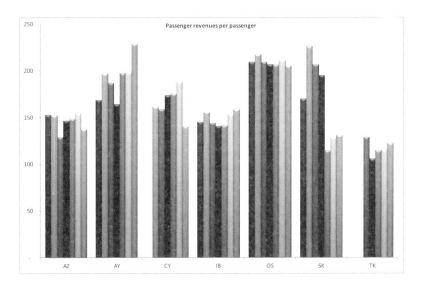

Figure 6.8   Average revenues from ticket sales per passenger in Euros

Source: Jacobs Consultancy, 2008

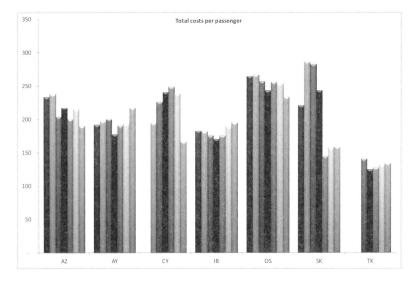

Figure 6.9   Total costs per passenger in Euros

Source: Jacobs Consultancy, 2008

    In conclusion, the analysis revealed that AZ has been performing negatively in terms of profits over the last decade. The carrier lacks cost control and a cohesive route structure. Furthermore, the literature confirmed the carrier's low efficiency performance. However, it is difficult to find easy answers and explanations in simple ratios, albeit this was not the aim of this section. In order to

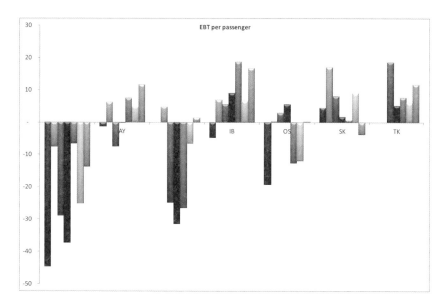

Figure 6.10   EBT per passenger in Euros
Source: Jacobs Consultancy, 2008

explain AZ's poor performance one must look beyond cost comparisons and operational indicators. The next section aims at outlining those factors that explain AZ's failure.

4. What Explains Alitalia's Failure?

To an outsider a number of managerial mistakes appear to have been the main causes of AZ's failure: the lack of a consistent hub and alliance strategy, efficient cost control, issues around ownership control and political influence, etc. This raises the question of why both the Italian government and the carrier's management have been either unable or unwilling to redress these mistakes in due course. This section investigates the mistakes being made in more detail in order to provide a more holistic explanation of AZ's demise.

4.1 Default Strategy

The literature on the economics of strategy provides some necessary conditions for the profitable management of firms (Porter, 1985; Besanko et al., 2003). These theories state that in order to earn sustained profits, firms can either decide to differentiate their product, to find a niche in which to operate or to become the cost leader. Each option entails a very different set of strategies that the firm needs to follow to be successful. Failure to decide on either option results in an inconsistent 'straddling strategy', which sends confusing signals to the market and ultimately leads to the firm's demise.

These strategies (or lack thereof) should be read in more general terms of the relationship between management behaviour and government directions. It will be asserted that AZ failed at developing a clear success strategy and ended up in the worst case scenario of straddling the market.

In particular it appears that pervasive State intervention in AZ's managerial decision making led to a loss of responsibility amongst AZ's management team.

4.1.1 Hub strategy   In terms of product differentiation a carrier might decide to offer a high-quality product by providing broad geographic coverage and high frequencies, most probably by adopting a Full Service Carrier model (FSC). FSCs rely on hub-and-spoke (H&S) networks to create economies of scale, scope and density. Smaller network carriers should operate one single hub in order to reap the full benefits (Wojahn, 2001). Before 1998 AZ had no fully integrated H&S network. However, with the opening of MXP and the KLM partnership, the carrier tried to restructure its network by focusing on a mono-hub structure from MXP. At that time the AZ's flight schedule was based on four hub waves per day in MXP (Burghouwt and de Wit, 2005). However, between 2000 and 2008 AZ's strategy changed radically by moving back a significant part of its supply to Rome and creating a peculiar two semi-hubs (MXP and Fiumicino) network (Beria and Scholz, 2010). The majority of long-haul flights (17 routes) remained in MXP together with the feeder routes structured into a three waves timetable, whereas many domestic and European flights moved to Rome. This led to a duplication of short-haul connections that decreased productivity (Bergamini et al., 2008). Hence AZ had lower load factors on feeder routes, especially in MXP, which also affected long-haul routes. Competing airlines specialized in their Italian routes (especially northern) to catch the demand not served, in favour of their hubs. In other words, separating point to point traffic from feeder traffic in two different routes and airports made the existence of a hub nonsensical.

The situation was worsened because of the existence of a third important network airport: Milan Linate, which connected north Italy to southern Italian cities. This irrational and unsustainable configuration, partially due to the bipolar Italian economic geography, made economies of scale impossible. Rather, this inefficient duplication is the outcome of a politically biased management imposed on AZ by national and local politicians (Macchiati, 2006; Beria and Scholz, 2010; Giuricin, 2009). It is worth noting that AZ's hub MXP, had it been managed differently, could have become dominant in northern Italy.[10] This would have been an effective, competitive strategy capable of consolidate the rents that in the past monopolistic flag carriers were legally entitled to. In other words, the original idea of closing Linate, boosting MXP and building an alliance with KLM would have created a truly powerful local monopolist, as happened in other European countries, particularly France and Germany.

4.1.2 Alliance strategy   Instead of becoming a FSC itself, AZ could have opted to become a niche carrier, operating in regional markets and feeding traffic to other larger airlines. Such small network carriers generally team up with alliances in order to reap network economies and to take advantage of frequent flyer programmes and branding. From 1999 to 2001 AZ was among the first airlines pursuing such a strategy by trying an alliance that would have led to a merger with KLM. However, the Italian airline was not able to create a stable relationship with its partner, which in the end withdrew its collaboration. The Dutch airline justified its withdrawal decision as follows. First, they questioned the failure in setting MXP up as a hub, which had been caused by the behaviour of numerous stakeholders, for example the local authorities that vetoed the closure of the well-located Linate airport. Furthermore, many competing airlines complained that this new

---

10   The topic of regional dominance through hubbing was described ten years before the opening of MXP for the Northern American market by Bailey and Williams (1988) and later reconsidered by Oum et al. (1995).

hub was an anticompetitive action in favour of AZ, an assertion which was later confirmed by the EU (Giuricin, 2009). The second element which drove KLM to separate from AZ was the lack of full privatization of the Italian carrier by June 2001. Apart from political motivations, KLM also suffered under the political uncertainty regarding AZ's ownership and market positioning. This political opposition and the changed political context made other allies such as AF and SkyTeam more attractive (Giraudi, 2008). Further uncertainty was caused by the lack of agreement among Italian political bodies and unions. As had been the case in the past, no party was willing to curtail its control over the flag carrier strategies. In due course KLM, less politically committed than AZ and free to pursue industrial strategies, recognized that the political risks involved were too high. They finally preferred to pay a fine[11] and retreat rather than staying involved with an overly politicized partner.

4.1.3 Lack of cost control   According to Porter (1985), cost leadership is another strategic option to guarantee long-term profits. Yet after the failure to form an alliance with KLM AZ remained a small FSC, which made it problematic to develop the airline as a cost leader. Nevertheless, it would not have been impossible to try to transform AZ into a low-cost carrier just as for example Aer Lingus had done previously. Also, after 1993 a number of other European airlines had adapted themselves successfully to the new competitive threats of LCCs, especially by improving operational efficiency (Oum and Yu, 1998). AZ failed on all counts.

Although many strategic elements, such as the heterogeneity of its fleet, were not correctly addressed by AZ's management, labour issues, such as too favourable labour conditions, are most often used in the literature to explain the carrier's poor financial performance. In 2007, AZ cost per employee amount approximately to €66,000 Euros (Jacobs Consultancy, 2008). That is higher than easyJet's or Ryanair's staff costs, which amount to €54,000 and €50,000 respectively. However, AZ's average wages are aligned with AF, LH or OS, AZ's direct competitors. The specific situation of crews was different, as Doganis (2001) reports. In 1998 AZ's pilots were the best paid amongst Western countries' carriers. In 2002 cockpit crew accounted for 29 per cent of staff costs, just below OS and with KLM, AF and British Airways counting 22 per cent or less (Doganis, 2006).

However, as shown in Table 6.1, productivity in terms of ASK per employee is comparable or even better than other legacy carriers.[12] The cost problems of AZ cannot be explained *only* in terms of high wages.[13]

A number of other facts help in better understanding why the airline became the worst financially performing carrier in Europe. Despite the downgrade in 1998 of Rome airport in favour of the new hub in Milan, the majority of the labour force remained in Rome, due to union pressures. According to Cavalli et al. (2004), only 6.6 per cent of the labour force (1,400 of 21,000) was based in Milan, implying that approximately 250 workers were moved *daily* from their Roman base to

---

11   KLM had to pay €150 million plus interest due to breaking the contract in December 2002.

12   Yet productivity is very dependent on network structure. AZ, except for a few intercontinental routes, has a network focused on Italy and Europe, where employees' turnarounds are shorter and productivity could in fact be more similar to that of an LCC. This should be taken into account to correctly compare labour productivity.

13   It should also be noted that careful consideration should be applied to compare productivity measures of airlines which are highly integrated (e.g. having their own maintenance) with other airlines that have outsourced parts of their value chain. Although the data by Jacobs Consultancy (2008) were promised to account for differences in the value chain, possible drawbacks remain and therefore limited conclusions can eventually be drawn from this table.

Table 6.1   ASK (m) per employee (2007)

Air Berlin	AF	*AZ*	British Airways	Ryanair	Iberia	Lufthansa	OS	SK	easyJet
7.1029	2.3413	*4.7449*	3.4096	10.7068	2.4318	3.5470	3.3062	2.1969	7.9194

Source: our elaborations on Jacobs Consultancy (2008)

their workplace in Milan (*La Repubblica*, 2007). Faced with competitive pressures by LCCs, such an organization is clearly inefficient and unsustainable in the long run.

4.1.4 Weak competitive response   As shown above, AZ failed to meet competition and continued with a strategy that was clearly not fit for the requirements of a liberalized market. A comparison of market indexes shows the effects of following such a policy.

The strong growth of the Italian market separated in 1996 to 1997 from the trend of AZ, which shows that the strategic response of the airline to a change in consumer demands was not sufficient. AZ's passenger numbers either declined or remained constant from 2001 onwards, which cannot be attributed to the 9/11 effects in 2001 only, since these were soon recovered in the rest of Italian market. AZ's competitive response, especially to LCCs was inadequate, because the airline was unsuccessful at reducing its costs. In contrast the carrier might have been more successful with respect to FSCs if it had focused on quality and network structure. However, as the airline could not renew its fleet, lacked proper incentives and worked with a politically imposed double-hub structure, it also failed in the FSC market. AZ only succeeded in preserving market shares where it was politically and/or legally protected. This was the case on domestic routes (Linate–Rome, for example) and some of the long-haul routes, where bilateral agreements prevented new entrants.

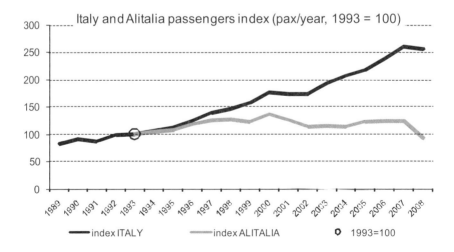

Figure 6.11   Air sector indexes in Italy. Passenger volumes (1993=100)

Sources: CNIT, various years; ENAC, 2007; Alitalia website

4.2 Ownership, Incentives and Subsidies

Privatization as such can, but does not necessarily, increase efficiency. It does not directly[14] change the nature of product competition, but reduces the weight of objectives other than the purely financial ones. This generally leads to less well-performing public firms (Backx et al., 2002). A common explanation is the change in the principal–agent relationship between the owners of a firm and its management. While public owners have a variety of at times conflicting financial and social objectives such as employment and regional competitiveness, private owners are assumed to have a singular objective: profit maximization. However, given the imperfections of capital markets, labour markets for managers and incomplete contracts between management and owner, incentives cannot be devised perfectly for managers. Nevertheless, a privately owned firm should have a strong incentive to reduce costs and increase revenues (Vickers and Yarrow, 1998). The following section argues that based on how AZ was privatized, the carrier's management never had strong incentives to improve efficiency.

4.2.1 Different purposes of privatization   AZ's privatization process has been long and complex, with four different attempts. Despite apparently being similar, these privatization attempts had actually very different characteristics, implicit goals and outcomes.

The first attempt took place in 2006 and can be considered a true privatization, aiming at maximizing the value of the firm without compromising the previous configuration. However, AZ was not valuable for its industrial assets, but for its monopolistic stronghold on the Italian market and its political protection. These intangible assets could not be guaranteed at the time and hence the privatization failed. The second attempt in 2007 was aimed at finding a stronger partner to merge with. Again, political protection and guarantees regarding slots and bilateral agreements were necessary. The ambiguity of political decision makers on these points and the forthcoming general elections did not give sufficient assurances to the buyers, leading to a second failure. The third privatization attempt took place in May 2008 and was characterized by AZ's bankruptcy. It was largely dominated by a strong political clash, focused on the 'Italian character' of the former flag carrier. The debate developed during the electoral campaign that finally saw the right-wing parties headed by Berlusconi winning, partly owing to the nationalistic argument of keeping AZ Italian.

The last and finally successful privatization process was driven by the prevalence of large private interests, in addition to political motivations and labour protection. A compromise was made possible because almost all the interests were fulfilled. The labour unions obtained extraordinary conditions for the redundancy fund;[15] the politicians succeeded in '*defending the Italian character of the flag-carrier*'[16] as promised before the elections; the private investors obtained control of the carrier nearly for free and without any industrial or and financial risk (Giuricin, 2009). Finally AF-KLM took control of AZ on January 2009 spending only one-fifth of what previously planned. Politically seen this was a 'win–win' result. Only the Italian taxpayers and competitors, such as small regional carriers and big LCCs, were at a loss, as they had not been represented in the political

---

14   According to Oum et al. (1989) privatization might change the objectives of airlines, forcing the management to choose products that are profit maximizing. This might reduce the generally too broad product line of public firms, force the firm to choose profit-maximizing products and thereby change the intensity of competition.

15   Seven years at 80 per cent of last year's wage instead of two or three years at 80–60 per cent.

16   *La Repubblica*, 29 August 2008.

arena where the battle about AZ had taken place. Table 6.2 summarizes the main aspects of the second and of the last bid, showing how conditions for the Italian state and workers worsened.

4.2.2 The conflict of interests and the role of the state   The role of the state may be seen, over the entire AZ history, as the main driver of company behaviour. Management never had any incentives to turn the airline into an efficient and competitive operation, because it was an instrument for political rent-seeking serving particular interest groups. No serious attempt was ever made to depoliticize air transport and leave AZ to the forces of competition. This introduced a never-ending political protection, leading to a 'soft budget constraint' impeding efficiency and growth (Ponti and Ragazzi, 2005), disempowering management and discharging the political decision makers of their responsibilities (Boitani, 2008b). AZ did not evolve its business model because it simply did not have to.

The last events surrounding the privatization process confirm past experiences and raise even more questions. First one can determine a conflict of interests that dominated AZ's recent history. CAI, in which the bank BancaIntesa holds a significant share, was chosen as the best by the privatization advisor, which again was BancaIntesa. In other words, the advisor found itself to be a good potential buyer of the bankrupted company. Moreover, BancaIntesa was also the main lender of AirOne, whose critical financial situation does not foresee the payment of debts (Giuricin and Falasca, 2008). The merger with AZ, in fact, is granting not only a quasi-monopoly in the domestic market, but also the disappearance of AirOne debts with the bank.

Another issue is the role of the State. Once the sole decision maker on all aspects of AZ choices, the State formally retires once AZ is in receivership, leaving all decisions (including decisions on property) to the administrator and, rhetorically, in the 'market'. As the bid by CAI is accepted, the public excluded itself from decision making, although politicians continue to interfere in at least two ways. First by media manipulation with ongoing open political debate on the fate of the carrier that is duly reported by the media. Second and more subtly, politicians interfere by taking on a more substantial role of mediator between numerous stakeholders interests (e.g. unions, CAI, banks, local authorities, etc.).

Table 6.2   Characteristics of two of the four privatization attempts

Privatization trial	Offer	Estimated job losses	Other conditions
2nd (AF-KLM)	€1.7b (of which €1b approx. for recapitalization), plus 1.4% of AF-KLM shares	2,100	Guarantee of all traffic rights of AZ (slots, bilateral agreement, etc.)
4th (CAI)	€1.05b (partially cash and partially taking off AZ debt)	>10,000*	AirOne becomes part of the group Guarantee of all traffic rights of AZ and AP (slots, bilateral agreements, etc.)

* According to ANSA (10/12/2008) the workers admitted to the redundancy fund are 12,500 (10,000 AZ and 2,500 AirOne).

Source: our elaborations

5. Summary: Alitalia, a Political Tool in a Competitive Market

This chapter analysed the long and persistent decline of the former Italian flag carrier. Although AZ faced only mild competition in the 1990s, it nevertheless needed €1.6 billion capital injection. As plans to shift the hub from Rome to MXP and to merge with KLM failed in 2001, AZ faced intense competition from LCCs and began losing market share during positive phases. Moreover, it was unable to reorganize its business as some of its competitors did. The causes of AZ's bad performance are:

- low productivity and relative high costs largely due to an odd route structure;
- the lack of a strategy;
- the presence of two semi-hubs (MXP and Fiumicino) and a third important airport, Linate, that led to many duplicate routes;
- the partial withdrawal from the long-haul segment, concentrating on the scarcely profitable and harshly contested domestic and European markets;
- the presence of very favourable working conditions, obtained over time by powerful labour unions; and
- the political protectionism, together with 'soft budget constraints' typical to the former flag carrier and the discharging of both management and the political decision makers of their responsibilities.

The causes of AZ's demise can hence be categorized as both internal (management and inefficiencies) and external (the competitive environment). The internal causes are driven by an exogenous element: the influence of political bodies and of specific interest groups that 'used' the carrier for at least 15 years as a source of rents and political consensus. Hence it is impossible to conclude that competitive forces alone undermined AZ, but some of the cause are found in improper external influences inside a liberalized context. The traditionally invoked causes for the airline's failure (inefficiency, insufficient dimension, competition by LCCs, etc.) are in fact the outcomes of bad political choices. At first these political choices appear irrational or short-sighted because they amplified the carrier's problems and led to further political repercussions. Future research should address these political choices together with their economic implications and analyse them in more depth. The analysis could be broadened by including comparisons of the political economy of failures of a former flag carrier such as Olympic Airways with successful reorganizations of carriers such as AF.

Acknowledgements

The authors wish to thank Peter Forsyth, David Gillen, Bernard Wieland, Henning Schmidt and seminar participants of the 2009 ATRS World Conference in Abu Dhabi for their useful comments and Christoph Prühn for excellent research assistance. Special thanks go to Nathalie McCaughey for excellent and extensive editing as well as thorough discussion and constructive feedback. Financial support by the German Ministry of Education and Research and the DAAD is gratefully acknowledged.

References

Arndt, A. (2004) *Die Liberalisierung des grenzüberschreitenden Luftverkehrs in der EU*. Frankfurt: Lang Publishers.

Backx, M., Carney, M. and Gedajlovic, E. (2002) Public, private and mixed ownership and the performance of international airlines. *Journal of Air Transport Management*, 8, 4, 213–220.

Bailey, E.E. and Williams, J.R. (1986) Sources of economic rent in the deregulated airline industry. *Journal of Law and Economics*, 31, 1, 173–202.

Barbot, C., Costa, A. and Sochirca, E. (2008) Airlines performance in the new market context: a comparative productivity and efficiency analysis. *Journal of Air Transport Management*, 14, 5, 270–274.

Barros, C.P. and Peypoch, N. (2009) An evaluation of European airlines' operational performance. *International Journal of Production Economics*, 122, 2, 525–533.

Bergamini E., Gitto S. and Mancuso P. (2008) *La produttività totale dei fattori di Alitalia dopo la liberalizzazione del trasporto aereo in Italia.* Studi e ricerche in ingegneria. Rome: Università Tor Vergata.

Bergamini, E., Gitto, S. and Mancuso, P. (2010) Restructuring the Alitalia business model. *Journal of Air Transport Management*, 16, 16–19.

Beria, P. and Scholz A. (2010) Strategies for infrastructural development of airports. A comparison between Milan Malpensa airport and Berlin Brandenburg International airport. *Journal of Air Transport Management*, 16, 65–73.

Besanko, D., Dranove, Shanley, M. and Schaeffer, S. (2003) *Economics of Strategy*, 3rd edn. Hoboken, NJ: Wiley.

Boitani, A. (2008a) Alitalia: destinazione finale. *laVoce.info*, 20 March.

Boitani, A. (2008b) L'insostenibile leggerezza dell'irresponsabilità. *laVoce.info*, 4 April.

Boitani, A. (2009) Alitalia. Paradossi tra le nuvole. *laVoce.info*, 8 January.

Burghouwt, G. and de Wit, J. (2005) Temporal configurations of European airline networks. *Journal of Air Transport Management*, 11, 3, 185–198.

Cavalli F., Gazzoletti F. and Nepoti D. (2004) Come si dice Malpensa in cinese? *laVoce.info*, 27 May.

CERTeT (2003) Analisi del mercato del trasporto aereo in Italia: un quadro sistematico e aggiornato. Final report. Rome: ASSAEREO

CLAS (2005) *Gli effetti economici dello sviluppo dell'aeroporto di Milano – Orio al Serio*. Bergamo: SACBO.

Corriere della Sera (2009a) Crollo dei voli. E i conti Sea entrano in crisi. *Corriere della Sera*, 9 January 9.

Corriere della Sera (2009b) Nuova Alitalia, dal cda sì ad Air France. Colaninno: 'Malpensa hub strategico'. *Corriere della Sera*, 12 January.

Crocioni C. and Newton, C. (2007) State aid to European airlines. A critical analysis of the framework and its application. In D. Lee (ed.), *Advances in Airline Economics, Vol. 2*. Amsterdam: Elsevier, pp. 147–170.

Doganis, R. (2001) *The Airline Industry in the 21st Century*. London: Routledge.

Doganis, R. (2006) *The Airline Business*, 2nd edn. London: Routledge.

ENAC (2008) *Dati di traffic 2007*. Rome: ENAC.

Fisconelmondo (2008) Sulla ricapitalizzazione Alitalia la Corte Ue dice si alla Commissione. *Fisconelmondo*, 9 July.

Giraudi, G. (2008) Italy and regulatory policy. In S. Fabbrini and S. Piattoni, *Italy in the European Union. Redefining National Interest in a Compound Polity*. USA, Plymouth: Rowman and Littlefield Publishers, pp. 67–86.

Giuricin, A. (2009) *Alitalia. La privatizzazione infinita*. Torino: IBL Libri.

Giuricin, A. and Falasca, P. (2008) Alitalia ultima fermata: correggere l'incorreggibile. *IBL Focus*, 104.

Jacobs Consultancy (2008) *Airline Performance Indicators*. London: Jacobs Consultancy.

La Repubblica (2007) L' aereo pazzo che brucia 10mila euro l'ora. *La Repubblica*, 8 October.

La Repubblica (2008) Alitalia, resta solo la bandiera. *La Repubblica,* 29 August

La Repubblica (2009a) Roma-Milano, il treno in vantaggio. *La Repubblica*, 27 March.

La Repubblica (2009b) 'Noi marziani per i sindacati Alitalia e Malpensa non sarà mai un hub. *La Repubblica*, 7 May.

Macchiati, A. (2006) La privatizzazione di Alitalia. *laVoce.info*, 4 December.

Morrison, S.A. and Winston, C. (1995) *The Evolution of the Airline Industry*. Washington, DC: The Brookings Institution.

Oum, T., Gillen, D. and Tretheway, M. (1989) Privatization of Air Canada: why it is necessary in a deregulated environment. *Canadian Public Policy*, 15, 285–299.

Oum, T., Zhang, A. and Zhang, Y. (1995) Airline network rivalry. *Canadian Journal of Economics*, 27, 836–857.

Oum, T. and Yu, C. (1998) An analysis of profitability of the world's major airlines. *Journal of Air Transport Management*, 4, 4, 229–237.

Oum, T., Fu, X. and Zhang, A. (2009) *Air Transport Liberalization and its Impacts on Airline Competition and Air Passenger Traffic*. Paris: The International Transport Forum.

Ponti, M. (2007) Dov'è il valore di Alitalia. *laVoce.info*, 31 May.

Ponti, M. and Boitani, A. (2004) Alitalia dopo gli accordi. *laVoce.info*, 21 October.

Ponti, M. and Ragazzi, G. (2005) Alitalia, una sopravvivenza politicamente garantita. *laVoce.info*, 18 November.

Porter, M. (1985) *Competitive Advantage*. New York: Free Press.

Scarpa, C. (2004) Alitalia: bene così, ma non facciamoci illusioni. *laVoce.info*, 29 September.

Scarpa, C. (2007) Alitalia: un prezzo troppo elevato. Per il paese. *laVoce.info*, 03 July.

Spagnuolo, A. (2000) *Concorrenza e deregolamentazione nel mercato del trasporto aereo in Italia*. Working paper 3.96. Salerno: Dipartimento di Scienze Economiche, Università degli Studi di Salerno.

Vickers, J. and Yarrow, G. (1988) *Privatization: An Economics Analysis*. Cambridge, MA: MIT Press.

Wojahn, O.W. (2001) *Airline Networks*. Frankfurt: Lang Publishers.

Chapter 7

Airline Liberalization and Implications for Safety:
A Theoretical and Empirical Conundrum

Andreas Papatheodorou, Konstantinos Polychroniadis
and Jakub Tomasz Kapturski

1. Introduction

The initial period post market deregulation in the USA and liberalization of the air-transport system in the EU was marked by a considerable degree of enthusiasm about the superiority of market forces in delivering optimal outcomes. In fact, the low-cost revolution on both sides of the Atlantic has brought about the democratization of the airline industry and the freedom, of those previously unable, to fly for the cost of 'a pair of jeans'. Many airlines at least on short-haul routes moved away from the bold, luxurious and formal context to offer a rather informal, relaxed and minimalist service where the core product is offered for a low price and ancillary services are available for an additional payment. Nonetheless, the relaxation of tight regulatory supervision and the freedom of the private sector to provide new B2B (business to business) and B2C (business to customer) services within the system of air transport has been also associated with headline incidents and accidents, which acted as the stepping stone for traditional carriers to defend their existence over the ever-increasing low-cost sector. For example, aircraft accidents such as the August 2005 Helios Boeing 737-300 in Greece, where everybody on-board died, have raised concerns over the potential adverse effects of the airline deregulation on aviation safety as a result of the cost minimization practices used by the profit-maximizing, cost-reducing commercial operators (Papatheodorou and Platis, 2007).

Still, recent statistics provided by the International Civil Aviation Organization (ICAO) have demonstrated supportive arguments against this view (International Civil Aviation Organization, 2005; Morrison and Winston, 2008). By monitoring the accident rate since 1980 when deregulation was gradually deployed on a global scale, a negative trend seems to emerge. In 1986, 24 fatal accidents were reported, amounting to 0.04 fatalities per 100 million passenger-kilometres. Ten years down the line, the accident rate remained the same yet the same statistic in 2006 was down to just six fatal accidents. Noting that in 2002 14 accidents were recorded, a rate of 0.01 fatalities per 100 million passenger-kilometres seems to be an outperformance of the supervisory framework and airlines themselves. In addition, the annual number of deaths on aircraft accidents has been sliding since 2005 from 1,050 to 863, 744 and 583 (Flight Global, 2010). Along the same line, the International Air Transport Association (IATA) announced that 'the 2010 global accident rate (measured in hull losses per million flights of Western-built jet aircraft) was 0.61', i.e. the lowest in history (*Air Transport News*, 2011).

On the other hand, studies by Elvik (2003) and Raghavan and Rhoades (2005) have revealed that accident and incident numbers have risen in the US and EU; yet these studies provide gross data that do not distinguish between fatal and non-fatal incidents/accidents. Although both studies argue that market deregulation has been directly linked to an increase in safety and security problems, Flight Global (2010) suggests that only 17 per cent of total aircraft accidents occurred in civil (as opposed to other types such as general) aviation in that year and only 11 per cent of those accidents were caused by technical or maintenance inefficiency. Nonetheless, as safety inadequacies one may also consider inefficient cabin crew and pilot training; lack of control crew expertise; and inability of secondary airports to provide the necessary safety facilities that a potential emergency landing would require. Hence there might be evidence that a liberal economic environment can lead to safety perils. As a consequence and asserting the existence of market failure to maximize social welfare, safety accreditation becomes of major importance in a self-regulated environment. As such, since 2005 the European Commission has been aggressively listing on its website all airlines that do not conform to the required safety standards and hence are banned from flying over European airspace. Moreover, the European Union gradually centralizes safety and certification operations through the active involvement of the European Aviation Safety Agency (EASA). At the same time, ICAO has been urging regulators to classify airlines into five distinct categories according to their safety implementation as part of their total quality management strategy (Fisher, 2005).

In what follows, this chapter aims at contributing to the discussion of the theoretical and empirical conundrum regarding the liberalization–safety nexus in the airline industry. Section 2 discusses the evolution of market liberalization and contestability conditions primarily in the EU by highlighting issues related to safety. Then section 3 discusses the main determinants of safety in the airline industry and the possible implications of market deregulation/liberalization for safety. Subsequently, section 4 shows the results of secondary data research regarding the evolution of aircraft incidents and fatalities in selected European countries. Finally, section 5 summarizes and concludes.

2. Liberalization and Contestability in the Airline Industry

The economic liberalization of an industry may be expressed as the removal of formal regulations limiting entry to the sector, giving potential entrants the freedom to operate in the market at their own risk (Moses and Savage, 1989). In a regulated industry, new entry and pricing strategies by incumbent firms are subject to approval by an authorized public body. As such, the main purpose of public policy in deregulating an industry is to promote competition and allow the market mechanism to function freely. Despite economic liberalization, antitrust laws prohibit price collusion or mergers that threaten to monopolize the industry. Moreover, health and safety standards have never been subject to relaxation, at least in the airline industry. In fact, airlines continue to be subject to a number of regulations, including:

- Safety standards for aircraft and their minimal maintenance;
- Safety regulations for traffic operations (air traffic control and minimum spacing between aircraft);
- Regulation of working conditions for employees (maximum length of working hours, minimum rest periods for cabin crew between flight segments, physical characteristics).

Air transport liberalization within the European Union (EU) was carried out in four distinct stages. The first step was reached in December 1987: the Council of Ministers agreed on the Directive and the decisive regulatory framework. The second step was agreed in June 1990 and was concerned with increasing fifth-freedom traffic within the EU, hence broadening the opportunity for airlines to offer discounted tariffs and expand their own competitive share of route capacity. Moreover, the second step included acceptance by the EU Member States that their national carriers would no longer be subject to favourable treatment against new entrants. The third step was agreed in 1993 and introduced three types of regulatory reform, i.e. the rights of establishment for new entrants; complete stop-over rights for all airlines within the member states; and the abolition of fare control by the government on all airlines licensed to offer services. Since April 1997, all cabotage restrictions have been removed allowing airlines to freely compete on any route within the EU leading to the completion of the European Common Aviation Area (ECAA).

In spite of market opening, both the EU and the US examples of deregulated air transport have been characterized by oligopolistic and in some cases monopolistic structure at a route level. The competitive conduct at a regional and international level has been shaped by the strong forces of concentration. This has led to increased market power by dominant carriers over parts of or their entire network of city pairs. Several researchers argue that the increased degree of concentration has been subject only to modest regulatory monitoring: regulators have been misled by the belief that the contestability element of deregulated environments has been brought forward (Butler and Huston, 1989; Baumol, 2003). Levine (1987) supports the argument that contestability has only been considered in the light of low-cost airlines leasing aircraft and adopting a 'hit and run' strategy. Longer term empirical evidence (Butler and Huston, 1989) has demonstrated that in the US and EU alike there may be entry and exit barriers in the form of bold terminal leases and availability of prime slots. Most importantly, excessive predatory pricing has been exercised by incumbent firms and has been signalled by non-rational overcapacity. Potential competition may restrain the power of incumbent firms. Bain (1956) showed that an incumbent might sacrifice current profits to discourage entry and potential future profit erosion.

Levine (1987) suggests that 'deregulated airline markets cannot be modelled by any pure model of contestability theory'. According to the contestability theory (Baumol, 1982), firms that operate in a given city pair will necessarily reduce their prices to match the levels of new entrant competition to prevent the addition of capacity which would, in the long run, deny market share and profitability. However, on both sides of the Atlantic, it has been evident that incumbent airlines did not adequately prepare for deregulation and liberalization. The majority of them still face higher labour costs than low-cost carriers and they prefer to maintain route structures endowed by the regulated era and in most cases do not meet the increased need for point-to-point travel (Papatheodorou and Platis, 2007). Moreover, some of them have kept pricing philosophies originally structured under the safety and protectionism of regulation in spite of the wide current use of sophisticated revenue management systems (Papatheodorou, 2002). According to Levine (1987), suboptimal pricing policies had led to the purchase of capital which drained their profit and loss account and proved inadequate under a deregulated environment. An example of that would be British Airways' ageing fleet of Boeing 767s which are used to compete against easyJet's brand new Airbus A319 on the intra-European routes. If market reflected the principles of contestability, British Airways would have had no survival advantages over easyJet and Ryanair, which seem to have been 'tailor-made' to meet the needs of competing based on cost leadership in a liberal environment.

Furthermore, transaction costs related to contractual commitments with employees and suppliers and long-term lease of inefficient capital have all contributed to considerably higher costs incurred by traditional airlines compared to those faced by the no-frills sector. Consequently, these committed transaction costs should have been eliminated by the incumbents to provide successful competitive pressure on the low-cost sector. Nonetheless, any attempts by European and US legacy carriers to be partly transformed or establish a subsidiary low-cost carrier have proved hasty (e.g. KLM and Buzz; and Delta Airlines and Song) as very few such ventures have resulted in a long-term sustainable business model. Over 15 years of deregulation in the EU and 30 in the US have shown that the majority of dominant firms managed to survive even if they had to change their cost and operational structure to adapt to the challenge. In other words and although the theoretical framework of deregulation does not suggest that incumbency is a requirement for survival, in most of cases this is valid. Certainly, traditional carriers have been urged to change their strategic vision and there are now examples of alliances between legacy and low-cost carriers (e.g. American Airlines and jetblue).

Moreover, Levine (1987) suggests that traditional carriers have been good in dealing with above-market costs by pursuing revenue-earning strategies that generate rents, especially in long-haul international markets still governed by regulatory impediments. Although long-haul markets have been significantly liberalized in the last 25 years as a result of the implementation of open skies policies at both bilateral and multilateral level (e.g. the creation of the Open Aviation Area between the EU and the USA), most low-cost carriers have not been willing to enter long-haul markets as such a strategy is not deemed compatible with their business model. In related terms, fatal accidents which could occur as a result of inadequate maintenance provision by cost-cutting 'hit and run' new entrants have been avoided. Based on the fact that the contestability theory has found little application into the deregulated airline sector, it can be bearably considered that the dynamic efficiencies enjoyed by the established dominant firms provide the necessary resources to ensure safety. In fact, as competition in the point-to-point market increased, passengers faced increased choices and ample different options of air travel. With the number of airlines climbing by 40 per cent between 1995 and 2005 (International Civil Aviation Organisation, 2005), consumers have made selections of different new carriers with alluringly low prices yet an untraceable safety history. Fatal accidents such as that of Helios Airways in 2005 in Greece signalled that some new entrants at least had in fact sacrificed safety for profitability. Yet passengers were not aware of the maintenance inefficiencies when booking their seat online. The prevailing lack of contestability has led to the minimization of transaction costs between the principal (i.e. passenger) and the agent (i.e. airline) as market consolidation has resulted in dominant existing brands with a wider network.

3. Determinants of Airline Safety and Implications of Liberalization[1]

According to Rose (1992), airline safety is a function of two sets of factors: investments on safety and operating conditions. The former consist of actions that an airline deploys to increase the level of safety on its flights. For instance, more intense and frequent scheduling of maintenance; the use of newer equipment featuring more advanced safety technology (i.e. low-cost carriers moving from the older B737s to newer A319s) to reduce the probability of failure; reliance on more experienced personnel and implementation of intensive training programmes. Furthermore, the operating conditions in which an airline functions may greatly affect the level of safety and the potential for failure. Adverse climatic conditions may increase the probability of accidents such as those of Air France A330 in 2008; variations in airport equipment may also entail risks. Systemic traffic congestion as experienced in the EU skies may increase certain hazards and associated costs; nonetheless, advances in aircraft and air traffic control technology may improve safety over time. Rose (1992) suggests that if there is a learning curve with respect to airline safety or operating efficiency, an airline's cumulative operating experience may reduce its risk or allow it to achieve the same level of safety with fewer resources. Such factors determine the characteristics of the probability distribution function of a flight being subject to an incident. Not surprisingly, airlines

---

1   This section relies on material originally published in Papatheodorou and Platis (2007).

conclude on a certain level of safety investment having carried out first a cost–benefit analysis. In particular, they balance the cost of additional safety-enhancing investment with the benefits of reducing accident or incident risk. Consequently, risk reduction may lead to lower insurance premia, higher customer loyalty, and ultimately in higher prices (Papatheodorou and Platis, 2007).

Different stakeholder interests such as airline passengers, management and insurance companies are all induced to monitor safety levels and to penalize airlines that seem to under-invest in safety. In the case where the management of a carrier has better information about its safety level than other stakeholders such as passengers, the difference between private and social incentives may lead to suboptimal levels of investment as a result of adverse selection (Akerlof, 1970) and/or moral hazard. As such, financial conditions may influence safety investments. There has been a variety of economic models that prove how inefficiencies may be generated. These include models of liquidity or financing constraints on investment, models of decision making near bankruptcy under limited liability rules, and models of reputation formation and quality choice (Gibbons, 1992). Although these models suggest that financial conditions may influence airlines on the level of investment, theory is not always applicable in practice. Empirical research is necessary to ascertain whether such linkages are substantively important.

Although not very extensive, the available academic literature discusses several issues regarding the implications of air transport liberalization for safety. First, there are various arguments, which underline the possible negative effects of liberalization on the safety of airline services. Competition may induce carriers to overlook maintenance standard operating procedures and checks to reduce their cost base; outsourcing of maintenance and technical training programmes may also lead to a loss of direct control on quality; shorter turnaround times, longer flying hours and inadequacy in staff numbers may lead to mechanical failures, labour fatigue and pilot mistakes as well as low morale and nervousness among cabin crew due to problematic rostering (Icon Consulting et al., 2001). In addition, the commercial requirement to raise aircraft utilization factors to achieve economies of density may lead airlines to operate smaller aircraft and/or rely on a hub-and-spoke network (Rose, 1992). These business choices may lead to a rise in airport congestion and overload of air traffic control management at the expense of safety. Passengers deprived of direct services between their point of origin and final destination as a result of network restructuring may now be required to make a stop-over at a hub airport; hence, the traveller's individual risk of experiencing an accident at some stage may rise as the number of flights taken increases. Occasionally, the abolition of certain direct air services may also lead to transport mode substitution primarily to the benefit of trains and cars; however, if these modes are less safe than the aircraft, then airline deregulation may again have a negative effect on passenger safety (Rose, 1992).

In any case, it is important to consider the converse argumentation before reaching specific conclusions. On these grounds, the emergence and commercial success of low-cost carriers mostly in the United States and Europe (but also increasing in Asia and the Middle East) belies those who argue that a low fare pricing strategy is only financially viable at the expense of safety. Carriers such as Southwest, Ryanair and easyJet own new aircraft and employ experienced and respected cabin crew to minimize training costs. They use regional and satellite airports reducing congestion at major airports; in addition, their point-to-point, direct services offer a credible substitute to those passengers willing to avoid hub airports (Papatheodorou, 2002). Moreover, their emphasis on outsourcing has not proved a detrimental practice. Over time, specialist firms have emerged in MRO (maintenance, repair, overhaul), catering and other functions: by achieving economies of scale and scope and moving fast on their learning curve, these firms can successfully produce reliable outsourced services at a low cost and without reducing safety standards (Hirshman *et al.*, 2005). In reality, however, not all low-cost carriers have been as profitable as Southwest, Ryanair and easyJet; in fact, bankruptcies and market exit through mergers and/or acquisitions in the sector are not unusual: Sky Europe in Slovakia and Virgin Express in Belgium and are just some recent examples. Still, there is no clear evidence that the low-cost or charter carriers experience systematically increased rates of incidents or accidents compared to legacy airlines. What seems to play a primary role here is the implementation of a strict regulatory and transparent framework in both the USA and the EU, which guarantees compliance to safety standards. Conditions may be different, however, in other parts of the globe, where incidents and accidents occur no matter what the actual airline business model is. Korean Airlines, the country's flag carrier, was threatened with expulsion from the Sky Team alliance in 1999 because of concerns regarding its safety record (Icon Consulting et al., 2001).

Market liberalization may also trigger mechanisms to discourage carriers from deliberately disregarding safety matters: the popular expression 'if you think safety is expensive, then try having an accident' communicates this message in a bold way. The Folk Theorem of game theory (Gibbons, 1992) may be used to highlight the implications of an accident for an airline's financial position. More specifically, a carrier's management team should balance the short-term cost savings resulting from poor maintenance against the longer-term damage if an accident occurs. The consequent loss in that airline's reputation and brand name will most probably result into a major drop in its future sales and a significant rise in the insurance premia it pays (Rose, 1992); moreover, it may have a very adverse effect on the carrier's share price and market capitalization (Chance and Ferris, 1987; Borenstein and Zimmerman, 1988). This happens especially when carriers prove unable to handle accident crises efficiently (Siomkos, 2000). For this reason, even if a carrier is fully covered against indemnities, it may opt not to under-invest in MRO and other safety-related activities. Moreover, and to avoid the transmission of bad publicity beyond the level of the suffering carrier, airline associations such as the International Air Transport Association (IATA) require their members to abide by strict guidelines and participate in safety certification schemes such as the IATA Operational Safety Audit (IOSA).

Still, there are occasions when a carrier may discount the future so heavily to rationally reduce MRO and safety provision at present. For example, if a carrier is close to bankruptcy or has serious liquidity problems, then meeting safety standards may either expedite market exit or deny the savings that are necessary to achieve organic growth in the future; consequently, the opportunity cost of reducing safety levels becomes relatively low. Unfortunately, this line of argumentation may be used by financially healthy incumbents in the market to discourage successful entry of new airlines, which in most cases are unlikely to achieve good borrowing terms in the financial markets. On these grounds, meticulous and expensive certification schemes on airworthiness can play a decisive role. As in the case of bonding in the tour operations business, such schemes lead to the erection of institutional entry barriers; given the sunk nature of related set-up costs, only committed and rich investors would be prepared to fund an airline start-up. This very willingness should then convince the financial markets (to some extent at least) that it is makes sense to offer better lending conditions. Similarly, destructive price competition in a liberal environment may induce certain carriers to exit the market and engage in malpractice. To pre-empt this adverse result, and in addition to monitoring the efficient use of airport and other related infrastructure (Moses and Savage, 1989), civil aviation (and/or competition) authorities should heavily penalize strategies of predatory (i.e. often below average cost) pricing and undertake financial investigations on a regular basis.

4. Analysis of Accidents in Germany, France, Spain and the United Kingdom

A quantitative analysis of the correlation between the level of regulatory supervision, degree of corporate rivalry and the number of airline incidents could provide strong supporting evidence to the theoretical framework discussed earlier in the chapter. In practice, however, the collection of such data is a very difficult and complicated task. As a second-best alternative, therefore, the following empirical analysis aims at studying the patterns of commercial aviation aircraft accidents and involved fatalities in major European countries over the period 1990–2010; data related to general aviation and military aircraft accidents are excluded from the analysis as there is no reason to believe that any observed trends in them are related to the liberalization of the prevailing civil aviation regime. The relevant statistics have been retrieved from the Ascend World Aircraft Accident Database, one of the most reliable databases available worldwide. Accidents are reported by location of occurrence and not by the place of aircraft registration or the nationality of airlines: this may be regarded as a potential caveat of the analysis as the reasons behind the accident may lie in poor management and regulation in the home country of the airline and not related to the civil aviation conditions prevailing in the country where the accident occurred. Still, this caveat is largely tackled in practice by the analysis given its focus on Germany, France, Spain and the United Kingdom. First, these countries jointly represent a very significant share of the total air traffic in the ECAA market. Second, a very substantial number of aircraft movements over their skies are related to intra-ECAA flights and performed by operators and aircraft registered in ECAA countries which share a common liberal civil aviation regime.

Figure 7.1 shows the evolution of the number of commercial aviation aircraft accidents in the four countries over the examined period, whereas Figure 7.2 shows the evolution in the associated

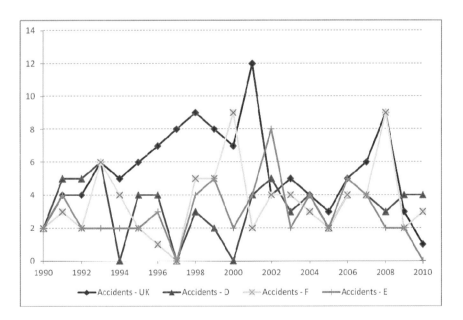

Figure 7.1   Number of commercial aviation aircraft accidents in UK, Germany, France and Spain over the period 1990–2010

Source: Ascend (2010). Note: D is for Germany, F for France and E for Spain number of fatalities. From the diagrammatical analysis, it is evident that there is no systematic pattern or clear trend either in the number of accidents or in the number of involved fatalities over time. There are 'good' years where no accidents and fatalities are reported (as in the case of Germany in 1994 and 2000), while in other cases the number of annual accidents in one only country exceeds eight or even ten (as in the United Kingdom in 2001). Interestingly, a high number of accidents is not necessarily associated with a large number of fatalities: illustratively the 12 accidents which took place in the UK in 2001 resulted in only two fatalities; conversely, the two accidents which occurred in Spain in 2008 had the loss of 154 lives as a consequence – all related to the Spanair Douglas MD-82 accident.

In fact, from a statistical perspective, the correlation between the number of accidents and the number of fatalities at a country level is usually positive but relatively low to be considered as seriously statistically significant: more specifically, the relevant Pearson coefficient is +0.29 for the UK; +0.39 for Germany; +0.39 for France and –0.08 for Spain; whereas for the pooled sample (consisting of $4 \times 21 = 84$ observations), the coefficient is +0.11. Most importantly, however, for the purpose of this chapter, the correlation between the simple time line trend and the number of accidents and fatalities in the four countries is usually negative but too low to be considered as statistically significant. In particular, for the UK the relevant values of the Pearson coefficient are –0.06 and –0.19 for accidents and fatalities respectively; for Germany the values are +0.05 and –0.12; for France +0.20 and –0.23, and for Spain +0.05 and +0.28. In terms of the pooled sample (where accidents and fatalities every year across the four countries are accordingly summed up to produce again 21 observations), the coefficient is +0.10 for accidents and –0.01 for fatalities. In

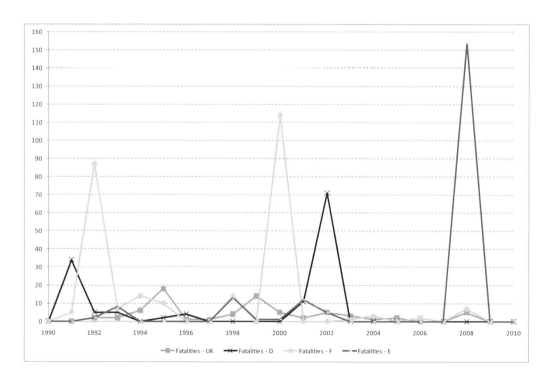

Figure 7.2   Number of fatalities in commercial aviation aircraft accidents in the UK, Germany, France and Spain over the period 1990–2010

other words, it appears that the liberalization of the air transport market in Europe is not associated with a systematic increase in the number of reported accidents and fatalities; conversely, however, it is not associated with a systematic decrease either. Although it would be rather superficial to argue that the efforts of the European safety regulatory authorities have been unsuccessful in this context, it may be the case that further emphasis should be put on ensuring that a liberal civil aviation environment can safeguard better aviation safety.

5. Summary and Conclusions

This chapter aimed at highlighting the relationship between airline market deregulation and safety from both a theoretical and empirical perspective. The end result is rather inconclusive because theoretical arguments exist in different directions: parts of the literature seem to support the view that liberalization had adverse effects on safety while other authors believe that the implications have been largely positive. Likewise, the empirical analysis is not suggestive of the existence of a systematic statistical pattern. Whether this is the result of relying on data which do not reveal the full complexity of the issue or is just the ultimate truth is not known. To complicate things even further a lack of systematic behaviour may just be the result of countervailing powers (i.e. positive and negative implications) acting in the same intensity... In any case, the issue of the liberalization–safety nexus is too serious and sensitive to ignore from both an economic and social perspective. Researchers of the aviation sector are, therefore, strongly encourage to shed more light in this surprisingly underexplored area.

References

Air Transport News (2011) *IATA: Aircraft Accident Rate is Lowest in History,* http://www.airtransportnews.aero/article.pl?categ=organisations&id=28416, accessed 25 February 2011.

Akerlof, G.A. (1970) The market for lemons: quality, uncertainty and the market mechanism. *The Quarterly Journal of Economics*, 84, 3, 488–500.

Ascend (2010) *World Aircraft Accident Summary*, CAA CAP479, Issue 160, London: Ascend.

Bain, J. (1956) *Barriers to New Competition*. Cambridge, MA: Harvard University Press.

Baumol, W.J. (1982) Contestable markets: an uprising in the theory of industry structure. *American Economic Review*, 72, 1–15.

Baumol, W.J. (2003) *Growth, Industrial Organization and Economic Generalities*. Cheltenham: Edward Elgar Publishing.

Borenstein, S. and Zimmerman, M.B. (1988) Market incentives for safe commercial airline operations. *American Economic Review*, 78, 5, 913–935.

Butler, R. and Huston, J. (1989) Merger mania and airline fares. *Eastern Economic Journal*, 1, 7–16.

Chance, D.M. and Ferris, S.P. (1987) The effect of aviation disasters on the air transport industry. *Journal of Transport Economics and Policy*, 21, 2, 151–165.

Elvik, R. (2003) Assessing the validity of road safety evaluation studies by analysing causal chains. *Accident Analysis and Prevention*, 35, 5, 741–748.

Fisher, B. (2005) Regulators must oversee companies and people that reflect the entire safety spectrum. *ICAO Journal*, 60, 4, 4–6.

Flight Global (2010) *Global Airline Accident Review of 2009*, http://www.flightglobal.com/articles/2010/01/11/336920/global-airline-accident-review-of-2009.html, accessed 10 April 2010.

Gibbons, R. (1992) *A Primer in Game Theory*. Hempstead: Harvester Wheatsheaf.

Hirshman, B., Cords, R. and Hunter, B. (2005) Strategic direction. *Airline Business*, 21, 10, 59–62.

Icon Consulting, Human Reliability Associates and IATA Aviation Information and Research (2001) *The Human Factors Implications for Flight Safety of Recent Developments in the Airline Industry: A Research Study for the JAA*, http://www.icon-consulting.com/study_reports/human_factr_stud.html, accessed 7 March 2005.

International Civil Aviation Organisation (2005) *The World of Civil Aviation 2003–2006*, Circular 307-AT/129. Montreal: ICAO.

Levine, M.E. (1987) Airline competition in deregulated markets: theory, firm, strategy, and public policy. *Yale Journal on Regulation*, 4, Spring, 158–166.

Morrison, A. and Winston, C. (2008) The effect of FAA expenditures on air travel delays. *Journal of Urban Economics*, 63, 2, 669–678.

Moses, L. and Savage, I. (1989) *Transportation Safety in an Age of Deregulation*. Oxford: Oxford University Press.

Papatheodorou, A. (2002) Civil aviation regimes and leisure tourism in Europe. *Journal of Air Transport Management*, 8, 6, 381–388.

Papatheodorou, A. and Platis, N. (2007) Airline deregulation, competitive environment and safety. *Rivista di Politica Economica*, 97, I–II, 221–242.

Raghavan, S. and Rhoades, D.L. (2005) Revisiting the relationship between profitability and air carrier safety in the US airline industry. *Journal of Air Transport Management*, 11, 283–290.

Rose, N.L. (1992) Fear of flying? Economic analyses of airline safety. *Journal of Economic Perspectives*, 6, 2, 75–94.

Siomkos, G.J. (2000) Managing airline disasters: the role of consumer safety perceptions and sense making. *Journal of Air Transport Management*, 6, 101–108.

PART B
Liberalization and Low-cost Airline Competition

Chapter 8

Liberalization of Air Transport in Europe and the Evolution of 'Low-cost' Airlines

Keith Mason, William G. Morrison and Ian Stockman

1. Introduction

Liberalization of air transportation in Europe during the period 1992–1997 relaxed pre-existing constraints on where airlines could fly and at what prices. In the late 1990s a dramatic growth in air travel occurred in Europe, in response to the implementation of the 'third package' of liberalization measures and the emergence and growth of what have become known as 'low-cost carriers' (LCCs).

In the debates prior to liberalization, there were concerns that new airlines would focus on major trunk routes and that competition would create incentives to cut costs that could impact safety.[1] Neither of these concerns became a reality. Rather, LCCs opened new routes and created air travel markets that had previously not existed. Through the use of smaller secondary airports, air travel through LCCs became more regional than before. However, a third concern – that national carriers would not fare well in a more market-based environment – came at least partially true, although not for the reasons originally envisaged. Pre-liberalization fears of reduced service and job cuts by national carriers were based on the notion that regional services deemed uneconomical would become abandoned and that prices would rise. The reality that emerged was that indeed national carriers ultimately were pressured to cut costs and in many cases staff, but as a result of competitive pressures from LCCs.

The timing of liberalization in Europe also coincided with the emergence of the Internet as a means of consumer commerce. This allowed LCCs to enter an expanding market with a general business model, derived from Southwest Airlines in the USA, which was made all the more powerful by technology that connected LCCs directly with their customers. LCCs could keep the Internet interface simple because of the point-to-point composition of their route structure, and one-way pricing policies.

The short duration of many flights within Europe and the availability of many small secondary airports made it feasible for LCCs to combine a streamlined 'no-frills' or 'low-frills' service over sets of city pairs with a much lower cost structure than the traditional flag carriers. In general, LCCs were able to provide a price–service quality combination that consumers found very attractive for short-haul flights. LCCs could offer safe, on-time service at significantly lower fares than full service incumbents.

Then, as the twentieth century drew to a close, the airline industry faced a series of major challenges beginning with the macroeconomic downturn caused by the bursting of the stock-market bubble in 1999, followed by another macro downturn in 2001 along with the effects of the 9/11 terrorist attacks. These were quickly followed by SARS, the war in Iraq and an escalation of jet fuel prices. However, LCCs with lower cost structures and flexibility to adapt quickly were better positioned to withstand and gain from these negative shocks, largely at the expense of traditional full-service carriers.

---

1 See ICAO (2003), for example.

Nevertheless the creation of an LCC airline did not guarantee success, nor did it necessarily imply the uniform application of a single business model. Indeed, while there are general similarities in the approach of LCCs, there are also important differences. The nature of these differences is crucial to our understanding of the competitive landscape and the evolution of market structure in this sector, with potentially important implications for competition policy and regulation. In section 2, we examine entry and exit in the period 1995–2011 in the LCC sector, looking not only at the growth of airlines competing in the LCC sector over time, but also distinguishing between newly created airlines and those that evolved into LCCs from pre-existing airlines. In section 3 we summarize a system of indices that help explore the potential areas of similarity and differentiation in LCC business models and use this methodology to outline two distinct conceptual business models. We then relate these conceptual models to real indices for dominant LCCs Ryanair and easyJet. In section 4, we examine whether LCCs business models have been evolving over time and we conclude in section 5 with some speculations concerning the future evolution of airline business strategies.

2. Entry and exit in the European Low-cost Carrier Sector

To date, empirical studies of entry and exit in air transportation have defined the market in terms of city pairs. Under this definition, exit occurs when an airline 'exits' a single city pair market even though it may continue to exist as an airline, serving other city pairs. By contrast, we examine entry (exit) from the LCC sector in terms of the start (end) of all operations by an airline. That is, by our definition, 'exit' means that an airline no longer operates at all in the LCC sector. We present data for the period 1995–2011. In 1995, Ryanair was the only airline operating in the LCC sector in Europe. Full liberalization that allowed cabotage came into force in 1997 and the sector was poised for a 15-year period in which there would be dramatic growth but also a great deal of both entry and exit.

Table 8.1 summarizes entry and exit in the sector between 1995 and 2011.[2] As the table indicates, the European LCC sector has grown from a single airline (Ryanair) prior to 1995, to 32 airlines in operation as of February 2011. However, a total of 110 airlines entered the sector during this period. Of the 78 airlines that exited the LCC sector over the 15-year period, 30 airlines (38.5 per cent) existed for less than one year and in some cases never flew a single flight. Some examples include Swedish start-up Gothia Airlines, which began selling tickets in 2002 even though they did not have a lease agreement in place for a single aircraft; Now Airlines, (2004) which intended to offer one-way fixed prices from Luton; Hop Airways (2005), which planned to provide 'show up and go' service within the UK; and Flyforbeans (2008) which was based in Cardiff but never got off the ground.

Factoring out all airlines that were in existence for less than a year, the average (median) duration of airlines in the sector was 3.4 years (3 years).

Approximately half of all the entry into the European LCC sector over the period has been from airlines based in the UK, Italy, Germany or Sweden, with the largest single contingent coming from UK-based airlines (17.4 per cent). Table 8.2 gives a complete breakdown of entry by country of origin.

---

2   Data for this section was obtained with the kind permission of David Lyall, who maintains the website http://www.airlinehistory.co.uk. The raw data received from Mr Lyall was screened and checked against other sources, including www.rati.com, to ensure the greatest possible accuracy.

Table 8.1   Entry, exit and market duration in the European LCC sector 1995–2011

Total number of airlines entering LCC sector	110
Number of airlines remaining active in 2011	32
Total no. exits by LCCs in Europe 1995–2011	78
Number of LCCs that 'existed' for less than one year	30
Average duration of airlines that exited during the period*	3.4 years
Median duration of airlines that exited during the period*	3 years

Ryanair is included as the only European LCC that existed prior to 1995. * Excludes airlines that existed for less than one year.

Table 8.2   Entry into the European LCC sector by country of origin (1995–2011)

Airline country of origin	No. airlines entering European LCC sector	Airline country of origin	No. airlines entering European LCC sector
Albania	4	Ireland	4
Austria	3	Italy	13
Belgium	2	Lithuania	1
Bosnia-Herzegovina	1	Netherlands	3
Bulgaria	2	Norway	2
Croatia	1	Poland	3
Czech Republic	3	Portugal	1
Denmark	3	Romania	1
France	6	Slovakia	1
Germany	12	Spain	2
Gibraltar	1	Sweden	10
Greece	2	Switzerland	3
Hungary	2	Turkey	3
Iceland	1	UK	19

Given that the fundamental elements of liberalization were not fully implemented until 1997, it is instructive to look at the overall time-trend in entry and exit. Given the long announcement effect of the 'third package' dating back to 1992, we might expect to see large-scale entry around or shortly after 1997. However, although the number of entrants started to increase in the late 1990's the real jump in growth actually began in 2002, continuing until 2006, with the number of exits also increasing significantly in 2003.

Thus while liberalization may have been a necessary condition for such dramatic increases in entry and exit, there does not appear to be a direct link between the spikes in entry/exit and the implementation of liberalization. Note however that a lag between the implementation of liberalization and the numbers of airlines entering the LCC sector could be caused in part by the

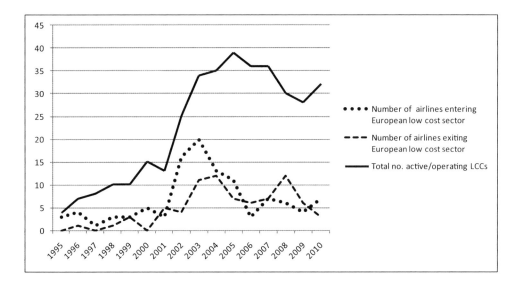

Figure 8.1   Entry, exit and surviving incumbents in the European low-cost sector

amount of time it took pre-existing airlines to react to the changing market environment and either implement an LCC strategy or create a new LCC subsidiary (more on this later).

Because our definition of entry and exit hinges on airlines beginning and ending operations in the LCC sector, care must be taken when inferring new entry from the creation of an LCC airline. In particular, one must be careful to account for low-cost carriers created from or by pre-existing non-LCC airlines. LCCs that 'evolved' from pre-existing non-LCC airlines potentially represent a change of strategy for an airline rather than new entry into the sector per se. For this reason, Table 8.3 shows the entry and exit summary data with separate columns for 'newly created' and 'evolved' LCCs.

As Table 8.3 indicates, approximately 36 per cent of entry into the European LCC sector during the period was by airlines that evolved from pre-existing airlines. This includes airlines that changed from being, say, regional or full-service carriers into LCCs and also airlines created as LCC subsidiaries of full service airlines, such as 'Buzz' (KLM) and Go (BA). While 32 per cent of newly created LCCs entering the sector remain in operation, only 23 per cent of the evolved LCCs that entered remain. Looking at duration in the sector, we see that 31 per cent of newly created LCCs existed for less than a year compared with 21 per cent for evolved LCCs. Further, the average and median duration in the sector for newly created LCCs is lower than for evolved LCCs.

Figures 8.2 and 8.3 show the trend in entry/exit by LCC type. What we observe is that entry and exit patterns are similar for newly created LCCs. Liberalization lowered entry barriers for all airline types, both at the route level but also for the incorporation of airlines. While this was true for all carriers operating in the liberalized market it was particularly relevant for LCCs as these could be established and enter routes with relatively minimal investment.

Considering airline exits, the data show that LCCs evolved from other carriers tended to survive longer than the newly created LCCs. One possible explanation for this difference is that entry by newly created LCCs is more likely to be based on entry into a small number of city pair markets. If those markets do not prove profitable then it is harder for the airline to find other city pair markets and financing to continue operations. In contrast, evolved LCCs are more likely to have access to

Table 8.3   Entry, exit and market duration by LCC type in the European LCC sector (1995–2011)

	Newly created LCCs	'Evolved' LCCs
Total number of airlines entering sector	71	39
Number of airlines remaining active in 2011	23	9
Total no. exits by LCCs in Europe 1995–2011	48	30
Number of LCCs that 'existed' for less than one year	22	8
Average duration of airlines that exited during the period*	3 years	4 years
Median duration of airlines that exited during the period*	2 years	3 years

*Excludes airlines that existed for less than one year.

a larger number of existing routes and city pairs and in some cases access to more financing either from parent airlines or because their tenure provides additional access to capital funds. These airlines may also have pre-existing knowledge of the markets they are seeking to serve. Lastly, LCCs derived from pre-existing airlines may be slower to respond to negative market signals, either because of a more cumbersome organizational structure inherited from non-LCC days or due to an LCC being part of an overall strategy dictated by a parent airline (such as a 'fighting brand' strategy, for example).

There can be little doubt that liberalization was a necessary condition for the growth in the number of LCCs in Europe over the last 15 years, however the patterns of entry and exit do not show a clear direct causal relationship between the implementation of liberalization and growth of LCC sector incumbents. Other factors, such as the growth and prominence of the Internet, improved access to aircraft leases, the growth and development of secondary European airports and acceptance of the viability of the LCC business model by financial institutions and investors have also played a part.

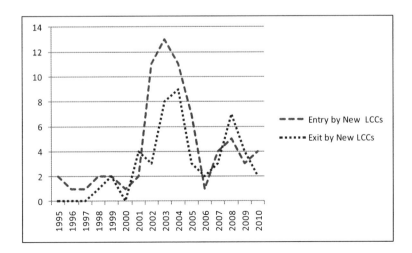

Figure 8.2   Entry and exit in the European low-cost sector by newly created LCCs

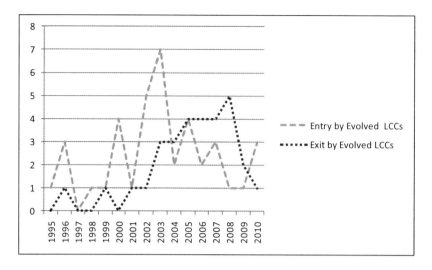

Figure 8.3   Entry and exit in the European low-cost sector by LCCs evolved from pre-existing airlines

3. Fine-tuning our Understanding of LCC Business Models

Mason and Morrison (2008) provide a structured way to understand the strategies of low-cost carriers in more detail by constructing a set of indices designed to capture the interrelationships between the architecture of a core product, the organizational architecture used to deliver that product and the market structure and competitive environment. These descriptors of the business strategy are then related to the overall cost structure and the ability to generate revenues and ultimately profits. Ten market, performance and product indices are built using thirty-seven individual data items for each of the airlines incorporated in the benchmark analysis (see Appendix A for details). What emerges is a representation of each airline's business strategy, relative to other benchmarked LCCs.

With regard an airline's core product bundle, Mason and Morrison focus on three key sets of elements that create consumer value: connectivity, convenience and comfort. Connectivity refers to the type and extent of the airline's route network. Increased connectivity holds value for consumers but can also increase costs. Mason and Morrison measure a connectivity index using three components: network density (departures per airport per day), number of routes offered and all destinations offered at airports served. These three indices thus measure the value proposition inherent in the service that an airline elects to provide for its customers.

The Mason–Morrison convenience index is composed of the following elements: average weekly frequency per route, average distance of airports from the nearest population centre, the percentage of flights from 'primary' airports (defined as having ten or more network carriers operating from the airport, see Mason and Morrison, 2008 for discussion), punctuality (percentage of on-time departures and arrivals) and a baggage service quality rating (provided by Skytrax).[3]

---

3   The term 'primary airport' is defined as having 10 or more network carriers operating from the airport. Examples of primary (secondary) airports include; Frankfurt (Frankfurt-Hahn), Hamburg (Hamburg-Lubeck), Glasgow (Glasgow-Prestwick), London-Luton, and Paris CDG (Paris-Orly).

Lastly, the comfort index is composed of four elements: average number of passengers per flight, number of cabin crew per flight, economy seat width and economy seat pitch.

In addition to these indices, Mason and Morrison also construct indices for aircraft productivity, labour productivity, airport attractiveness, distribution and market structure. Finally, indices are also calculated for overall costs, revenues and profitability.[4]

For this analysis, a database of a number of low-cost airlines incorporating 2005 and 2006 data that had previously been developed (see Mason and Morrison, 2008) was updated. This database incorporates all available data up to and including 2010 financial, network and traffic. Data are mainly drawn from the various airlines' annual reports, and then combined with OAG network and various published data from airports to allow the construction of all the index items listed in Appendix A. The airlines included in the benchmarking analysis and the years of data available are as follows: easyJet (2005–2010); Ryanair (2005–2010); Norwegian (2005–2009);[5] FlyBe (2005–2009); SkyEurope (2005–2008)[6] and Air Berlin (2005–2010).

The methodology adopted to calculate the 11 index scores per airline is based on 'best in class' performance by the sample airlines for each item benchmarked. For most benchmarks the highest score represents the best in class – e.g. average seat kilometers (ASKs) per employee – if each employee produces a large number of ASKs, the performance of the airline's employee productivity is likely to be high. In some cases the best in class is the lowest score – e.g. the airline that achieves the lowest unit costs per ASK in the benchmark pool is clearly the best in class. In some cases the directional preference of the benchmark is not clear and a value judgement is required. For example, when considering network density it is not clear whether the best airline is the one that has the highest or lowest network density. In this case the best in class is considered to be the airline with the highest benchmark statistic and the aggregate index is used to see further examine the impact of the network decisions on the performance of the airline. Correlation coefficients between individual elements in each index and operating profits are calculated and used as weights in the construction of each overall index value.

Finally Mason and Morrison benchmark each airline's index scores to the best in class (top scoring) airline scores in each category. The best-in-class score is normalized to a value of 10.[7]

All of the index values can be summarized visually in the 'spider web' diagram shown in Figure 8.4. The outer perimeter of the web represents the best in class score for each index category. This representation of the key elements of an airline's business model allows us to consider the trade-offs between product architecture, organizational structure, the competitive environment, costs, revenues and profitability facing LCCs.

When the Mason–Morrison index was developed the original concept was to highlight that airlines that called themselves 'low cost' did not necessarily have the lowest costs, and that within the sector a number of different business models were being pursued. The concept was extended to see whether any one model was more successful than any other. In an earlier working paper we concluded that more than one LCC model might be possible, however, the benchmarking database was limited to a couple of years' data, and this did not allow the conclusion to be verified. With six years' data it is possible to identify two distinct LCC business models.

---

4   A full listing of the indices and their components is shown in Appendix A.

5   Financial and traffic data for Norwegian and FlyBe in 2010 were not available at the time of writing.

6   SkyEurope went into liquidation in 2009, but its last publically available data were for 2008.

7   Complete details of the methodology and calculation of indices can be found in Mason and Morrison (2008).

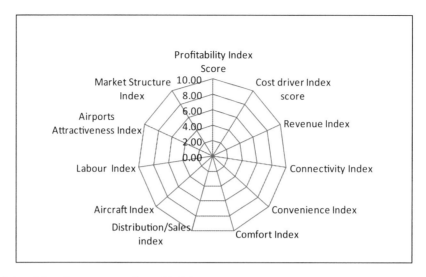

Figure 8.4   Visual representation of LCC business model indices

4. Two Distinct LCC Business Models

Analysis of the index scores for the benchmark airlines identifies two distinct stylized LCC business models, which we term 'the truly low-cost' (TLC) model and the 'full-service carrier competitor' FSAC model. These are described below.

4.1 The 'Truly Low-cost' Model

The driving force behind the TLC model is cost minimization and commodity provision of air travel. A commodity approach to airline service provision places minimal emphasis on customer service, focusing instead on cost efficiency. If the model is implemented successfully, customers who become dissatisfied with the level of service are offset by those who are willing to trade-off service quality in return for lower prices. The objective of this strategy is to be the lowest-cost competitor, and consequently this provides an overriding influence on everything from the core product bundle to labour productivity, pricing and revenues. The airline following this model will not expect to be the best in class on the indices related to service quality – convenience, connectivity and comfort: rather these elements will provide a basic level of value that will lead consumers to expect low prices in return. Consequently, the airline is not expected to be best in class for revenue generation, although passenger volumes in response to low prices will offset this. Where the TLC carrier expects to dominate competitors is in the other indices – aircraft and labour productivity, airports attractiveness and market structure. The choice of secondary airports (where airport bargaining power is lower, where there is little or no direct competition from other carriers and where airport congestion is low) translates into high aircraft utilization, low airport fees and increased market power (on a city pair basis). The combination of low costs with a high volume of sales at low prices means that although revenues may be lower than other carriers, profit margins can still be high.

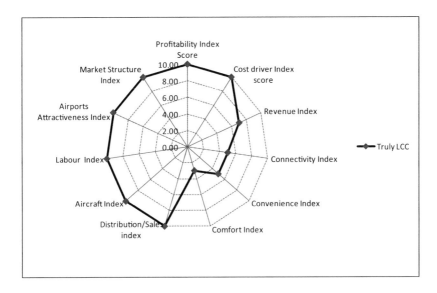

Figure 8.5   A stylized 'truly low-cost' business model

4.2 The 'Full-service Airline Competitor' Model

Unlike the previous model, the full-service airline competitor model does not strive to have the lowest costs. Rather the model is designed to be an effective competitor with comparable service quality to full-service carriers while maintaining a relatively low cost structure, allowing price discounts over full-service carrier competitors. In the short-haul markets where LCCs and full-service carriers compete, LCCs have had several important advantages, including a simplified Internet pricing system and interface with customers that was extremely difficult for full-service carriers to respond to initially. While in recent years full-service airlines have responded and adopted several aspects of the LCC business (including an improved Internet interface), LCCs still hold a significant cost advantage given their point-to-point network design, which in comparison to full-service competitors is far less complex and less costly than the hub-and-spoke system.

Thus, the FSAC model seeks to provide enhanced connectivity, convenience and comfort relative to the TLC model in order to compete on service quality. This means that while revenues can be enhanced (if consumers find their product a close substitute for the full-service product), costs will also be higher. LCCs who adopt the FSAC approach are likely to choose fewer secondary airports, opting instead to fly into primary airports. This does help provide higher levels of connectivity and convenience but it comes at a higher cost. Primary airports will have higher bargaining power and fees, there will be more direct competition and congestion will affect aircraft utilization and costs. Onboard service quality may necessarily also have to be higher than the TLC model which again supports higher prices and revenues, but costs more to provide. In the stylized figure the profitability of the model is lower than that of the truly low-cost model. This is based on the recognition that seat costs will be higher for this type of airline, but the revenues it will be able to earn, per seat, will be largely limited by the prices set by their full service network competitors.

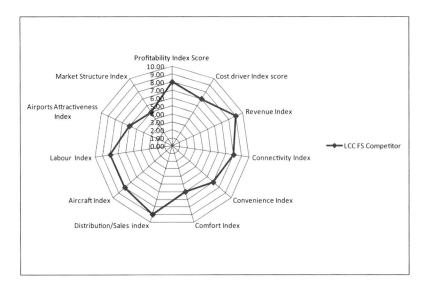

Figure 8.6   A stylized 'full-service airline competitor' business model

5. Ryanair and easyJet

Ryanair and easyJet have dominated the LCCs in Europe and as it turns out, they each appear to operate business models that are close in design to the stylized models outlined in the previous section. Each has a strong position in the market and have both grown into large successful carriers, Ryanair at the low-cost end of the market, and easyJet competing directly with network carriers. Ryanair enjoys first-mover position in the TLC position, restricting the opportunity for other carriers to pursue such a model. EasyJet's strategy of offering value on business-oriented routes leaves the airline more vulnerable to competition from start-ups than Ryanair.

Mason and Morrison (2008) calculated indices for Ryanair and Easyjet in 2005 in a group of six LCCs. The results (see Figures 8.7 and 8.8) show that Ryanair's index values closely approximate the stylized TLC model, while those of easyJet closely match the stylized FSAC model.

As our earlier description of entry and exit suggests, not all LCCs have been successful, and there is perhaps an argument to be made that once there are dominant incumbents implementing the TLC and FSAC models it becomes harder for other LCCs to gain and sustain sufficient market share to survive in the industry. Airlines can either try to replicate the TLC and FSAC models of Ryanair and easyJet, or they must try to define some other differentiated business strategy. In the former case, FlyBe has adopted a version of the FSAC model, while in the latter case it becomes hard to identify sustained success with alternative business models. Rather, one can identify attempts at other business models that have ended in failure. For example, looking at the Mason–Morrison indices for SkyEurope in 2005 (see Figure 8.9) we can see a business strategy with quite a different shape than that of either Ryanair or easyJet. SkyEurope ultimately failed in 2009 and perhaps we can infer some clues from their Mason–Morrison indices. One can see in Figure 8.6 that SkyEurope was generating a high degree of convenience and comfort relative to competitors, but that this was not translating into high revenues. Furthermore, in addition to the costs implied by their core product, labour productivity and airport attractiveness scored poorly. The airline ended up with relatively high costs and low revenues, and thus low profitability.

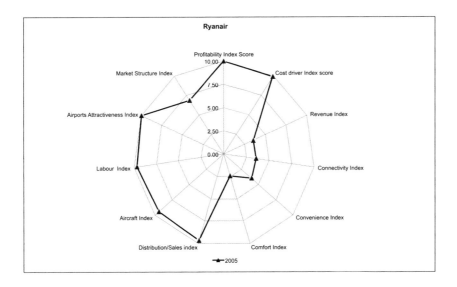

Figure 8.7   Estimated Mason–Morrison indices for Ryanair (2005)

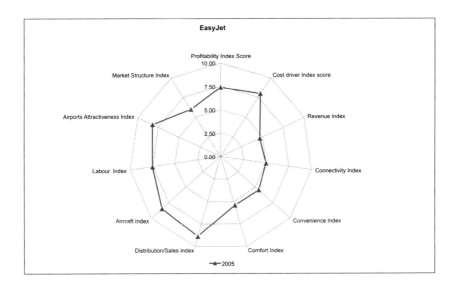

Figure 8.8   Estimated Mason–Morrison indices for EasyJet (2005)

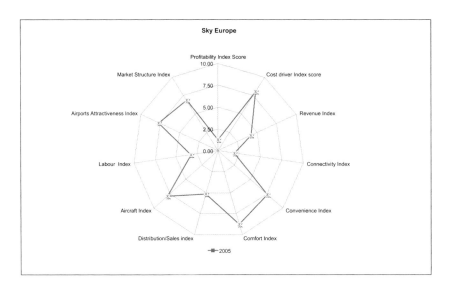

Figure 8.9   Estimated Mason–Morrison indices for Sky Europe (2005)

5.1 Are European LCC Business Models Evolving over time?

Perhaps the commercial air travel industry airline sector's dominant characteristic is its dynamic nature. The industry has witnessed a great deal of change, in part brought about by liberalization, deregulation and in some cases re-regulation of airports and airlines. The dynamic nature of the industry suggests that business models may evolve over time in order to adapt to changing market circumstances. Consequently, it is interesting to explore whether, using the Mason–Morrison indices, we can observe an evolution in the business models of LCCs over time. Figure 8.10 shows calculated index values for Ryanair for the years 2006 and 2010.

What is evident is that there is little deviation from the overall TLC strategy. The shape of the spider web is largely unchanged, with the very clear exception of the connectivity index, which we shall return to. The airline's profitability has been reduced a little, perhaps as an effect of the economic turndown in 2009 and 2010. In a number of the productivity indices the airline is little less strong: labour, aircraft and airport attractiveness. While the productivity of the labour force has remained high, or increased against some measures, the salaries paid have increased costs into the business.

This would seem to be a legacy cost. As companies age, their wage bill tends to increase, and for Ryanair this may be a concern. Another reason the labour productivity index has fallen is due to the increase in sector length and concomitant fall in number of sectors achieved during a day's operation, meaning that the number of passengers handled by cabin crew has fallen. Furthermore, as the sector length has increased the numbers of sectors per day and the aircraft utilization has fallen somewhat. This is a concern as one of the key findings from Mason and Morrison was that both Ryanair and easyJet achieved advantages over their competitors by achieving around one additional sector per day. As Ryanair has grown the average size of the airport it serves has increased, meaning that its airport attractiveness index has fallen.

By far the most remarkable change in Ryanair's spider web is the vastly increased index score for connectivity. The index is measured by the departures per airport per day, the number of routes

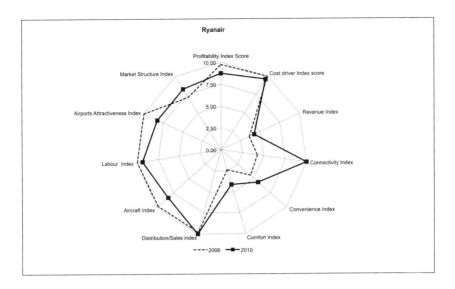

Figure 8.10   Estimated Mason–Morrison indices for Ryanair; 2005 and 2010

offered and the number of all destinations at the airports and average frequency per route. The large number of routes offered (rising from 206 in 2005 to 940 in 2010) and with departures per airport, at 7.6, similar to easyJet (7.7 in 2010 down from 9.8 in 2005) and a move to larger airports (weighted average number of passengers of 8.04 million in 2010 up from 2.07m in 2005), Ryanair has become the benchmark leader in this index. We would consider this a result and effect of network density as the airline has become, by some degree, the largest LCC in Europe.

By contrast, Figure 8.11 shows calculated index values for easyJet for the same years. Here we see some evidence of an evolution towards higher levels of service quality and revenue generation with a small increase in costs and profitability largely unchanged. Changes to the airline's network, as it has grown, has meant that its connectivity index has increased, while its choice to serve principal airports (rising from 36 per cent in 2006 to 54 per cent in 2010), with higher airport costs has had a detrimental impact on its airports attractiveness index, but a simultaneously positive impact on its convenience index. Here the move towards becoming an effective competitor for network carriers can be seen, however, the success of this strategy is somewhat surprising when it has allowed its average frequency drop to double-daily service from triple-daily, a key demand for business travellers.

These figures suggests that the TLC model tends not to change significantly over time – if Ryanair's lowest cost structure can be maintained, then it can sustain profitability over the long term by sticking to the TLC model. However, the FSAC model appears to have a tendency to gravitate towards the full-service model of legacy carrier competitors. In order to capture significant market share in the business travel market, airlines like easyJet must offer the comfort, convenience and connectivity that business travellers value and are willing to pay for. As LCCs operating the FSAC model approach the levels of service quality offered by full-service airlines we might expect closer institutional ties between LCCs and full-service airlines. Indeed code-sharing and interlining agreements between LCCs and full-service airlines are already taking place in North America. In Canada, Westjet Airlines have recently announced a code-sharing agreement with Delta Airlines and with Singapore Airlines. GOL have also announced a code-sharing agreement with American

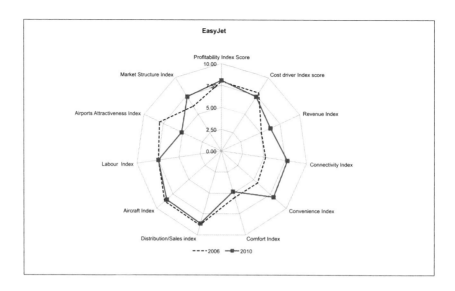

Figure 8.11   Estimated Mason–Morrison indices for easyJet; 2005 and 2010

Airlines and there has been mention of GOL joining oneworld. When announcing its initial public offering (IPO) in the UK, FlyBe stated that the IPO would provide a strengthened cash position that will allow the airline strategic flexibility to pursue additional growth opportunities such as the expansion of code-share arrangements and strategic arrangements with other European airlines.[8]

6. Conclusion

The event of liberalization in European air transport set the stage for the emergence of the LCC business model. Data on entry and exit from the LCC sector for the period 1995–2011 indicates that the real jump in growth began in 2002, continuing until 2006, with the number of exits also increasing significantly in 2003. Thus, while liberalization was a necessary condition for the growth of LCCs in Europe, the patterns of entry and exit are not closely correlated with key events in the liberalization process. Our analysis of LCC business models also shows that LCCs are not one variety. Rather there are at least two definable stylized business models – the 'truly low-cost' model and the 'full-service airline competitor' model – both of which seem to be successful strategies. Ryanair and easyJet, who have sustained dominance in the LCC sector, have implemented business models that closely follow the TLC and FSAC models. While the TLC model does not appear to change much over time, the FSAC model has more potential to evolve, bringing the LCC product closer to that of their full-service competitors at the expense of cost efficiency. Scale effects seem to be having some influence over the business models as these two large carriers take ownership of a rapidly growing fleet, and place these aircraft across the European arena. There is a question as to whether small niche low-cost players can survive in the long term in competition, not only with network competitors but also the two dominant low-cost carriers. The airline industry has always been a network industry and it is perhaps not surprising to conclude that liberalization, for

8   Buyck (2010).

all its benefits of competition, cost saving and some removal of underperforming legacy carriers has not changed fundamentally. Airlines, be they full service or low-cost, need networks to become significant players in the long term.

Acknowledgments

We wish to thank David Lyall for providing us with raw entry and exit data for European airlines.

References

Buyck, C. (2010) *Flybe to proceed with long awaited IPO*. ATW, http://atwonline.com/airline-finance-data/news/flybe-proceed-long-awaited-ipo-1130.

ICAO (2003) *European Experience of Air Transport Liberalization*, http://www.icao.int/icao/en/atb/ecp/CaseStudies/EuropeLiberalization_En.pdf.

Lyall, D. (2011) *Airline History*, http://www.airlinehistory.co.uk.

Mason, K. and Morrison, W.G. (2008). Towards a means of consistently comparing airline business models with an application to the 'low cost' airline sector. *Transportation Economics*, 24, 1, pp. 75–84.

Appendix A:
Mason–Morrison indices for Comparing Airline Business Strategies

Index items
Cost drivers weighting
Unit cost (per ASK) GBP pence
Revenue weighting
Yield per RPK (GBP pence)
Operating revenue per sector (GBP)
Average fare paid (GBP) (Including ancillary revenues)
Connectivity weighting
Network density – departures per airport per day
Routes offered
Average flight frequency
All destinations available at airports served
Convenience weighting
Average frequency per route
Airport location – average distance from nearest population centre (km)
Flights at primary airports
Punctuality
Baggage service (Skytrax rating)
Comfort weighting
Passengers per flight
Passengers per flight and cabin-crew members
Economy seat width
Economy seat pitch
Distribution/sales weighting
Ticketing, sales, promotion per passenger (GBP)
Internet distribution (%)
Aircraft productivity weighting
Aircraft utilisation (aircraft hours per day)
Most populous aircraft type/mark accounts for fleet
Aircraft sectors per day
Labour productivity weighting
Passenger per employee
Passenger per employee adjusted by % employee cost/total cost
Employees per aircraft
Personnel cost per ASK
Flight and cabin crew/total employees
ASK per employee ('000)
Airports weighting
Percent of city pair routes are monopolies
Weighted average annual passenger at airports served (m)
No of full service airlines at destination
Airport/en-route costs per passenger (£)
Market structure weighting
Median HHI on capacity (seat)
Average HHI on capacity (seat)
Average no of competitors per route
Capacity share of seats
Average city size served

Source: Mason and Morrison (2008).

Chapter 9

Low-cost Carrier Services in Germany and Europe – from Novel to Normal

Dieter Wilken and Peter Berster

1. Introduction

It is only a few years back that traditional network carriers in Europe were convinced that low-cost carriers (LCCs) could successfully operate in some niche markets only. Their real development has told another story: LCCs entered the European market in the late 1990s and achieved a market share of about 34 per cent by 2008, while full-service network carriers (FSNCs) provided 58 per cent of seats available at European airports in that year, and charter and regional carriers had a share of almost 5 and 3 per cent respectively (DLR, 2009). These days, FSNCs are thinking about converting their European product into low fare, no-frill services in order not to lose more market share and to compete more successfully with LCCs. Much of the traffic growth in Europe since the year 2000, when air traffic was hit globally by an economic crisis and terrorism, was due to the proliferation of LCCs, while traditional network carriers lost market share and were forced to reduce capacity, both on feeder routes to their hubs as well as on non-hub routes.

The main objective of this chapter is to provide an overview on the characteristics of low-cost carriers, their development in Europe – with a special emphasis on Germany – in terms of supply features such as networks, routes, flights and seats offered and, to a lesser degree, of passenger demand such as passengers carried, and on-demand generation.

2. Main Characteristics of Low-cost Carriers

Although there is no exact definition of LCCs we can state that, in general, they offer no-frills services between mainly European and US airports at low prices, as regarded in absolute terms as well as compared with fares of established network carriers on similar routes. The main business objective of LCCs is to produce seat-kms at very low unit costs in order to be able to offer services at prices well below those of traditional network carriers. As we have seen, these low-fare services, with average fares ranging from about €40 to €120 per flight, have attracted many new passengers, partly coming from other carriers and partly newly generated.

Herb Kelleher and Rollin King invented the idea of no-frills air services in the US by founding the airline Southwest in 1971. Southwest has been the predominant example of a sustainably successful LCC, it is the only airline in the US that has always produced positive annual incomes in its history, and Southwest has now become the fourth-biggest airline in the US, offering nearly 100,000 flights per month. Ryanair, the first LCC in Europe, adopted and copied the Southwest concept; the airline has always been successful in commercial terms and is the biggest LCC in Europe, offering about 35,000 flights per month (in April 2010).

Prior to the year 1998 low-fare services in Europe were offered only by charter carriers, to primarily Mediterranean destinations and by FSNCs on some intercontinental routes, primarily to the US and Asian destinations. Typically, charter flights were not available as flights only, but as part of a holiday package, so that passengers did not necessarily know the price that was charged for the flight as such.

In 1998 a small start-up carrier, Debonair, was the first airline to offer low-fare flights in Germany, from Mönchengladbach to three European destinations, the airline, however, was bought up by Lufthansa and disappeared from the market fairly soon. Ryanair came to Germany in 1999 and began to offer very low-fare services from Hahn airport to Ireland and the UK. Hahn airport is located in the western part of Germany, with primarily rural areas in the vicinity. The next major conurbation area is the Rhine/Main area with Frankfurt as the main city, which is more than 120 km away from Hahn. Nevertheless, Ryanair succeeded in attracting many passengers from places far away from the airport. The airport was formerly used as a military base which was converted into a civil airport and Ryanair has been the major carrier there ever since, building up its main base in Germany at that airport.

Despite this, in 2000 LCCs did not play a strong role in Germany: only eight routes – compared with seven routes in 1998 – between the UK and Germany were offered by Buzz, an airline that doesn't exist any more, and Ryanair. It was in 2002 that the picture really changed when carriers from other countries, like GO but mainly start-ups from Germany, entered the market. Even so, in July 2002 only 26 routes were served by five LCCs (see Figure 9.6), however, in October the newly formed carriers Germanwings and Hapag Lloyd Express opened up lines from their base at Köln/Bonn airport in addition to the routes already served by the incumbent LCCs. In 2003 more LCCs entered the market, so that in 2004 more than 150 routes were served by five German and two British carriers. LCC development continued dynamically, in 2010 low-cost and low-fare services were offered on almost 700 domestic and international routes from Germany. Although the pace of growth has been slower in recent years, in particular in 2009 when LCCs had to cut back flights due to the economic downturn, we can still expect network expansions in the future with, however, some consolidation of LCCs and approximation of business models of LCCs and FSNCs.

To achieve low unit costs, and thus low prices, LCCs must exercise strict cost control in all phases of operations. Simplicity of all processes is the key factor. The operating model of LCCs includes several components, all of which are focused on reducing and keeping costs down. They are:

- Network structure with point-to-point services of relatively short and medium-haul (non-intercontinental) routes, with a preference of using secondary airports because of lower charges and slot availability, allowing high aircraft utilization, quick turnaround times and easier operations.
- Uniform fleet, with typically one aircraft type, like A 320 or B 737, single class configuration and high seating density.
- Direct marketing of services, typically via the Internet and Internet-based booking.
- Price strategy of low fares, including very low promotional fares, on a one-way basis, however, with increasing fare levels in relation to the time span between booking and flying and the probability of seat availability (which is partly correlated with the time span), incorporating yield management systems.
- No frills preceding, during and after the flight, including services in and infrastructure of the airport terminal.

Studies (e.g. Doganis, 2001, and Hansson et al., 2002, 2003) have shown that LCCs have successfully operated commercially at 40–50 per cent of the unit costs of FSNCs. At least one-third of the cost gap comes from the typical lean LCC production with simple shuttle-like flights between high-demand destination areas, resulting in a considerably higher productivity of aircraft and crew (see also Franke, 2004). A case study (Kurth, 2004) on the cost reduction potential of a German LCC, Hapag Lloyd Express (HLX), has shown the amount of cost savings by cost type compared with a traditional network carrier (see Figure 9.1).

In total, Hapag Lloyd Express has been operating at unit costs which are 50 per cent below those of a typical FSNC, with the main savings coming from lower aircraft and airport capacity costs. More than half of the total cost saving is caused by these two components. In reducing importance, the other factors are distribution costs through direct sales, high aircraft utilization – LCCs operate their aircraft more than 12 hours per day – simple or no on-board services, and no CRS fees. Only marginal cost savings are coming from outsourcing of maintenance, fewer cabin crew and lower overheads.

The commercial success of LCCs has caused traditional network carriers to reconsider their business model and adopt more of their features, i. e. reduce costs in order to be more competitive and regain market penetration. The comparison of unit costs of some major FSNCs and LCCs in the US between 2005 and 2009 (see Figure 9.2) has shown that FSNCs have succeeded in reducing costs whereas LCCs were not able to keep their costs at the original low levels. Delta and United airlines lowered unit costs from about nine–ten US cents to seven–eight US cents, unit costs of Southwest airlines and JetBlue grew at the same time from five–six to about seven US cents. These cost increases were caused by more expensive products geared to business travellers, higher staff costs and growing complexity of operation. On the other hand, FSNCs lowered their costs through restructuring and consolidating production and cutting back on services and quality.

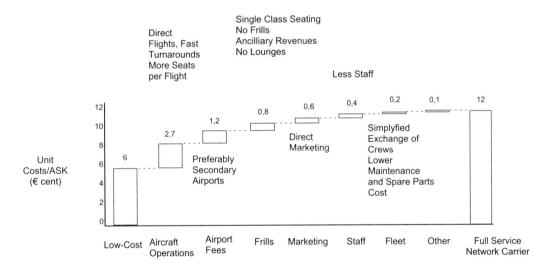

ASK: Available Seat-kilometers

Figure 9.1   Cost savings by a German LCC compared to a FSNC
Source: Kurth (2004).

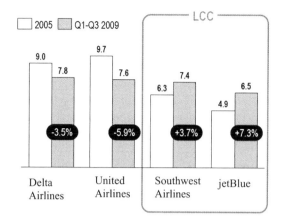

Figure 9.2   Comparison of unit costs (excluding fuel costs) of US airlines 2005/2009. US-cents/seat miles offered, growth p.a. in per cent

Source: Albrecht (2009).

The key factor in attracting potential passengers to LCC flights is the low prices. The marketing of LCCs has been successful in making people believe that their fares are very cheap, in the order of some €20 or €30. LCCs have successfully advertised very low fares and charged, in reality, higher fares by adding additional fare components which have not been part of the marketing of their services. These additional fares are charged for airport fees, taxes, surcharges, e.g. for kerosene, luggage, reserved seats and other services, which have, so far, been part of fares charged by FSNCs. An analysis of prices charged by LCCs offering services within and from Germany has shown that prices vary considerably between LCCs, by a factor of about two, and with the time span between booking date and flight date, by a factor of three to five.

For autumn of 2010 we have analysed prices offered by the most important LCCs serving the German market. Average prices have been calculated by considering all routes and time spans between booking and flying day. In addition, price variation over the time has been retained. The main carriers serving the German low-cost market are:

- Ryanair (FR) with a fleet of 250 aircraft (B 737-800),
- easyJet (U2) with a fleet of 178 aircraft (A 319/320/321, B 737),
- Germanwings (4U) with a fleet of 32 aircraft (A 319, B737),
- Air Berlin (AB) with a fleet of 117 aircraft (A 319/320/3121, B 737) which are used both in normal scheduled services and low-cost services, depending on the route,
- Intersky (3L) with a fleet of 5 aircraft (D 8, ATR 42), and
- Wizz (W6) with a fleet of 29 aircraft (A 320).

In Table 9.1 we show the average one-way prices as advertised (net prices) and charged (total prices) by these LCCs.

Table 9.1   Average fares of low-cost carriers in the German market 2010

	Average net fare (flight fare only, €)	Average total fare (including taxes, levies, surcharges, €)
	For selected days	
Ryanair (FR)	30.48	41.50
Easyjet (U2)	n/a	59.17
Germanwings (4U)	70.10	84.28
Air Berlin (AB)	55.62	95.36
Intersky (3L)	n/a	144.08
Wizz (W6)	22.52	35.46

Source: DLR.

While average net prices vary between €22 and €70 among airlines, total prices vary between €35 and €144. The difference between net and total prices varies thus between €7 and €27 on average: in specific situations the difference may be much greater. The price variation due to the time between booking and flight date is shown in Figure 9.3. As can be seen, prices decrease substantially between booking and flight date. Really low fares, in the order of about €10 to €50 per flight, are offered only for flights booked several months in advance. If low-cost services are booked only one day before flying prices may well reach levels of €100 to €200 per flight and thus not differ much from prices charged by FSNCs.

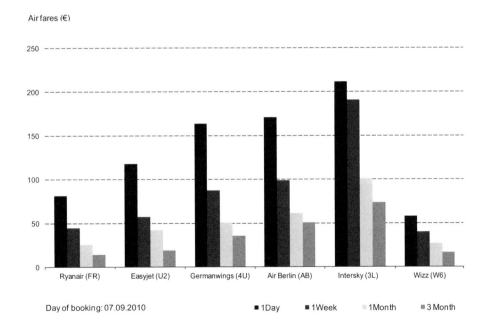

Figure 9.3   Average fare of low-cost carriers in relation to the time span between booking and flight date in 2010

Source: DLR.

Although LCCs offer low-fare services across Europe today which vary greatly in price, service and networks, their main innovation has been to develop business with the objective of reducing cost as a means of driving profit and increasing ancillary revenues, as opposed to the traditional objective of maximizing revenues. The cost reduction principle has gone, in some instances, so far that the European Commission has questioned the profitability of airport operations when the airports are served almost exclusively by LCCs. It was argued that the airports attracted airlines in order to increase traffic, under conditions which were very favourable for the airlines, however, they required public subsidies in order to cover the costs. Up to now, no such case has been proven.

3. Low-cost Carriers in Europe and Germany in 2010

Carriers active in the low-cost business produce their services in different ways and offer them at different fares. Due to this inhomogeneity there are few common criteria suited for assigning carriers either to the low-cost segment or to traditional full-service network carriers. These criteria are, first of all, generally available low prices and direct purchasing possibility and accessibility of service information via the Internet. Some airlines follow mixed supply strategies and offer both classical scheduled and low-cost services, as for instance Air Berlin in Germany. Their number is in fact increasing. In describing the low-cost market we have included only those services for which the criteria mentioned before apply. In some cases, however, the distinction between traditional network carriers, holiday charter airlines and LCCs becomes even more complicated because the same services are marketed through several channels as both low-cost and classical scheduled services. Consequently the analysis of LCC services cannot be considered to be very accurate, but is intended to approximately inform on the extent and structure of the German and European low-cost market.

In autumn of 2010, there were 19 airlines (of all airlines operating in Germany) which completely or partly provided low-cost services to and from airports in Germany:

- Aer Lingus (EI) (www.aerlingus.com), fleet: 35 airplanes (A320: 29, A321: 6)
- Air Baltic (BT) (www.airbaltic.com), fleet: 32 airplanes (B737: 17, F50/70: 12, D8: 3)
- Air Berlin (AB) (www.airberlin.com), fleet: 117 airplanes (A319/20/21: 53, B737: 64)
- Blue Air (0B) (www.blueair-web.com), fleet: 13 airplanes (B737: 10, S: 3)
- Corendon (CAI) (www.corendon.com), fleet: 7 airplanes (B737: 7)
- easyJet (U2) (www.easyjet.com), fleet: 178 airplanes (A319: 141, A320: 25, A321: 4; B737: 8)
- Flybe (BE) (www.flybe.com), fleet: 69 airplanes (D8: 55, E: 14)
- Germanwings (4U) (www.germanwings.com), fleet: 32 airplanes (A319: 32)
- Iceland Express (5W) (www.icelandexpress.com), fleet: 5 airplanes (B737: 3, B757: 2)
- Intersky (3L) (www.intersky.biz), fleet: 5 airplanes (D8: 4 ATR: 1)
- Jet 2 (LS) (www.jet2.com), fleet: 27 airplanes (B737-300: 17, B757-200: 10)
- Niki (HG) (www.flyniki.com), fleet: 17 airplanes (A319: 2, A320: 9 A321: 2, E: 4)
- Norwegian (DY) (www.norwegian.no), fleet: 53 airplanes (B737: 53)
- Ryanair (FR) (www.ryanair.com), fleet: 250 airplanes (B737: 250)
- Transavia (HV) (www.transavia.com), fleet: 31 airplanes (B737: 31)
- Vueling (VY) (www.vueling.com), fleet: 37 airplanes (A320: 37)
- Windjet (IV) (www.windjet.it), fleet: 12 airplanes (A319: 5, A320: 7)
- Wizz (W6) (www.wizzair.com), fleet: 29 airplanes (A320: 29)

- Wizz Ukraine (WU) (www.wizzair.com), fleet: 2 airplanes (A320:2)
  (A: Airbus, B: Boeing, C: Canadair, D: Dash, E: Embraer, F: Fokker, MD: B/McDonnell, S: Saab)

In total the number of LCCs operating in the German market was constant compared with the preceding year. Clickair, which merged with the Spanish budget airline Vueling, disappeared from the German market. However, it now operates under the name of Vueling. TUIfly has left the low-cost segment and has ceded the city links to Air Berlin, who were then able to considerably extend their market share. The airline Myair lost its operating licence in summer 2009. Flights offered by CONDOR or the former LTU are not considered in this analysis, because these airlines indeed also offer several low-cost-flights, but their distinct allocation to the low-cost sector is considered to be difficult, since only selected flights can be booked directly, with low fares. This contradicts the actual LCC concept of booking the majority of flights online and of pricing according to the booking period, respectively the day of travel. In a broad sense, Lufthansa flights of the 'Better-Fly' segment also have to be considered, but here also no distinct allocation can be made. Air Berlin, which is running several business models, can be allocated to a grey zone. For this former charter airline, which was an early actor in the LCC market by launching the Cityshuttle, the identification of low-cost routes has become much more complicated due to mergers with DBA, Gexx and LTU as well as cooperation with Walter airline (LGW). Thus, only the present low-cost routes served by these airlines, as well as the corresponding ones, are considered, however, flights to typical holiday destinations like North Africa are excluded. Air Berlin has recently added the city links previously operated by TUIfly. Furthermore, in the autumn of 2010 and before 2008, Windjet provided flight services from Germany.

Most airlines have kept their fleet size relatively constant. Only Ryanair shows a strong increase of 44 aircraft on the previous year and holds a fleet of 250 aircraft, all Boeing 737-800s, equipped with about 190 seats each.

Besides the carriers operating in the German low-cost market there are another 13 European airlines active in the European market, thus bringing the number of European LCCs to 32:

- Air Italy (I9) (www.airitaly.it), fleet: 8 airplanes (B737: 5, B767: 3)
- AviaNova (AO) (www.avianova.com), fleet: 5 airplanes (A320: 5)
- Blu Express (BV) (www.blu-express.com), fleet: 3 airplanes (B737: 3)
- Bmibaby (WW) (www.bmibaby.com), fleet: 14 airplanes (B737: 14)
- Flybaboo (F7) (www.flybaboo.com), fleet: 5 airplanes (D8: 2, E190: 3)
- Jet4you (8J) (www.jet4you.com), fleet: 6 airplanes (B737: 6)
- Meridiana (IG) (www.meridiana.com), fleet: 30 airplanes (A319: 4, A320: 9, MD82/83: 17, ATR: 1)
- Skyexpress (www.skyexpress.ru), fleet: 9 airplanes (B737: 9)
- Star1Airlines (V9) (www.star1.aero), fleet: 1 airplane (B737: 1)
- Transavia France (TO) (www.transavia.com), fleet: 7 airplanes (B737: 7)
- Transavia Denmark (PH) (www.transavia.com), fleet: 3 airplanes (B737: 3)
- Volare (VA) (www.volareweb.com), fleet: 1 airplane (A320: 2)
- Wizz Bulgaria (8Z) (www.wizzair.com), fleet: 3 airplanes (A320: 3)

In addition, LCCs from abroad come into the European market with partly long haul services between Europe and Asia. They are:

- Air Arabia Maroc (3O) (www.airarabia.com), fleet: 3 airplanes (A320: 3)
- Air Asia X (D7) (www.airasia.com), fleet: 8 airplanes (A330: 6 A340: 2)
- Flydubai (FZ) (www.flydubai.com), fleet: 9 airplanes (B737: 9)
- Nasair (UE) (www.nasair.aero), fleet: 11 airplanes (A320: 7, E: 4).
  (A: Airbus, B: Boeing, C: Canadair, D: Dash, E: Embraer, F: Fokker, MD: B/McDonnell, S: Saab)

4. Supply of Low-cost Carrier Services

Germany, a country with a population of about 82 million people and a size of nearly 360,000 km,[2] has a rather dense network of classified airports. There are 17 international airports which – together with some ten regional airports – serve primarily the public air transport system with scheduled and non-scheduled services on domestic and international traffic routes, provided by FSNCs and to a growing degree by LCCs. The international airports handle most of this traffic, although at some of the regional airports traffic volumes are exceeding one million passengers per year.

In 2009, the international and regional airports handled a traffic volume of about 181 million passengers, enplaned and deplaned, and of almost 2.1 million air transport movements (ATMs) in commercial traffic, on mainly scheduled services (ADV, Arbeitsgemeinschaft Deutscher Verkehrsflughäfen). Since 1992, the second year after the reunification of East and West Germany, passenger traffic has more than doubled (corresponding to an average annual growth of 4.4 per cent) and the ATM volume has grown by half the pace of the passenger volume, that is by 51 per cent (2.5 per cent annually). Air transport has thus grown much faster than the classical car and rail mode, however, the growth came to a halt in 2001 for three years, among other things influenced by the 11 September incident in New York, and in 2008 due to the international financial and economic crisis.

Germany has two hub airports, Frankfurt and München, with both origin–destination (O-D) and feeder traffic concentrations, while all the other airports handle mainly origin–destination traffic to domestic and European destinations and in addition feeder traffic to the German and some European hub airports. The biggest airport is Frankfurt (FRA) with 50.6 million passengers and 458,000 commercial flight movements in 2010, of which almost 60 per cent belonged to the 'home carrier' Lufthansa, which operates its primary hub there. More than 50 per cent of all passengers in Frankfurt use transfer flights.

Following the criteria of low fares and general availability of low fares via the Internet we have identified 32 European LCCs and four LCCs from overseas offering domestic, intra-European and – to a small degree – intercontinental, low-cost services in the European market. In the following we describe supply characteristics of these carriers in terms of number of flights and seats offered and of routes served, by airline, country and airport, and the development of networks.

4.1 Flights and Seats Offered

In Table 9.2 we have put together the number of departures, seats and routes served by airline in the German low-cost market, ranked by the number of flights (departures), for one week in July of 2010 and 2009.

Table 9.2   Departures, seats and routes of low-cost carriers in the German market 2009 and 2010 by airline

Rank	Airline	07/2010			07/2009			Change (%)		
		Flights	Seats	Routes*	Flights	Seats	Routes*	Flights	Seats	Routes*
1	Air Berlin	2,590	399,716	230	2,100	323,390	148	23.3	23.6	55.4
2	Germanwings	1,037	154,152	160	883	126,668	132	17.4	21.7	21.2
3	Ryanair	832	157,248	174	791	149,499	150	5.2	5.2	16.0
4	Easyjet	357	55,871	48	302	47,185	40	18.2	18.4	20.0
5	Intersky	178	9,416	21	110	5,500	22	61.8	71.2	-4.5
6	Flybe	111	8,436	13	108	8,424	12	2.8	0.1	8.3
7	Wizz	75	13,500	20	54	9,720	12	38.9	38.9	66.7
8	Air Baltic	63	6,294	6	51	6,293	6	23.5	0.0	0.0
9	Aer Lingus	53	9,222	6	67	11,658	9	-20.9	-20.9	-33.3
10	Norwegian	34	5,590	7	32	5,023	7	6.3	11.3	0.0
11	fly Niki	32	4,568	2	24	3,396	2	33.3	34.5	0.0
12	Wizz (Ukraine)	17	3,060	5	11	1,980	3	54.5	54.5	66.7
13	Corendon	13	2,090	9	0	0	0	100.0	100.0	100.0
14	Blue Air	10	1,404	3	10	1,360	4	0.0	3.2	-25.0
15	Iceland Express	7	1,036	3	6	888	3	16.7	16.7	0.0
16	Jet2	6	888	1	10	1,480	2	-40.0	-40.0	-50.0
17	Transavia	4	488	1	4	552	1	0.0	-11.6	0.0
18	Vueling	3	540	1	0	0	0	100.0	100.0	100.0
19	Windjet	2	322	1	3	540	1	-33.3	-40.4	0.0
20	Myair	0	0	0	1	50	1	-100.0	-100.0	-100.0
21	TUIfly	0	0	0	557	85,792	112	-100.0	-100.0	-100.0
		5,424	833,841	711	5,124	789,398	667	5.9	5.6	6.6

*Routes served by several carriers are subject to multiple counting.
Source: DLR.

The 19 LCCs active in the German market offered, in one week of summer 2010, nearly 5,400 departures with 830,000 seats on over 700 domestic and border-crossing routes. Since July 2009 the number of departures has grown by 300 flights. The number of flights has increased by 6 per cent, as did the number of seats offered, while the number of routes has grown by 7 per cent. On the 5,400 flights on average 154 seats have been made available per flight, which is a similar value to the preceding year. It shows clearly that low-cost carriers have established a typical average aircraft capacity of more than 150 seats. Thus, these flight-specific seat capacities continue ranging distinctly higher than those of traditional European scheduled airlines. When considering the fleet composition of individual airlines the tendency of disposing of small-scale aircraft is revealed. Typical aircraft are Airbus 320 and Boeing 737. Only a few airlines, such as Intersky or Flybe, are holding small-scale propeller-driven airplanes in their fleet.

According to the number of flights served (departures) in one week in July 2010 the Air Berlin low-cost segment, covering almost 2,600 departures after the takeover of the city lines of TUIfly, is the major supplier in Germany; as opposed to summer of the year before when 2,100 departures had been performed, an increment of almost 23 per cent. Together with the 500 flights served by TUIfly both airlines performed approximately 2,650 flights in July 2009, too. Thus the total number of flights did not change much. During the six years to 2008 high yearly growth rates have been achieved in this sector: the change had started by summer 2008 when the growth rates dropped distinctly, and this decline continued until summer 2009. After a further consolidation phase in spring of 2010 positive growth rates have been seen again for most airlines. According to the ranking, Germanwings (1,037 flights) and Ryanair (832 flights) follow. Obviously, Ryanair continues its expansion strategy. They have been able to increase the number of flights through the period of economic crisis in 2009, whereas almost all other major LCCs had to decrease their services. Also, easyJet increased their services again. This is due to extension of services in Munich and Hamburg and the newly served routes departing from Duesseldorf. On places 5 and 6 in the ranking are Intersky and the British airline Flybe. While Intersky has increased frequencies on existing routes, Flybe has only marginally grown. All other LCC flights range below 100 flights per week.

Taking the number of departures as an index of the position of an airline in the market we can see that the six major LCCs, of a total of 19 airlines, in the German market cover about 94 per cent of the low-cost market (see Figure 9.4). Just Air Berlin, with 48 per cent, covers almost half of all flights. In the market share ranking following are Germanwings (19 per cent), Ryanair (15 per cent), and easyJet with 7 per cent. This is a considerable growth in market share by Air Berlin, due to its takeover of the city links formerly served by TUIfly.

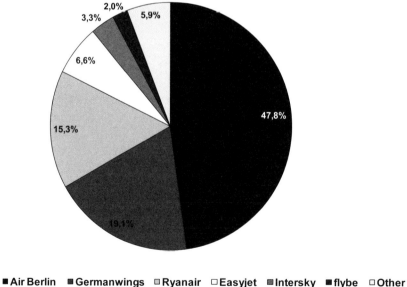

Figure 9.4   Low-cost carrier market share in Germany 2010 (according to number of flights performed during one week in July 2010)

Source: DLR.

The market success of LCCs shows clearly when the developments of flights of both FSNCs and LCCs are compared. Figure 9.5 shows the number of flights offered by FSNCs and LCCs in the German market from 2001 to 2010 (flights per week in July).

As can be seen, the flight offer of traditional network carriers in the German market has gone down from about 17,000 departures per week in 2001 to below 14,000 in 2010, while at the same time the LCC offer developed from almost non-existence to about 5,400 weekly flights. The reduction of FSNC flights was particularly strong in the years of crises, 2001–2003 and 2008–09, whereas the number of LCC departures typically went up in the whole period, with some signs of saturation since 2008 and one exception in 2009, when a small decline in services was recorded. Since that year, both FSNCs and LCCs have increased their services again. LCCs have thus reached a share in the German market of about 28 per cent of the total flight offer.

In the European market of summer 2010, 36 LCCs have, together, offered more than 41,000 departures with 6.5 million seats on almost 6,800 routes in Europe and to other non-European destinations, particularly to North Africa, as can be seen in Table 9.3.

The major European low-cost airline is Ryanair, with more than 10,000 departures in July 2010. They have exceeded their values of July 2009 by more than 1,000 departures or 12 per cent and have been able – like most major European low-cost airlines – to extend their services despite the financial crisis. Number two is easyJet with almost 8,000 departures thus serving, Europe-wide, 8 per cent more flights than in the preceding year. While Ryanair has added more than 200 new city pairs to the network, easyJet has increased the number of city pairs by almost 80. At a distance follow Air Berlin and Flybe with about 3,000–3,500 departures each per week. Then there is a big gap: Norwegian, Vueling, Aer Lingus, Germanwings, Wizz, Air Baltic and Meridiana follow with a number of flights between 1,000 and 2,000. Whereas Wizz too has considerably

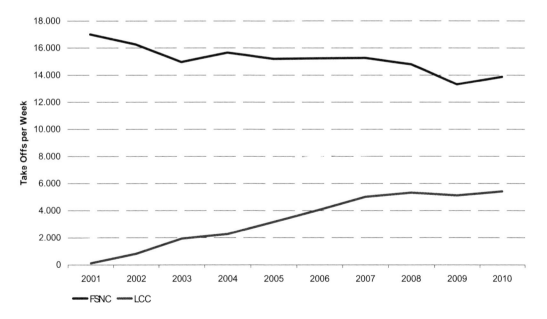

Figure 9.5   Development of flights offered by FSNCs and LCCs in the German market
Source: OAG.

extended its service, Clickair was taken over by Vueling. Thus the consolidation in the LCC market is continuing. While some airlines, such as Clickair, are integrated into major LCCs like Vueling others, such as Air Italy, are taken over by former national carriers such as Alitalia and others, such as Sky Europe, had to file for bankruptcy. Opposed to this there is a group of airlines, in particular Ryanair, who have been permanently expanding until the year 2010. A large number of airlines which have reduced their services in the last year of crisis show again positive growth tendencies in 2010.

Low-cost traffic in Europe is not as strongly concentrated on just a few airlines as in Germany, however, the three top-ranked LCCs, Ryanair, easyJet and Flybe, provide more than half (52 per cent) of all departures, and almost 90 per cent of the European low-cost traffic (in terms of flights) is concentrated on 12 airlines (33 per cent) out of 36 airlines in total.

The LCC market share of total European air traffic increased slightly to 27 per cent in summer 2010. Seventy-three per cent of the flights are mainly served by the traditional scheduled airlines and holiday airlines. Another part of the market is served by smaller regional airlines, which mostly cooperate with a big airline.

Table 9.3   Departures, seats and routes of low-cost carriers in the European market 2010

Low-cost carrier market in Europe

07/2010

Rank	Airline	Flights	Seats	Routes
1	Ryanair	10,069	1,903,041	2,006
2	Easyjet	7,936	1,263,888	951
3	Flybe	3,532	264,052	375
4	Air Berlin Euro Shuttle	2,960	463,301	299
5	Norwegian	2,187	359,715	421
6	Vueling	1,984	356,940	193
7	Aer Lingus	1,701	283,919	200
8	Germanwings	1,610	238,954	288
9	Wizz	1,360	244,800	364
10	Air Baltic	1,262	120,030	151
11	Meridiana	1,175	166,087	197
12	Jet 2	756	128,621	220
13	Transavia	618	81,692	173
14	bmybaby	594	85,566	96
15	fly Niki	513	80,210	105
16	Windjet	431	71,348	83
17	Blu Express	388	69,730	84
18	Corendon	353	56,374	145
19	Air Italy	265	39,502	30
20	Blue Air	251	42,584	46

Table 9.3   *Concluded*

Low-cost carrier market in Europe

07/2010

Rank	Airline	Flights	Seats	Routes
21	Intersky	224	11,900	34
22	Sky Express	211	25,320	17
23	Volareweb	184	26,986	20
24	Transavia.France	182	33,852	52
25	flybaboo	166	14,516	34
26	Iceland Express	132	19,432	65
27	Transavia Denmark	89	11,236	29
28	Wizz Ukraine	88	15,720	22
29	jet4you	84	14,532	20
30	AviaNova	62	9,300	14
31	Air Arabia Maroc	45	6,750	12
32	Star1 Airlines	34	5,032	14
33	AirAsiaX	9	2,160	1
34	Wizz Bulgaria	8	1,440	2
35	flydubai	4	720	1
36	Nasair	4	833	3
	Total	41,471	6,520,083	6,767

Source: DLR.

4.2 Networks: Routes Served, Competition

In total, the low-cost airlines considered in the German market cover 675 different domestic and cross-border routes in a summer week of 2010 (see Table 9.4). This is nearly 50 routes more than in summer 2009, which equals a growth rate of more than 7 per cent. After stagnation and having abandoned routes early in 2009 the growth of route development has returned and the levels of 2008 and 2009 have been surpassed. The number of flights has increased by 6 per cent and has exceeded the level of former years.

Since the emergence of the low-cost market eight years ago, in the first six years about 100 routes were added per year. In 2002 LCCs began to build up networks with domestic as well as border-crossing services; in July 2002 flights were offered on only 26 routes, one year later the number of routes served had increased to 128 (Wilken and Berster, 2007). In the following three years the summer LCC network was enlarged by about 100 new routes until summer 2006. More than 140 routes were added in summer 2007 compared with 2006. The financial crisis was already looming in summer 2008, when only around 50 routes were newly opened by LCCs. In spring 2009, for the first time there was a decline as opposed to the reference period. In summer 2009 a positive development of routes started again, which continued over the spring of 2010 and reached a new high level with 675 routes in summer of 2010. As opposed to the period of dynamic growth in the years of forming and building up LCC networks when, each year, about 100 new routes were opened, it took a further three years, from 2007 to 2010, to add the same number of routes to the network. The development of LCC routes of German airports over the period 1998–2010 is shown in Figure 9.6 (DLR, 2010).

The new growth of LCC route networks seems to indicate the overcoming of the financial and economic crisis, which forced some carriers to reduce services. Whereas some small airlines have even left the market, Ryanair has extended their network of routes from summer 2008 (112 routes), summer 2009 (150 routes) to summer 2010 (174 routes) by an additional 62 routes. The Niederrhein, Berlin-Schoenefeld, Bremen and Memmingen airports were mainly affected by this network extension, in particular Memmingen airport has been added to the Ryanair network of routes. However, flight service to London Stansted from Zweibruecken has ceased. In Cologne and Stuttgart Air Berlin has been able to considerably extend their service by taking over the TUIfly routes. Germanwings, too, was able to exceed the values of 2008 (before the crisis) with 160 destinations in summer 2010. EasyJet has enlarged its network by almost 20 per cent and thus achieved the level of 2008. For domestic flight routes double counting (outward MUC-DUS and return DUS-MUC) should be taken into account.

Some new destinations in middle and Eastern European countries have been added to the route networks of LCCs operating from airports in Germany. In addition, countries in the Near East and North Africa have been served for the first time by LCCs from Germany. As usual during summer, typical warm-weather regions such as Spain and Italy are served more frequently than in winter seasons.

If the network development is followed airline-by-airline one can observe a strategy of avoiding direct competition with other low-cost airlines. In fact, direct competition among LCCs has been very low and has even decreased, if the number of routes with two or more airlines is taken into account. Only on 34 (5 per cent) of the total number of 675 routes are two airlines competing. There is just one route left with more than two airlines competing directly and 640 routes – the majority – are served by a single airline.

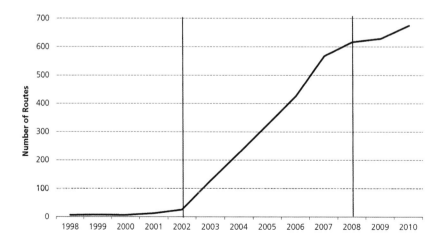

Figure 9.6   Development of the LCC route network of German airports

Source: DLR.

4.3 Countries Served

In 2010 German LCCs have served, in total, destinations in 33 countries (see Table 9.4). Compared with the preceding year Israel has become a destination, whereas destinations in Macedonia and Slovakia are not served any more. The country of destination ranking reveals the big market share of domestic traffic: in this market about 40 per cent of all LCC flights departing from German airports have been offered on more than 120 routes, corresponding to 60 airport pairs, which account for just 20 per cent of all routes. Compared to the summer flight schedule in 2009 the number of German domestic routes served has remained relatively constant. During the summer months Spain and Great Britain range on the second and third place of the ranking list (about 730 and 510 flights respectively): Italy ranks ahead of Austria and Switzerland in fourth place. In places 7 to 9 France, Greece and Poland (offering five new routes) follow; ahead of Sweden and Ireland where service is stagnating and, respectively, decreasing. Low-cost carrier services to destinations in Great Britain and Ireland have been decreased, whereas almost all other countries show double-digit growth rates. This is, among other things, due to administrative reasons such as a more rigid charging policy: both countries have implemented an air traffic tax and have raised taxes drastically. Consequently, several airlines have reduced their service in these markets.

In the European LCC market Great Britain remains 'country of destination' no. 1, according to the LCC flight destination ranking (see Table 9.5). The network of this country covers more than 1,100 routes from all over Europe, including domestic traffic. Here, too, a slight growth of routes has taken place as opposed to the preceding year, however, a slight decrease in flights offered has occurred, which might be due to the rise in the air traffic tax in this country. Almost 10,000 flights have been performed in the period monitored. Then Spain, Italy and Germany follow (more than 5,000 flights): places 5 to 7 are occupied by France, Ireland and Norway (more than 1,000 flights).

As in the German market, LCCs avoid direct competition in the European network: 92 per cent (5,800 routes of 6,200 different routes in total) is covered by a single low-cost carrier.

Only 453 routes are covered by two carriers and on 25 routes more than two low-cost carriers are competing. The number of routes where direct competition is taking place has decreased markedly since last year.

Table 9.4   Departures, seats and routes of low-cost carriers in the German market 2009 and 2010 to destinations in Europe

Rank	Country of Destination	Low-cost carrier market in Germany								
		07/2010			07/2009			Change (%)		
		Depart.	Seats	Routes	Depart.	Seats	Routes	Depart.	Seats	Routes
1	Germany	2,139	308,246	123	2,002	288,646	119	6,8	6,8	3,4
2	Spain	734	133,507	89	764	136,818	75	-3,9	-2,4	18,7
3	Great Britain	513	73,426	54	518	74,387	60	-1,0	-1,3	-10,0
4	Italy	491	80,397	112	475	77,973	108	3,4	3,1	3,7
5	Austria	304	40,518	23	232	33,062	23	31,0	22,6	0,0
6	Switzerland	145	22,610	9	122	19,008	8	18,9	18,9	12,5
7	France	94	13,182	20	96	13,304	18	-2,1	-0,9	11,1
8	Greece	94	14,922	34	76	11,682	29	23,7	27,7	17,2
9	Poland	93	16,011	24	79	13,169	19	17,7	21,6	26,3
10	Sweden	83	14,274	15	86	14,773	15	-3,5	-3,4	0,0
11	Irleand	82	14,586	11	97	17,448	15	-15,5	-16,4	-26,7
12	Croatia	79	11,719	29	84	12,034	30	-6,0	-2,6	-3,3
13	Latvia	74	8,373	9	64	8,750	9	15,6	-4,3	0,0
14	Norway	69	11,794	13	60	10,199	12	15,0	15,6	8,3
15	Russia	61	9,910	10	54	8,626	9	13,0	14,9	11,1
16	Turkey	53	8,036	18	35	5,040	12	51,4	59,4	50,0
17	Portugal	52	9,065	13	45	7,294	12	15,6	24,3	8,3
18	Denmark	37	5,895	4	33	5,163	3	12,1	14,2	33,3
19	Finland	34	5,764	5	40	6,460	5	-15,0	-10,8	0,0
20	Hungary	34	5,170	6	35	5,200	6	-2,9	-0,6	0,0
21	Romania	33	5304	10	29	4456	9	13,8	19,0	11,1
22	Serbia	24	3,792	11	15	2,160	6	60,0	75,6	83,3
23	Ukraine	20	3,510	5	14	2,412	3	42,9	45,5	66,7
24	Morocco	16	3,024	6	10	1,890	3	60,0	60,0	100,0
25	Bulgaria	14	2,394	5	11	1,830	4	27,3	30,8	25,0
26	Lithuania	14	2,646	4	6	1,134	2	133,3	133,3	100,0
27	Czechia	11	1,806	2	9	1,386	2	22,2	30,3	0,0
28	Iceland	10	1,486	5	9	1,320	5	11,1	12,6	0
29	Belgium	6	936	1	6	936	1	0,0	0,0	0
30	Bosnia	4	600	2	5	720	2	-20,0	-16,7	0,0
31	Netherlands	4	488	1	4	552	1	0,0	-11,6	0,0
32	Israel	2	300	1	0	0	0	100,0	100,0	100,0
33	Albania	1	150	1	1	144	1	0,0	4,2	0,0
34	Macedonia	0	0	0	2	288	1	-100,0	-100,0	-100,0
35	Slovakia	0	0	0	6	1,134	2	-100,0	-100,0	-100,0
	Total	**5,424**	**833,841**	**675**	**5,124**	**789,398**	**629**	**5,9**	**5,6**	**7,3**

Source: DLR.

Table 9.5   European country ranking according to number of departures

		Low-cost carrier market in Europe		
		07/2010		
Rank	Country	Flights	Seats	Routes
1	GB	9,883	1,369,683	1.173
2	ES	6,074	1,066,297	846
3	IT	5,615	926,937	860
4	DE	5.424	833,841	675
5	FR	2.413	391,483	428
6	IE	1,634	289,241	195
7	NO	1,425	236,596	215
8	NL	887	134,994	152
9	PT	800	137,109	118
10	PL	722	128,497	198
11	CH	676	101,164	101
12	LV	637	68,940	79
13	SE	586	97,159	118
14	DK	487	78,534	92
15	BE	474	84,691	83
16	GR	445	74,026	164
17	RO	436	79,076	92
18	AT	425	61,900	74
19	TR	374	60,197	118
20	RU	365	46,722	48
21	HR	245	39,943	88
22	FI	221	24,969	36
23	LT	180	22,131	35
24	HU	172	29,022	37
25	CZ	169	28,497	36
26	BG	108	18,623	34
27	MT	99	17,884	29
28	EE	95	6,036	10
29	SK	80	15,120	21
30	CY	72	13,378	22
31	UA	71	12,098	16
32	IS	69	10,290	31
33	RS	47	6,807	17
34	MD	11	1,310	3
35	SI	9	1,452	2
36	BA	8	1,180	4
37	BY	7	322	1
38	GI	7	1,092	1
39	AZ	6	1,004	2
40	GE	6	842	1
41	AM	2	240	1
42	LU	2	296	1
43	MK	2	310	1
44	AL	1	150	1
	Total	41,471	6,520,083	6,259

Source: DLR.

4.4 Airports Served

The most frequented German airport – Frankfurt – continues to play a minor role in the low-cost segment in Germany, due to its distinct hub function in traditional scheduled airline traffic and the already high utilization of airport capacity (see Figure 9.7). Thus only 150 flights, or around 3.3 per cent, have been performed as low-cost flights by Air Berlin and Flybe. Cologne/Bonn is still number one in the list of airports serving low-cost flights (646 departures, which correspond to 64 per cent of the flight traffic), although LCC traffic went down by 5 per cent compared with the preceding year. Berlin-Tegel airport, where the low-cost share continued to increase in the preceding year, follows with an LCC share of about 40 per cent and 585 departures. Low-cost carrier traffic has considerably increased at Friedrichshafen airport, where LCC service has been extended from 77 flights in summer 2009 to 121 flights (50 per cent) in summer 2010. Growth is also reported by Bremen, Karlsruhe/Baden-Baden and Niederrhein airports. Decreasing is the low-cost traffic at Hahn and Luebeck airport where the number of low-cost flights dropped by more than 20 per cent. This is a severe loss for airports featuring almost entirely LCC flights, provided primarily by one carrier, Ryanair. Hahn, Niederrhein, Luebeck, Altenburg, Dortmund, Memmingen and Karlsruhe/Baden-Baden airports are almost exclusively served by LCCs (90 per cent), likewise, but to a somewhat smaller extent, the Berlin-Schoenefeld airport.

Due to easyJet's considerable route extension London Gatwick has become the major European LCC airport with 1,417 LCC departures per week in July 2010 (see Figure 9.8); immediately

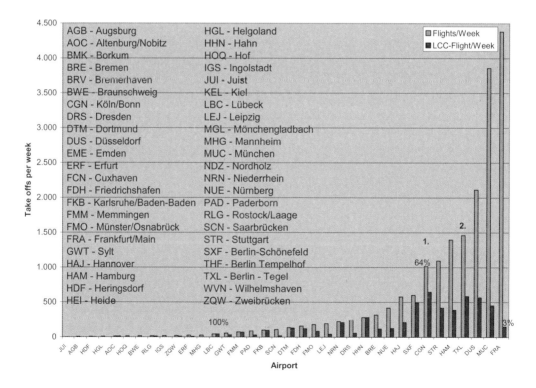

Figure 9.7   Passenger flights on German airports per week in July 2010
Source: DLR.

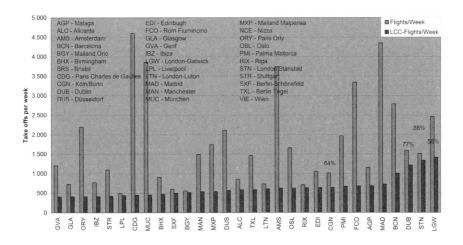

Figure 9.8   Major LCC airports in Europe according to flights per week in July 2010
Source: OAG.

followed by London Stansted (1,336 departures) and Dublin (1,214 departures). Barcelona is in fourth place (1,008 departures). Cologne is at number 9 (646 departures), the third London airport – Luton – is number 14 (609 departures). In total 3,300 low-cost flights have been served at London airports – more than in any other European agglomeration in summer 2010. Berlin-Tegel (place 15), Duesseldorf (place 17), Berlin-Schoenefeld (place 21), Munich (place 23) and Stuttgart (place 26), among other German airports reporting more than 400 LCC departures per week, range among the 30 major European LCC airports. This reveals that LCC service provided at German airports has only changed slightly since the summer 2009 ranking when compared from a European point of view.

As to European traffic, the LCC market share has grown to 27 per cent of the flights: 73 per cent of the flights are mainly performed by traditional scheduled and holiday airlines. Another market share is covered by smaller regional airlines, however, most of them cooperate with major airlines.

5. Demand for Low-cost Carrier Services in Germany

Low-cost Carriers began to enter the German market in 2001/02 at a time when the overall demand for air services was declining or stagnating, due to a general economic crisis, regional wars and terror attacks. However, LCCs managed to capture a growing part of the total demand and, more importantly, generated new demand segments, in particular short-stay personal journeys, with dynamics that were unknown before.

Since demand data for LCC services are generally not as easily available as supply data the growing demand for LCC services is typically reflected against the increase in the number of flights, seats and routes offered (see Chapter 4). Special analyses of statistical data of the Federal Statistical Office of Germany (Statistisches Bundesamt) allow us to quantify the demand for LCC services in the German market in terms of passengers carried for some years.

5.1 Passengers Carried and Market Share in the Low-cost Segment

In 2009, the most recent year for which statistical demand data are available, the 22 international and 4 regional airports in Germany (Berlin is counted as one site) handled 53 million passengers which emplaned or deplaned flights of LCCs (see Table 9.6). The total traffic volume was 181 million passengers, the LCC market share in terms of passengers carried was therefore almost 30 per cent. In 2006, three years before, 40 million LCC passengers (23 per cent) were counted, out of a total of 173 million. About half of all LCC passengers were using domestic services. In 2009, the year of overall demand reduction, domestic LCC traffic was the only segment which did not follow the general trend: it grew by over 1 per cent. The reason behind this was that many business travellers chose LCC services at much lower fares instead of normal scheduled flights. The market share of LCCs grew therefore to over 55 per cent; this means that on short domestic links about every second passenger is now using low-cost flights. In border-crossing LCC traffic almost all flight destinations lie within Europe. The market share of LCCs in the original European traffic (without transfer passengers) amounted to over 40 per cent in 2009.

Since the market entry of LCCs in Germany they have succeeded in growing faster than the total market and taking passengers away from FSNCs. In addition, by opening up new routes and offering much lower fares than the established carriers, LCCs have generated new demand that otherwise would not have travelled by air.

As can be seen in Table 9.6, not all airports are participating equally in low-cost traffic: the LCC share of total airport traffic varies substantially between airports. Some airports, such as Hahn and Niederrhein, depend almost solely on LCCs, while others, both airports with high and lower traffic volumes like Frankfurt and Paderborn, favour FSNCs. As in the preceding years, regional airports have shown the highest growth in low-cost traffic, due to the preference of LCCs for these airports, which are often underutilized and prepared to yield favourable charging and operating conditions to carriers. Looking at the historic development of LCCs in the US and in Europe we can assume that they will not only stay in the market but continue to grow with the market and grow even faster. This means that all airports have an interest in offering low-cost services in addition to 'normal' scheduled and charter flights. The concentration of LCCs on a few airports will then probably lessen and more airports will offer low-cost services.

Table 9.6   Low-cost passenger traffic by airport and market share in the German market 2009

Low-cost carrier market in Germany				
Airport **Total**	**Passengers 2009**		**Change of LCC traffic (%)**	**LCC share of total (%)**
	Total	**LLC**		
Berlin (total)	20,933,602	11,061,937	–4.3	52.8
Köln/Bonn	9,709,987	6,793,096	–6.0	70.0
Düsseldorf	17,755,982	5,224,064	–3.4	29.4
München	32,628,791	5,040,402	–1.4	15.4
Stuttgart	8,896,518	3,818,473	–12.6	42.9
Hahn	3,743,281	3,734,640	–3.9	99.8
Hamburg	12,206,130	3,509,974	–9.7	28.8
Niederrhein	2,395,544	2,306,444	54.1	96.3
Frankfurt	50,615,550	1,944,351	11.5	3.8
Hannover	4,925,828	1,603,455	–13.6	32.6
Dortmund	1,711,157	1,451,493	–25.3	84.8
Nürnberg	3,939,067	1,210,512	–9.3	30.7
Bremen	2,440,085	1,055,568	5.1	43.3
Karlsruhe/Bad.-Bad.	1,078,034	836,683	–1.3	77.6
Lübeck	688,066	682,987	29.7	99.3
Dresden	1,686,691	558,551	1.1	33.1
Münster/Osnabrück	1,364,682	450,122	–14.0	33.0
Leipzig/Halle	1,865,247	396,486	0.0	21.3
Saarbrücken	405,899	203,613	73.1	50.2
Friedrichshafen	570,490	140,767	–8.2	24.7
Paderborn	959,926	83,963	–18.0	8.7
Erfurt	259,932	–	–	–
Total IVF	180,780,489	52,107,581	–3.1	28.9
Memmingen		621,424	172.3	
Zweibrücken		167,413	24.4	
Altenburg-Nobitz		133,409	10.1	
Rostock		53,090	221.0	
Total RVV		975,336	94.9	
IVF + RVV		53,082,917	–2.2	

Source: ADV, DLR.

In the early years of low-cost offers, LCCs enlarged their networks substantially from season to season – as we have seen by about 100 new routes in the German market alone – it seems that these growth steps belong to the phase of generally building up the low-cost business. Growth rates of LCC traffic in Germany and Europe have come down drastically and have become more or less normal, as can be seen in Figure 9.9, which shows the growth rates of passenger demand for low-cost services in Germany from 2002 to 2009. While in the first years the growth of LCC traffic was characterized by annual rates of more than 50 per cent, they are now comparable to those of the total market, although on some airports with LCC concentration and new carriers high growth of passenger demand can still be the case.

The fact that LCCs are becoming an established segment in the total spectrum of air traffic services can be demonstrated by following the market shares of the main components of the market, that is FSNCs, traditional charter carriers and LCCs. Figure 9.10 (Source ADV, DLR) shows the development of market shares in these segments in the German market since 2002. Without LCCs, until around 2000, the market was dominated by traditional scheduled carriers, and holiday charter carriers supplemented the total air transport supply by flight chains to mainly summer resort areas. With LCCs in the German market the share of FSNCs has come down to less than 60 per cent, and charter airlines carry not more than 13 per cent, while LCCs have gained significant market share over time and reached a level of nearly 30 per cent in 2009. However, as can be seen, the change in market share of the three service types was narrowing in recent years, due to fare reactions of FSNCs and the slow-down of network extensions of LCCs. It seems that FSNCs, LCCs and charter carriers are reaching a new equilibrium of market penetration and changes occur only marginally, depending on successful marketing initiatives by carriers in each market segment.

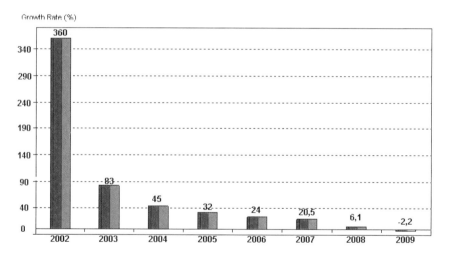

Figure 9.9   **Growth rates of passenger demand for low-cost carriers in Germany 2002–2009**
Source: ADV.

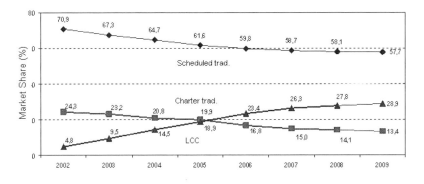

Figure 9.10   Development of market shares of airline types in the German market
Source: ADV, DLR.

5.2 Demand Generation

Based on passenger surveys and demand statistics there is reason to assume that LCCs have succeeded in generating substantial new demand for their low-fare services, nevertheless, depending on the specific route, about 40 to 60 per cent of all LCC passengers come from other airlines or other modes of transport. With the gain in market share LCCs not only captured passengers from other airlines in direct competition and transfer passengers from hub services in a more indirect competition with FSNCs, but in particular gained newly generated passengers who otherwise would have not travelled by air or not travelled at all. In a strict sense, only the latter category belongs to the demand generated by LCC services.

There is probably no way of finding an exhaustive answer to the question of newly generated demand in air transportation, since one can think of many activities in daily, weekend or weekly life that could be subject to substitution by low-fare air services. Among those are certainly car and non-LCC air trips. What can be clearly shown from statistics is the total demand attracted by new LCC services. The portions coming from other flights or other modes or substituted by other activities have to be estimated case-by-case since the competitive conditions vary from airport to airport and from route to route.

In order to show the demand attracted to new LCC services we have depicted two examples of domestic routes – from the Rhineland to Hamburg and to Berlin. The first is a short distance route (of around 400 kms) used mainly by business travellers, the second is a route with a distance of 600 kms, used by both private and business travellers. Day return trips are, practically, not feasible by car or train on both routes.

In Figure 9.11 we show the development of passenger demand on the two routes from Köln (CGN) and Düsseldorf (DUS) to Hamburg (HAM) from 2002 to 2009. The two airports in Köln and Düsseldorf are only about 60 km apart, so that we can assume that passengers coming from the region of these conurbations will choose either of the two airports depending on the personal utility of the air service. The demand on the DUS–HAM route has grown from about 10,000 passengers per month in 2002 to nearly 20,000 in 2009. Flight service has been offered by Lufthansa and Air Berlin, and prices have been higher than offered by typical LCCs. At the beginning of 2006, Lufthansa introduced a Better Fly ticket as a response to low LCC fares with a round trip fare of €99. The market reacted immediately, 2,000–3,000 new passengers were attracted by the new, low-fare service.

Market reaction was much more profound on the CGN–HAM link, when low-cost services by Hapag Lloyd Express (HLX) were introduced in early 2003; more than 10,000 new passengers per month used the new service, resulting in a doubling of the number of passengers on that link. As can be seen, the negative effect on the parallel route from Düsseldorf was very small. The new demand has partly modally switched from train services, as was reported by passenger counts in trains, and from the car, which has been reported by air passengers asked in surveys. In addition, the newly generated demand does not only consist of business travellers, as was formerly the case, but also of travellers with a non-business trip purpose. When HLX opened this route Lufthansa, as the incumbent carrier, matched the new low fares, at least for a limited number of seats, thus also causing an additional generating effect. The true demand generation effect of the introduction of low fare services is not known, nevertheless, the overall effect was immediate and strong; demand had doubled on that link. In the following years demand did not grow, HLX services were taken over by Air Berlin, and as a consequence average prices increased. In October 2009 another LCC, Germanwings, entered that market with lower prices, and the demand generation followed again immediately: Another 8,000 passengers per month used the new low-fare service.

The second example (Figure 9.12) shows the demand development on the Rhineland (CGN, DUS) to Berlin route. The demand for air services on this route has traditionally been strong, and both business and private purpose travellers have been using flights between the Rhineland and the three airports in Berlin, Tegel (TXL), Schönefeld (SXF) and until 2008 Tempelhof (THF). Most flights have been offered to Tegel, however, flights have then been added or switched to Schönefeld und Tempelhof and also partly abandoned again; Tempelhof was closed as an airport in October 2008.

While on the Düsseldorf to Berlin link no spectacular changes in air services occurred, such changes have taken place on the Köln to Berlin route. The most important change in supply was the introduction of LCC services by Germanwings as well as HLX in 2002. Within a few months the demand grew from about 35,000 passengers per month to around 55,000. Demand changes in the following years were mainly caused by flight transfers to Schönefeld and Tempelhof or by

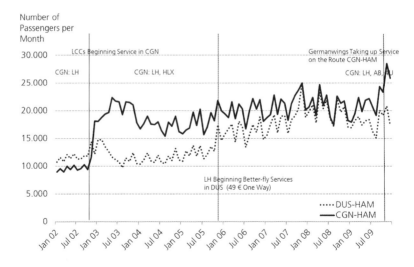

Figure 9.11   Demand development on the Rhineland–Hamburg route
Source: DLR.

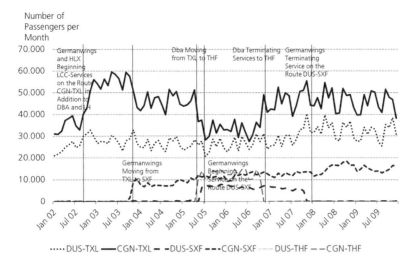

Figure 9.12 Demand development on the Rhineland–Berlin route

Source: DLR.

discontinuation of services to these airports respectively. As has been shown by the Rhineland to Hamburg example, the introduction of LCC services causes demand to react strongly and price elasticity is accordingly high, in particular in the segment of private purpose travel. Moreover, the market reaction occurs in a short period of time, say a few months: after that the development pattern follows the former trend. This type of demand effect has been observed on almost all links where LCCs have taken up service.

In concluding we can state that the introduction of LCC services on a link where normal scheduled services had already been available, or the opening up of such services on a new route, has a great impact on demand, that is on passengers substituting for traditional air services and services of other modes as well as on new passengers substituting for other activities, including non-travel activities. There have been numerous examples where the effect on demand was in the order of more than 10,000 passengers per month attracted to the new LCC services. Second, the impact occurs immediately after the introduction of new services and lasts only a short time, say a few months; the development of demand then follows the former trend. This means that the generation effect of LCC services is strongly correlated with the extension of LCC networks. If networks are only marginally extended, as was the case since 2008, then the generation effect is equally marginal. Low-cost carriers will only succeed in further increasing their market share if they can add new routes with strong demand potential. This may cause them to look more for tourism markets, e.g. in the Mediterranean region, and perhaps intercontinental markets.

6. Summary and Conclusions

Low-cost carriers entered the European market in the late 1990s and have achieved a market share of about 34 per cent in 2008, while FSNCs provided 58 per cent of seats available at European airports in that year, and charter and regional carriers had a share of almost 5 per cent and 3 per cent respectively (DLR, 2009). Much of the traffic growth in Europe since the year 2000, when air traffic was hit globally by an economic crisis and terrorism, was due to the proliferation of LCCs, while traditional network carriers lost market shares and were forced to reduce capacity, both on feeder routes to their hubs as well as on non-hub routes.

Although there is no exact definition of LCCs we can state that in general they offer no-frills services between mainly European and US airports at low prices, as regarded in absolute terms as well as compared with fares of established network carriers on similar routes. The main business objective of LCCs is to produce seat-km at very low unit costs in order to be able to offer services at prices well below those of traditional network carriers.

To achieve low unit costs, and thus low prices, LCCs must exercise a strict cost control in all phases of operations. Simplicity of all processes is the key factor. The operating model of LCCs includes several components all of which are focused to reduce and keep costs down. They are:

- Network structure with point-to-point services, with a preference of using secondary airports because of lower charges and slot availability, allowing high aircraft utilization, quick turnaround times and easier operations.
- Uniform fleet, with typically one aircraft type, like A 320 or B 737, single class configuration and high seating density.
- Direct marketing of services, typically via the Internet and Internet-based booking.
- Price strategy of low fares, incorporating yield management systems.
- No frills preceding, during and after the flight, including services in and infrastructure of the airport terminal.

Studies (e.g. Doganis, 2001, and Hansson et al., 2002, 2003) have shown that LCCs have operated commercially successful at 40–50 per cent of the unit costs of FSNCs. On the other hand, FSNCs lowered costs through restructuring and consolidating production and cutting back on services and quality. The commercial success of LCCs has thus caused traditional network carriers to reconsider their business model and adopt more features of LCCs, i.e. reduce costs in order to be more competitive and regain market penetration.

For autumn of 2010, we analysed prices offered by the most important LCCs serving the German market. While average net prices vary between €22 and €70 among airlines, total prices, including taxes, levies and other surcharges, vary between €35 and €144.

The 19 LCCs active in the German market offered in one week of summer 2010 nearly 5,400 departures with 830,000 seats on over 700 domestic and border-crossing routes. On these 5,400 flights, on average, 154 seats were made available per flight. It shows clearly that LCCs have established a typical average aircraft capacity of more than 150 seats. Thus, these flight-specific seat capacities continue to range distinctly higher than those of traditional European scheduled airlines.

According to the number of flights offered (departures) in one week in July 2010 the Air Berlin low-cost segment covering almost 2,600 departures is the major supplier in Germany. In the ranking of airlines, Germanwings (1,037 flights), Ryanair (832 flights) and easyJet (357 flights) follow. Taking the number of departures as an index of the position of an airline in the market we can see that the six major LCCs, of a total of 19 airlines in the German market, cover about 94 per cent of the low-cost market.

In the European market of summer 2010, 36 LCCs have altogether offered more than 41,000 departures with 6.5 million seats on almost 6,800 routes in Europe and to other non-European destinations, particularly to North Africa. The major European low-cost airline is Ryanair with more than 10,000 departures in July 2010, followed by easyJet with nearly 7,000 flights. Low-cost traffic in Europe is not as strongly concentrated on just a few airlines as in Germany, however, the three top ranked LCCs, Ryanair, easyJet and Flybe, provide more than half (52 per cent) of all departures, and almost 90 per cent of the European low-cost traffic (in terms of flights) is concentrated on 12 airlines (33 per cent) out of 36 airlines in total.

The low-cost airlines considered in the German market cover altogether 675 different domestic and cross-border routes in a summer week of 2010. Since the emergence of the low-cost market in 2002, about 100 routes were added per year during the first six years. As opposed to the period of dynamic growth in the years of forming and building LCC networks it took three years, from 2007 to 2010, to add the same number of routes to the network.

If the network development is followed airline-by-airline one can observe a strategy of avoiding direct competition with other low-cost airlines. In fact, direct competition among LCCs has been very low and has even decreased, if the number of routes with two or more airlines is taken into account. Only on 34 (5 per cent) of the total number of 675 routes are two airlines competing. There is just one route left with more than two airlines competing directly: 640 routes – the majority – are served by a single airline.

In 2010, LCCs of Germany have served in total destinations in 33 countries. The country of destination ranking reveals the big market share of domestic traffic: in this market 40 per cent of all LCC flights departing from German airports have been offered on more than 120 routes, corresponding to 60 airport pairs, which account for just 20 per cent of all routes. In the European LCC market, Great Britain remains the number one destination, according to the LCC flight destination ranking. The network of this country covers more than 1,100 routes from all over Europe, including domestic traffic. The most frequented German airport – Frankfurt – continues to play a minor role in the low-cost segment in Germany, due to its distinct hub function in traditional scheduled airline traffic and the already high utilization of airport capacity. Köln/Bonn is still number one of the airports serving low-cost flights (646 departures, which correspond to 64 per cent of the flight traffic). Due to easyJet's considerable route extension London Gatwick has become the major European LCC airport with 1,417 LCC departures per week in July 2010, immediately followed by London Stansted (1,336 departures) and Dublin (1,214 departures): Barcelona is in fourth place (1,008 departures).

In 2009 German airports handled 53 million passengers which emplaned or deplaned LCC flights. The total traffic volume was 181 million passengers, the LCC market share in terms of passengers carried was therefore almost 30 per cent. About half of all LCC passengers were using domestic services. The market share of LCCs in the original European traffic (without transfer passengers) amounted to over 40 per cent in 2009.

Growth rates of LCC traffic in Germany and Europe have come down drastically and have become more or less normal. While in the early years the growth of LCC traffic was characterized by annual rates of more than 50 per cent, they are now comparable to those of the total market, although at some airports with LCC concentration and new carriers, high growth of passenger demand can still be the case.

Low-cost carriers have succeeded in generating substantial new demand for their low-fare services. Depending on the specific route, about 40–60 per cent of all LCC passengers come from other airlines or other modes of transport. There have been numerous examples where the effect on demand was in the order of more than 10,000 passengers per month attracted to the new LCC services. Second, the impact occurs immediately after the introduction of new services and lasts only for a short time, say a few months: the development of demand then follows the former trend. This means that the generation effect of LCC services is strongly correlated with the extension of networks of LCCs. If networks are only marginally extended, as was the case since 2008, then the generation effect is equally marginal. Low-cost Carriers will only succeed in further increasing their market share if they can add new routes with strong demand potential. This may cause them to look more for tourism markets, e.g. in the Mediterranean region, and perhaps intercontinental markets.

References

ADV (Arbeitsgemeinschaft Deutscher Verkehrsflughäfen), *Airport Traffic Statistics* of various years, Berlin: ADV.

Albrecht, D. (2009) Marktumfeld im Luftverkehr im internationalen Vergleich (Market environment in an international comparison). Paper presented at an IHK Conference in Dortmund, 23 November.

DLR (2009) *Analyses of the European Air Transport Market, Annual Report 2008. A Study Carried out for the European Commission*. Cologne: DLR.

DLR (2010) *Low-cost Monitor 2/2010*. Köln: German Aerospace Center.

Doganis, R. (2001) *The Airline Business in the 21st Century*. London, New York: Routledge.

Franke, M. (2004) Competition between network carriers and low-cost carriers – retreat battle or breakthrough to a new level of efficiency? *Journal of Air Transport Management*, 10, 15–21.

Hansson T., Ringbeck, J. and Franke, M. (2002) Flight for survival; a new operating model for airlines. *Strategy + Business*, *Enews*, 12 September.

Hansson T., Ringbeck, J. and Franke, M. (2003) Flight for survival; a new business model for the airline industry. *Strategy + Business*, 31, 78–85.

Kurth, W. (2004) *Stimulanz der Nachfrage schafft Wachstum – Das Marktpotential der Niedrigpreisairlines* (Stimulating demand creates growth – the market potential of low-fare airlines). Bensberg: Thomas Morus Akademie.

Statistisches Bundesamt, Federal Statistical Office, *Air Transport Statistics* of various years, published and unpublished data, Wiesbaden: Statistisches Bundesamt.

Wilken, D. and Berster, P. (2007) *The Impact of New Type Services, i.e. Low-cost Services, on the Transfer Passenger Market in Germany – Some New evidence*. ATRS 2007 Conference, Berkeley, California.

Chapter 10

À la Carte Pricing to Generate Ancillary Revenue: The Case of Ryanair

Richard Klophaus

1. Introduction

Ancillary revenue has become a key revenue component for low-cost carriers (LCCs) in Europe, but airlines throughout the world are following the ancillary revenue movement. This chapter focuses on ancillary revenue generated by à la carte pricing. It describes the practice of à la carte pricing among European LCCs using the example of Ryanair, the leading LCC in Europe. Ryanair is often considered as the pioneering airline of the à la carte business model, unbundling its services into core air travel, charging very low base fares while offering an increasing list of optional services at a fee.

In view of its practical significance it is surprising that no published research exists on the optimality of unbundling air travel services. However, the advantage of unbundled sales of components of a composite product by one firm has been the subject of research on bundling in economics and marketing. Today, a plethora of normative guidelines can be found for the bundling of two or more products and/or services to specially priced packages as reviewed by Venkatesh and Mahajan (2009). Unbundling services into core product and à la carte items is the opposite of pure bundling. Hence, building upon previous research on bundling this chapter evaluates the impact of à la carte pricing with checked baggage as an add-on service to basic air transport on airline's revenues.

The chapter is structured as follows: Section 2 illustrates the current practice among airlines to generate ancillary revenue through à la carte pricing. Section 3 analyses the economic rationale for à la carte pricing and unbundling of air travel services based on a methodological framework provided by Guiltinan (1987). The purpose of the analysis is to identify conditions under which à la carte pricing and unbundling lead to higher total revenues for carriers. Section 4 applies this framework to the case of Ryanair's unbundling of checked baggage using data from the carrier's annual report (Ryanair, 2010). The closing section 5 summarizes the chapter's results.

2. Ancillary Revenue and À la Carte Pricing

Ancillary revenue has been defined as revenue beyond the sale of tickets (Ideaworks, 2009). Further, three categories of optional services leading to ancillary revenue have been differentiated:

- À la carte features: seat selection, priority check-in, on-board sales of food and beverages, etc.
- Commission-based products: commissions earned on the sale of hotel accommodation, car hire, travel insurance, etc., primarily via the airline's website.
- Frequent flyer programme: sale of miles or points to programme partners.

This chapter focuses on ancillary revenue generated by à la carte pricing. This label is taken from the hospitality industry. If you eat à la carte, you choose each dish from a separate list instead of eating a fixed combination of dishes at a fixed price. Each item on the menu has a separate price. À la carte pricing clarifies the value of optional services.

The success of à la carte pricing depends not only on the proper control of price variables but the right combination of marketing tools, that is the entire offering to consumers often referred to as the '4 Ps' of the marketing mix. À la carte pricing in the airline industry first involves decisions on the product, for example, how to unbundle air travel services into basic air transport and optional services in order to meet the needs of specified target markets. Internet websites are the dominant distribution channel for ticket sales of LCCs. The sale of optional services does not necessarily occur at time of booking (via website, call centre, travel agent) but also during travel at places like the airport or on board during the flight. This adds complexity to LCCs' processes. With regard to promotion of unbundled services, an important question is how and when information concerning add-ons and the respective fees is communicated to the target audience. From the consumers' perspective à la carte pricing can be beneficial. More specifically, there is a plausible argument that consumers who do not book add-ons only pay for basic air transport without cross-subsidizing other consumers.

The present chapter exemplifies à la carte pricing among airlines using the example of Ryanair. It is not only the leading LCC in Europe but has also become the world's largest international scheduled airline by passenger numbers. At the end of the fiscal year 2009 Ryanair operated a fleet of 181 Boeing 737-800s and transported 58.6 million passengers. The average number of employees was 6,369 leading to 9,195 passengers per employee (Ryanair, 2010). High labour productivity contributed to an adjusted net profit after tax of €105.0 million in the fiscal year 2009, an *annus horribilis* by many of Ryanair's competitors.

Ryanair's ancillary revenue increased 22.5 per cent from €488.1 million in the 2008 fiscal year to €598.1 million in the 2009 fiscal year (Ryanair, 2010). This represents 20.3 per cent of Ryanair's total operating revenue of €2,942.0 million. The ancillary revenue stream from so-called non-flight scheduled operations amounted to €425.8 million and includes revenues from excess baggage charges, debit and credit card transactions, sales of rail and bus tickets, accommodations and travel insurance. In-flight sales of beverages, food and merchandise led to €83.2 million and Internet-related sales, that is commissions received from products sold on websites linked to Ryanair's website, to another €56.9 million. A contract with Hertz car rental added €32.2 million revenue (Table 10.1).

Table 10.1   Ryanair's ancillary revenues (fiscal year end march 2009)

Category	Revenue (€m)
Non-flight scheduled operations	425.8
In-flight sales	83.2
Internet-related sales	56.9
Car rentals	32.2
Total	598.1

Source: Ryanair.com, visited 15 April 2010.

Ancillary revenue per booked passenger was €10.22. It is not difficult to generate test bookings on Ryanair. com where à la carte fees are a multiple of the base fare even without fees charged for travel extras like sporting equipment. Ryanair's ancillary revenue earned from à la carte pricing alone cannot be estimated from the published components of ancillary revenue. The category of non-flight scheduled operations as the primary source of ancillary revenue contains revenue from à la carte features but also from commissions. On the other hand, Ryanair does not count fees on checked baggage as ancillary revenue. These are added to the so-called scheduled revenue of €2,343.9 million in the 2009 fiscal year.

Some of Ryanair's à la carte items and associated fees are published on the airline's website (Table 10.2). The price list for on-board sales of drinks, snacks etc. is not available on the website.

Table 10.2   Ryanair's à la carte items (excerpt)

Item	Description	Fee
Online check-in	Unavoidable charge except for some promotional fares	€5 online €10 call centre
Administration	For payments made with credit card; per passenger/per one-way flight	€5
Priority boarding	Per passenger/per one-way flight	€4 online €5 other*
1st checked bag	15 kg allowance/per one-way flight	€15 online[†] €35 other*
2nd checked bag	15 kg allowance/per one-way flight; maximum 2 bags per passenger permitted	€35 online[†] €70 other*
Excess baggage	Per kilo, can only be purchased at airport	€20

* Booked via call centre or at airport; [†] Higher fees during peak period July/August; Source: Ryanair.com, visited 15 April 2010.

It is arguable whether online check-in should be listed as an à la carte item: all passengers need to check-in. Since October 2009 airport check-in is no longer available for Ryanair's customers. Hence they can avoid the check-in fee only on some promotional fares when online check-in is not charged by Ryanair. Further, only some passengers are holders of a Mastercard Prepaid Debit Card, the only payment form to avoid an administration fee of €5 per passenger and one-way flight. This administration fee is challenged as illegal in court. The fees for priority boarding and checked baggage are lower when booked via the Internet in comparison to sales via call centre or at airport. Approximately 99 per cent of Ryanair's flight reservations are made through its website (Ryanair, 2010). The lower online fees further strengthen the Internet as predominant distribution channel.

The communicated success of à la carte pricing has created an ancillary revenue movement within the airline world not confined to European LCCs. Major US-based carriers like American, United or Delta implemented à la carte baggage fees. However, implementation of à la carte pricing is more difficult for network carriers than for LCCs due to connections via hubs with through-checking baggage, interlining, code-sharing and integration in global airline alliances. Further obstacles for network carriers are multi-channel distribution and higher product expectations of their passengers. These difficulties may be sufficient to explain why European network carriers like Air France, British Airways or Lufthansa have not introduced à la carte pricing for checked baggage. However, the following section questions the economic rationale of unbundling checked baggage from basic air transport.

3. Economic Rationale for à la Carte Pricing

Ryanair sells a wide range of à la carte items, from priority boarding to on-board sales of food and beverages. The commonality of these à la carte items is that they are complementary to basic air transport. Consumers can enjoy air travel without paying for priority boarding or food and beverage, but à la carte items have no value to them except when used together with the basic product. Therefore, à la carte items can be considered as one-way complements.

This chapter focuses on the economic rationale for LCCs charging a separate fee for checked baggage, that is, items of luggage delivered to an airline for transportation in the hold of an aircraft. The analysis does not cover excess baggage, that is, baggage exceeding the allowance in size, weight and number of checked items that is charged additionally per kilo. Checked baggage fees are common among LCCs. Eight out of the ten largest European LCCs by seat capacity charge for checked baggage (Table 10.3).

Table 10.3   Checked baggage fees among the 10 largest European LCCs

LCC	Checked baggage fee (Y/N)?
Ryanair	Y
Easyjet	Y
Air Berlin	N
Norwegian	Y
Flybe	N
Wizz	Y
Germanwings	Y
Vueling	Y
Clickair*	Y
Jet 2	Y

* Merged with Vueling; Source: LCC's websites, visited 15 April 2010.

Economic justification of à la carte pricing to date is rather vague. No published research exists on the optimality of unbundling air transport services. Unbundling air transport services into basic air transport and optional à la carte items like checked baggage turns bundling, defined as the practice of selling two or more products in a single package, to its opposite. Hence, the existing literature on bundling can be applied to analyse when and how airlines benefit from à la carte pricing.

The literature identifies three alternative bundling strategies (Venkatesh and Mahajan, 2009):

- Pure bundling: the seller offers the bundle alone.
- Mixed bundling: the seller offers the bundle as well as the individual products.
- Pure components (or unbundling): the seller offers only the individual products.

In his widely cited paper about the comparative properties of commodity bundling and unbundled sales, Schmalensee (1984) concludes that the advantage of pure bundling is its ability to reduce heterogenity in consumers' willingness to pay, while the rationale for unbundling is to collect a high price for each good from some customers who care very little for the other good.

In order to analyse the economic rationale for à la carte pricing with checked baggage as an add-on service to basic air transport, the present chapter applies the methodological framework provided by Guiltinan (1987).

Let

A	= basic air transport (core product)
B	= checked baggage (add-on service)
P_{A+B}	= price of bundle with components A and B
P_A, P_B	= prices of unbundled products A and B
RP_{A+B}	= reservation price for bundle
RP_A, RP_B	= reservation prices for individual products
$RP_{B/A}$	= reservation price for B given A
X_O	= number of bundle buyers
X_N	= number of non-customers of bundle
α	= share of X_O who become buyers of A only
ß	= share of X_N who become buyers of A

with $0 < α, ß < 1$.

The parameters α and ß recognize that the success of an airline's decision to unbundle air transportation services and apply à la carte pricing will depend on:

- revenue losses due to customers who become non-buyers of the add-on service, and
- the generation of new customers for the core product who have previously been non-customers (e.g. buyers of competitors' products).

Reservation prices stand for the maximum amounts consumers are willing to pay. This chapter does not assume any distribution of reservation prices among the buyers and non-customers of the individual products and the bundle respectively. If A and B are independent in demand, the reservation price for the bundle equals the sum of the individual reservation prices (i.e., $RP_A + RP_B = RP_{A+B}$).

After unbundling, checked baggage as an add-on service B has no value to consumers (i.e., $RP_B = 0$) except when used together with basic air transport A. Some consumers might not appreciate checked baggage at all. For the others checked baggage as a one-way complement B is worth more if A is purchased (i.e., $RP_{B/A} > 0$). Let us assume positive reservation prices satisfying:

$$RP_A + RP_{B/A} = RP_{A+B} \tag{1}$$

and no price discount on the bundle, i.e.,

$$P_A + P_B = P_{A+B} \tag{2}$$

(1) and (2) together rule out the possibility that unbundling leads previous non-customers to become buyers of A and B. If $RP_{A+B} < P_{A+B}$ than also $RP_A + RP_{B/A} < P_A + P_B$ holds. Similarly, bundle

buyers cannot turn into non-customers. Figure 10.1 shows the possible customer flows resulting from unbundling B (checked baggage) from A (basic air transport).

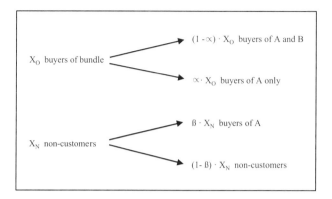

Figure 10.1   Possible customer flows resulting from unbundling checked baggage from basic air transport

For bundle buyers who become buyers of A only as well as for new buyers of A the following conditions hold: $RP_A > P_A$ and $RP_{B/A} < P_B$. The customer flows depicted in Figure 10.1 increase the carrier's total revenue if

$$(P_A + P_B) \cdot (1 - \alpha) \cdot X_O + P_A \cdot \alpha \cdot X_O + P_A \cdot \beta \cdot X_N$$
$$-P_{A+B} \cdot X_O > 0 . \tag{3}$$

With $P_A + P_B = P_{A+B}$ that is excluding the impact of a higher sum of the two prices for the unbundled products A and B, the condition for a revenue gain resulting from unbundling can be restated as

$$-\alpha \cdot P_B \cdot X_O + \beta \cdot P_A \cdot X_N > 0 \tag{4}$$

If the revenue loss associated with former buyers of checked baggage is compensated by revenue gains through new buyers of basic air transport the total revenue impact is positive. Rearranging (4) leads to

$$-\alpha \cdot \frac{P_B}{P_A} \cdot \frac{X_O}{X_N} + \beta > 0 \tag{5}$$

Equation (5) allows us to identify conditions under which à la carte pricing increases the airline's revenue even without specifying distributional assumptions for consumers' reservation prices:

- Low share α of bundle buyers who become buyers of A only.
- Low price ratio P_B/P_A
- Low ratio of bundle buyers to non-customers X_O/X_N

- High share ß of non-customers who become buyers of A.

These intuitively plausible conditions lead us to conclude that if airlines sell individual service components instead of air transportation services as a bundle, their revenue may not increase. This conclusion depends largely on the assumption made in equation (4) that the bundle price equals the sum of prices for the components. Hence, revenue gains reported by airlines practicing à la carte pricing may not be the result of unbundling services but of price increases (i.e., $P_{A \text{ new}} + P_{B \text{ new}} > P_{A+B \text{ old}}$).

4. The Case of Ryanair

The previous analysis is now applied to the case of Ryanair. In August 2007 Ryanair started charging for first checked baggage. In the meantime, the online fee for first checked baggage rose to €15 representing additional ancillary revenue created through à la carte pricing. Ryanair even increased this fee to €20 for flights during the two peak months of Summer 2010. During the period from 2007 to 2009 Ryanair's average base fare decreased from €44 to €40. Further, before charging checked baggage, some 80 per cent of Ryanair's passengers were travelling with checked-in luggage. That figure fell to 30 per cent in 2009 (Ryanair, 2010).

Let us assume that the decline in Ryanair's average base fare is determined by the carrier's decision to unbundle checked baggage. Then with the notation defined above the price variables take the following values: $P_{A+B} = 44$, $P_A = 40$, $P_B = 15$, $P_A + P_B = 55$. In the fiscal year 2009 Ryanair transported $X_O = 58.6$ million passengers. Approximately $\alpha = 30\%$ of these passengers checked-in luggage. The value for ß cannot be directly taken from Ryanair's annual report or other published information by the carrier. Instead the price elasticity of 1.96 on intra-European short-haul routes derived in a synoptic study (Intervistas, 2007) is used to calculate the effect of unbundling checked luggage on Ryanair's sales of its core product A. Hence, lowering the average base fare for air transport by 9 per cent from $P_{A+B} = 44$ to $P_A = 40$ created approximately ß = 18% new customers buying product A. This allows us to calculate the minimum X_N required for unbundling to increase Ryanair's total revenue. Solving equation (5) for X_N leads to a required sales potential of 36.6 million non-customers. This value of X_N depends on the price elasticity of demand. The lower the price elasticity the higher is the required X_N.

In view of approximately 200 million passengers carried by the ten largest European LCCs in the year 2009, the actual sales potential for Ryanair beyond 58.6 million already-transported passengers may or may not be higher than 36.6 million. Therefore it is not clear whether Ryanair increases its total revenue through unbundling checked baggage. This result is in line with the general conditions under which à la carte pricing increases total revenue derived in the previous section. Whereas the strong reduction in checked in baggage penetration rates reflected by high $\alpha = 30\%$ and the high price ratio P_B/P_A seem to make gains in total revenue due to unbundling impossible, the relatively low ratio of bundle buyers to non-customers X_O/X_N in combination with a high share ß = 18% of non-customers who become buyers of A tend to increase total revenue.

As the empirical example of Ryanair illustrates gains in total revenue from à la carte pricing and unbundling air transportation services are far from certain. In the case of Ryanair the potential cost savings due to reduced checked baggage may be the primary reason for implementing a separate checked baggage fee.

5. Conclusions

Business decisions on unbundling previously bundled products require estimates of distributions of reservation prices including conditional reservation price distributions. However, the methodological framework presented above allows to derive conditions under which unbundling air travel services is likely to increase airlines' revenues without specifying such distribution of reservation prices.

These conditions were applied to the case of Ryanair. This leading low-cost carrier decided to unbundle checked baggage from basic air transport some years ago. With the empirical data available it is uncertain whether unbundling checked baggage led to an increase in Ryanair's total operating revenue because of a high share of previous bundle buyers with reservation prices for the optional service below the charged fee and a high ratio of the checked baggage fee compared to the base fare. Hence, the primary motivation for Ryanair's decision to charge a separate fee seems not to be revenue maximization but cost savings.

In general, revenue gains reported by airlines practicing à la carte pricing may not be the result of unbundling services but of higher prices. Hence, the often proclaimed benefit of unbundling for consumers to pay only for services required may be offset by price increases. In order to ensure à la carte pricing becomes a successful marketing strategy, airlines are likely to reduce the ability of consumers to compare air fares. Hence, consumers may accept increases in total air fares not transparent to them. This asks for regulatory efforts to ensure clarity of airlines' websites and other advertising to allow consumers to compare total fares. Within the European Union under Article 23 of Regulation 1008/2008 on common rules for the operation of air services each carrier – when operating from an airport located in the territory of a Member State – should indicate the final ticket price from the beginning of the booking process. To be in accordance with Article 23, services that are in fact unavoidable should be correctly specified and included in the basic air fare and add-on services shown in the booking process should be on an opt-in basis. The EU commission launched a 'ticket sweep' in September 2007 to check that 386 websites selling airline tickets are complying with consumer protection laws. One in three websites surveyed had to be followed up with enforcement action for breaches of consumer law. However, efforts to regulate airlines' price information and to avoid misleading pricing need to keep in mind that today's complex fare structures are an outcome of the deregulation process of removing price restrictions in the airline industry.

During recent years many airlines have proudly reported increases in ancillary revenue (Ideaworks, 2009). However, what really counts is total revenue and eventually profits. This chapter questions the economic rationale for unbundling air travel services. The recent re-bundling of à la carte items (e.g. Southwest's Business Select fare) may be a sign that the aviation industry as well is re-evaluating unbundling.

The present analysis was limited to airline's revenues and did not consider the impact of unbundling on costs. The case of Ryanair shows that cost savings may be the primary reason for charging fees for checked baggage. If unbundling of components of air travel services lead to reduced demand for optional services as in Ryanair's case with checked luggage, the question is how much cost savings are possible without abusing bargaining power vis-à-vis airports or handling service providers. This exemplifies that an in-depth analysis of à la carte pricing and unbundling air travel services on carriers' profitability is an interesting issue for further research, airline executives as well as for policy makers.

References

Guiltinan, J.P. (1987) The price bundling of services: a normative framework. *Journal of Marketing*, 51, 74–85.

Ideaworks (2009) *The Guide to Ancillary Revenue and a la Carte Pricing*. Shorewood, Wisconsin: Ideaworks.

Intervistas (2007) *Estimating Air Travel Demand Elasticities, Study Commissioned by IATA*. Vancouver: Intervistas.

Ryanair (2010) *Annual Report 2009*. Dublin: Ryanair.

Schmalensee, R. (1984) Gaussian demand and commodity bundling. *Journal of Business*, 57, 211–230.

Venkatesh, R. and Mahajan, V. (2009) The design and pricing of bundles: a review of normative guidelines and practical approaches. In V.R. Rao (ed.), *Handbook of Pricing Research in Marketing*. Cheltenham: Edward Elgar, 232–257.

PART C
Liberalization and Airline Cooperation

An Assessment of the Success of Cross-border Airline Mergers and Acquisitions in Europe

Karsten Fröhlich, Wolfgang Grimme, Julia Hellmers, Martin Holtz, Adél Németh
and Hans-Martin Niemeier

1. Introduction

While the airline business is international, access to foreign markets is generally regulated by a restrictive framework that is more than 60 years old. In comparison to other sectors, even other services industries, foreign direct investment, be it either as the establishment of a new subsidiary or the acquisition of foreign companies, is in most cases subject to strict ownership caps and other regulations. Even where it is not explicitly prohibited, the takeover of a foreign airline is usually associated with a loss of international traffic rights within the current framework. The potential loss of traffic rights in case of mergers or acquisitions has led to the emergence of international airline alliances. International mergers and takeovers seldom occurred in the past. However, merger activity is growing with a number of examples in recent years, predominantly in Europe. This growth in mergers and takeovers is potentially triggered by a changing regulatory environment. As more and more horizontal aviation agreements between the EU and third countries come into effect, a common community of national airlines based in the EU is being accepted. In contrast, transactions in the past had relatively complicated holding structures with a division of economic voting rights and effective ownership and control had to be created, for instance in the case of the merger of Air France and KLM.

There is a broad literature on airline alliances and their ramifications, but rarely can a discussion be found on the advantages and disadvantages of mergers and acquisitions, in comparison to strategic alliances, as a business strategy for internationalization. This issue is of particular interest because alliances are sometimes seen as second-best solutions to circumvent restrictive bilateral agreements, which generally restrict cross-border mergers or acquisitions. Alliances therefore have been characterized as 'virtual mergers' (Li, 2000). In the light of developments that suggest further liberalization of ownership clauses in the future, an interesting question is will alliances develop further towards fully fledged mergers? Based on cross-border mergers that have occurred in the recent past, this chapter will try to answer the question, 'have these mergers have proved successful, as initially envisaged by the management?'. Success is here defined purely from the perspective of the firm. Any merger that has temporarily, and preferably permanently, increased the competitive position of the merged firms is seen as successful, although the success might stem from the abuse of market power with negative welfare effects. This success should also be valued by capital markets and should show up in event studies.

In Section 2 of the chapter, general theories explaining the internationalization of firms will be applied to the special case of airlines to answer the question, 'why are mergers the preferred management strategy?' In Section 3, a sample of cross-border airline mergers in Europe will be analysed in depth, and an attempt to assess their success is made in Section 4 with the event study method. Given the complexities and lack of data, only preliminary results can be derived. Finally, the main results of our analysis will be summarized in Section 5.

2. Theories on the Internationalization of the Firm and Applicability to the Airline Industry

When an airline chooses its internationalization strategy, either to engage in an alliance, or to merge with or acquire a foreign airline, owners or the management must evaluate the advantages and disadvantages of these two different business strategies. So the question is: which advantages/ disadvantages do mergers or acquisitions have in comparison to strategic alliances? What are the factors driving airline management's decisions on which strategy to choose? In the case where a merger or an acquisition is chosen, what competitive advantages can be exploited?

These questions have been discussed broadly in the literature with respect to multinational corporations (e.g. Aharoni, 1966; Dunning, 1981; Forsgren, 2008; Glaum, 1996, Morck and Yeung 1992). However, the discussion and literature on airlines, in light of the changing international environment of airline ownership clauses, has yet to be focused on. Existing literature explains the diverse forms of airline alliances (e.g. Doganis, 2006) and the competitive advantages that can be achieved within an airline alliance without a merger/acquisition (e.g. Hanlon, 2003). Competitive advantages can be classified into two categories, one efficiency-seeking, and the other market-oriented (Kleymann and Seristö, 2001). Among the efficiency-seeking advantages, one could mention joint use of resources, such as maintenance facilities, ground handling facilities and staff, or pooling for aircraft and fuel purchasing. Among the market-oriented advantages, one could mention code-sharing/blocked space agreements to extend the network, seamless connections for passengers, and the integration of frequent flyer programmes.

To date, airline-related literature seems to have neglected a discussion on the advantages that can be generated with a merger as compared to an alliance. The following discussion may help to shed some light on this question.

2.1 Resource-based/Efficiency-oriented Theories

Resource-based or efficiency-oriented theories can help to explain international mergers or acquisitions in the airline industry. This group of theories is based on the assumption that transnational firms are set up in order to exploit imperfections in markets involving inputs and outputs (Glaum, 1996). In the airline industry, such imperfections can be seen in the existence of market power, economies of scale, the scope and density of airline networks and the access to airport slots. These factors have been intensively studied in the literature on airline alliances. One important result is that economies of scale vanish at a rather early stage, and therefore cannot be used to explain mergers in the air transport industry (Caves et al. 1984, Laaser, 2001). More important are economies of scope and density. Gellman Research Associates emphasize 'carriers enter into transnational alliances to take advantage of economies of scope and density by increasing the size and reach of their networks' (1994: 7). This point is shared by numerous researchers (see for example Oum et al., 2000). There is no doubt that these types of network economies have been one of the major driving forces of alliances and mergers. Brueckner and Spiller (1991) differentiate between parallel and complementary integration. Parallel integration occurs if the networks of the partners strongly overlap, while complementary integration increases the size of the network. In the real world, alliances and mergers are a mixture of both the complementary and parallel types of network integration in markets with different degrees of competition and different potentials for economies of scale, scope and density. Most studies have found that alliances have positive effects on productivity, airfares and profits. Oum et al. (2000) found positive effects for what they call major alliances[1] like KLM/NWA and insignificant effects for minor alliances. Major alliances increase total factor productivity by 4.9 per cent, lower revenues (due to lower fares) per output by 1.5 per cent and increase profitability by 1.5 per cent.

While network economies can be exploited within existing alliances, direct access to an alliance partners' resources, such as slots at capacity-constrained airports, would only be possible with a takeover. This argument is strengthened by the fact that even under a regime that allows slot trading, slot pairs are rarely traded between competing carriers or alliances due to strategic considerations. The possession of slots is seen as a key business asset and even at airports that are not used as hubs, such as New York La Guardia, new entrants have had difficulties obtaining slots from incumbents (Ball et al., 2007). Therefore the acquisition of complete airlines, or major parts of their assets for the sake of gaining control over slots, could be observed in the past. One example is the divestiture of Pan Am after its bankruptcy in December 1991, when Delta Airlines bought a major part of Pan Am's transatlantic and domestic network in the north-east for US$416 million and the assumption of its liabilities (MacNeille, 1992) and United acquired Pan Am's Latin American network for US$160 million (Salpukas, 1991). The transactions included the transfer of route authorities, slots, staff and other assets.

The realization of economies of scale in marketing (Hanlon, 2003) is limited within an alliance, as the focus of the alliance partners is likely to be on the promotion of their own brands, instead of the alliance brand. However, it is still questionable, whether the creation of a single global airline brand is desirable, as airline passengers seem to have a preference for their national carrier(s), expressing the respective national identity. For instance, when British Airways introduced a multicultural branding strategy at the end of the 1990s, a strongly negative public opinion was provoked, finally resulting in the restoration of the 'British' image (Thurlow and Aiello, 2007). The national identity of a carrier can be interpreted as part of a unique selling position, which therefore is a valuable asset in the market. The creation of the pan-European brands Thomas Cook and – more recently – TUIfly have shown that it seems to be very difficult to exploit economies of scale in marketing due to the cultural diversity in Europe. In the former case, the experiment of renaming the traditional German brand Condor into Thomas Cook was reversed after less than two years. Although Thomas Cook is a brand with a tradition of more than 160 years in the UK, it was virtually unknown in Germany. A more positive example is the presence of the Virgin brand in different markets all over the globe, although the independent operation of Virgin-branded companies in totally different geographical markets (UK, Australia and USA) and with different business models (short-haul low-cost services in Australia and the USA, long-haul low-cost operations from Australia and a full-service long-haul operation based in the UK) seems to reduce the possibility of achieving economies of scale (Altman, 2009).

Besides greater airport access through slots, a further element of the resource-based theory is the access to cheaper labour with an international acquisition. With the foreign acquisition, it may be possible to offshore some of the acquiring airline's functions, such as data processing, weight and balance calculations or maintenance.

A famous branch of efficiency-oriented theories is the internalization theory. This approach follows Coase (1937), who extensively described the determinants of the boundaries of firms, using the transaction costs occurring for market transactions, and internalization or hybrid forms of interaction. Following this theory, a merger may lead to a reduction in transaction costs when compared to an alliance. It is also reasonable to assume that within an alliance, a certain level of rent seeking over the alliance partners occurs and that alliance partners have to bear transaction

---

1   The term major alliances does not refer to size but to the scope of cooperation (Oum et al., 2000).

costs, in the form of costs for monitoring and control, to avoid the possible opportunistic behaviour of their alliance partners. Anecdotal evidence from recent events may illustrate such intra-alliance rivalries: while both Singapore Airlines and Lufthansa are members of Star Alliance, the early morning departure of Singapore Airlines from Frankfurt to New York does not bear the Lufthansa code and is therefore not sold by Lufthansa. Moreover, starting with the winter schedule 2007, Lufthansa scheduled their own all-business-class service to New York, five minutes ahead of the departure of Singapore Airlines. Lufthansa's service was discontinued in 2008, but Lufthansa still does not cooperate with Singapore Airlines on this particular flight. Another example of intra-alliance competition was provided by Christian Hylander, the Germany-based Country Manager for Scandinavian Airlines (SAS), who characterized the relation to alliance partner Lufthansa as 'friendly competition' (Jegminat, 2007). Elements of this include the unilateral introduction of one-way fares (which in fact has the potential to erode yields for Lufthansa), the reintroduction of Scandinavian Airlines' group sales and travel agent support in Germany, and the termination of both the joint call centre use and the joint corporate volume discount programme (Jegminat, 2007).

These examples show that even within alliances, opportunistic behaviour cannot be avoided and that the behaviour of alliance partners is in many instances beyond the control of the other partners. In the presented instances, neither 'deterrence-based trust' nor 'familiarity' within the alliance seems to be working (Kleymann and Seristö, 2001). Kleymann and Seristö further sum up the problems and disadvantages associated with alliances, among them uncertainty, ambiguity and market dynamics that need to be adapted to, and may destabilize alliances in the long run. Here, one could argue that these elements are likely to have a discouraging effect on alliance-specific investments that are needed to increase the operational efficiency of the alliance, while on the other hand, Kleymann and Seristö argue that such specific investments provide for a commitment to the relationship, and thus an element of deterrence against opportunistic behaviour, stabilizing the relationship between the partners.

In the case where alliance partners were to be integrated into one firm under a single management, it can be expected that transaction costs could be reduced, for instance when frequency or destination decisions can be made unilaterally and not by bi- or multilateral negotiations.

Part of every successful strategy is to gain market power, and alliances might be a very effective instrument. Youssef and Hansen (1994: 416) point out that 'alliances may create virtual monopolies in markets between the hubs of alliance partners'. Competition authorities treat alliances and mergers similarly, but in some cases do not allow for price fixing among alliance partners. The advantage of a merger approved by the competition authorities is that it allows for practices which otherwise would not have been allowed by these authorities.

2.2 Management-oriented and Behavioural Theories

The behaviour and the objectives of a firm's management can help to explain international mergers and acquisitions. Based on the managerial theory of the firm and the principal agent theory, it is perceived that the primary objective of managers is not to increase shareholder value, but to pursue their own personal objectives, such as increasing their personal power or salary. An extensive analysis on this subject can be found in Glaum (1996). A promising strategy for managers to achieve these objectives can be the pursuit of mergers and acquisitions, resulting in 'empire-building'. As mergers and acquisitions seem to be more promising than alliances as a way to achieve the personal objectives of the management, managers may underestimate the risks associated with the integration of the acquired firms and they may overestimate the chances of success, as explained by Roll's 'hubris-theory' (1986). The failure of some transnational mergers in other industries (such as Daimler-Benz and Chrysler) may provide some anecdotal evidence for this theory, but the airline industry also provides some examples, where cross-border equity investments (although no completed mergers) have failed (e.g. Swissair's investments in Sabena, Air Outre Mer, Air Europe and South African Airways to name just a few).

A number of other theories explaining the internationalization of the firm can be found in the literature, among them the behavioural theory of internationalization (Aharoni, 1966). This theory describes the firm as a network of interacting stakeholder groups, which each influence the decision-making processes of the firm with their own objectives. Internationalization of the firm often occurs not along a strategic rationale, but instead is influenced by coincidental events, trends and fashions ('merger & acquisition waves') or the interests and opinions of the leaders within the firm (typically higher management, board members or consultants).

3. Major Cross-border Airline Mergers and Acquisitions

In this section, the mergers of Air France (AF) with Royal Dutch Airlines (KLM), Lufthansa with Austrian, British Midland International (BMI), Brussels Airlines and Swiss, and British Airways (BA) with Iberia are presented. Followed by a short overview of the merger itself, each subsection will look at the benefits that were claimed when the merger was explained to shareholders, and how the managers justified the proposal.

Figure 11.1 provides a geographical overview of airline mergers in Europe since 2004. There were other cases (like SAS/Spanair in 2002, KLM/Martinair in 2008, Iberia/Vueling/Clickair in 2009 or AF/KLM/Alitalia in 2010 (Beria et al., 2011) in the recent past, but at least the first two were mergers on a much smaller scale. Therefore we will not be concerned with them in this chapter.

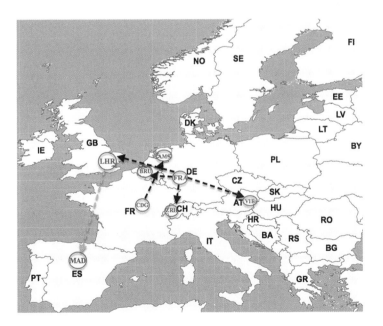

Figure 11.1   Hub connections after the major mergers in Europe

Source: Own figure.

3.1 Air France/KLM

In 2003 the two airlines, Air France and the Dutch KLM, merged and became one group or holding with two separate operating companies and three main business arms (passenger, cargo and maintenance). The merger was completed through a swap of shares and the establishment of a common holding company. A rather complex procedure was needed for this merger so that no air traffic rights were lost.[2] The holding's management is coordinated by the strategic management committee (SMC), which represents Air France and KLM members equally. Both companies remain independent and are largely self-responsible for their commercial and operational management. The SMC is responsible for the group's overall strategy. It coordinates the network and the hub strategy, and is responsible for the overall budget and mid-term planning. The SMC also oversees the fleet and the investment strategy as well as the alliance strategy.

To make the merger possible, several conditions had to be met: first, the Dutch government made it compulsory that the merged company had to pursue a two-hub strategy which meant that Schiphol Amsterdam Airport had to be maintained as a hub for the new airline group and a minimum number of direct international connections had to be maintained. It was also obligatory that both Air France and KLM brands and identities had to be kept as they were before the merger. Finally, it was enforced that existing labour and wage schemes could not be changed, and a labour guarantee was set in place for the next five years. Thus, the merged companies largely cooperated via code-share agreements, harmonization of flight plans and optimization of revenue management (Iatrou and Oretti, 2007). Thus, the realized benefits of the AF/KLM merger reached the same level as a merger with a true integration of resources. There is reason to speculate (see Iatrou and Oretti, 2007) that the merger was only put forward by Air France so as to secure KLM as an alliance partner, because British Airways made several efforts to buy KLM in an attempt to secure attractive slots at the Amsterdam airport. Suspicion arises that Air France wanted to eliminate the risk of losing an important alliance partner. Another factor might be to gain or secure market power on the North Atlantic market. According to Brueckner and Pels (2005) the merger between Air France and KLM posed a threat to economic welfare. The integration of KLM and its alliance partner Northwest Airlines into the SkyTeam alliance introduced a dominant position for SkyTeam in the North Atlantic market. The merger was nonetheless permitted by European Competition authorities, subject to the restriction that Air France and KLM had to surrender 94 slots at Amsterdam Schiphol and Paris Charles de Gaulle.

The management of Air France tried to justify the merger and its particularities. The labour agreement for example was explained to be strategic, because the merged company wanted to be active in a larger market (all of Europe) rather than the two separate companies operating jointly (own national markets). Since the company's strategy relied on growing market share and revenues, cost-cutting and downsizing was less of an issue. Suspicion remains as to whether this was actually an intentional strategic move or whether rigid labour rules were enforced by strong union intervention. Furthermore, it was claimed that the merged company would have higher bargaining power for negotiations with airframe manufactures. However, Air France's fleet consists mainly of Airbus aircraft, while KLM's fleet has predominantly Boeing aircraft. Thus, unless the strategy was to swap either Air France's or KLM's fleet completely, the proposed bargaining power was non-existent, since bargaining power increases largely if a greater number of aircraft is ordered. Another source of synergies that was claimed to be feasible was the alignment of IT systems.

---

2   A special holding structure was needed up until 2007, where the Dutch government held parts of the voting rights and a special option. After 2007, the holding's structure was converted into a more simplified structure.

However, such synergies always go hand in hand with substantial investment requirements and only materialize after a long period of time. Theoretically synergies from a common IT system should only start materializing about ten years after the merger. Other than that, the management of Air France-KLM claimed that synergies could be realized through combined fares, a common frequent flier programme and integrated flight plans. It should be noted however that all these latter synergies could also have been realized through an alliance. The merger was, in fact, less of a merger, but rather a case of deeper integration. To this day, both carriers operate largely independently of each other. Both AF and KLM have individual brands, operate two hubs and they cooperate to a degree that occurs in some alliances as well. All in all, the merger seems to be an example where one alliance partner wants to secure another alliance partner by merging with it. The actions that were put forward through the merger could, to a large degree, have been realized by an alliance.

3.2 Lufthansa's European Mergers

Over the past few years, Lufthansa (LH) has acquired a number of European airlines such as SWISS, BMI, Austrian and Brussels. They all have in common that they have faced severe financial problems. In the following subsections we present the cases in chronological order.

3.2.1 Lufthansa/SWISS   Lufthansa bought 85 per cent shares in the airline in 2005. SWISS began operations on 31 March 2002 as a follow-up of the former Swissair. Its hub airport in Zurich is a slot-coordinated airport with high barriers to entry for new airlines. The proposed synergies of the merger with Lufthansa were high because SWISS had already signed code-share agreements with the rival oneworld alliance members, American Airlines and Finnair. Lufthansa and SWISS benefited from the new code-share agreement, which affected 563 weekly services between Germany and Switzerland. The merger was supposed to add value for the consumers in the form of more frequent flights, more destinations, better timetables, and more efficient connections at the hubs Frankfurt, Munich and Zurich.

Since 1 July 2007 SWISS has been fully integrated into the Lufthansa Group. The merger was not only driven by synergies but also formed to achieve other objectives. The latter becomes obvious from the following statement of Christoph Franz, at that time President and CEO of SWISS: 'The Integration Agreement ensures fair development of the Zurich hub, the size of our long-haul fleet, the quality brand SWISS, and the continued existence of SWISS as an operating airline based in Switzerland' (SWISS, 2005). This is evidence of the limited synergy effects, because if the airlines have to keep their hubs there is only limited network optimization possible. Despite the limited potential, the airlines claimed to be able to create €470 million in synergies in three years, €465 million of which they could successfully achieve (see Table 11.1). SWISS is still profitable; in 2010 Lufthansa forecast an additional €230 million in efficiency gains for the year 2011.[3]

The LH/SWISS merger had one specific reason for its creation: SWISS entered its second bankruptcy after restructuring efforts failed. Lufthansa took advantage of the opportunity to expand traffic flows and hub structure. Pursuant to Morgan Stanley Research (2010a) €233 million in synergies had already been reached by the second year of the merger. Thus SWISS had been successfully restructured, and the airline outperformed the average peer EBIT margin (Morgan Stanley Research, 2010b). SWISS had an operating result of €93 million in 2009.

---

3   As it is in the interest of management to demonstrate that the merger was a success, one should take these figures as the upper bound of what has been realized.

Table 11.1   Synergies generated by the LH/SWISS merger (in € million)

Year	Forecast by LH in 2005		Forecast by LH in 2006		Realized according to annual report/press release
Source	Revenue	Costs	Revenue	Costs	
2005	15	15	14	18	32
2006	32	40	77	73	200
2007	86	70	80	94	233

Source: Deutsche Lufthansa AG (2005, 2010), SWISS (2005, 2007).

3.2.2 Lufthansa/BMI   After BMI chairman Sir Michael Bishop exercised his option to sell his shares to Lufthansa in October 2008, Lufthansa bought 50 per cent plus one share in the loss-making British airline. Lufthansa did not want to pay the high price (£298 million) agreed to in a contract in 1999, but Bishop resorted to the High Court and Lufthansa agreed in an out-of-court settlement to pay Sir Michael £175 million to give up his option and pay £48 million for the BMI shares.[4] Stephan Gemkow, Lufthansa chief financial officer, commented on the purchase: 'There are options that put us in the position to acquire the majority of BMI over a foreseeable timeframe. We are determined to exercise these options. Beyond that there is no need to hold talks' (Osborne, 2008). The quote shows that the airline did not expect substantial synergies, because it was a 'must-takeover'.

At the same time, Lufthansa also made an agreement with SAS to buy its remaining 20 per cent share in BMI (Done and Wiesmann, 2009). Thus Lufthansa took full ownership of BMI and obtained 11 per cent of all of the slots at London Heathrow, becoming the second-largest airline at the airport and improving its position in this capacity-constrained market. The takeover has strengthened BMI's position in the Middle East as well (Prock-Schauer, 2010). Even so, the European Commission had no objections concerning the possible anti-competitive effects of the merger (EU COM, 2009a). Lufthansa's former CEO Mayrhuber (2009) argues that due to the multiple hub strategy, passengers would have higher network quality, more choices and increased flexibility

The track record of BMI since the takeover is still bleak: operating profits (EBIT) since 2007 have been negative, and BMI still reported high net losses of €78 million in 2009. However, the airline shows a slow recovery, especially after selling Heathrow slots for £100 million and thus reducing the total number of slots from 87 to 66 (Morgan Stanley Research, 2010b). More cost synergies can be achieved by reducing BMI's fleet by 10 aircraft in the following years. Loss-making routes were immediately cancelled after the merger with Lufthansa, thus capacity was cut by 20 per cent in 2009. All in all, the synergy potentials are €20 million yearly (Morgan Stanley Research, 2010b). The next step is to restructure the network and focus on niche markets.

3.2.3 Lufthansa/SN Brussels Airlines   Only a few weeks after the BMI deal, Lufthansa purchased a 45 per cent share in SN Brussels Airlines.[5] At that time, SN Brussels Airlines did not belong to any major airline alliance. Viscount Etienne Davignon, Chairman of the Board at Brussels Airlines, proposed that 'a joint future with Lufthansa provides us with the best chance of operating

---

4   Compared to this, in 1999 Lufthansa paid £91.4 million for a 20 per cent share package in BMI.

5   SN Brussels Airlines was the former Sabena, which went bankrupt in 2001.

successfully against the competition. Lufthansa's multi-hub and multi-brand strategies constitute the best prerequisites for stability and future growth' (Brussels Airlines, 2008). Post-merger activities included code-sharing, a common frequent flyer programme (FFP) and the introduction of business class at (renamed) Brussels Airlines on all European routes. The network of Brussels Airlines was to be expanded by 18 new destinations in Africa (Mayrhuber, 2009). Morgan Stanley estimates potential yearly synergies of €60 million at Brussels Airlines, compared to a €12.2 million loss in 2008. Nevertheless, Lufthansa announced the sale of BMI in September 2011. The main reason was that BMI's losses since the takeover, only in 2010 and the first half of 2011, achieved £233 million (€268 million). BMI's operating margin dropped back to –26 per cent in the first half of 2011. After all, without BMI, Lufthansa's share of aircraft movements at Heathrow would fall by 8 per cent down to 5.5 per cent (anna.aero, 2011).

The EU COM concluded that 'it is not likely that the merger would benefit consumers on the affected routes to such an extent that they could counter-balance the competitive harm' (EU COM, 2009b: 112). Despite this the EU COM approved the full takeover by the end of 2011. In order to mitigate anti-competitive effects and enable entry, the merging airlines were forced to make slots available on four routes from Brussels, specifically those from Brussels to Munich, Hamburg, Frankfurt, and Zurich.

3.2.4 Lufthansa/Austrian In August 2009 Lufthansa took over the loss-making alliance partner, Austrian Airlines. The parties argued that the merger would lead to cost efficiencies and benefits to the consumers, up to €80 million a year, though at the end of 2008 Lufthansa CEO Wolfgang Mayerhuber reported only €70 million for that year (Die Presse, 2008). Almost 40 per cent of the synergies are from revenue gains, another 40 per cent stem from operating cost savings and the remaining 20 per cent from other cost savings, for example common sales offices with Lufthansa (Deutsche Lufthansa AG, 2010). According to Lufthansa the efficiencies will stem from network effects, namely from the extension of hub connections, feeder and transit services, resulting in more destinations, higher traffic and better capacity utilization. During the investigation process, Lufthansa and Austrian ensured the EU COM that ticket prices would decline due to network effects (EU COM, 2009c). However, according to the EU Commission, Lufthansa has not put forward any evidence in support of such efficiencies (EU COM, 2009c). The airlines had many overlapping routes with a very high joint market share from Vienna to Stuttgart, Cologne/Bonn, Frankfurt, Munich, and Brussels and had to give up slots at Vienna airport. However, in the last two years only one competitor, Air Berlin, has entered the Vienna–Cologne/Bonn route, but withdrew in 2011.

The total costs of the acquisitions of Austrian were €500 million. In 2009 Lufthansa paid €366,269 million for Austrian Airline's shares and up to the financial improvements of both airlines Lufthansa will pay a debtor warrant of maximum €162 million until the end of 2012. Austrian still suffered losses in 2010, however, on the other side €100 million in synergies have been identified due to integrations in cargo and sales (Morgan Stanley, 2010a).

In the (2010) annual report, Lufthansa announced the following forecasted synergies: €230 million from SWISS, €130 million from Austrian Airlines, €60 million from Brussels and €30 million from BMI. However, these are the forecast synergies in 2010, without any timeframe. The synergies are mainly related to the common route network, but they are also derived from IT services, catering, and maintenance, repair and overhaul (MRO).

Table 11.2   Forecast and realized synergies in the LH cases (in € million)

Airline	SWISS (2004/2005)	BMI (2008/2009)	Brussels (2008/2009)	Austrian (2008/2009)
Forecast by LH (EU COM decisions)	470 In three years	127 Annual	'Mid-double-digit annually within three years'	80 Long-term annual
Forecast by LH in 2010 (annual report)	230	30	60	130
Realized synergies in the first year (Morgan Stanley)	233 By the second year	20	60	100
Claimed reason for synergy	Restructuring	Route optimization by 20% Capacity cut	Bilateral cooperation	Integrations in cargo and sales
Loss of the airline in the year of merger	n.a.	78	12.2	31

Source: EU COM, Annual Reports and Morgan Stanley.

Concerning the market power of the airlines, the Lufthansa mergers affected 25 overlapping city pairs, where the merger could have led to a monopoly situation. In 2011, Lufthansa has a monopoly on 13 of these routes, while a new competitor has entered on seven of the routes. It thus seems to be the case that Lufthansa has gained market power on some routes due to takeovers and acquisitions, which might have been a reason behind the mergers. If and to what extent Lufthansa can abuse this market power remains open.

3.3 British Airways/Iberia

British Airways is a leading partner in the oneworld alliance. This alliance was launched in 1999 and Iberia was a founding member along with American Airlines, Finnair, Qantas, Canadian Airlines and Cathay Pacific. BA is the British flag carrier and had revenues of almost £8 billion in 2010 and an EBIT of £231 million. The BA hubs are the two London Airports, Gatwick and Heathrow.

Iberia's revenues amounted to €4.7 billion with an EBIT of €162 million in 2010. The company operates two hubs, one in Madrid and one in Barcelona. Iberia gathered experience in cross-border mergers during its 1990 takeover of 85 per cent of Aerolinas Argentinas. The activities of Iberia in South America[6] ended in disaster, caused by management problems, rising costs and the general economic situation in South America (Iatrou and Oretti, 2007: 33). This resulted in a buy-out of Iberia shares by three Spanish businessmen. Despite these failures, 30 per cent of Iberia's operations are still to South America. This is largely due to Spanish cultural heritage in South America. Iatrou and Oretti (2007) conclude that Iberia's strong presence in this market is its strength for any upcoming merger.

---

6   Iberia held also a 45 per cent share in VIASA (Venezuela) and a 37 per cent share in LADECO (Chile). Both companies failed.

The merger between Iberia and BA is the final episode of an intensifying cooperation which started as an alliance in 1999. While speculation on a full merger has endured since then, the merger was repeatedly postponed, due to financial turmoil in the industry and the discussions of alternative alliance or merger partners. The success of Air France/KLM and Lufthansa eventually put pressure on Iberia to seek a major partner and on BA to expand into Europe. The BA–Iberia merger was announced in April 2010, approved in July by the European Commission and confirmed in October 2010 by stock owners.[7] Iberia and BA consolidated into a merged entity on 21 January 2011.

The BA–Iberia merger is a complementary network expansion. There is overlap only on a single route (Madrid to London Heathrow) and strong complementarities on the intercontinental route network, as Iberia is relatively strong in traffic between Europe and Latin America, while BA has an extensive network between Europe and North America and Asia (see Figure 11.2).

The European Commission (2010: 8f.) approved the merger without any remedies. Monopolistic tendencies were not seen and no slots had to be abandoned. As the major hubs of BA are in London, there is a lot of competition from the low-cost carriers Ryanair and easyJet within Europe. easyJet offers several connections every day from London Gatwick to Madrid and Barcelona. Ryanair also has many connections from Stansted, Luton and Gatwick to the two major cities in Spain.

The merged BA–Iberia company is called International Airline Group with its operational headquarters at Heathrow. It is too early to assess the success of the merger, as this will depend largely on how well the management will be able to transform the long-haul network of Iberia to British Airways' customers, and vice versa. At the same time there is a €400 million cost saving and revenue increasing target set for 2015, a similar amount as seen in the AF/KLM merger. This target should be reached within the first five years of the collaboration. Figure 11.3 outlines the major tasks for this five-year period.

- - - - - Routes operated by British Airways
———— Routes operated by Iberia

Figure 11.2   Route networks of British Airways and Iberia in July 2010

Source: Own representation based on OAG.

---

7   At the beginning of October 2010, BA's market capitalization was €3,267 million compared to Iberia's €2,707 million. Due to a one to one exchange of shares, the former BA-stock owner will receive a 54 per cent stake in the new enterprise.

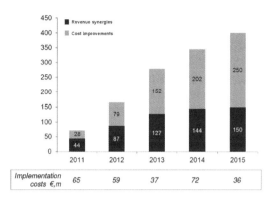

Figure 11.3   **Estimated synergies of the British Airways–Iberia merger**

3.4. Comparison of the Mergers

First, a summary of the nature of synergies (Table 11.3) is provided, followed by an overview of unit cost developments for Air France, British Airways, Lufthansa, Iberia, SWISS and Austrian Airlines.

Despite the fact that SWISS airlines had negative operating results and a very high debt at the time of the takeover, Lufthansa succeeded in reshaping the business concept and implementing a common strategy after the merger. Compared to the forecasted synergies at the time of the LH–SWISS merger, SWISS seems to have performed well, but the beneficial effects from the LH BMI takeover were greatly overestimated. One reason behind the limited synergies might be the forced takeover of the British airline after the put option of Sir Michael Bishop was exercised.

Austrian Airlines is in the process of dramatically restructuring after facing high operating losses. In the first half of 2011 Austrian operated with 18 aircraft less than in 2008. Moreover, Lufthansa announced that it would cut the number of employees by 6000 in the next few years, translating into a 75 per cent decrease in employees at Austrian Airlines. As a comparison, it might be interesting to recall the words of the Management Board of Austrian before the takeover:

> For a stand-alone solution more than 1,000 jobs would have to be reduced and more than 15 aircrafts would have to be sold. The Offer Price of € 4.49 per Share significantly exceeds the equity value per Share of Austrian Airlines on 31.12.2008 … The Management Board of Austrian Airlines therefore recommends that the shareholders accept the Offer. (Austrian Airlines, 2009)

The merger between Iberia and British Airways differs from the other mergers in that there is an attempt to build a new branded corporation, where none of the two brands is mentioned. Furthermore, the two networks seem to be more complementary than the networks of KLM and Air France and Lufthansa and Swiss, because Iberia focuses on South America and BA on North America.

The reason for the AF–KLM merger seems to result from the attempt to secure a valuable alliance member against a takeover by a rival alliance, rather than the realization of synergies. Furthermore, these synergies could have also been realized through an alliance because AF and KLM did not combine their business structures, but kept them separate despite the full merger, meaning that the realization of cost synergies was limited.

Turning to unit costs, Figure 11.4 indicates that Air France could not generate significant cost savings after the merger with KLM compared to other major carriers. Austrian Airlines (OS) costs showed the sharpest increase among the sample. The unit costs of SWISS have increased the least of all of the carriers in the sample, which could indicate the synergies realized from the merger with Lufthansa.

Table 11.3   Overview on synergies

	AF/ KLM	LH/ SWISS	LH/BMI	LH/ Brussels	LH/ Austrian	BA/ Iberia
Improving technical efficiency	–	XX	XX	XX	X X	
Cost reduction by complimentary network	X	–	–	–	–	XX
Reducing transaction costs to consumers (i. e. joint branding, coordinate schedule)	X	–	X	–	–	XX
Overcoming regulatory restrictions	–	X	x	X	X	–
Getting access to resources	–	X	XX	–	X	–
Lessening of competitive pressure	X	X	X	X	X	–

XX, strong; X, weak; – hardly relevant.

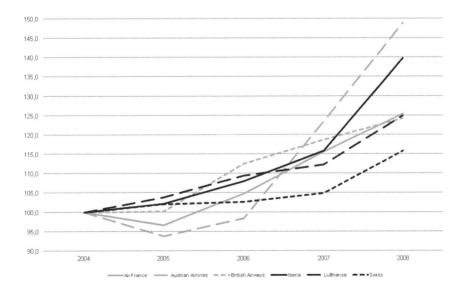

Figure 11.4   Unit costs of major airlines between 2004 and 2008

4. An Assessment of the Success of Cross-border Airline Mergers and Acquisitions

Kay (1993) differentiates between four methods to evaluate the performance of mergers. The subjective method, based on the personal opinions of managers, is the simplest one, but also the most biased. A second method is the long-term method. In the long-term method, analysing whether the acquired company is retained in the long term is not feasible in our context as the mergers are still progressing. A third method is to compare overall profitability before and after the merger, which faces a similar problem with mergers that are still ongoing. Furthermore, the industry has been subject to exogenous shocks several times, complicating the profitability comparison method. This leaves us with the fourth method, the effects on stock market valuation. However, using this fourth method also presents some severe methodological problems. We decided to use the stock market valuation method with care and add a qualitative analysis illustrating how investment bankers evaluated the mergers in their reports.

4.1 Short- and Long-term Performance on Capital Markets

Capital markets can be considered as a rather good indicator for either the generation or destruction of shareholder value followed by merger announcements. Based on the assumption of efficient capital markets, new information related to any publicly listed company will be reflected, in a short time frame, in company share prices (Fama, 1969). In the case where a merger or acquisition announcement is perceived by the capital markets to create value, positive abnormal returns following the announcement should be observed. In the case where the capital markets react negatively to merger/acquisition announcements, negative abnormal returns would be the consequence.

   In order to assess the initial reaction of capital markets on merger announcements, event studies are considered an established methodology. Usually, a sample of companies is created, which have all communicated the same type of event to the capital markets (e.g. merger or acquisition plan) and then the average abnormal return, in reaction to this event, is tested for statistical significance. Unfortunately, in the airline industry, only a very limited number of large-scale merger/acquisition events can be observed. Therefore, the sample for a convincing cross-sectional event study analysis is too small. Nevertheless, it is possible to gain some anecdotal evidence by an analysis of share price development in reaction to new information on airline mergers. The methodology described in the following paragraphs is based on Brealey and Myers (2000) and Goerke (2008).

   In the following, the share price reaction to merger/acquisition activities for British Airways, Iberia, Lufthansa and Air France will be analysed. The analysis follows a three-step approach:

1. Modelling the expected daily returns for each share based on market returns
2. Calculation of the abnormal returns as a consequence of merger/acquisition announcements
3. Calculation of cumulative abnormal returns.

The expected returns on the shares are modelled using a linear regression estimating α and β parameters, which determine the relationship between the market return and the return of each share:

$$R_{it} = \alpha_i + \beta_i R_{mt} + \varepsilon$$

Where R_{it} denotes the daily return of share i and R_{mt} the daily market return. In our model, we use the main national indices as a benchmark for the estimation of the parameters α_i and β_i, which are the

FTSE100 in the case of British Airways, the IBEX35 in the case of Iberia, the DAX30 in the case of Lufthansa and the CAC40 in the case of Air France. The national leading stock market indices were chosen for comparison, as the only 'global' airline index, NYSE Airline Index, includes, apart from Ryanair, only North and South American airlines. Moreover, relatively narrow industry indices are problematic in the calculation of abnormal returns, as the event itself influences the valuation of the index (Goerke, 2008).

The estimation window for the calculation of the parameters is chosen as the time frame from 20 trading days before the event to 220 trading days before the event.[8] R_{it} and R_{mt} are calculated based on adjusted daily closing prices obtained from Yahoo Finance.

The expected daily return of share $_i$ is then modelled as

$$E(R_{it}) = \alpha_i + \beta_i R_{mt}$$

The abnormal return AR_{it} is then calculated using the formula

$$AR_{it} = R_{it} - E(R_{it})$$

The event window considered here was defined as $t - 3$ to $t + 3$, therefore covering the three days before and three days after the announcement. In Table 11.4, the cumulative abnormal returns, starting from $t - 3$ are shown. The cumulative abnormal returns (CAR) are calculated as

$$CAR_{i[t-3,y]} = \sum_{t=t-3}^{y} AR_{it} \ with \ y = [-3, -2, -1, 0, 1, 2, 3]$$

The seven[9] investigated events are shown in Table 11.4.

The merger of British Airways and Iberia was seen as strongly positive, as a positive cumulative abnormal return can be observed by the financial markets after the merger announcement. In fact, the day before the announcement, a significant positive reaction can be observed, which leaves scope for speculation that information on the merger leaked before the official announcement. Overall, as the following figure shows, the positive effects for Iberia were estimated to be stronger than for British Airways. The positive CAR for BA, in the order of +8 per cent, remained stable at least until three days after the announcement.

In the case of Lufthansa, none of the acquisition activities (Swiss, JetBlue, SN Brussels) were regarded by the capital markets as significantly positive or negative. In the case of the LH acquisition of a stake in SN Brussels, the slightly positive $CAR_{-3;+1}$ and $CAR_{-3;+2}$ in the order of +3 per cent vanished completely on the third day after the announcement ($CAR_{-3;+3}$).

The strongest reaction can be observed following the announcement that Sir Michael Bishop, then owner of BMI, had exercised his put option, forcing Lufthansa to take a majority stake in the carrier. This extremely negative reaction is puzzling, as through 'forced' acquisition of BMI, which is the second-largest carrier at London Heathrow, Lufthansa had the prospect of gaining a large number of valuable slots. However, the financial markets apparently assumed that the turnaround process of the loss-making carrier would be difficult and costly.

---

8   Except Air France, where share price information was only available from 1 January 2003, resulting in the calculation of the parameters based on t-5 and t-189.

9   We have added the 19 per cent acquisition of Jet Star by Lufthansa.

Table 11.4   Merger/acquisition events and cumulative abnormal returns for British Airways, Iberia, Lufthansa and Air France

			Cumulative abnormal return, days before/after event						
Airline	Date	Event	−3	−2	−1	0	1	2	3
British Airways	30.07.2008	Announcement of merger with Iberia	2.4%	−1.4%	4.6%	8.0%	5.4%	8.6%	8.1%
Iberia	30.07.2008	Announcement of merger with British Airways	1.8%	0.9%	19.4%	26.7%	20.0%	22.8%	18.6%
Lufthansa	22.03.2005	Lufthansa announces Swiss acquisition	−1.1%	−1.5%	−1.1%	−1.2%	−1.6%	−0.3%	−1.0%
Lufthansa	13.12.2007	Lufthansa announces takeover 19% of JetBlue	1.0%	0.6%	1.1%	0.8%	0.4%	0.1%	1.4%
Lufthansa	28.10.2008	Lufthansa announces that Sir Michael Bishop had exercised BMI put option	−2.4%	−2.5%	−10.3%	−31.8%	−25.1%	−19.7%	−20.5%
Lufthansa	15.09.2008	Lufthansa announces to take 45% stake in SN Brussels	0.0%	−0.7%	−1.0%	0.6%	3.4%	3.7%	0.4%
Air France	30.09.2003	Announcement of merger with KLM	−0.6%	−5.1%	−3.0%	−5.3%	−11.9%	−7.6%	−13.3%

Source: Own calculation, based on Yahoo Finance data.

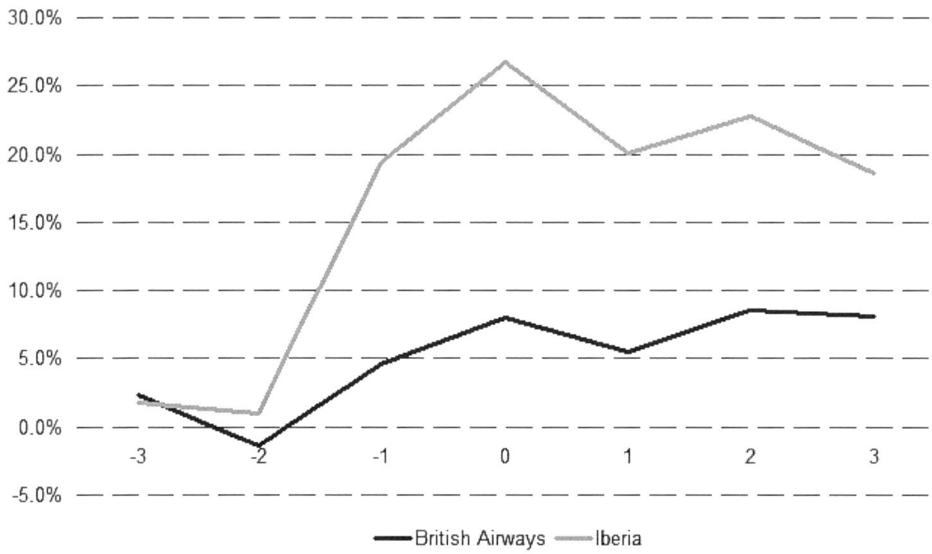

Figure 11.5   Cumulative abnormal returns for British Airways and Iberia around the merger announcement on 30 July 2008

Source: Own calculation, based on Yahoo Finance data.

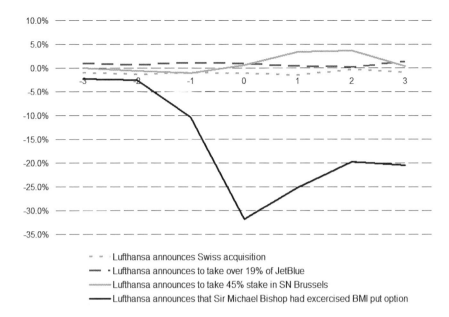

Figure 11.6   Cumulative abnormal returns for Lufthansa around the announcement dates of acquisitions

Source: Own calculation, based on Yahoo Finance data.

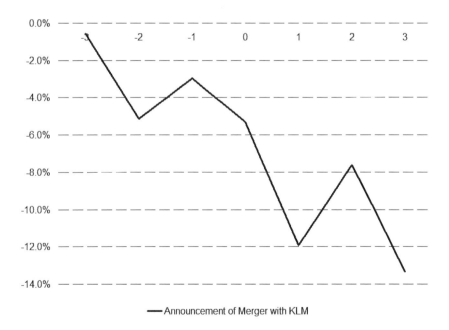

Figure 11.7   Cumulative abnormal return for Air France around the announcement date of the merger with KLM

In the case of Air France, a negative reaction on capital markets can be observed, with a $CAR_{-3;+3}$ of −13.3 per cent.

In summary, the results of the analysis of the short-term market reactions to merger announcements are inconclusive. In the case of BA–IB, a positive response on capital markets can be observed. In the case of Lufthansa, with its strategy to acquire smaller network carriers, the markets reacted neither positively or negatively, with the exception of the 'forced' takeover of BMI, which was considered to be highly negative. In the case of Air France–KLM, a negative response for Air France followed the merger announcement.

After this view on the short-term method perspective, Figure 11.8 shows the long-term performance of British Airways, Iberia, Lufthansa and Air France from 2003 to 2010.

Over the 2003 to 2010 time period, a very high correlation of share price development can be observed for each carrier. None of the four carriers outperformed each other over this time period. Although the short-term reaction of Air France's share price, after the announcement of the merger with KLM, was negative (previously mentioned), the airline was outperforming the other carriers until mid-2007. Nevertheless, in the time frame 2007 to 2010, Air France was the worst performer with a price only 37 per cent higher in mid 2010 than in January 2003. Apparently, the promised synergies from the merger could not be converted into shareholder value when compared to the other carriers.

4.2 Evaluation by Analysts and Investment Banks

According to the reports by Morgan Stanley (2010a, 2010b), airlines do have strong financial incentives to merge, but airlines have generally underestimated the complexity and effort to integrate IT systems.

For Lufthansa, Morgan Stanley (2010a) forecast an overall €1 billion cost savings and synergies, in part due to the mergers and better leverage on cargo for 2011 and 2012. Figure 11.9 shows the

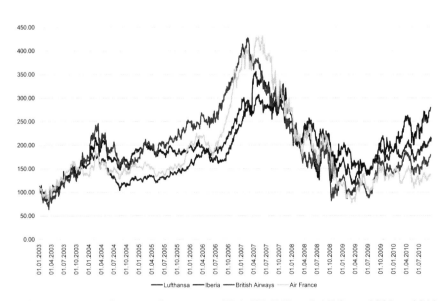

Figure 11.8   Long-term share performance of BA, IB, LH and AF from 2003 to 2010

Source: Own calculation, based on Yahoo Finance data.

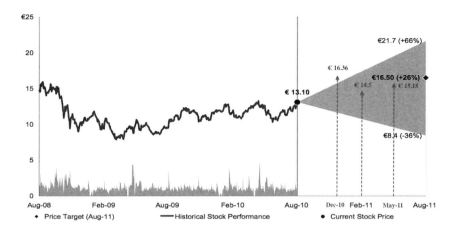

Figure 11.9   Impacts of synergies from acquisitions on share price data

Source: Morgan Stanley (2010b, p.2), dotted lines: Lufthansa company website.

forecast share prices by Morgan Stanley and the real prices (dotted lines) according to Lufthansa's webpage. As displayed in the figure, the actual price development was broadly in line with Morgan Stanley's fair value range, indicating that capital markets agree with Morgan Stanley's assessment of synergy potentials.

Analysts viewed the merger between Air France and KLM as positive for KLM, but negative for Air France. Analysts believed that Air France was paying too high a price, considering the low level of synergies. According to the firms' management, synergy effects of €385 to 495 million per year were realizable, allegedly starting from 2008 (Flottau and Fischer, 2003). Morgan Stanley was also very critical concerning the merger. In 2003 an equity research report stated that the merger was very risky and would not resolve the basic industry problem of excessive cost structure and excess capacity (Morgan Stanley, 2003). The report went on to say that the expected synergies were too low and subject to execution risk.

About a year after the AF–KLM merger, the carrier announced even higher synergies than expected and claimed synergies of €600 million per year until (sic) 2008 (Flottau, 2004). In the coming years pessimists were proved wrong by Air France KLM and the company achieved higher than expected profits. However, only about €300 million in synergies were realized in 2005 (Fischer and Genger, 2005). In 2006 Morgan Stanley issued equity research reports indicating that synergies from the merger were on track and that the management had the potential to extract more synergies than originally expected (Morgan Stanley, 2006).

Another view on the merger by analysts was that the achieved synergies needed to be contrasted with the high cost base of both companies and that most achievements were due to KLM's efforts to cut costs. The company had the lowest operating margin, high debts and an aggressive investment programme. Thus, prospects were regarded as unclear (FAZ, 2005).

5. Conclusion

The application of internationalization theories and the firm is helpful in explaining internationalization strategies for airlines. While alliances provide several distinctive advantages in accessing international markets, some of the disadvantages of alliances can only be overcome by mergers or acquisitions. With mergers or acquisitions it is possible to avoid the instability inherent to alliances. Furthermore, potential efficiency losses due to intra-alliance competition can be avoided. However, to transform the apparently more stringent structure of having several airlines in a single holding company, with one management, into a structure with cost advantages seems to be rather difficult. In the cases studied, airlines have great difficulty in reaping these potential synergies (see Table 11.5) and in turning them into a better competitive position. This is in particular true of the Air France and KLM merger. Due to complicated traffic rights as well as national and international laws, a rather complex holding structure was necessary to accomplish this merger. The governments of France and the Netherlands, as well as the labour unions, enforced strong restrictions on the management of AF–KLM. Our analysis of the financial markets shows that the merger had no positive effect. This is a plausible, but due to data problems, not a fully conclusive result. However, investment reports are also critical on the value of this merger, and in the long term performance comparison, this merged company was the worst underperformer.

Lufthansa performed better than AF–KLM with their strategy to buy loss-making, small- to medium-sized former national carriers, but overall the markets were neutral to the mergers with the exception of BMI. Lufthansa was able to buy valuable slots at Heathrow airport, but did not benefit from network economies and was forced into a costly restructuring process, which ended in the sale of BMI to IAG. Although the management claims synergies, the restructuring of Brussels and Austrian does not add value to the company. This seems to be different with SWISS where synergies were reaped through centralizing functions, staff reduction and joint frequent flyer programmes. Lufthansa gained an important brand name in one of the richest regions of Europe. Lufthansa, in addition, gained market power in particular on high-density routes between its hubs.

The financial markets also valued the merger of BA and Iberia. This merger differs to some degree because BA and Iberia have worked together for a long time in an alliance, and the networks are largely complementary. The expectations are that the merged airline will be able to reap these synergies. However, this remains to be seen as the integration process is in its infancy.

What emerges from this analysis is the picture that European airline mergers have difficulties reaping the synergies and reducing costs, but have gained market power. Overall, this does not change the competitive position of the airlines much, so that the financial markets are in general neutral to this strategy. Further research should focus in particular on the institutional obstacles that

Table 11.5   Characteristics of synergies in the presented airline merger cases

Case	Network	Other synergies	Markets/scarce resources
AF/KLM	AF: southern Europe KLM: northern Europe + UK	Joint purchasing, IT synergies, Joint FFP	None
LH/Swiss	Parallel		Brand name, Swiss market
LH/SN	SN: Africa, complementary	Centralizing functions, staff reduction, joint FFP	African market
LH/AUA	AUA: Eastern Europe, complementary		East European market
LH/BMI	None	BMI as platform for decentral LH routes	LHR slots
BA/IB	BA: North Atlantic IB: South America, complementary	IT synergies	South America

reduce synergies which could be passed on to the passenger, if they had not prevented by market power. Of course, the latter also demands detailed analysis at the route and network level.

References

Aharoni, Y. (1966) *The Foreign Investment Decision Process*. Cambridge, MA: Harvard University Press.

Altman, W. (2009) Branson – the global brand builder. *Engineering & Technology*, 31 January–13 February, 80–81.

anna.aero (2011) http://www.anna.aero/2011/09/08/lufthansa-reconsidering-bmis-future-after-latest-financial-results/, accessed 8 September 2011.

Austrian Airlines (2009) *Statement of the Management Board of Austrian Airlines of the Voluntary Public Takeover Offer of ÖLH Österreichische Luftverkehrs-Holding-GmbH*. Vienna: Austrian Airlines.

Ball, M.O., Ausubel, L.M., Berardino, F., Cramton, P., Donohue, G., Hansen, M. and Hoffman, K. (2007) Market-based alternatives for managing congestion at New York's La Guardia airport. *Proceedings of the 1st Annual Airneth Conference, The Hague*, http://www.garsonline.de/Downloads/070413/Ball-et-al-AirNeth2007.pdf, accessed 8 October 2007.

Beria, P., Niemeier, H.-M. and Fröhlich, K. (2011) Alitalia – the failure of a national carrier. *Journal of Air Transport Management*, 17, 215–220.

Brealey, R.M. and Myers, S.C. (2000) *Principles of Corporate Finance*, 6th edn. McGraw-Hill, Boston.

Brueckner, J.K. and Pels, E. (2005) European airline mergers, alliance consolidation, and consumer welfare. *Journal of Air Transport Management*, 11, 27– 41.

Brueckner, J.K. and Spiller, P.T. (1991) Competition and mergers in airline networks. *International Journal of Industrial Organization*, 9, 323–342.

Brussels Airlines (2008) http://corporate.brusselsairlines.com/en_be/corp/alliances/brussels-airlines-and-lufthansa.aspx, 15 September 2008, accesed 17 January 2011.

Caves, D.W., Christensen, L.R. and Tretheway, M.W. (1984) Economies of scale: why trunk and local service airline costs differ. *The RAND Journal of Economics*, 15, 4, 471–489.

Coase, R.H. (1937) The nature of the firm. *Economica, New Series*, 4, 16, 386–405.

Deutsche Lufthansa AG (2005) *Annual Report 2005*. Cologne: Deutsche Lufthansa AG.

Deutsche Lufthansa AG (2010) *Annual Report 2010*. Cologne: Deutsche Lufthansa AG.

Die Presse (2008) AUA Verkauf besiegelt: Kranich soll Flügel verleihen (AUA sale confirmed: Crane should give wings), http://diepresse.com/home/wirtschaft/economist/435595/AUAVerkauf-besiegelt_Kranich-soll-Fluegel-verleihen, 5 December, accessed 11 2011.

Doganis, R. (2006) *Airline Business in the 21st Century*, 2nd edn. London, New York: Routledge.

Done, K. and Wiesmann, G. (2009) Lufthansa to take control of BMI http://www.ft.com/cms/s/0/89e38e7e-5f37-11de-93d1-00144feabdc0.html, accessed 23 January 2011.Dunning, J. (1981) *International Production and the Multinational Enterprise*. London: Allen & Unwin.

EU COM (2009a) *Case No. COMP/M. 5403 – Lufthansa-BMI*. Luxembourg: Office for Official Publications of the European Communities.

EU COM (2009b) *Case No. COMP/M. 5335 – Lufthansa – SN Brussels Airlines*. Brussels: Official Journal of the European Union.

EU COM (2009c) *Case No. COMP/M. 5440 – Lufthansa/Austrian Airlines*. Brussels: Official Journal of the European Union.

Fama, E.F. (1969) Efficient capital markets. A review of theory and empirical work. *Journal of Finance*, 25, 2, 383–417.

FAZ (2005) Die sanfte Fusion. *Frankfurter Allgemeine Zeitung*, 15 March.

Fischer, H. and Genger, J. (2005) Air France–KLM deklassiert Rivalen (Air France-KLM declasses rivals). *Financial Times Deutschland*, 24 November.

Flottau, J. (2004) Air France spart mehr ein (More savings at Air France). *Financial Times Deutschland*, 25 November.

Flottau, J. and Fischer, H. (2003) Air France zahlt 784 Mio. Euro für KLM (Air France pays €784 million for KLM). *Financial Times Deutschland*, 1 October.

Forsgren, M. (2008) *Theories of the Multinational Firm*. Cheltenham: Edward Elgar.

Gellman Research Associates (1994) *A Study of International Airline Code Sharing*. Washington, DC: Office of Aviation and International Economics, Office of the Secretary of US Department of Transportation.

International Airlines Group (IAG) (2010) *IAG results presentation 2010*. London, http://media.corporate-ir.net/media_files/IROL/24/240949/IAG_results_2010.pdf.

Glaum, M. (1996) *Internationalisierung und Unternehmenserfolg* (Internationalisation and Business Success). Wiesbaden: Gabler.

Goerke, B. (2008) Event studies. In S. Albers, D. Klapper, U. Konradt, A. Walter and J. Wolf, eds, *Ergänzungen zur Methodik der empirischen Forschung* (Supplements to the Methodology of empirical Research), 3rd edn. Kiel: Gabler.

Hanlon, J.P. (2003) *Global Airlines: Competition in a Transnational Industry*, 2nd edn. Amsterdam: Butterworth-Heinemann.

Iatrou, K. and Oretti, M. (2007) *Airline Choices for the Future: From Alliances to Mergers*. Ashgate: Aldershot.

Jegminat, G. (2007) Spannungsvolle Partnerschaft (Suspenseful Partnership) *FVW*, 41, 8, 68–70.

Kay, J. (1993) *Foundations of Corporate Success*. Oxford: Oxford University Press.

Kleymann, B. and Seristö, H. (2001) Levels of airline alliance membership: balancing risks and benefits. *Journal of Air Transport Management*, 7, 303–310.

Laaser, C.-F. (2001) Vor- und Nachteile globaler Allianzen im Luftverkehr. In A. Knorr, ed., *Europäischer Luftverkehr. Wem nützen strategische Allianzen* (European Air Transport: Who Benefits from Alliances). Frankfurt: DVWG, 70–111.

Li, M. (2000) Distinct features of lasting and non-lasting airline alliances. *Journal of Air Transport Management*, 6, 65–73.

MacNeille, S. (1992) Redrawing the international air map. *New York Times*, http://query.nytimes.com/gst/fullpage.html?res=9E0CE0D81339F932A35750C0A964958260, 1 March 1992, accessed 10 October 2007.

Mayrhuber, W. (2009) On solid strategic track in turbulent times. Company presentation 25 June 2009. Seeheim, Germany: Lufthansa Training.

Morck, R. and Yeung, B. (1992) Internalization. An event study test. *Journal of International Economics*, 33, 33–56.

Morgan Stanley (2003) *AF–KLM Deal: Where is the Value? Equity Research Report*, 22 October. London: Morgan Stanley.

Morgan Stanley (2006) *Air France–KLM, Equity Research report*, 7 February. London: Morgan Stanley.

Morgan Stanley Research (2009) *Deutsche Lufthansa AG*, 28 October. London: Morgan Stanley Research.

Morgan Stanley Research (2010a) *Deutsche Lufthansa AG*, 18 March. London: Morgan Stanley Research.

Morgan Stanley Research (2010b) *Deutsche Lufthansa AG*, 6 August. London: Morgan Stanley Research.

Osborne, A. (2008) Bmi set for takeover by Lufthansa, http://www.telegraph.co.uk/finance/newsbysector/transport/2788938/Bmi-set-for-takeover-by-Lufthansa.html, accessed 22 January 2011.

Oum, T.H., Park, J.-H. and Zhang, A. (2000) *Globalization and Strategic Alliances: The Case of the Airline Industry*. New York: Pergamon.

Prock-Schauer, W. (2010) Lufthansa Investor Day. Frankfurt, Germany. From 28 June.

Roll, R. (1986) The hubris hypothesis of corporate takeovers. *Journal of Business*, 59, 2, 197–216.

Salpukas, A. (1991) United bid gets assets of Pan Am. *New York Times*, http://query.nytimes.com/gst/fullpage.html?res=9D0CE3D61E3CF933A25751C1A967958260, 10 December 1991, accessed 10 October 2007.

SWISS (2005) SWISS startet mit Lufthansa in eine neue Zukunft, press release, http://www.SWISS.com/web/EN/about_SWISS/media/press_releases/2005/Pages/pr_20050322.aspx, 22 March 2005, accessed 25 January 2011.

SWISS (2007) Integration von SWISS in den Lufthansa Konzern erfolgreich abgeschlossen, press release, http://www.swiss.com/web/EN/about_swiss/media/press_releases/2007/Pages/pr_20070621.aspx, 21 June 2007, accessed 10 August 2011.

Thurlow, C. and Aiello, G. (2007) National pride, global capital. A social semiotic analysis of transnational visual branding in the airline industry. *Visual Communication*, 6, 3, 305–344.

Youssef, W. and Hansen, M. (1994) Consequences of strategic alliances between international airlines: the case of Swissair and SAS. *Transportation Research Part A*, 28, 415–431.

Chapter 12

Open Skies and Antitrust: Do We Need Them Both?
A Review of the Air New Zealand Cases

Tim Hazledine

1. Introduction

How does competition operate in the passenger aviation market? Does it differ from other service industries? And what types of policy instruments might be needed to ensure that airline customers receive good service at competitive prices? In particular, is easing actual or potential entry, as through an 'open skies' treaty, a good substitute for actual competition 'in the air' between incumbent operators? These are questions addressed in this chapter, using a case study of a particularly interesting aviation market: the set of routes linking cities in New Zealand with cities in Australia, these being approximately 2,500 kilometres apart, across the Tasman Sea.

The Tasman market is unusually open, designated as a 'Single Aviation Market' (SAM) reinforced by a 2002 open skies agreement between the two countries. Any locally owned airline can compete freely on any Tasman route, as well as any foreign airline flying long-haul into either Australia or NZ, who are granted fifth freedom rights to carry trans-Tasman passengers. It is particularly interesting because this open regime has been the setting of three major antitrust cases over the past decade, each involving the national carrier of NZ, Air New Zealand, attempting to gain authorization from the antitrust authorities for a cartel-like arrangement with one of its major competitors.

In many, probably most, antitrust situations the regulator focuses on the effect on competition and prices of a merger or other arrangement between a subset of the existing firms supplying the market. This approach will definitely be appropriate in the majority of aviation cases, because of prohibitions on foreign competition in most domestic markets, and bilateral treaties limiting entry onto international routes.

However, the openness of the Tasman market gives real possibility to the relevance of potential competition from new entrants on any route. This is reinforced by a possibly unique characteristic of the airline business: its main piece of capital equipment is – quite literally – mobile, and all the other inputs it needs (fuel, maintenance, ground facilities, labour) can easily be purchased almost anywhere. It was, of course, precisely these characteristics that encouraged the founders of 'contestability theory' – the ultimate in potential entry doctrines – to predict that it would be the newly deregulated US domestic airline market where the theory would first bear empirical fruit. Although these hopes were to be disappointed in the United States (Levine, 1987), we will see below that a modified contestability concept gained considerable traction in the Tasman antitrust cases. In this, the main innovation was proposed to be the importance for competition across aviation markets of possibly the most significant innovation in passenger aviation of the past quarter century, namely, the low-cost carrier (LCC) business model.

In the 2002 and 2006 attempts by the 'legacy carriers' Air New Zealand and Qantas to in effect merge their operations in the Tasman markets – despite holding joint market shares on these routes of around 80–100 per cent – the airlines argued that consumers would be protected by actual or potential low-price competition from Virgin Blue, which had already successfully set up as an LCC within Australia, and was also serving a few Tasman routes at the time. They actually carried this case with one local competition authority, but the proposal was vetoed by others. The third, 2010, case involved Air New Zealand in alliance with the LCC, and was eventually granted regulatory approval.[1]

In this chapter I will first recount the narrative of the antitrust cases, and then report the results and implications of some empirical work I carried out in response to these striking proposals. I will conclude with some general assessment of the open skies/antitrust issue as it applies to air transport.

2. The Tasman Antitrust Cases

First, some legal background: competition policy in Australia and (especially) New Zealand is based on Acts of Parliament which have been interpreted as requiring the regulatory authorities to impose a total surplus, or 'efficiency' standard, not the consumer surplus standard relied on in the US and Europe (Hazledine, 2004). This means, in particular, that a finding of a likely substantial lessening of competition (SLC) from, say, a merger, resulting in a significant increase in consumer prices, is not here of itself determinative. Transfers of surplus from consumers to shareholders cancel out – only the allocative efficiency 'deadweight triangle' loss from the reduction in output that drives the price increase is counted as a detriment.

This would seem to open the door to the use of the Williamson 'Efficiencies Defence', under which even a quite small 'rectangle' of production efficiency gains (e.g. from economies of scale) resulting or predicted to result from a merger could easily outweigh the allocative inefficiency triangle (Hazledine, 1998). Given the relatively small size of New Zealand and even Australian markets, one might expect efficiencies defences to be quite common in the region. However, claimed scale economies or other production efficiencies were not important in these airline cases, and indeed are not generally prevalent in Australasian antitrust. Further, the authorities have often focused on 'dynamic efficiencies' – in particular, incentives to innovate – which (although we don't really have a lot of good empirical evidence) can quite plausibly be linked to competitive pressure in product markets. Thus, in Australia and (especially) New Zealand, the effect on competition of a structural change in a market does still hold sway in regulatory decisions, even if by a rather longer chain of reasoning than through a simple SLC test. So we focus now on how the airlines argued that their proposals would not significantly lessen competition, and how the regulatory authorities responded.

2.1 The Two Air New Zealand/Qantas Cases

The November 2002 proposal for a 'strategic alliance' between Air New Zealand and Qantas was very close to a takeover of the smaller airline by the larger, and in particular proposed full operational integration (cartelization) of their activities in the three large market sectors within which they competed directly with each other: domestic New Zealand, trans-Tasman, and their duopoly over the Auckland–Los Angeles route.

---

1   The author was involved in the first two cases, making independent submissions opposing the airlines' proposals, and (in the first case) as an expert witness commissioned by a corporate travel agency who also opposed the Alliance. I did not take a position on the third case.

The proposal was rejected in full in first draft then final determinations by both countries' competition agencies – the Australian Competition and Consumer Commission (ACCC) and the New Zealand Commerce Commission (NZCC), holding independent hearings in 2003. The grounds were, not surprisingly, likely significant lessening of product market competition with little in the way of plausible offsetting benefits.

The airlines appealed: to the High Court in New Zealand, and to the Australian Competition Tribunal (ACT). The High Court hearing was supposedly limited to matters of law: specifically, whether the NZCC was legally justified in coming to the decision it is made on the basis of the evidence available to it. The Court quite quickly decided that the Commission was so justified, issuing its Judgment in September 2004, following its hearing in July.[2]

ACT proceedings, however, are in the way of a re-hearing, not an appeal, with new evidence and argument admissible. Also, the Australian public interest in the case was just about limited to the trans-Tasman routes (i.e. to routes heavily used by Australian consumers), with little or no concern for the domestic New Zealand market (and not much interest in the Auckland–Los Angeles sector).[3]

The applicants took effective advantage of both these features, mounting a strong new case in support of the proposal that differed substantively from its earlier submissions to the Commissions;[4] now relying heavily on qualitative analysis stressing the actual and potential competitive constraint mounted in trans-Tasman markets by the LCC Pacific (Virgin) Blue and the fifth freedom carrier Emirates flying three wide-body jets daily into Auckland and one into Christchurch.[5] In testimony quoted by the Tribunal a Qantas executive claimed that

> under the Alliance, Qantas would be compelled to respond to the fare categories offered by Virgin Blue, albeit with a price premium … as Pacific Blue grew, the Alliance would be able to command less and less of a price premium … if Pacific Blue reached a market share of above 15 percent, average fares on trans-Tasman routes would be dictated by the fares set by Pacific Blue.[6]

Air New Zealand in its submission to the Tribunal told a similar story, that:

> most of its pricing focus and tactical pricing activity had been driven by Fifth Freedom Carriers and Virgin Blue … since Virgin Blue commenced promoting its services [i.e., even before its actual entry], Air New Zealand had responded … by offering similar fares to those offered by Virgin Blue.[7]

---

2   See ACCC (2003), NZCC (2003), High Court of New Zealand (2004).

3   Thus, these countries do not operate a true 'total' surplus regime, since their concern is limited to the interests of their own citizens. So, for example, higher prices paid by Australian consumers to fly on Air New Zealand services (and thereby accruing to the NZ shareholders of Air NZ) would not be cancelled out, in either jurisdiction.

4   In particular, the quantitative (but not empirical) merger simulation oligopoly models introduced into the case in December 2002, and responded to both by the NZCC and by me, were abandoned for the Australian ACT Hearing.

5   Due to trade-mark restrictions, Virgin had to brand its Tasman operations as Pacific Blue. Other fifth freedom carriers are (currently) Aerolineas Argentina and Lan Chile, but these and others who have for a time used these rights, fly only one route and this daily or less.

6   ACT (2005), at paragraph 334.

7   ACT (2005), at paragraph 330.

That is, the two legacy carriers claimed that, operating independently, their pricing on the Tasman routes was in effect constrained by Virgin (Pacific) Blue, as well as by Emirates (i.e., not by each other), and that this constraint would continue, more or less unchanged, under the proposed cartel.[8]

So why would this happen? Here the applicants introduced, through the oral testimony of one of their expert witnesses, Professor Janusz Ordover, the concept of the price-sensitive 'marginal customer', which would come to have a hugely influential – perhaps paramount – impact on the Tribunal's decision. The following passage is representative of the Tribunal's findings on the matter:

> Professor Ordover's view was that fares in airline markets were driven generally by the competition for customers at the margin, and that this competition was provided by new entrants and other airlines seeking either to fill scarce [sic] capacity by marginal cost pricing or by introducing a new set of competitive strategies generally to which incumbent airlines were compelled to respond … entry and expansion barriers were so low that the market was … 'workably contestable', that is that any attempt by the Alliance … to raise average fares would divert so many passengers to its rivals that it would not be profitable to do so. His evidence, which we accept, was that a 10 percent fare increase would divert so many passengers away from the Alliance that such an elevation in fares would be unsustainable.[9]

The Tribunal found in favour of the applicants, giving authorization to the cartel for a period of five years. Although this was in effect a dead ruling, because of the veto exercised by the earlier New Zealand High Court Decision, which Air New Zealand and Qantas had already decided to not appeal, it did encourage them to come back to the authorities in 2006 with a proposal for a 'Tasman Networks Agreement' (TNA), which would again be a cartel, but this time restricted to the trans-Tasman routes. The impetus for this was claimed to be the incidence, since 2003, of 'significant excess capacity on the Tasman, driven by the growth of Virgin Blue and Emirates, as well as by Air NZ and Qantas as they strive to maintain comparable network offerings'.[10]

The airlines provided a detailed proposed schedule which the ACCC calculated would in the first instance reduce market capacity (seats flown) by around 6 per cent.[11] Thus we have here an interesting twist: the cartel would indeed reduce potential supply (with consequent costs savings to be claimed as public benefits), but not actual output, because the capacity eliminated was actually 'excess'. And, in any case, as the ACT had in effect agreed:

> The lower cost airlines – Emirates … and Virgin Blue – effectively set fare levels on the Tasman, with intense competition occurring for price sensitive travellers (or 'marginal' passengers).

8   Emirates is of course a full-service airline, not an LCC, but it is generally accepted that because the opportunity cost of a daily trans-Tasman return trip is leaving the aircraft sitting on the tarmac in Australia (given that the long-haul flights arrive in the morning and leave in the evening), it can price on the basis of variable costs, which enables it to offer economy tickets at prices similar to those set by Pacific Blue.

9   ACT (2005), at paragraph 353.

10   Air New Zealand and Qantas Airways Limited (2006), at paragraph 1.4. This reference is to the airlines' Application made to the NZ Ministry of Transport, which by a quirk of the Civil Aviation Act 1990 has regulatory jurisdiction over trans-Tasman aviation matters. A similar application was made to the ACCC, which body took the lead in assessing the competitive implications of the proposal.

11   ACCC (2006) at paragraph 9.311. The ACCC did predict that in the 'counterfactual' – i.e. business as usual with no TNA – the airlines would unilaterally find ways of reducing capacity, but by less than 6 per cent because of the spillover problem (paragraphs 8.47–8.49)

Competition for marginal passengers is not confined to those customers and extends to all passengers … The conduct and business models of Emirates and Virgin Blue keep Air NZ and Qantas on constant competitive alert.[12]

Submissions by interested parties opposing the TNA expressed some scepticism about the extent of truly 'excess' capacity, but even granting the existence of low capacity utilization, the economist's natural question is to ask why individual airlines offering 'too many' seats cannot independently act to reduce such without the need for any coordinated cartel arrangement. The applicants had anticipated this objection:

When faced with a choice between network airlines (such as Air NZ and Qantas) consumers (particularly business passengers) are more likely to choose the network airline that offers more destinations and frequencies … if Air NZ decided to reduce capacity unilaterally, this would simply spill customers to its network competitor, Qantas.[13]

In its Draft Determination proposing to decline authorization, the ACCC jumped on this distinction:

The importance of the time-sensitive [i.e., business passenger] segment on the trans-Tasman … is clear from the Applicants' argument as to why the TNA is necessary in the first place; namely, that they cannot unilaterally act to reduce capacity because these passengers would spill to their network rival. This also provides the compelling insight that the Applicants do not view Virgin Blue and Emirates as viable alternatives for these passengers over the authorisation period.[14]

The ACCC was not here just scoring debating points – it continued to maintain the view that it had come to in the earlier strategic alliance case that indeed, as it now put it:

In the first instance … a lessening of competition in the time-sensitive segment of the market under the TNA is likely to provide the Applicants with scope to increase prices for fares typically directed at these types of passengers. Given their current trans-Tasman schedules and barriers to expansion, Emirates and Virgin Blue would appear to have a limited ability to contest for these passengers.[15]

And not just for the business passenger market. The Commission also implicitly rejected the 'marginal customer' doctrine:

Secondly, by planning to reduce capacity, the TNA is likely to have the effect of reducing the number of 'low fare' seats Qantas and Air NZ make available on their aircraft … the TNA is likely to result in a cascading effect on the composition of 'fare buckets' that are made available … average prices are likely to increase … and it will be more difficult to get a 'cheap seat'.[16]

Application provisionally declined. Faced with the ACCC's Draft Determination, Air New Zealand and Qantas gave up their attempts to cartelize aspects of their operations, and continued to compete independently with each other, as they have done with some success ever since. Interestingly, both

---

12   Air New Zealand and Qantas Airways Limited (2006) at paragraphs 1.2 and 1.3.
13   Air New Zealand and Qantas Airways Limited (2006) at paragraphs 4.10 and 4.11.
14   ACCC (2006) at paragraph 9.298.
15   ACCC (2006) at paragraph 9.304.
16   ACCC (2006), at paras 9.305 and 9.307.

Qantas and Air New Zealand quickly reduced their capacity, thereby rather vitiating their claims in the 2006 TNA proposal that they could not eliminate 'excess' capacity unilaterally.[17]

2.2 The 2010 Air NZ/Virgin Blue Proposal

On May 4, 2010, Virgin Blue and Air New Zealand jointly submitted to the ACCC and to the New Zealand Ministry of Transport requests for authorization of an 'Alliance', this being another cartel arrangement across the Tasman, with ancillary agreements; in particular to code-share on connecting flights within New Zealand and Australia (and beyond).

In the four years since the Tasman Network Agreement proposal, there had been evolution but no radical change in the Tasman markets. No new carrier had entered, although Qantas had handed over (beginning in 2005) a number of routes or time-slots on routes to its wholly owned 'fighting brand' LCC subsidiary Jetstar, here focusing, as it does in domestic Australian markets, on bracketing Virgin where this airline is strongest.[18] Air New Zealand had quietly closed down its own LCC subsidiary, Freedom Air, which had previously served some smaller regional New Zealand cities (Hamilton, Dunedin).

Despite competition from Jetstar, Virgin (Pacific) Blue achieved quite impressive increases in market share at the expense of Air New Zealand and Qantas, with this more than doubling over the Tasman routes in total from 7.5 per cent to 16 per cent. The latter was achieved by (a) some increases in weekly frequencies on existing routes; (b) introduction of new leisure destinations in Queensland for NZ travellers; (c) entering the major Auckland–Sydney and Auckland–Melbourne routes with daily service.[19]

It might seem potentially embarrassing for Air New Zealand, having previously made much of the competitive discipline imposed by an independent Virgin Blue,[20] to now turn around and claim that the loss of independent LCC competition would not significantly affect pricing (especially given the increase in Virgin's market presence on the Tasman), but it managed to achieve this quite smoothly, depending on three main new arguments. First, the applicants claimed an invigorated competitive effect from the expansion onto Tasman routes since of Jetstar. Second, and more creatively, they argued that an Air New Zealand/Virgin alliance could actually strengthen competition and improve the product, not just across the Tasman, but also in the Australian domestic market, in which the time-sensitive (business traveller) segment in particular was still dominated by Qantas. And third (and this must be seen as resiling somewhat from the earlier position) they

---

17   Indeed, Air New Zealand announced cuts to its offerings within a week of its decision with Qantas to not challenge the ACCC Draft Determination. See 'Air NZ slashes capacity on Tasman route' by Liam Dann, *NZ Herald*, 24 November 2006. Capacity and market share data are given in ACCC (2010), Tables 4.2 to 4.6, pages 18–21.

18   Virgin's head office and main base is in Brisbane, and it is strong on leisure routes serving Queensland resort cities. Accordingly, Qantas handed over Christchurch–Brisbane and Auckland–Gold Coast routes to Jetstar.

19   Pacific Blue's entry onto the crowded Auckland–Sydney route in October 2008 may (or may not) have had something to do with a gaffe made by the Virgin Group's founder, Sir Richard Branson, on a visit to Auckland the previous year. In an interview, Sir Richard claimed that Pacific Blue currently did fly Auckland–Sydney direct. (See 'Work dressed up as fun' by Michele Hewitson, *NZ Herald*, January 20, 2007.)

20   Recall the assertion (quoted above) to the ACT from Air New Zealand's fellow applicant Qantas that Pacific Blue with 15 per cent of the Tasman markets would be 'dictating' average airfares.

conceded that 'Air New Zealand and Qantas are well recognized as each other's closest competitor on the Tasman.'[21]

Code-sharing would give the Alliance something that no Australasian carrier had enjoyed since Air New Zealand's brief and disastrous ownership of Ansett in 2000–01: full access to regional air travel markets in both Australia and New Zealand, through Air New Zealand's and Virgin's domestic networks.[22] As for the Tasman market; integrating operations would deliver more frequent and convenient service offerings, especially on the thinner routes such as those connecting Wellington with Australian cities and resorts.[23] The result would be an operator providing stronger competition to the Qantas/Jetstar group, to everyone's benefit (except possibly Qantas):

> The applicants' commercial assessment is that Qantas is currently able to maintain a yield premium on the Tasman, which the Alliance will challenge, leading to greater fare and service competition for time sensitive passengers.

and

> From Air New Zealand's perspective this Alliance is very different from its previously proposed alliances with Qantas [of which a core aspect was] the removal of capacity from the market in order to reduce costs … In contrast, the Alliance is about growing Air New Zealand's and Virgin Blue's combined market presence and not about reducing capacity.[24]

In summary, what was being proposed in this case was that the Alliance would:

- Make Virgin a more effective competitor to Qantas in the duopolistic Australian business travel market;
- Give New Zealand and other business and leisure travellers better choices and frequency of services trans-Tasman with little penalty from loss of an independent competitor.

The ACCC issued a draft Determination in September 2010 broadly accepting the airlines' position, but nevertheless proposing to decline authorization, mainly on the grounds of competitive concerns on particular smaller routes (including those ex-Wellington, which cannot be served by wide-body aircraft) on which Qantas/Jetstar could not be expected to prevent loss of Pacific Blue/

---

21   Virgin Blue and Air New Zealand (2010) at paragraph 6.3.

22   Qantas flies in New Zealand, but only on main trunk routes servicing airports from which it also flies to Australia, so there is no regional feeder traffic generated.

23   Although each airline would continue to fly its own aircraft, marketing would be 'metal neutral', such that a passenger flying on, say, an Air New Zealand ticket would likely neither know nor care whether they were carried on an Air New Zealand or Pacific Blue aircraft. This neutrality would be achieved through a 'middle of the road' coming together of on- and off-plane service: Virgin continuing its rebranding strategy to move from being an LCC to the self-styled 'New World Carrier' (with premium economy seating, frequent flier programme and airport lounges), while Air New Zealand would go down-market to meet Virgin by removing the business class seating from its A320 aircraft.

24   Virgin Blue and Air New Zealand (2010), at paragraphs 6.3 and 2.5(f). Qantas did not take a public position on the proposed Alliance, though its CEO Mr Alan Joyce could not resist taking a dig at its competitor Virgin Blue's attempts to please both leisure and business travellers, claiming that those following such a 'middle of the road' strategy could end up as 'road kill' (quoted in the ACCC's Draft Determination at paragraph 5.178, but not included in the [final] Determination referenced here).

Air New Zealand competition from substantially lessening competition. Having then negotiated undertakings with the applicants to maintain scheduled seat capacity on these routes, the ACCC's final (2010) Determination granted approval, which was not challenged in New Zealand or elsewhere.[25]

3. The Economics of the Airline Cases

The economist seeking to evaluate a possible structural change in a market seeks first to establish a 'theory of the case' – an understanding of the current situation, based on mainstream assumptions of rational, profit-seeking behaviour by the players in the market. With the implications of this in mind, and maintaining still the assumption of rationality, we go on to predict, and evaluate, the likely outcome of the proposed change.

In the case of the Tasman air travel market, we identify this as a small-number oligopoly, with the incumbent firms most likely competing independently. In this situation, it is very hard to write down a plausible model in which the 'marginal customer' proposition would be valid. That is, even assuming a homogeneous product, so that no price differentials across suppliers are sustainable, it does not follow that attempts by an Air New Zealand/Qantas cartel to raise the price by pulling seats off the market would be vitiated in full by equivalent expansions of capacity offered by Pacific Blue and/or Emirates. The latter are oligopolists too, and in most models would be predicted to benefit from an overall increase in market price, and accordingly be prepared to limit their own output increases to permit this to occur, to some extent.

The problem is exacerbated by the inference that the observed rather small market shares of both Pacific Blue and Emirates (each around 10 per cent, at the time), despite their lower costs of supply, signal significant limits on the cross-price sensitivity of demand: that is, it seems that for many – perhaps most – customers, the products of these carriers are not in fact perfect substitutes for the offerings of either Air New Zealand or Qantas, and as such the competitive constraint of Pacific Blue and/or Emirates' pricing will be softened further.

These are, of course, quite mainstream propositions, and were in essence accepted by the ACCC, the NZCC and the (New Zealand) High Court. However, they had failed to carry the day in the Australian Competition Tribunal, and it seemed worthwhile investigating the situation further. It was a rather regrettable fact that none of the large sums of money spent on pursuing these cases[26] had gone into actual empirical research into the nature of competition in the affected markets,[27] and this seemed like an interesting and useful gap to fill.

Lacking data on actual prices paid for air travel, I used the airlines' websites to observe prices offered, at various times before flight date. This in particular would track the intertemporal price discrimination used by airlines everywhere to sort low willingness to pay leisure travellers (who are prepared to purchase tickets well in advance) from high-value business customers whose decisions

---

25   We could note that seats can be flown empty, so that capacity guarantees in themselves do not prevent a cartel or alliance from choosing to increase prices.

26   Informal estimates are that Air New Zealand and Qantas themselves disbursed more than $NZ50 million to lawyers, consultants etc.

27   The US-based experts employed by the airlines seemed to have been heavily influenced by the impact of the LCC Southwest Airlines on domestic competition. There are, however, many differences between the US and Tasman markets; notably the much stronger cost and market positions of the national legacy carrier incumbents Air New Zealand and Qantas.

tend to be made soon before the date of travel – i.e., sorting 'price-sensitive' from 'time-sensitive' sub-markets, as had been made much of in the cartel cases.

I reported my results in a number of papers; most recently Hazledine (2010, 2011). The basic bottom line is that structural competition, as proxied by the standard Hirschman-Herfindahl Index HHI measure of the size (measured by seat capacity) distribution of airlines actually serving a route, does appear to matter for average fares offered, such that removing competition between the two largest carriers, Air New Zealand and Qantas, might reasonably be expected to result in a significant (from the lessening of competition perspective) upward shift in the price structure.

I did however find that structural competition was less important in the leisure travel segment of the Tasman market, though probably not sufficiently so to justify the 'workably contestable' proposition that Virgin and/or Emirates would adequately constrain an Air New Zealand/Qantas cartel from raising prices.

Turning to the 2010 case, involving the proposed alliance or cartel between Air New Zealand and Virgin (Pacific) Blue, we find that at last the authorities have undertaken some serious empirical analysis. The ACCC modelled pricing econometrically, using data on Air New Zealand's airfares from 2002 to 2010, supplied to it on a confidential basis by the airline. Unfortunately, the Commission has chosen not to document its modelling strategy and just reports some results in summary, so we have to take these on faith.[28]

The ACCC reports[29] that (i) Jetstar's presence on a Tasman route has little effect on Air New Zealand's prices; (ii) Emirates' presence has an 'at least' 3 per cent impact (more on Auckland–Sydney with the A380 super-jumbo); (iii) Pacific Blue's presence has 'had the effect of reducing Air New Zealand's average economy fares by around 6–8 per cent, on a significant number of routes'. It is not clear whether a 'significant number' is with reference to all routes, or to just the subset of routes served by Pacific Blue.

On the basis of these findings, the ACCC evidently reached its conclusion that Pacific Blue has behaved as a maverick on the trans-Tasman, wielding price influence that is disproportionate to its market share.

It is doubtful that the term 'maverick' is justified.[30] The standard LCC business model is based on assessing each route or potential route on its merits (i.e. with no concern for the 'network' effects that interest legacy carriers): it will be served if and only if the LCC expects to do so profitably. Prices will be 'low', but these are justified by low costs. Indeed, it is the responses by some (US) legacy carriers of desperately slashing prices to defend market share when an LCC such as Southwest Airlines enters, while doing little to reduce their cost base, which might more reasonably deserve the epithet maverick.[31]

---

28   As we have had to take on faith modelling done for the applicants by their consultant Dr Tretheway using a QSI (Quality Service Index) model calibrated to the US market to predict stimulus to passenger demand resulting from the Alliance. The extent to which 'Public' versions of applications and determinations are scarred by massive deletions on the purported basis of commercial confidentiality needs to be reassessed. No doubt it serves the private interests of both applicants and regulator to jointly monopolize this information.

29   See ACCC (2010) at paragraph 5.258.

30   Air New Zealand and Qantas used the word 'maverick' to describe Pacific Blue in their 2006 TNA application. This was noted by the ACCC in its Draft Determination (2006, 9.80) but apparently without comment or judgement as to the term's appropriateness. Thus it is quite odd to find it reproduced by the ACCC in its 2010 Determination, with no real justification given.

31   So, Virgin Blue 'confirmed that because of the strategy of its competitors, there needs to be a "very strong" profitability case for entering a certain route' (ACCC (2010, paragraph 9.234)). The (claimed)

In any case, despite in effect tacitly conceding that it and others (including me) had previously rather underestimated the competitive threat posed by Virgin Blue to the legacy carriers on the Tasman routes, the ACCC determined on balance that loss of Virgin as an independent competitor would not substantially lessen competition on most routes, and was compensated by improvements in service quality (e.g. from the Air New Zealand/Virgin code-share), which in particular would strengthen Virgin's ability to compete with Qantas in the domestic Australian market.

4. Summary and Implications

Overall, it seems reasonable to conclude that appropriate regulatory decisions were finally made in all three merger or cartel cases covering the trans-Tasman passenger air travel market over the 2002–2010 period. Allowing the large incumbent legacy carriers Air New Zealand and Qantas to cartelize their operations would most likely have had a seriously detrimental effect on competition, as mainstream analysis would predict. Allowing Air New Zealand to combine forces with the LCC Virgin is perhaps less clearly justifiable, but at least at the time of writing (early 2012), problems in the market have not manifested themselves.

The attempt to resurrect the doctrine of contestability in the form of the 'all-important marginal customer' notion lacks theoretical and empirical plausibility and should be deemed to have failed. Arguments in 2010 about the strengthening of competition in an unequal duopoly (the Australian domestic market) through allowing Virgin to work more closely with Air New Zealand are interesting and developments in this market will be followed with interest.

As for the performance of the various regulatory authorities, I make two observations. First, it was unfortunate that the local markets were not subjected from the beginning to focused empirical (econometric) investigation, rather than relying (as it happened) on possibly inappropriate and misleading transplants from the ample literature on competition and the role of low-cost carriers in US airline markets.

Second, the capturing (in effect) of the Australian Competition Tribunal by determined advocacy in the actual hearings of the workably competitive/marginal customer doctrine may illustrate the dangers of allowing these complex matters to be adjudicated by a Court with no recourse to the institutional knowledge and analytical capability of an established agency or secretariat (such the NZCC or ACCC).

As for the question raised in the title of this chapter – *antitrust and open skies: do we need them both?* – my answer must be that, yes, definitely we do, at least under the present regulatory regime. The trans-Tasman air travel market operates under an unusually liberal set of open skies treaties (allowing up to fifth freedom rights of access), but such has not gainsaid the need for complex activist antitrust intervention as in the three cases studied here. 'Openness' simply is not sufficient to safeguard competition.

However, we should note the aviation sector's notion of openness is still highly restrictive compared to openness in other service and commodity trade sectors, in which free trade generally permits a much wider range of sources of supply than the locally owned carriers permitted under most open skies treaties. Perhaps if domestic and international markets could be freely supplied by any of the hundreds of technically competition commercial aviation operators around the world –

---

competitor strategy was for Air New Zealand and/or Qantas to respond aggressively (as a maverick?) by increasing their own capacity following Pacific Blue's entry to a route.

that is, extending access up to the ninth freedom of the air – then contestability theory would finally get its chance to shine.[32]

References

ACCC (Australian Competition and Consumers Commission) (2003) *Final Determination: Applications for Authorisation A30220 etc, lodged by Qantas Airways Limited and Air New Zealand Limited, 9 September*.

ACCC (Australian Competition and Consumers Commission) (2006) *Draft Determination: Applications for authorisation A91001, A91002, A91003, lodged by Qantas Airways Limited and Air New Zealand Limited, 3 November*.

ACCC (Australian Competition and Consumers Commission) (2010) *Determination: Application for authorisation lodged by Virgin Blue Airlines Pty Ltd and Others, 16 December*.

ACT (Australian Competition Tribunal) (2005) *Determination Qantas Airways Limited [2004] ACompT 9, 16 May*.

Air New Zealand Limited and Qantas Airways Limited (2006) *Application to the Minister of Transport pursuant to Part 9 of the Civil Aviation Act 1990*.

Hazledine, T. (1998) Rationalism rebuffed? Lessons from modern Canadian and New Zealand competition policy. *Review of Industrial Organization*, 13, 243–264.

Hazledine, T. (2004) Application of the public benefit test to the Air New Zealand/Qantas case. *New Zealand Economic Papers*, 38, 2, 279–298.

Hazledine, T. (2010) Pricing, competition and policy in Australasian air travel markets. *Journal of Transport Economics and Policy*, 44, 37–58.

Hazledine, T. (2011) Price discrimination in Australasian air travel markets. *New Zealand Economic Papers*, 45, 3, 311–324.

High Court of New Zealand (2004) *High Court of New Zealand, Auckland Registry: Judgement (No. 6) of Rodney Hansen J and Kerrin M. Vautier CMG (Lay Member), 17 September*, Auckland

Levine, M.E. (1987) Airline competition in deregulated markets: theory, firm strategy, and public policy. *Yale Journal on Regulation*, 4, 393–494.

NZCC (2003) [New Zealand Commerce Commission]: *Final Determination in the matter of an application for authorization of a business acquisition involving Air New Zealand Ltd and Qantas Airways Ltd*, Wellington.

Virgin Blue and Air New Zealand (2010) *Submission in support of the Application for Authorisation of the Virgin Blue and Air New Zealand Airline Alliance, (to ACCC), 4 May*.

---

32   The domestic NZ air travel market may be the only (?) example of ninth freedom rights granted when there is an incumbent domestic carrier. Since the late 1980s a competent stand-alone operation can be mounted with no international links, and such indeed was provided for more than a decade by Ansett NZ. However, the provisions of the Single Aviation Market treaty rule out such an operator contesting the Tasman unless it satisfies the requirements for Australian or NZ ownership and control.

Chapter 13

The Impact of Liberalization on Cross-border Airline Mergers and Alliances

Dr Kostas Iatrou and Lida Mantzavinou

Airline alliance evolution has been influenced by, and has itself had an impact on, the course of deregulation in many domestic markets and regional blocs, much as it has both felt the effects of and contributed towards the gradual liberalization and relaxation of the international air transport industry. Together, intergovernmental agreements and inter-firm strategies have created a new environment that is offering new opportunities and challenges and have paved the way towards the much-awaited and needed consolidation of the air transport industry in the form of cross-border mergers.

Airlines, like other firms in other sectors, have resorted to alliances because an alliance is a flexible organizational form offering rapid growth potential. It is the modern engine for growth, and in the case of airlines, growth takes the form of increased network coverage and entrance to new markets. Because of the peculiarities of the air transport industry and the regulatory framework governing it, which strictly prohibits cross-border mergers, alliances represented the only business arrangement that would allow airlines from different countries to serve the global market together.

1. The Impact of Liberalization on Alliances

International and national aviation policies and corporate strategies are acting upon each other in ways that have serious implications for the structures of international aviation, a symbiotic relationship which becomes even more obvious when observing how domestic deregulation, bilateral and regional liberalization have moved hand in hand with airline alliances. A distinctive feature of the current mega-alliances is that a US airline and a European airline form the core partnership in each. This pairing is by no means a coincidence, but instead answers the specific needs of the airlines from these geographical regions and their corporate strategies. These two geographical regions represent the world's most important aviation markets. In 2008, passengers carried on transatlantic flights represented 13.5 per cent of all passengers transported by air worldwide, partly because transatlantic flights connect the world's two largest domestic air transport markets, Europe and the US, which account for 9.1 per cent and 17.8 per cent respectively of global air traffic (IATA, 2009).

The industry re-concentration that followed deregulation (1978) left the US air transport industry with six major airlines, three of which – American Airlines, Delta Air Lines and United Airlines – controlled 58 per cent of domestic traffic. They developed hub-and-spoke networks to effectively cover the entire nation. These so-far domestic airlines turned to international routes, which were attractive because they were more profitable than domestic flights.

The main obstacle was regulatory. Newcomers had to obtain authority under the existing ASA (Air Service Agreement) to operate international routes. They took over traffic rights from Pan Am and TWA and pushed US authorities to renegotiate less restrictive air transport services agreements, the so-called 'open skies', that would enable them to operate more flights from more points in the

US at higher frequencies and capacities, inaugurating the move towards the gradual liberalisation of international air transport.

At the European level, liberalization, as part of the European Union single market programme, has resulted in cabotage restrictions being removed and bringing about increased competition in the regional airline market. There was initial uncertainty about the external consequences of liberalization and fears about the effects that deregulation would have on the international stakes of European Union airlines. After US airlines began their aggressive international expansion programme, European airlines resisted bilateral agreements allowing unrestricted capacity increases and route expansion.

Since 1992, when the liberalization package in the EU was agreed on and further completed in 1997 on both sides of the transatlantic market, the major European Union and US airlines were essentially facing the same dilemmas: both had very large stakes in North Atlantic routes, both had been hit by the slump in traffic caused by the Gulf War and both were anxious to draw more directly on traffic within the other's home markets. In addition, the Single European Aviation Market further hindered the attempts of US airlines to create hub-and-spoke systems within Europe, as its establishment resulted in the loss of some of their fifth freedom rights. For example, a US airline could no longer fly from Rome to Paris once the European Aviation Market was considered to be unified, because such a flight required cabotage rights the Americans lacked. US airlines were therefore forced to enter into alliances with European airlines operating in these markets, to preserve such flights through code-sharing.

In the wake of deregulation, with a more competitive environment, the airline industry became increasingly concentrated. The best solution for both US and European airlines was to establish alliances, which represented the mechanism that could provide indirect access to restricted markets. Although they were now liberalized, US and EU airlines were looking for ways to get government support in either securing their position in their domestic markets or gaining access to new markets through alliances and open skies agreements. Once this support was obtained, the appropriate national or regional authorities would then give the go-ahead to the alliance efforts.

Parallel to the consolidation trend affecting full service carriers, new low-cost, value-based airlines were starting to emerge. The development of hub-and-spoke networks, improvements in technology, the growth of frequent flyer schemes and the role of computer reservation systems all contributed to the proliferation of alliances.

Liberalization has been the great catalyst behind the formation of airline alliances. Without liberalization it would have been impossible for airlines to cooperate closely enough to find the common ground enabling them to reap mutual benefits. Full deregulation in the European Union, at least concerning the internal market, in combination with open skies agreements, has enabled airlines to access new markets, a process that could never have occurred within the confines of the Chicago bilateral regime, which was not as such restrictive, rather restrictions were imposed through ASAs between countries.

2. Open Skies

As the new US majors started out on a path of vigorous international expansion they came up against the restricted international bilateral system of traffic rights, a stumbling block which made it difficult for them to operate outside their national markets. Only liberal ASAs providing for full market access without restrictions on designation, route rights, capacity, frequencies, code-sharing and tariffs between the participating countries could enable the large US players to become more actively involved in the international scene by flying to new markets. The US government therefore started pressing for less restrictive ASAs – known as open skies – which would provide access to all routes between two given countries, by removing the restrictions on designation, capacity, fares and frequency, meanwhile maintaining ownership rule limitations (Toh, 1998). Even these open skies agreements, however, required the airlines designated by each of the states in the bilateral agreement to be 'substantially owned' and 'effectively controlled' by nationals of the designating state.

From 1992 onwards, the United States began to sign a series of open skies bilateral air services agreements with various European and Asian countries, and by December 2012 some 104 open skies agreements had been concluded (Air Transport News, 2012).

Even with complete deregulation, European Union airlines are operating under a regulatory regime divided into two parts – one governing flights within the European Aviation Area, the other governing international aviation outside the European Union, where rigorous tests of nationality are still applied.

3. EU–US Open Skies

One of the main consequences of the EU–US Open Skies agreement is that it enables EU carriers to consolidate and merge and it enhances alliance cooperation. Furthermore, the model of the EU–US Open Skies is very important because it accounts of 60 per cent of global civil aviation output and will set a model for aviation liberalization worldwide (for example open skies agreement between the EU–Canada in 2009).

Through this agreement the US allows the development of multinational EU carriers that are at least 50 per cent owned and are effectively controlled by citizens of any EU member state. In addition, they give some form of seventh freedom rights by allowing a European carrier to establish itself in any other Member State and to operate from any city in the EU to any city in the US.

Furthermore, the agreement makes Heathrow available to any US or EU carrier wanting to fly from there to the US. According to the previous Bermuda II agreement, only four airlines had this advantage (American Airlines, British Airways, United Airlines and Virgin Atlantic). The first EU carrier to grab the opportunity was Air France-KLM which launched a daily service from Los Angeles to Heathrow, code-sharing with Delta, at the end of March 2008. However, they decided to cease the operation in November in order to enhance the Heathrow–New York route. In addition, British Airways launched a route from Paris (Charles de Gaule) to New York. Currently, Paris–New York flights are operated by the OpenSkies subsidiary of British Airways. Additionally, Aer Lingus took advantage of the EU–US open skies agreement and started serving the Madrid–Washington route on behalf of United Airlines.

In exchange for a country signing the Open Skies agreement, the US will grant antitrust immunity to the designated carriers from the two respective states, enabling them to make joint decisions on pricing, scheduling, capacity provision and service quality. Without such immunity airline alliances would be very restricted in terms of what aspects of their businesses they can jointly undertake. For example, oneworld did not have such immunity, mainly because the UK did not have open skies agreement with the US, which limited the ability of oneworld's members to fully exploit synergies in their business. BEcause British Airways and American Airlines did not have antitrust immunity, they were at a disadvantage compared to Lufthansa and United Airlines, members of Star Alliance, and Air France-KLM and Delta, members of SkyTeam. With the EU–US open skies deal, approval of an antitrust immunity between British Airways and American Airlines was of a much higher likelihood and would enable them to cooperate more fully in the oneworld alliance. On the other hand, the EU–US agreement had already seen the UK and US authorities agree to antitrust immunity for bmi and its US Star Alliance partner United Airlines. Finally, in July 2010, British Airways and American Airlines received antitrust immunity.

Another benefit arising from the EU–US agreement is that carriers from both sides are able to make transatlantic investments, but of less than 50 per cent. For example, Lufthansa took 19 per cent stake of JetBlue in February 2008.

In a liberalized market competition increases, therefore airlines are likely to merge or form alliances in order to achieve cost savings, price reduction and output expansion. Through consolidation air carriers would be able to exploit size-related economies, leading to further efficiency gains. Two carriers involved in a merger or an alliance can take advantage of economies of scale by spreading their fixed costs over more passengers. They can also take advantage of economies of scope and achieve added savings by reconfiguring their combined network to connect more flights to certain hub airports and also share costs on marketing and distribution of different types of products. They are able to exploit the advantages of a density economy by achieving higher utilization, e.g. by combining traffic to raise load factor. The costs of production per unit will decrease as the density of the region in terms of geography and production increases. The per-unit cost will be lower.

By facilitating deeper forms of integration between US and EU carriers, liberalization would allow improved price coordination on transatlantic interline routes, for example routes that require passengers to fly on two or more airlines to reach their destination. Within their coordination, each carrier is motivated to set a lower fare in order to increase combined profits. Economists Jan Brueckner and W. Tom Whalen analysed fares on US international routes to assess whether alliances result in lower fares on interline routes as a result of improved price coordination. The authors found that alliance partners charge interline fares that are between 18 and 28 per cent below the prices charged by non-allied airlines on the same route. They concluded that when allied airlines are allowed to share revenues or profits and engage in coordinated fare-setting, consumers benefit from lower interline prices (Brueckner and Whalen, 2000).

It is expected that the agreement will lead to a large increase in passengers travelling annually between the EU and the US. However, Pitfield's research in 2007 showed that open skies agreement does not seem to result in either a significant growth or in increased competition. He argues that the strength of airline alliances could act as a barrier to entry. In addition, Peter Morrell and Barry Humphreys in their study 'Potential impact of the EU/US Open Sky Agreement: What will happen at Heathrow after spring 2008?' (Morrell and Humphreys, 2009) stated that benefits of the EU–US agreement and the impact in terms of traffic growth and lower fares predicted by several studies seem overly optimistic. Airlines may not achieve the level of profitability that they had expected by the agreement because of high prices paid for Heathrow slots, combined with the economic downturn and higher oil prices. They observed a net increase of seven services per day between London and US between the years 2007 and 2008, which represents less than double the rate of annual growth that would be expected. Furthermore, they do not predict similar level of expansion in the future due to slot shortages in Heathrow (Pitfield, 2007).

In addition, huge potential of this agreement has is being restricted by the US cabotage. European carriers can not serve the US market internally and directly compete with the US airlines. However, the US has made a franchise proposal in order to balance the fact that US airlines can freely serve the internal European market. Under the franchise proposal an EU airline can effectively make use of a US carrier's fleet and fly under its own colours, while the US carrier remains under US ownership.

The transatlantic agreement does little to resolve the congestion issues either at airports or regarding the air traffic management. Therefore the increase in traffic between the EU and the US is likely to face difficulties in being served, hence alliances may face restricted growth. Another problem that alliances will have to face is the environmental implications, which will result in further restrictions and charges that the additional traffic is going to generate, despite the new technology implemented on aircraft for lowering the level of CO_2 emissions. For example, currently US airlines strongly object to the introduction of the EU emissions trading scheme for CO_2 emissions.

Giovanni Bisignani, CEO and Director General of IATA stated:

> We are absolutely moving from alliances to consolidations. We have seen success stories of EU (Air France-KLM-Lufthansa) and US (Delta-Northwest) consolidations. I welcome every merger (Qantas-BA). I would like every merger to take place. Consolidation does not certainly create profits and enhance liquidity but gives the opportunity to build synergies that could help to develop aviation. The industry should be able to operate as the other industries (telecommunications, car manufacturers, banks, oil), (*Air Transport News*, 2009a)

Observing the way forward, Daniel Calleja, Director of the Directorate of Energy and Transport of European Commission, has emphasized the need to achieve successful second-stage negotiations until 2010, otherwise either party may serve notice of suspension of some of the rights contained in the original agreement. Europe continuously challenges the US ownership status quo, but the US resists loosening US ownership restrictions and lifting cabotage rights (*Air Transport News*, 2009b).

4. Air Transport after Deregulation and Airline Alliances: A Brave New Reality

The aim of domestic deregulation and bilateral and/or multilateral liberalization was to create 'more competitive air services', or in other words to foster competition among airlines by removing regulatory constraints. The idea was that by promoting an international aviation market with unrestricted entry and competition amongst the most efficient carriers on a multilateral and global level, unprofitable companies would fall by the wayside and this would lead to greater efficiency and, ultimately, falling air fares, higher flight frequency and greater customer choice.

At the same time, domestic deregulation and bilateral and/or multilateral liberalization have changed the rules of the game by allowing entry to some new players, mostly in the form of low-cost carriers (LCCs). LCCs constitute the only credible threat of new competition, although in reality they offer a somewhat different product which does not perfectly substitute the air service of the established airlines. Nevertheless, their entry has been the main factor in driving airfares downward, especially on intra-continental, point-to-point service.

Airline alliances that exploited the opportunities offered by the still partially deregulated international routes often softened competition for partner airlines, and according to some even raised the existing entry barriers. As Mr Michael Gremminger of the European Commission put it, certain alliances seem to have been formed not only to achieve the necessary scale to compete globally – but also for less noble causes: to control certain markets, especially those protected by entry barriers, to preside over slots at congested airports and to exploit traffic rights. Seen from a regulator's point of view, airline alliances have made it possible for the partners they link together to enjoy a kind of monopoly. This view is strongly contested by the airlines themselves, and this conceptual dispute has been at the heart of the controversial relationship between members of alliances and antitrust authorities for the past ten years.

Airline alliances have enabled carriers to increase their dominance at their respective hubs. In major hub airports, there is a clear tendency towards single-carrier dominance, which means that significant portions of the passenger movements are accounted for by a single airline. In 9 of the top 25 airports, the dominant carrier is responsible for over 50 per cent of the enplanements at the airport (OECD, 2006).

Another important consequence of the airline crisis is that both governments and the public – at least in Europe – have accepted that airlines should cease to be regarded as national status symbols. Most countries are now convinced they are better off with a smaller airline securely harboured in an alliance – or better still in a merger – than with a larger airline that guzzles away at public money to survive. People have given up their 'romantic' ideas, to use Gantelet (European Commission) and Windmuller's (IATA) expression, about their national flag carriers, especially when these are poorly managed and do not provide the service expected of them. Consumers nowadays are much more interested in reliable service and lower fares. Chris Tarry (CTAIRA), however, raises an interesting point when he mentions that the demise of an airline is a rather complicated issue, as it may bring about a financial blow to the main airport of the country of the flag carrier, with the resulting consequences in employment, procurement in the area, etc. Brussels is an often cited example of a hub airport that was badly hurt by the demise of its main client, Sabena. This is especially true for the airports of Central Europe, where the proximity of many airports may eventually lead, in the eventuality of mergers, to their closure or downgrading. This may explain why the Dutch government and KLM management have insisted on making certain in the Air France-KLM deal that Amsterdam airport will retain all its services for a period of ten years.

Another issue that airlines and alliances will have to deal with are the developments in aircraft technology. Large aircraft such as the Airbus A380, destined to be used on international high-density routes, will expand capacity and reduce costs by raising the overall number of passengers per flight. At the same time, new smaller aircraft such as Airbus A350s and Boeing 787s will allow competing alliances or merged airlines to provide direct services on long-distance, thin city pairs such as San Francisco and Copenhagen or Hong Kong and Oslo. Today, no airline would dream of undertaking such a service, because it would require a Boeing 777 the carrier would be unable to fill.

5. Reasons Pushing Airlines to Merge

Global airline alliances have developed in response to the increasing liberalization of aviation markets and the drive for efficiency in international commercial activity. However, with deregulation and liberalization completed and airline alliances formed and established, carriers have still been facing a number of serious problems: overcapacity, reduced yields and uncompressed costs. After the events of 9/11 almost all airlines began to carry out massive capacity adjustments and cost-cutting programmes, personnel and wages reductions, but regardless of these measures most of them have been unable to prevent losses. Under the emerging realities and new threats, the need to limit costs and achieve efficiencies becomes even more compelling.

Alliances were promising to bring down costs, but the true magnitude of their effects in this sense appears to have been small. Analysts and airlines believed that alliances would achieve efficiency through synergies, since many of the elements which are present in a merger also appear in alliances, at least in theory. However, a decade of alliance cooperation has shown that while alliances may have succeeded in increasing traffic and expanding networks they do not seem to have scored highly in the area of cost reduction and operational synergies. Perhaps the main reason they have fallen short of the mark is due, as Chris Tarry (CTAIRA) believes, to a reluctance of small carriers to integrate, because of fears that becoming too dependent on alliances is tantamount to being bought out. Airline managements started wondering whether alliances are the right medium to deliver on costs and whether mergers and consolidations is the only way to secure a sustainable future for the airlines and a viable and competitive airline system. The European Commission officially supports the view that consolidation among its majors may be inevitable and even desirable if they are to retain a leading role on the world stage.

The attractiveness of mergers lies precisely in the promise they hold, that is to deliver the efficiency that may result from commercially powerful and financially viable airlines as well as from a far more competitive and supple global airline industry.

Given the novelty of the phenomenon, there is still no widely and/or officially accepted definition of airline cross-border mergers. Mohamed Elamiri of ICAO (International Civil Aviation Organization) has defined cross-border mergers as 'acquisitions or operational integration of airlines of different countries under a single holding company'.

The main difference between alliances and mergers has to do with ownership and control: mergers lead to a single entity, whereas alliances do not affect legal ownership and are based on revenue-sharing and capacity-coordination with loose links, with each company remaining independent.

Airlines, like all global companies today, need to be fast, efficient, profitable, flexible, adaptable and future-ready, with a strong market position. As most experts agreed in a series of interviews, the main drive behind mergers in the airline industry is 'control', whereas alliance partners have to 'negotiate, compromise, convince'. According to Gilles Gantelet, of the European Commission, the main drive behind mergers is the need for 'full operational and commercial control' in order 'to face the global situation at the global market', because in a merger you have 'one strategy, one executive board and you are developing all the products in the same way'. Mergers seem the only safe way to achieve synergies and secure a single strategy. Mohamed Elamiri, of ICAO, believes mergers provide 'a better control of operations', whereas Michael Gremminger, of the European Commission, expressed the opinion that the main reason behind mergers is the need to achieve efficiency by reducing the cost base and improving the network. The main difference between alliances and mergers is that although they actually have the same aims, mergers offer a better level of control and achieve efficiency more quickly. A merger potentially allows 100 per cent consolidation, while in alliances integration is much more limited.

In other words, mergers can better achieve the objective for which alliances were formed. Alliances do not seem to have provided an efficient enough vehicle for the growth in earnings which the capital markets could require. Furthermore, such control could reduce airlines' vulnerability to economic and competitive pressures and increase their flexibility to design a range of services. As Chris Tarry suggested, airlines need to come up with 'more tailored products' that will provide customers with choice, customization and flexibility. The three alliances essentially differ only in identity and membership – otherwise they can be seen to be pursuing the same objectives. From a product point of view there is no real reason to prefer one alliance/airline over the other, since they are competing with similar tools and offering comparable products. Chris Tarry has often stressed that a strong financial performance will only be achieved when airlines align their products to the price passengers are prepared to pay. A merged entity with one strong management structure which decides 'we are going in that direction' seems to be in a better position to proceed towards redesigning products and services.

Another survey (Iatrou, 2006) indicates that the major problems alliances are facing could be solved through mergers. Management difficulties, governance hurdles, troubles in identifying a common ground – all such factors limit partners' ability and flexibility to respond to a changing, dynamic market.

There is no real precedent in cross-border mergers which enables researchers and analysts – or the carriers themselves – to assess their potential. The only close alternative is the background of US consolidation, and this is because of the sheer size of the US domestic market and that of the airlines involved in it. But US carriers did not have to bother, when merging, with issues such as national identity, state ownership or the possibility of losing traffic rights. Still, the merger experience in the US has certainly brought about two important results: market power produced through the exit of a competitor and cost savings from scale and scope economies. In the US, airline mergers also resulted in greater concentration at a reduced number of large hubs and the closing down or reduction of activity at smaller hubs, reallocating flights to the large hub. A merger wave in Europe could lead to the eventual closing down of second-tier hubs such as Zurich, Rome, Copenhagen or Vienna. US major airlines operate multiple hubs but they are geographically dispersed throughout the US, which enables them to serve different flows with each hub. Ordinarily, it makes sense for a merged company to focus on one hub, avoiding the hurdles of managing two airports situated as closely together as Paris is to Amsterdam, or Frankfurt is to Munich. But European airports suffer from capacity restrictions, the territory is densely populated and the closing down of airports seems less viable.

6. Airline Executive Opinion about Airline Alliances and Mergers

In 2006 the executives of the airlines that are part of the alliances were asked to express their opinion regarding alliance performance, the potential evolution and development of cross-border mergers and how such developments can influence not only their own airline but also the future air transport structure.

All executives agreed, at the time that the survey was conducted, that the aim of alliances was the creation of a global network that serves many destinations without the airlines incurring extra cost. In this way, passenger traffic increase was observed in combination with the creation of a global FFP (Frequent Flyer Program). This has resulted in a rise of revenues and a corresponding reduction in operating cost. Even if this cost reduction has not been achieved yet, or achieved at the desirable degree, it is certainly one of the major future goals of alliances. In essence, the airlines can through alliances, as they state, 'satisfy customer demand with more global products' and achieve 'global presence without global cost structure'. In parallel, alliances permit airlines to increase their competitiveness and gain market share.

In general accession and participation in the alliances is considered successful. While one-third of participants rate their alliance cooperation as 'excellent', the rest believe that the course and operation of the alliances has so far been 'good'.

Almost all participants believe that joining the alliance grouping has led to an increase in traffic, load factor and revenue. While two-thirds of participants expressed the opinion that fares have not been influenced, the rest declared that fares on routes operated jointly by partners have increased. A large proportion of participating airlines affirm that costs have registered some reduction.

5.1 Airlines' Perception of the Drive Towards Consolidation

Airline executives were also asked to assess how the airlines view the potential of mergers, that is, to identify whether they believe that there is indeed an imminent wave of cross-border mergers and a consequent restructuring of the air transport system. While 75 per cent of the airlines say that consolidation is slowly but surely gaining momentum, only 13 per cent believe that there is a strong drive towards a more consolidated industry.

Despite the fact that the respondents agree that mergers do gain momentum, 37 per cent stated that alliances will stay as they are and 26 per cent believe that alliances will continue to develop and move to closer integration without proceeding to mergers. These answers may seem contradictory on the surface, but on a deeper level they may simply mean that mergers and alliances will co-exist. Finally, 17 per cent say that the merged airlines will focus more on mergers than alliances. This low percentage clearly shows that mergers will not disturb the smooth functioning of alliances and there will be no reaction from the other partners in the alliance. However, what is apparent from these answers is that further integration, whether it takes the form of mergers or of closer cooperation between allied partners, is the new rule of the game in the air transport arena.

Alliances play a very important role in the strategic plans of airlines, but what is much more intriguing is that 36 per cent also believe that mergers are a crucial part of their strategy and 6 per cent of the carriers give precedence to mergers over alliances as a significant strategic move. That gives us 42 per cent, which means that almost half of the airlines participating in alliances are, one way or the other, contemplating the possibility of mergers. At the same time, 36 per cent of the respondents believe that cross-border mergers are somewhat more marginal and put a premium on alliances, and this finding is confirmed by the fact that 65 per cent mention that cross-border mergers are a choice for the airlines and not a necessity.

5.2 The Impact of Alliances and Cross-border Mergers on Airline Performance

Mergers as a form of airline cooperation largely outweigh alliances in the production of positive effects on airline operations. The only category in which alliances present more positive aspects is economies of scope and more specifically in the subcategory of new market growth; a plausible finding because a merged carrier, no matter how large the merged airlines are, cannot match the network reach of a eight, nine, or sixteen-member alliance. After all, the main drive behind alliance formation was, as the airlines themselves stated, the desire to expand their geographic scope of their network so as to achieve global scale (Iatrou, 2004). With regard to hubbing, the results do not give a clear precedence in one form of cooperation over the other. Alliances thus far operated in such a way as to take the most out of the hubbing system and the resulting economies of density, with each partner feeding traffic to the other. A merger will probably entail network integration, even network rationalization, which may mean that the overall network structure may change and some airports lose connections while others have more connections. Although it is much more efficient to close a duplicating hub and concentrate resources on the stronger one (Duedden, 2005), it is not certain that the merged airline will reduce the number of hubs: other aviation experts claim that mergers would lead to an increase in the use of the hubs of the two merged carriers.

The most positive aspects of mergers appear, according to the respondents, in the area of economies of scale: corporate planning synergies followed by financial, IT and maintenance synergies. It seems that a strategic alliance does not allow the same type of cost synergies as a full merger. This result clearly shows that alliances have not been able to produce significant benefits in the area of cost synergies. None of the three major alliances have yet engaged actively in joint purchase of aircraft or in joint investments in IT systems and customer databases, all those cooperation aspects that promise cost-effectiveness. All respondents agree that only cross-border mergers can more effectively bring about scale benefits and synergies as well as better-quality decision making.

It is not the positive but the negative aspects of mergers that are far greater than those of alliances, with the reduction of personnel being the most negative, according to the respondents. Labour costs are certainly the single most important component of total airline costs, accounting for 25–30 per cent of total operating costs, and all airline managements would like to reduce it but they know very well that, given the unique leverage airline unions enjoy, this cannot be achieved without serious social and even political reaction. The second most adverse negative aspect of mergers is the threat posed to the existence of the acquired airline, as the mergers of two airlines would result in the demise of the smaller carrier. Next in ranking as the most negative aspect of mergers is the reduction of traffic in certain hubs, because it is expected that the new merged entity will concentrate on exploiting the traffic out of the hub that will be the most profitable for the new company. Interestingly, the idea of brand dissolution does not appear to be considered a serious problem by the respondents, whether in the case of alliances or mergers.

5.3 The Possible Evolution of Mergers

Most of the respondents (44 per cent) consider that in the short term (1–2 years, 44 per cent of respondents) and medium term (3–5 years, 52 per cent) new cross-border merger will be effected.

The most serious problems a merger initiative might face, according to the respondent airlines, would arise from the competition authorities followed by labour issues. Mergers will certainly raise regulatory concern in terms of potential adverse impact on competition and consumers. Competition authorities will consider mergers on the case by case basis taking into account the current network structure of the prospective merger partners as well as the actual and potential competition on the routes involved. Another issue they will certainly consider and will bend their reaction to consolidation is whether an airline – whether flag carriers or not – can survive without being acquired.

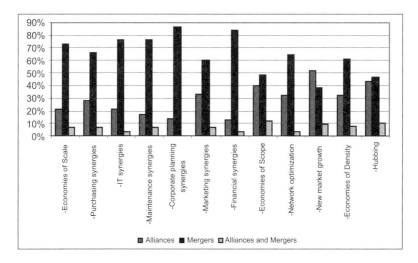

Figure 13.1   Benefits of alliances and cross-border mergers on airline operations

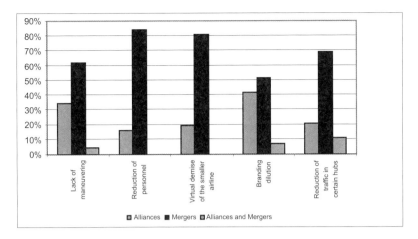

Figure 13.2   Negative impact of alliances and cross-border mergers on airline operations

Even though a cross-border merger between smaller- or medium-sized airlines would give the merged partners the possibility to strengthen the position of the new entity in the market and inside the alliance, 70 per cent of the respondent airlines have stated that cross-border mergers will take the form of a major airline acquiring a smaller one. Thus it seems that it is the big players that pull the strings of the consolidation game. This does not mean, however, that the possibility of a 'confederation' of smaller regional carriers should be excluded.

Fifty-nine per cent of the respondents believe that cross-border mergers would strengthen the position of the merged carrier inside the alliance, but whether this will affect the other airlines of the alliance depends on the case by case basis: this is why 28 per cent mention that there will be no impact. Alliances are made up of a significant number of allies, thus any merger will not significantly alter the balance of power. After all, majors were and are the centres of gravity of all three alliances and it is they who will determine the course of both alliances and mergers.

Although cross-border mergers so far, such as those between Air France/KLM and Lufthansa/ Swiss, have been effected between airlines that did not participate in the same alliance, 68 per cent of the respondents stated that future cross-borders will be effected between airlines belonging to the same alliances and such mergers will result in the strengthening of the merged entity within the alliance. It is certainly easier for two airlines that already cooperate on a bilateral level within the alliance to proceed to merger, as they have built some level of trust and compatibility of operations. Furthermore, alliance membership seems to a large extent to have been fixed, thus no major realignments are expected.

As far as the question of multilateral cross-border mergers is concerned, answers diverge greatly: only 55 per cent of the respondents dismiss such a possibility. Some of the respondents that rejected this eventuality stated that the creation of a cross-border merger between two airlines is already too challenging a task and difficult to achieve, which makes even more difficult to visualize mergers of three carriers. Efforts within the framework of a tripartite attempt would be further hampered by the challenge of naming the new entity and by the concerns of competition authorities and the increased cultural differences.

More than two-thirds of the airlines said that there will be cross-continent mergers: 75 per cent of the airlines did not accept the statement that alliances are hard to govern, lack promised synergy benefits and have to a large extent failed. From the analysis of the questions it seems that alliances have failed to deliver the expected synergies only on the scale level. Airlines are proceeding to mergers not out of dissatisfaction from the performance of alliances, but because they want to attain growth and have better control over their operations.

6. Conclusion

Global airline alliances have developed in response to the economic demand of global markets and to the opportunities provided by deregulation and liberalization initiatives. These cooperative agreements initially took the form of simple code-share agreements; but as deregulation started to take effect in the European Union, a Single Internal European Aviation Market was created and the US authorities pursued more 'open' and less restrictive bilateral air services with other countries, the horizontal links between carriers took the form of deeper and more complex cooperation.

International alliances appear to be crystallizing around three major international groupings and these have expanded to include virtually all the major European and US airlines flying across the North Atlantic as well as an increasing number of airlines in other continents.

There are many that have argued that airline alliances are simply a second-best solution, the only viable alternative, because had it not been for the regulatory constraints which make a carrier's traffic rights dependent on the nationality of its ownership, airlines would have moved to mergers which seem to hold the promise of efficiencies, synergies, cost reductions, scale benefits and better control over operations. With a worsening financial environment and with restrictive bilateral agreements being gradually replaced by multilateral agreements between groups of countries, usually on a regional level, airlines are reassessing their priorities and considering whether mergers and consolidations is the only way to secure a sustainable future for themselves and a viable and competitive airline system.

It seems that there will be some merger activity within the next five years on an intra-regional level – and more probably within EU – but the early stage of consolidation does not allow predictions on how the future landscape will look. It is probably going to be a long process.

What is certain is that whether the air transport industry moves toward greater liberalization or not, the impact of such liberalization will depend as it did in the past on the continuous interaction between airlines – and their strategies – and the public bodies and the regulatory framework they impose.

References

Air Transport News (2009a) Giovanni Bisignani, Director General and CEO – IATA. http://www.airtransportnews.aero/analysis.pl?id=616&keys=, updated 1 September 2009.

Air Transport News (2009b) Daniel Calleja, Director Air Transport Directorate – European Commission. http://www.airtransportnews.aero/analysis.pl?id=586&keys=, updated 1 September 2009.

Air Transport News (2012) *United States, St. Christopher and Nevis Sign Open-Skies Aviation Agreement.* http://www.atn.aero/article.pl?&id=33836.

Brueckner, J. and Whalen, T.W. (2000) The price effects of international airline alliances. *Journal of Law & Economics*, 43, 2, 503–545.

Duedden, J.-C. (2005) Consolidation and its implications for long haul direct travel. Given at the ninth Annual ATRS World Conference in Rio de Janeiro, Brazil, 2005. Unpublished, available from 7 July 2005.

IATA (2009) *World Air Transport Statistics*, 53rd edn. Montreal: International Air Transport Association.

Iatrou, K. (2004) *The Impact of Airline Alliances on Partners' Traffic*. Bedford: Cranfield University.

Iatrou, K. (2006) Airline Choices for the Future: From Alliances to Mergers. Given at the 10th Annual ATRS World Conference in Nagoya, Japan, 2006, unpublished, available from 28 May 2006.

OECD (2006) *Airline Mergers and Alliances*. http://www.oecd.org/dataoecd/1/15/2379233.pdf, updated 1 October 2006.

Morrell, P and Humphreys, B. (2009) The potential impacts of the EU/US Open Sky Agreement: What will happen at Heathrow after spring 2008. *Journal of Air Transport Management,* 15, 72–77.

Pitfield, D.E. (2007) The impact on traffic, market shares and concentration of airline alliances on selected European–US routes. *Journal of Air Transport Management*, 13, 192–202.

Toh, R. (1998) Toward an international open skies regime: advances, impediments, and impacts. *Journal of Transportation World Wide*, 3, 1, 61–71.

Chapter 14

Economic Effects of Antitrust Immunity for Airline Alliances: Identification and Measurement

Volodymyr Bilotkach and Kai Hüschelrath[1]

1. Introduction

The last ten to fifteen years witnessed a substantial increase in the size and depth of airline alliances in international air transportation. From the size perspective, more and more individual airlines have decided to join one of the three remaining global airline alliances – Star, SkyTeam, or oneworld. For example, while the respective alliances were founded between 1997 and 2000 by in sum 14 airlines, the number of member airlines grew to 52 in 2010 – 27 in Star, 13 in SkyTeam and 12 in oneworld. This growth is reflected in basic transportation statistics. For example, in 2008 the three 'mega alliances' together transported about 59 per cent of the roughly 2,271 million airline passengers world-wide.[2] Airline alliances have particularly high market shares (at least 70 per cent, based on network capacity) on intercontinental markets, such as the market between North America and Europe.

From the depth perspective, members of all three global alliances receive increasingly more freedom in coordinating various aspects of joint operations, including scheduling and pricing decisions, as well as the right to form revenue-sharing joint ventures in international markets. On the transatlantic market in 2008, for example, seven out of ten flights involved at least one airport used as a hub by an airline participating in airline alliances with so-called antitrust immunity.[3] The granting of antitrust immunity by the respective antitrust authorities is a precondition for the implementation of airline agreements, which involve cooperation on essential competition parameters such as pricing or scheduling.

Given the identified increase in the size and depth of international airline cooperation, the question whether such a development is in the interest of the consumer immediately suggests itself. Although it is undisputed that consumers gain from airline alliances, it is unclear whether the observed increase in the degree of cooperation is necessary to reap the largest part of these benefits. Furthermore, a detailed understanding of the competitive effects of granting airline immunity is pivotal for an overall assessment of the respective costs and benefits for society.

Against this background, this chapter aims to develop an understanding of the economic effects triggered by granting antitrust immunity to airline alliances. Differentiating between a competitive effects assessment and an efficiencies assessment, our approach not only identifies the key economic factors but also provides guidance on how to measure their respective sizes in antitrust investigations.

---

1   We are grateful to an anonymous reviewer for valuable comments and suggestions. Parts of this chapter make use of earlier research of both authors published in Bilotkach and Hüschelrath (2011) and Bilotkach and Hüschelrath (2012).

2   Data sources: International Civil Aviation Organization, websites of Star Alliance, SkyTeam and oneworld.

3   Data source: US Department of Transportation T-100 Dataset for International Airline Services.

The chapter is organized as follows. The second section gives a brief introduction into the general economics of airline alliances, followed by a characterization of the competitive effects of antitrust immunity in the third section. This section differentiates between the general effects on key competition parameters on the one hand, and specific theories of anti-competitive effects of antitrust immunity on the other. The subsequent fourth section focuses on the identification and measurement of efficiencies triggered by antitrust immunity. As efficiency arguments are usually brought forward by the alliance members in antitrust investigations as a counterweight to potential anti-competitive effects, an analysis of potential efficiencies triggered by the respective agreement is a compulsory part of an integrated assessment of the economic effects of antitrust immunity. The fifth section concludes the chapter by reviewing the key results and identifying further research needs.

2. Airline Alliances: Characterization and Economic Effects

An important precondition for an assessment of antitrust immunity for airline alliances is an understanding of the key business motivations and key economic effects of airline alliances generally. The following two sections briefly characterize both complexes.

2.1 Characterization of Airline Alliances

The airline industry – defined here as commercial scheduled passenger transportation – deals with moving people and their luggage from point A to point B. The production process is rather complex and involves many aspects such as ticketing, luggage handling, passenger catering, fuelling, air traffic control, and aircraft maintenance. The airlines differ in many ways, from pricing policies, the fleet mix and the degree to which they choose to vertically integrate the various parts of the production process. Yet there is one thing in common for all the carriers: no single airline's network encompasses all possible 'point A to point B' combinations. This fact forces many passengers to 'interline' or change an airline during their journey.

Given these specifics of air transport, the first joint ventures between airlines on deregulated markets have appeared as a way to tackle this interlining problem more efficiently, making the 'joint' product more attractive to the customer compared to other possible interlining options. At the perhaps most primitive level, the passenger would be more attracted to an interline service – other things being equal and assuming no online service is available – which allows them to check their luggage through to the final destination, thus not having to worry about the checked bags beyond the customs requirements.

An advanced form of cooperation among airlines is called code-sharing. Code-sharing refers to including an airline's flights into the partner airlines' schedules. Thus, an airline via a code-sharing arrangement is able to enlarge its network without having to service additional flights. Moreover, it can sell tickets for the interline flight as its own. For this arrangement to work, however, the partner airlines need to set up a mechanism for placing the interline passengers on each other's flights. There are, roughly speaking, two such mechanisms. First, airline A can sell the ticket for the entire journey involving airlines A and B, and pay airline B a certain fee accepting the interline passenger (so-called 'free flow' or 'free sale' agreement). Second, airline B can appropriate some of the seats on its flight for airline A to sell at the price it sees fit – a set-up known as the 'blocked space arrangement'. Doganis (2001) states that code-sharing agreements may or may not involve blocked space arrangements. Code-sharing-related joint ventures are often complemented by agreements to jointly use airport facilities (e.g., gates). Additionally, sharing of customer loyalty (i.e., frequent flier) programmes is very common.

A further degree of cooperation is reached if the alliance partners enter into some form of revenue sharing and joint price-setting arrangements that typically also imply a joint coordination of scheduling (i.e. departure times and flight frequencies). Although such partnerships are increasingly being referred to as 'joint ventures' in the literature and the business community, the discussion in this section shows that revenue-sharing arrangements are only one of the many forms of cooperation among airlines. In fact, given the price-fixing nature of such agreements, antitrust laws typically prohibit the implementation of this kind of joint venture and granting antitrust immunity is a precondition for a legally sound implementation of such strategies.

2.2 Economic Effects of Airline Alliances

A number of studies, both theoretical and empirical, evaluate the economic effects of international airline partnerships.[4] Most of these studies analyse motives for and effects of a single airline alliance, outside of the broader context. The issue of competition between alliances is considered by Brueckner and Whalen (2000), Bilotkach (2005), and Flores-Fillol and Monquer-Colonques (2007). The general conclusion from those studies is that airline consolidation benefits interline passengers due to the complementary nature of the product and the removal of double marginalization. However, as soon as consolidation decreases competition, consumers may lose depending on the relative sizes of the cost-saving effect and the market power effect.

Generally, the size of the cost-saving effect is influenced to a great extent by the realized benefits of higher traffic due to cooperation between airlines reflected in the so-called economies of traffic density (i.e. falling average cost with higher load factors). Furthermore, airline alliances are expected to realize further alliance-specific efficiencies due to cost reductions via shared back office functions, maintenance facilities and operational staff as well as joint purchasing and marketing advantages through integrated frequent flyer programmes. These incremental advantages for consumers need to be traded off against the market power effect of airline consolidation. This effect is basically driven by the possibility that airline alliances might eliminate horizontal intra-alliance competition, thereby causing higher fares and a reduced choice on certain routes (see, e.g., Reitzes and Moss, 2008). The existence and magnitude of the market power effect is dependent on various competition parameters. For example, as argued by Oum et al. (2000) the degree of overlap between the respective networks typically is a key determinant because the higher the overlap, the more severe are the competition concerns and the more likely are price increases as a consequence of cooperation. Furthermore, the participating airlines may use alliances to reduce competitive pressures by facilitating collusive behaviour or restricting entry through the implementation of foreclosure strategies (see Section 3 for a detailed assessment).

Empirical analyses of the effects of international airline alliances have been offered by Oum et al. (1996), Park and Zhang (2000), Brueckner and Whalen (2000), Brueckner (2003), Whalen (2007) and Bilotkach (2007c).[5] All of these papers confirm that airline alliances benefit interline

---

4   Theoretical models of international airline consolidation include studies by Oum, Park and Zhang (1996), Park (1997), Brueckner (2001), Brueckner and Whalen (2000), Heimer and Shy (2006), Bilotkach (2005, 2007a, 2007b), Barla and Constantatos (2006), Chen and Gayle (2007) and Flores-Fillol and Monquer-Colonques (2007).

5   There is also an older set of empirical papers available which study the effects of airline alliances on airline costs, revenues or profits, passenger traffic, passenger fares, convenience and service quality. However, given the significant changes in the degree of cooperation among airlines we omit a detailed discussion of the

passengers by offering lower fares. Park and Zhang also find evidence for increasing market power of the alliance members at their hubs, even though they suggest that this effect is offset by the cost savings that the alliance brings about. While finding that alliances decrease interline fares, Brueckner and Whalen (2000) fail to observe a statistically significant increase in fares due to airline consolidation where such appears to decrease the number of competitors.

In general, the consensus of research on the economic effects of airline alliances is that interline partnerships benefit consumers thanks to the removal of double marginalization and economies of traffic density. These benefits might partly come in the form of lower ticket prices, but could also include higher flight frequency, more destinations within easy reach, or shorter travel times. All these factors tend to have a stimulating effect on demand and traffic growth. However, what needs to be investigated closer in the following are the relative costs and benefits of several degrees of cooperation between airlines. In particular, an understanding needs to be developed as to whether granting antitrust immunity is necessary to realize the key benefits for consumers, or whether lower degrees of cooperation can reach comparable benefits levels (while avoiding the incremental costs).

3. Airline Alliances and Antitrust Immunity: Characterization and Competitive Effects

In this section, the analysis is narrowed down from airline alliances in general to granting antitrust immunity for airline alliances in particular. In addition to a brief characterization of antitrust immunity in Section 3.1, an overview of the key competitive effects – discussed in the theoretical and empirical literature – is provided in Section 3.2. Complementary to such a foray though academic research, Section 3.3 focuses on the treatment of competitive effects in a real antitrust immunity investigation, namely the most recent investigation of the immunity application of members of SkyTeam at the US Department of Transportation.

3.1 Characterization of Antitrust Immunity

Airline partnerships in their modern form started appearing in the early 1990s, with airlines coordinating their handling of interline passengers via agreements of various types. The most common and policy-relevant form of such agreements involves code-sharing, whereby flights are assigned the partner airlines' flight number(s), and are effectively incorporated into those carriers' networks. As already explained above, such services are oftentimes jointly marketed by the partner airlines, and are sometimes supplemented with blocked-space arrangements, whereby a certain number of seats on the flight are sold directly by the partner airline. Multi-airline code-sharing agreements led to emergence of the global airline alliances, each of which started from the partnership between a US and an EU carrier. Oneworld developed around the partnership between American Airlines and British Airways; Skyteam evolved from the Delta Air Lines–Air France alliance; and the current Star Alliance is the expanded United Airlines–Lufthansa partnership.

Looking for more freedom to coordinate various aspects of their joint operations, the partner airlines sought antitrust immunity, or the right to jointly set fares throughout their international networks, as well as to establish revenue-sharing agreements. Generally, antitrust immunity represents a higher degree of cooperation than code-sharing agreements, and changes the airlines'

results here as they might not be that relevant for contemporary alliances (see generally Button and Drexler, 2006, and Morrish and Hamilton, 2002, for overviews).

incentives with respect to the acceptance of interline passengers. While code-sharing – either with or without antitrust immunity – does not technically preclude an airline from accepting interline passengers from the non-partner airlines, immunity makes market foreclosure more likely. An airline accepting an interline passenger on its flight both increases its revenue and lowers the per passenger cost via economies of traffic density. Antitrust immunity, when supplemented with a revenue-sharing agreement, effectively induces joint profit maximization,[6] and makes accepting interline passengers from outside airlines an inferior choice. Even in case of antitrust immunity without explicit network-wide revenue sharing,[7] partner airlines can share the revenue from the interline fares in such a way as to factually foreclose the market for outside carriers. Effectively, antitrust immunity allows the partner airlines to set 'transfer prices' for the interline itineraries within the alliance. As an example, suppose airline A can feed its traffic to either carrier B or C and the total fares for the A–B and A–C interline trips are the same. Then, if airlines A and B have antitrust immunity, they can split the interline fares in such a way that airline A obtains a disproportionately large share of the total interline fare for feeding its passengers to its partner carrier B. This arrangement can be reciprocal, so that airline B will recoup the losses by receiving the disproportionately large share of the total fare for feeding traffic to airline A. This kind of 'transfer price' can eliminate the non-alliance airline C as a competitor.

Note that with simple code-sharing the above-described agreement is not feasible, as explicit coordination of prices for the interline trips is not allowed. Besides, it should be noted that the non-acceptance of the interline passengers from carriers outside of the immunized alliance increases the respective airlines' cost due to lower load factors, again working through economies of traffic density.

3.2 Competitive Effects of Antitrust Immunity

Given the brief characterization of antitrust immunity, this section focuses on its key competitive effects. According to the International Competition Network (2006: 16), competitive effects analysis aim at assessing 'whether [an agreement] is likely to harm competition significantly by creating or enhancing the .. firm's ability or incentives to exercise market power, either unilaterally or in coordination with rivals'. With respect to airline alliances, the following sections will address the effects of antitrust immunity on key competition (i.e. prices and non-price) parameters, complemented by a closer look at specific theories of potential anti-competitive effects of antitrust immunity.

3.2.1 General effects on key competition parameters   Any investigation of the economic consequences of a certain business strategy requires an identification and assessment of the key competition parameters in the respective industry. In the airline industry, the effects on market price and market output are typically of the greatest concern: however, as shown in the following, non-price parameters cannot be ruled out from an integrated assessment.

---

6   For more details on revenue-sharing agreements within airline alliances, see Brueckner and Proost (2010).

7   With revenue-sharing, partner airlines may split revenue not only from the interline, but also from the online (i.e., single-airline) passengers.

3.2.1.1 Effects on market price

The most imminent effect of airline alliances is the effect on market price. The basic line of reasoning found in the literature is that cooperation between airlines, given the complementary nature of the product, removes double marginalization, thereby reducing the price for the interline trip as compared to the no cooperation scenario. The double marginalization argument has also been used as a rationale for antitrust immunity.

The key benefits of airline cooperation are straightforward to show in a very simple airline network in which airlines 1 and 2 provide complementary services, e.g. a trip from city A to city C via city B without a direct flight option, where airline 1 is serving the AB route, and airline 2 operates on the BC route. In such a framework, it is straightforward to show theoretically that moving from no cooperation to full cooperation creates benefits for both firms and consumers due to the removal of double marginalization. However, this general argument would work just as well in case of a complete merger instead of the immunized alliance. The trick of applying the above double marginalization argument to airline partnerships lies in the fact that they are modelled in the same way as mergers. However, it is not correct to treat code-sharing without antitrust immunity as the case of no cooperation. In fact, as shown by Bilotkach and Hüschelrath (2011), code-sharing without antitrust immunity may lead to equivalent pricing outcomes. Although the argument admittedly is derived in a very simple network structure, it suggests that antitrust immunity cannot automatically claim the removal of double marginalization as incremental benefit as this goal might already be reachable by lower degrees of cooperation.[8]

A more realistic airline network for the study of the price effects of antitrust immunity is a partially overlapping network, i.e. airline 1 is providing services between cities AB and CB while airline 2 flies between cities CB and BD. Focusing on the overlapping route CB, allowing coordination between the partner airlines would eliminate competition on this route while still bringing the identified benefits to interline passengers identified above. In his seminal theoretical paper, Brueckner (2001) investigates the relative sizes of the two effects and finds that although the welfare impact on consumers is generally ambiguous the welfare increases in the interline markets are likely to offset the potential negative effects in non-stop markets.

Although this theoretical result suggests likely positive welfare effects of airline coordination in a partially overlapping network, a still preferred option would be to keep the benefits of cooperation in interline markets while avoiding the elimination of competition on the overlapping routes. In general, a regulator concerned about reduced competitive interaction on the overlapping part of the airlines' networks following a cooperative agreement by the airlines basically has three options. First, antitrust immunity to the partnership can be denied. Second, antitrust immunity can be granted anyway (e.g., as the benefits are expected to dwarf the costs) and third, antitrust immunity can be granted, but made applicable only to joint setting of the interline fares. The latter scheme is known as carve-out set-up, as routes within the overlapping part of the alliance partners' network are 'carved out' of the deal.

On the surface, carve-outs appear to be an attractive option. However, recent theoretical research by Brueckner and Proost (2010) shows that carve-outs may yield lower welfare than simple

---

8   However, it has to be kept in mind that this result relies on a very simple network structure and ignores possible additional cost efficiencies triggered by antitrust immunity (but not by simple code-sharing agreements). Nevertheless, the caution in claiming the entire benefits of the elimination of double marginalization to antitrust immunity is justified by Bradshaw and Patel (2009: 7) who argue that '[p] redictably, though some reduction in negative double marginalization externalities may possibly be achieved through code-sharing, full antitrust immunity ensures its elimination as it makes carriers truly indifferent between carrying a passenger itself versus a partner'.

immunized alliances where airline partners set up a revenue-sharing agreement. The difference between the non-immunized alliance and the revenue-sharing partnership is effectively that with the latter partner airlines enjoy more freedom over pricing and cost aspects of their operations. This basically suggests that the real issue in point is whether joint operation of the alliance partners brings higher benefits via cost synergies and economies of density on the overlapping part of the network relative to the cost it may impose via increased market concentration and joint price-setting.

From an empirical perspective, Brueckner's (2003) research shows that antitrust immunity decreases fares for interline trips to a greater extent than the code-sharing without such immunity. Whalen (2007) confirms these findings in a time-series analysis of the effects of international airline partnerships. In contrast, Bilotkach (2007c) suggests, admittedly by analysing a smaller sample of routes than Brueckner (2003), that antitrust immunity does not decrease fares by more than consolidation via code-sharing already does. Additionally, an empirical study by Wan, Zou and Dresner (2009) found that cost synergies are large enough on parallel routes to avoid price increases as a consequence of joint price-setting. Interestingly, they find that oneworld business class fares are lower than fares between non-alliance hubs. Given the fact that oneworld do not have antitrust immunity to coordinate fares, this result can be interpreted in the sense that alliances without antitrust immunity may produce the greatest consumer benefits. Most recently, an econometric study by Willig, Israel and Keating (2009) challenged the results of a US Department of Justice (DOJ) study on the price effects of antitrust immunity. Contrary to the results of the DOJ, the authors are unable to find – across a range of model variations – any evidence that antitrust immunity causes an increase in fares on gateway-to-gateway routes. Part of the explanation can most likely be seen in the incentives to expand capacity on gateway-to-gateway routes after receiving antitrust immunity and the thereby triggered downward pressure on price.

3.2.1.2 Effects on non-price parameters
It is a well-established fact that price is not the only product characteristic taken into account by consumers in making their choices. Firms therefore typically also compete in non-price characteristics and usually work hard to differentiate their product from those of their competitors, aiming at charging a premium for the associated distinguishing features. With respect to passenger airline markets, frequency and convenience of service are arguably the most important (and closely related) non-price features consumers will care about. Higher frequency of service means lower schedule delay, and better scheduling coordination between partner airlines implies more benefits for interline passengers via shorter total travel time, other things equal. Airlines also use their frequent flier programmes to create horizontal product differentiation via brand loyalty.

The issue of choice of non-price characteristics under airline joint ventures has received limited attention in the literature. Bilotkach (2007a) offers a model which allows a purely complementary alliance to choose prices and the degree of scheduling coordination; Lederman (2007) provides some empirical evidence on demand effects of international frequent flier programme partnerships. Modelling choice of price and frequency is generally a complex affair. We actually do not see how interline partnerships will affect individual members' frequency choice beyond the obvious implication that higher traffic due to a joint venture may yield higher frequency of service on spoke-to-hub routes, creating additional benefits to passengers travelling point-to-point on those markets.

The issue of frequent flier programme partnerships which go hand in hand with airline alliances appears much more interesting for at least three reasons. First, where such partnerships are alliance-wide, airlines entering a global alliance may end up sharing frequent flier programmes on markets where they compete with each other (e.g., United and US Airways – both Star Alliance members – on the US domestic market). Recent empirical evidence (Bilotkach, 2009) suggests that such competing partners will reduce their frequency of service as a cost-cutting measure in response to an otherwise higher substitutability between their services. Second, there is strong evidence (Lederman, 2008) that airlines flying into airports dominated by their frequent flier programme partners are able to get under the umbrella of what is known as the airport dominance effect. For practical purposes this means that frequent flier programme partnerships may increase average fares for flying into some important airports. Third and perhaps most important, the size of alliance-wide frequent flier programmes creates an additional potentially important entry barrier. In this respect, we refer not only to the need for any new alliance to attain certain scale to be able to compete with the incumbents. Frequent flier programme partnerships within the alliance can create entry barriers on individual airlines' home markets because new entrants will have to either attain certain scale, or join one of the global alliances. Alternatively it can, like Ryanair in Europe, decide not offer any loyalty programme and to solely rely on attracting customers via lower fares.

3.2.2 Specific theories of anti-competitive effects of antitrust immunity Probably the biggest drawback of the models that have been used in the literature to address effects of airline partnerships is that they tend to focus on benefits of the removal of double marginalization and economies of traffic density on one or several markets, without putting the markets being modelled into a broader context. Given an increasing role of the only three global airline alliances remaining in the industry and the tendency among the responsible authorities to allow more coordination between alliance members, it is crucial to see what we can find in that broader context. Therefore, the following sections concentrate on the derivation of more specific theories of potential anti-competitive effects triggered by antitrust immunity.

3.2.2.1 Potential for market foreclosure
Market foreclosure involves denying actual or potential competitors' access to either an essential input or customers, and thereby preventing them from competing. The tools in the foreclosing firm's toolbox include vertical integration with competitors, refusal to deal, exclusive arrangements and price discrimination. In either case, the visible outcome of such interaction is lower quantity (market share) of the firm being foreclosed on.

The possibility of foreclosure in airline partnerships has been suggested in models of Chen and Gayle (2008) and Bilotkach (2007a). Both papers effectively model alliances with antitrust immunity and profit-sharing. In either model, where an airline can choose from a variety of potential alliance partners, the airline not chosen as a partner is unable to carry its passengers beyond its network. Think of a simple airline network in which route AB is offered by airlines 2 and 3 while the BC route is only provided by airline 1. In such a framework, airline 1 has the possibility to foreclose the A–C market to airline 3 upon setting up the alliance with airline 2. To see why and how this can be a rational strategy, suppose that before the creation of the alliance airline 1 charges the same sub-fare or interlining fee to either airline 2 or 3. After the partnership between airlines 1 and 2 is concluded, airline 1 will decrease the fee for accepting the interline passengers from airline 2 (due to the removal of double marginalization). Given this advantage, in theory, airline 1 does not need to increase the interlining fee for airline 3 for that carrier to lose market share and the change in relative sub-fares or interline fees can already yield foreclosure of the A–C market to airline 3. In practice, however, foreclosure can also be facilitated either via a direct refusal to deal, or by setting prohibitively high fees for accepting interlining passengers. Doing so might be perfectly rational for the alliance members, as it not only increases their revenue but also lowers their cost via economies of traffic density (and increases the rivals' cost for the same reason).[9] Whatever the exact mechanism, the end result will be higher traffic by partner airlines with antitrust immunity and lower traffic by the outside airlines on routes to/from the partner airlines' hub airports.

As noted by Reitzes and Moss (2008), foreclosure will be more successful the higher the gateway's reliance on connecting traffic and the fewer the options for channelling passengers via alternative hub airports. They also suggest that the current structure of the transatlantic airline industry appears more conducive to foreclosure at EU rather than US gateways, due to the relative dominance of the individual EU countries' flag carriers on the respective domestic markets. Furthermore, although foreclosure may not reduce overall competition between alliances (as they will still channel their interline passengers via respective hubs, and will not technically exit any city pair markets), non-stop competition on some important routes may be reduced. This fact is indeed acknowledged by some industry experts (Kasper and Lee, 2009), however, they claim that any losses due to foreclosure are more than offset by higher traffic through alliance members' main hubs. Whether this is so is an empirical question. One thing we can say for sure is that the likelihood of market foreclosure as we described it here is the highest in case of the revenue-sharing joint venture (requiring antitrust immunity).[10]

3.2.2.2 Potential for collusion

Generally and *ceteris paribus*, the potential for collusion among firms or alliances increases with shrinking numbers of competitors as it is easier to reach and maintain a tacitly or overtly formed agreement. The general argument is not new to the economic analysis of the airline industry and often studied in direct relation to the theory of multi-market contact.

For example, for the domestic US airline industry there exists substantial evidence consistent with the so-called mutual forbearance hypothesis. This hypothesis states that a firm will be less reluctant to compete aggressively on any given market against the firms with which it also competes on other markets (Bernheim and Whinston, 1990). An empirical investigation by Evans and Kessides (1994), for example, found that fares are higher in city pair markets served by carriers with extensive inter-route contracts. The authors argue that airlines seems to follow a 'golden rule', i.e. airlines refrain from initiating aggressive pricing actions on a given route for fear that competitors might react in other jointly contested routes. Furthermore, Gayle (2008) investigates the question of whether the effects on price and traffic levels triggered by the approval of the Delta/Continental/Northwest code-share alliance supports a collusive behavior hypothesis. In 64 per cent of the cases, the evidence fails to support this hypothesis.

Taking these results for the US domestic airline industry into account, it can be argued that the higher the extent of cooperation within airline alliances, the higher the extent of multi-market contact in the global airline industry. Additionally, the recent inclusion of more than one US airline into the same alliance certainly has the potential to aggravate the general issue.[11] However, the

---

9   On the margin, if a connecting passenger comes from within your alliance rather than from the outside, your load factor increases, and that of your rival falls, which – due to economies of traffic density – increases the difference between your per passenger cost and that of your rival.

10   Based on an enlarged network structure, an empirical investigation by Bilotkach and Hüschelrath (2013) finds for the sample period from 1992 to 2008 that granting antitrust immunity leads to a decrease in flight frequency of up to 6 per cent by the non-alliance carriers serving a newly immunized hub. The effect on passenger volumes is even greater (a drop of up to 8.5 per cent), suggesting excluded airlines switch to smaller aircraft and/or end up with lower load factors on their services to the newly immunized hubs.

11   In 2009, the announcement of Continental and United to build a common IT platform that will serve as a backbone of their joint operations in international markets triggered a discussion in US media

current literature on airline partnerships does not pay particular attention to the extent of multi-market contact and possible negative effects on competition intensity between the three global alliances.

3.2.2.3 Impact on network development

The issue of the impact of airline partnerships on network development boils down to the question of whether alliances affect any individual airline's incentive to enter with non-stop services. The above discussion on foreclosure suggests that airlines will have less incentive to enter into markets involving hubs of competing alliances. As for entry into other markets, recent literature suggests both theoretically (Bilotkach, 2009) and empirically (Dunn, 2008) that an airline will be less likely to enter with a non-stop service on a market where it already is present with a one-stop service. Alliance membership increases the number of such markets, thereby hindering development of individual alliance members' networks. Whether the effect will be the same with or without antitrust immunity is not clear. To the extent we can say partnership with antitrust immunity involves a higher degree of commitment on part of the individual members, we will be able to claim it also hinders entry of the member airlines with new non-stop services.

3.3 The Treatment of Competitive Effects in Antitrust Immunity Investigations: The Case of Members of SkyTeam

Given the discussion of key competitive effects of airline alliances and antitrust immunity from a theoretical and empirical perspective, this section investigates the treatment of competitive effects in recent antitrust immunity investigations. Due to the fact that there is currently no published final decision from the European Commission on the antitrust immunity applications of any of the three global alliances, the forthcoming sections concentrate on the applications and decisions of the responsible authority in the United States, the Department of Transportation (DOT).[12] In particular, the most recent investigation of the immunity application of members of SkyTeam is reviewed in greater detail.[13] In addition to a characterization of the alliance members' perspectives on competitive effects as documented in their joint application for approval of antitrust immunity,

---

as to whether such a platform facilitates collusion in national markets. 'The IT cooperation according to Continental and United is only for international endeavors, but that is hard to believe. The algorithms and inside information to create a blended IT system goes far beyond the limited antitrust immunity currently in force' (Leocha, 2009: 1).

12   As a consequence of the Airline Deregulation Act of 1978, the Antitrust Division of the DOJ is responsible for the review of domestic airline mergers and acquisitions. Granting antitrust immunity to agreements between US and foreign carriers is, however, the responsibility of the US Department of Transportation. The statutory basis can be found in the 1979 International Air Transportation Competition Act, which allows international inter-carrier agreements to be filed before the DOT for approval and antitrust immunity. For a detailed assessment, see Bilotkach and Hüschelrath (2011).

13   Given the comparable sizes and depths of the joint venture agreements of the three remaining global alliances, it can be expected that the general competitive effects and efficiency arguments brought forward are quite similar. Therefore, it appears to be sufficient for a high-level characterization of the respective analyses to concentrate on one particular alliance application. Given the fact that only the most recent Star and SkyTeam applications have already been decided (and approved), those two alliances are the prime candidates for a detailed assessment. In the following, the most recent SkyTeam approval will be characterized in greater detail, as this decision of the DOT refers to the earlier Star investigation and decision (DOT-OST-2005-22922; Submission, Nov. 4, 2005; Final Order, Order 2007-2-16, Feb. 13, 2007), and therefore incorporates the key arguments from this investigation as well. Furthermore, the case of SkyTeam is particularly interesting,

the section also gives an overview of the authority's perspective and analysis of the competitive effects reflected in the documented investigation and decision respectively.

3.3.1 The joint applicants' perspective　An obvious starting point of a study on the role of competitive effects in antitrust investigations is an analysis of the perspective of the alliance members in their joint application. Although it is fairly obvious that alliance members have incentives to water down potential anti-competitive effects (and to overestimate potential efficiencies), the arguments brought forward nevertheless have to address the key potential competition problems in order to increase the credibility of the entire application. In other words, given the previous experiences with immunity investigations of the DOT, it would not be a sensible move to ignore potentially anti-competitive effects completely in the application.

In its most recent investigation, SkyTeam applied[14] for antitrust immunity in 2007, and in May 2008 the DOT decided[15] to grant members of the SkyTeam alliance four-way antitrust immunity (see the following section for more details on the case). In its joint application, the applicants generally argue that they have entered into the alliance agreements – including the four-way joint venture agreement[16] – to 'expand and deepen their coordination, strengthen their transatlantic services, expand and fully develop their global network, enhance their ability to compete with other global airlines, and exploit synergies resulting from more complete integration among the joint applicants' (DOT-OST-2007-28644, p. 16). Unsurprisingly, a large part of the entire application concentrates on the exposition of arguments why an approval and grant of antitrust immunity for the alliance agreement would be in the public interest and would produce substantial benefits (see Section 4.2 for a detailed assessment). Subsequently, the applicants argue why they think that the grant of antitrust immunity will not substantially reduce or eliminate competition in any relevant market. The assessment differentiates between the following relevant markets: global alliance competition, US–Europe/Africa/Middle East/India Market, US–Europe, country pairs, city pairs and US domestic competition and concludes with respect to the transatlantic market that

> there are few non-stop overlap routes. Given the highly competitive transatlantic market for non-stop and connecting passengers (made even more competitive by the EU.-U.S. Open Skies Agreement), there will be no reduction in competition as a result of the proposed Alliance. (DOT-OST-2007-28644, p. 50)

Investigating the arguments for several of the identified relevant markets a little closer, with respect to global alliance competition, the applicants argue on the one hand that combining Northwest/KLM (the two key members of the former 'Wings' alliance) with SkyTeam does not eliminate a global alliance, basically because Wings has never been a global or branded alliance. In fact, the lack of global scope and reach led KLM to merge with Air France and become a member of SkyTeam (DOT-OST-2007-28644, p.52). Second, the inclusion of Wings into SkyTeam would permit the applicants to compete more effectively against the other major alliances and therefore will enhance inter-alliance competition as a whole (DOT-OST-2007-28644, p. 51).

---

as its first application for antitrust immunity was denied by the DOT (DOT-OST-2004-19214; Submission, September 24, 2004; Final Order, Order 2006-2-1, February 6, 2006).

14　DOT-OST-2007-28644 (Submission, June 28, 2007). All page numbers of the quotations in the main text in this section refer to the Submission.

15　DOT-OST-2007-28644 (Final Order), Order 2008-5-32 (May 22, 2008).

16　The four-way joint venture between Delta, Northwest, Air France and KLM is the core of the entire SkyTeam application.

With respect to the US-Europe market, the applicants argue that this market 'is intensely competitive and will be even more so as a result of the EU-U.S. Open Skies Agreement' (DOT-OST-2007-28644, p. 55). In particular, the applicants not only identified at least 8 US and 40 foreign scheduled passenger carriers currently provide scheduled service between 33 airports in the US and 55 airports in the EU, but also presented evidence of several new carriers that entered the market recently. They conclude that intense competition will continue 'as airline and alliances compete on fares, service, schedules, and routings. For example, transatlantic passengers have the option to travel to, from, and through a large number of gateways on each side of the Atlantic' (DOT-OST-2007-28644, p. 56). They further argue that a grant of immunity for SkyTeam 'will not materially change this competitive balance' (DOT-OST-2007-28644, p. 57), as no single carrier or alliance will have a dominant share of the market.

On the country pairs level, the applicants bring forward the argument that the proposed alliance will not reduce or eliminate competition in relevant country pairs because there is significant non-stop, one-stop, online and interline service between the US and the Netherlands, France, Italy and the Czech Republic so the applicants will not be able to impose and sustain supra-competitive prices or reduce service below current competitive levels (DOT-OST-2007-28644, p. 64). The large homeland market shares as such are not considered as anti-competitive, particularly in those markets where open entry permits other competitors to offer non-stop and online options to travellers (DOT-OST-2007-28644, p. 62).

On the city pairs level, the applicants identify overlapping non-stop transatlantic service on three routes (Atlanta–Amsterdam, Detroit–Paris, New York–Amsterdam). However, the applicants argue that much of the traffic on the respective routes is flow traffic and therefore, local Origin&Destination (O&D) passengers in these markets have a substantial number of one-stop connecting options (DOT-OST-2007-28644, p. 65). In order to avoid the creation of unnecessary inefficiencies, the applicants strongly suggest that no routes should be excluded from the grant of antitrust immunity (see Section 4.2 below for a detailed assessment).

Finally, with respect to US domestic competition, the applicants bring forward the argument that the agreement will not affect the US domestic market as it only refers to international routes and Delta and Northwest will remain fully accountable under US antitrust laws with respect to those markets (DOT-OST-2007-28644, p. 66). In order to ensure that international coordination has no anti-competitive effect on domestic markets, Delta and Northwest developed detailed antitrust compliance protocols in which they '(1) restrict the exchange of competitively sensitive information regarding domestic service; (2) restrict joint conduct with respect to domestic service; and (3) require periodic antitrust compliance training, and to submit to the Department for review any revisions to the antitrust protocols' (DOT-OST-2007-28644, p. 67).

3.3.2 The authority's perspective   Given the overview of the competitive effects assessment by the members of SkyTeam in its most recent successful application for antitrust immunity, the consequential next step is an investigation of the economic arguments brought forward by the DOT. Focusing again on SkyTeam, a first landmark investigation out of several applications of members of SkyTeam was the first attempt to receive antitrust immunity for the consolidation of core SkyTeam (Delta/Air France) and Wings (Northwest/KLM) in 2004.[17] The investigation was of particular importance for at least two reasons. First, it was the first time that two large airline alliances planned to merge, and members of both alliances applied for antitrust immunity. Second, it was the first time that two US airlines applied for immunity on international markets

---

17   DOT-OST-2004-19214 (Submission, September 24, 2004).

within the same alliance (although forced to continue competing in the US domestic market). Given the applicants' failure to show that sufficient public benefits would be produced by the agreement, together with the fear that the close cooperation on international markets might have spillover effects on US domestic competition, the DOT first denied antitrust immunity for the enlarged SkyTeam alliance.[18] Anticipating the introduction of the US–EU open skies agreement, and following the development of a more sophisticated integration concept, SkyTeam members reapplied[19] for antitrust immunity in 2007 and the DOT (in its Show Cause Order DOT-OST-2007-28644[20]) in April 2008 'tentatively find that the proposed alliance is consistent with the public interest, will produce public benefits, and will not substantially reduce competition' (DOT-OST-2007-28644, p.1).

From a procedural perspective, the review of immunity applications by the DOT has to proceed in two steps. The first is approval of the agreement under 49 U.S.C. § 41309, for which it has to be shown that the agreements are not adverse to the public interest and do not violate the statute (DOT-OST-2007-28644, p. 4). Factually, following the content of the statute, the DOT can even approve agreements that substantially reduce or eliminate competition as long as it can show that they are necessary to meet a serious transportation need or achieve important public benefits.

If the agreements are approved, the second step is a grant of immunity under 49 U.S.C. § 41308. This statute gives the DOT the authority to exempt airlines from the antitrust laws to the extent necessary to allow the transaction to proceed, provided that the DOT determines that the exemption is requires by the public interest (DOT-OST-2007-28644, p. 5). A compulsory part of such an overall assessment is a competitive effects analysis in which the DOT has to answer the essential question whether the alliance agreement is likely to substantially reduce competition such that the joint applicants would be able to exercise market power. To determine whether this is likely to be the case, the DOT primarily considers

> whether the alliance would significantly increase concentration, whether the alliance raises concerns about potential anticompetitive effects in light of other factors, and whether entry into the market would be timely, likely, and sufficient either to deter or counteract a proposed alliance's potential for harm. (DOT-OST-2007-28644, p. 5)

Given this delineation, the DOT separates its investigation into the US–Europe market, country-pair markets, city-pair markets and domestic competition. With respect to the US–Europe market, the DOT analyses the non-stop market shares among competitors offering services between the US and the countries of the EU and basically concludes that the agreement does not significantly increase overall market share or change the competitive landscape. The same conclusion is basically drawn from the analysis of country-pair markets for which the DOT concludes that the high identified market shares (of up to 79.8 per cent in the US-Netherlands market) do not reflect some important aspects of the competitive environment (DOT-OST-2007-28644, p. 12) and should therefore not generally foreclose a possible clearance of the alliance agreement.

---

18   DOT-OST-2004-19214 (Final Order), Order 2006-2-1 (February 6, 2006). Other reasons to deny the initial request for antitrust immunity were the potential reduction of competitive pressures in gateway-to-gateway markets and the foreclosure of competitor's access to alliance hubs.

19   DOT-OST-2007-28644 (Submission, June 28, 2007).

20   The following analysis of the decision is largely based on the Show Cause Order (DOT-OST-2007-28644, April 9, 2008) as it provides a much more detailed assessment of the key arguments compared to the relatively brief Final Order. All page numbers of the quotations in the main text in this section refer to the Show Cause Order.

On a city-pair level, the DOT identified the above mentioned three overlapping non-stop markets on which both Delta and KLM operate. However, the DOT acknowledges that these overlaps inevitably happen when two global network carriers combine their operations and that

> potentially serious anticompetitive effects of reducing competition on hub-to-hub routes may be offset to some extent if the affected city pairs are served on a connecting basis by competing carriers. Additionally, efficiencies created by the transaction in other markets may ... be considered if an appropriate remedy is not available to preserve the benefits of the transaction. (DOT-OST-2007-28644, p. 9)

A discussion of whether carve-outs can be considered as such an appropriate remedy is provided in Section 4.2 below as part of a discussion of immunity-specific efficiencies.

The final category of the DOT investigation refers to the potential effects of the agreement on US domestic competition. Given that the proposed alliance includes two US carriers – Delta and Northwest – that compete in domestic markets, the DOT is concerned

> about the potentially serious competitive harm that may result from the immunized cooperation of two U.S. carriers, even if the cooperation is limited to the provision of foreign air transportation. However, because we are not willing to arbitrarily limit the number of U.S. carriers that may join an immunized alliance, we must assess the risk of harm on a case-by-case basis, and weigh it against the potential public benefits. (DOT-OST-2007-28644, p. 11)

Given the antitrust protocols submitted by Delta and Northwest together with the absence of any specific competitive harm, the DOT decided that it is in the public interest to allow both Delta and Northwest to participate in the proposed alliance (DOT-OST-2007-28644, p. 11).

3.4 Identification and Measurement of Immunity-specific Competitive Effects

Based on the identification of competitive effects of antitrust immunity from a merely academic perspective in Section 3.2, and the review of experiences with the most recent SkyTeam investigation by the DOT in the United States in Section 3.3, this subsection aims at bringing both complexes together to derive a framework for an assessment of competitive effects of antitrust immunity. An initial comparison of the main insights of both sections already suggests that such an endeavour is challenging. While the academic research identifies various channels of how granting antitrust immunity may harm competition, the investigation of the DOT largely seems to concentrate on an analysis of concentration figures and rather anecdotal evidence. As a consequence, it cannot be ruled out that the DOT investigation misses important aspects in its competitive effects analysis. However, given the fact that the insights of academic research often turn out to be difficult to implement in practical antitrust investigations – last but not least due to the often severe time and data constraints – the demands of both sides have to be taken into account in the development of an implementable framework for an assessment of antitrust immunity applications by airline alliances.

Thinking about the general structure of such a framework, it is proposed to subdivide the analysis into two stages: identification and measurement. In the first stage, theoretical, empirical, and case-specific arguments are applied to identify the channels of possible anti-competitive effects. In the second stage, empirical techniques need to be applied to receive ball park figures on the likely dimension of the identified competitive effects.

With respect to the *identification of competitive effects*, the existing merger guidelines can provide guidance on the necessary steps of such an investigation. Although airline alliances apparently differ from airline mergers,[21] the antitrust literature tends to argue that alliances or joint ventures can factually be investigated as mergers as soon as competition in consumer markets is directly affected (which certainly is the case with airline alliances).[22] The general structure of the merger guidelines in the US and the EU is very similar and reflected in the *Merger Guidelines Workbook* that was compiled by the International Competition Network (2006: 14ff.). This workbook separates a merger assessment into the following seven stages: 1. Market definition; 2. Market structure and concentration; 3. Unilateral effects; 4. Coordinated effects; 5. Market entry and expansion; 6. Efficiencies; and 7. Failing firm.

The first step focuses on the definition of the relevant market(s),[23] followed by an assessment of market structure and concentration in the second step. With respect to airline alliances, the description of the DOT investigation, on the one hand, showed the various levels of relevant market (e.g., networks, countries, cities) that need to be investigated to capture all key types of competitive effects. On the other hand, the investigation showed that the interpretation of concentration measures (derived on the basis of market delineation) might not be particularly helpful as these figures do not reflect some important aspects of the competitive environment.

The third step concentrates on the possible anti-competitive effects of horizontal mergers and differentiates between non-coordinated (unilateral) effects and coordinated effects. With respect to the unilateral effects, the horizontal merger guidelines of the European Commission, e.g., mention six factors which may influence whether significant unilateral effects are likely to result from a merger: the merging firms have large market shares, the merging firms are close competitors, the customers have limited possibilities of switching suppliers, the competitors are unlikely to increase supply if price increases, the merged entity is able to hinder the expansion by competitors and, finally, the merger eliminates an important competitive force. With respect to airline alliances, the academic contributions analyse especially specific channels of unilateral effects while the DOT in its SkyTeam investigation tries to investigate the practical relevance with a clear focus on market share and 'switching supplier' analysis (in the sense of inter-alliance competition).

With respect to the non-coordinated effects, the Horizontal Merger Guidelines of the European Commission, e.g., mention six factors which may influence whether significant coordinated effects are likely to result from a merger: reaching terms of coordination, monitoring deviations, deterrent

---

21   Technically, an airline alliance should be considered as a vertical merger rather than a horizontal merger. However, as the non-stop route overlap typically is the major concern in alliance investigations, the horizontal merger guidelines are – in this respect – the most relevant source. As soon as exclusionary effects analysis comes into play (as described in Section 3.2.2.1), 'vertical' or 'non-horizontal' merger guidelines certainly are a valuable source to guide the respective assessment.

22   The typical joint venture from an antitrust perspective is formed by companies with complementary resources to pool their research and development efforts. In such joint venture projects not only are the created efficiencies often obvious and undisputed but also the assessment of competitive effects is often obsolete given the pre-market characteristics of the agreements. However, as soon as joint venture projects include agreements with respect to product development or even the marketing of the products, an antitrust assessment of such joint ventures becomes virtually identical to that of a merger. See generally Werden (1998) for a detailed treatment.

23   Market definition in airline markets usually refers to routes or bundles of routes. Furthermore, the time sensitiveness of passengers, airport substitution or substitution between other transport modes must be taken into account. See Straiger (2001) for a detailed description of the policy followed by the European Commission.

mechanism, reaction of outsiders, evidence of past coordination and, finally, the structural features of the markets concerned. With respect to airlines, the academic as well as the DOT investigation acknowledge the general relevance of the argument; however, both do not provide a detailed thinking on the identification of such an effect.

Following an assessment of the competitive effects, the guidelines propose to study the presence of countervailing buyer power and the analysis of entry (likelihood, timeliness and sufficiency of entry). Both aspects are important for putting the results of the analysis of market concentration and the competitive effects into perspective. Subsequently, merger-related efficiencies need to be investigated by focusing on benefits to consumers, merger specificity and verifiability (see Section 4.1 for a detailed assessment). Finally, the sixth step of the framework outlines special conditions for mergers which involve a 'failing firm'.

The identification of the various components of competitive effects needs to be complemented by a *quantification* of these effects. Although it is fairly obvious that an exact calculation of the effects cannot be expected, the responsible authority should at least try to get an idea of the broad dimension of the competitive effects. Generally, quantitative techniques such as price correlation analysis, stationarity analysis, price elasticity analysis, critical loss analysis, switching analysis, simulation, price/concentration analysis, shock analysis or bidding studies have the potential to help in the derivation of estimates for the sizes of the competitive effects (see Lexecon 2003 for a general overview). Although most of these methods apparently have not been used in the SkyTeam investigation, the controversial DOJ/DOT investigation of the Star Alliance saw a couple of high-level econometric studies on both sides which try to investigate the price effects of antitrust immunity in non-stop overlap markets (see especially Willig et al., 2009).

Based on the importance of the identification and the measurement of competitive effects, Table 14.1 presents an overview of the respective identification and measurement strategies for two different levels of analysis: Network/Country and City-Pair. Generally, the key aim of Table 14.1 is to provide a basic framework for an assessment of the competitive effects. The actual (relative) sizes of the respective types depend on the characteristics of the alliance under investigation. Furthermore, it must be remembered that every identification and measurement of competitive effects has to be complemented by an analysis of immunity-specific efficiencies achieved by granting antitrust immunity. Only an identification and measurement of these potential benefits allows a comparison of the overall costs and benefits of granting antitrust immunity and therefore provides a well-founded basis for the decision of the antitrust authority.

4. Airline Alliances and Antitrust Immunity: Efficiencies

Although it is virtually undisputed that consumers gain from airline alliances, the high degree of cooperation facilitated by granting antitrust immunity demands a detailed assessment of the incremental costs and benefits. While the competitive effects analysis in the preceding section focused on the potential incremental costs of granting antitrust immunity, this section concentrates on a complementary assessment of the incremental benefits. A sound investigation of these so-called immunity-specific efficiencies is important for at least two reasons. First, as efficiency arguments are usually brought forward by the alliance members in antitrust investigations as a counterweight to potential anti-competitive effects, an analysis of potential efficiencies triggered by the respective agreement is a compulsory part of an integrated assessment of the economic effects of antitrust immunity. Second, an antitrust authority that does not have a clear picture on the respective efficiencies triggered by different degrees of cooperation will have a hard time evaluating the welfare consequences of the implementation of suitable approval conditions (that aim at healing the competition concerns without unnecessarily reducing the incremental efficiencies achieved by the cooperation).

Given the strategic importance of a sound assessment of efficiencies, this section aims at identifying and quantifying immunity-specific efficiencies. As already explained in Section 3.4 above, the assessment is guided by the belief that antitrust immunity applications can factually be treated as mergers. Therefore, the forthcoming Section 4.1 identifies the building blocks of an antitrust assessment of merger efficiencies, followed by an overview of the treatment of efficiencies in recent antitrust immunity investigations of members of SkyTeam in Section 4.2. The assessment of efficiencies is closed by a discussion of the identification and measurement of immunity-specific efficiencies in Section 4.3.

Table 14.1   Identification and measurement of immunity-specific competitive effects

Level of analysis	Identification and measurement
Network/country	Identification: theoretical and empirical research suggests that higher prices and/or lower quality can be caused by alliance members to foreclose markets for interlining passengers; (2) reduced inter-alliance competition due to 'mutual forbearance'; and (3) reduced individual airline's incentives to enter new non-stop routes. The SkyTeam investigation suggests that (A) inter-alliance competition might be enhanced through the creation of three large global alliances; (B) a large number of potential competitors (together with evidence on successful entry attempts) might mitigate potential anti-competitive effects; and (C) large homeland market shares should not per se be viewed as anti-competitive as they do not reflect some important aspects of the competitive environment
	Measurement: (1/A/C) descriptive analysis of the extent and scope of overlap of networks (non-stop service overlap, overlap where only one party operates a direct flight, overlap between indirect services), simulation of the effects of changes in the alliance structure on competition; (2/B/C) assessment of various criteria which ease coordination among airlines/alliances, e.g. analysis of competitor reactions to price changes, customer switching behaviour, changes in market shares, stability of costs and demand, analysis of new routes/product introductions; (3/C) assessment of the gateway's reliance on connecting traffic and the options for channelling passengers via alternative hubs; simulation of the effect of foreclosure strategies on competition
City pair	Identification: theoretical and empirical research suggests that the routes with a non-stop service overlap become monopolies, potentially causing harm for consumers in the form of higher prices and/or lower quality; indirect services as potential (lower-quality) substitute gain importance with increasing travel distances; the SkyTeam investigation suggests that only a relatively small number of non-stop overlap routes exist and that an analysis of concentration measures is typically of limited value as these figures do not reflect some important aspects of the competitive environment (especially the various connecting options)
	Measurement: simulations, natural experiments or econometric analyses (e.g. regression analysis, demand estimation, critical loss analysis, price correlation analysis, switching patterns) focusing on the price and quality effects of either a '2 to 1 merger' or 'immunity routes vs. non-immunity routes' on the respective (overlapping) non-stop routes and connecting routes; assessment of the significance of potential competition (e.g. can a new service generate sufficient point-to-point and connecting traffic to reach minimum efficient scale?, is aircraft/airport capacity available?)

4.1 Characterization of Efficiencies

This section aims to provide an overview of an antitrust assessment of merger efficiencies. A characterization of the types of efficiencies in Section 4.1.1 is followed by the identification of efficiencies in the everyday work of an antitrust authority in Section 4.1.2.

4.1.1 Types of efficiencies   The antitrust literature has studied merger efficiencies quite intensively. One universal finding of these studies is that the direct effect of a reduction in a product's marginal cost on its own price is an important channel of merger efficiencies. However, there is also consensus that merger efficiencies can be delineated more broadly. While some efficiencies may indeed translate directly into marginal cost reductions (e.g. economies of scale), others rather lead to a reduction in fixed costs (e.g. R&D expenditures). The question whether only the former or both types of efficiencies should be considered within a merger efficiencies assessment ultimately depends on the underlying welfare approach followed by the respective antitrust authority. Additionally, the realization of efficiencies differs with respect to the time window in which they are scheduled to materialize. For example, while a reallocation of production can be accomplished fairly quickly, efficiencies in R&D might only materialize in the medium or long term by, for instance, improving new product development.

    In practice, merger efficiencies can take many forms. This is reflected in the development of several taxonomies of merger efficiencies. For example, Kolaski and Dick (2002) provide a taxonomy of possible efficiencies based on the traditional differentiation between allocative efficiencies, productive efficiencies, dynamic efficiencies, and transactional efficiencies. Röller et al. (2001: 42ff.) differentiate between a typology based on the concept of the production function (rationalization, economies of scale, technological progress, purchasing economies and slack) and another typology based on the alternate distinctions of real cost savings vs. redistributive (or pecuniary) cost savings, fixed costs vs. variable costs, firm-level efficiencies vs. industry-level efficiencies and, finally, efficiencies in the relevant market vs. efficiencies in other markets. Finally, Evans and Padilla (2003) point out that every merger efficiencies assessment has to consider both supply-side efficiencies (referring to the cheaper production of existing products) and demand-side efficiencies (referring to new or better products, such as increased network size or product quality). This separation will be of particular value below in the assessment of immunity-specific efficiencies.

4.1.2 Identification of efficiencies   Given the identification of possible types of efficiencies, the major problem for an antitrust authority with respect to merger efficiencies is to evaluate their plausibility, their likelihood of realization, and their likely effects on post-merger competition. From a microeconomic perspective, it is straightforward to identify substantial informational advantages on the side of the merging firms about the existence and size of merger efficiencies. Amir et al. (2004) show in a Cournot oligopoly context that firms have an incentive to 'overestimate' the efficiencies achieved by the merger with respect to both the antitrust authority (in order to get the merger through), and the rivals (in order to influence their beliefs on the competitiveness of the new merged entity). They therefore conclude that antitrust authorities should be cautious to accept cost-reducing arguments, as there is a high probability that the estimated efficiencies are smaller or even non-existent in reality, leading to higher prices in the post-merger world. The results of empirical studies which show a very moderate success of horizontal mergers in terms of realized efficiencies support such an argument (see, e.g. Gugler et al., 2003, analysing mergers between 1981 and 1998). As a consequence, antitrust scholars such as Farrell and Katz (2006) have argued that it may be optimal to follow a pure consumer welfare approach in merger control as some kind of counterweight to the firm's informational advantages and to possible lobbying activities during the merger control procedure (see Neven and Röller, 2006).

The question of an appropriate standard for 'acceptable' merger efficiencies is – among others – assessed by Farrell and Shapiro (2001). Having in mind their own theoretical finding that not just a reallocation of production but real merger synergies – that is, the integration of specific and hard to trade assets which create output/cost configurations that would not be feasible otherwise – are necessary to avoid welfare-reducing horizontal mergers, they propose a simple, three-step decision tree to extract merger-specific synergies. The first stage of the framework investigates whether the merged entity would likely achieve the claimed efficiencies. Given the fact that every merger purports to be motivated by substantial efficiencies, an antitrust investigation has to assess whether such calculations are sound and plausible. If this is found to be the case, the second step asks whether the merging firms would likely achieve the efficiencies unilaterally. This question tries to find out whether the efficiencies are merger-specific or not. If this is found to be the case, in a third step it is asked whether the efficiencies could be achieved unilaterally. Only if such a question is denied, can we call the merger-specific efficiencies synergies, which are relevant for an antitrust assessment following the Farrell–Shapiro approach. Applying the framework would, for instance, allow the conclusion that economies of scale are typically not accepted as synergies, because they can be achieved unilaterally by 'simply' extending the production capacities (see Farrell and Shapiro, 2001, for a discussion of additional implications).

Based on these general theoretical considerations and on practical experiences (see especially Everett and Ross, 2002, for an overview), three conditions for 'acceptable' merger efficiencies have been identified (see International Competition Network, 2006: 64):

1. *Verifiability* – only those efficiencies which have a high probability of realization within a reasonably short period after completion of the merger will be taken into account.
2. *Benefit to consumers* – some share of the expected benefits of the merger efficiencies are likely to be passed on to consumers in the form of lower prices. Factually, this condition rules out a pure total welfare standard as appropriate for merger control.
3. *Merger specificity* – the efficiency gains must be merger-specific, that is, they are unlikely to be produced or available absent the merger.

Only efficiencies which satisfy all three conditions should be considered during (or alternatively following) the competitive assessment of a proposed horizontal merger. However, as reported by Scheffman (2004) for the United States, the practical role of efficiencies is more understood as a sort of 'sliding scale', in which the stronger the anti-competitive case, the less weight is given to efficiencies. In other words, in practice, there seems to be no weighting of the magnitude of efficiencies against the magnitude of anti-competitive effects.

4.2 The Treatment of Efficiencies in Antitrust Immunity Investigations: The Case of Members of SkyTeam

Before an identification and measurement of immunity-specific efficiencies is commenced, it adds value to cast an eye on the treatment of efficiencies in recent antitrust immunity investigations. As already stated in the section on the competitive effects above, due to the fact that there is currently no published final decision from the European Commission on the antitrust immunity applications of any of the three global alliances, the forthcoming sections concentrate on the applications and decisions of the responsible authority in the United States, the Department of Transportation. In addition to a characterization of the alliance members' perspectives on immunity-specific efficiencies as documented in their joint application for antitrust immunity, the section also gives an overview of the authority's perspective on immunity-specific efficiencies reflected in the documented investigations and decisions respectively.

4.2.1 The joint applicants' perspective   An obvious starting point of a study on the role of efficiencies in antitrust investigations is an analysis of the efficiencies claimed by the alliance members in their joint applications. Although the preceding paragraph has shown that alliance members have obvious incentives to 'overestimate' the efficiencies achieved by the alliance/ antitrust immunity, the arguments brought forward nevertheless have to make use of logically sound lines of economic reasoning to have a chance to be accepted by the responsible authority.

As already mentioned in Section 3.3.2 above, in its most recent investigation, SkyTeam applied[24] for antitrust immunity in 2007, and the DOT in May 2008 decided[25] to grant members of the SkyTeam alliance four-way antitrust immunity. In its joint application, the applicants generally argue that they have entered into the alliance agreements – including the four-way joint venture agreement – to 'expand and deepen their coordination, strengthen their transatlantic services, expand and fully develop their global network, enhance their ability to compete with other global airlines, and exploit synergies resulting from more complete integration among the joint applicants' (DOT-OST-2007-28644, p. 16).

Following the detailed argumentation in the application, the immunized alliance agreements will enable the Joint Applicants to produce the following substantial public benefits:

> A broader and fully optimized joint network with unfettered code-sharing, improved economies of scale and scope and density that will promote new flying, lower fares for consumers as a result of the elimination of incentives for each carrier to build in separate profit margins on non-[antitrust immunity] code-sharing and enhanced service options for consumers. (DOT-OST-2007-28644, p. 18)

The applicants continue by discussing the key drivers of immunity-specific efficiencies, and provide evidence for their likely realization following antitrust immunity. Table 14.2 gives an overview of the key types of efficiencies claimed and the key arguments for their relevance.

The conjunctive element of all types of efficiencies is that the applicants believe that they can only be realized to a full extent by 'creating a common economic interest among the joint applicants' (DOT-OST-2007-28644, p. 6), i.e. by granting of antitrust immunity. In particular, the applicants argue that they need to be able to 'agree on service and capacity, jointly plan schedules/ routes, align economic incentives, work together toward common economic interests, jointly establish prices and fares, jointly determine inventory allocations, and share revenues, among other activities' (DOT-OST-2007-28644, p. 6f.). Standard code-sharing or other forms of non-immunized collaboration will – according to the applicants – not generate comparable efficiencies as

---

24   DOT-OST-2007-28644 (Submission, June 28, 2007). All page numbers of the quotations in the main text in this section refer to the Submission.

25   DOT-OST-2007-28644 (Final Order), Order 2008-5-32 (May 22, 2008).

each carrier strives to maximize its own economic benefit and is unwilling to disadvantage itself for the benefit of the other alliance participants. The closer cooperation made possible through the immunized [joint venture] agreement removes the incentives for the [joint venture] participants to act opportunistically in ways which inure to the short-term financial benefit of one carrier, but which reduce the efficiency and consumer benefits of the transatlantic alliance as a whole. (DOT-OST-2007-28644, p. 20)

The arguments brought forward by the applicants were supported by a (commissioned) LECG study on the consumer benefits of an expanded SkyTeam antitrust immunity. In this study (published as Appendix E in DOT-OST-2007-28644), Jorge Padilla and Matthew Bennett find that consumers benefit from the granting of antitrust immunity more than from simple code-sharing agreements for basically two reasons:

First, antitrust immunity facilitates code-sharing on routes where carriers previously did not have an economic incentive to do so ... Second, with [antitrust immunity], carriers eliminate the 'double mark-up' charged by code-sharing partners ... which results in lower prices for passengers. (DOT-OST-2007-28644, Appendix E, p. 2)

Table 14.2   Types of immunity-specific efficiencies claimed by SkyTeam members

Type of efficiency	Relevance
Expansion of non-stop flights	The network synergies from immunized coordination enable the participants to expand their joint network by providing new non-stop international flights (hub-to-hub and hub-to-spoke) as well as increased frequencies on routes that currently receive non-stop service.
Improved online service options	Approval of immunity will enable schedule coordination in ways that will result in improved time-of-day coverage, improved elapsed travel times, additional flexible routings and travel paths for passengers, and more efficient use of hub networks.
Elimination of double marginalization	Granting antitrust immunity and the gained possibilities to fully coordinate pricing, fares and inventory/yield management will eliminate inherent inefficiencies to pricing and enable the members to offer more attractive fares to customers.
Cost reductions*	Approval of immunity will allow members enhanced coordination and therefore cost reductions though joint marketing, promotion distribution, procurement and development and coordination of accounting and information systems and data.

Source: own collection based on the Joint Application of SkyTeam members (DOT-OST-2007-28644).

* Interestingly, in Appendix A of the joint application the applicants admit that it is difficult to forecast precisely the exact amount of cost savings that will be produced through the improved integrative efficiencies enabled by the proposed alliance. However, they refer to the following estimates in the Star application (which were accepted by the DOT): sales, marketing and distribution (20–50 per cent), price and fare filing (10–50 per cent), revenue management (50–70 per cent), IT systems harmonization/integration (10–30 per cent), joint/shared airport operations and facilities (10–40 per cent) and inter-carrier communications and decision making (10–30 per cent).

In addition, the report compares the consumer benefits of the granting of 'basic' [antitrust immunity] and an enhanced form of [antitrust immunity] in which the airlines establish so-called 'metal-neutrality'. Following the concept of metal-neutrality, the granting of antitrust immunity as such is seen as not sufficient to reap the identified immunity-specific efficiencies because each carrier still has an incentive to maximize its own revenue. Only a closer cooperation based on metal-neutrality, i.e. an indifference as to which airline actually carries the customer, will allow a full realization of these efficiencies because it removes each carrier's incentive to act opportunistically by increasing its own short-term financial benefit at the expense of the efficiencies delivered by the alliance as a whole. For example, after the granting of a metal-neutral form of antitrust immunity, every member will focus on winning the customer's business by booking the optimal routing in the entire alliance network. Technically, in a metal-neutral agreement, the participating airlines agree to pool revenues and costs which leads to the indifference as to which aircraft ('metal') actually operates the flight. In such an enhanced form of cooperation, it is assumed that the following three kinds of additional benefits for consumers are created:

1. Incentives to implement more efficient code-sharing because the risk of passenger diversion is neutralized,[26]
2. Incentives to jointly optimize schedules in a way that optimizes passenger convenience, and
3. Incentives to route passengers over the joint network in the most efficient manner.

4.2.2 The authority's perspective   Given the detailed characterization of the efficiencies claimed by members of SkyTeam in its most recent successful application for antitrust immunity, the consequential next step is an investigation of the economic arguments accepted by the DOT. Focusing again on SkyTeam and the two landmark decisions already sketched in Section 3.3.2 above, the DOT (in its Show Cause Order[27]) in April 2008 'tentatively find that the proposed alliance is consistent with the public interest, will produce public benefits, and will not substantially reduce competition' (DOT-OST-2007-28644, p. 1).

However, in the Show Cause Order as well as the Final Order[28] in May 2008, the DOT also found that granting antitrust immunity should be subject to conditions. In addition to standard conditions, such as the obligation to submit origin and destination survey data, the DOT proposed and later implemented the following special conditions designed to preserve competition and ensure the realization of public benefits:

First, we clarify that the Joint Applicants will at all times remain subject to the antitrust laws for purely domestic air transportation and international air transportation that is beyond the scope of the Alliance Agreements. Second, pending full implementation of the joint venture, we propose to preserve limited 'carve outs' of the Atlanta-Paris CDG and Cincinnati-Paris CDG markets to prohibit the coordination of fares for time-sensitive travellers. Third, we propose to require the Joint Applicants to fully implement the joint venture within 18 months, as planned, in order for the antitrust immunity to remain effective. (DOT-OST-2007-28644, p. 1)

---

26   The argument assumes that carriers have incentives to behave opportunistically in standard code-share agreements to avoid the cost of traffic diversion on routes where they have a competitive advantage. These problems often lead to code-share agreements with a suboptimal narrow scope.

27   The following analysis of the decision is largely based on the Show Cause Order (DOT-OST-2007-28644, April 9, 2008) as it provides a much more detailed assessment of the key arguments compared to the relatively brief Final Order. All page numbers of the quotations in the main text in this section refer to the Show Cause Order.

28   DOT-OST-2007-28644 (Final Order), Order 2008-5-32 (May 22, 2008).

With respect to efficiencies, comparing the first and second application for antitrust immunity of SkyTeam members, the first application lacked a convincing concept which showed the public benefits of granting antitrust immunity. In particular, the DOT argued that the degree of cooperation of the two alliances was too different to create such benefits without a detailed concept to realize these benefits:

> Northwest/KLM was a highly integrated, common bottom line arrangement with joint decision making on pricing and capacity, and pooling of all revenues from transatlantic flights. SkyTeam, on the other hand, was a less integrated alliance in which only Delta and Air France had agreed upon limited revenue pooling for incremental changes in capacity that arose from immunized cooperation. (DOT-OST-2007-28644, p. 2)

In the second application for antitrust immunity, the joint applicants especially introduced the concept of 'metal neutrality' which refers to the practice that the airlines of the joint venture pool revenues and costs of their operations and are therefore indifferent as to which airline actually provides the service. For the DOT, this agreement was essential for the decision to grant antitrust immunity, as only such a merger-like joint venture is likely to generate operating efficiencies and cost reductions on a significant and sufficient scale. In particular, the DOT argued that '[t]he proposed alliance is likely to result in the introduction of new capacity and greater availability of discount fares across the entire joint network' (DOT-OST-2007-28644, p. 15). However, despite its conclusion that the efficiencies realized by the agreements are substantial and cannot be realized otherwise, the DOT is relatively skeptical with respect to certain demand-side efficiencies claimed by the applicants:

> The networks of each alliance overlap to a large extent ... The public benefits that could result from the proposed overlapping alliance are attributable more to rationalization and integration of the networks than to the number of cities that could be newly served on an online basis. (DOT-OST-2007-28644, p. 14)

4.3 Identification and Measurement of Immunity-specific Efficiencies

Based on the characterization of merger-specific efficiencies in section 4.1, and the review of experiences with the most recent SkyTeam investigation by the DOT in the United States in section 4.2, this subsection aims at bringing both complexes together to assess the immunity-specificity of various types of efficiencies. Generally, such an assessment can be subdivided into two stages: identification and quantification. In the first stage, theoretical, empirical, and case-specific arguments are applied to identify those types of efficiencies that are immunity-specific. In the second stage, empirical techniques need to be applied to receive ball park figures on the likely dimension of the identified efficiencies.

The *identification of efficiencies* has to start with some kind of structured thinking on the types of possible efficiencies. In this respect, section 4.1 above has shown that several typologies have been developed to guide such an analysis. With respect to airline alliances, Table 14.2 in section 4.2.1 provided a selection of demand-side efficiencies (e.g. expansion of non-stop flights, improved online service options, elimination of double marginalization) and supply-side efficiencies (e.g. cost reductions). Following the collection and structuring of possible efficiencies, the next step needs to identify the relevant (i.c. immunity specific) efficiencies. In this respect, section 4.1 above has shown that such an investigation needs to focus on 1. Verifiability; 2. Benefit to consumers; and 3. Specificity.

With respect to verifiability, this criterion basically must be assessed on a case by case basis, and it is therefore difficult to provide any general guidance. The same conclusion is basically true for the 'benefit to consumers' criterion, where the analyst must assess on a case by case basis whether the prevailing market structure and the state of competitive interaction will ensure that the consumers get 'a fair share' of the cost advantages realized by airline cooperation (e.g. through a reduction in ticket prices). With respect to airline alliances, it is important to note that an assessment of the 'benefits to consumers' is non-trivial as soon as different types of airline customers are taken into account. For example, a leisure traveller might not care that much about increases in flight frequency (as long as the price remains unchanged), while a business traveller might value more flight options as it helps them to optimize their work schedule. In other words, the benefits to consumers of the implementation of a certain alliance agreement may be distributed unevenly between different types of airline customers.

With respect to the specificity question, Section 2.1 above showed that an alliance agreement including scheduling and pricing decisions is only one out of various types of airline cooperation agreements. As a consequence, the crucial question is to what extent the efficiencies realization potential changes with an increasing degree of cooperation. In other words, if efficiencies can already be realized with interline or code-share agreements, these efficiencies cannot be used as an argument for agreements that include the coordination of scheduling and pricing decisions.

The identification of immunity-specific efficiencies needs to be complemented by a *quantification of these efficiencies*. Although it is fairly obvious that an exact calculation of efficiency realization cannot be expected, the responsible investigatory authority should at least try to get an idea about the broad dimension of immunity-specific efficiencies. Generally, simulations, natural experiments, as well as empirical techniques such as regression analysis or descriptive statistics have the potential to help in the derivation of estimates for the respective efficiencies (see Copenhagen Economics 2006 for a comprehensive overview).

Based on the importance of identification and quantification of immunity-specific efficiencies, Table 14.3 presents an overview of important types of efficiencies together with descriptions of the respective identification and quantification strategies. Generally, the key aim of Table 14.3 is to provide a basic framework for an assessment of immunity-specific efficiencies. The actual (absolute and relative) sizes of the respective types of efficiencies depend on the characteristics of the alliance under investigation. Furthermore, it must be remembered that every identification and quantification of efficiencies has to be complemented by an analysis of the potentially anti-competitive effects of a higher degree of airline cooperation. Only an identification and quantification of these potential costs allows a comparison of the overall costs and benefits, and therefore provides a well-founded basis for the decision of the antitrust authority.

5. Conclusion

The development of international airline markets has led to the dominance of three global airline alliances – Star, SkyTeam and oneworld. At the same time, members of these alliances receive increasingly more freedom in coordinating various aspects of joint operations, including scheduling and pricing decisions as well as the right to form revenue-sharing joint ventures in international markets. Although the significant consumer benefits generated by airline cooperation are undisputed, the recent developments raise antitrust concerns. Against this background, this

Table 14.3 Identification and quantification of immunity-specific efficiencies

Type of efficiency	Identification and quantification
Demand-side	
Elimination of double marginalization	*Identification*: theoretical and empirical research suggests that this efficiency may partly be realized already in a code-share alliance. Furthermore, the larger the degree of price discrimination, the lower the double marginalization effect. The SkyTeam investigation suggests that merger-like integration is necessary to fully exploit the efficiency. *Partly immunity-specific*.
	Quantification: simulation or econometric analysis focusing on price differences between competitive spoke-to-hub and spoke-to-spoke routes after the granting of antitrust immunity to an alliance; estimation of price reductions for interline connections; assessment of the role of price discrimination. Potentially *significant impact* (due to a large number of interline connections).
Expansion of route network	*Identification*: from a theoretical perspective, incentives for network expansion depend on the complementarity of the networks, and the intensity of inter-alliance competition. The SkyTeam investigation suggests that a large part of this efficiency is already realized by interline or code-share agreements. *Largely not immunity-specific*.
	Quantification: descriptive analysis of entire route network; comparisons with route networks of competing alliances; market simulations; valuation of incremental benefits for different customer groups. Potentially *small impact* (due to relatively small number of affected routes).
Expansion of flight frequency	*Identification*: theoretical and empirical research suggests that this efficiency may partly be realized already in a code-share alliance. The SkyTeam investigation suggests that merger-like integration is necessary to fully exploit the efficiency. *Partly immunity-specific*.
	Quantification: Descriptive analysis of hub-to-hub markets; descriptive analysis of aircraft capacities; market simulations; valuation of incremental benefits for different customer groups. Potentially *small impact* (due to relatively small number of affected routes).
Improved online service options	*Identification*: theoretical and empirical research suggests that this efficiency may partly be realized already in an interline alliance. The SkyTeam investigation suggests that especially scheduling coordination contributes to the improved exploitation of the efficiency. *Partly immunity-specific*.
	Quantification: descriptive statistics on various service options; valuation of increased service options for different customer groups. Potentially *significant impact* (due to relatively large number of affected routes).
Supply-side	
Marginal cost reductions though economies of traffic density	*Identification*: theoretical and empirical research suggests that this efficiency may partly be realized already in a code-share alliance. The SkyTeam investigation suggests that merger-like integration is necessary to fully exploit this efficiency. *Partly immunity-specific*.
	Quantification: (regression) analysis based on internal cost data from the airlines; estimation of cost reductions for every hub-to-hub route; estimation of traffic increase on spoke-to-hub routes. Potentially *medium impact* (due to dense but relatively small number of hub-to-hub connections).
Cost reductions through coordination of *second*-degree competition parameters	*Identification*: by definition, second-degree efficiencies can already be realized by interline or code-share agreements. Examples are cost reductions through the sharing of maintenance facilities, sales offices, check-in desks, baggage handling, airport lounges or catering services. *Not immunity-specific*.
	Quantification: not applicable
Cost reductions through coordination of *first*-degree competition parameters	*Identification*: by definition, first-degree efficiencies can be realized by merger-like integration only, i.e. by cooperation on key competition parameters such as pricing, yield management and schedules. *Fully immunity-specific*.
	Quantification: (regression) analysis based on internal cost data from the airlines; analysis of the potential to realize marginal costs reductions and/or savings in fixed costs (time frame assessment; compatibility and capacity assessments of facilities). Potentially *high impact* as the entire alliance network is the focus of cost reductions.

Source: Bilotkach and Hüschelrath (2012).

chapter on the one hand, aimed at developing an understanding of the key competitive effects triggered by granting antitrust immunity. On the other hand, it focused on an assessment of the question how immunity-specific efficiencies can be identified and quantified.

Our conclusions are the following. First, granting antitrust immunity triggers both potentially anti-competitive effects (the 'cost' side) and potentially immunity-specific efficiencies (the 'benefits' side). As a consequence, an assessment of the responsible authority has to identify and quantify the drivers and sizes of both groups of effects in order to receive meaningful conclusions on the net welfare effect of granting antitrust immunity. This implies that even the realization of significant immunity-specific efficiencies as such might not be sufficient as long as the anti-competitive effects are found to be of comparable size. Second, the competitive effects analysis conducted by the DOT in the SkyTeam investigation seems to rely to a large extent on an assessment of changes in market concentration, the strength of inter-alliance competition and the existing threat of potential competition. Theoretical approaches of harm potentially caused by granting antitrust immunity – such as market foreclosure or reduced incentives of individual airlines to further develop their networks – were apparently not investigated. Third, in contrast to 'average' antitrust investigations, efficiencies seem to play a larger role during immunity investigations. In fact, in the SkyTeam investigation antitrust immunity was first denied because the alliance members did not demonstrate the full benefits from close cooperation. Fourth, given the significant degree of asymmetric information between the responsible authority and the alliance members, antitrust immunity should probably be denied in cases in which the potentially anti-competitive effects are of comparable size as the immunity-specific efficiencies. Fifth, any robust assessment of competitive effects and immunity-specific efficiencies should consist of two subsequent steps: identification and measurement. While the former step has to answer the question of what types of effects/efficiencies are relevant, the latter step has to quantify the likely impact in the world in which immunity has been granted (compared to the counterfactual of the denial of antitrust immunity). Sixth, the above analysis has shown that a significant part of the efficiencies realized by airline cooperation are not immunity-specific, as they can in fact be realized by interline or code-share agreements already.

The two important steps in an assessment of the competitive effects and immunity-specific efficiencies – identification and quantification – also delineate two major areas in which further economic research would be desirable. With respect to the identification question, more theoretical and empirical research is certainly needed to receive a better understanding on the types and the general impact of competitive effects as well as the immunity-specificity of certain efficiencies such as, e.g., the removal of double marginalization. With respect to the quantification question, a deeper knowledge of the effects/efficiencies demands more econometric studies, both ex-ante and ex-post. Ex-ante, a fruitful research area would be the development of implementable tools to quantify certain effects/efficiencies. Ex-post, it seems particularly interesting to investigate, on the one hand, the actual size of competitive effects and, on the other hand, the successfulness of airline alliances in the realization of the efficiencies claimed in their joint applications for antitrust immunity.

References

Amir, R., Diamantoudi, E. and Xue, L. (2004) *Merger Performance under Uncertain Efficiency Gains*. Nota di Lavoro 79.2004. Venice: Fondazione Eni Enrico Mattei.

Barla, P. and Constantatos, C. (2006) On the choice between strategic alliance and merger in the airline sector: the role of strategic effects. *Journal of Transport Economics and Policy*, 40, 409–424.

Bernheim, D. and Whinston, M. (1990) Multimarket contact and collusive behavior. *RAND Journal of Economics*, 21, 1–26.

Bilotkach, V. (2005) Price competition between international airline alliances. *Journal of Transport Economics and Policy*, 39, 167–189.

Bilotkach, V. (2007a) Complementary versus semi-complementary airline partnerships. *Transportation Research Part B*, 41, 381–393.

Bilotkach, V. (2007b) Airline partnerships and schedule coordination. *Journal of Transport Economics and Policy*, 41, 413–425.

Bilotkach, V. (2007c) Price effects of airline consolidation: evidence from a sample of transatlantic markets. *Empirical Economics*, 33, 427–448.

Bilotkach, V. (2009) A framework for modeling 'real-life' airline networks. *Review of Network Economics*, 8, 255–270.

Bilotkach, V. and K. Hüschelrath (2011) Antitrust immunity for airline alliances. *Journal of Competition Law and Economics*, 7 (2), 335–380.

Bilotkach, V. and Hüschelrath, K. (2012) Airline alliances and antitrust policy: the role of efficiencies. *Journal of Air Transport Management*, 21, 76–84.

Bilotkach, V. and Hüschelrath, K. (2013) Airline alliances, antitrust immunity and market foreclosure. Review of Economics and Statistics, forthcoming

Bradshaw, B. and Patel, B. (2009) Final descent? The future of antitrust immunity in international aviation. *GCP: The Antitrust Chronicle*, September, 1, 1–8.

Brueckner, J. (2001) The economics of international codesharing: an analysis of airline alliances. *International Journal of Industrial Organization*, 19, 1475–1498.

Brueckner, J. (2003) International airfares in the age of alliances: the effects of codesharing and antitrust immunity. *Review of Economics and Statistics*, 85, 105–118.

Brueckner, J. and Proost, S. (2010) Carve-outs under airline antitrust immunity. *International Journal of Industrial Organization*, 28(6), 657–668.

Brueckner, J. and Whalen, T. (2000) The price effects of international airline alliances. *Journal of Law and Economics*, 43, 503–545.

Button, K. and Drexler, J. (2006) The implications on economic performance in Europe of further liberalization of the transatlantic air market. *International Journal of Transport Economics*, 31, 45–68.

Chen, Y. and Gayle, P. (2007) Vertical contracting between airlines: an equilibrium analysis of codeshare alliances. *International Journal of Industrial Organization*, 25, 1046–1060.

Copenhagen Economics (2006) *Practical Methods to Assess Efficiency Gains in the Context of Article 81(3) of the EC Treaty. Final Report to DG Enterprise and Industry*. Copenhagen: Copenhagen Economics.

Doganis, R. (2001) *The Airline Business in the 21st Century*. London: Routledge.

Dunn, A. (2008) Do low-quality products affect high-quality entry? Multiproduct firms and non-stop entry in airline markets. *International Journal of Industrial Organization*, 26, 1074–1089.

European Commission (2004) Guidelines on the Assessment of Horizontal Mergers under the Council Regulation on the Control of Concentrations between Undertakings (2004/C31/03). Brussels: European Commission.

Evans, W. and Kessides, I. (1994) Living by the 'golden rule': multimarket contact in the US airline industry. *Quarterly Journal of Economics*, 109, 341–366.

Evans, D. and Padilla, J. (2003) Demand-side efficiencies in merger control. *World Competition*, 26, 167–193.

Everett, A.-B. and Ross, T. (2002) *The Treatment of Efficiencies in Merger Review: An International Comparison*. Vancouver: Delta Economics Group.

Farrell, J. and Katz, M. (2006) *The Economics of Welfare Standards in Antitrust*. Competition Policy Center, Working Paper CPC-06-061. Berkeley.

Farrell, J. and Shapiro, C. (2001) Scale economies and synergies in horizontal merger analysis. *Antitrust Law Journal*, 68, 685–710.

Flores-Fillol, R. and Moner-Colonques, R. (2007) Strategic formation of airline alliances. *Journal of Transport Economics and Policy*, 41, 427–449.

Gayle, P. (2008) An empirical analysis of the competitive effects of the Delta/Continental/ Northwest codeshare alliance. *Journal of Law and Economics*, 51, 743–766.

Gugler, K, Mueller, D., Yurtoglu, B. and Zulehner, C. (2003) The effects of mergers: an international comparison. *International Journal of Industrial Organization*, 21, 625–653.

Heimer, O. and Shy, O. (2006) Code-sharing agreements, frequency of flights, and profits under parallel operation. In D. Lee (ed.), *Advances in Airline Economics, Vol. 1: Competition Policy and Antitrust*. Amsterdam: Elsevier, 163–181.

ICN (2006) *Merger Guidelines Workbook*. Prepared for the Fifth Annual ICN Conference, Cape Town.

Kasper, D. and Lee, D. (2009) Why airline antitrust immunity benefits consumers. *GCP: The Antitrust Chronicle*, September, 1, 1–5.

Kolaski, W. and Dick, A. (2002) The merger guidelines and the integration of efficiencies into antitrust review of horizontal mergers. *Antitrust Law Journal*, 71, 207–251.

Lederman, M. (2008) Are frequent flyer programs a cause of the 'hub premium'. *Journal of Economics and Management Strategy*, 17, 35–66.

Lederman, M. (2007) Do enhancements to loyalty programs affect demand? The impact of international frequent flyer partnerships on domestic airline demand. *RAND Journal of Economics*, 38, 1134–1158.

Leocha, C. (2009) Wait a second! Continental/United IT deal is flat-out collusion. *Consumer Traveler*, 29 July, accessed 5 June 2010.

Lexecon (2003) *An Introduction to Quantitative Techniques in Competition Analysis*. London: Lexecon.

Morrish, S. and Hamilton, R. (2002) Airline alliances – who benefits? *Journal of Air Transport Management*, 8, 401–407.

Neven, D. and Röller, L.-H. (2006) Consumer surplus vs. welfare standard in a political economy model of merger control. *International Journal of Industrial Organization*, 23, 829–848.

Oum, T., Park, J. and Zhang, A. (2000) *Globalization and Strategic* Alliances: *The Case of the Airline Industry*. London: Emerald.

Oum, T., Park, J. and Zhang, A. (1996) The effects of airline codesharing agreements on firm conduct and international air fares. *Journal of Transport Economics and Policy*, 30, 187–202.

Park, J.-H. (1997) The effect of airline alliances on markets and economic welfare. *Transportation Research, Part E*, 33, 181–195.

Park, J.-H. and Zhang, A. (2000) An empirical analysis of global airline alliances: cases in the north Atlantic markets. *Review of Industrial Organization*, 16, 367–384.

Reitzes, J. and Moss, D. (2008) Airline alliances and systems competition. *Houston Law Review*, 45, 294–332.

Röller, L.-H., Stennek, J. and Verboven, F. (2001) Efficiency gains from mergers. In *The Efficiency Defence and the European System of Merger Control*, European Economy No. 5. Brussels: European Commission.

Scheffman, D. (2004) Efficiencies – Dynamic Analysis – Integrated Analysis. LECG Presentation, Boston.

Straiger, J. (2001) Airline Alliances and Mergers – The Emerging Commission Policy. Speech given to the European Air Law Association, 9 November 2001, Zürich.

Wan, X., Zou, L. and Dresner, M. (2009) Assessing the price effect of airline alliances on parallel routes. *Transportation Research, Part E*, 45, 627–641.

Werden, G. (1998) Antitrust analysis of joint ventures: an overview. *Antitrust Law Journal*, 66, 701–735.

Whalen, W. (2007) A panel data analysis of code sharing, antitrust immunity and open skies treaties in international aviation markets. *Review of Industrial Organization*, 30, 39–61.

Willig, R., Israel, M. and Keating, B. (2009) Competitive effects of airline antitrust immunity. Working Paper, Washington.

Chapter 15

Parallel Frequent Flier Programme Partnerships: Impact on Frequency

Volodymyr Bilotkach

1. Introduction

This chapter analyses the effect of frequent flier programme (FFP) partnerships between the major US carriers on the choice of frequency of service. Since FFP partnerships make airlines' services more substitutable, potentially leading to fiercer price competition, a natural response by the carriers will be to cut costs, which can lead to lower frequency of service on routes where partner airlines compete directly. We find support for this contention in the data.

About a decade ago, airline companies on the US market started employing a new strategy: partnering with their competitors. These partnerships consisted of code-sharing agreements (including partner airlines' flights into your schedule), as well as near unification of FFPs. Frequent-flier programme partnerships have been almost a default feature of international airline alliances; joining the FFPs is in this case a way to reinforce the complementary alliances between the carriers.[1]

On the other hand, the benefits of domestic FFP partnerships for US carriers are not obvious. Even though US carriers may not be directly competing on many non-stop routes (since most large network carriers have their hubs in different airports), they do compete on many city pair markets. So FFP partnerships between the US carriers appear more parallel than complementary (with the exception of alliances involving carriers operating on Alaska and Hawaii markets).

As Lederman (2008) correctly points out, such partnerships are likely to increase substitutability between the partner airlines' services, which is not a result carriers would be happy with. Moreover, the practice of domestic FFP partnerships has survived up to now. American Airlines is currently the only major network airline in the US staying out of partnering with other US carriers.[2] We therefore wonder whether there is any way in which carriers can actually benefit from parallel FFP partnerships, even though such are likely to reduce the substitutability between their services.

It is possible that the carriers join their FFPs to compete with other similar airline partnerships. In this case, a consumer choosing between two joint FFPs may value the one which gives them more earning and redemption options higher. This may positively affect joint market share of the partner airlines. Yet fiercer price competition between the partner airlines due to higher substitutability between their services can lead to adverse consequences for carriers' profits. One should keep in mind that while airlines on the US domestic market can form partnerships and join their FFPs, they are not allowed to jointly set prices or frequency of service.

---

1   Being able to earn and (especially) redeem miles for international flights with the partner airlines increases the value of the airline's frequent flier programme to domestic customers. A business traveller could now redeem miles earned traveling domestically with, for example, Delta, for a vacation abroad to locations where Delta does not fly but its partners do.

2   While Continental and Northwest customers can earn miles on a limited number of American Eagle's services to/from Los Angeles international airport, American Airlines does not allow its frequent fliers to earn or redeem AAdvantage® miles on flights by any other US carrier.

There is only limited support for the supposition that FFP partnerships could be precursors to full-scale mergers. This can be seen from a glance at Figures 15.1 and 15.2. Clearly, partnership between Delta and Northwest preceded the merger between the two airlines.[3] At the same time, Continental Airlines ended up merging with United, despite the long-term FFP partnership with Delta and Northwest. Moreover, United opted for merging with Continental after the merger talks between United and US Airways fell apart, despite the fact that formal merger announcement had been made earlier.

When your revenue can take a hit due to fiercer price competition, your natural response will be to cut your costs. A cost-cutting strategy that can be easily seen in the data is reduction in frequency of service. We suppose that such a strategy will be easier to implement when your competitor is also your partner. Data analysis shows that airlines offer lower frequency on routes (10 to 30 per cent, depending on the specification employed) where they compete with carriers with whom they have a FFP partnership, as compared to markets where the airlines that have no partner relationships compete. At the same time, we find no evidence that this effect of the FFP partnerships on frequency is immediate; nor do we detect that partnerships lead to a significant decrease in the total frequency offered at the market level. Our results thus show that FFP partnerships are not as harmful to consumers as the simple correlation between them and the frequency of service might suggest.

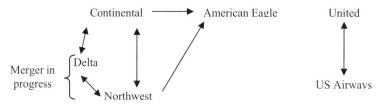

Excludes largely complementary partnerships with Alaska and Hawaiian. Continental-American Eagle and Northwest-American Eagle partnerships are limited to selected routes and not reciprocal (American Eagle customers cannot earn/redeem miles on Continental or Northwest)

Figure 15.1   FFP partnerships involving US network carriers, June 2009

Excludes largely complementary partnerships with Alaska and Hawaiian. Partnerships involving American Eagle are limited to selected routes and not reciprocal (American Eagle customers cannot earn/redeem miles on partner airlines' flights)

Figure 15.2   FFP partnerships involving US network carriers, February 2011

---

3   Note that earlier merger between America West and US Airways (concluded in 2005) was also preceded by the FFP partnership between the two airlines.

Prior empirical analysis of FFP partnerships can be found in works by Mara Lederman. Lederman (2007) examines to what extent FFP partnerships on US domestic market are parallel and how they affect demand. She finds that, first, partnerships do increase earning and redemption opportunities for some passengers; and second, partnerships appear to affect partners' demand positively (airline's market share at an airport increases with an increase in size of operation by the partner carrier). This finding is not inconsistent with fiercer price competition between partner airlines due to increased substitutability. Lederman (2008) shows that the airline flying into an airport dominated by a certain carrier can gain from partnering with that dominant airline.

Also related to our work are studies of airline partnerships on the US domestic market. This growing literature yields no clear consensus as to whether such partnerships benefit consumers. Bamberger et al. (2004) and Ito and Lee (2007) document lower prices following domestic code-sharing agreements and suggest consumers did benefit from consolidation; Gayle (2007, 2008) also concludes that the Northwest–Continental–Delta alliance has had no apparent anti-competitive effects. However, Armantier and Richard (2005) suggest ambiguous competition effects, while Armantier and Richard (2006) find that consumer surplus actually fell as a result of the Northwest–Continental alliance. All these studies look at the price effects of airline partnerships.

2. Empirical Analysis

The data for our analysis comes from databank T100 Segment, collected monthly by the US Department of Transportation and publicly available at the Department's website. This dataset provides information on (among other things) frequency of service at the airline-airport-pair-market level.

To focus on peak travel period with stable configuration of airline partnerships, we chose July of 2004 for our analysis. The frequent flier programme partnerships scheme presented in Figure 15.1 was established around 2002–2003 (see Bamberger et al., 2004). Focusing on the peak travel month of the year with robust demand for air travel (July 2004), we effectively look at the time period where airlines have otherwise little incentive to reduce frequency, making the data work against us.

We included into our analysis only those airport-pair markets on which two or more carriers offered non-stop services (for a total of 393 markets); this allows for the direct comparison of frequency choices on markets where partners compete versus routes where airlines without partner relationships are the competitors. Our observations are at the airline-airport-pair-market level; with regional carriers'[4] services lumped with those of the corresponding major carrier. We ended up with 874 observations. Natural logarithm of carrier's frequency is the dependent variable.

The variable of interest is PARTNER dummy, taking value of 1 if a carrier with which the airline has a FFP programme partnership is also offering non-stop service on the same airport-pair market. As a clarifying example, consider Boston–Los Angeles airport-pair market. On this route, non-stop services in July of 2004 were performed by American Airlines, United Airlines and

---

4   On the US market, some of the commercial passenger services (particularly on thinner markets) are performed by so-called regional carriers, effectively operating as agents of major airlines. Those can be either independent companies (SkyWest, Atlantic Southeast); or fully owned subsidiaries of major carriers (American Eagle). Several such airlines perform services for more than one major airline (e.g., SkyWest flies as Delta, United, and Midwest agent). Where a regional carrier was known to perform flights for more than one major airline, classification was made according to the hub airport to/from which the service was performed; airlines sharing hub airports have not been found to share a regional carrier.

America West Airlines. Since United had an FFP partnership with America West; the PARTNER variable will take on value of one for observations for United and America West, and zero for observation corresponding to American Airlines. Our model suggests coefficient on this variable should be negative and significant. Of 393 airport-pair-markets included into our analysis, partner airlines compete on 102; PARTNER dummy takes on value of 1 for 206 cases, or in almost quarter of all observations.

The set of control variables we employ is standard and includes carrier dummies; carrier–hub[5] indicator variables; natural logarithm of distance; geometric averages of endpoints' metropolitan areas population and per capita income; and quantity (not frequency) based airport-pair-market Herfindhal–Hirschman index (HHI). The latter is also instrumented by the number of airlines offering non-stop service due to its potential endogeneity with the explanatory variable.

Table 15.1 presents results of the following specifications. First, we report OLS regression with White robust standard errors; then, two-stage least squares results with number of carriers as the instrument for HHI are presented; finally, regression with airport-pair-market fixed effects to control for unobservable market-specific heterogeneities is shown. Note that all airport-pair-market controls we used are absorbed by fixed effects; therefore, the only control variables available in that specification are airline and airline-hub indicator variables, coefficients on which we do not report to save space. It is evident from the table below that there is support for our hypothesis in

Table 15.1   Estimation results

Regressor	Least squares	Two-stage least squares	Fixed effects
Constant	6.1403* (0.3133)	6.2931* (0.3277)	5.2708* (0.0919)
Partner	−0.1003[†] (0.0572)	−0.1095* (0.0578)	−0.2951* (0.1296)
Log (distance)	−0.3089* (0.0325)	−0.3141* (0.0323)	–
Geometric average of population	8.22E–08* (1.18E–08)	7.49E–08* (7.29E–06)	–
Geometric average of per capita income	3.10E–05* (7.15E–06)	3.22E–05* (7.29E–06)	–
HHI	−0.8840* (0.1986)	−1.1771* (0.3103)	–
Adjusted R-squared	0.3601	0.3576	0.4717

Dependent variable is natural logarithm of frequency, at airline-city pair-market level; number of observations is 874; white heteroscedasticity-consistent standard errors are reported; all regressions include airline dummies and airline–hub interactions, which are not reported; variables absorbed by airport-pair-market fixed effects are not reported; statistical significance: * – 5%; [†] 10%.

---

5   The main airline–hub combinations are: Chicago O'Hare, Dallas Fort Worth and Miami for American Airlines; Houston Intercontinental, Newark and Cleveland for Continental Airlines; Atlanta, Salt Lake City and Cincinnati for Delta Air Lines; Memphis, Minneapolis, and Detroit for Northwest; Denver, Chicago O'Hare, Washington Dulles and San Francisco for United Airlines; Philadelphia, Charlotte and Pittsburgh for US Airways; Phoenix and Las Vegas for America West; Phoenix and Chicago Midway for Southwest Airlines.

the data: when a partner airline serves a market, carriers tend to lower their frequency of service. The size of the effect, however, varies; fixed effects regression suggests effect that is three times that implied by OLS and two stage least squares specifications. In either case, the magnitude of the impact is non-trivial. As an illustration, consider an airline offering three daily services (21 weekly flights) between two airports. Our results suggest that, other things being equal, upon joining its FFP with that of a competitor on the same route, our hypothetical carrier will adjust its schedule from operating three flights on weekdays and only two services on the weekend (OLS estimate) to dropping the third flight altogether – maybe flying three times only on one of the days of the week (fixed effects estimate).

Control variables exhibit expected behaviour: frequency is higher on thicker markets and on those where consumers have deeper pockets; longer routes are associated with lower frequency of service, other things being equal; and airlines choose lower frequency of service on more concentrated markets. These outcomes are consistent with theoretical study by Brueckner and Flores-Fillol (2007), as well as with empirical evidence by Pai (2010), and Bilotkach, Fageda, and Flores-Fillol (2010). It also pays to note that airline–hub interactions, not reported in the table, all have positive and significant (with exception of that for Continental Airlines) coefficients associated with them.

Results reported above suggest there is a correlation between the airlines' participation in FFP partnerships and choice of frequency of service on the routes where the carriers compete with their partners. To further assess the effects of the partnerships on competition, we report results of the following two exercises. First, using our data for July 2004 and collapsing all observation to the airport-pair-market level, we investigate whether presence of competition between the partner airlines affects *total number of flights offered on the market*. Indeed, partners may reduce frequency to eliminate redundant flights (channelling, for instance, traffic to their hubs using partner airlines' flights rather than their own); and other competitors may respond by increasing their frequency of service. As the relevant explanatory variable, we use PARTNERSHARE, or share of traffic by the partner airlines on the market. Results (reported below) show that while the coefficient on PARTNERSHARE is negative as expected, it is not very significant, undermining the proposition that FFP partnerships are detrimental to consumer welfare, as our earlier results seem to have indicated.

Further, we have made use of the fact that United Airlines–US Airways partnership was formed in late 2002; whereas Delta joined the Continental–Northwest alliance in the summer of 2003 to examine the effect of *establishing* the FFP partnerships on frequency of service. Taking the T-100 segment data for July 2002, and matching it to July 2004 data used up to now; we are able to examine whether and how changes in the partnership status affect changes in frequency of service, chosen by the airlines. Specifically, matching airport-level airline observations for the two years (we were able to obtain 549 such matches), we have constructed the indicator variable for those observations which represented frequent flier partners competing with each other with non-stop services in both 2002 and 2004; as well as for those which did not represent the partner airlines in 2002, but did in 2004. Using natural logarithm of the ratio of 2004 to 2002 frequency as the dependent variable; we examined the relationship between change in frequency choice and change in partnership status. Results are presented in Table 15.3. We have been unable to estimate fixed effects regression, since the indicator for observations representing partner airlines' services in both 2002 and 2004 is absorbed by the fixed effects. Both random effects and instrumental variables specifications yielded similar results to those reported overleaf.

Table 15.2   Market-level regressions

Regressor	Least squares	Two-stage least squares
Constant	6.9611** (0.4056)	8.5162** (0.5262)
Partnershare	−0.0752 (0.0772)	−0.0899 (0.0939)
Log (distance)	−0.3469** (0.0462)	−0.3812** (0.0383)
Geometric average of population	2.85E–05** (9.09E–06)	4.34E–05** (1.06E–05)
Geometric average of per capita income	9.04E–08** (1.46E–08)	8.63E–08** (1.38E–08)
HHI	−0.6842** (0.2075)	−3.2564** (0.5725)
Adjusted R-squared	0.4646	0.2594

Dependent variable is natural logarithm of frequency, at airport-pair-market level; number of observations is 393; white heteroscedasticity-consistent standard errors are reported; all regressions include airline dummies and airline–hub interactions, which are not reported; statistical significance: ** –5%.

Table 15.3   Effects of partnerships in dynamics

Regressor	Least squares
Constant	−0.1721** (0.0231)
Partnership in 2002 and 2004	−0.1494** (0.0094)
No partnership in 2002, partnership in 2004	0.0482 (0.0918)
Log (distance)	−0.0105 (0.0264)
Logarithm of ratio of geometric average populations in 2004 and 2002	2.7904** (0.245)
Logarithm of ratio of geometric average per capita income in 2004 and 2002	0.6501 (0.4425)
Logarithm of ratio of HHI in 2004 and 2002	−0.2836** (0.0934)
Adjusted R-squared	0.0657

Dependent variable is natural logarithm of ratio of frequencies in 2004 and 2002, at airline-airport-pair-market level; number of observations is 549; white heteroscedasticity-consistent standard errors are reported; all regressions include airline dummies and airline–hub interactions, which are not reported; results for random effects and IV models are similar; statistical significance: ** –5%.

We can see from the above reported results that airlines which were partners in 2002 decreased their frequency of service more substantially than carriers which have not been partners in either of the two years. At the same time, airlines which became partners between 2002 and 2004 (as we mentioned above, the US Airways–United partnership was concluded in this time window, and Delta joined the Continental–Northwest alliance) changed their frequency in line with airlines which have never been partners. Our results effectively suggest that any effects of the FFP partnerships take time to materialize.

4. Concluding Comments

At the first glance, it appears airlines should derive little benefit from alliances involving FFP partnerships in the US domestic markets. Since fare coordination by alliance members is illegal, and partners compete on a number of city-pair markets (even though not necessarily with non-stop services), one can suspect that FFP partnerships may lead to consumers perceiving airlines' services as closer substitutes compared to the case without such a partnership. This may lead to fiercer price competition and lower revenue. We however suggest that partner relationships may enable the airlines to respond to this higher substitutability by reducing costs, which can be reflected in the data via lower frequency on routes where an airline competes with a partner as opposed to otherwise identical markets where the same airline's competitors do not have any partner relationships with it.

The data analysis finds support for the alleged effect of FFP partnerships on frequency choice by airlines on the US market. Competing with a partner, the airline will offer 10–30 per cent fewer flights compared to otherwise similar markets where the airline does not have any partnership with its competitors.

At the same time, further analysis suggests that frequency changes by the partner airlines are compensated for by other market players; leading to no significant effect of partnerships on frequency at the airport-pair-market level. Further, analysis of the dynamic effects of FFP partnerships shows that any effects on frequency we eventually observe take time to materialize.

Our chapter thus shows that even though FFP partnerships appear to lead the involved airlines to lower frequency of service (as either a way to compensate for closer substitutability between their products, or a measure to increase efficiency); they have a limited effect on competition at the market level. At the same time, we find that established partnerships have rather robust longer-term dynamic effects on frequency choice. Coupled with some previous evidence suggesting airline partnerships on the US market could have had anti-competitive price effects, our study suggests adverse price effects of parallel airline partnerships can be potentially exacerbated on the product quality side. This is an issue that regulators should take into account when evaluating future proposed partnerships in airline and potentially other industries.

References

Armantier, O. and O. Richard (2005) *Domestic Airline Alliances and Consumer Welfare*. Working paper.

Armantier, O. and O. Richard (2006) Evidence of pricing from the Continental Airlines and the Northwest Airlines code-sharing agreement. In D. Lee (ed.), *Advances in Airline Economics*, pp. 91–108 Elsevier, Amsterdam.

Bamberger, G., Carlton, D. and Neumann, L. (2004) An empirical investigation of the competitive effects of domestic airline alliances. *Journal of Law and Economics*, 47, 195–222.

Bilotkach, V., Fageda, X. and Flores-Fillol, R. (2010) Scheduled services versus private transportation: the role of distance. *Regional Science and Urban Economics*, 40, 60–72.

Brueckner, J. and Flores-Fillol, R. (2007) Airline schedule competition. *Review of Industrial Organization*, 30, 161–177.

Gayle, P. (2007) Airline code-share alliances and their competitive effects. *Journal of Law and Economics*, 50, 781–819.

Gayle, P. (2008) An empirical analysis of the competitive effects of the Delta-Continental-Northwest code-share alliance. *Journal of Law and Economics*, 51, 743–766.

Ito, H. and Lee, D. (2007) Domestic codesharing, alliances and airfares in the U.S. airline industry. *Journal of Law and Economics*, 50, 355–380.

Lederman, M. (2007) Are frequent flyer programs a cause of the 'hub premium'? *Journal of Economics and Management Strategy*, 17, 35–66.

Lederman, M. (2008) Do enhancements to loyalty programs affect demand? The impact of international frequent flyer partnerships on domestic airline demand. *RAND Journal of Economics*, 38, 1134–1158.

Pai, V. (2010) On the factors that affect airline flight frequency and aircraft size. *Journal of Air Transport Management*, 16, 169–177.

PART D
Liberalization and Infrastructure

Chapter 16

Airport Traffic Growth
and Airport Financial Performance

Zheng Lei and Romano Pagliari

1. Introduction

Since liberalization of the European aviation market, completed in 1997, the nature of air travel in Europe has changed dramatically. One of the most important outcomes is the emergence of low-cost carriers (LCCs). These LCCs have driven down the cost of air travel and forced a fundamental restructuring of many existing full-service airlines as well as charter carriers (Njegovan, 2006; Papatheodorou and Lei, 2006). Intensified price competition between airlines has stimulated demand for short-haul air travel, leading to phenomenal growth of traffic at regional airports. Increased traffic appears to have had a significant impact on the financial performance of the airport industry because profitability is to a large extent dependent on the volume of traffic (Graham, 2003).

The airline liberalization in Europe coincided with airport commercialization and privatization. Accordingly, the airport business evolved from a traditional model, where the airports' only tasks were to meet the basic and essential needs of passengers, airlines, freight forwarders and other direct customers or users, to a more customer- and market-oriented commercial model. By adopting the latter, improving financial performance has become a primary business goal for airport management: hence understanding the impact of traffic growth on financial performance is vitally important from an airport's perspective. This chapter seeks to address the above issue and is structured as follows. Section 2 reviews past studies on airport traffic and financial performance. Section 3 describes the data used in the empirical study. Section 4 discusses the results, and finally, Section 5 provides concluding remarks.

2. Past Studies

As a result of airport commercialization and privatization, greater attention has been placed on the commercial aspects of running an airport, with a particular focus on commercial revenue generation (Graham, 2003). Attracting LCCs has become an appealing way for airports, particularly under-utilized regional ones, to increase passenger throughput to reach a critical mass for the sustainable financial operations of their facilities (Lei et al., 2010). Yet LCCs operate a different business model in which cost minimization is a top priority. Doganis (2002) noted that having pushed all other cost inputs to minimal levels, the only cost variable that LCCs could further squeeze was airport charges. Lei et al. (2010) observed that a common strategy used by regional airports was to trade off a reduction in aeronautical revenues in return for an increase in the commercial income. In a case study of two European regional airports, Francis et al. (2003) found that both airports offered significant concessions on aeronautical charges to attract LCCs. The relationship between the LCC and one airport was regarded as mutually beneficial: the average expenditure of an LCC passenger was approximately €8, compared to an average of €5.5 for all passengers. For the other airport, to cover the revenue shortfall resulting from aeronautical revenue concession and marketing support, it needed to extract €6.50 from each LCC passenger; nonetheless, this was not achieved and the airport finally had to abandon its deal with the LCC.

Using a larger sample of 17 UK and Irish airports, Graham and Dennis (2007) analysed the relationship between airport traffic and financial performance. Airports were divided into three groups, depending on the extent to which they were dependent on low-cost traffic. Their research revealed that airports highly dependent on LCC traffic (Group 1) had the lowest aeronautical revenue per work load unit[1] (WLU), compared to airports with some dependence on LCC traffic (Group 2), and little or no dependence on LCC traffic (Group 3). Although airports in Group 1 generated slightly more commercial revenue per WLU than airports in Group 2, it was much less than airports in Group 3. In terms of total revenue, there was a marked difference among the three: £8.37 for Group 1, £10.29 for Group 2; and £13.42 for Group 3. Interestingly, the authors also found that airports in Group 1 had the lowest costs per WLU (£6.01) as opposed to airports in Group 2 (£7.04), and in Group 3 (£11.33). Overall, airports in Group 1 had 25.9 per cent of operating margin, compared to 31.5 per cent for airports in Group 2 and 15.2 per cent in Group 3.

In a recent study, Lei and Papatheodorou (2009) measured the effect of LCCs on 21 UK regional airports' commercial revenue using panel data econometrics. They found that passenger traffic had a significant impact on an airport's commercial revenue, but LCC passengers made a much smaller marginal contribution to airport's revenue than passengers carried by other types of airline. Holding other variables constant, on average, each additional LCC passenger raised airport commercial revenue by £2.87, while each additional other carrier passenger boosted airport commercial revenue by £5.59. The results were relatively stable across the three different models (pooled ordinary least squares, fixed effects and random effects).

3. Data Issues

This research has no intention of duplicating previous efforts. Instead, we focus on the relationship between airport traffic and airport financial performance at individual airport level. The empirical study is based on the UK market as this is arguably the biggest and most competitive market for LCCs in Europe. Its level of maturity and experience of deregulation presents opportunities to study the long-term impact of LCC market penetration on airport financial performance. A total of 23 UK airports over the period of 1996/97 to 2007/08 are used using airline traffic data provided by the UK Civil Aviation Athority (CAA). LCCs in the data set are defined by the UK CAA as comprising Ryanair, easyJet, easyJet Switzerland, Bmibaby, Go, Mytravelite, Jet2, Flyglobespan, Flybe, Astraeus (Iceland Express), Air Berlin, Deutsche BA, Norwegian Air Shuttle, Sky Europe, Basiq Air, Hapag-Lloyd Express, Air Polonia, Smartwings, Central Wings and Volare. Airport financial data was collected from annual Airport Statistics published by the Centre for the Studies of Regulated Industries (CRI), UK. All traffic data was adjusted to airports' reported financial years. Furthermore, the financial data was deflated using the UK Retail Price Index to make them comparable across different years.

A total of 28 airports are included in the CRI's Airport Statistics. Among these, London Biggin Hill, Norwich, Southend had few scheduled flights; Highlands and Islands and Prestwick had considerable missing data in the observation period. Therefore these airport operators were excluded from the analysis, reducing the sample size to 23. Using a sample that consists of financial

---

1   A work load unit (WLU) is defined as a passenger or 100kg of freight.

data from 23 airports over a 12-year period creates a volume of statistical observations that is sufficiently large enough to observe the dynamic effects of traffic growth on airports' financial performance.

4. Empirical Results

From 1996/97 to 2007/08, passenger throughput at sample airports increased from 133 million to 231 million, of which 86.4 per cent of the traffic growth was generated by LCCs, 0.4 per cent was attributable to charter airlines and 13.2 per cent to full-service carriers. The traffic impact of LCCs on UK airports is best demonstrated by looking at individual airports. For illustrative purposes, airports are categorized as large-, medium- and small-sized based on the number of terminal passenger throughput.

Figure 16.1 shows how passenger traffic mix at four major UK airports has changed over the observation period. We can see that Heathrow Airport experienced marginal passenger traffic growth (1.7 per cent) during the 1996/7–2007/08 period due mainly to the presence of runway capacity constraints at the airport. In contrast, there was faster passenger traffic growth experienced at Gatwick and Manchester (3.3 and 3.8 per cent, respectively), mainly due to the effects of increased LCC activity. In fact, 75 per cent of the passenger growth at Manchester and 83 per cent at Gatwick were attributable to LCCs. Stansted experienced a considerable growth in traffic, with passenger throughput increasing from 4.9 million in 1996/97 to 23.8 million in 2007/08, i.e. 15 per cent average annual growth rate. Virtually all traffic growth was due to LCCs: their share of passengers increased from 26 per cent in 1996/97 to 93 per cent in 2007/08.

Traffic growth at four medium-sized UK airports is illustrated in Figure 16.2. Luton, Birmingham and Glasgow all experienced a decline in the number of passengers carried by full-service carriers. Although Edinburgh Airport managed to increase its full-service carrier passengers from 3.4 million to 3.7 million over the observation period, this only represents 0.7 per cent average annual

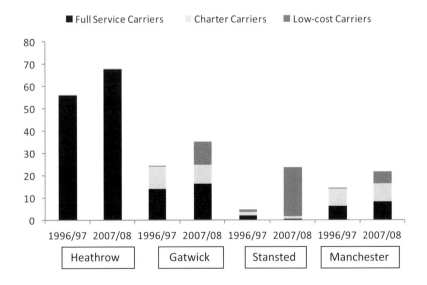

Figure 16.1   Change of passenger traffic mix at large-sized airports

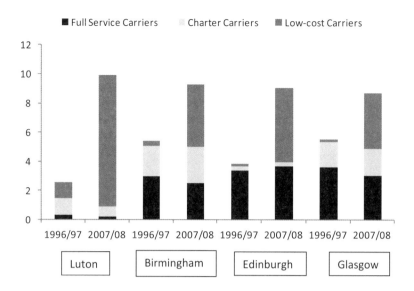

Figure 16.2   Change of passenger traffic mix at medium-sized airports (1)

growth. As for charter traffic, the average annual growth rate was small for Glasgow (0.6 per cent), Edinburgh (0.6 per cent) and Birmingham (1.4 per cent), and negative for Luton Airport (–4.4 per cent). By contrast, the growth of low-cost traffic at these four airports was phenomenal: 21.1 per cent average annual growth rate for Luton, 25.5 per cent for Birmingham, 33.4 per cent for Glasgow, and 34.4 per cent for Edinburgh. Consequently in 2007/8, 91 per cent of the traffic at Luton, 56 per cent at Edinburgh, 46 per cent at Birmingham, and 44 per cent at Glasgow was accounted for by LCC activity.

Figure 16.3 shows there was a dramatic increase in low-cost traffic at Bristol, Newcastle, East Midlands, Liverpool and Belfast airports. At Liverpool Airport, since easyJet set up a base there in 1997, growth has been quite phenomenal, with LCC passenger traffic volume increasing from 0.1 million to 5.1 million over the observation period. By contrast, charter traffic remained static at all these airports, while there was a decline in the number of passengers carried by full-service carriers. From modest beginnings, LCCs quickly came to dominate these airports' traffic. In 2007/08, 93 per cent of the passengers at Liverpool airport were carried by LCCs, while the share was 84 per cent for Belfast International airport, 70 per cent for Bristol and East Midland airports, and 49 per cent for Newcastle airport.

According to Figure 16.4, London City airport recorded the fastest average annual growth in traffic (13.4 per cent), followed by Southampton (12.1 per cent), Leeds Bradford (9.3 per cent), Cardiff (6.7 per cent) and Aberdeen (3.3 per cent). Due to its close proximity to London's main financial centre, City Airport has managed to attract a range of full-service carriers seeking to exploit the high-yield business market potential of its catchment area. Traffic growth can be largely attributed to network expansion by regional carriers such as Cityjet, BA Cityflier and VLM; all three of them affiliated to Air France, British Airways and KLM, respectively. At Leeds Bradford and Southampton airports, the number of passengers carried by full service and charter airlines declined substantially. This is in stark contrast to the dramatic increase in low-cost traffic at these airports. Consequently, both airports came to be dominated by low-cost traffic; 89 per cent at Southampton and 72 per cent at Leeds Bradford in 2007/08. By contrast, the more modest traffic growth at Cardiff and Aberdeen airports appeared to be the result of a much less dramatic increase in low-cost activities. Having said that, LCCs still accounted for 69 per cent of traffic growth at Aberdeen airport, and 53 per cent at Cardiff.

Finally, Figure 16.5 shows the change of traffic types at five small-sized UK airports (Blackpool, Bournemouth, Exeter, Humberside and Teesside). Growth was fastest at Blackpool, Bournemouth and Exeter; all three airports dominated by LCCs. By contrast, Humberside airport, which did not have sizable presence of LCCs, had the lowest average annual traffic growth. For Teesside airport, virtually all its traffic growth was the result of increased LCC activities.

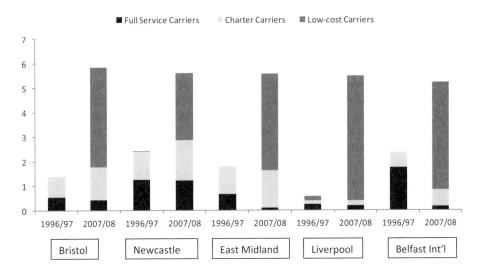

Figure 16.3   Change of passenger traffic mix at medium-sized airports (2)

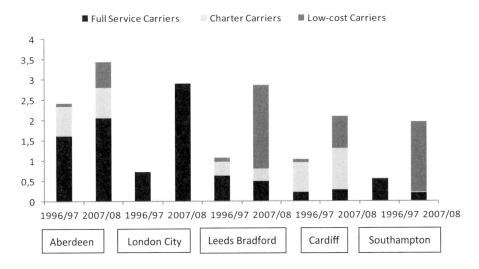

Figure 16.4   Change of passenger traffic mix at medium-sized airports (3)

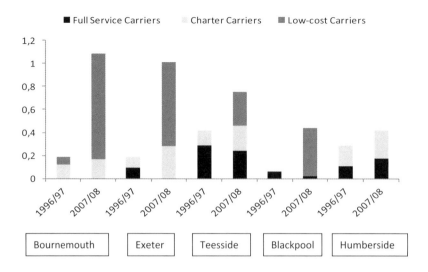

Figure 16.5   Change of passenger traffic mix at small-sized airports

In summary, the examination of 23 UK airports demonstrated that over the 12-year period, types of passenger traffic at these airports underwent fundamental changes. Starting with very low level, LCCs quickly became dominant forces at a number of regional airports. In the majority of cases, airport traffic growth was generated by LCC activities.

The above analysis reveals that airports managed to attract substantial LCC operations experienced a dramatic increase in traffic. But does increased traffic necessarily mean improved financial performance for airports? To answer this question, we first need to understand what the impact of passenger traffic growth has been on the airport's financial performance. In this study, we use operating profit as an indicator for financial performance because it embeds revenue and cost.

A correlation analysis was conducted between the passenger traffic and airport's operating profit in 1996/97 and 2007/08, and the results are shown in Figure 16.6. A Pearson's product moment correlation coefficient was calculated between the two variables on the assumption that there is a linear relationship between them. The computed correlation coefficient is 0.98 for 1996/97 and 0.97 for 2007/08. The high, stable and positive correlation coefficients suggest that a strong and predictable linear relationship exists between passenger volume and airport operating profit over time.

A visual inspection of the scatter diagram for 1996/97 and 2007/08 illustrates the dominance of a few large airports. To better understand how each individual airports deviate from the regression line, we drop the four largest airports – Heathrow, Gatwick, Manchester and Stansted – and plot passenger traffic against airport operating profit (Figure 16.7). The calculated correlation coefficient for 1996/97 data is 0.96, indicating positive and near perfect correlation between passenger traffic and airport operating profit.

However, there is a marked reduction in the correlation coefficient (0.78) when we use 2007/08 data, suggesting a much weaker relationship between these two variables. Closer observation of Figure 16.8 reveals an interesting pattern. In 2007/08, Luton had more terminal passengers than Edinburgh, Glasgow and Birmingham, but its operating profit was much lower. In fact, the operating profit per passenger at Luton was £1.66, compared to £2.60 at Birmingham, £3.01 at Glasgow, and £3.91 at Edinburgh. The marked difference can be explained by the different traffic

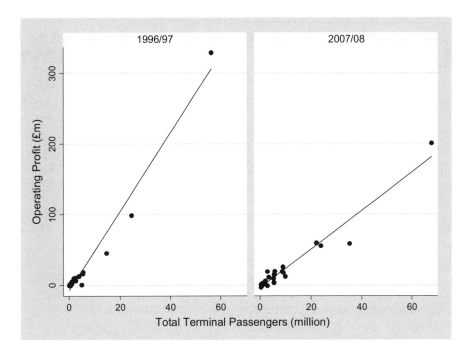

Figure 16.6   Correlation between passenger traffic and airport operating profit in 1996/97 and 2007/08

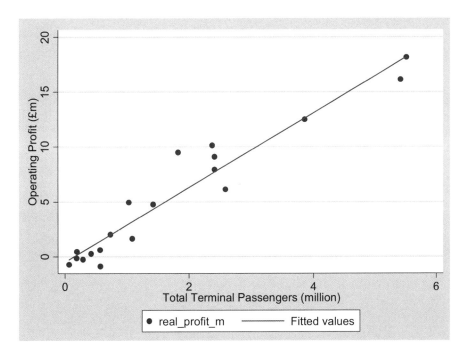

Figure 16.7   Correlation between passenger traffic and airport operating profit in 1996/97

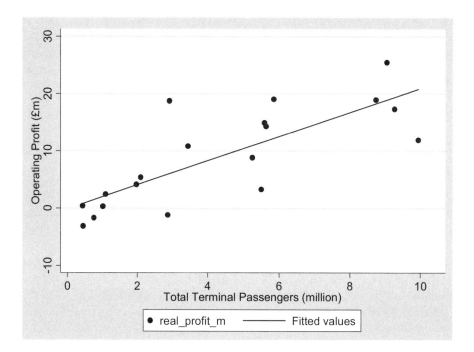

Figure 16.8   Correlation between passenger traffic and airport operating profit in 2007/08

mix at these airports: 91 per cent of traffic at Luton Airport in 2007/08 was carried by LCCs, while the corresponding figure for Edinburgh, Glasgow and Birmingham was 56, 44 and 46 per cent, respectively. The results seem to suggest that LCC passengers make a much a lower marginal contribution to an airport's operating profit.

This observation also holds for Bristol, East Midlands, Newcastle, Belfast and Liverpool airports. All five airports recorded similar volume of passenger traffic in 2007/08, but Liverpool's operating profit per passenger of £0.83 was much lower than that of Belfast (£2.34), Newcastle (£3.52), East Midlands (£3.71) and Bristol (£4.52). Liverpool airport's below-average performance is likely due to its overdependence on LCC traffic (i.e. 93 per cent).

This finding is reinforced when examining London City, Aberdeen and Leeds Bradford airports. With 2.87 million passenger throughput in 2007/08, Leeds Bradford incurred an operating loss of £1.7 million – equivalent to the loss of £0.60 per passenger. By contrast, with a similar volume of passenger traffic, Aberdeen airport generated operating profit of £4.37 per passenger, while London City airport's operating profit per passenger was £8.94. A closer look into Leeds Bradford's operating profit shows that the airport was actually consistently profitable during 1996/97 to 2006/07. Its loss in 2007/08 is due to the effects of an asset revaluation which doubled depreciation costs. From 2004/05 to 2006/07, the airport's operating profit was £1.6m, £1.4m, and £1.4m, respectively. To avoid a biased comparison, we used Leeds Bradford's data in 2006/07 and the calculated operating profit per passenger is £0.53 – a figure which is still much lower than that of Aberdeen and London City airports. Aberdeen's enhanced financial performance is to a large extent a reflection of its mix of traffic. This airport operates as a base for helicopter traffic to North Sea oil installations and is in receipt of premium oil-related traffic from extensive scheduled flights to the Norwegian airports of Bergen and Stavanger. As for London City airport, its aeronautical charges are known to be very high which makes a significant contribution to its operating profit. By contrast, Leeds Bradford's much higher dependence on LCC traffic (72 per cent) would have had the effect of depressing yields from aeronautical charges.

The above analysis examined the correlation between passenger traffic and airport operating profit in two separate years, but it is unable to reveal the relationship between traffic growth and airport operating profit growth. To overcome this problem, we use compound average growth rate (CAGR) to calculate the annual growth rate for each airport over the period of 1996/97 to 2007/08. As operating losses were recorded at several sample airports – Exeter, Humberside, Leeds Bradford, Liverpool and Teesside – in various years, this renders the computation of CAGR impossible for those airports.[2] To satisfy the mathematic condition, for the above airports only those years when they made operating profit were taken into account in computing the CAGR.[3] Figure 16.9 shows the relationship between passenger growth and airport operating profit growth. The calculated correlation coefficient is quite low (i.e. 0.45) which is likely due to the presence of three outliers: Stansted, Liverpool and Blackpool.

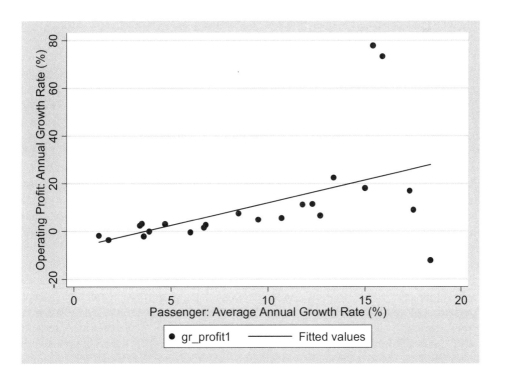

Figure 16.9   Airport passenger growth and operating profit growth

---

2   The mathematical formula only applies to positive numbers in order to avoid taking the root of a negative product, which would result in imaginary numbers.

3   The years taken to compute CAGR for these airports are as follows: Exeter: 1998/99–2007/08 (10 years); Humberside: 1999/00–2007/08 (9 years); Leeds Bradford:1995/96–2007/08 (12 years); Liverpool:2001/02–2007/08 (7 years); and Teesside: 1996/97–2000/01 (6 years).

We now examine each of these outliers in detail. With passenger traffic growing at a CAGR of 15 per cent between 1996/97–2007/08, Stansted airport's operating profit increased at a staggering CAGR of 78 per cent. For Liverpool airport, the period under consideration is from 2001/02 to 2007/08. Its annual average growth rate of passenger traffic and operating profit was 16 and 73 per cent, respectively. The much higher rate of operating profit growth at both airports is likely due to dramatically increased passenger traffic, which helped both airports achieve a critical mass of traffic volume, thereby resulting in disproportionately higher rates of commercial revenue growth. Moreover, during the sample period, Stansted airport undertook a significant renovation of its terminal retail estate which enabled higher sales penetration and improved commercial yield for the airport. Likewise the new passenger terminal built at Liverpool provided the opportunity to exploit commercial revenue spend from a rapidly expanding traffic throughput. Another reason, though less significant, is probably due to the fact that both airports started from a very low base (i.e. Stansted's operating profit in 1996/97 was £0.10m, while Liverpool was £0.14m in 2001/02).

By contrast, the financial performance of Blackpool airport continued to deteriorate even as traffic volume was increasing at an average annual rate of 19 per cent. The airport incurred an operating loss of £0.76m in 1996/97 which grew to £4.3m in 2007/08, equivalent to a 14 per cent (in constant value) year on year reduction. One possible explanation relates to the likely nature of the contractual relationship with its only airline customer, Ryanair. Based on experience elsewhere in Europe it is likely that Ryanair was able to negotiate a significant discount on aeronautical charge; recognizing of course the rather speculative nature of this assertion. Indeed, Blackpool is not known to have expanded and renovated its terminal facilities and commercial outlets during the observation period, leaving it with insufficient capability to enable a meaningful leverage of the potential additional spend from higher traffic volumes generated by Ryanair. The airport appears in a classic sunk cost expansion quandary; should it expand and renovate facilities, in the hope that commercial spending will mitigate the loss in aeronautical income, or is there too great a risk that Ryanair may withdraw services, leaving the airport with stranded under-utilized assets?

It appears that the presence of Stansted, Liverpool and Blackpool airports seriously distorted the correlation analysis. When the influence of these three airports was removed, the correlation coefficient increased to 0.78 at the 1 per cent level of significance, suggesting a positive and quite strong relationship between passenger traffic and airport operating profit.[4] It can be seen from Figure 16.10 that airports with higher traffic growth, in general, tend to have higher growth rate in operating profit. Another interesting observation is that airports dominated by LCC traffic tend to have a below-average growth rate in operating profit. Airports in this category include Exeter, Luton, East Midlands, Leeds Bradford, Belfast International, though there is a notable exception – Southampton. Eighty-nine per cent of the passenger traffic at Southampton in 2007/08 was carried by Flybe. However, it is questionable whether the Flybe operation at Southampton represents a classic LCC case. The airport has a high proportion of business traffic, a market that is generally quite price inelastic. Moreover, being a member of BAA, it is unlikely that Southampton offers discounts to Flybe that are on a similar scale to that agreed between Ryanair and Blackpool, for example.

---

4   As mentioned before, different periods were used to compute CAGR for a few airports. To ascertain whether this has distorted the correlation analysis, we dropped these airports and found the effect was pretty similar to that in Figure 16.10.

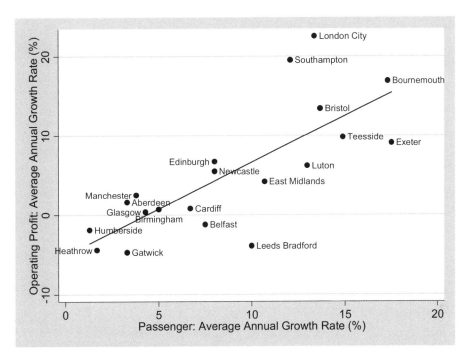

Figure 16.10 Airport passenger growth and operating profit growth (excluding Stansted, Liverpool and Blackpool airports)

5. Concluding Remarks

In this chapter, we found that airports which embraced LCCs all experienced a dramatic increase in traffic. A cross-sectional correlation analysis revealed that there was a positive and strong relationship between passenger traffic and airport financial performance. In general, airports with more passenger throughput tended to have higher operating profit. This was especially the case at the start of the observation period in financial year 1996/97. However, the strength of the correlation weakened in 2007/08 when LCCs became dominant players at many airports. By looking into the average annual growth rate, we also found there was positive and strong correlation between passenger traffic and airport operating profit after removing the influence of the outliers. Higher operating profit growth was generally associated with higher passenger traffic growth. Nevertheless, airports dominated by LCCs experienced below average growth in operating profit, though there were several exceptional cases, notably Stansted and Liverpool airports.

   To attract LCCs, especially Ryanair, significant discounting of aeronautical charges is generally expected and required. While this may lead to significant traffic growth, it does not necessarily translate into the higher commercial revenue that one would intuitively expect. Only those airports with adequately developed retail estates will benefit from the increased traffic. Nevertheless, terminal expansion or refurbishment of facilities are, to a large extent, irreversible commitments and would both represent a significant sunk cost to regional airport operators. In the short- to medium-term, these airports may have to sustain losses. This may not be a particular problem for regional airports in large metropolitan areas because there is potential for future traffic growth, but it could be particularly problematic for smaller ones like Blackpool that have limited catchment areas as LCCs can withdraw air services just as quickly as they established them. While the promise of substantial traffic volume may seem particularly alluring to airport managers and planners, a significant degree of caution would need to be exercised in establishing the business case for attracting LCC services. Having said that, this study only examines the correlation between traffic and airport profitability, while co-founding factors have not been analysed. Further research based on a rigorous econometric model is required to test the robustness of these conclusions.

References

Doganis, R. (2002) *Consultancy Advice on Aviation Issues for the Department of the Taoiseach, Ireland.* London: Rigas Doganis & Associates.

Francis, G., Fidato, A. and Humphreys, I. (2003) Airport–airline interaction: the impact of low-cost carriers on two European airports. *Journal of Air Transport Management*, 9, 267–273.

Graham, A. (2003) *Managing Airports: An International Perspective*, 2nd edn. London: Butterworth Heinemann.

Graham, A. and Dennis, N. (2007) Airport traffic and financial performance: a UK and Ireland case study. *Journal of Transport Geography*, 15, 161–171.

Lei, Z. and Papatheodorou, A. (2009) Measuring the effect of low-cost carriers on regional airports' commercial revenue. *Research in Transport Economics*, 26, 1, 37–43.

Lei, Z., Papatheodorou, A. and Szivas, E. (2010) The effect of low-cost carriers on regional airports' revenue: evidence from the UK. In P. Forsyth, D. Gillen, J. Muller and H. Niemeier (eds), *Airport Competition: the European Experience.* Farnham: Ashgate, pp. 311–320.

Njegovan, N. (2006) Elasticities of demand for leisure air travel: a system modelling approach. *Journal of Air Transport Management*, 12(1), 33–39.

Papatheodorou, A. and Lei, Z. (2006) Leisure travel in Europe and airline business models: a study of regional airports in Great Britain. *Journal of Air Transport Management*, 12, 1, 47–52.

Chapter 17

Deregulating Ground Handling Services in Europe – Case Studies on Six Major European Hubs

Cornelia Templin

1. Introduction

The liberalization of the airline industry during recent decades led to far-reaching changes in market structure, both horizontal and vertical – including a strong impact on the ground handling business.

Ground handling activities describe the aviation-related services that take place on the ground between arrival and departure of an aircraft. They include elements such as passenger check-in, handling of cargo, transportation of luggage and also airline catering, fuelling, fresh water and toilet services.

Service quality on the ground is essential for airlines due to the increasing competition for passengers. The potential for an airline to differentiate their products 'in the air' is low. Competitive advantages lie, to a great extent, in pre- and post-flight activities such as convenient check-in procedures, punctuality, fast and efficient transfer processes and short baggage delivery times.

Ground handling markets in Europe were regulated to a great extent when liberalization in the airline industry took place. Carriers were more and more exposed to full competition and did not want to limit their choice to the few and highly regulated suppliers on the ground. The pressure from airlines ultimately led to a deregulation of ground handling services and the implementation of Council Directive 96/67/EC on access to the ground handling market at Community airports.[1]

This chapter focuses on the deregulation of airside handling services at European airport hubs.[2] A brief introduction of the handling industry is followed by the reasons for the opening of ground handling markets and the description of the contents of Council Directive 96/67/EC. The effects of deregulation at six major European hubs are then analysed. The chapter concludes with the outlook for future developments in the industry.

2. The Ground Handling Industry

Providers of ground handling services can be airlines, airports or independent handling companies. Many airlines service their own aircrafts (self-handling) and may also provide this service to other carriers (third-party handling). Additional third-party handling can be provided by airport operators and independent handling companies.

Before deregulation took place in Europe, airlines usually self-handled flights at their home base airports. To improve the utilization of resources, they regularly offered their services to other airlines, commonly on a reciprocal basis between airlines at their respective hubs. Airports at times provided third-party handling for historical reasons. For example, in Germany, only airport authorities were allowed to offer handling services after the Second World War, supervised by

---

1   See European Council (1996).
2   Concentrating on baggage and ramp handling.

the Allies. Independent handlers at that time were largely restricted to local markets and had only modest market shares.[3]

Due to the growing competition in handling markets, industry structures began to change. Some airlines started to outsource their handling activities in order to concentrate on their core competencies. Airlines also chose third-party handling because of cost-oriented make or buy decisions. Furthermore, several airports ceased their handling activities due to decreasing market shares or because of more favourable cost structures of competing independent third-party handlers. Subsequently, independent handlers started to grow with the opening of handling markets in Europe. A lot of them now offer their services at numerous airports, either worldwide or in certain regions of the world.[4]

The world market of ground handling had a volume of about €31 billion in 2007.[5] At the beginning of the last decade, airlines used to dominate the market (59 per cent), the remaining handling volume was split between independent handlers (24 per cent) and airports (17 per cent). The share of independent handlers increased to 45 per cent of the total volume by 2012,[6] leading to further consolidation throughout the industry, which is still very fragmented. The eight largest companies hold only 14 per cent of the total market volume of €31 billion.[7]

The industry consists of local, regional and global ground handling companies. In addition to over 100 small, mostly local, handlers worldwide there are a few large international companies that offer their services at a number of airports in various countries.[8] Global players serve up to about 180 airports in 40 countries and have revenues up to €1.3 billion.[9] They usually have fairly small market volumes at these airports, with an estimated average of 20,000–30,000 turnarounds per year.[10] From this perspective, Fraport is in a different league as the third-largest independent supplier, serving over 200,000 turnarounds a year at one single airport.[11]

3   See KPMG (2002: 2), Nana (2003: 21–22) and Piper (1994: 51).

4   Alaska Airlines was one of the first airlines to outsource ramp operations at their hub in Seattle with 140 daily flights, see Anon. (2006: 31). Aeroporti di Roma sold their handling activities in 2006 to independent handler Flightcare, see FCC (2006).

5   See Cartwright (2008: 2) estimate for 2007. The evaluation of the total market volume varies largely. Experts estimate the volume between €32 and €35 billion (or about US$40 billion), see Swissport (2005: 5), Smith (2004: 6) and Nana (2003: 21). The World Trade Organization calculates a volume of only €22 billion (approximately US$27 billion), see WTO (2005: 2).

6   See KPMG (2002: 2), ACI Europe (2004: 16), Cartwright (2008: 2) and ACI Europe (2013). Swissport estimated the market share of independent handlers at about 30 per cent in 2005, see Swissport (2005: 5).

7   See Conway (2005: 48) and Fraport (2009). The 'Big 8' are Swissport, Servisair, Fraport, Worldwide Flight Services, Menzies Aviation Group, Aviapartner, Aviance UK and SATS. Besides Fraport (airport operator at Frankfurt) and SATS (a subsidiary of Singapore Airlines) the large suppliers are independent third-party handlers. The consolidation process in the handling industry between 1998 and 2005 is illustrated in Templin (2007: 33–34).

8   See Walker (2000: 7).

9   See Swissport (2009).

10   An average volume to successfully operate at a hub is estimated at 20 to 30 sometimes even up to 55 turnarounds per day. This leads to 7,000–20,000 turnarounds per year, depending on the operating costs and pricing structures at the relevant airport, see Templin (2007: 145).

11   See Fraport (2009) and Templin (2005a: 1).

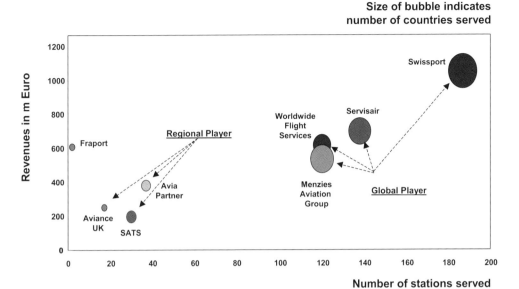

Figure 17.1   The largest ground handling companies worldwide[12]

3. The Need to Deregulate

Many ground handling services such as landside cargo and passenger handling are generally completely open to competition. Airside baggage services and most services on the ramp are provided in different market structures throughout the world. In North America for example, ground handling markets are fully liberalized. Airlines dominate the market, providing self- and third-party handling. In addition, several independent ground handlers offer handling services to the remaining airline customers. In Asia, the markets are still quite regulated and it is mainly airlines who provide handling. Normally only one additional independent handler serves as a competitor in a sort of 'regulated duopoly'.

European airports, in contrast, still have heterogeneous market structures for airside handling services. Before the deregulation process for ground handling in Europe started, the market structure at European airports on the ramp was often monopolistic. Sometimes ground handling was provided by the flag carrier of the respective country, at other airports the sole supplier was the airport company. Even if there were more suppliers active at an airport, market entry was often restricted to only a few handlers.

When competition for airlines increased in the early 1990s, airlines lobbied for more competitive structures for their suppliers. They were no longer willing to accept regulated market structures for their most important business partners and wanted to improve the influence on their own competitive situation. Several carriers complained to the European Commission about the abuse of market dominating positions at certain airports. Neil Kinnock, EU Commissioner for Transport at that time, therefore asked on behalf of the airlines:

---

12   See Fraport (2009) for a diagram; for revenues, number of stations and countries served, see company home pages.

It is essential for them to be able to choose which handler they want, including handling for themselves, rather than just having to accept the price and service of the monopoly handler. That is the situation now in most airports.[13]

In addition to the specific cases of the abuse of market dominating positions at certain airports, the Member States themselves were accused to have granted special or exclusive rights to handlers that led to these artificial monopoly situations at a large numbers of European airports. Consequently, not only the handlers' behaviour but also regulatory frameworks led to a lack of competition in the handling industry.[14] The European Commission realized the need for horizontal actions and started the process to open the handling markets in all Member States. The establishment of neutral tender and approval procedures as well as transparent terms of access to airports were initially asked for in the European Commission consultation paper in 1994.[15]

In 1996, the Council Directive 96/67/EC on access to the ground handling market at Community airports came into force. The particular aims of this directive were to help reduce the operating costs of airline companies and improve the quality of service provided to carriers.[16] It set standards for all Member States of the European Union. The opening-up of the ground handling markets pursues and completes the liberalization of the aviation industry within the Single European Market. Moreover, the aim to deregulate the markets traces back to the efforts of the European Union to break up existing monopolistic structures.[17]

4. Implementing Council Directive 96/67/EC

Council Directives are addressed to all Member States of the European Union who are committed to transform them into national law. Primary legislation of European competition regulations are still applicable, Directives as a secondary legislation provide an additional framework that has to be complied with.[18]

The Directive essentially guarantees effective and fair competition by setting rules for the number of competitors as well as the selection process of handlers. All in all, the access to the ground handling market according to the Directive should be introduced gradually and take the specific requirements of the sector into account.[19] Therefore, the EU acknowledged the special circumstances of airside services and provided for the possibility of restricting the number of competitors for ramp, baggage, fuel and oil handling as well as some parts of freight and mail handling. Member States (not airports themselves) could ask for an additional limitation, which was only granted under special conditions such as lack of capacity or security problems. If the number

---

13   Kinnock (1996: 11).

14   See Soames (1997: 83). The Directive is based on Article 80 (2) of the Treaty establishing the European Community (at the time of the introduction of the Directive Article 84 (2), see European Council (1996), Introduction to Recitals and von Einem (2000: 104).

15   See van Miert (1994: 62–63), European Commission (1993: 87–88) and European Commission (1994).

16   See European Council (1996), Recital 5.

17   See von Einem (2000: 30).

18   See European Council (1996), Recital 28 and Deselaers (1996: 264). This chapter only discusses some aspects of the Directive are discussed, e.g. analysis of cargo airports is omitted.

19   See European Council (1996), Recital 10.

of handlers was limited, a tender process had to be carried out. The tender process described in the Directive had to be non-discriminatory and licences could be given out for up to seven years.[20]

4.1 Number of Competitors

Unrestricted competition is not always possible or desirable. The scale of competition and thus the number of competitors that offer handling services at an airport might depend on several aspects. Limiting factors include:[21]

- The actual situation at the relevant airport, e.g. capacity and security aspects, technical feasibility, necessary investments
- The effects on quality of a market opening on airlines as customers, e.g. guarantee of minimum connecting times, impact on passenger service
- The problems occurring for market entrants, e.g. high start-up investments for new handling companies.

As a result, duopolistic or even monopolistic market structures can still be possible in some situations. The heterogeneity of services can lead to different degrees of competition, and circumstances have to be assessed at every airport individually. The following analysis concentrates on airside services for baggage and ramp handling.[22] These services are characterized as sensitive concerning security issues, have a high level of technical requirements and investments and are capacity intense. Furthermore, there is no direct contact to passengers – subsequently, these services belong to the Directive's exemptions described above where market access can be limited. The scale of deregulation depends on the handling volume at the relevant airport and the fact if self- and / or third-party handling is offered.[23]

Airlines conducting self-handling only perform services for themselves.[24] Since 1998, self-handling has to be allowed on all community airports. Member States may limit the number of self-handlers at an airport, without a reason, to no less than two carriers (so called 'airport users') for the exempted services mentioned above.[25] While this regulation for self-handlers has existed for airports with more than 1 million passengers a year since 1998, the regulation for third-party handlers was gradated. Originally, the regulations were applicable from 1999 on for airports with more than 3 million passengers. Since 2001, airports with more than 2 million passengers have to implement them; at least two handlers have to offer airside handling services there.[26] Furthermore, one of the handlers has to be independent from the managing body of the airport and the dominant carrier; each airline now has to have the chance to choose between two handlers.[27]

For the initial implementation of the Directive in 1998, there was a possibility to temporarily limit the number of handlers to one or even prohibit self-handling due to capacity reasons. This

---

20   See European Council (1996), the Directive also allows to keep facilities of the central infrastructure in one hand.

21   See European Commission (1994), pp. 4–5, for an intense analysis see von Einem (2000: 147–149).

22   See European Council (1996), annex List of Groundhandling services, Articles 3 and 5.

23   See ibid., Articles 6 and 7.

24   According to the Directive, majority-owned subsidiaries are allowed, see ibid., Article 2 (f).

25   See ibid., Article 1 and 7.

26   See European Council (1996), Article 1, Para. 1(c) and 2. The limitation to two handlers does not have to be justified.

27   See ibid., Recital 12 and Article 6.

exemption was limited in time and had to be explained in detail including measures to eliminate the problem.[28] Since January 2003, at least two handlers for airside services have to offer their services at the relevant community airports.

4.2 Selection Process

If the number of handlers at an airport limited, self- and third-party handlers have to be selected using relevant, objective, transparent and non-discriminatory criteria in a transparent procedure.[29] Third-party handlers are selected through a public tender process for a maximum period of seven years: the selection process is not regulated in detail. Airport operators offering third-party handling have a privilege and are exempted from the tender process and can offer their services without being subject to the selection process.[30]

The decision about the selected handlers is generally carried out by the airport operator, as long as they are not providing handling services themself. In this case, an independent competent authority of the Member State has to decide about the market entrants. Either way, airlines as airport users have to be consulted before the decision. They are represented by the Airport Users' Committee that must be set up at every affected airport.[31]

To ensure high-quality performance at the airports, Member States may be required to establish standard conditions or technical specifications after a consultation with the Airport Users' Committee. The selection criteria must be relevant, objective, transparent and non-discriminatory.[32] In addition, Member States may request approval from an independent public authority concerning general solidity of an applicant before granting a licence to a new handler. The criteria for an approval include for instance a sound financial situation and sufficient insurance coverage, security and safety issues as well as environmental protection and compliance with the relevant social legislation. The necessary regulation concerning the selection of handlers has to ensure the proper functioning of the airport, relate to the preservation of quality standards and must not try to limit competition.[33]

4.2.1 Non-discrimination   Self- and third-party handlers need access to the airport and its facilities and the permission to use it to ensure fair competition. Terms of conditions for access and use have to be appropriate, objective, transparent and non-discriminatory.[34]

In this context, the so called centralized infrastructure at airports needs closer attention. Infrastructure necessary for the supply of ground handling services such as baggage sorting systems, de-icing facilities and water purification and fuel distribution systems may be reserved for and managed by one single provider, often the airport operator. Because of the complexity, cost or environmental impact, a division or duplication of these facilities is not efficient. To ensure the access of ground handlers and self-handling airlines, the management of this infrastructure has to be transparent, objective and non-discriminatory. On the other hand, Member States may even

---

28   See ibid., Article 9.

29   See ibid., Recitals 11 und 16.

30   See ibid., Article 11.

31   See ibid., Recital 17, Articles 5 and 11. For a more detailed analysis of the selection process see von Einem (2000: 185–186).

32   See European Council (1996), Article 11, Para. 1(a). This regulation is relevant for third party handlers and not applicable for self-handlers.

33   See ibid., Recital 22 as well as Article 14–15.

34   See ibid., Article 16.

make it compulsory for suppliers to use these infrastructures.[35] Furthermore, prices for using this infrastructure always have to be cost-related and also transparent, objective appropriate and non-discriminatory.[36]

To ensure non-discriminatory competition, ground handling services may not be cross-subsidized with revenues that derive from its role as an airport authority. They are required to keep separate accounts for their infrastructure management and regulatory activities on the one hand and for the supply of ground handling services on the other. The same transparency applies to all third-party handlers. The separation of accounts and the absence of financial flows has to be checked and approved by an independent examiner on an annual basis.[37]

Besides possible obstructions concerning the access to airport infrastructure and the threat of cross-subsidies, an additional potential for discrimination exists, when incumbents are allowed to transfer employees to new entrants according to market volume shifts. Article 18 was supposed to protect the rights of workers: some Member States, for instance Germany, Italy and Spain, transferred this article into the respective national regulations for opening the ground handling markets in Europe. Workers could be transferred to the new entrants, keeping the same working conditions they had with the previous incumbent.[38] After successful law suits against Germany and Italy, their regulations were deemed to be in breach of the Community law and therefore invalid.[39]

Another enhancement of the Directive since it was implemented was the abolition of fees for the use of airport facilities according to article 16, paragraph 3. When the Directive came into force, this fee could be imposed in addition to the charges for the use of the infrastructure as an equivalent for the possibilities to generate business opportunities at an airport. Since 2003 such a fee is no longer permitted, only a cost-related charge for the use of the infrastructure is allowed.[40]

5. Effects and Consequences of Deregulation

By the beginning of 1999, almost all Member States had implemented the Directive and started opening up their markets at airports with more than 2 million passengers per year.[41] At some European airports, market structures according to the Directive already existed before it came into force. A few markets exceeded the requirements of the Directive, for instance the airports in Amsterdam, London Heathrow, Manchester or Stockholm. Some countries anticipated the changes and adapted their national legislation in advance, as happened in Greece and Spain.[42] According to Council Directive 96/67/EC, 161 airports should be open to competition in 2009 in Europe:

---

35   See ibid., Recital 13 and Article 8. Elements of the centralized infrastructures differ from airport to airport. They are defined as being a preliminary product of ground handling services. Elements of ground handling services as defined in the annex of the Directive can never be elements of the central infrastructure. See Knospe and Neumann (1996: 9–13).

36   See European Council (1996), Articles 8 and 16, Para. 3 and Knospe and Neumann (1999: 9–13, 25). The Council Directive does not give a specific regulation for the level of fees for the use of the centralized infrastructure.

37   Ibid., Recitals 19–21 and Article 4.

38   Ibid., Article 18. Some countries already had regulations in their national Employment Laws and did not implement Article 18, for instance France and Great Britain, see SH&E (2002a: 43, 49).

39   See European Court of Justice (2004, 2005) and European Commission (2007), Article 5.

40   See European Court of Justice (2003).

41   See SH&E (2002a: 40).

42   See von Einem (2000: 34–35) and SH&E (2002b: 29, 43, 48, 52, 54).

112 of them with more than 2 million passengers and 49 with more than 1 million passengers.[43] Nevertheless, competition is still limited at most of the European airports. At present, there is a predominance of handling oligopolies, with the exception of a few completely open markets and some handling duopolies.

The European Commission mandated the consultancy firm SH&E in London to compose an analysis on the first market results after the Directive came into force, including opinions, findings and developments concerning the application and the consequences of the implementation.[44] Hereafter, these results are summarized and replenished with additional insights of experts at six European hubs, interviewed in 2005 as part of a doctoral thesis. The airports visited were London Heathrow (LHR), Paris Charles de Gaulle (CDG), Frankfurt (FRA), Amsterdam Schiphol (AMS), Madrid Barajas (MAD) and Rome Fiumicino (FCO).[45] The following in-depth analysis will concentrate on these six essential European airports. It is important to note that not all of the described effects can be directly traced back to the deregulation process. Other developments like economic problems, consolidation processes and general setbacks in aviation like crises and pandemics also influenced the ground handling markets.

All of the airports visited are hubs of their national carrier and the respective alliance. They handled volumes between 28 and 67 million passengers and 150,000 to 260,000 aircraft turnarounds[46] in 2004. On the demand side, the customer structures are very different. Focusing on alliances, CDG, AMS and FCO are Sky Team hubs, LHR and MAD serve as oneworld hubs and FRA is the only Star Alliance hub. This might be the reason why Lufthansa and Star Alliance have the dominant position at their hub with 72 per cent of the movements compared to the presence of the other alliances at their hubs with oneworld having only 50 per cent at LHR and Sky Team 61 per cent at CDG (and the other three hubs with a figure in between), Star Alliance in Frankfurt is by far the most powerful customer group.[47]

5.1 Handling Structures

On the supply side, all airports had different market structures in their ground handling business. In 2004, 24 different ground handling companies offered their services at these 6 airports. LHR and AMS had a completely deregulated market, the others had restricted the number of providers. The numbers ranged from 11 airside ground handling companies at LHR and only two third-party handlers at FRA and MAD. Three of the six airport companies offered ground handling themselves (at CDG, FCO and FRA), while the others left ground handling to airlines and third-party handlers. At most airports, at least the home carrier and sometimes also other airlines provided self-handling, usually combined with third-party handling. Only at two airports (AMS and MAD) did self-handlers not offer additional third-party handling. At another airport (FRA) not even the home

---

43   See European Commission (2009).

44   See SH&E (2002a, 2002b). Interviews were conducted at 33 European airports, a further 48 airports filled in a questionnaire. Opinions of airport operators, airlines, airport user committees as well as handlers were analysed, including the comments of unions representing airlines, handlers and airports like AEA, IAHA and ACI Europe. See SH&E (2002a: 5–8).

45   See Templin (2007: 16–20). Qualitative semi-structured interviews had been carried out with several airport experts in the relevant markets to learn from their experiences about market entry and competition on the ramp. The interview partners represented between 50 and 100 per cent of the ground handling community at the respective airports. All experts were responsible for the sales of handling products.

46   Half the aircraft movements, a figure commonly used in ground handling.

47   Data analysis based on OAG (2005).

carrier used the possibility to self-handle. The volume of third-party handling ranged from 27 per cent in Madrid with four self-handlers, to 100 per cent in Frankfurt, with no self-handlers.[48] At the majority of all airports in Europe where the number of handlers changed an increase of third-party handlers was reported. The number of self-handlers has either remained stable or decreased.[49]

5.2 Administrative Market Entry Barriers

A few administrative entry barriers for third-party handlers still existed at the observed hubs, even after deregulation was implemented in Europe. Market entry is regulated according to either Directive or local rules. Amsterdam and London Heathrow had minimum standards that new handlers had to comply with before starting their handling business on these completely deregulated markets. Self-handling was generally not restricted, but airports were allowed to limit the number of self-handlers. In reality, not all offered licences were occupied when the markets were opened. In Frankfurt, no airline was self-handling and in Rome, only two out of three licences were used.

Airport operators like ADP in Paris and Fraport in Frankfurt, were de facto selected as third-party handlers according to the airport privilege in the Directive.[50] In Paris and Frankfurt, there were additional temporary restrictions for market entrants at Terminals 2 and 3 (Paris) and Terminal 2 (Frankfurt), granted by the European Commission due to capacity constraints. According to the Directive, these exemptions had to be well-grounded; they both expired in 2000.[51]

London Heathrow still serves as a role model concerning competitive market structures, with more than ten airside ground handling companies. However, administrative entry barriers existed for handlers when it came to moving around the terminals at the airport. If a handler wanted to provide services to an airline at a terminal he was not serving yet, he had to complete an approval process set up by the airport authority. The motivation was to protect active handlers and airlines operating at the respective terminal,[52] and a case study to evaluate the effects of an additional handler at that specific airline had to be conducted. First, the minimum handling volume to be shifted had to represent at least 5 per cent of the terminal volume. Moreover, the additional infrastructure needs of the potential new handler (check-in counters, equipment parking or baggage belts) were weighed against the released infrastructure of the former handler. In the end, the airport authority had to decide if a handler was allowed to offer its services at the terminal.[53]

---

48   See Templin (2007: 34–38). The analysis was carried out in 2004. In the interim, the ground handling markets at some of these airports has changed dramatically. For instance, the airport operator in FCO no longer offers handling anymore and the market is fully open. In MAD one additional licence was given and one of the incumbent independent handlers did not receive a new licence.

49   See European Commission (2007), article 12.

50   See European Council (1996), article 11. The same rule applied to Aeroporti di Roma Handling, they ceased their handling activities a few years after the Directive was implemented.

51   See SH&E (2002a: 11–12) and European Commission (2007), Article 6.

52   See Templin (2007. 161).

53   Usually, the requests are granted, but there has been at least one case, where the transfer was not allowed by BAA, see Templin (2007: 161).

5.3 New Entrants

After the opening of the markets, new entrants had the opportunity to start ground handling operations at these airports.[54] This was usually through application for an operating licence in completely open markets or the participation in a tender process in markets with a limited number of entrants. Additionally, they had the possibility to enter markets through the acquisition of active handlers. Technical entry barriers were fairly low in open markets, but ground handlers still had to fulfil certain institutional criteria set by the airport before they could start operations.[55] Disputes on licensing new competitors occurred at several airports where there was a limit on market entrants. Some handlers that were not approved for a licence filed objections against the tender process or the final decision, which then postponed market entries for up to one year.[56]

The regulated markets in Rome, Madrid, Paris and Frankfurt were especially attractive for new handlers, up to 16 companies applied at these airports. But new companies also entered the already open markets London and Amsterdam, however, these two airports also have had market exits since the Council Directive came into force.[57] Market changes since then are shown in Figure 17.2.

Airport	Company	Entry	Comments
LHR	Plane Handling	1999	operating permit
	GlobeGround	1999	operating permit (now Servisair/GlobeGround)
	Swissport	1999	acquisition (Aer Lingus handling), exit in 2004
	Aviance UK	2001	acquisition (British Midland handling)
	Menzies	2005	operating permit, after Swissport´s exit
CDG	Servisair/GlobeGround	2000	tender
	Groupe Europe Handling	2001	tender
	Swissport	2000	tender
FRA	Acciona	2000	tender
AMS	AviaPartner	1999	operating permit
	Dutchport	1999	operating permit, exit 2002
	Servisair/GlobeGround	2000	acquisition (Aero Ground)
	Menzies	2000	acquisition (Ogden)
MAD	Ineuropa	1997	tender
FCO	Alitalia Airports	2001	outsourcing / tender
	EAS	2001	outsourcing / tender

Figure 17.2   Market dynamics since the opening of the markets[58]

---

54   Additionally, airlines now have the opportunity to start self-handling.

55   For example, the presentation of statements concerning the financial situation and business plans, evidence for quality and security of operations including insurance coverage as well as experience and qualification of employees, see Templin (2007: 160).

56   See ibid., p. 163.

57   See SH&E (2002a: 25–26) and Templin (2007: 69–70).

58   See Templin (2005b: 38).

To start operations at open handling markets, potential new entrants had to fulfil the relevant requirements at these airports. Entering still-restricted airports, the interested handlers first had to convince airport operators, labour unions and airlines as the stakeholders[59] to obtain a licence. When newcomers finally obtained a licence at a certain airport, their entry was usually accompanied by a slow gain of market share in the first few years of operation. Airlines frequently used the emergence of new competitors to increase their negotiating power to receive price reductions with their long-term handling partners.

The start-up at a new airport called for a solid financial backing and some handling experience. To win the customers trust and make them change their supplier, the new company has to offer an attractive value for money package. Besides competitive prices, the entrant had to make sure that the services offered were provided at the promised quality right from the start. This required qualified workers and ground handling equipment before operation started, leading to high fixed costs in advance.[60] However, within five years of operations new competitors gained in all of the six markets studied – up to one third of the market volume in the case of LHR, and at FCO almost two-thirds of the total traffic (see Figure 17.3).

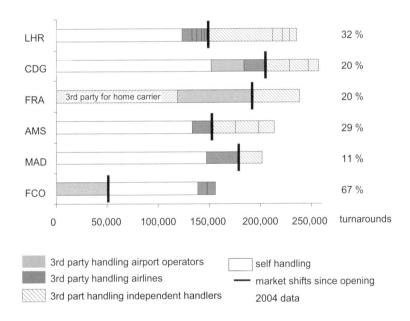

Figure 17.3   Shifts in market share after deregulation (1999–2004)[61]

General success factors for new entrants were their competitive cost structures compared to the incumbent handlers. They also had lean and flexible organizational structures and short decision processes as well as a very strong customer orientation. Also very important for new entrants was a good reputation and their handling expertise obtained in their international operations. Entrants

59   See Templin (2007: 85–86).
60   See Templin (2007: 85–86).
61   See ibid.: 76.

that were part of global handling companies used this as an additional competitive factor. Their customers could compare service levels between airports at which they operated or even combine contracts for two or more stations, which offered networking advantages.[62]

5.4 Incumbent Suppliers

The shifts in market share due to new competitors were the most serious change for incumbent suppliers. In particular airport operators like Aeroporti di Roma, Aéroports de Paris and Fraport lost significant market shares. While airlines changed their supplier in Frankfurt and Paris, the two major airlines in Rome decided to self-handle. Incumbent airlines also lost third-party handling volume, for instance Air France in Paris but especially Iberia in Madrid (being the former monopolist) as well as British Airways in London who decided to cut back third-party handling for strategic reasons.[63] The market in Amsterdam was described as very dynamic, but not in the sense that certain handlers lose and others gain customers, airlines were switching their handlers back and forth. Two of the three new entrants in Amsterdam acquired incumbent suppliers including their customers and employees.

New competitors entered the markets with quite low prices to gain customers and quickly reach the critical mass for production. Therefore, incumbent handlers had to lower their prices to adapt to the new pricing levels and hold their customers.[64] The decrease of absolute handling volumes, accompanied by significant price reductions, led to considerable revenue losses. In consequence, the experienced ground handlers had to adapt their cost structures and to increase their flexibility and productivity. The decrease in absolute handling volumes could not always be balanced out with general market growth in aviation. Unstable performance due to several crises in the aviation industry during the last decade reinforced this problem. Adaptations of resources could sometimes compensate for the loss of market share; but to deal with the price declines, all incumbent handlers had to go through broad restructuring processes concerning their cost structures to ensure sustainable profitability.

Incumbent companies first looked for possibilities to optimize processes in order to generate efficiency gains. A better use of resources led to cost reductions, but inflexible cost structures set boundaries to savings through mere re-engineering of processes. The main focus here is labour costs, which can account up to 8 per cent of the total costs of handling companies.[65]

National labour laws limit the possibilities for more flexible labour conditions for permanent staff, therefore a lot of handling companies adapted their organizational structures to find new solutions to stay competitive. In particular the former monopolists offering ground handling started to change their structure. In Frankfurt all handling activities were consolidated under one roof, but still within the airport authority. Iberia in Madrid also restructured their handling activities within the existing company. In Rome the airport operator had to cope with more severe changes, the former vertically integrated monopolist had to be split in three because the two major airlines, Alitalia and Air One, decided to start self-handling. Therefore, the ground handling division was

---

62   See Templin (2007: 85–86).

63   Additionally, some airlines gave up self-handling in London and switched to third-party handlers, see ibid.: 75–76.

64   In general, pricing levels of handling companies are not transparent. However, especially in open and dynamic markets it seems as if the level for negotiation is down to the lower price limit. None of the airline customers is willing to pay more, at the most according to the development of the consumer price index and the increase of tariffs for workers. See ibid.: 78–79.

65   See SH&E (2002a: 97).

first outsourced as the subsidiary Aéroporti di Roma Handling and then divided into three companies according to the handling volumes.[66] The airport operator in Paris started to use subsidiaries before competition was introduced in Paris and is still shifting permanent staff to the new companies. Air France as the second incumbent in Paris is also changing its structures, but the airline preferred the use of subcontractors to outsource services.[67]

Furthermore, due to the increasing negotiating power of airlines, incumbents had to reconsider their customer relationships and adjust their pricing and product strategies to offer competitive services. The satisfaction of customer needs started to play a more important role than it did before the introduction of competition. Customer care turned out to be an essential task to actively keep airlines and fulfil their individual needs. Incumbents started to sharpen their profile and worked on their competitive advantages as airline third-party providers or independent airport suppliers or third-party handlers in order to be attractive to clients. Besides these typical features, other aspects like qualification of workers and flexibility, modern equipment or process innovations and compliance with security measures as well as handling experience, were also seen as being relevant when choosing a service provider. In addition, handlers tried to extend contracting periods to gain more planning reliability.[68]

According to the demands of airlines the portfolio of handling products changed over time, some handlers offered a greater variety of different products, some also proposed different quality levels airlines could choose from. Quality standards including ISO certifications were introduced and customer service centres implemented.

5.5 Processes and the Use of Resources

The downsides of deregulation were the emergence of inefficient processes and an unproductive use of resources. More operating companies per airport led to an increase in interfaces and occasionally more complex handling procedures and divided responsibilities. The more parties involved, the more coordination was necessary to ensure safe and seamless handling processes.[69]

To ensure smooth operations, interfaces are usually defined in cooperation between the airport and handlers. In London for instance, a so-called aircraft turnaround plan describes all handling processes with all involved parties having clearly defined responsibilities. In Frankfurt, general processes are defined and quality objectives are given. Additionally, regular meetings between all parties are held to solve problems and to optimize processes.[70]

Especially at the considered hubs, handling of transfer baggage is very important. One crucial factor for the success of transfer handling seems to be the structure and operations of the baggage facilities at each airport. Rome reported an increase of interface problems after introducing competition because all handlers were allowed to use the baggage conveyer system after the opening of the market. In London and Amsterdam, baggage facilities were reported to be insufficient, also leading to quality problems. Amsterdam therefore implemented a Baggage

66   Both airlines later also received third-party licences; in 2006, the airport itself sold its shares to third-party handler FCC.

67   See Templin (2007: 80–82). For information on subcontracting in Paris see SH&E (2002b: 18).

68   Usually, contracts are negotiated for one to three years. Some long-term contracts between three to six years were questionable, but discriminating long-term contracts are difficult to trace, see Anon. (2004: 36).

69   See Templin (2007: 81–85).

70   See ibid.: 81–82.

Handling Group to solve trouble with interfaces directly. In Frankfurt, Madrid and Paris, processes stayed stable compared to the situation before the opening of the markets.[71]

Furthermore, capacity and space constraints at airports sometimes interfered drastically with handling operations. Originally, airports were not made for the vast amount of traffic today and the current number of handlers. There was always a lack of office space for handlers as well as on the ramp, which led to competition for the necessary space.

Benefits from economies of scale and scope were often reduced because more personnel and equipment serviced the same amount of traffic as before. On the one hand, the amount of handling equipment as well as personnel is determined by the individual traffic peaks of handlers. Each handler uses its own resources, but most of the time it cannot be optimally utilized due to the structure of traffic. On the other hand, the constraints were increased by a suboptimal allocation of resources between handlers. New entrants brought along their own equipment and workforce whereas incumbents usually did not reduce their existing resources according to the loss of market share. The opening of markets consequently led to an increase of resources.[72]

As a result, incumbents sometimes had to give up space in favour of the new competitors. In Frankfurt for instance, four gates had to be closed to accommodate the handling equipment of the market entrant. In Amsterdam there even seemed to be an unofficial market for office space where companies rented space out to each other. Capacity constraints were also the reason for the complex admission process in London; as described above, handlers had to make sure that their commencement of handling in a certain terminal did not disturb the competitors in their operations. Customers switching handlers increased the problems due to the fact that the amount of equipment and workers were generally not very flexible.[73]

One possibility to optimize the use of resources would be the pooling of handling equipment. So far, hardly any examples exist for such cooperation between handlers. Established operators with a large handling volume do not find this possibility attractive, they think needs and standards of handlers are too different. In particular, handlers with high-end equipment fear the risk of losing a competitive advantage, whereas handlers with less sophisticated equipment fear the potentially high prices. Interestingly, on completely open markets in London and Amsterdam, companies share equipment on an informal basis: employees sometimes use the equipment that is closest to their handling position.[74] It will be interesting to see if the pooling concept with white-tailed equipment will materialize one day, maybe for the use of new and expensive devices, for instance when handling A380 flights in the future.

As seen in the case of ground service equipment, the circumstances for the staff were similar. Human resources were often not fully used to capacity. On some airports personnel has been transferred from the incumbent handler to the new entrant according to the rules and the shift in market share.[75] A flexible adaptation of the workforce on a short-term basis remains more difficult. In particular time-consuming and expensive qualifications limit the flexibility of handlers. Handling

---

71   See ibid.: 82–83.

72   See Templin (2007: 83).

73   See SH&E (2002a: 52, 88–90); SH&E (2002b: 23, 44) and Templin (2007: 83–84).

74   Ibid.: 84. The airport in Amsterdam reported that there is cooperation on the use of ground power units.

75   Implementing the Directive into national law, Spain, Italy, and Germany integrated a rule to protect the workforce allowing the transfer of personnel. The laws in Germany as well as in Italy were judged to be illegal in the meantime. Great Britain and France had national laws that were independent from the directive and allowed shifts of workforce according to transferred functions. Only the Netherlands did not allow transfers, companies had to adjust the volume of their workforce by themselves. See Templin (2007: 68, 87).

companies responded with the increased use of temporary workers and short-term contracts. Nevertheless, in some cases layoffs could not be avoided.[76]

5.6 Other Effects on all Ground Handlers

Besides operational and competitive issues, the industry nowadays also has to cope with administrative challenges and related additional costs. The implementation of the Directive imposed expenses on all participants. The participation in selection processes, the provision of separate accounts for integrated companies and the costs for supervising and coordinating interfaces and processes put even more pressure on the profits of handling companies and airports.[77]

5.7 Effects on Employees

Since ground handling is a very labour-intensive industry, the implementation of the EU Directive consequently had significant impact on employees. As mentioned earlier, costs for personnel might account for up to 80 per cent of the total costs of ground handling companies, the efforts to reduce costs to be competitive therefore concentrate on labour costs.

The loss of market share, as well as productivity increases due to process re-engineering, led to a decreasing demand for workers for incumbent handlers.[78] To lessen the negative impact on employees, the Directive envisaged measures to protect employment rights.[79] In Madrid, Rome, London and Paris, legal possibilities to transfer workers to new entrants were used. In Frankfurt, no transfer was necessary. However, in Amsterdam employees had to be laid off.[80]

In addition to the shift of workforce volumes, the pressure on costs led to significant changes for handlers and their employees. The more recently a handling company started operations at an airport, the lower the average wages generally were. New entrants paid sometimes up to 30 per cent lower salaries, moreover working times were longer and more variable than for employees working for incumbent handlers.[81] Incumbents therefore searched for in-house solutions together with unions and workers' councils to make cost structures more flexible and competitive to avoid dismissals.[82] Contracts and collective agreements were adapted to meet the needs for more flexible working conditions. Nowadays, new employees sometimes have different contracts than long-established colleagues, with unfavourable working conditions, lower salaries, less vacation and longer working hours.[83]

The most serious changes occurred concerning the composition of the workforce. These new structures were adapted by most of the handlers and apply to the whole industry today. To increase

---

76   Ibid.: 85.

77   See SH&E (2002a: 59–60, 2002b: 98–99) and Anon. (2004: 39).

78   The unions report that the increase in traffic volumes during the last years has been met by a meer 50 per cent increase in workforce. See SH&E (2002a: 97).

79   See European Council (1996), Article 18.

80   See Templin (2007: 87). Although working and payment conditions stayed the same, the acceptance of these changes was difficult for a lot of workers.

81   See Bender (2005: 8). In addition, new independent handling companies do not have the expensive benefits that airlines and airport handlers offer their employees.

82   The operator of Frankfurt Airport negotiated an arrangement together with the workers council to lower personnel costs and at the same time prevent layoffs, see Templin (2000:15).

83   See Templin (2007: 88–89). Split shifts are common at smaller airports but have not been reported from the visited six large hubs thus far.

productivity and to manage a profitable handling company, resources have to be used as efficiently as possible. To meet the needs for flexible and less expensive workers, both incumbents and new entrants relied to a greater extent on part-time and temporary workers. They also used more limited contracts to be able to facilitate the termination of employment relationships according to the shift in handling volumes. Furthermore, there was a tendency to employ less qualified staff or keep qualification to a minimum to lower costs.[84]

Full-time permanent employees were regularly reduced in favour of workers with limited contracts. In addition, the share of part-time workers increased. They sometimes work four to six hours a day or have seasonal shift patterns to adapt to the peak structures at the relevant airport. Limited contracts, on the other hand, provide the flexibility to react to shifts in market share from season to season.

While these strategies help to increase the productivity and synchronize the workforce and the airlines' demand for the actual traffic volume, they also limit the flexibility to react to shifts of market shares on short notice. Possibilities for creating more flexible structures and lower costs were the use of temporary workers to cover peak traffic periods as well as the subcontracting of complete activities to other handling companies. Security and qualification standards can limit the use of temporary workers at certain airports.[85]

For employees, these changes led to less attractive and sometimes unstable working conditions, including transfers to new entrants or unemployment.[86] Due to increasing competition, the workers had to be seen as the stakeholders with the strongest negative impact. In particular the employees of incumbent handlers had difficulties in adapting to the new, competitive situations. Handlers tried to inform their workers in advance about the challenges and tried to proactively improve their attitude towards competition but the acceptance and adaptation of employees occurred only very slowly.

5.8 Effects on Airlines and Passengers

As described above, the airlines, as the ground handlers' customers, were the target group to benefit from the Directive. In general, the implementation was seen as successful concerning the development of prices and quality. Nevertheless, airlines believed that changes did not come fast enough and further improvements had to be made.

It was not only the deregulation of handling services had changed the industry. Competition and the tight financial situation of most airlines as well as worldwide crises with volatile traffic developments and increasing security needs also lead to increasing cost pressure with a direct impact on ground handling services. Cause and effect of the development in the industry cannot clearly be distinguished.

Unanimously, stakeholders describe a considerable decrease in prices since the opening of the markets.[87] Between one and four new handlers entered the markets at the observed airports. The change in prices ranges from 5–50 per cent for the airport sample analysed (see Figure 17.4). On completely opened markets, handling prices fell by as much as 50 per cent and at airports

---

84 Ibid.: 88–89. Even though temporary workers sometimes have higher average wages than the permanent workers, the flexibility to take them up on demand makes the use of temporary workers attractive.

85 In Frankfurt for instance, temporary workers with low-level salaries are used to lower average wages. In Paris, temporary workers are more expensive than permanent workers, and flexibility leads to higher costs here. See Templin (2007: 89–90).

86 See European Commission (2007), Article 22.

87 See ibid., Article 8.

with limited competition prices dropped about 30 per cent. Possible reasons for this effect were said to be quite aggressive competitors entering the open markets on one hand and fairly small handlers there on the other hand, who had to fight hard for shares to stay in the market.[88] However, price changes were not only caused by pressure on prices due to competition, changes in scope of services and modified contracting periods were just as important.[89]

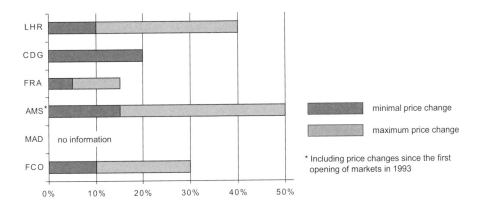

Figure 17.4   Price development after deregulation, 1998–2002[90]

Altogether, the market was more and more driven by demand. Airlines exploited their growing negotiating power, combined with more detailed service-level agreements to strengthen the commitments of handlers. The more dynamic a market was, the shorter the contracting periods became.[91] In markets with a small number of ground handlers, long-term contracts were generally rewarded with price reductions. In more competitive markets, airlines preferred to discuss contracts more often to take advantage of the competitive pressure and reduce their handling costs even further.

Compared to new pricing levels, the development of quality after the implementation of the EU Directive was less transparent. It differed from airport to airport as well as from handler to handler. On one hand, there were lots of different opinions when defining and measuring quality in the first place. In addition, quality was often seen as mandatory; the willingness to pay for quality was therefore limited. On the other hand, the pressure to reduce costs due to competition was intense for handlers. To provide low production costs while experiencing an expensive increase in interfaces and complexity challenged all ground handlers.[92] Combined with enhanced customer

---

88   See SH&E (2002a: 21–23).

89   Airline alliances and hubbing as well as the emergence of low-cost carriers change the needs of airlines. Multi-station contracts, complex transfer processes as well as 'light' handling services become increasingly more important issues when negotiating ground handling contracts.

90   See SH&E (2002a: 21–23, 2002b: 43). A change in prices was a clear specification in Spain when tendering the licences, see SH&E (2002b: 51).

91   In deregulated markets contracting periods generally were one to three years, in partly deregulated markets the periods vary between two and five years, see Templin (2007: 173).

92   Pressure on costs can lead to a more efficient use of resources, but also to leaner service levels, lower reserve capacity and the use of too little resources such as personnel and equipment to maintain a certain

awareness and a wider variety of products to choose from, the introduction of competition led to a mixed picture for the development of quality aspects. [93]

In general, stakeholders had the impression that quality stayed the same or improved.[94] An initial decrease in quality was reported for airports that are completely open to competition. Unsatisfactory quality levels balanced out again when airlines realized that insufficient handling services had an impact on their own quality.[95] Some other quality improvements were quite obvious; customer orientation and flexibility improved and superior, more differentiated products were being offered.[96] The number of service level agreements to constitute agreements on the quality offered increased, sometimes even combined with financial impact due to *bonus malus* systems.[97]

Another positive effect for airlines besides decreasing costs and – at some airports – increasing quality, was the additional variety when choosing handlers. As mentioned before, even if an airline was satisfied with the current handler, the enhanced negotiating power helped to improve the airlines' position and to lower handling prices.[98] However, the overall number of handlers at an airport was not crucial for the assessment of the negotiating power since not all handlers could offer their services at all of the terminals at the respective airport. The number of handlers for airlines to choose from varied from two to six. For the distribution of handlers according to terminals, see Figure 17.5.

In Paris for instance, airlines did not have a choice between all five handlers but between two or three, depending on the terminal they were located at. Only the airport operator ADP offered handling at all three terminals. Air France operated at terminals 1 and 2. All three new, independent handlers received licences for only one terminal each.

Market	Terminal	Airport operator	Airline	Independent Handlers	Total no. of Handlers
LHR	1		3	3	6
	2		2	2	4
	3		2	3	5
	4		1	1	2
CDG	1	1	1	1	3
	2	1	1	1	3
	3	1	1		2
FRA	1, 2	1		1	2
AMS	1, 2, 3		1	3	4
MAD	1, 2, 3		1	1	2
FCO	A, B, C	1	2		3

**Figure 17.5	Third-party competition per terminal in 2004**[99]

service level.

93	See SH&E (2002a: 23–24).

94	Stakeholders have different views, mostly according to the perspective of their respective competitive positions, see European Commission (2007), Article 9.

95	The air carriers have used their negotiating power mainly to play off the various suppliers against one another in order to get the best price, while putting less emphasis on the quality of service. See European Commission (2007), Article 9.

96	See SH&E (2002a: 106, 2002b: 98–99).

97	See SH&E (2002a: 51, 66) and Templin (2007: 74).

98	See SH&E (2002a: 52).

99	See Templin (2007: 212).

The larger choice of handlers with an increased negotiating power could be seen as one of the reasons why airlines did not make much use of the new possibilities to self-handle. Another motivation for airlines to rely on the services of third-party handlers and sometimes even give up their self-handling activities were unfavourable traffic structures with peaks that led to inefficient and costly production structures. In addition, increasingly airlines tend to concentrate on their core competencies rather than offering the full scope of aviation services.[100]

As successful as the deregulation was for airlines, the direct impact on end users – the passengers – was quite small. Passengers had a higher chance of noticing a difference in quality changes than that of observing reduced costs. The time spent for check-in and baggage claim and the quality of service regarding the delivery of transfer baggage were directly perceptible for travellers. However, the provided service level depended mainly on the airlines' strategy and willingness to pay and had to be agreed upon between airlines and handlers. Changes of handling quality therefore depended less on the competitive situation of the handlers than on the airlines' objectives and the capabilities of the chosen handler. Price decreases between handlers and airlines did not cause substantial price reductions for passengers; ground handling costs represent only 4–7 per cent of the total costs of airlines.[101]

5.9 Effects on Airports

Airports as stakeholders were also impacted by the deregulation, but the effects were less significant than expected. In the beginning, most airport operators were afraid of decreasing quality concerning airport performance and security as a consequence of liberalization. In the end the overall performance of the airports studied was not reduced, decreases were short term or did not occur at all. One of the reasons for this smooth transition to more competition in ground handling markets was certainly the gradual deregulation process that the European Commission implemented with the Directive, allowing the Member States to limit the number of new entrants.[102]

Nevertheless, a temporary decrease in safety due to the increase of personnel and equipment, combined with considerable space limitations were reported at several airports.[103] A number of factors have to be considered when assessing the development of safety standards on the apron.

Workers of one or more handling companies may obstruct each other's processes when working side by side in one of the many capacity-restricted areas. Moreover, increasing pretensions of airlines put more pressure on workers, for instance a reduction of ground times or additional requirements agreed upon in service level agreements. These requirements were often accompanied by equipment that was not parked properly due to time pressure on workers. A lack of concentration and too much haste might have increased the number of accidents on the apron.[104]

Handlers thought that thorough and timely qualification of workers would help to reduce these safety risks but, directly after the opening of the markets, they were very sensitive to costs and

---

100   Ibid.: 74–75.

101   According to a study conducted at the Cranfield University, station and ground handling costs together represented about 17 per cent, see AEA (1998), attachment 2. Concerning mere ground handling costs the estimates vary according to the airlines' business model between 4 and 7 per cent, see Smith (2004: 11) and Schmitz (2004: 277).

102   See Templin (2007: 90–92).

103   As described above, incumbents usually did not reduce their workforce and equipment according to the loss of market share, while new competitors entered the market with new personnel and equipment.

104   See Templin (2007: 90–92).

focused too much on the saving or gaining of market share to be concerned about qualifications. Later, the skills of workers gained the status of a selling proposition and were again more important to employers. In addition, handlers pushed the claim to increase the supervision of conduct on the apron and adapt processes to increase safety on the ramp.[105]

6. Evaluation of the Status Quo and Outlook

The decline of monopolistic structures in ground handling markets was considered to be a positive development by airlines and also independent ground handlers. Nevertheless, some improvements are still to be made, in the opinion of various stakeholders. Essentially, Council Directive 96/67/EC had the following positive effects on the situation at community airports in Europe:[106]

- an introduction of competition at numerous formerly closed or static handling markets;
- greater pressure on prices and better value for money spent on ground handling services;
- a decent change in market shares at the most important European airports;
- no evidence of an overall reduction of jobs, but impact on employment conditions in the industry;
- a reluctant implementation of the Directive by some Member States.[107]

The implementation and expansion of competition had a sustainable impact on production processes, costs and also on the sales and revenues of ground handlers. Changes in the overall market structure with a consolidation of ground handling companies is certainly one of the repercussions for the industry, besides market entries and exits on individual handling markets. The most extensive adjustments occurred to former monopolistic service providers. Declining revenues and sometimes increasing costs led to shrinking profits for incumbents that could only partly be compensated with efficiency gains. Many of these previously large handlers nowadays struggle with their financial survival because inflexible cost structures are difficult to adapt to the new market requirements.[108]

For new entrants, market access was not possible at many airports before the deregulation came into force. Even though they gained considerable market share at a number of airports, the situation for independent handlers still seems to be difficult from their point of view. One reason for their complaints is the selection process of handlers when entering still-regulated markets with a licence. To assure a non-discriminating selection procedure, the entity that finally decides on new handlers must not be a potential competitor at this airport but has to be an independent authority. In reality, this neutrality and objectivity cannot be assured in all occasions. Sometimes, Member States have financial stakes in airport operators that provide handling services. In this case, the Member States

---

105   In Rome for instance, a permanent committee was introduced to deal with accidents and measures to reduce risks, see ibid.: 90–92.

106   The 'new' Member States entering the EU in 2004 have limited experience with the Directive so far, see European Commission (2007), Article 7.

107   See European Commission (2007), Article 29 and SH&E (2002b: 98–99).

108   Generally high wages are difficult to cut down to meet competitive cost structures; tariffs and the influence of unions as well as workers' councils including regulations about codetermination limit the scope of actions for management.

have a direct interest in the profitability of the airport company and might not always decide in favour of the airport users.[109]

Other reasons for criticism are potential limitations of commercial opportunities for new entrants such as the small size of the so-called 'contestable market' at some airports and the limitation of licenses to seven years. The contestable market describes that part of the market that is free to be captured by independent handlers and is not occupied in the long run by any other supplier. This is often the case for self-handling hub carriers that also provide third-party handling for their alliance, code-share or franchise partners on the basis of reciprocal agreements at the respective airports.[110] While this condition is historically driven and not an outcome of the deregulation process, the limitation of licences is directly determined by the Directive. Airlines and handlers consider this limit to be too short to build up solid handling activities with strategic perspectives. The constraint may work like an administrative barrier to access for new entrants because they are afraid that they are not able to recover the necessary investments in staff and equipment. In addition, close to the expiration of the licence, airlines might hesitate to contract with the handler because no long-term commitment can be ensured.[111]

Another concern of airlines and independent handlers is the role of airports. While the stakeholders acknowledge the efforts of airports to accommodate new handlers despite capacity restrictions, their attitude towards airport operators offering ground handling is still apprehensive. They fear a distortion of competition when airport operators act as direct competitors, because they are landlord, operator of infrastructure, ground handler and sometimes regulator at the same time. Moreover, airport handlers often have a strong market position, which makes it even more difficult for new entrants to gain market share.[112]

In a sustainable market, no additional supplier wants to enter the market, because they do not see a chance to succeed. Looking at the six airports, the situation is as varied as described above. The markets in Amsterdam and London are fully liberalized and appear to be sustainable. Nevertheless, one supplier in Heathrow was replaced, whereas a departing handler in Schiphol was not substituted. At airports with limited access sustainability still has to be proven. With a large market volume, only two third-party handlers, and no self-handlers operating, the market at Frankfurt seems to be very attractive for additional handlers from the competitive point of view. Problems concerning the size of the market exist in Paris and Madrid as well as Rome. Paris might be interesting for new handlers but because it has limited the scope of the licences to certain terminals, there might not be enough handling volume for another handler if this artificial barrier to entry remains.[113] In Madrid and Rome self-handling companies considerably reduced the handling volume for third-party handlers.

The EU is working on a revision of the Directive. The changes concentrate on increasing competition. Some of the possible changes are:[114]

---

109   See European Commission (2007), Article 14.

110   Ibid., Article 13. For slightly different definitions of the contestable market see ibid. and SH&E (2002a: 26–27). Different stakeholders perceive the contestable markets differently, see ARC (2009: 81–87).

111   See European Commission (2007), Article 15, for a discussion on the advantages and disadvantages of a seven year limit see Templin (2007: 235–237).

112   See European Commission (2007), Articles 16, 17 and 21. Airports, on the other hand, argue that airline handlers and independent handlers have other competitive advantages, see ibid., Article 17.

113   Although the distance between the terminals and the efficiencies of probably necessary split operations have to be considered carefully.

114   See Templin (2007: 207–208). Between 2003 and 2006, the Commission was working on a revision of the Directive. Inter alia, they published a consultation paper and held a hearing with all relevant

- An increase of the minimum number of third-party handlers at airports with more than 10 million passengers per year => four instead of two third-party handlers at airports with over 20 million passengers.
- A wider definition of self-handling which would allow airlines to 'self-handle' their alliance partners => decreasing market volume for third-party handlers but greater chance to self-handle due to the increased handling volume.
- Legal unbundling of airports and airlines and their ground handling business => forced outsourcing of ground handling for vertically integrated airport and airline handling companies.
- Abolition of the airport privilege => airport operators offering third-party handling would have to apply for a licence like the other third-party handlers.
- An implementation of minimum quality standards for ground handlers => to protect performance standards.
- an implementation of social standards for workers => to protect the workforce from excessive disadvantages due to competition.

The first proposals for the revision were postponed and further studies on the effects of the deregulation were assigned. In 2007 the EU published a report on the application of Council Directive 96/67/EC, based on the Study conducted by SH&E in 2002, concluding that a large number of stakeholders recognized the need for an improvement in terms of simplification and clarification of provisions of the Directive. In addition, a future proposal should provide further deregulation as well as some sort of reregulation including new aspects like insurance and quality standards.[115]

Moreover, the research and consultancy firm Ecorys was engaged to assess the impact of changes in the aviation industry on employment, wages and working conditions in the air transport market, with a qualitative evaluation on the relation between these developments and the deregulation of the industry, including ground handling. They observed that an increase in competitiveness has direct consequences in the type of contracts and working conditions.[116]

At the same time, the EU Committee on Transport and Tourism (TRAN), published its report on airport capacity and ground handling. It called for a new impact analysis on the implementation of the Directive, assessing its final benefits and disadvantages for users, employees and passengers, before making any proposal that would lead to further liberalization. Changes to be made should concentrate on the quality of handling and social standards for employees.[117] Airport Research Center (ARC), was mandated in 2008 to conduct this new impact study on the implementation of the EU Directive in all Member States of the EU as a preliminary to a revision of the Directive. The study was meant to update the findings of SH&E in 2002, including the development in the new

---

stakeholders, see European Commission (2007), Article 27.

   115   See SH&E (2002a), and European Commission (2007), Article 28.

   116   See Ecorys (2008).

   117   See TRAN (2007). Further suggestions concerning the revision amongst others dealt with the role of subcontractors, the minimum number of handlers per airport, minimum quality requirements for licences, minimum level of training and social protection for employees as well as levels for security and safety for all airport users, see ibid.

EU Member States since 2004, and additionally focus on working conditions and security aspects in the industry.[118]

Despite remaining entry barriers, ground handlers gain new opportunities to expand their businesses in deregulated markets. They have a chance to develop international strategies and to offer their services at various airports within the EU and globally. This multi-station strategy offers new competitive advantages to other handlers and allows them to adapt to the needs of airlines that increasingly ask for multi-station contracts.[119] For now, the revision of the Directive is still on hold.

References

ACI Europe (2004) *Agreed Service Levels Required: E-communiqué ACI Europe*. September/ October 2004, Issue 157, www.aci-europe.org, 1 June 2009.

ACI Europe (2013) *Ground Handling*, www.aci-europe.org/policy/position-papers.html?view= group&group=1&id=8, 20 January 2013.

AEA (1998) *Benchmarking of Airport Charges, Information Package*. February 1998, AEA, Brussels.

Anon. (2004) Seven year hitch? *Ground Handling International*, 9, February, 32–39.

Anon. (2006) World analysis – the US and Canada. *Ground Handling International*, 11, 1, 30–34.

ARC (2009) *Study on the Impact of Directive 96/67/EC on Ground Handling Services 1996– 2007, Final Report*, February, www.ec.europa.eu/ transport/air/studies/doc/airports/2009_02_ ground_handling.pdf, 1 June 2009.

Bender, W. (2005) Mitarbeiter Dialog: Wir machen Fraport fit (Employee dialogue: we limber up Fraport), Management Conference Fraport AG, 19 January, lecture unpublished.

Cartwright, R. (2008) *International Ground Handling – Financial Overview*. Presentation by KPMG, 10th Annual Ground Handling International Conference, October 2008, Dublin.

Conway, P. (2005) Revolution delayed. *Airline Business*, January, 46–48.

Deselaers, W. (1996) Liberalisation of ground handling services at community airports. *Air & Space Law*, xxi, 6, 260–266.

Ecorys (2008) *Social Developments in Employment, Wages and Working Conditions in the Period 1997–2007, Summary*, www.ec.europa.eu/transport/ air/studies/doc/internal_market/2008_01_ social_study_summary.pdf, 1 June 2009.

Einem, A. von (2000) *Die Liberalisierung des Marktes für Bodenabfertigungsdienste auf den Flughäfen in Europa (Liberalisation of the ground handling market at airports in Europe), Europäische Hochschulschriften, Vol. 2, No. 2962*. Frankfurt: Lang.

24.1.2007, www.eurlex.europa.eu/LexUriServ/LexUriServ.do?uri=CELEX:52 006DC0821:EN: HTML:NOT, 1 June 2009.

European Commission (1993) *XXIII Bericht über die Wettbewerbspolitik 1993 (XXIII Report on competition policy 1993)*. Luxemburg: Publications Office.

European Commission (1994) *Bodenabfertigungsdienste auf Flughäfen: Konsultationsunterlage 94/C 41/02 (Ground handling services at airports: Consultation document 94/C 41/02)*, Abl. EG Nr. C41 vom 11.2.94, pp. 2–8, Luxemburg: Publications Office.

---

118 See ARC (2009). According to European Commission (2007), Article 24, the Directive was correctly applied in the majority of these new Member States.

119 Economies of scale and scope are believed to be negligible. Transaction cost savings may explain this trend, but this topic has to be researched further.

European Commission (2007) *Report from the Commission on the application of Council Directive 96/67/EC of 15 October 1996*, COM(2006) 821 final, Luxemburg: Publications Office.

European Commission (2009) Commission communication concerning the procedure laid down by Article 1, paragraph 4 of Council Directive 96/67/EC. *Official Journal of European Union*, C 97, 28 April, 10–13, www.ec.europa.eu/transport/air/airports/ground_handling_market_en.htm, 1 June 2009.

European Council (1996) Council Directive 96/67/EC of 15 October 1996 on access to the groundhandling market at Community airports. *Official Journal of the European Union*, L 272, 25 October, 0036-0045.

European Court of Justice (2003) *Judgement of the Court of 16 October 2003 in the Case C-363/01: Flughafen Hannover–Langenhagen GmbH v Deutsche Lufthansa AG. (Air transport – Access to the groundhandling market in Community airports – Directive 96/67/EC – Article 16 – Collection of a fee for access to airport installations – Conditions.)*. European Court reports 2003 Page I-11893.

European Court of Justice (2004) *Judgement of the Court of 9 December 2004 in Case C-460/02: Commission of the European Communities v Italian Republic. (Air transport – Groundhandling – Directive 96/67/EC)*. European Court reports 2004 Page I-11547.

European Court of Justice (2005) *Judgement of the Court of 14 July 2005 in Case C-386/03: Commission of the European Communities v Federal Republic of Germany (Failure of a Member State to fulfil obligations – Airports – Groundhandling – Directive 96/67/EC)*. European Court reports 2005 Page I-06947.

FCC (2006) FCC acquires Aeroporti di Roma Handling (ADRH), the leading independent handling operator at Rome's airports, 7 August 2006, press room, http://www.fcc.es/fcc/corp/ing/sdp_n_ddln_255.htm, 25 April 2009.

Fraport (2009) Fraport Ground Services – Master Presentation. Fraport AG, April, unpublished.

Kinnock, N. (1996) The liberalisation of the European aviation industry. *European Business Journal*, 8, 4, 8–13.

Knospe, M. and Neumann, H. (1999) Die Liberalisierung der Bodenabfertigungsdienste und der Zugang zu zentralen Infrastruktureinrichtungen auf deutschen Verkehrsflughäfen (Liberalisation of groundhandling services and access to centralized infrastructure facilities), Legal opinion, Bruckhaus Westrick Heller Löber, unpublished.

KPMG (2002) *Handling Pressure: A Snapshot of the Aviation Ground Handling Industry*. KPMG Corporate Finance.

Miert, K. van (1994) Luftverkehr und Wettbewerbspolitik – Gestaltung oder Bürokratie? In *DVWG: Erstes Forum Luftverkehr der DVWG: Luftverkehr im Wandel – Chancen und Risiken der Zukunft (First Aviation Forum of the German Society for Transport Science: Aviation Changes - Chances and Risks in the Future)*, vol. B, no. 171. Bergisch-Gladbach, 58–63.

Nana, J.-P. (2003) Assistance au sol: conjuguons nos talents. *Aéroports Magazine*, 335, Janvier–Fevrier, 20–26.

OAG (2005) *Official Airline Guide*, OAG Worldwide Limited, June 2005, Vol. 6, No. 12.

Piper, H.P. (1994) Deregulierung im Flughafenbereich: Bodendienste der deutschen Verkehrsflughäfen (Deregulation in Aviation: Groundservices at German Airports). *Internationales Verkehrswesen*, 46, 1+2, 51–52.

Schmitz, P. (2004) Liberalisierung der Bodenverkehrsdienste um jeden Preis? (Liberalisation of groundhandling services at all costs?), *Internationales Verkehrswesen*, 56, 6, 276–278.

SH&E (2002a) *Final Report: Study on the Quality and Efficiency of Ground Handling Services at EU Airports as a Result of the Implementation of Council Directive 96/67/EC. Report to European Commission.* SH&E International Air Transport Consultancy, London.

SH&E (2002b) *Appendices: Study on the Quality and Efficiency of Ground Handling Services at EU Airports as a Result of the Implementation of Council Directive 96/67/EC. Report to European Commission.* SH&E International Air Transport Consultancy, London.

Smith, C. (2004) A valued business? A financial overview. Presentation SH&E International Air Transport Consultancy, 6th Annual Ground Handling International Conference, 30 November 2004, Budapest.

Soames, T. (1997) Ground handling liberalization. *Journal of Air Transport Management*, 3, 2, 83–94.

Swissport (2005) *Profile 2005*, Swissport, www.swissport.com/download/publications/profile_05.pdf, last accessed 7 June 2009.

Swissport (2009) *The Swissport profile*, http://www.swissport.com/corpo-rate/index.php, last accessed 25 April 2009.

Templin, C. (2000) Unternehmensreport Flughafen Frankfurt Main AG: Marktanteilsverluste und Beschäftigungssicherung – wie passt das zusammen? (Company Report Frankfurt Airport: Loss of Market shares and protection of jobs - how does that work together?) In: P. Knauth and A. Wollert (eds), *Human Resource Management: neue Formen betrieblicher Arbeitsorganisation und Mitarbeiterführung (Human Resource Management: new forms of internal work organization and personnel management), 25.* supplement, section 9.19, November. Köln: Dt. Wirtschaftsdienst, 1–21.

Templin, C. (2005a) *Deregulation of Ground Handling on Six European Airports*, www.garsonline.de/Downloads/050609/Templin_paper_new.pdf, 7 June 2009.

Templin, C. (2005b) *Deregulation of Ground Handling, Empirical Analysis of 6 European airports – Management Summary.* November 2005, unpublished.

Templin, C. (2007) Deregulierung der Bodenabfertigungsdienste an Flughäfen in Europa – Konsequenzen für Märkte und Wettbewerber (Deregulation of groundhandling services at airports in Europe - consequences for markets and competitors), Dissertation. Cologne: Kölner Wissenschaftsverlag.

TRAN (2007) *Airport Capacity and Groundhandling: Towards a more Efficient Policy.* TRAN, Committee on Transport and Tourism, TRAN/6/48857, Ref. INI/2007/2092, www.europarl.europa.eu/oeil/file.jsp?id=5479492, 1 June 2009.

Walker, S. (2000) *The Liberalisation of Ground Handling Services: The Impact and Implementation of the European Directive.* Global Aviation Reports. London: SMi Publishing Ltd.

WTO (2005) *Communication from Australia, Chile, the European Communities, New Zealand, Norway and Switzerland – Trade in Services to the Aviation Industry: A case for commitments under the GATS.* World Trade Organization, Council for Trade in Services, TN/S/W/29, Geneva.

.

Chapter 18

Comparative Inefficiencies of Various Air Navigation Service Systems

Kenneth Button

Introduction

Modern commercial air transportation revolves around airlines, airports and the air navigation service providers (ANSPs).[1] The latter, our focus here, are responsible for supplying a number of services; they not only control aircraft movements and separate planes on the ground and in flight, but also offer information on such things as weather conditions and communication facilities. They may be seen as providing and managing the links of the air transportation system with airports as the hubs and air corridors as the links.

In terms of economics, an air navigation system is naturally a 'private good' because it is both rival, in the sense that it can get congested, and excludable, in that the operators of the system can exclude use of it. It is not, however, normally a service that is provided in an unconstrained market context but is highly regulated, and often there is a degree of public ownership. There are a number of reasons put forward for this including that air traffic control has a strategic, military purpose, that there is a need for operational and technical coordination, because of economies of scale, ANSPs are natural monopolies, and that safety and other social considerations should transcend the profit motive. In these conditions, it is argued the normal commercial pressures for economic efficiency do not pertain, and this makes it rather more challenging to assess just how efficient or otherwise the various ANSPs are than would be the case in a purely commercial environment.

This chapter does not seek to provide some sort of ranking of the economic inefficiency of national ANSPs,[2] or indeed the various generic forms that they may take: rather it considers how the different models of ANSs have performed over the recent past in fairly general terms.[3] This provides some guidance as to the elements of relative efficiency of systems, although it says nothing about the absolute levels of efficiency. It could well be that they are all manifestly inefficient; there is simply no counterfactual to make such judgements. We also largely, but certainly not exclusively,

---

1   The chapter focuses on commercial, civil aviation and says little about either military or general-purpose aviation, although both can be significant in some countries and can pose particular challenges in the provision of efficient ANSs from a narrow economic perspective.

2   Button and Neiva (2013) offer some guidance on this.

3   Economic inefficiency can take several forms. In the context of ANSPs, allocative, or Harberger (1959) inefficiency is when some degree of monopoly power on the part of the ANSP allows it to charge a price that exceeds marginal costs and thus reduce the utilization of the system. If there is perfect price discrimination then there will be no inefficiency but simply an accumulation of all net benefits to the provider. X-inefficiency exists when the incentives confronting an ASNP are insufficient to encourage it to provide services at minimum costs (Leibenstein, 1966). Technical inefficiency occurs when there is a normally short-term shortage of a particular input, often management skills, that leads to a ranking of providers with some unable to reach the maximum efficiency level (Farrell, 1957). Rent-seeking inefficiency is when there are incentives for an ANSP to use economic surpluses gained to protect its market position (Tullock, 1967). We touch, either explicitly or implicitly, on all of these.

focus on the efficiency of the ANSPs in North America and Europe. This is partly to keep the task manageable, but these geographical areas are also large air transportation markets, especially when the North Atlantic is included, and they also embrace systems that we have the most information about. As a further boundary, much of the consideration of efficiency is with respect to the economic aspects of ASNP actions rather than such things as safety or the environment, although these not entirely neglected.[4]

There are also broader issues that cross into matter of efficient delivery of services, and the pricing of those services. An ANSP may be efficient in providing navigation and control services given the constraints it is confronted with, but overall the system is suboptimal in welfare economic terms because of the imposition of institutional boundaries. In particular, the pricing of the services an ANSP supplier may be suboptimally regulated, affecting both its own activities and ultimately the signals its customers, the airlines, respond to. There may also be other elements of the air transportation supply chain, such as airports, that have suboptimal economic regulations imposed on them or that operate in non-competitive conditions, that affect the demand for, and *ipso facto* the overall efficiency of, ANS provision. While we consider some of these types of issues, inefficiencies due to distortions in other elements in the supply chain are not given much attention, although they may quantitatively be important.[5]

The Role of Air Navigation Service Providers

Most of the public's perception and debates regarding ANSs focus on their role as air traffic controlling agencies, and often on their perceived failures in that role – e.g. regarding delays and safety levels, and reactions to unexpected events of the type seen in the US on 11 September 2001 or in Europe when an erupting volcano in Iceland in the spring of 2010 produced high altitude dust clouds. These debates, however, although naturally of interest to the travelling public, only reflect some of the functions that ANSPs generally serve, and ignore that providers are also major suppliers of information to potential aircraft users and airports that transcend the strict control function.

At the global level, under the 1944 Chicago Convention, each country has sovereignty over its own air space and can in effect use it as it sees fit. Thus most countries provide and regulate the ANSs that are available in their airspace, but coordinate their provision for safety and economic efficiency reasons, often through agreements reached at the United Nations International Civil Aviation Organisation (ICAO).[6]

Air navigation systems embrace a number of separate elements in their roles as air traffic controllers and information providers (Nolan, 1998). These can broadly be divided into three activities (Figure 18.1). Ground control involves moving aircraft and other 'vehicles' around an airport to avoid conflict, and to direct them to appropriate runways, holding areas, gates, etc. Tower

---

4　There is nothing, for example, on security although the efficiency with which ANS are protected from attack is generally treated as a matter of national security. This omission is quite simply because there is, and rightly so, little information on the resources devoted to security. Further, since a major objective of security is to prevent incidents, there is by definition no information on how successful the deterrence function has been.

5　An ASNP provider in the second-best situation where markets for complements do not deliver marginal cost pricing should ideally pursue a second-best strategy. The conditions for what this action ought to entail are inevitably case-specific and beyond our objectives in this chapter.

6　In some cases, as with COCESNA in Central America, and, to a more limited extent, EUROCONTROL in Europe, countries have relinquished parts of their sovereignty to larger national groupings.

control is responsible for the active runway surfaces at an airport, clearing aircraft for take-off or landing, and ensuring for safety reasons that prescribed runway separation exists at all times. Flow or flight control is responsible for ensuring that both traffic controllers and pilots have the most current information: pertinent weather changes, outages, airport ground delays/ground stops, runway closures, etc. It issues clearances and instructions for airborne aircraft that pilots are required to comply with.

From an operating perspective, each of these three elements of ANS provision can be managed and operated separately, although in many cases countries combine all, or some of the functions. The various ANSPs can differ quite considerably in the technologies that they use and the approaches that they adopt for each of the various ANS required. In part this is due to geographical conditions, for example terrain or local weather conditions need particular attention at the take-off and landing stages of an aircraft movement. There may also be institutional constraints imposed by such things as noise restrictions around airports, and airspace restrictions imposed on flow control associated with such things as military air space segregation. Legacy effects, in term of the technology available, can also affect then ways ANSPs function.

There are, for example, quite significant differences in the way that flights are handled within Europe and the US, although they both cover roughly the same space. The segmentation of airspace by national boundaries has resulted in numerous ANSPs in Europe compared to just the Federal Aviation Administration in the US (Table 18.1). Air traffic management in the European Union is largely undertaken by member states, cooperating through an intergovernmental organization, EUROCONTROL that includes both Union members and most other European states. The US by contrast is a single nation that has a unitary federal administration that provides ANS. Partly as a result of this we also note the larger number of en route centres in Europe.

In terms of the traffic handled by the ANSPs, the European traffic density is much less than that of the US system, with more routes at maximum configuration; a fact driven largely by the great amount of flights in America where the geography makes air travel a much more attractive mode of transportation for many. Additionally the type of traffic handled is somewhat different, with general aviation being a very small part of the total in Europe compared to the US. The European air system also has slot controls at many of its airport that require structured coordination of traffic and limits aircraft movements whereas the US system, with a few exceptions, does not control airport slots.

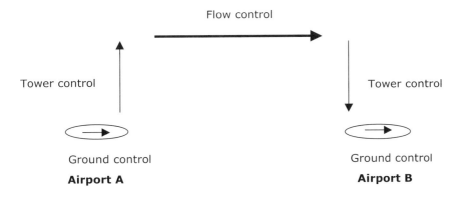

Figure 18.1   The elements of air traffic control

Table 18.1   United States and European ATM systems (2008)

	Europe	USA	Difference USA vs. Europe (%)
Area (million km²)	11.5	10.4	–10
Number of ASNP	38	1	
Number of air traffic controllers	16,800	14,000	–17
Total staff	56,00	14,00	–40
Controlled flights (million)	10	17	+70
Share of flights to/from top 34 airports	68%	64%	–5
Share of general air traffic	4%	23%	+450
Flight hours controlled (million)	14	25	+80
Relative density (flight hours per km)	1.2	2.4	+100
Average length of flight (within respective airspace	541NM	497NM	–8
Number of en-route centres	65	20	–70
En-route sectors at maximum configuration	679	955	+40
Number of airports with ATC services	450	263	–42
Slot-controlled	>73	3	

Sources: EUROCONTROL; Federal Aviation Administration.

Problems in the 'Benchmarking' of Systems

To look at just how well various ANSPs are performing, we need to establish a basis of comparison and a methodology for making comparisons. Benchmarking is the standard, generic empirical method for considering the relative efficiency of any organization. It does not provide any indication of absolute efficiency because, for a variety of reasons, the sample of ANSPs in the comparison may have no supplier that is absolutely efficient. In the simplest sense, benchmarking just means comparing the performance of different suppliers in terms of salient characteristics. In a pure market context, profits are the obvious metrics to consider, but in the case of ANSPs the objective function is multifaceted because of the range of public service requirements involved – safety, access, environment, etc. – as well financial performance indicators. This poses challenges of comparisons between objectives and the implicit weight to consign each. Nevertheless, this is a common approach adopted, for example, by the EUROCONTROL Performance Review Commission (2010a) in its annual reviews, and periodically by the US Federal Aviation Administration (2009) in transatlantic comparisons.

This form of benchmarking is normally cross-sectional and normalizing for background differences in systems – for example fluctuations in local demand, local climate and the nature of services offered by airlines – can be difficult. An alternative is trend analysis that benchmarks an ANSP's own current performance against its performance in previous periods, although as with cross-sectional benchmarking there remains the matters of what dimensions of output are to be considered.

The types of comparison that are made are of the form seen in Figure 18.2 that compare the on-schedule performances at a major European and US airports as an aggregate proxy for ANSP's efficiency in those two geographical markets. The data clearly show trends, and indicate relative efficiency between systems and for each, efficiency differences through time. This sort of analysis can provide some insights but is poor at taking into account background effects, such as fluctuation in demands for services over time due, for example, to macroeconomic cycles, and offers little by way of explanation for spatial and temporal patterns, for example the US system has a single ANSP whereas there are a multiplicity of different types of provider in Europe. Additionally, the use of a 15-minute deviation from schedule to indicate poor performance is not only an arbitrary cut-off point, but can lead airlines to adjust their schedules to minimize their 'delayed' flights. Delays are also a function of other factors than air traffic control, including the capacity of airports and the time of day an initial delay occurs – a delay early in the day has knock-on, ripple effects on schedules for the rest of that day.

Benchmarking their activities against predefined performance targets can also be used to assess efficiency of ANSP providers; e.g. there are proposals to extend the benchmarking that is done in Europe, where currently there is some assessment in terms of safety, capacity, cost-effectiveness and flight efficiency, to embrace notions of sustainable development and to allow a more complete assessment of the create of the Single European Sky (EUROCONTROL, 2010b). As with all forms of satisficing analysis, which targeting essentially is, the devil is in the detail and in this case it is a matter of what targets to use – both in terms of the targets themselves but also their thresholds – and how to handle cases where some targets are exceeded handsomely but there is a small falling short on others.

Whether using cross-section, time series data, or using targets, most analysis normally just involves the type of eyeballing of data done above, but there are more rigorous programming

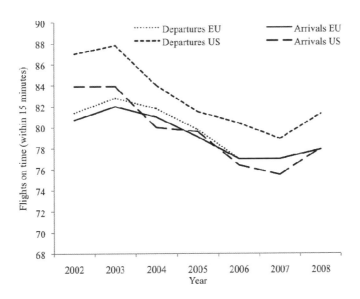

Figure 18.2   On-time performance compared to schedule

Note: the data relates to 34 main airports in each market.

Sources: US Federal Aviation Authority (2009).

and econometric approaches that are slowly beginning to be considered in the context of ANSPs. In particular non-parametric techniques, especially data envelopment analysis (DEA), have been widely used across a wide range of applications, and stochastic frontier analysis in various forms has been deployed. Neither of these broad techniques, however, has been widely used to assess the efficiency of ANSPs, although they have increasingly been adopted in examining airline and airport efficiency. DEA techniques require a series of external assumptions to be made regarding such things as the presence of scale effects, and ideally require data to be in physical units. They also have difficulties in handling outliers and, although there are bootstrapping methodologies available, their non-stochastic nature makes it difficult to test the impacts of exogenous variables on the efficiency frontier. Econometric methods allow testing for causal linkages but require pre-specification of the production or cost function involved.[7]

The Regulatory Environment

Given their strategic importance, their high fixed costs and thus their decreasing cost economics, and their public visibility, the market for ANSs has always been the subject of government manipulation. In terms of managerial economics, the areas of interest usually focus around the structure, conduct and performance of the institutional structure in which ANSs are provided, and particularly the regulatory environment, and the efficiency of the outcome. The regulation of ANSs varies quite considerably between countries, and there have been quite important changes since the 1980s in the approaches to regulation that have been pursued.

Table 18.2 provides a brief overview of some of the key features of 11 of the main ANSPs. Regulation comes in two broad forms, economic (or quantity) regulation that affect such things as the fees charged to users of a ANS and reflect the financial objectives set providers, and social (or quality) regulation that is to do with such things as safety and the use of less environmentally intrusive flight paths. We look at some of the more important elements of these forms of regulation in more detail.

Ownership

The majority of the world's ANSPs have traditionally been state-owned and operated with objectives akin to those of public utilities; namely safety, common carrier obligations, allocation by need, etc. Recent trends from the mid-1990s have seen moves to engender more commercial approaches to the supply of ANSs (Charles and Newman, 1995). Table 18.2 provides in footnotes, details of the existing ownership structures of 11 major ANSPs together with some information of when structures have been created and modified. The institutional structures in which they operate vary by form of ownership and by the nature of prevailing rate controls – see Button and MacDougall (2006) or Oster and Strong (2008) for more details. From a financial risk-taking

---

7   NERA Economic Consulting (2006) is an example of the use of stochastic frontier analysis is the ANSP context. There have been no major explicit efforts to apply non-parametric techniques to assess the relative efficiency of ANSPs, although it has been widely used to look at airports and within some of these studies there are inputs that reflect the characteristics of local air traffic control services, e.g. congestion levels. In general, however, they are focused on local airport efficiency and the ways things like ANS delays reflect on that rather than then the wider inefficiencies in ANS provision. There have been some attempts to apply econometric analysis, for example in EUROCONTROL (2010b), but this has been been rather incomplete, in part because of data and specification issues.

perspective, there are also differences as to whether State debt guarantees are offered; in fact they are not except in the cases of Australia, France and Switzerland and the issue is not applicable in the US where taxes are the current mode for finance.

There has been a gradual but perceptible shift away from state ownership with a variety of institutional structures emerging.[8] Ownership is clearly, from the political economic perspective, not seen as a neutral matter.

As we see below, corporatization has become a popular option in an effort to distance government from the operations of ASNPs and their financing, although the formulation varies;

Table 18.2   Basic features of selected air navigation service providers

Country	ANSP name	Ownership	Rate regulation[*]
Australia[1]	Airservices Australia	Government corporation	Commission oversight
Canada[2]	NAV CANADA	Not-for-profit private corporation	Legislated principles/ appeals
France[3]	Direction des services de la navigation Aérienne (DSNA)	State department	Approved by transport ministry
Germany[4]	Deutsche Flugsicherung GmbH (DFS)	Government corporation	Approved by transport ministry
Ireland[5]	Irish Aviation Authority	Government corporation	Regulatory commission
Netherlands[6]	Luchtverkeersleiding Nederland (LVNL)	Not-for-profit government corporation	Approved by transport ministry
New Zealand[7]	Airways Corporation of New Zealand	Corporation	Self-regulating/ appeals
South Africa	Air Traffic and Navigation Services Ltd.	Not-for-profit joint-stock corporation	Transport ministry committee
Switzerland[8]	Skyguide	Not-for-profit government corporation	Approved by transport ministry
United Kingdom[9]	National Air traffic System, Ltd.	Public/private partnership	Price capping
United States	FAA's Air Traffic Organization	State department	Financing from taxation

Note: [1] Corporatized in 1988; [2] Corporatized in 1996; [3] Consolidated in 2003; [4] Established in 1993 and was to be privatized in 2006 but since aborted; [5] Corporatized in 1993; [6] Corporatized in 1993; [7] Corporatized in 1987; [8] Incorporated in 2001, predecessor established in 1921 [9] Public/private partnership in 2001; [*] Excluding national, generic anti-trust and similar regulations. All ANSPs are financed by user fees except for the US Federal Aviation Administration which is funded by taxation.

Source: Button and Dougall (2006).

---

8   Although there are numerous particular circumstances, the trend has partly been because of the need to upgrade and update ANS and the public sector and its sources of revenue are often not seen as sufficient, or at least not consistent enough over time, to do this. Linked in is a perception that state ownership generally results in excessive political intervention that both slows change and reduces static and dynamic efficiency.

in some cases it involves the creation of a free-standing entity whereas in others the undertaking remains linked, albeit at arm's length, to the state. The shift in the focus of ownership can be seen as a reflection of wider national approaches to the topic with some countries having a tradition of preferring particular types of corporate entities and have experiences of their workings. In some cases there are explicit rate-of-return conditions – namely non-profitability – built into the terms under which the corporation is established. In other cases, the reforms have been within the context of existing state owned entities, as with the U S, or towards more private sector, market based models, as with the UK. Each model reflects national priorities, and the national willingness to accept varying degrees of economic inefficiency to meet other, wider political objectives.

Rate Setting and Finance[9]

Rate of return regulation in various guises was a characteristic of US industrial policy and that of many other countries until the 1980s. It largely became discredited because of manifest evidence of X-inefficiency when it has been applied and the longer term effects of over capitalization that accompanied it – the so-called Averch–Johnson effect.[10] The X-inefficiency arises largely because of the ability of the regulated enterprise to capture the system through control over information flows about costs and allowed them to enjoy significant inert areas without the pressure for full cost efficiency. The Averch–Johnson effect comes about because rate of return regulation creates a bias that leads to excessive capital intensity. Nevertheless, a number of countries now practice this explicit form of rate of return regulation (e.g., Canada, Netherlands, South Africa, and Switzerland) over their ANSPs by adopting either private or public 'not-for-profit' regulation. New Zealand also practices a variety on the zero rate of return regulation whereby the ANSP returns money to users once costs have been recovered and an agreed 'profit' has been paid to the government.

Price-capping, as developed in the UK by Littlechild (1983) for the newly privatized telecommunications sector, has been preferred more recently because of its lower informational needs and because it is directly aimed at minimizing X-inefficiency, both static and dynamic. It entails the setting of a maximum average price across a bundle of outputs that is related to changes in general price levels. In the transport context it is the preferred method for regulating the BAA in the UK, and is now to be applied to the privatizedNATS (Goodliffe, 2002; Steuer, 2010) and was to be used as the tool to regulate the now aborted public-privatization of the German ANSP provider (Classen, 2007). Whether price-capping is appropriate for regulating ANSPs (or, for that matter, airports) depends on a number of factors. The simplicity of price-capping diminishes as X-inefficiency is driven from the system; as this occurs it effectively converges on a rate-of-return regulation. But it is also most effective when supply is highly flexible. If there are shortages, as does occur at airports and in airspace because of invisibilities or other rigidities in supply, price should be used as a 'congestion' charge. A price-cap regime to bring down the cost of use over time is not the instrument to use in these conditions and its rigidity reduces the ability to allocate scarce supply effectively. Indeed, most of the early advocates of price-capping seem to have viewed it as a

---

9   Internationally, the United Nations International Civil Aviation Organisation has sought to establish fees and charges for monopoly ASNPs that are non-discriminatory and are cost-based, with users bearing their full and fair costs. The definition of 'fair' is problematic, but is interpreted by many countries as in the Chicago Convention that prohibits discrimination between foreign and domestic airlines and between the same aircraft type.

10   In the particular context of its use for airports, Tretheway (2001) also points to its complexity, high administration costs and lack of responsiveness.

short-term expedience where there was rapidly expanding capacity and while genuine competition built up; hence its use in telecommunications and energy.

Other countries have adopted less structured forms for regulating their ANSPs. Some have commissions that monitor the rates that are levied; a government ministry fulfils this role in a number of cases. In the case of Canada, there are appeals procedures that effectively lead to regulation by a judicial process that can review changes in the rates levied by ANSPs to assess whether they violate a set of specific charging principles. The Australian Competition and Consumer Commission that regulates the prices of Airservices Australia does not have powers of price-capping, only of giving opinions as to the appropriateness of the price increases. In South Africa the ANSP is prohibited from levying or increasing an air traffic service charge unless it has permission from the Economic Regulatory Committee. New Zealand and Ireland largely leave it to the market.

Financing investment in expanding and modernizing ATC systems also takes a variety of forms. The US Federal Aviation Administration (FAA) is largely funded from a variety of taxes, notably the federal ticket tax and the federal flight-segment tax, with no explicit user charges being levied. It has no access to the private capital market.[11] The French ANSP provider operates in a more commercial way by levying user charges and by having recourse to the private capital market, although there is oversight as to investment levels. NATS, Deutsche Flugsicherung (DFS), NAV CANADA, and Airservices Australia, for example, borrow extensively in the market.

Safety Regulation

While safety generally comes under the umbrella of social regulation, it can have significant economic implications. Air transportation is a remarkably safe way of travelling or moving goods; for example between 1995 and 2008 1304[12] died on US aircraft compared to 336,153 on US roads over the same period. Globally, the chances of being killed in an air crash per kilometre flow has consistently fallen (Table 18.3).[13] Nonetheless, because individual air accidents often involve large numbers of people, air traffic control safety is continually being scrutinized, even through many of the fatalities are associated with adverse weather conditions, pilot error, or failure of aircraft.[14]

The ICAO has sought to improve safety standards by establishing technical standards, but also institutional arrangements to enhance safety management. The approach includes the concepts of a state safety programme, which is a set of regulations and activities aimed at improving safety, and safety management systems that are a systematic approach to managing safety, including the necessary organizational structures, accountabilities, policies and procedures. In particular, members have agreed to separate out the regulation of safety from its enforcement. A number of approaches have been adopted in doing this, some implying a greater separation than others (Button and McDougall, 2006).

---

11   Gloaszewaki (2002) outlines the nature of the US ANS and also gives a comparative analysis of the interactions between ANSP and airport regulations in the US and Europe.

12   The small number of fatal air crashes has tended to result in much analysis of air transportation safety being done in terms of changes in near accidents, such as incursions into the designated safety zones of other airplanes. The correlation, at least at the aggregate level, between the air misses and actual accidents is, however, extremely lean (Button and Drexler, 2006).

13   To give a more direct comparison for a traveler in the US, in 1997 there was a fatal crash for every 2 million departures but this ratio fell to one fatal crash for every 4.5 million departures in 2006, and certainly part of the credit for this is due to improved air traffic control

14   There were, for example, only seven commercial air transport accidents in EUROCONTROL's air space between 1992 and 2009 that were attributable directly to air traffic management.

Table 18.3   Global airline accidents

Year	Fatal accidents	Passenger deaths	Death rate*
1986	24	641	0.07
1987	25	900	0.09
1988	29	742	0.07
1989	29	879	0.08
1990	27	544	0.05
1991	29	638	0.06
1992	28	1,070	0.09
1993	33	864	0.07
1994	27	1,170	0.09
1995	25	711	0.05
1996	24	1,146	0.07
1997	25	921	0.06
1998	20	904	0.05
1999	21	499	0.03
2000	18	757	0.04
2001	13	577	0.03
2002	14	791	0.04
2003	7	466	0.02
2004	9	203	0.01
2005	17	712	0.03
2006	23	755	0.02
2007	11	587	0.01
2008	11	439	0.01

*Rate per 100 million passenger kilometres performed.

Source: International Civil Aviation Organization (annual).

The Move to Greater Commercialization

Concern over both the potential problems of both allocative and X-inefficiency has led to a variety of initiatives to move away from the state-provided, public-enterprise model of an ANSP. The demonstration effects from airline deregulation and privatizations (in particular the fact that safety was not adversely affected) and that of other transportation modes led to considering alternative means of stimulating ASNP managements to be more efficient, and, in some cases, to seek out alternative sources of revenue. The efforts of the European Union, and its moves towards more efficient ways of regulating ANS charges, also reflects a wider review of the way that efficiency in ANS provision may be improved by taking note of lessons learned in other sectors, such as telecommunications. Here we focus mainly on matters of inefficiencies in ownership structures.

Corporatization

The past 15 years has seen many countries trying to enhance the efficiency of their ASNPs by injecting at least a degree of commercial-style incentive into their activities without turning systems entirely to the market.[15] The aim was first to provide those running systems with a clearer set of incentives and objectives without, in most cases, exposing them to the full rigours and penalties of the market, and second to link more closely those that run the system with their sources of finance. One approach that has gained favour in a number of slightly different forms is corporatization.

One should use the term corporatization with some caution. The traditional notion of a corporation is that of a very large commercial, rent-seeking enterprise, but more recently it has come to mean in some countries a not-for-profit government or private organized business. Although it was not the first system to undergo the move, there has been a steady move towards corporatization of ANSPs since Canada's change in the mid-1990s. The experiences of NAV CANADA, as well as some of the other systems with similar organization structures, after the terrorist attacks in the US in 2001, and the subsequent dramatic decline in air traffic shows one of the limitations of the underlying business model. Figure 18.3 provides a very simplified stylization of the problem.

The ANSP is assumed to have the optimal scale of activities for current, pre-crisis demand levels of D_1. Its LRMC curve is taken as constant, and the prevailing SRMC curve is assumed constant to the point where the optimal capacity, traffic T_1, is reached when it becomes vertical. The pre-crisis condition where LRMC intersects with both the prevailing $SRMC_1$ curve and demand D_1 gives a cost-covering charge of C* and revenues that cover full costs for that period; the provider meets its non-profit remit.

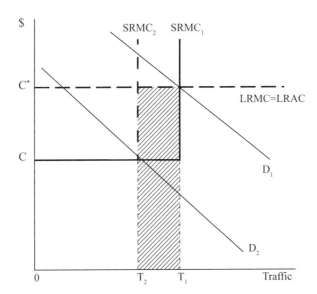

Figure 18.3   The economics of corporatized ANSPs

---

15   An oft-cited concern about not for-profit entities is that they can be prone to X-inefficiency because of their near monopoly status in many cases. This issue has not been rigorously examined in the context of corporatized ANSPs.

Although the diagram inevitably has to present the argument in terms of comparative statics and not as dynamics, we can see what happens if there is a sudden reduction in the level of demand to D_2. If the provider were to retain C* as its charge, there would be a significant reduction in traffic to the point where C* meets D_2. If there are economies of scale or scope in the provision of ANSs then the charge would have to rise for full cost recovery. Irrespective of whether C* remains the same, or increases because of scale effects, the use of the system would decline significantly and its short-term use would be suboptimal.

A welfare-maximizing approach in the constant LRAC case illustrated, in contrast, would entail rates falling to C with the existing capacity being used optimally until replacement of capital is needed, and capacity is reduced to T_2. At this later capacity, a charge of C* again allows both long- and short-run costs ($SRMC_2$) at the new capacity to be recovered. In the interim, however, as capacity is adjusted the ASNP will incur losses; these are shown as the shaded area. A profit-driven undertaking would deal with this by drawing on reserves acquired during previous periods of high demand, or in the extreme, as de facto happened with NATS after the events of 2001, have its finances restructured, normally through some form of bankruptcy. A not-for-profit corporation breaks even in the short term and has limited reserves designed to cover short-term, minor fluctuations in revenue flows, and cannot normally seek bankruptcy protection if it is a public corporation. Hence, the only available internal option is to raise charges at a time when welfare theory indicates that charges should decline to make optimal use of existing capacity, and to draw down what reserves it has.[16] An alternative that violates the notion of autonomy of corporatized ANSPs is that the transition cost of adjusting to a shock in the system is borne by the government and direct subsidies are awarded.[17]

There is some evidence of this happening following the inward shift in demands for ANSs after 2001. Figure 18.4 shows both en route and terminal charges levied by a large group of providers and systems such as those in the Netherlands and Ireland increased their charges.

Corporatized ANSPs also have the potential for suffering from Averch–Johnson type effects (Averch and Johnson, 1962) because their not-for-profit status is a de facto form of rate of return regulation; a zero return. Rate of return regulation offers a strong incentive for companies to over-invest and have a suboptimally high capital labour ratio.[18] While this is a problem normally seen as affecting profit-driven companies, the managerial motivation for efficiency in a non-profit organization should be identical if constrained welfare maximization is to be achieved.

The Public–private Approach

The UK has the only ANSP that is essentially designed around the concept of a private company (Goodliffe, 2002). The previous state-owned and operated system came under review in the late 1990s, in part because of the budget limitations under which it operated and in part because the regulatory regime to which it was subject could give perverse incentives; e.g. there were controls

---

16   NAV CANADA, for example, not only increased charges after the events of 2001 but also drew its rate stabilization fund down from its normal level of $80–100 million to zero very rapidly.

17   There are also unexpected surpluses when traffic at prevailing charges exceeds those projected. In some case, as with New Zealand, this can lead to rebates to airlines.

18   This is often embodied in the notion of 'gold-plating' whereby airports' management provides excessively high-quality services within a zero profit framework. It can also be seen in a different context in the form of X-inefficiency whereby the rate of return controls allow any cost increases to be passed on to users thus reducing the incentive for management to minimize costs. This problem can be compounded if the ANSP has control over information flows about costs.

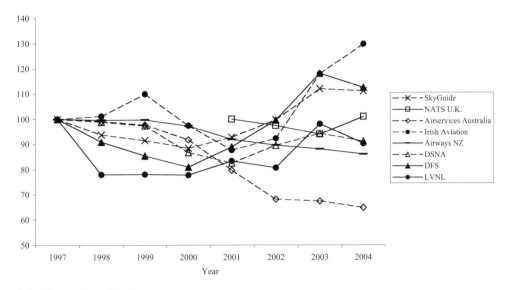

(a) En route unit rates

Note: All data based on 1997 except for NATS UK 2001=100.

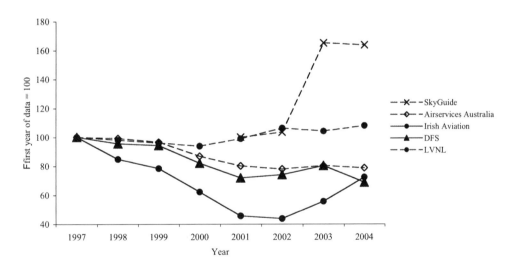

(b) Terminal unit rates

Figure 18.4   Charges for en route and terminal services in constant 2004 prices

Source: Button and McDougall (2006).

on capital expenditure but very little inbuilt to control operating expenditures. Enabling legislation for privatization was passed into law in December 2000 and in a consortium of seven UK airlines, the Airline Group was appointed to be the private sector strategic partner with the public–private partnership completed in July 2001. The crisis following the terrorist attacks in 2001 led to modification of the structure of what transpired to be an under capitalized undertaking: £130 million of additional investment was required, £65 million coming each from the UK government and the British Airports Authority (BAA), that received 4 per cent of the company in return; the government has 49 per cent of shares.

The NATS experience is too new to offer any long-term insights into its efficiency, not only because of the events of 2001, but also because the privatization also coincided with a pre-planned, phased physical move of operations from West Drayton to Swanwick. One challenge that has emerged is the role of economic regulation in overseeing a largely private, monopoly ANSP. The former nationalized undertaking was subjected to quite stringent cost-plus regulations essentially stemming from EUROCONTROL, but from 1999 price-capping became possible and was initiated for non-competitive markets – essentially UK en route and Oceanic routes.[19]

The Single European Sky and NextGen Initiatives

Most of the efficiency analysis of ANSPs has been static in the sense that they have focused on the past and future performance of systems, but changes are taking place and the efficiency, not only of what they entail but also the efficiency of transition mechanisms, is important in this context. Air traffic control systems are not easily modified or updated because their network nature makes it impossible to just close down the old and replace it with the new. In other cases, as with the European Union, there is not a level playing field to begin with, making the phasing in of new any system all the more difficult.

Single European Sky

European air space is some of the busiest in the world, and the current system of air traffic management suffers by using air traffic control boundaries that follow national borders, and having large areas of airspace reserved for military use. The European Commission initiated the move to a Single European Sky with the aim that design, management and regulation of airspace be coordinated throughout the European Common Aviation Area (ECAA); this is very much a matter of long-term interoperability.[20] Airspace management is planned to move away from the previous domination by national boundaries to the use of 'functional airspace blocks', the boundaries of which are designed to maximize the efficient use of airspace. Air traffic management, while continuing to have safety as its primary objective, will also be driven by the requirements of airspace users and the need to provide for increasing air traffic.

---

19   NATS's price cap is broadly determined by $M_t = SC_t - S_t + K$, where M_t is the maximum permitted average charge per service unit in year t. SC_t is the base charge per service unit uplifted each year by (RPI$_t$ $- X_t$), S_t is a quality of service term (delay), K_t is a technical correction term for when NATS over- or under-recovers in a previous period. Initially, charges were subject to a revenue yield price cap set at (RPI –2.2 per cent) in 2001 followed by (RPI –3 per cent), (RPI –4 per cent) and thereafter, (RPI –5 per cent) up to 2005.

20   The ECAA came about though the signing of bilateral agreements in May 2006 in Salzburg whereby the EU and some external countries created a single market in aviation services.

In October 2001, the Commission adopted proposals for the Single European Sky, to create a Community regulator for air traffic management within the European Union, Norway and Switzerland.[21] The Community regulator will merge upper European airspace, currently divided into national regions, and organize this airspace uniformly, with air traffic control areas based on operational efficiency, not national borders. It will also integrate civil and military air traffic management.

In June 2008 a revision of the SES regulations were adopted, called SES-II. This focuses on:

- The existing Single Sky legislation is sharpened to deal with performance and environmental challenges.
- The Single European Sky ATM Research programme to provide future technology.
- The competence of the European Aviation Safety Agency is extended to aerodromes, air traffic management and air navigation services.
- The 'action plan for airport capacity, efficiency and safety' is to be implemented to provide ground capacity.

NextGen

There have been a number of efforts to significantly upgrade the American ANS.[22] In contrast to the European long-term phased approach to reform, the US has been pursuing a much more sudden and once for all change – the Next Generation Air Transportation System (NextGen). The US$40–45 billion programme was initiated in 2003 and is due for implementation across the US in stages between 2012 and 2025. It has five elements:

- Automatic dependent surveillance-broadcast will use the global positioning system (GPS) satellite signals to provide air traffic controllers and pilots with more accurate information that will help to keep aircraft separated in the sky and on runways. Once fully established, pilots and air traffic controllers will see the same real-time display of air traffic.
- System-wide information management will provide a single infrastructure and information management system deliver high-quality, timely data to users. It will reduce data redundancy and better facilitate multi-user information sharing, and also enable new forms of decision making as information is more easily accessed.
- Current communications between aircrew and air traffic control, and between air traffic controllers, are largely through voice communications. Initially, the introduction of data communications will provide an additional means of two-way communication for air traffic control clearances, instructions, advisories, flight crew requests and reports. With the majority of aircraft data link equipped, the exchange of routine controller–pilot messages and clearances via data link will enable controllers to handle more traffic.
- The next generation network enabled weather is aimed at cutting weather-related delays by

---

21   There are discussions about enlarging the initiative to cover the Balkan and Mediterranean states.

22   Prior to NextGen, the US has made a number of previous efforts to upgrade and update its ANSs but with limited success (Dillingham, 2003). While the costs of failure in these efforts has not been fully assessed, if for no other reason than that developing reasonable counterfactuals is difficult, Robyn (2007) does produce data showing that the productivity of the system had not improved in the 25 years up to 2005 while production costs rose considerably. Morrison and Winston (2008) take a more micro perspective, and find a loss of US$1 billion in travellers time and airline costs because FAA expenditures had not been focused on the most congested tower controls at the most congested airport.

at least 50 per cent by fusing thousands of global weather observations and sensor reports from ground-, airborne- and space-based sources into a single national weather information system, updated in real time.

- There are currently 17 voice-switching systems in the NAS, some in use for more than 20 years. The NextGen voice system will replace these with a single air/ground and ground/ground voice communications system.

Comparing the efficiency of these approaches is challenging; indeed, given the different contexts, objectives, and constraints they may both be efficient.[23] One clear distinction relates to the method of charging for using the systems; the EUROCONTROL system will have something at least akin to cost-based user fees whereas there are no firm plans to move from the tax-based financing regime of the FAA in the US. Linked to this, there is no formal plan to move away from the first come first served allocation of airport slots in the US, thus there will remain little incentive for the system to be used economically efficiently. Further, modern information systems and pricing mechanisms offer an opportunity for slot auctions and secondary spot-markets that could prioritize the slot user in an genuinely economic fashion.

Conclusions

There is no pretence that the material here is either original or that it covers all aspects of the inefficiency with which ANSs suffer. It also does not relate those elements of inefficiency that have been discussed with those in other forms of inefficiency in the air transport supply chain with which they interact and which may compound or reduce their economic welfare implications. It has been an overview of much of the available material on the functioning of ANSPs in America and Europe, with some specific focus on elements of the subject that are either the most important or the most topical from an economic policy perspective.

There is probably no such thing as an optimal air traffic control system in the economic sense. The services provided by ANSPs are contextual in that they need to meet the technical requirements of the geographical area that they serve, to provide the portfolio of services that the users of the air space that they cover seek, and to meet societal demands for safety, security and environmental protection. Added to this there is considerable governmental intervention for strategic reasons in the market for ANPS services that makes commercial-based efficiency criteria inappropriate for evaluating the various institutional systems that exist. A wider, multi-criteria approach is, therefore, generally accepted as necessary in assessing the relative efficiencies of ANSPs.

But even if we could be more precise as to the relative inefficiencies of ANSPs, there remains the challenge of moving towards best practices in terms of developing new institutional structures and technical standards. Changes are taking place, but the dynamics of change and the most efficient transition mechanisms for bringing them about have hardly been thoroughly considered. The US, for example, is tending to pursue a big-bang approach as it introduces the NextGen Strategy whereas the Single European Sky initiative is incremental in its orientation, but comparative analysis of the two options are in short supply and the implicit focus tends to assume that transferability of insights is of limited use.

---

23   Robyn (2007) offers some comparative points that bear on the relative efficiencies of the two approaches.

References

Averch, H. and Johnson, L.L. (1962) Behavior of the form under regulatory constraint. *American Economic Review*, 52, 1052–1070.

Button, K.J. and Drexler, J. (2006) Are measures of air-misses a useful guide to air transport safety policy? *Journal of Air Transport Management*, 12, 168–174.

Button, K.J. and McDougall, G. (2006) Institutional and structural changes in air navigation service-providing organizations. *Journal of Air Transport Management*, 12, 236–252.

Button, K.J. and Neiva, R. (2012) Economic efficiency across national air navigation systems, paper o the *American Economic Association 124th Annual Meeting*. San Diego.

Charles, R.A. and Newman, H.K. (1995) Public policy and technology management: changing the role of government in the operation of air traffic control. *Transportation Journal*, 35, 39–48.

Classen, A.B. (2007) Privatization of Air Navigation Services in Germany – an Up-to-date Case Study. Paper presented to the 11th World Conference on Transport Research, Berkeley.

Dillingham, G. (2003) Air Traffic Control, FAA's Modernization Efforts – Past, Present, and Future. Statement before the Sub-committee on Aviation, Committee on Transportation and Infrastructure, US House of Representatives, GAO-04-227T, Washington, DC.

EUROCONTROL Performance Review Commission (2010a) *An Assessment of Air Traffic Management in Europe during the Calendar Year 2009*. Brussels: European Union, EUROCONTROL.

EUROCONTROL (2010b) *Performance Scheme: Initial EU-wide Targets Proposals, A Consulation Document*. Brussels: EUROCONTROL.

Farrell, M.J. (1957) The measurement of productive efficiency. *Journal of the* Royal Statistical Society, 120, 253–281.

Gloaszewaki, R. (2002) Reforming air traffic control: an assessment from the American perspective. *Journal of Air Transport and Management*, 8, 3–11.

Goodliffe, M. (2002) The new UK model for air traffic services – a public private partnership under economic regulation. *Journal of Air Transport and Management*, 8, 13–18.

Harberger, G. (1959) Using the resources at hand more effectively. *American Economic Review Papers and Proceedings*, 59, 134–147.

International Civil Aviation Organization (annual) *Civil Aviation Statistics of the World*. Montreal: ICAO.

Leibenstein, H. (1966) Allocative efficiency vs 'X-efficiency', *American Economic Review*, 56, 392–415.

Littlechild, S. (1983) *Regulation of British Telecommunication's Profitability*. London: Department of Industry.

Morrison, S.A. and Winston. C. (2008) The effect of FAA expenditure on airport delays. *Journal of Urban Economics*, 63, 669–678.

NERA Economic Consulting (2006) *Cost Benchmarking of Air Navigation Service Providers: A Stochastic Frontier Analysis: Final Report*. London: NERA.

Nolan, M.S. (1998) *Fundamentals of Air Traffic Control*, 3rd edn. Pacific Grove CA: Wadsworth.

Oster, C.V. Jr. and Strong, J.S. (2008) *Managing the Skies: Public Policy, Organization, and Financing of Air Navigation*. Aldershot, Ashgate.

Robyn, D. (2007) *Reforming the Air Traffic Control System to Promote Efficiency and Reduce Delays*. Washington, DC: The Brattle Group.

Steuer, M. (2010) The partially private UK system for air traffic control. *Journal of Air Transport Management*, 16, 26–35.

Tretheway, M.W. (2001) *Airport Ownership Management and Price Regulation, Report to the Canadian Transportation Review Committee*. Ottawa, Transport Canada.

Tullock, G. (1967) The welfare costs of tariffs, monopolies and theft. *Western Economic Journal*, 5, 224–232.

US Federal Aviation Administration (2009) *US/Europe Comparison of ATM-related Operational Performance*. Washington, DC: FAA.

PART E
Liberalization and Public Policy

Chapter 19

Economic Impact of Aviation Liberalization

Ian Kincaid and Michael Tretheway

Preface

In October 2008, the International Air Transport Association (IATA) held the Agenda for Freedom Summit in Istanbul with representatives of 14 nation states and the EU. The purpose of this summit was to discuss the further liberalization of the aviation industry. The participants agreed that further liberalization of the international aviation market was generally desirable, bringing benefits to the aviation industry, to consumers and to the wider economy. To explore the effects of further liberalization, the participants asked IATA to undertake studies to examine the impact of airline liberalization on the aviation industry, air passengers and the wider economy, focusing on 12 countries that participated in the summits. IATA commissioned InterVISTAS to undertake these studies, with aim of investigating two forms of liberalization: market access (i.e., liberalizing bilateral agreements) and foreign ownership and control.

This chapter draws on the research commissioned by IATA. The authors would like to thank IATA for commissioning InterVISTAS to undertake this study and for allowing the findings to be published in this book.

1. Introduction

In most parts of the world, international air services between countries operate under the terms of a bilateral *air service agreement* (commonly referred to as a bilateral) negotiated between the two countries. These agreements are generally of treaty status and are enforceable in international law (although some operate under, or are modified by, a less formal Memorandum of Understanding arrangement). The framework for these bilateral air service agreements was established towards the end of the Second World War in 1944, when 52 countries came together at the International Civil Aviation Conference held in Chicago, USA, which established the *Chicago Convention*.[1]

The Chicago Convention stipulated that two nations seeking to be linked by commercial air services would negotiate the terms through concluding a bilateral air service agreement. This would specify the conditions under which the proposed services would operate in terms of the privileges granted by either signatory country to the airline or airlines of the other country.

The Chicago Convention stipulated that two nations seeking to be linked by commercial air services would negotiate the terms through concluding a bilateral air service agreement. This would specify the conditions under which the proposed services would operate in terms of the privileges granted by either signatory country to the airline or airlines of the other country. The agreement would cover such items as:

---

1   The Chicago Convention framework clearly distinguishes between international and domestic services. Domestic services are considered strictly a matter for the respective national government.

- **Traffic rights**. Also known as *Freedoms of the Air*, these are a standard set of nine distinct air rights over which the two countries will negotiate. For example, the first freedom of the air is the right to overfly the territory of a country without landing there, the second freedom is the right to stop in a country to refuel (or other technical reasons), the third freedom is the right to carry passengers (or cargo) from one's own country to the other country and the fourth freedom is the right to carry passengers (or cargo) from the other country to one's own. A summary of the freedoms of the air are provided in the box which follows. Virtually all the bilaterals will allow freedoms one to four.[2] However, bilaterals differ in their treatment of fifth-freedom rights – the ability of a carrier from Country A to carry traffic from Country B to a third country as an extension of a service between Countries A and B. Some bilaterals do not permit this type of traffic while others do, or some variant of it.
- **Authorized points**. The allowable routes that could be operated. This could range from a general statement such as 'any point in Country A to any point in Country B' to a detailed specification of individual airports (or routes), and what points could or could not be combined on a particular flight and in what order.
- **Capacity**. The number of flights or seats that could be operated between the two countries.
- **Pricing**. The method for setting fares on the route. The agreement would specify the conditions necessary for a fare proposed by the airline of one country to become operative. Some agreements require airlines reach agreement on prices, and/or to submit ticket prices to aeronautical authorities for approval. Others effectively allow the airlines to set prices without restriction.
- **Designation**. The number of airlines the bilateral partners can nominate to operate services and the ownership criteria airlines must meet to be designated under the bilateral agreement (e.g., the airlines designated by Country A must be majority owned by residents of Country A).
- Other clauses related to operative agreements (e.g., code-sharing) and various 'doing business' issues such as repatriation of currencies, the ability to select handling agents at foreign airports and the use of computer reservations systems.

Freedoms of the Air

When countries negotiate air services agreements, they grant traffic rights to airlines that are referred to as 'freedoms of the air'. These rights are:

- First freedom. The right to fly over another nation's territory without landing.
- Second freedom. The right to land in a foreign country for non-traffic reasons, such as maintenance or refuelling, without picking up or setting down revenue traffic.
- Third freedom. The right to carry people (or cargo) from the airline's own country to the other country.
- Fourth freedom. The right to carry people (or cargo) from the other country to the airline's own country.
- Fifth freedom. The right to carry traffic between two foreign countries with services starting or ending in the airline's own country (also known as beyond rights).

---

2   For many countries, the first two freedoms (known as technical freedoms) are enshrined in a multilateral agreement known as the International Air Services Transit Agreement signed at the Chicago Conference.

- Sixth freedom. The right to carry traffic between two countries via the airline's own country.
- Seventh freedom. The right to carry traffic between two foreign countries on a service that does not involve the airline's own country.
- Eighth freedom. The right to carry traffic between two points within a foreign country (i.e., domestic traffic) as an extension of a service starting or ending in the airline's own country (also known as tag-on or fill-up cabotage).
- Ninth freedom. The right to carry traffic between two points within a foreign country with no requirement to start or end the service in the airline's own country (also known as pure or stand-alone cabotage).

Further details on the freedoms of the air can be found in Appendix A.

Historically, many bilaterals have been fairly restrictive. One of the earliest agreements was the 'Bermuda I' agreement between the US and the UK signed in 1946 which specified limits on pricing, capacity, designated airlines and routes operated. This restrictive agreement acted as a template for a great number of subsequent bilaterals between various countries.[3] As a result, the development of international air service has been as much a function of government policy as it has been a function of commercial considerations.

In addition to the bilaterals, most countries have also placed foreign *ownership and control* restrictions on the airlines (although in many cases airlines were, and sometimes still are, government owned). In part, this was to ensure that the airline complied with the national ownership requirements in the bilateral – in order for an airline to be designated by a country in the bilateral, it typically needed to be majority owned and controlled by citizens of that country. However, these ownership restrictions were also justified for various strategic, safety and defence reasons, e.g., governments wanted the ability to control the airlines in times of national emergency.

Typically, the ownership restrictions specify the maximum percentage of airline shares (stocks) that can be owned by foreign nationals. For example, the United States requires that foreign ownership of domestic and international US airlines is restricted to no more than 25 per cent of voting shares (stocks).[4] Other countries set the ownership limit at 20 per cent (e.g., Brazil), 33 per cent (e.g., Japan and Taiwan), 35 per cent (e.g., China), 40 per cent (e.g., India), 49 per cent (e.g., Peru, Kenya, Australia and New Zealand for international carriers), or 50 per cent (e.g., South Korea).

2. The Trend Toward Liberalization

Arguably, the international framework of the Chicago Convention has proven to be durable and fairly flexible, allowing a wide range of market regimes, from highly restrictive agreements with rigidly defined descriptions of allowable city pairs, capacity and pricing to more liberal agreements that allow free entry of airlines of either signatory nation to any route, unrestricted capacity and full pricing freedom.

---

3   Bermuda I was replaced by a slightly less restrictive Bermuda II agreement in 1977. Bermuda II has now been replaced by the US–EU Open skies agreement which came into force in 2008.

4   It is possible for foreign investors to hold up to 49 per cent equity stake in a US airline provided it can be proven that the airline is under the control of US citizens and the CEO is a US citizen, based on criteria set out by the US Department of Transport.

Nevertheless, a number of shortcomings have been identified with this form of regulation:

- The regulation is slow-moving and unresponsive – under restrictive bilaterals, changes in capacity, number of airlines, pricing, etc. would require negotiation by diplomats creating delays of several years in some cases before the changes can take place.
- The bilateral negotiations are often narrowly focused on the benefits to the airlines. The benefits to passengers, shippers, tourism and the wider economy are given less weight, often because they are more difficult to quantify.
- The industry has undergone considerable transformation which is not always reflected in the bilaterals. Technological improvements have allowed a great range of services at much lower cost and many countries have privatized previously state-owned air carriers.

Recognizing these shortcomings and the potential economic benefits of a more liberal aviation sector, many governments have moved to deregulate various aspects of aviation. This has included the privatization of airlines and airports, deregulation of domestic markets and liberalization of bilateral agreements.

One of the earliest instances of liberalization was the deregulation of the US domestic air market in 1978. Prior to deregulation, the pricing, routes and capacity operated on air services within the US was tightly controlled by government. Deregulation removed all of these controls and allowed market forces to determine service and price levels. There has also been a trend towards the liberalization of international air services. Since 1992, the US has pursued 'open skies' bilaterals with other countries.[5] The term 'open skies' is somewhat loosely defined but the US government defines it as allowing the carriers of the two nations to operate any route between the two countries without restrictions on capacity, frequency or price, and to have the right to operate fifth and sixth freedom services.[6] It also allows cooperative marketing arrangements such as code-sharing and liberal all-cargo operations (e.g., seventh freedom operations). The US definition of open skies does not include seventh freedom passenger services, cabotage or liberalization of ownership and control restrictions, although other definitions of open skies do (e.g., the European Union considers cabotage to be part of open skies). To date, the US has signed over 90 open skies agreements. Other countries, such as New Zealand, Chile and Morocco, have also pursued similar open skies arrangements. For example, in 1996 Australia and New Zealand signed a Single Aviation Market agreement which now allows carriers from the two countries to operate without restriction between the two countries (the Trans-Tasman market) and also allows fifth freedom and cabotage rights.

A number of multilateral agreements have also developed, most notably the European Union (EU) single aviation market. Between 1987 and 1993, the EU introduced three packages of reforms that almost fully deregulated the EU air market. Carriers from within the EU are now free to operate any route within the EU without restriction on price or capacity, including cabotage (i.e., domestic air travel within a member state), which has been permitted since 1997. In addition, all restrictions on airline ownership have been removed for EU citizens (e.g., an air carrier operating from Italy can be 100 per cent owned by investors from the UK; however, investment by non-EU citizens is restricted to 49 per cent). The EU is also negotiating open skies bilateral agreements as

---

5   In fact, the US had started pursuing more liberal bilaterals since the late 1970s, but the policy was only formalized as open skies in the 1990s.

6   Some controls on pricing remain through a double disapproval mechanism, i.e., if both governments concur to disallow the fare.

a block with other countries, for example, the EU–US Open Skies agreement in 2008. Another less extensive example of a multilateral agreement is the *Multilateral Agreement on the Liberalization of International Air Transportation* (MALIAT) between Brunei, Chile, New Zealand, Singapore and the US. The MALIAT signatories have granted each other unlimited traffic rights between each other under third, fourth, fifth and sixth freedoms, as well as unlimited seventh-freedom traffic rights for cargo-only flights. National majority ownership is not a requirement for being designated between MALIAT countries, only a principal place of business is required. New Zealand, Chile, Singapore and Brunei have gone even further and granted each other seventh and eighth freedom rights for passenger flights.

In the area of ownership and control, there has been some liberalization but considerable restrictions still apply in most cases. Chile is one of the few examples of countries that do not place any restrictions on the foreign ownership and control of its domestic and international airlines. However, the airlines are required to have their principal place of business in Chile (i.e., the airline must be primarily based in Chile). In part, this is to ensure that the airline can reasonably be designated as a Chilean carrier under the terms of Chile's international bilateral. However, most countries apply some limit on ownership that typically ranges from 20 to 50 per cent of voting shares (stocks). Some countries apply different restrictions on domestic and international carriers. For example, both Australia and New Zealand allow 100 per cent foreign ownership of domestic carriers but only 49 per cent ownership of international carriers.

3. Impact of Liberalization

In many ways, the liberalization of the aviation industry can be seen as part of a fairly global trend of market deregulation and privatization which has also been applied to the the telecommunications, utilities, railway and other industries.[7] It is generally accepted that this deregulation has on the whole been beneficial to these industries and, more importantly, to the consumers they serve. Indeed, empirical research has found deregulation/privatization of many industries has often led to lower prices for consumers, higher service quality, improved access to services (greater take-up by consumers, in part due to lower prices and increased levels of investment). This section focuses on the empirical research into the economic impact of liberalization in the airline industry both of bilaterals and airline ownership and control.

3.1 Liberalization of Air Service Bilaterals

As the examples below illustrate, liberalization of bilaterals has generally fostered greater competition, resulting in lower fares for travellers, greater numbers of people travelling, greater choice of airlines and routes and improved service levels (higher frequencies, etc.). A 2003 study by the European Union found that the liberalization of the EU air market (the single aviation market) had resulted in the following:[8]

---

7   However, it is worth noting that many of the remaining restrictions placed on the operation of international air service and the ownership and control of airlines are fairly unique to the industry. Today, there are very few industries subject to such a large degree of government control. Major industries such as pharmaccuticals, energy and even parts of the defence industry have been allowed to merge across borders and have no restriction on their foreign ownership.

8   See European Union and the European Civil Aviation Conference (2003).

- **Changes to industry structure**. The total number of scheduled airlines increased 6 per cent between 1992 and 2000, increasing from 124 to 131 airlines. However, this understates the degree of change in the industry. The EU reports that just over half the airlines present at the start of 1993 were still operating by the end of 2000. Between 1992 and 2000, 144 new airlines entered the market, of which 64 were still operating in 2000.
- **Increased routes and capacity**. There was a strong rise in the number of city pairs served and in overall capacity provided in the EU market. The total number of intra-EU city pairs increased 74 per cent, while the number of domestic city pairs increased 12 per cent between 1992 and 2000. Both the number of flights and seats operated increased by an even greater amount, indicating that overall capacity has increased substantially.
- **Increased route competition**. The number of carriers competing for traffic on European routes has increased substantially. The number of domestic city pairs served by more than one carrier increased 88 per cent, while the number of intra-EU city pairs served by three or more carriers increased 256 per cent.
- **Reduced fares**. In real terms (i.e., after adjusting for inflation), average fares have declined substantially for most passengers. Discount economy fares, which represent the vast majority of tickets purchased, declined 34 per cent in real terms between 1992 and 2000. Full economy fares declined somewhat (5 per cent), while business fares actually increased by 26 per cent. A 2006 study by InterVISTAS-ga^2 also found a substantial stimulation of traffic resulting from the liberalization of the EU air market.[9] It found that as a result of liberalization the rate of traffic growth doubled from an average of 4.8 per cent per annum in 1990–1994 to 9.0 per cent per annum in 1998–2002.

The stimulatory effect on traffic of liberalizing individual bilaterals is illustrated in Figure 19.1, which provides a comparison of traffic levels in the year immediately preceding inauguration of the new bilateral to volumes in the first full calendar year after inauguration. These examples result from changes in bilateral air service agreements, or from specific government decisions to relax the restrictive provisions of current agreements. The figure shows that just one year after liberalization, traffic increased by as much as 174 per cent. This may understate the stimulus impacts as traffic can take several years to fully mature.

Similarly, the UK Civil Aviation Authority (CAA) examined the impact of the liberalization of the UK–India bilateral which took place in 2004.[10] The study found that two years afters liberalization, the number of direct services between the UK and India had increased from 34 to 112 services per week (an increase of 229 per cent). While most of these new services were operated between the two countries' main airports (Heathrow in the UK and Delhi and Mumbai in India), services connecting secondary points in the UK and India also arose. In addition, the number of carriers operating between the two countries increased from three to five. This increased competition resulted in average fares declining by 17 per cent for leisure passengers and by 8 per cent for business passengers. The lower fares and increased service caused passenger traffic between the two countries to increase by 108 per cent.

---

9   InterVISTAS-ga^2 (2006).
10   UK CAA (2006a).

City-Pair	Service	Liberalisation Event	Increase
Vancouver-Phoenix	America West 1995	1995 Canada-U.S. Bilateral	146.4%
Toronto-Minneapolis	Air Canada 1995, Northwest	1995 Canada-U.S. Bilateral	55.3%
Toronto-New Orleans	Air Canada 1998	1995 Canada-U.S. Bilateral	41.2%
Ottawa-Chicago	Air Canada/ American 1995	1995 Canada-U.S. Bilateral	109.7%
Montreal-Atlanta	Delta 1995	1995 Canada-U.S. Bilateral	55.5%
Atlanta-San Jose CR	Delta 1998	1997 U.S.-Costa Rica	118.5%
Chicago-Hong Kong	United 1996	U.S.-Hong Kong Bilateral	21.1%
Chicago-London	United 1995	U.S.-U.K Mini Deal, 1995	42.1%
Chicago-Sao Paulo	United 1997	U.S.-Brazil, 1996	80.4%
Chicago-Buenos Aires	United 1998	Reassignment of routes	41.1%
Houston-Sao Paulo	Continental 1999	U.S.-Brazil, 1997	120.5%
Atlanta-Guadalajara	Delta 1999	U.S.-Mexico, 1991	169.5%
Detroit-Beijing	Northwest 1996	U.S.-China, 1995	174.3%
Houston-Tokyo	Continental 1998	1998 U.S.-Japan	116.6%
Atlanta-Rome	Delta 1999	1998 U.S.-Italy	110.8%
Dallas/Fort Worth-Zurich	American 2000	1995 Open Skies	115.3%

Figure 19.1   Air service agreement liberalization and traffic growth

Source: 'The Economic Impact of Air Service Liberalisation', InterVISTAS-ga2, June 2006.

3.2 Ownership and Control Liberalization

The removal of restrictions on ownership and control is anticipated to have a number of impacts on the airline industry:

- Airlines will obtain access to a wider pool of capital rather than being largely restricted to their home markets.[11] In many cases this will lower the cost of capital due to the increased supply available, particularly in countries with less developed capital markets. In addition, struggling or start-up airlines with weak credit ratings can obtain access to capital that would otherwise be unavailable. Airlines may also benefit from the expertise of the investor as many investors will likely have a specialized interest in the sector (e.g., other airlines).
- In many countries the ownership and control restrictions also limit foreign representation on the airline board and in airline management (e.g., the US requires the CEO to be a US citizen in some cases). With liberalization, airlines would be free to seek the best expertise available from around the globe.

---

11   As Cosmas, Belobab and Swelbar (2008) note, while ownership laws restrict equity, the same also applies to the debt markets. Debtors often seek a level of control in their investments which may not be permitted under current ownership and control laws.

- The lifting of ownership and control restrictions would lead the way to cross-border integration and merger of airlines (mergers would still be subject to scrutiny by competition authorities). This would enable airlines to exploit cost efficiencies and network synergies with considerable benefits for consumers. Studies in other industries show mergers provide efficiency gains of 1.5–2.7 per cent.[12]

A 2002 study on the potential economic impact of an US–EU open aviation area estimated that removal of ownership and control restrictions had the potential to produce cost savings of 4.2 per cent in US and EU air carriers, leading to lower fares for consumers and stimulating additional demand.[13] A recent study by the World Trade Organization (WTO) also examined the impact of ownership and control restrictions on international air traffic, and estimated that the removal of such restrictions could stimulate a 34–39 per cent increase in traffic, depending on the degree of control already in place and the measurement methodology used.[14]

The issue of ownership and control is closely linked to bilateral agreements due to the nationality requirements for the designated airlines. This further restricts the ability of airlines to merge across borders. Consider the case of Air France/KLM which merged in 2004. As both airlines were within the EU, they were free to merge subject to the approvals of the EU and national competition authorities. However, in order to comply with the nationality requirements in the French and Dutch bilaterals, the merged airline had to develop a complex 'two-headed' structure to maintain French and Dutch control for the relevant bilaterals. When eventually the EU is able to replace all member state bilaterals with a single EU-wide bilateral, the complex structure of Air France/KLM may no longer be required (it is possible the structure will be maintained for other reasons).[15] One way around this issue is to replace the ownership and control requirements in the bilateral with principal place of business requirements, as has been done by Chile.

3.3 Impact on the Wider Economy

The impacts of liberalization extend beyond just reduced fare levels and increased traffic volumes. The increase in air services and traffic volumes stimulated by liberalization has been found to increase employment and benefit the wider economy. This arises in a number of ways:

- **Aviation sector**: additional economic activity in the aviation sector is generated by the servicing, management and maintenance of the additional air services. This includes activities at airlines, airports, air navigation and other businesses that support the aviation sector. The impact can 'spin-off' into the wider economy (called indirect or multiplier impacts) – e.g., food wholesalers that supply food for catering on flights, trucking companies that move goods to and from the airport, refineries processing oil for jet fuel, etc.

---

12   UK CAA (2006b).
13   Brattle Group (2002).
14   Piermartini and Rousová (2008).
15   The EU is addressing this issue in two ways. In the short-term, it is negotiating 'horizontal agreements' which amend the airline designation clause in the existing bilaterals between member states and third countries to allow all qualifying EU carriers to be designated, as well as other adjustments to bring the bilateral into compliance with EU law. Longer term, the EU is seeking to negotiate a single EU-wide (open skies) bilateral to replace those of the member states. The most significant example of this to date is the EU–US Open Skies agreement in 2008.

- **Tourism sector**: air service facilitates the arrival of larger numbers of tourists to a region or country. This includes business as well as leisure tourists. The spending of these tourists can support a wide range of tourism-related businesses: hotels, restaurants, theatres, car rentals, etc. Of course, air service also facilitates outbound tourism, which can be viewed as reducing the amount of money spent in an economy. However, even outbound tourism involves spending in the home economy, on travel agents, taxis, etc. In any case, it is not necessarily the case that money spent by tourists flying abroad would be spent on tourism at home if there were no air service.
- **Catalytic impacts**: also known as wider economic benefits. Air transportation facilitates employment and economic development in the national and regional economy through increased trade, attracting new businesses to the region and encouraging investment. Industries and activities that would otherwise not exist in a region can be attracted by improved air transport connectivity. In particular, catalytic effects can include some or all of the following:
  - Trade effects – air transport liberalization opens new markets to many businesses as a result of new destinations, better flight connections and higher frequencies offered. This leads to a broader demand for existing products.
  - Investment effects – a key factor many companies take into account when taking decisions about location of office, manufacturing or warehouses is proximity of an international airport.
  - Productivity effects – air transportation offers access to new markets which in term enables businesses to achieve greater economies of scale. Air access also enables companies to attract and retain high quality employees.

A 2004 study by the UK CAA examined the impact of liberalization of the EU market on employment in the aviation sector.[16] It found that between 1991 and 2001 (i.e., before and after liberalization) employment in the aviation sector had increased by 38 per cent in the UK. The study found similar results across Western Europe with employment increasing by 6–84 per cent, except in a few countries where the government-owned national carrier had collapsed or been restructured (e.g., Switzerland, Belgium, Greece).

More broadly, a number of studies have examined the link between air service levels and general employment or economic growth (the catalytic impacts):

- A study by Irwin and Kasarda (1991) examined the relationship between the structure of airline networks and employment growth at 104 metropolitan areas in the US.[17] Using data for a 30-year period, the researchers conducted statistical analysis which found that expansion of the airline network serving a region had a significant positive impact on employment in that region, particularly in service sector employment.[18]
- Button and Taylor (2000) examined the link between international air service and economic development.[19] Using data for 41 metropolitan areas in the US, the authors statistically analysed the link between high-tech employment and the number of direct routes to Europe offered by airports in the region. The analysis found that there was a strong and significant

---

16 UK CAA (2004).

17 Irwin and Kasarda (1991).

18 The analysis was conducted using non-recursive models which confirmed that increases in the airline network were a cause rather than a consequence of this employment growth.

19 Button and Taylor (2000).

relationship between employment and air services to Europe, such that increasing the number of European routes served from three to four generated approximately 2,900 high-tech jobs.

- In a similar study, Brueckner (2003), also looked at the impact of air service on employment in the US.[20] The analysis found that a 10 per cent increase in passenger enplanements in a metropolitan area leads to an approximately 1 per cent increase in employment in service-related industries. Frequent service to a variety of destinations, reflected in the high levels of passenger enplanements, was found to both attract new firms to the metro area and stimulate employment at established enterprises. However, the analysis found that there was no impact on manufacturing and other goods-related employment, suggesting that air travel is less important to these industries than it is to service-related industries.

- Cooper and Smith (2005) examined the contribution of air transportation to tourism, trade, location/investment decisions and productivity.[21] The study estimated that the net contribution of air transportation to trade (i.e., export minus imports) to be €55.7 billion in 2003 across the 25 current EU members, or approximately 0.6 per cent of Gross Domestic Product (GDP).

- A 2006 study by InterVISTAS Consulting Inc. found that a 10 per cent increase in a nation's air connectivity (a measure of international air service) increased GDP by 0.07 per cent.[22]

- Hansen and Gerstein (1991) investigated the relationship between Japanese air service to the US and Japanese direct investment in the US.[23] Using data from 1982 to 1987, the analysis related the amount of Japanese investment in each US state to measures of level of air service operated between Japan and that state (and other background factors). The analysis found a significant positive relationship between investment and air service. The results also suggested that the amount of service provided by Japanese carriers had a larger impact on investment than service provided by US carriers. The issue of causality is also addressed (i.e., does more air service lead to greater investment or does greater investment lead to more air service?), with the authors determining that the evidence indicates that air service impacts on investment rather than the other way around. The authors concluded that greater air service supports the input needs (i.e., labour and materials) of the Japanese ventures in the US and enable greater awareness and information flows in Japan of those regions in the US with direct service.

- Bel and Fagenda (2008) analysed the relationship between international air service and the location of large firm's headquarters across major European urban areas.[24] The authors found that supply of non-stop intercontinental flights was a significant factor in determining headquarter locations (along with other economic, business, labour and tax factors). Empirical research indicated that a 10 per cent increase in supply of intercontinental air service was associated with a 4 per cent increase in the number large firm headquarters location in the corresponding urban area.

The research summarized in this section provides evidence of the way in which liberalization leads to increased air service levels and lower fares, which in turn stimulates additional traffic volumes, and can bring about increased economic growth and employment, as illustrated in Figure 19.2.

---

20   Brueckner (2002).
21   Cooper and Smith (2005).
22   InterVISTAS Consulting Inc. (2006).
23   Hansen and Gerstein (1991).
24   Bel, G. and Fageda, X. (2008) 'Getting There Fast: Globalization, Intercontinental Flights and Location of Headquarters', *Journal of Economic Geography*, 8, 4.

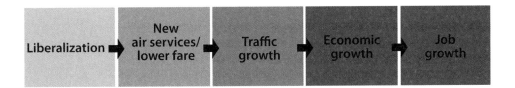

Figure 19.2   Contribution of Liberalization to Economic Growth

Source: InterVISTAS-ga2, 'The Economic Impact of Air Service Liberalisation', June 2006.

4. Measuring the Economic Impact of Liberalization Utilizing a Gravity Model

As noted previously, the InterVISTAS was commissioned by IATA to investigate the economic impact of aviation liberalization on 12 countries. These countries were Australia, Brazil, Chile, India, Mauritius, Morocco, Peru, Singapore, Turkey, United Arab Emirates, Uruguay and Vietnam.
Two forms of liberalization were considered in this analysis:

1. **Market access liberalization**. This refers to liberalization in terms of the bilateral air service agreements relating to airline designation, capacity restrictions, pricing restrictions, authorized points, fifth freedom rights and cooperative arrangements. The analysis considers the impact if all restrictions on these terms were removed from all of a country's bilaterals (e.g., all airlines of the home country, and those of the other country, were free to operate any route between the two countries without restriction on capacity, frequency or price and with the ability to operate fifth freedom services and enter into code share arrangements).

2. **Ownership and control liberalization**. This refers to liberalization of the ownership and control restrictions placed on the country's airlines operating international services. The analysis considers the impact if these restrictions were removed (e.g., no restrictions on foreign ownership). As this form of liberalization is considered separately to market access liberalization, it is assumed that a principal place of business requirement replaces the national ownership requirements within the bilaterals.

In addition, the two forms of liberalization are also considered in combination. It should be noted that governments typically require reciprocity when negotiating the terms of a bilateral. In this analysis it is assumed that reciprocity is reached in the liberalization of these agreements.

4.1 The Gravity Model

The impacts of liberalization (or further liberalization) was estimated using a gravity model which forecast traffic between any two countries based on the economic characteristics of the two countries, trade levels between the two countries, their geographic relationship and the characteristics of the bilateral between the two countries as in Figure 19.3:

$$\text{Traffic}_{AB} = F(\text{GDP}_{AB}, \text{ServiceTrade}_{AB}, \text{Intervening}_{AB}, \text{BilateralFactors}(0,1)_{AB})$$

Where.

Traffic$_{AB}$ is the total Origin/Destination (O/D) passenger traffic between countries A and B in both directions.

GDP$_{AB}$ is the product of the GDP of the two countries, capturing their economic size.

ServiceTrade$_{AB}$ is the total amount of trade in service (i.e., not goods) between the two countries in US dollars.

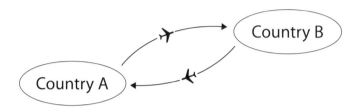

Figure 19.3   The Gravity Model

Intervening$_{AB}$ captures the intervening opportunities for closer travel than between two countries. Traffic between two countries was found to be less if there were opportunities for travel to closer countries. The intervening variable is calculated as an index of the sum of GDPs of every country that is 10 per cent or less distant than the distance between countries A and B.

BilateralFactors$(0,1)_{AB}$ are dummy variables capturing the presence or absence of specific restrictions on the bilateral. For example, if bilateral allows flights only to named points then the dummy variable takes the value 1 or else, if carriers are unrestricted in the airports/cities they can fly to, the dummy variable takes the value 0. The dummy variables also have 'modifiers' to reflect the circumstances of the individual bilateral. For example, the *named points* dummy is multiplied by a variable derived from the product of the geographic area of the two countries. This captures the fact that liberalizing this term will have minimal impact on geographically small island nations with only one major airport (e.g., the bilateral for Singapore–Mauritius) than on large countries with multiple airports (e.g., the bilateral for Australia–US). Each of the dummy variables are described below:

1. **Permitted number of airline designations**. Bilateral agreements usually specify the number of airlines permitted to fly any route between the two countries. A '0' denotes a dual or multiple designation; a '1' otherwise. This digit is then multiplied by the distance between the two countries. A country pair can only benefit from a multiple designation if one or both countries have more than one airline fit, willing and able to operate the route. Furthermore, each such country must be willing to allow its own airlines to compete. An airline seeking to operate long-distance services must usually use wide body aircraft. It will require a network of feeder services using smaller aircraft. In contrast, many short-haul services use much smaller aircraft, and can serve strictly point-to-point markets. The airline operating long-haul services requires very substantial physical and financial resources. Comparatively few countries have more than one airline operating long-distance services. Many are more conservative in allowing competition between their airlines on intercontinental routes, compared to shorter and highly fragmented regional markets. A single-designation rule would therefore be more onerous to short distance services than to longer flights.

2. **Capacity controls**. Many experts consider capacity controls as particularly inimical to market growth, and a key trait of a restrictive agreement. Sometimes the limits are written directly in the agreements. Lengthy negotiations are often necessary to increase the limits. In other instances, such as 'Bermuda' agreements, the capacities are subject to a regular process of consultation. In either case, the airlines flying between the two nations have many opportunities to curb capacity growth and maintain high fares. Two variables were employed to model the impact of capacity controls. The first variable was a '1' if capacity was fully predetermined by the agreement (which corresponds to the most inflexible form of capacity clause), and zero otherwise. A second 1-0 dummy applied if a Bermuda-type clause was in force. Both dummy variables were multiplied by GDP, reflecting a hypothesis that capacity controls become proportionately more detrimental to competition as the size of the market grows.

3. **Pricing**. This variable is assigned a '0' if the bilateral allows free pricing without significant government control. It was assigned the value '0.5' if the bilateral included a double-disapproval (a more permissive form of pricing enforcement). A '1' indicates another regime, such as country of origin or single disapproval pricing. The resultant quantity was then modified by the product of the per capita GDPs of both countries. This reflected the belief that countries with a large per capita GDP would be most likely to generate large volumes of leisure travellers. They would be especially affected by any price rigidities. Furthermore, airlines are most likely to offer incentive fares on routes with considerable leisure traffic. A restrictive pricing regime, which limits their flexibility, would be a proportionately large obstacle to growth in affluent country pairs.

4. **Fifth freedom rights**. A '1' indicates the absence of any fifth freedom rights in the bilateral. A '0' depicts an agreement with such provisions. The data did not permit a more precise delineation of fifth freedom rights, such as between 'intermediate' and 'beyond' rights. Fifth freedom rights can be most valuable for long-haul services, for which intermediate stops may be technically necessary. An ability to 'top-off' a long-distance flight with incremental short-haul revenue, or serve a minor centre as part of a longer flight to a more significant destination may be necessary for a profitable route. These factors suggest that a fifth freedom provision may be more important to nation pairs that are relatively distant. Furthermore, other significant markets should occur either in close proximity to the great circle flight path between the two nations (for intermediate fifths) or reasonably close to either nation. The 0-1 variable is therefore multiplied by the product of the *intervening destinations* variable (described earlier) to measure the significance of fifth freedom services for each country pair observation.

5. **Named points**. Some bilateral agreements limit services to a very few rigidly defined destinations; others, following a more liberal approach, allow services to any operationally feasible combination. In many situations, bilateral agreements will stipulate a fixed number of 'roving points', for which each nation can choose the precise destinations at a later date. A very flexible definition of permissible routes is most conducive to competition when it involves nations with large areas and many potential destinations. This variable was assigned a value of zero for country pairs with broad route definitions. Those observations with specific point restrictions were assigned a value equal to the product of variables representing the area of the country.

6. The gravity model was developed and calibrated as part of a previous study by the InterVISTAS group.[25] The model was estimated using cross-sectional data on over 800 country pairs. The endogenous variable, country pair origin-destination traffic, was sourced from IATA for the year 2005.[26] The exogenous variables were sourced from World Bank, International Monetary Fund, World Tourism Organization and the United Nations for the same year.

The cross-sectional analysis assumes that a particular relationship between traffic, the extent of liberalization and socio-economic conditions applies to every market. Each country pair will display unique traffic volumes, socio-economic variables, airline industry conditions and degrees of liberalization in the air service agreements. Through correcting for variations in economic activity and other extraneous factors, this approach seeks to explain variations in the passenger traffic between different country pairs to variations in their bilateral agreements. In theory, this method should isolate the separate impacts of route definitions, single/multiple designations, pricing controls, the presence or absence of fifth freedom permissions and other attributes of air service agreements. Through using a very large sample involving all regions of the world, nations in all stages of development, and countries with a wide range of approaches to international aviation, the process should yield a robust estimate of the impacts for any arbitrary country pair.

The preliminary estimation process used an ordinary least squares algorithm on a double-log specification. This reflects the assumption that many of the processes being modelled are multiplicative. For example, a restrictive bilateral would cause a greater absolute loss of traffic in a large market than in a small one. As is common with many cross-sectional models, the preliminary specification showed problems with heteroscedasticity, as determined by a significant Goldfeldt Quandt statistic. A general least squares procedure, using the GDP variable as a weighting factor, produced the final estimates shown in Figure 19.4.

The regression provided a reasonable 'fit' (adjusted R-squared of 0.67) and the signs are consistent with expectations. The coefficient on the bilateral-related variables are all negative

Variable	Coefficient	T Statistic
Intercept	-0.42345	-1.52
GDP Product	0.240543	5.92
Commercial Flows	0.14279	4.30
Intervening Opportunities	-0.05739	-11.19
Single Designation	-0.02101	-2.87
Predetermined Capacit	-0.03687	-3.63
Bermuda Capacity	-0.02578	-2.74
Single Disapproval Pricing	-0.03629	-3.37
Fifth Freedoms	-0.00036	-3.11
Authorized Points	-0.05866	-3.14

Figure 19.4   Gravity model estimates

25   The results of that study can be found in the report by InterVISTAS-ga² (2006).
26   Based on data in International Air Transport Association (2005).

providing evidence that the artificial constraints posed by bilateral air service agreements constrain the growth of traffic. Furthermore, these obstacles operate not only between well-studied country pairs such as the US and the UK, but also in a huge variety of markets, involving countries of all sizes, stages of economic development and political systems in every part of the world. These results therefore support the hypothesis that restrictive bilateral agreements constrain traffic development.

4.2 Using the Gravity Model

The impacts of liberalization were estimated by specifying changes to the terms of the bilateral. So, where the current bilateral is restricted in regard that factor, the BilateralFactors(0,1) dummy was switched from 1 to zero.[27] The gravity model then calculates the growth in international traffic stimulated by this change.

To avoid extreme results whereby unrealistic increases in traffic were forecast, the model 'tests' the stimulus predicted by the removal of each restriction. Should the predicted stimulus exceed a particular critical value, the stimulus is reduced to that particular value. Furthermore, a 'grand limit' capped the total growth resulting from a full liberalization.

The limits were estimated by taking a sample of 600 country pairs in various stages of liberalization. Each attribute of the relevant bilateral agreements was examined in turn and subject to a step-by-step liberalization. The model calculated the conditional expectations of traffic resulting from each perturbation of the bilateral for each observation, generating a series of calculated stimuli. For each attribute in the bilateral, a maximum limit on the traffic gain from an incremental liberalization was calculated using Chebyshev's Inequality.[28] The process yielded, for each attribute and for a total liberalization, a level of stimulation that would be exceeded by only 10 per cent of the observations. To eliminate the risks of overestimating the stimulus from liberalization, the model superimposed the limits shown in Figure 19.5 on any extrapolation produced by the gravity model.

Liberalisation Measure	Maximum Permissible Traffic Growth
Single to Multiple Designation	50.7%
Predetermined Capacity to Open Capacity	25.0%
Bermuda Capacity Control to Open Cap	17.8%
Single Refusal to Double Refusal Pricing	4.1%
Including Fifth Freedom Rights	8.8%
Named Point Route Annexes to Open Routes	97.3%
Fully Restrictive to Fully Liberal ("grand limit")	166.4%

Figure 19.5 Maximum allowable liberalization impacts in the benefits model

27 Where the specific bilateral is already liberalized in regards to a certain factor (e.g., the bilateral allows fifth freedom services), there is no change to the dummy variable as it is already set to zero.

28 Chebyshev's Inequality describes very broad characteristics that govern any statistical population. It is 'distribution free' in that it does not require any prior knowledge of the population, except that it have a mean and variance.

Furthermore, in estimating the traffic, the model takes account of the fact that liberalization is a necessary but not a sufficient condition for traffic growth. No new services will result if there is no underlying demand to support them. The model therefore examines the air services already operating between each country pair (the model contains up-to-date information on air services from OAG schedule data). If any such flights already operate, it is assumed that capacity can expand to accommodate demand. If no such flights exist, the model algorithm determines the aircraft most appropriate for a route of that length. If the traffic available is insufficient to support a reasonable level of service, the model assumes that no direct service will arise. The model then examines the bilateral agreement to ascertain if fifth freedom rights are available. If so, it then allocates the traffic to an appropriate indirect service, reducing the estimated traffic due to the undesirability of the indirect service. If no fifth freedom rights are available, then the model assumes that there will be no increase in traffic level despite the liberalization of the bilateral.

Having estimated the incremental traffic stimulated by liberalization, the model then calculates the employment and GDP generated by this traffic. The model contains economic multipliers to estimate the employment and GDP stimulated by increased air service at both ends of each country pair. These multipliers capture the employment and GDP generated by unit increases in traffic based on data collected from around the world and are broken down into different types of impacts (aviation industry, tourism, catalytic). The model contains 14 sets of multipliers reflecting differing levels of stimulation that occur in different types of countries. For example, increased air service can have a larger employment impact in developing countries than in developed countries due to the greater use of technology in developed countries.

To set a baseline, the model was populated with 2007 traffic and economic data (the most recent available on a global basis at the time of the study).[29] In addition, information was collected on all the major bilaterals impacting the 12 counties of interest.

4.3 Comment on Modelling Ownership and Control Liberalization

The gravity model developed did not contain any parameters relating to ownership and control. Therefore, an additional parameter was developed which could address the impact of this form of liberalization using results obtained by other researchers. After conducting an extensive literature review, two items of research were found to provide information in this area:[30]

- The Brattle group report estimated that liberalization of ownership and control in the EU–US market could stimulate traffic by 5–11 per cent.[31] This estimate is based on a specific market which has already seen significant liberalization, especially on the EU side. Furthermore, the estimate is based on airline cost analysis to determine potential cost savings which then get passed onto passengers in fare savings.
- Research by the WTO indicates that full liberalization of ownership and control could stimulate 34–39 per cent growth in traffic.[32] The findings were based on the estimation of a gravity model similar to that described above, which included dummy variables related to ownership and control. The authors also conducted cluster analysis (grouping Air Service

---

29   The economic data was sourced from the World Bank's World Development Indicators. The traffic (and fare) data was sourced from IATA's PaxIS data product.
30   In general, there is very little empirical research on this form of liberalization.
31   Brattle Group (2002).
32   Piermartini and Rousová (2008).

Agreements based on their degree of liberalization), which also provided a means to determine the impact of ownership and control restrictions.

Based on the available research, it was decided to incorporate a parameter which allowed for a maximum traffic impact from ownership and control liberalization of 34 per cent (the lower end of the research from the WTO). However, the impact was scaled by the degree of ownership restriction already in place. For example, liberalizing ownership when the original limit was 49 per cent foreign ownership would have a smaller impact than if the original limit was 25 per cent, which itself had a smaller impact than if the original limit was 0 per cent.

4.4 Results from the Gravity Model

4.4.1 Traffic impacts   The traffic impacts of liberalization estimated by the gravity model are summarized in Figure 19.6. These represent the long-term increase in international traffic manifesting 1–2 years after liberalization is enacted, and based on 2007 traffic levels. As noted previously, the analysis assumes each country is able to obtain reciprocity with other countries (liberalization is not unilateral).

Across the 12 countries examined, the traffic impact of market access liberalization (i.e., going to open skies bilaterals) ranged from an increase in international traffic of 9 per cent (Morocco) to an increase of 47 per cent (Brazil), with a median impact across the 12 countries of 33 per cent growth. To a great degree, impact of market access liberalization was affected by the degree of liberalization already undertaken (economic and geographic conditions were also contributory factors). For example, Morocco had a low impact as it has already signed an open skies agreement with the EU, which accounts for 80 per cent of Morocco's international traffic. In contrast, Brazil, India and Mauritius have high impacts (40%+) as they have restrictive bilaterals (little or no open skies agreements have been signed).

Ownership and control liberalization generally generated somewhat lower levels of traffic stimulation, with the impact ranging from 0 per cent (Singapore and Chile) to 33 per cent (Brazil) and averaging 22 per cent. As Singapore and Chile impose no restriction on foreign ownership and control, the impacts of liberalization were set to zero.[33] Brazil is estimated to experience the largest impact from liberalization as it current has the most restrictive controls on foreign ownership and control (foreign ownership is restricted to 20 per cent).

Combined liberalization is estimated to stimulate traffic by 21 per cent (Singapore) to 79 per cent (Brazil) and averages 53 per cent across the 12 countries. Not surprisingly, countries with the most restrictive controls on aviation, such as Brazil, Vietnam, India and Mauritius, are projected to have the largest traffic gains from liberalization. However, even countries that have already significantly liberalized their industries, such as Singapore, Chile and Morocco, are projected to see traffic growth of 20–35 per cent if they pursue complete liberalization.

---

33   Although the Singapore government places no restriction of airline ownership and control, Singapore Airlines maintains a corporate policy to restrict foreign ownership to less than 50 per cent.

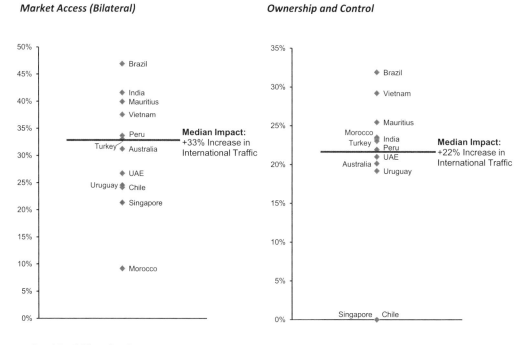

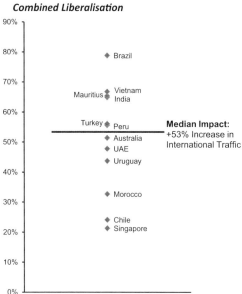

Figure 19.6   International traffic impact of liberalization

4.5 Economic Impacts

Some of the broader economic impacts of combined market access and ownership and control liberalization are presented in Figure 19.7.[34] The following impacts are provided:

- **Percentage reduction in the average fare**. With liberalization, it is expected that international fares would decline due primarily to increased competition in the marketplace (efficiency gains may also contribute to fare reductions, although even here the pass-through of these gains to consumers is due to competitive conditions). This is supported by the research discussed previously. As can be seen in Figure 19.7, the estimated fare reductions range from 17 to 50 per cent over the 12 countries and averaged 38 per cent.[35] The potential fare reductions are greatest for those countries with the most restrictive controls on the aviation industry, and consequently the largest estimated traffic stimulation impacts.

- **Increase in GDP**. As described previously, growth in aviation has been shown to contribute to economic growth through increased employment in the aviation sector and related sectors of the economy (e.g., tourism) and through increased trade, investment and productivity. The estimated GDP impact was a function of the size of the economy, the structure of the economy and stage of development (e.g., tourism-dependent economies experienced larger impacts; impacts were generally larger in developing countries) and the size of traffic impact from liberalization. Across the 12 countries, the estimated GDP impact on each country represented between 0.34 per cent (Singapore) to 1. 35 per cent (Vietnam) of national GDP and summed to US$ 67.6 billion (at purchasing power parity). While the impact on the overall economy is relatively small, the contribution to economic growth could be substantial.

- **Employment generated**. The employment generated in the aviation and tourism industry were estimated for each of the 12 countries, as well as the employment generated by catalytic effects (through increased trade, investment and productivity). Similar to the GDP estimates, the estimated level of employment was the result of a combination of factors including the scale of traffic stimulated by liberalization, the size of the workforce and the structure of the economy and stage of development (e.g., developing countries had larger employment impacts). The employment impacts include both the direct and indirect impacts. For example, direct employment in the aviation sector relates to the servicing, management and maintenance of additional air services, which includes activities at airlines, airports, air navigation and other aviation-related businesses. The indirect employment relates to spin-off activities, for example food wholesalers that supply food for catering on flights, trucking companies that move goods to and from the airport, refineries processing oil for jet fuel, etc.

---

34   In the interests of brevity, only the impacts of the combined liberalization are presented here. Separate impacts for market access and ownership and control liberalization were estimated in the study.

35   The fare reductions were estimated on the basis of the traffic increases estimated by the gravity model. Through the application of fare elasticities, it was possible to estimate the fare reduction associated with the traffic increase, as follows: % Fare Reduction$_{AB}$ = % Traffic Increase$_{AB}$/Fare Elasticity$_{AB}$. However, it was assumed that not all the traffic stimulation was due to fare reductions – improved service levels (increased frequency, new direct service, etc.) also had an impact, which had the effect of reducing the estimated fare reduction.

Across the 12 countries, the total employment generated is estimated to be nearly 2.4 million full-time equivalent (FTE) jobs. While this is a substantial figure, the estimated employment impacts represented only 0.21 per cent (India) to 4.06 per cent (Mauritius) of the total workforce of each country.[36]

Country	Average Fare Reduction	GDP Increase (US$ PPP)*	Employment Generated (FTEs) †			
			Aviation	Tourism	Catalytic	Total
Australia	-37%	5.5 Billion (0.75%)	20,200	37,200	33,100	90,500 (0.82%)
Brazil	-48%	17.6 Billion (0.96%)	72,900	173,300	158,400	404,600 (0.41%)
Chile	-17%	1.2 Billion (0.51%)	4,700	19,000	11,500	35,200 (0.48%)
India	-49%	26.6 Billion (0.86%)	241,200	393,900	275,000	910,100 (0.21%)
Mauritius	-50%	136 Million (0.96%)	3,200	10,900	3,400	17,500 (4.06%)
Morocco	-26%	1.2 Billion (0.95%)	8,400	54,700	29,700	92,800 (0.80%)
Peru	-35%	2.1 Billion (0.95%)	8,200	40,600	28,800	77,600 (0.59%)
Singapore	-15%	875 Million (0.34%)	8,800	22,000	13,100	43,900 (1.23%)
Turkey	-46%	7.7 Billion (0.83%)	75,600	250,200	59,600	385,400 (1.54%)
UAE	-37%	1.5 Billion (0.76%)	23,700	67,200	34,200	125,100 (3.02%)
Uruguay	-26%	306 Million (0.82%)	2,000	8,400	3,800	14,200 (0.87%)
Vietnam	-47%	3.0 Billion (1.35%)	42,000	131,900	25,400	199,300 (0.85%)
Total	-38%	67.6 Billion	510,900	1,209,300	676,000	2,396,200

Note: In the case of Chile and Singapore, the figures represent the impact of just market access liberalisation since ownership and control have already been liberalised in these countries.

* For comparison across countries, the Gross Domestic Product figures are in 2007 US$ are purchasing power parity (which controls for cost-of-living differences). The figures are in parenthesis are the estimated GDP increase as a percentage of national GDP in 2007.

† Employment figures are in Full-Time Equivalent jobs (FTEs). The figures in parenthesis are total employment generated as a percentage of the country's total workforce in 2007 (sourced from the World Bank Economic Development Indicators).

Figure 19.7   Economic impact of combined market access and ownership and control liberalization

36   The model does not address whether this employment would be sourced from the national workforce or would require some of the labour requirements to be met through immigration.

5. Impact on Home Carriers

One of the issues arising from liberalization of the aviation sector is the impact on the home carriers of the country pursuing liberalization. Across the 12 countries examined, the home carrier accounted for 31 to 59 per cent of international traffic to/from the country.

In general, liberalization of bilaterals is expected to have a number of impacts on home carriers. Undoubtedly, liberalization exposes the home carriers to greater competition. Many of the benefits of liberalization discussed previously, such as fare reductions and increased service levels, are driven by the competitive forces unleashed when markets are deregulated. While this increased competition has the potential to weaken the market position and profitability of the national carriers, liberalization also offers a number of offsetting benefits to national carriers:

- Access to new markets – liberalizing bilaterals can offer home carriers access to new routes that previously were unavailable. In addition, fifth freedom rights can provide opportunities to serve markets that previously had been uneconomical.
- Improve access to capital – removing ownership restrictions will allow home carriers to access a wider range of investment options at lower cost.
- Access to world-class expertise – removal of ownership and control restrictions will provide home carriers with greater access to managerial and technological knowledge and best practice.
- Improved efficiency – liberalization will enable home carriers to achieve efficiencies through greater access to investment and expertise, and through consolidation and mergers (providing economies of scale and scope benefits). This will aid home carriers in remaining competitive and exploiting new opportunities in the deregulated market.

There is little empirical research into the impact of liberalization on home carriers. This is due in part to the widely varying circumstances of the home carriers (in terms of public ownership, financial strength, managerial excellence, etc.), making it difficult to produce generalized findings from the research. Instead, a number of case studies are provided below to provide some insight into the impact of liberalization on home carriers:

5.1 UK–US Liberalization, 1995

In 1995, the UK and US governments agreed amendments to the existing Bermuda II agreement allowing access to a greater number of airports which essentially deregulated much of the UK–US air market, with the exception of Heathrow and Gatwick airports, allowing carriers to operate any city pair, and at pricing that was commercially determined. The impact of this liberalization was a significant increase in transatlantic traffic with capacity (seats) growing by 7.8 per cent per annum between 1995 and 2000 compared with 3.9 per cent per annum between 1990 and 1995.[37] Liberalization also led to a shift in market share, with the share of capacity operated by UK carriers (largely British Airways and Virgin Atlantic) declining from 52 per cent in 1990 to 42 per cent in 2000 (a greater share of capacity was operated by the larger US carriers).[38] Despite the loss of market share, UK carriers still experienced an increase in total traffic of approximately 4.5 per cent per annum between 1990 and 2000.

---

37   Source: InterVISTAS-ga^2 (2006).
38   Ibid.

5.2 European Union Single Aviation Market, 1987–1993

Section 3 provided an overview of the impact on fares and traffic of the deregulation of the EU air market which occurred between 1987 and 1993. Another major impact of deregulation was the rise of low-cost carriers (LCCs). The market share of LCCs rose from 1.6 per cent in 1996 to 20.2 per cent in 2003.[39] This placed considerable pressure on the traditional national carriers, many of which responded by reducing capacity on intra-EU markets and focusing on long-haul markets.[40] The increased competition resulting from the liberalization of the EU was certainly a factor in the failure or weakening of a number of (generally smaller) national carriers, such as Sabena (Belgium), Swissair (Switzerland) and Alitalia (Italy). However, a greater number of national carriers have managed to restructure and continue operations, and a number of new carriers have become established in the market (Ryanair, easyJet). Furthermore, liberalization has facilitated greater consolidation, such as the Air France–KLM merger, and Lufthansa's takeover of Swiss International Air Lines and controlling stakes in BMI and Austrian Airlines.

5.3 UK–India Liberalization, 2004

As part of its review of the liberalization of the UK–India bilateral, the UK CAA conducted a modelling exercise to estimate the impact on the revenues and profits of UK carriers.[41] The CAA estimated that liberalization had resulted in an increase in revenues of approximately £30 million but a reduction in profits of £46 million. In short, UK carriers carried greater numbers of passengers but at a lower per passenger yield. The CAA notes that the analysis may overstate the profit reduction as their analysis assumes fixed unit costs when in fact greater traffic volumes could yield economies of scale benefits, and does not take account of the increased connecting traffic (connecting in the UK) also stimulated. In addition, the CAA found that all the incumbent carriers had remained in the market after liberalization and that they had increased the number of routes and capacity operated between the UK and India. While three new carriers entered the market after liberalization, two of these exited within a year.

5.4 EU–Morocco, 2006

In 2006, an open skies agreement between the EU and Morocco came into force. The agreement allows EU carriers to serve any point in Morocco without restriction on price or capacity while allowing Moroccan carriers the same freedom to operate to any point in the EU, and provides fifth freedom rights for carriers from both sides. The impact on the home carrier, Royal Air Maroc, and its LCC subsidiary, Atlas Blue, is illustrated in Figure 19.8. In 2005, the combined market share of Royal Air Maroc and Atlas Blue peaked at 66 per cent of the total seat capacity operated between Morocco and the EU. By 2008, after the open skies agreement, that share had declined to 47 per cent. This was the result of entry by European LCCs easyJet and Ryanair as well as other European carriers. However, while the market share of the home carriers declined, total traffic carried increased by 25 per cent between 2005 and 2007 (by 46 per cent between 2004 and 2008). In addition, the number of routes to the EU operated by the two home carriers increased from 26 in 2004 to 40 in 2008.

---

39   Source: European Commission (2005).
40   Ibid.
41   UK CAA (2006a).

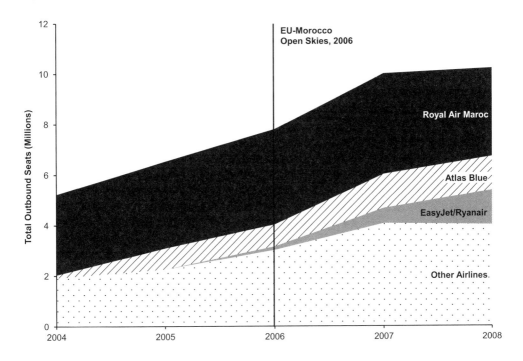

Figure 19.8 Impact of EU–Morocco open skies on the market share of Royal Air Maroc total seat capacity between Morocco and EU destinations

Source: OAG Max Airline Schedule data 2004–2008.

The evidence on the impact to home carriers of liberalization is mixed. A common result is that liberalization leads to loss of market share as new competitors enter the market. However, the stimulatory impact of liberalization also means that the incumbent home carrier often still experiences a growth in traffic volumes despite this loss of market share. While increased competition has the potential to weaken the viability and profitability of home carriers in some instances, liberalization also offers a means to restructure the carriers and protect profitability by expanding into new markets, accessing a wider pool of investment and through consolidation. Ultimately liberalization per se does not set off an inevitable chain of events. Whether the home carriers prosper or suffer under liberalization will depend in greater part on the quality of management of the carrier and how the carrier chooses to respond to liberalization.

6. Conclusions

Based on over 30 years' worth of 'experiments' with liberalization in the aviation industry, a considerable body of research has developed into the impacts of liberalization both to the industry itself and to the wider economy. This chapter provides a summary of the pertinent research into the liberalization of the international air market.[42] It is the hope of the authors that the analysis of the 12 countries summarized here further contributes to this body of research. In line with much of the previous research, our analysis suggested that liberalization of market access (bilaterals) and ownership and control could bring about significant increases in traffic, substantial fare reductions for passengers, and economic and employment gains for the wider economy. These benefits were found for a diverse mix of countries, although the scale of the impact differed depending on the economic structure and development of the country, its geographic situation and the degree of liberalization it has already undertaken. The impact of liberalization on home carrier is less clear-cut although it is not necessarily the case that liberalization is harmful to those carriers. In any case, the potential harm to select carriers has to be weighed against the wider benefits that may accrue to passengers, to tourism and to the general economy.

It should be noted that while liberalization will in many cases bring about major changes within the aviation industry, it is not being argued that liberalization of aviation alone would have a transformative impact on the overall economy. The GDP impacts of liberalization are in the billions of US dollars, but generally represent less than 1 per cent of the national GDP. Furthermore, our analysis is based on an idealized situation where the government of a country is not only able to achieve wide political support for extensive liberalization but is also able to obtain full reciprocity with its bilateral partner countries. In reality, this is incredibly difficult to achieve.

Recognizing these difficulties, IATA, through its *Agenda for Freedom* initiative, has sought to develop a pragmatic and fast approach to progressing liberalization.[43] The approach involves the signing of a multilateral Statement of Policy Principles around ownership restriction, market access and pricing. In short, the Statement of Policy Principles would allow the waiver of certain aspects of bilateral agreements. For example, Country A could waive the ownership clause of a bilateral with Country B, while still maintaining ownership restrictions on its own airlines, thereby allowing Country B to pursue a more liberal policy towards to airline ownership. While not providing full liberalization, this approach does allow some progress towards liberalization and in a fairly short time frame.

In November 2009, IATA held a second Agenda for Freedom summit in Quebec, Canada where the results of InterVISTAS' analysis were presented along with the formalized Statement of Policy Principles developed by IATA. At the end of the summit, seven countries signed the Statement, promoting the adoption of more liberal terms in bilateral air service agreement negotiations. The Statement was also endorsed by the European Commission and, since the summit, another five signatories have been added, bringing the total to 12 as of August 2010.[44]

References

Bel, G. and Fageda, X. (2008) Getting there fast: globalization, intercontinental flights and location of headquarters. *Journal of Economic Geography*, 8, 4, pp. 471–495

Brattle Group, The (2002) *The Economic Impact of an EU-US Open Aviation Area*, Prepared for the European Commission, The Brattle Group, London, December 2002.

---

42   An even larger body of research exists around the impacts of the deregulation of the US domestic market.

43   For more details on the Agenda for Freedom, go to http://www.agenda-for-freedom.aero.

44   The 12 signatories are: Bahrain, Chile, the European Commission, Kuwait, Lebanon, Malaysia, Panama, Qatar, Singapore, Switzerland, United Arab Emirates and the United States of America.

Brueckner, J. (2003) Airline Traffic and Urban Economic Development, *Urban Studies*, 40, 8, pp. 1455–1469

Button, K. and Taylor, S. (2000) International air transportation and economic development. *Journal of Air Transport Management*, 6, 4, pp. 209–222

Cooper, A. and Smith, P. (2005) *The Economic Catalytic Effects of Air Transport in Europe*, Document EEC/SEE/2005/004, EUROCONTROL, Brussels.

European Commission (2005) *DG TREN: Analysis of the European Air Transport Industry 2005*, European Commission, Brussels.

European Union and the European Civil Aviation Conference (2003) European Experience of Air Transport Liberalisation. Joint Presentation by the to the Fifth Worldwide Air Transport Conference (ICAO), 24–29 March 2003.

Hansen, M. and Gerstein, R. (1991) Capital in flight: Japanese investment and Japanese air service in the United States During the 1980s. *Logistics and Transportation Review*, 27, 3, pp. 257–276.

International Air Transport Association (2005) *Passenger Forecast 2005–2009*, reference 9261-05. Geneva: International Air Transport Association.

InterVISTAS Consulting Inc. (2006) *Measuring the Economic Rate of Return on Investment in Aviation*. Prepared for IATA by InterVISTAS Consulting Inc., Vancouver,

InterVISTAS-ga² (2006) *The Economic Impact of Air Service Liberalisation*. InterVISTAS-ga², Washington DC.

Irwin, M. and Kasarda, J. (1991) Air passenger linkages and employment growth in U.S. metropolitan areas. *American Sociological Review*, 56, 4, pp. 524–537.

Piermartini, R. and Rousová, L. (2008) Liberalisation of Air Transport Services and Passenger Traffic. Staff Working Paper, December, World Trade Organization.

UK CAA (2004) *The Effect of Liberalisation of Employment*. 16 March. UK Civil Aviation Authority, London.

UK CAA (2006a) *UK–India Air Services: A Case Study in Liberalisation*. 22 November. UK Civil Aviation Authority, London.

UK CAA (2006b) *'Ownership and Control Liberalisation: A Discussion Paper*. October. UK Civil Aviation Authority, London.

Chapter 20
European Liberalization: A View From Afar

John King

Introduction

This chapter will trace the development of Australia's aviation relationship with European countries including showing how new European carriers, over time, have entered and exited the market. Traffic rights and the emergence of the code-share as a substitute for own aircraft operations will be demonstrated, as will the 2008 and 2009 negotiations concerning the establishment of a horizontal agreement with the EU. Future negotiations are discussed and obstacles identified.

A brief review of the agreements and physical operations between the ASEAN states and Europe will also be undertaken as will a similar review for New Zealand. While there are several aviation relationships between ASEAN states and EU states, and burgeoning relationships with the EU as an entity, ASEAN as an institution has little current capability to negotiate a comprehensive agreement with the EU. New Zealand, on the other hand, which has a very small operating relationship, has entered into an EU horizontal agreement.

1. Australia's Aviation Relationship with Europe

1.1 Introduction

Australia now depends upon very few third and fourth freedom airlines to maintain and develop its aviation relationship with Europe. Considerably more direct and indirect service is offered by sixth freedom carriers than is offered by third and fourth freedom carriers. The only European carriers to physically service the Australian market are British Airways, who operate 14 flights a week to Sydney in a joint service arrangement with Qantas, and Virgin Atlantic Airways who operate an Airbus A 340–600 daily to Sydney. Qantas is the only Australian carrier to serve Europe. The Australia–Europe aviation relationship has been a long one: though for many years it was built on British Empire and later Commonwealth ties, the first European airline to operate an aircraft to Australia was KLM who operated a Fokker Trimotor in the 1931 London to Melbourne air race, with scheduled service between Australia and the Netherlands commencing in 1938.

As seen in Table 20.1, 16 different European airlines have provided, at various times, scheduled service to Australia. In addition there have been scheduled charter services, with Britannia Airways operating a service under Australia's liberal 'test and development' charter policy which allowed fifth freedom rights on intermediate points, carriage of cargo and passenger own stopover rights within Australia.

A number of these carriers no longer exist, while others have exited the market in face of costs and sixth freedom competition. Those carriers which still seek a presence in the market generally do so by means of code-share operations. Table 20.2 shows code-share operations as at January 2009.

Table 20.1   Historic EU carrier operations to Australia

Passenger carrier	Country	From	To	Aircraft types operated
AOM French Airlines	France	Nov. 1995	Nov. 2000	DC-10-30
Aeroflot Russian International A/I	Russia	May 1993	Mar. 1996	767-200
Air France	France	Jan. 1993	Oct. 1995	B747-300
Alitalia	Italy	Unknown	Oct. 2000	DC-8/DC-10/747
Austrian Airlines	Austria	July 2005	Mar. 2007	777-200 IGW/A340-300
British Airways	UK	July 1938	Current	VC-10/707/747/777
Cargolux Airlines	Luxembourg	Sep. 1999	Current	747F
KLM Royal Dutch Airlines	Netherlands	1st – 1938 then 1960	Mar. 2001 In Jet Era	DC-8/DC-10/747
Lauda Air	Austria	May. 1988	June 2005	777-IGW
Lufthansa German Airlines	Germany	Oct. 1965 Pax	Oct. 1996	707 /DC-10-30/747
Olympic Airways	Greece	Dec. 1984	Nov. 2002	707
Union de Transports Ariens	France	Unknown	Dec. 1992	DC-8/DC-10-30
Virgin Atlantic Airways	UK	Dec. 2004	Current	A340-600
Yugoslav Airlines	Yugoslavia	Apr. 1975	May 1992	707/DC-10
Cargo carriers				
Cargolux	Luxembourg	Sep. 1999	Current	747
Martinair	Netherlands	Sep. 1996	Dec. 2008	DC-10/747

Source: Department of Infrastructure and Transport Schedule Filings 2011.

Table 20.2   European carriers offering code-share services as at January 2012 (not including BA)

European carrier	Operating carrier	Frequency of European carrier
Air France	Qantas	48 in/48 out
Air Malta	Qantas	14 in/14 out
Alitalia	Thai Airways/Malaysia	12 in/12 out
Austrian	Thai International	17 in/16 out
Finair	Cathay Pacific	19 in/19 out
KLM	Malaysia	41 in/41 out
Lufthansa	Singapore Airlines	70 in/63 out
SAS	Thai International	14 in/12 out

Source: Department of Infrastructure and Transport Schedule Filings 2011.

Table 20.3   Australian/European carrier services (January 2012)

Carrier	European departure point	Frequency	Aircraft type	No. of seats	Total weekly seats
QF	LHR	5	380	450	2,250
QF	LHR	23	744	353	8,119
QF	FRA	7	744	412	2,884
BA	LHR	7	744	351	2,457
BA	LHR	7	772	291	2,037
VS	LHR	7	346	213	1,491
Total weekly seats (all carriers)					**18,384**

Source: Department of Infrastructure and Transport Schedule Filings 2011.

Capacity levels are subject to change, especially as some airlines move up to the A380 on some services and downscale on others by replacing B747 aircraft with B777-200 or 300 or even smaller A330 aircraft. As an example, at an earlier time Cathay Pacific Airways replaced B747-400 with a heavy A330-300 on its Melbourne and Sydney service. Table 20.3 shows actual physical own aircraft operations by European Carriers as at April 2009 between Europe and Australia. This level of service has been constant for two years, with market changes being met by sixth freedom carriers. Singapore Airlines has in early 2009, introduced A330-300 aircraft on Brisbane and Perth services as a replacement for the less economic but larger B777-200.

1.2 Air Service Agreements: Australia–Europe

There are 19 air service agreements with EU states and two with European non-EU states (Switzerland and Norway). In some cases (Netherlands and Germany) the basic Air Services Agreement (ASA) dates from the 1950s, however the important Memoranda of Understanding (MoUs), which govern capacity and traffic rights, inter alia, are of a more recent date. The most recent ASA was agreed with the Czech Republic in 2008. Australia has adopted a conscious policy of endeavouring to 'collect' as many ASAs as possible prior to the negotiation of a horizontal agreement with the EU in 2008/2009. As of 2012, this had still not occurred.

1.3 Australian Carrier Operations to Europe

1.3.1 Physical operations   Qantas is the only Australian designated carrier to operate its own aircraft to Europe. In 2009 Qantas operated 28 flights per week between Australia and London (Heathrow): 14 operated via Singapore and seven via each of Bangkok and Hong Kong. The B747-400 aircraft is used on the via Hong Kong and Bangkok services, while Singapore has a mixture of A380 and B747 aircraft. As Qantas receives further A380 deliveries it will increase London service by that type to daily from five weekly.

The only other European-owned aircraft services are to Frankfurt which is operated daily by Qantas with B747-400 aircraft configured in business, premium economy and economy. All London services are operated with four-class aircraft. The Frankfurt services operate via Singapore. In 2011 Qantas announced it would withdraw service from Bangkok to London and Hong Kong to London but maintain connecting flights to British Airways at both points.

1.3.2 Code-share operations   Qantas, as marketing carrier performs a number of code-share operations. The most significant relationship is with British Airways (BA), where, as a result of the Joint Services Agreement, it has 14 code-share flights to London on BA as operating carrier with extensive code-share connections beyond London. The seven weekly BA flights operating via Singapore are on B777-200 ER aircraft and the seven via Bangkok are on B747-400 aircraft.

Qantas also acts as marketing carrier with Cathay Pacific from Hong Kong to Rome (and vice-versa) on daily flights and with Air France to Paris via both Singapore and Hong Kong. One short-haul code-share flight is operated within Europe to Budapest, on Malev, from Frankfurt. Details of these code-shares are given in Table 20.5.

In 2011 Virgin Australia established a comprehensive agreement with Etihad Airlines of the United Arab Emirates (Abu Dhabi) which among other things permitted code shares to points in Europe where a third country code share facility is available.

Virgin Australia both code-share on Etihad and operate flights to Abu Dhabi in order to service code-share to and from Europe.

Table 20.4   Australia's air service agreements with Europe

ASA	Capacity available	Treaty	MoU
Austria	Yes	1967	1999, 2003 2005
Croatia	Yes	2007	Interim effect
Czech Republic	Yes	2008	Interim effect
Denmark	Yes	1998	Interim effect
Finland	Yes	1999	Interim effect
France	Yes	1965	1997, 1996
Germany	Yes	1957	MoU 1998, 1996
Greece	Yes	1971	MoU 1998
Hungary	Yes	2006	Interim effect
Ireland	Yes	1957	MoU 2005
Italy	Yes	1960	At 1996
Luxembourg	Yes	Interim effect	Initialled
Malta	Yes	1996	
Netherlands	Yes	1951	MoU 1997
Norway	Yes	Interim effect	As for Sweden
Poland	Yes	2004	
Spain	Yes	Initialled	13/02/2007 Initialled int
Sweden	Yes	New treaty interim effect	16/10/1998 Initialled int
Switzerland	Yes	1990	
UK	Yes	1956	2006

Source: Author research and Department of Infrastructure and Transport Schedule Filings 2011.

Table 20.5   Code-share: Qantas marketing carrier to points in Europe

Operating carrier	Points served	Originating point	Frequency (in)	Frequency (out)
AF	Paris	HKG	14	11
	Paris	SIN	7	7
BA	Vienna	LHR	21	14
	Copenhagen	LHR	13	13
	Paris	LHR	17	17
	Lyon	LHR	14	14
	Nice	LHR	14	14
	Germany (various cities)	LHR	141	117
	Amsterdam	LHR	21	19
	Zurich/Geneva	LHR	21	21

Operating carrier	Points served	Originating point	Frequency (in)	Frequency (out)
CX	Rome	HKG	1	7
EY	Athens	Abu Dhabi	7	7
EY	Brussels	Abu Dhabi	8	8
EY	Dublin	Abu Dhabi	10	10
EY	Dusseldorf	Abu Dhabi	2	2
EY	Frankfurt	Abu Dhabi	14	14
EY	London	Abu Dhabi	21	21
EY	Manchester	Abu Dhabi	14	14
EY	Munich	Abu Dhabi	7	7
EY	Paris	Abu Dhabi	14	14
MA	Budapest	FRA	7	7
MK	Malta	LHR	4	14

Source: Department of Infrastructure and Transport Schedule Filings 2011.

2. European Carriers to Australia

2.1 The History

KLM was the first European carrier to operate to Australia, even before Imperial Airways, the predecessor of British Airways, by operating a Fokker VII Trimotor aircraft in 1931 to Melbourne via Karachi and Batavia. The initial flight carried only mail and participated in the MacRobertson Air Race. MacRobertson was an Australian chocolate manufacturer (subsequently acquired by Cadbury), who was fascinated by aviation. He not only used the air race to market his products, he established an airline in Western Australia which became MacRobertson Miller Airlines and, eventually, part of the now defunct Ansett group. It was not until 1938 that KLM was able to obtain traffic rights for regular flights, as a result of the Imperial Airways/Qantas consortium requiring Dutch East Indies (now Indonesia) landing rights for their joint flying boat service. The initial KLM route was via Leipzig, Budapest, Athens, Alexandria, Lydda, Baghdad, Basra, Jusk, Karachi,

Jodhpur, Alla Hakjad, Calcutta, Rangoon, Bangkok, Penang, Malacca, Singapore, Palembang and Batavia (now Jakarta) and Lombok before reaching Australia at Darwin.

A scheduled air service was established between the UK and Australia by use of Imperial Airways flying boats in July 1938. The focus of the service was the carriage of mail rather than passenger or cargo. The flight departed Southampton, England on 28 July 1938 and arrived in Australia at Darwin on 8 August 1938, and Sydney at Rose Bay two days later on 10 August 1938. The thrice-weekly service was discontinued with the outbreak of the Second World War. E.A. Crowe's book '*Qantas Aeriana*' is a useful source of Qantas and Imperial early operational history on 'Kangaroo Route'.

The post-war migration boom to Australia led to a spate of carriers entering the Australia–Europe market. The carriage of visiting friends and relatives (VFR) passengers was the mainstay of these operations although all carriers endeavoured to a greater or lesser extent to access tourism markets.

As the European markets reduced and the sixth freedom carriers developed their services (initially Singapore, Malaysian, and Thai Airways but subsequently Cathay Pacific and later Emirates) the European carriers withdrew their services. Today, as noted, it is sixth freedom carriers that dominate the Australia–Europe routes.

2.2 Current Operations

Following the withdrawal of Austrian Airlines in 2007, only the two UK carriers, British Airways and Virgin Atlantic, continue to provide online service, though an Indian Ocean-based French carrier, Austral Air, commenced services in 2009 and was to terminate in 2012; however a later announcement says that the route will be continued. Austral Air are based on Reunion Island, which is legally part of France unlike the French Pacific Territories, but it can hardly be regarded as a European carrier, not withstanding its use of external French traffic rights. Australia has a Tripartite Air Service Agreement with France, it is in three parts; Part One deals with routes to/from metropolitan France, Part Two deals with New Caledonia and Part Three deals with French Polynesia (Tahiti). The extensive code-share services by European carriers are shown in Table 20.2.

3. Cabotage and Fifth Freedom Rights

As will be seen, one of the apparently contentious issues between Australia and the EU is the question of new fifth freedom rights and cabotage. While Qantas does not operate any flights which exercise intra-European fifth freedom rights, it does, of course, exercise fifth freedom rights from points in Asia (Bangkok to London, Singapore to London and Frankfurt, Hong Kong to London – there is a capacity restriction of 50 per cent of aircraft capacity on HKG-LHR-HKG), and this service is to be withdrawn in March 2012. The only European carriers who exercise fifth Freedom Rights into and out of Australia on their own aircraft are British Airways to/from Bangkok and Singapore, and Virgin Atlantic to/from Hong Kong.

Australia does have air service agreements which give its carriers fifth freedom rights within Europe, as do a number of South East Asian (ASEAN) countries. Qantas, as an Australian designated carrier, as observed earlier, code-shares on a number of European carriers within Europe. The code-share relationship with Air France crosses Alliance borders, Air France being a lead player in Sky Team, and Qantas being in oneworld. The relationship with Cathay Pacific Airways, an Asian

Table 20.6   Fifth freedom physical operation by EU carriers

Country	Airline	Route	Frequency	Aircraft type
UK	VS	HKG–SYD	7	360
UK	BA	BKK–SYD SIN–SYD	7 7	744 772

Source: Department of Infrastructure and Transport Schedule Filings 2011.

carrier, to Rome from Hong Kong is of course within the oneworld alliance. The largest code-share alliance is, unsurprisingly, with British Airways (BA): with code-share flights to five countries in Europe covering over 260 flights. As a consequence of availability of connecting flights, inbound and outbound code-share flights do not necessarily equate, i.e., a carrier often connects in one direction but not the other. The code-shares with BA derive from the Australian Competition and Consumer Commissions approval of the Joint Service Agreement (JSA) between Qantas (QF) and BA. This approval was renewed in 2009 for a further five years.

Qantas does not operate any cabotage nor have any cabotage rights within EU countries. However, as we will see, the EU would regard new requests for additional fifth freedom rights within Europe to be a request for cabotage and would expect reciprocation. The Australian Aviation Policy Green Paper of 2008 makes it clear that Australia will resist claims for cabotage rights.

4. The Sixth Freedom Operators – Australia to Europe

While the majority of all airlines who service Australia and UK offer sixth freedom carriage (and a range of fares to induce that traffic), the 'traditional' sixth freedom airlines – Singapore, Thai and Malaysian – have been challenged in their carriage in European markets initially by Emirates and then by the rapid growth of Etihad and by the subsequent commencement of online operations by Qatar Airways.

While in a legal sense the power of these airlines is irrelevant to a consideration of Australia's attitude to European liberalization, it is central to the consideration in an economic sense. Table 20.7 shows the medium-term formal growth prospects for the UAE Gulf State carriers. Capacity is expressed as frequencies of any type.

From the current operations and the growth opportunities (capacity available to be utilized) it is apparent that not only are third and fourth freedom carriers in a very difficult competitive position, but so are the Asian-hubbed sixth freedom carriers. The European networks of the Gulf State carriers are extensive: Table 20.8 shows and provides one-stop service to a significant number of European points, whereas the third and fourth freedom carriers provide one-stop service to only two points with their own aircraft.

Over 30 points are served in greater Europe and 26 in EU Europe by Gulf State carriers. The opportunity for carriage by both European carriers and Australian carriers is restricted . The European airlines have reacted by changing to code share flights using predominantly Asian based alliance partners. Qantas serves only London and Frankfurt and Air New Zealand serves only London (over Los Angeles).

Table 20.7   UAE Gulf State ASAs with Australia

ASA partner	Designated carrier	Online to Australia	2011 capacity – ASA	Capacity utilized	Growth capacity available
UAE–Abu Dhabi	Etihad	Yes	28	21	7
UAE–Doha	Qatar	Yes	14	7	7
UAE–Dubai	Emirates	Yes	84	70	14
Bahrain	Gulf Air	No	7	Nil	7
Kuwait	Kuwait Airways	No	2	Nil	2

Source: Department of Infrastructure and Transport Schedule Filings 2011.

Table 20.8   Gulf State carriers: European networks

Points in Europe	EK	EY	QR	GF	KU
Amsterdam	Y	N	N	N	N
Athens	Y	Y	Y	Y	N
Barcelona	Y	N	Y	N	N
Berlin	N	Y	Y	N	N
Birmingham	Y	N	N	N	N
Brussels	Y	N	Y	N	N
Bucharest	N	N	Y	N	N
Budapest	N	N	Y	N	N
Copenhagen	N	N	Y	N	N
Dublin	Y	Y	N	N	N
Düsseldorf	Y	Y	N	N	N
Edinburgh	N	N	N	N	N
Frankfurt	Y	Y	Y	Y	Y
Geneva	Y	Y	Y	N	Y
Glasgow	Y	N	N	N	N
Hamburg	Y	N	N	N	N
Istanbul	Y	Y	Y	Y	Y
Kiev	N	Y	N	N	N
Larnaca	Y	Y	N	N	N
London	Y	Y	Y	Y	Y
Madrid	Y	N	Y	N	N
Malta	Y	N	N	N	N
Manchester	Y	Y	Y	N	N

Table 20.8   *Concluded*

Points in Europe	EK	EY	QR	GF	KU
Milan	Y	Y	Y	N	N
Minsk	N	Y	N	N	N
Moscow	Y	Y	Y	N	N
Munich	Y	N	Y	N	N
Newcastle	Y	N	N	N	N
Nice	Y	N	Y	N	N
Oslo	N	N	Y	N	N
Paris	Y	N	Y	Y	Y
Rome	Y	N	Y	N	Y
Prague	Y	N	N	N	N
St Petersburg	Y	N	N	N	N
Sofia	N	N	Y	N	N
Stockholm	N	N	Y	N	N
Stuttgart	N	N	Y	N	N
Venice	Y	N	Y	N	N
Vienna	Y	N	Y	N	N
Zurich	Y	N	Y	N	N
No. of points served	28	13	25	5	6

Note: Y, physical operation; N, no operation; *non-EU points. QR to add Zagreb and Helsinki in 2012.

Source: Carrier schedules website 2012.

Table 20.9   **EU carriers – carriage to and from Australia 2007/8**

Airline	Australia (in)	UK (out)		Intermediate rights only (in)	Intermediate rights only (out)
British Airways	101,933	101,113	BKK SIN	48,597 28,055	45,777 30,005
Virgin Atlantic	45,942	45,419	HKG	37,379	31,614

Source: AVSTATS – Department of Infrastructure and Transport 2011.

5. The Market: Australia–Europe

In Qantas 2007/2008 carried 240,270 passengers into Australia from the UK and 246,836 out of Australia to the UK. British airlines carried almost 148,000 passengers. The predominance of carriage between UK and Australia is by sixth freedom carriers, not European carriers.

However, analysis of carrier data reported to the Commonwealth Government and analysed by Tourism Australia shows following results given in Table 20.10 for the two markets served by the third and fourth freedom carriers.

While this table is for 2008, the same table for 2003 would show Emirates having a 9 per cent market share ex UK and Germany, doubling over the six years in both markets.

Table 20.10   Carrier share of passengers UK/Germany to Australia, 2008

Carrier	Rank	UK share (%)	Carrier rank	Rank	Germany share (%)
Qantas	1	29	Qantas	1	34
Emirates	2	18	Singapore	2	15
Singapore Airlines	3	15	Emirates	3	14
British Airways	4	6	Jetstar/Lufthansa	4	6
Cathay Pacific	5	7	Cathay Pacific	5	7
Malaysian Airlines	6	4	Thai Airways	6	5
Others	7	21	Other	7	18
Total		**100**			**100**

Source: Tourism Australia 2012.

6. Air Cargo to and from Europe

While the two European specialist carriers operate their own aircraft to Australia, on circular (non-mirror image) routings, the majority of cargo between Australia and Europe is carried on sixth freedom carriers (e.g. Cathay Pacific and Singapore Airlines, both of whom operate their own freighters to Australia, as scheduled services) or as belly hold on the third and fourth freedom carriers (QF/BA/VS). The principal sixth freedom carriers also handle considerable amounts of belly hold cargo, however the carriage is not directly reported in available aviation statistics. Approximations can be drawn at the micro level by cross-referencing of city pair data but accurate specific sixth freedom carrier and cargo (not passenger) carriage data is not available. The use of A340-500 aircraft on non-stop service to Gulf hubs impacts negatively on cargo uplifts because of performance limitations. Table 20.11 demonstrates the current and immediate past cargo operators to and from Australasia by European and Australasian carriers.

7. New Zealand's Aviation Relationship with Europe

New Zealand has 11 bilateral air service agreements with European Member States and a further two with the non-EU states of Norway and Switzerland, as well as with Russia. Agreement has

Table 20.11   Cargo

Carrier	Routing	Weekly frequency
Cargolux	LUX – SIN – WEL – AKL – LAX – LUX	1
Air New Zealand*	AKL – MEL – PVG – GVD – FRA – ORD – HNL – AKL	2
Martinair	AMS – BKK – SYD – HKG – SHJ – AMS	2

* Wetlease aircraft.

been reached with the Netherlands, but the agreement has not been formally signed. It has been given provisional effect and services are in place (code-share only services are provided). There are no own aircraft operations by designated airlines of either country.

New Zealand signed a horizontal agreement with the EU in 2006 which has the effect of bringing all of the air service agreements with EU Member States into conformity with EU law.

7.1 New Zealand Service to Europe

The only New Zealand airline designated to operate to any point in Europe (EU States) is the majority state-owned Air New Zealand, who operate 12 times per week to London. Five services per week operate via Hong Kong, seven via Los Angeles (AKL-HKG-LHR was daily until September/ December 2009 when it was progressively reduced to five per week). The Los Angeles–London sector has unrestricted fifth freedom traffic rights, however, the London–Hong Kong routing is subject to a 50 per cent cap on uplift/discharge at Hong Kong. Aircraft used are the Boeing 747-400 and Boeing 777-300 ER.

7.2 European Operations to New Zealand

There are no physical operations to New Zealand by any European carrier. Neither the OAG nor the Air New Zealand schedule website show any code-share operations to/from European points in EU states, not withstanding Air New Zealand's participation in the Star Alliance, however further investigation established that the code-shares in Table 20.13 are available for sale.

7.3 New Zealand and Code-shares

While Air New Zealand is said to operate as partner in more code-share flights than it physically operates, it seems to operate very few to or within Europe. The New Zealand Ministry of Transport, unlike Australia, has not published its schedule filings on its website. The information in Table 20.13 is derived from the Air New Zealand website route map which shows code-share flights.

Table 20.12   ASAs with EU Member States and New Zealand

State	Commencement
Austria	2002
Belgium	1999
Denmark	2001
France	1964, 1967
Germany	1987
Ireland	1999
Luxembourg	1992
Spain	2002
Sweden	2001
United Kingdom	1982, 2005
ASAs with European non-EU Member States	
State	Commencement
Norway	2001
Russia	1993
Switzerland	1999

Source: New Zealand Ministry of Transport.

Table 20.13   Points served in Europe by code-share (NZ and partnering carrier)

Point	Operating carrier
Amsterdam	BMI
Belfast	BMI
Berlin	Lufthansa
Brussels	BMI
Dusseldorf	Lufthansa
Dublin	BMI
Copenhagen	SAS
Edinburgh	BMI
Frankfurt	Lufthansa
Glasgow	BMI
Hamburg	Lufthansa
Leeds (Bradford)	Lufthansa
Manchester	BMI
Munich	Lufthansa
Newcastle (Teesside)	BMI
Paris	BMI
Stockholm	SAS
Vienna	Austrian airlines

Source: Air New Zealand Route Map.

8. ASEAN Carrier Services to Europe

Singapore Airlines is the carrier offering the most capacity to Europe among the Asean carriers, serving 10 points in the EU (and Zurich) with 69 services per week across the 10 European cities. Four aircraft types are operated: Airbus A380; and three Boeing types: 747-400, the 777-300 ER or the 777-200 (a higher gross weight version). Appendix IV shows city pair frequency and weekly seat capacity. Singapore Airlines operates fifth freedom sectors beyond Europe: a daily FRA–NYC (JFK) A.380 and three times a week a B777 service between Barcelona and São Paulo.

Thai Airways (commonly known as 'Thai' or 'Thai International') is the second most active Asean carrier to Europe. Although Thai Orient Airways previously operated to Europe, Thailand currently has only the partially state owned Thai Airways Ltd operating to five points plus Zurich for a total of 45 frequencies per week, 14 of which operate to LHR.

Indonesia's flag carrier Garuda has been the subject of a 'black ban' by the European Union because of safety performance issues by the carrier and surveillance issues arising in Indonesia's safety surveillance authority. Indonesia expects that the ban will be lifted in 2009, in the meantime no Indonesian carrier operates to Europe, though European carriers operate to Indonesia. In July 2009 there were media reports that the ban was to be lifted, resumed service to Europe but with 'own metal operations' to Amsterdam only, other points being served by code-share.

Malaysian Airlines serves Paris, Frankfurt, London and Amsterdam. Stockholm was used as an intermediate point to New York though the route was suspended in October 2009. Rome has also been suspended.

Vietnam Airlines operates from two points in Vietnam, Ho Chi Minh City and Hanoi to each of Paris (CDG) and Frankfurt, with multiple flights each week by Boeing 777-200 aircraft.

Royal Air Brunei is the only other Asean carrier with European operations, linking Bandar Seri Begawan to London via Dubai. The carrier previously operated Boeing 767-300 ER aircraft, however it obtained a small fleet of B777-200 aircraft from Singapore airlines.

A summary of Asean frequency types and seat capacities is at Appendix VI. Points served in Europe from points in Asean by Asean countries are shown in Appendix VII.

Singapore and other ASEAN Country Agreements

Only three ASEAN countries have signed horizontal agreements with the EU: Malaysia, Singapore and Vietnam. Singapore has 30 open skies agreements, 16 of which are with European Union Member States. There is service by 83 scheduled airlines to Singapore providing 4,600 weekly services.

Recent Singapore liberal agreements include the major liberalization of the Kuala Lumpur route (to allow, inter alia the introduction of service by low-cost carriers). Other agreements are in place with Portugal, Romania and Czech Republic, though there are no physical operations to any of these countries.

Indonesia, obviously, will not agree to a horizontal agreement with the EU while its carriers remain subject to the EU blacklist because of ongoing issues in airworthiness by operators and airworthiness surveillance by government. Indonesia does have air service agreements with a number of European countries including its former colonial master, The Netherlands. The Philippines also has a number of ASAs with European countries though there is currently no Philippines carrier serving any European point. There is an ambivalent approach to open skies in the Philippines, a strong tourism lobby supported by the academic community strongly supports an open skies approach but the airlines, led by Philippine Airlines, are opposed.

Table 20.14 EU-ASEAN state horizontal agreements

State	Years signed
Malaysia	2007
Singapore	2006
Vietnam	2006

Source: EU website.

8.1 Air Service to ASEAN States by European Carriers

Service to ASEAN states is provided by the mainstream European carriers and by LTU in the LCC/ITC sector. Thailand receives the highest frequency of flights per week, followed by Singapore. Bangkok serves as a transit point for several carriers, e.g. KL to MNL and AF to SGN and HAN. Only six of the states receive European carriers while four further states are served by two or less carriers.

Table 20.15 European air service to ASEAN states: January 2012 (non code-share)

ASEAN State	European carrier service		
	Carrier	Frequency	Type
Brunei	Nil	Nil	Nil
Cambodia	Nil	Nil	Nil
Indonesia	KL	7	777
	LH	7	744
Laos	Nil	Nil	Nil
Malaysia	KL	7	74M
	LH	7	343
Mayanmar	Nil	Nil	Nil
Philippines	KL	7	77W
Singapore	AF	7	77W
	BA	7	777
	KL	7	777
	LH	7	380
Thailand	SK	7	343
	AF	7	777
	LH	4	744
	KL	7	74M
	BA	7	744
	AY	7	330/340
	LT	2	332
	OS	7	772
Vietnam	AF	5	777
	LH	3	744

Source: AOG 2012

8.2 ASEAN Carriers and Europe Fifth Freedom Operations

The ASEAN carriers have pulled back from fifth freedom operations within, to and from Europe. In 2009 the only ASEAN carrier flying an intra-Europe fifth freedom sector was Singapore Airlines (SQ) who operate four times a week SIN-MPX-BCN service with A.380 aircraft. SQ also operate a beyond Europe flights service from Frankfurt to New York with A.30 aircraft. There are no fifth freedom rights beyond Dubai used to EU Europe, but there are to Moscow and to Istanbul. Malaysian operates no fifth freedom sector within Europe but did fly a Stockholm–New York sector three times per week using fifth freedom rights beyond Europe, however, this flight has now been withdrawn.

9. The US–EU Open Skies Agreement

This agreement took effect on 30 March 2008. The impact of the agreement is that any EU airline can operate from any point in the EU to the US. The importance of this agreement is that it links the two largest markets in the world, in total they represent 60 per cent of the global aviation market where approximately 50 million annual passengers commute between the US and the EU. The March 2008 implementation represented the first stage of a multi-staged agreement process, the second stage negotiation took place in May 2008. The progress of the second-stage negotiations was slow, however the EU recognized that the deal would open up competition and potentially create 80,000 jobs and €12 billion in economic benefits.

Key elements of the agreement in addition to the lack of change in relation to cabotage are:

- Removal of restrictions on route rights
- Ability to purchase 'no voting' shares in US carriers but retention of 25 per cent voting limits
- A suspension clause requiring the US to open up its domestic market and foreign investment rules by 2010

Many European observers believe that the phased negotiation allows the USA too much 'wriggle room', especially in relation to foreign investment. The EU milestones are:

- 30 April 2007: EU and US leaders signed the so-called open skies deal during the EU–US Summit in Washington
- 30 March 2008: accord entered into force
- 15 May 2008: launch of second-stage negotiations
- 2009: EU due to review the progress of second-stage negotiations
- Mid 2010: deadline for achieving an 'Open Aviation Area'

The major outstanding item is that whereas US carriers have very extensive fifth freedom rights within Europe, there is no cabotage within the US. Furthermore the US seems intent on retaining its limit of 25 per cent foreign investment in US carriers.

9.1 European Regulation

Individual countries within the EU have developed bilateral air service agreements with a wide range of non-European states. There has been growth in new routes, especially between North America, Europe and the Middle East. Some of these agreements have open skies elements but few are of a full open skies nature. Traditional air service agreements have been based on the notion that ownership and control lies with individuals (personal and corporate) of the states of designation, and while there has been movement towards 'principal place of business' as the test, that movement is slow.

In 2002 the European Court of Justice concluded that bilateral air service agreements concluded with the US were discriminatory and this is a breach of European Union Community Law. The case had a major impact in that it clearly established that the Community (as differentiated from individual states) had exclusive responsibilities in external aviation relations. Following the 2002 decision the EU set about negotiating a new agreement with the USA which had a staged implementation. There were many barriers to this agreement including legislation concerning ownership and control, access to London's Heathrow airport (which is heavily slot constrained), and significant differences in the US and European approaches to cabotage.

The EU has developed an approach based on a two-party strategy: all existing air service agreements of EU Member States have to be amended so as to be in conformity to EU Law. It initially enters into a so-called 'horizontal agreement' to be followed by the creation of a Common Aviation Area. As an example, EU and Georgia entered into a horizontal agreement in 2007. The agreement came into force on 25 February 2008. The Common Aviation Area is proposed to remove the market restrictions and 'associate Georgia to', the EU internal market. In effect non-EU countries who subscribe to a Common Aviation Area with the EU are subscribed for the purposes of aviation (only) into the EU.

9.2 What is a Horizontal Agreement?

A horizontal agreement is one negotiated by the European Commission on behalf of Member States so as to bring bilateral air service agreements into conformity with European Law.

The 2002 landmark decision of the European Court of Justice decided that an ASA permitting designation only on the basis of carriers being owned and controlled by nationals of the signatory EU Members State was discriminatory; this is a breach of EU law. The practical implication is that any EU carrier can operate from any point in the EU to points outside the EU and existing (at that time) air service agreements had to be amended to reflect EU law. The EU law was contrary to the tradition of the bilateral air service agreement (which had its origins in the Chicago Convention of 1944). What the EU has achieved is to recognize that nationals of any EU State can establish, invest in and control airlines located in any EU State. An airline is not (for example) a German airline if it is established in Germany, but is a Community Airline. This concept is supported by the ability of an EU carrier to operate on any route within the EU, as well as the rules on licensing, security and safety are common throughout the EU.

The EU has developed two methods of bringing air service agreements into conformity with EU law. A state could amend all of its agreements on a separate bilateral basis, or there could be the negotiation of a single horizontal agreement, with the Commission acting on behalf of all the EU States.

The results of the approaches between July 2003 and December 2008 were 132 further bilaterals being altered with 60 states, and by means of the horizontal option, there have been three changes with 37 partner states and regional organisations. In total the process of horizontal negotiation led to changes to 651 bilateral agreements. The number of designated airlines remains controlled by the air service agreements. Traffic rights existing in the bilateral agreements remain, but new ones are subject to negotiation, with the EU taking the stance that the reciprocal of EU fifth freedom rights (e.g. FRA-CDG) is a cabotage city pair (e.g. MEL-SYD) in the partner country. This is because the EU no longer sees the city pair within the EU by a non-EU carrier as being a fifth freedom international sector.

The horizontal agreement and bi lateral dual systems may result in the EU being able to bring a large number of agreements into conforming to EU Law, but it does create a dual system of agreements, which adds to complexity.

The EU argues that meeting the objectives of bringing air service agreements into conformity with EU Community law is of vital importance to the EU member countries and third countries.

In doing so it, it has established that all community operators have the same rights through the principles of non-discrimination and freedom of establishment and there is legal certainty. The bilateral relations of a state are governed by Regulation EC 847/2004, which provides for standard clauses and which the EU believes facilitates the objectives of the EU. In the event that a state cannot reach an agreement with a bilateral partner on the insertion of the standard clauses, the EU may allow an agreement to be reached if it does not otherwise breach Community law, however, the Community designation clauses are sacrosanct and the EU will not allow a breach of these laws because it would be discriminatory. Horizontal agreements have the advantage of allowing third countries to avoid a large series of individual negotiations to meet Community Law.

9.3 The Barriers to an Open Skies Agreement: Australia and Europe

Australia has been in discussion with Europe on several occasions, most recently in 2008, 2009 and informally in 2011 concerning the creation of an open skies agreement to replace the 19 agreements that Australia has with countries in Europe. There are two major differences between the parties.

The first relates to traffic rights and the notion of a fair trade for intra-European rights. While Australia may retain the fifth freedom rights it has from one European country to another, in order to gain additional fifth freedom rights between European countries it would be necessary for Australia to recognize that the fair trade involves a grant of cabotage to foreign carriers. Australia does not

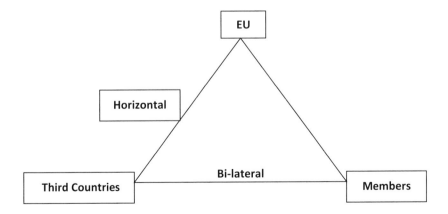

Figure 20.1   EU horizontal agreements and member/non-member states

grant scheduled, discrete or continuous cabotage, however there is a modified form whereby some countries have 'own stopover' rights, i.e. a carrier may uplift a passenger from a point in Australia and deposit it at another point if it brought that passenger to Australia, or will take it from Australia.

Australia has an extremely liberal approach to ownership of domestic airlines. A domestic airline maybe 100 per cent foreign owned. This policy is sometimes referred to as 'investment cabotage'. Cabotage for foreign carriers would seem to be not capable of being able to be agreed on between Europe and Australia. In the 2008 Aviation Green Paper, the process which leads to a White Paper, then finally a restatement of policy, the Australian Government has made it clear that the existing policy on cabotage will not be altered.

There is foreign investment in Australia's airlines: the Virgin Group through a company called Cricket SA owns 26 per cent of the Australian domestic carrier Virgin Blue (its Pacific Blue and V Australia subsidiaries, and Air New Zealand also owns 25 per cent of Virgin Group). In 2011 the carrier consolidated its various brands under the name Virgin Australia, Polynesian Blue was rebranded Virgin Samoa. Tiger Airways of Singapore has a 100 per cent owned low-cost operation in Australia, also known as Tiger, and there are significant Singapore owner share holdings in the regional carriers Sky West (Perth-based), and the NSW-based carrier Regional Express (also known as REX).

The second major area of difference is in environmental policies. In Europe 2007 prepared to include international aviation in the EU-ETS (Emission Trading Scheme). In the ETS effective 2011, operators would be required to surrender CO_2 allowances for inter EU-flights and from 2012 the scheme was imposed on all flights to and from European airports.

In February 2007 ICAO, a meeting of ICAO/CAEP, many countries said that such a scheme could only be applied by mutual consent. Both positions are argued from the basis of the Chicago Convention. In March 2007 the ICAO Council adopted an ICAO Guidance on Emissions Trading which includes a foreword expressing a view held by the majority of members that an ETS can only operate by mutual consent.

While European delegates to ICAO lodged formal reservations to the ICAO members' majority position, the ICAO position is evidentially advisory. In late 2009 the matter came before the European Parliament which proposed a more rapid and onerous regime than that proposed by the European Commission. In December 2007 there was a political agreement reached on flights by aircraft above 5700 KG MTOW (Maximum Take Off Weight) which will, from 1 January 2012 be required to surrender CO_2 permits. There are some exemptions: the '*de minimis*' rule applies and some essential air service flights are exempted as are various training and technical flights.

9.4 Australia's Approach to Climate Change and the EU Emission Trading Scheme

Australia is in the process of developing a climate change strategy with a member of the Ministry having climate change as a sole function. There is a long-term target of reducing year 2050 emissions by 60 per cent from year 2005 levels. An important element will be a Carbon Pollution Reduction Scheme (an ETS by another name) which will operate across all sectors of the economy. The Australian position is that it cannot act alone in managing emissions from international aviation. Australia is involved in international fora, including ICAO and APEC in seeking global cooperation. Industry-led voluntary offsetting schemes are supported.[1] The Australian Government is developing a tool for comprehensive carbon monitoring and footprinting. Australia's ETS was

---

1   Qantas gives persons making a booking on its website the option of making a voluntary additional payment to offset carbon emissions.

passed by the Parliament in November 2011 and comes into effect in July 2012. Eighteen pieces of legislation were enacted to set a floor price on carbon emissions of $23 (AUD) per ton. An important second, if unstated reason, is that on the European scheme, Australian carriers would be disadvantaged against Gulf state carriers because of the sector distances and flown and aircraft types operated.

In February 2009 European legislation came into force incorporating aviation into the EU Emissions Trading Scheme (ETS) as from 2012 (Directive EC/2008/101). Virtually all airlines with operations to, from and within the EU fall under the scope of the directive, including non-EU airlines.

In preparation for aviation's inclusion in the EU ETS, the European Commission (EC) is developing guidelines and CO_2 emissions. Under the guidelines, airlines captured by the EU ETS must meet certain requirements. In summary, these airlines will have to:

- submit monitoring plans by end of August 2009
- monitor tonne-kilometres and CO_2 emissions from 1 January 2010
- report tonne-kilometres data by 31 March 2011
- report CO_2 emissions data by 31 March 2011
- apply for free emissions allowances by 31 March 2011
- surrender allowances for 2012 emissions by 30 April 2013.

While distance at first glance may seem to advantage Gulf state carriers, their ability to use lighter aircraft increases the advantage, as the critical factor is not distance but tonne kilometres performed. One example suffices:

- Singapore Airlines operates a B747-400 aircraft FRA-SIN, tonne kilometres performed on one way trip are: weight of aircraft (316,895) × distance in km (10,270) 3,254,511 tonne kms
- Whereas Emirates operates a B777-300 aircraft over a lesser distance: weight of aircraft (297,500) × distance in km (4,841) 1,440,197 tonne kms.

It is clear that competitive carriers whose hub is more remote and who have to operate very heavy aircraft create more TKMs than the carriers with the nearer hub and who can operate a lighter aircraft.

If carbon credit prices relates to tonne kms performed then Emirates is clearly advantaged over Qantas (and of course, other Asian carriers including Cathay Pacific and Singapore Airlines). Australia's previous problem in negotiating an agreement which included acceptance of an ETS

Table 20.16   Comparative distances: Asia–Gulf State: the great circle route

From/To	Singapore		Dubai		Abu Dhabi
Frankfurt	5,546 nm 10,270 km		2,614 nm 4,811 km		2,617 nm 4,846 km
From/To	Singapore	Hong Kong	Bangkok	Dubai	Abu Dhabi
London	5,871 nm 10,873 km	5,205 nm 9,640 km	5,151 nm 9,540 km	2,899 nm 5,494 km	2,989 nm 5,498 km

Source: IATA World Air Distances 2003.

is that its ETS policy was not yet fully settled, however with the passing of the November 2011 legislation, an agreement has apparently had one obstacle removed. It is more likely that this matter will be dealt with in a way that is akin to the US–EU agreement in that it will be agreed that further discussions on the topic will be held in the future. The meeting that agrees this course of action will be in the category of meetings whose central rationale is to agree to another meeting. Australia continues to advocate a solution through ICAO as a global agency.

Conclusion

Australia and Europe have an aviation history dating from the 1930s. The beginning of service development was interrupted by the Second World War, however in the 1960s the advent of the long-range jet and the growth of the visiting friends and relatives market saw a strong growth in air service by European carriers including Lufthansa, Alitalia and Olympic Airways. Australia maintained a single designation policy until the 1990s, with the government-owned Qantas being the sole Australian international carrier.

One of the results of this policy as well as a growing commercialization of Asian national carriers was the strong growth of the so-called sixth freedom carriers – Singapore Airlines, Malaysian Airline Systems (as it then was), and Thai International. However, in the twenty-first century these carriers have found a new level of competition with the very rapid growth of the Gulf state hubs where airline, airports and policy are closely interrelated. As of 2009 Australia has service from Europe by only two British carriers and while Qantas serves only two points in Europe, code-share service on sixth freedom carriers is the dominant service offering.

Australia has collected a significant number of air service agreements with European countries and is engaged with the EU in the negotiation of a horizontal agreement, however major obstacles remain, particularly the application of the EU ETS to aviation and the consequent disadvantage to the Australian carriers and the issue of fifth freedom rights/cabotage. While there is no immediate practical impact, there are significant policy challenges in the cabotage issue.

New Zealand has no air service by European carriers, but its state-controlled carrier Air New Zealand offers service by both Eastern (USA) and Western (Hong Kong) routing to London.

In Asia, while the Asean states are liberalizing between themselves, ASEAN is ill-equipped as a body to negotiate either a horizontal agreement or an agreement to establish a common aviation area with the EU.

The Asia-Pacific region has a long aviation relationship with Europe but its future growth is heavily impacted by the rise of a new group of airlines, neither European nor Asia-Pacific in origin. The Gulf state carriers are rapidly optimizing their geographic position through rapid fleet growth, and active use of available rights.

Appendix I

European Carriers Using Fifth Freedom Rights on a Code-share Basis to Australia

Country of designation	Marketing carrier	Operating carrier	Fifth freedom sector	Frequency
Austria	OS	TG	VIE–BKK–MEL VIE–BKK–PER VIE–BKK–SYD VIE–BKK–BNE	7 3 in/2 out 7 6
Finland	AY	BA CX	HEL–BKK–SYD HEL–HKG–MEL HEL–HKG–SYD HEL–HKG–PER HEL–HKG–BNE HEL–HKG–ADL	7 7 in and out 7 7 4 in/3 out 3
France	AF	QF	CDG–HKG–BNE CDG–HKG–MEL CDG–HKG–SYD CDG–SIN–ADL CDG–SIN–BNE CDG–SIN–MEL CDG–SIN–PER CDG–SIN–SYD	4 7 14 3 7 7 7 7
Germany +	BA IB LH LH LH	QF QF SQ TG UA	LHR–FRA–SIN LHR–SIN–SYD MAD–FRA–SYD FRA–SIN–ADL FRA–SIN–BNE FRA–SIN–MEL FRA–SIN–PER FRA–SIN–SYD FRA–BKK–MEL FRA–BKK–PER FRA–BKK–SYD FRA–BKK–SYD–BNE LAX–SYD SFO–SYD	7 7 7 7 14 14 14 21 in/14 out 7 3 in/4 out 14 in and out 7 in and out 7 7
Greece	OA	EY	ATH–AUH–MEL ATH–AUH–SYD (Max 800 per week)	7 11
Hungary*	QF BA	MA QF	FRA–BUD BUD–LHR–SYD	7 7

European Carriers Using Fifth Freedom Rights on a Code-share Basis to Australia

Country of designation	Marketing carrier	Operating carrier	Fifth freedom sector	Frequency
Italy	AZ	MH	KUL–MEL	3
			KUL–PER	3
	AQ	EY	KUL–SYD	3
			ROM–AUH–SYD	11
			ROM–AUH–MEL	7
Malta	KM	QF	(LHR-BKK)–SYD	7
			(LHR-SIN)–MEL	7
			(LHR-SIN)–SYD	7
Netherlands	KL	MH	KUL–ADL	4
			KUL–BNE	7
			KUL–MEL	14
		CZ	KUL–PER	9
			KUL–SYD	7
			AMS–CAN–BNE	4
			AMS–CAN–MEL	7
			AMS–CAN–PER	3
			AMS–CAN–SYD	7
Scandinavian countries	SK	TG	BKK–MEL	7
			HKT–PER	4 in/3 out
		CA	BKK–SYD	7
			PEK–SYD	4
UK	VS‡	SQ	SIN–SYD	21
			SIN–ADL	0 in/7 out
			SIN–BNE	14
	BA	QF	SIN–MEL	21 in/14 out
			SIN–PER	21 in/14 out
			ADL–SIN	7
			BNE–AKL	7
			BNE–SIN	7
			MEL–AKL–LAX	7
			MEL–HKG–LHR	7
	NZ	VS	MEL–SIN–LHR	7
	VS	NZ	MEL–WLG	7
			PER–SIN	14
			SYD–AKL	7 in/14 out
			SYD–BKK–LHR	7
			SYD–CHC	7
			SYD–SIN–FRA	7
			SYD–SIN–LHR	7
			SYD–WLG	7 in/14 out
			SYD–ZQN	3
			LHR–HKG–SYD	7
			AKL–SYD	Free sale
			CHC–SYD	Free sale
			WLG–SYD	Free sale

* In addition, QF and BA mutually code-share on all services: QF 28 per week (in 2012 reducing to 21 per week)/BA 14 per week but reducing to seven.

† This carriage is entirely within Europe.

‡ VS is not in Star Alliance but SQ is a 49 per cent shareholder in VS.

Source: Department of Infrastructure and Transport Schedule Filings 2011.

Appendix II

Passenger Carriage Qantas–Europe 2010–2011

Airline	Australia (in)	UK (out)
Qantas	204,700	195,119
Airline	**Australia (IN)**	**Germany (OUT)**
Qantas	43,181	41,085

Appendix III

Cargo and Mail Carriage 2007/2008, EU Cargo Carriers to Australia

Carrier	Departure	Inbound	Destination EU cargo carriers	EU cargo carriers (outbound)
Cargolux	LUX SIN	3,886 925	LUX AKL USA	18.4 3,285 1,171
Martinair	AMS	8,061.8	BHH HKG AMS BKK UAE AKL	22.5 281.2 1,672.4 55.8 2,076 1.4

Appendix IV

ASEAN Nations, Flights to Europe

Country	Own carrier	Foreign carrier
Brunei	Yes	
Cambodia	No	No
Indonesia*	Yes	Yes
Laos	No	No
Malaysia	Yes	Yes
Myanmar	No	No
Philippines	No	Yes
Singapore	Yes	Yes
Timor Leste[†]	No	No
Thailand	Yes	Yes
Vietnam	Yes	Yes

* Anticipated resumption by GA in 2010.

[†] Not an ASEAN member.

Appendix V

Points Served in Europe by ASEAN Countries Carriers

From	To
Bandar Seri Begawan	LHR
Bangkok	ATH, CDG, FRA, LHR, STH, ZUR*
Hanoi	CDG, FRA
Ho Chi Minh City	CDG, FRA
Jakarta*†	AMS
Kuala Lumpur	LHR, LGW, CDG, FRA, AMS, ROM, STH
Manila	NIL
Phnom Pienh	NIL
Singapore	LHR, PAR, AMS, FRA, ROM, MXP, BCN, MAD, ATH
Yangon	NIL
Vientiane	NIL

*Non-EU

† see note in Appendix IV.

Appendix VI

ASEAN Carriers – Services to EU Member States and Switzerland

Royal Air Brunei

Departure	Destination	Frequency	Aircraft type	Seats	Weekly seats
BWN	LHR	7	772	285	1,995

Malaysian

Departure	Destination	Frequency	Aircraft type	Seats	Weekly seats
KUL	LHR	14	744	359	5,026
	AMS	7	744	359	2,513
	CDG	7	772	285	1,974
	FRA	5	772	282	1,410
	ROM	3	772	282	446
	IST	3	332	229	687

Air Asia X

Departure	Destination	Frequency	Aircraft type	Seats	Weekly seats
KUL*	LGW	5	343	325	1,625

* To terminate March 2012.

Air Vietnam

Departure	Destination	Frequency	Aircraft type	Seats in flight	Weekly seats
HAN	CDG	7	772	307	
HAN	FRA	4	772	307	
HCM	CDG	3	772	307	
HCM	FRA	4	772	307	

Singapore Airlines – European services

From Singapore	Destination	Weekly frequency	Aircraft type	Seats in flight	Weekly seats
	AMS	7	772		1,995
	ATH	2	772		570
	BCN* †	7	772		1,445
	CPH	3	772		855
	FRA	14	777/785/380		5,243
	LHR	21	7x77W/ 14x380		8,491
	MAN	4 5	380 772		1,425
	ROM	3	772		855
	MXP*	7	772		1,995
	CDG	7	380		3,248

* MXP and BCN – same flights, four times per week.

† Shared with first, three times per week SQ operate BCN–São Paulo (Brazil) with fifth freedom rights.

ASEAN Carriers – Services to EU Member States and Switzerland

Thai Airways

Departure	Destination	Frequency	Aircraft type	Seats	Weekly seats
BKK	CDG	7	744	375	2,625
BKK	CPH	10	747	375	3,750
BKK	FRA	7	744	375	2,625
BKK	LHR	14	744	375	5,250
BKK	STH	7	744	375	2,625
BKK	ZUR*	7	346	267	1,869

Source: AOG, carrier websites, 20 January 2011–2012.

*Non-EU.

Bibliography and Sources

Relevant EU Documents

Legislation
- 'Open skies' judgements of 5 November 2002 of the Court of Justice of the European Communities
- Communication from the Commission on relations between the Community and third countries in the field of air transport – COM (2003)94
- Regulation (EC) 847/2004 on the negotiation and implementation of air service agreements between Member States and third countries
- Information note: EU external aviation polity: why does the EU want to modify air service agreements between its Member States and partner countries?
- Draft Horizontal Agreement
- Commission Decision on approving the standard clauses for inclusion in bilateral air service agreements between Member States and third countries jointly lay down by the Commission and the Member States

Status of Amendment Bilateral Agreements:

- Bilateral ASA brought into legal conformity since ECJ judgments on 5 November 2002

Australian Government Sources:

- National Aviation Policy, Green Paper, December 2008

Department of Infrastructure and Transport and Regional Development website

- Aviation: Schedule Filings – Summary

OAG:

- Official Airlines Guide, January 2012

Tourism Australia

- Website

Grove, E.A. (1935). Qantas Aeriana 1920–1954. Francis J. Field Ltd, Sutton Coldfield, England.

A Detailed History of Qantas Flight Operations Including Aircraft Registrations, Crew Names Etc.

Aircraft

380	Airbus A380
744	Boeing 747-400
772	Boeing 777-200
773	Boeing 777-300
77W	Boeing 777-300ER
360	Airbus A340-600
332	Airbus A330-200
333	Airbus A330-300
343	Airbus A340-300
346	Airbus A340-600

Carriers

ADH	Abu Dhabi
AF	Air France
AY	Finnair
AZ	Alitalia
BA	British Airways
CX	Cathay Pacific Airways
EK	Emirates
EY	Etihad Airways
LH	Lufthansa
KL	KLM
KM	Air Malta
LT	LTU
MA	Malev (Hungary)
MH	Malaysian
OS	Austrian Airlines
QF	Qantas
QR	Qatar Airways
SK	Scandinavian Airlines System
SQ	Singapore Airlines
TG	Thai Airways
VS	Virgin Atlantic

City Codes

ADL	Adelaide
AKL	Auckland
AMS	Amsterdam
ATH	Athens
BCN	Barcelona

BUD	Budapest
BKK	Bangkok
BWN	Bandar Seri Begawan
CDG	Paris Charles de Gaulle
CHC	Christchurch
CPH	Copenhagen
DPN	Denpasar
FCO	Rome
FRA	Frankfurt
HEL	Helsinki
HKT	Phuket
HKG	Hong Kong
IST	Istanbul
KUL	Kuala Lumpur
LAX	Los Angeles
LGW	London Gatwick
LHR	London Heathrow
MAN	Manchester
MEL	Melbourne
MXP	Milan Malpensa
ORD	Chicago
PEK	Beijing
PER	Perth
PVG	Shanghai Pudong
SHJ	Sharjah
SIN	Singapore
SFO	San Francisco
STH	Stockholm
VIE	Vienna
WLG	Wellington
ZQN	Queenstown
ZUR	Zurich

General

ASA – Air Service Agreement
ICAO – International Civil Aviation Organisation
IATA – International Air Transport Association
MoU – Memorandum of Understanding
PKMs – tonne kilometre
KM – kilometre
NM – nautical mile

Chapter 21

Economic Evaluation of Air Services Liberalization: The New Calculus

Peter Forsyth

1. Introduction: The Changing Environment of Air Services Negotiations

The traditional approach to air services negotiations has been one steeped in mercantilist notions. Countries have emphasized access for their airlines to routes and capacity. Negotiations were excessively airline-centric – little attention was given to the passengers. Countries emphasized trading one route or rights for another. There has been an emphasis on not giving away rights – even though a country's travellers may gain from liberalization, countries have been proud to claim that they did not give anything away. As a consequence, countries would only liberalize when pushed to by others. It is not surprising that there has been slow progress in airline liberalization at the international level. This remains the case for most regions other than the US and the EU. Even with the US and the EU, it is notable that open skies agreements have only just recently been concluded – this is in sharp contrast to trade in most other goods and services.

Economists have been very critical of the prevailing orthodoxy in air services negotiations. They take a different perspective, and regard practice as a throwback to mercantilism, they consider that airline negotiations are dominated by producer interests, and that consumer interests have little say. Negotiations are seen as legalistic and bear little connection with a country's economic interests. A country will say no to a proposal which will be very much in its own economic interest.

Thus the economic approach to air service negotiations is very different. It begins by identifying what the country's economic interests are (and may be broadened by taking account of other interests, such as security). The approach seeks to determine how the country will fare under a proposal, for example, allowing additional services between it and another country. In particular, it seeks to find out how passengers and airlines will fare, though other aspects can also be taken account of. The objective is to determine the costs and benefits to a country – thus, one way to regard this approach is as the 'cost–benefit' approach to air services negotiations.

This approach is becoming much more accepted. Over the last 20 or so years there has been much more reliance on the economic approach. Economists have researched the pros and cons of liberalization. In some countries, this approach has had an effect on policy, both directly and indirectly. It is still not a dominant approach, except perhaps in some European countries and the US. Air negotiators and politicians still have a distinct say on what happens, but many countries now insist that economic aspects are taken into account.

Granted this, it is now time to review this approach. The building blocks of the approach are now established, but the airline market is changing. How do these changes affect the model? As an example, virtually all models of the cost–benefit approach assume that the home airline is fully home-country owned. This is no longer the case with many countries' airlines, granted that foreign ownership is now common.

The objective of this chapter is not so much to evaluate the cost–benefit approach, rather it is to take the approach, and assess how changes in air transport markets are affecting it. Which things will change the balance, and how and by how much? As will be seen, some factors can have a marked effect on the balance of benefits and costs, and these need to be accounted for in studies which take account of current market realities.

This chapter begins with a brief outline of the cost–benefit approach, before discussing the main sources of change – seven sources are identified. Then the impacts of these changes are put into perspective, and some concluding remarks are made.

2. The Cost–benefit Approach to Evaluating Liberalization

Over the past 20 or so years or so, there has been a growing and acceptance of what might be called the 'cost–benefit' approach to the evaluation of proposals for international and domestic liberalization of air routes. The approach involves specifying a range of cost and benefits that are expected to come about as a result of liberalization. These costs and benefits can be quantified and totals summed, and the net balance can be assessed. Other things being equal, if a proposal results in a positive balance of benefits less costs, it will be considered a good one. Most of the applications of this approach have been in international aviation, though some have been in domestic aviation – indeed, some of the pioneering studies were of domestic deregulation (e.g. the Morrison and Winston, 1986).

The costs and benefits from airline liberalization can be extensive; however, most of the gains and losses will accrue to the passengers and the airlines. Liberalization will be likely to lead to lower fares which will mean that passengers will gain. By contrast, lower prices will lead to lower profits in the hands of the airlines. These two elements of gain or loss will form the bulk of the gains and losses, though other effects could be moderately important – these include effects on frequency, connections and travel time taken. In economies for which there is unemployment jobs can be an issue, though it is difficult to measure the impacts of liberalization on jobs. Airlines will suffer a reduction in profits in the short run, though they may be able to claw back some or all of the profit reductions if they are able to increase productivity in the more competitive environment. Overall, the objective will be to measure the change in welfare coming through liberalization by assessing gains and losses.

The basic model is one which takes a home country, foreign country perspective (except for domestic liberalization). Normally, evaluation takes place from a home country perspective – home-country benefits count, while foreign-country benefits do not (though sometimes the welfare balance for all countries, home and foreign, are also measured). Typically, the home airline is assumed to be 100 per cent home-owned. The starting point is normally a restrictive bilateral agreement, and liberalization takes the form of a partial or complete removal of these restrictions. Liberalization could take many forms – it could involve granting partner airlines more capacity in terms of seats and services, less fare regulation, multiple designation or additional gateways.

The objective is to assess whether the proposal for liberalization gives rise to welfare gain for the home country. The home country's passengers gain, and the home country's airlines lose, though some of this loss may be reduced because there may be productivity gains. On balance, as a result of increased competition and the gains from trade, the overall welfare for all countries is likely to increase, the position of the home country could be worse. For example, if the home country has a high proportion of the airline traffic but a small proportion of the passengers, the consumer gains could be less than the producer's losses, and the country will be worse off as a result of liberalization. This has been the case for the Australia–Japan route, where the balance of traffic meant that it was not in Australia's interest to liberalize (Forsyth and Ho, 2003).

By now there are quite a number of studies which take a cost–benefit approach to evaluating liberalization. A cost–benefit approach has been used by Morrison and Winston (1986) to evaluate US domestic airline regulation. It has been used to set out a framework for international negotiations, and to evaluate liberalization of a route (Department of Transport and Communications, Australia, 1988), and specific options for reform have been evaluated using it (Street, Smith and Savage 1994; Gillen Harris and Oum 1996; Productivity Commission, 1998; Gregan and Johnson, 1999; Gillen et al., 2001). The approach has been used by courts and competition tribunals in evaluation of the effects of proposed airline alliances, such as the (now shelved) alliance between Qantas and Air New Zealand (Australian Competition and Consumer Commission, 2003; Commerce Commission, 2003). These studies identify a range of possible benefits and costs from a policy change, and attempt to measure them. Thus the gains to travellers from cheaper or more convenient travel are assessed, alongside implications for airline profits. These are the major direct benefits and costs – though in special circumstances there may be others. Typically, the largest benefits and costs are the direct ones, though other types of benefit and cost can be large in particular situations.

The cost–benefit approach to assessing air route liberalization is thus well established, though it must be recognized that the more traditional 'reciprocity' approach of air traffic negotiations being seen as a zero sum game still remains dominant. In this approach, where a country allows a foreign airline extra services it is seen as a loss to this country, and where the home airline gains additional services, it is a gain – gains or losses to passengers do not count. Essentially, this is a mercantilist approach which is at odds with the economic approach.

The economic or cost–benefit approach is gradually becoming more widespread. Significant reports in Australia, New Zealand, Canada and Germany have taken a Cost Benefit Analysis (CBA) approach, while countries such as the UK and the US have implicitly taken a more economic approach. Both government policy advisers (Productivity Commission, 1999) and competition authorities (Australian Competition and Consumer Commission, 2003; Commerce Commission, New Zealand, 2003) have adopted it. While other factors have been a factor in negotiations (for example, interest group lobbying is still very important) and policy makers have not been prepared to take a purely economic approach, this approach is having an effect on the policy stance taken by several countries.

3. Changing the Balance

As the cost–benefit approach has been adopted, the main parameters also become established. As noted, the main source of benefits has been increases in passenger fares, and the main source of costs has been reductions in airline profits. In addition, there have been a number of smaller sources. By and large, most studies of today are similar to studies of 20 years back. There have been a few changes, such as the recognition though not quantification of tourism effects, though the framework has been not changed by much.

In spite of this, there are several changes taking place in air transport markets, and some of these have the potential to change the cost–benefit balance. Some of these reflect new aspects – for example; climate change aspects of route negotiations, while others reflect changed perspectives of the problem, such as the greater importance being given to tourism aspects. It is useful to start with some changes which, though important, do not affect much the cost–benefit balance.

One is the move to airline alliances. While this is quite significant change, it does not make a large difference to the cost–benefit calculation – it is possible to analyse liberalization options involving alliances in much the same way as before: see, for example the studies of the proposed alliance between Qantas and Air New Zealand (Australian Competition and Consumer Commission, 2003; Commerce Commission, 2003). Another change has been the boom in low-cost carriers (LCC). Again, the same approach to evaluating liberalization options involving network carriers can be employed for LCCs.

What we need to do is to work out what changes in the market will have an impact on the ways which we evaluate options. Some of these changes could be quite small, but some could be very large, in particular circumstances. They are:

- changes in airline ownership;
- regionalization of negotiations;
- recognition of tourism benefits;
- the implications of airlines operating on a 6th and 7th freedom basis;
- implications of climate change policies;
- exchange rate changes; and
- recognition of frequency and agglomeration effects.

These can be analysed in turn.

3.1 Changes in Ownership

In years gone by, apart from the US, most international airlines had government owners. This meant that all of the profits accrued to the home country, along with all of the losses. Thus there was a one-to-one relationship between the country and equity interest in the home airline. While some countries had private international airlines, these airlines were mainly owned by domestic interests.

Privatization has changed this completely. There is no longer any necessary connection between the ownership of an airline and the home country in a negotiation. When privatizing airlines, many countries set out ownership restrictions, but full ownership in the home country is now rare – mostly, there is a significant level of foreign equity. For example, the Australian airline Qantas is now half owned by foreign shareholders – the Australian government has a limit on the foreign shareholding of 50 per cent, and for most of the time this limit is reached. In some cases, the capital structure of airlines means that while the airline is regarded as a 'home' airline for negotiations purposes, most of the airline's profits go to foreign shareholders – thus there might be a small number if shareholders who have 'A' shares in whom control is vested, but the bulk of the shares are in non-voting 'B' shares held by foreign interests. In some cases, these changes are recognized by countries changing to a 'Principal Place of Business' rather than ownership test as a criterion for the nationality of an airline (Doganis, 2006: Chapter 2).

Thus, if we are going to be assessing negotiations in which home countries benefits or welfare count, but foreign country benefits or welfare do not, we need to assess what proportion of the gains or losses to 'home' airlines go to home interests and what proportion of the gains or losses accrue to foreign interests. For national welfare purposes, home gains counts while foreign gains do not. Thus we need to determine what proportion of an airline's profits or losses can be attributed to the home country and what cannot. For many airlines this is straightforward, but for some it is not, and finding out what the beneficial interests on an airline can be a major research task. Mergers will also muddy the waters – to what extent is the merged Air France/KLM a French or Dutch airline?

While most profits accrue to the owners, some do not. Other entities may have a claim on the airlines profits. The most important of these will be the tax authorities. Airlines are typically subjected to corporate tax, which can be large – perhaps 20–40 per cent of profits. This means that the home country's share of the airlines profits will typically be greater than the share if equity.

The importance of this factor can be illustrated by means of a simple example. Suppose that a liberalization proposal results in a gain to the home countries share of passengers of $100 million, and that there is a reduction on the home countries' airline profit of $120 million – this could happen if the home country does not have a high share of airline passengers on this route. If there is no adjustment for where the airline profits go, this indicates that the country will lose from the liberalization option. However, suppose that the home airline is 50 per cent foreign-owned, and that there is a 40 per cent corporate tax. It means that the home country loses only 70 per cent of the reductions in airline profits. With the same gain to passengers, the home country will suffer a loss in airline profits and taxes of $84 million – overall the home country gains from liberalization. Many airlines have higher foreign ownership than this example supposes, and most tax rates are lower – if so this dilution of ownership can be much more significant than suggested here.

This result has strong implications for assessing whether a country gains or loses from a liberalization proposal. The most obvious one concerns the way in which the gains and losses can be calculated, as shown above – ownership matters. The second concerns the willingness of countries to liberalize – with the ownership of airlines becoming diluted, as has happened, countries will gain more from liberalization. Other things being equal, the benefits of liberalization will be unaffected, but the costs of liberalization will be reduced, sometimes quite substantially. Countries will be more prepared to liberalize because the costs of liberalization will be shared.

There are other implications which are worth noting. Countries may have a significant share in 'foreign' airlines, and this needs to be taken account of when assessing a liberalization proposal. This is especially true when countries are close neighbours, such the US and Canada, or Australia and New Zealand. Thus a country will share in the profits of foreign airlines. Airlines and their owners will be affected by the provision of infrastructure, such as airports, and they will be positively affected by improved facilities or negatively by airport congestion.

3.2 Regional Negotiations

Another factor which can affect the cost–benefit calculation is the move to negotiations on a regional basis. In this context what is meant by regional negotiations is that countries become part of a broader region, and need to take into account the interest of the whole region, not just themselves. The most important example of regionalization is with the EU, though ASEAN is developing an open sky initiative. Over the last decade or two Europe has become a single market for internal aviation, however, Europe had been a group of independent markets for international aviation. Until recently, France negotiated for France, Italy for Italy, and so forth. However, in recent years this has been changing. In some cases, the EU has been negotiating as a bloc – the best example of this has been the agreements with the US. However, another change has been that individual countries have been required to negotiate with other countries effectively on behalf of all EU carriers. Thus, if France were to conclude an agreement with another, non-EU, country such as Australia, it is required that all EU countries carriers, not just French carriers, have access to the route (see Chapter 20 in this volume). Thus German or British carriers could access the route. The idea is that EU countries will negotiate horizontal agreements covering all countries in the EU, rather than individual nationality-based agreements as in the past.

This may well be a step in the direction of the EU becoming a full single market for aviation. However, it does have important implications for how a country assesses liberalization.

Suppose there is a proposal to liberalize a route – say allowing more capacity – with a non-EU country. The new arrangements will affect how a country sees its interests. In particular, some capacity may go to non-home EU carriers, and the home airlines will lose profits, as a result of a reduction in market share and fare reductions. Thus liberalization will be less attractive to the home country under the horizontal agreement than before. This can create a conflict of interest between the home country and its peers in the community, because the gains from liberalization could be greater than with nationality-based negotiations.

This can be shown in an example in Table 21.1. The home country is shown as A, the foreign country is B and the home country is part of a regional bloc. Passenger benefits and airline profits can be summed to measure net benefits. Under the nationality-based negotiations, only home and the foreign airlines are allowed to access the route, while under the horizontal negotiations, airlines from the rest of the region are permitted.

Table 21.1 shows the position under nationality-based negotiations. In this case, liberalization is positive for both the home country and the foreign country. In addition, benefits accrue to the passengers from the rest of the region, though their governments have no say in the negotiations.

Under horizontal negotiations things change. Potentially, passenger benefits can be larger, because the market is more competitive. However, from the home country perspective, liberalization is less attractive – in fact, the home country loses from it. Home airline profits are reduced, because all airlines in the region can compete. Home airline profits are reduced, and overall, liberalization is negative from the home perspective. While overall benefits for the region and for the foreign country are increased, the home country loses. Thus, while it would agree to liberalization under nationality-based negotiations, it will refuse to liberalize under horizontal negotiations.

This does pose a problem for the regional authorities. It is in the interests of the region to encourage liberalization, but the approach of horizontal negotiations discourages it. The region could create incentives by subsidizing liberalization, though it might be difficult to develop a workable scheme for doing so. Others might suggest that members of the region should take a more

Table 21.1   Nationality Based Negotiations

	A	Rest of region	B
Passenger benefits	100	30	100
Airline profits	−80	0	−80
Net benefits	20	30	20

Table 21.1 shows the position under nationality-based negations. In this case, liberalization is positive for both the home country and the foreign country. In addition, benefits accrue to the passengers from the rest of the region, though their governments have no say in the negotiations.

Table 21.2   Horizontal Negotiations

	A	Rest of region	B
Passenger benefits	105	31	105
Airline profits	−110	30	30
Net benefits	−5	61	25

regional focus, and cease to be nationalistic. While this may be laudable, it is not very realistic. Countries in regions such as the EU still operate with their own economies, and still have a clear view of what constitutes their own interests. Thus when it comes to tax policies or welfare policies, the countries of the EU do not take a regional perspective. When it comes to evaluating options for airline liberalization; the move towards regionalization will result in another factor which changes the calculus.

3.3 Recognition of Tourism Benefits

In many of the earlier studies of the costs and benefits of liberalization, there was no explicit reference to the benefits of tourism. In more recent studies, tourism benefits have been recognized, though rarely explicitly measured. This is due to the limited research done on what tourism does for an economy – rigorous measures in the welfare gains from tourism have only recently been developed.

Liberalization encourages tourism in both directions, and countries will be affected by inbound and outbound tourism flows. Countries gain from increased foreign inbound tourism expenditure. Most countries now regard additional tourism expenditure as a benefit worth having, however they are unsure what weight should be put in it. Except in very special circumstances, the gain to the country will be less, and often a lot less, than the increase in expenditure (even though sometimes the gross increase in tourism expenditure is claimed as the benefit to a country). There is a need to provide the goods and services that the tourists consume, and these goods have a cost. The net welfare gain from increased inbound tourism expenditure will be much less than the expenditure itself. It will depend on such factors as whether there is full employment in the economy, and what taxes tourists pay. It is also the case that outbound tourism creates a cost, though this cost is not just the mirror image of inbound tourism.

In the various examples of the cost–benefit approach to assessing international aviation policy changes, tourism benefits are only sometimes taken into account. They were recognized in the Department of Transport and Communications study (1988), and noted though not evaluated in the Productivity Commission Study (1998). They have been measured using computable general equilibrium techniques by Forsyth and Ho (2003) and Forsyth (2006) and incorporated into the assessment of aviation policy options. Recently, they have been discussed extensively and measured in the context of the Qantas–Air New Zealand alliance proposal (Air New Zealand and Qantas Airways Ltd, 2002; Australian Competition and Consumer Commission, 2003; Commerce Commission, 2003). The relevance, and potential significance, of tourism benefits for the assessment of costs and benefits of aviation reforms has now been established. In addition to this, it should be recognized that tourism benefits have been an important driver of aviation policies, even where policy makers have not attempted to take a quantitative approach to assess how large the benefits and costs might be.

Measurement of the welfare gains or losses from inbound and outbound tourism is at its infancy, but some estimates have been made. Computable General Equilibrium (CGE) provide a rigorous way of measuring how much better off a country is from tourism expenditure. Australian studies suggest that the welfare gain from inbound tourism is about 5–10 per cent of expenditure (Forsyth, 2006). Australia has high employment, and a low tax rate on goods and services and motor fuel – i.e. in short, does not charge tourists high taxes. The welfare gain from tourism expenditure for a country such as the UK, with higher tourism taxes, would be larger.

One might suggest that since airline liberalization will encourage both inbound and outbound flows these will tend to cancel out, and that there need not be any explicit recognition of tourism benefits in assessing liberalization. However, there is an asymmetry that comes about from liberalization. This leads to the two countries liberalizing gaining more tourism and other countries gaining less – both countries become more competitive vis-à-vis their competitors. Thus there is redistribution towards the liberalizing countries and away from others. Other countries will gain tourism expenditure, and a net gain in welfare. This is much the same as the trade creating effects of a customs union – both countries gain in terms of net exports.

The recognition of tourism benefits in air service negotiations has several implications. One is that the results of evaluations are now less sensitive to the share of home country passengers on a route. This is because the country benefits from inbound tourism, not just its own passengers. Another implication is that liberalization will almost always lead to a net gain in welfare from the tourism flows.

The welfare gains from increased tourism can be measured, and they are likely to be significant. They will not be as large as the gains to home passengers, or the reductions in profits of the airlines, but they will be worth measuring and in some cases, they could sway the decision.

3.4 The Growth of Sixth and Seventh Freedom Traffic

Many and perhaps most of the applications of the cost–benefit approach to evaluating liberalization proposals have been done for third and fourth freedom routes. With these, the home and foreign countries and carriers are clearly identified. As markets are open up, there is pressure to examine fifth, sixth and seventh freedom routes. Most fifth freedom routes are allowed as add-ons – an airline serving country B on the way to country C is allowed to access traffic on a limited basis from B to C. It would be possible for country B to allow an airline to fly between B and C on an unlimited basis. Many airlines operate on a sixth freedom basis – it is difficult for countries at either end of a route to police the actions of airlines based in countries between them, and thus sixth freedom operations tend to grow up of their own accord. Seventh freedom traffic is rarer, though it does exist, and is probably growing as airlines seek new markets. The countries at either end of the route have control over this type of traffic because their approval is required. Thus, for example, Singapore is seeking to have Singapore Airlines permitted on to the Australia to US route – the US is willing to allow this, but Australia has rejected the request.

The presence of third country airlines had the effect of changing the balance of the equation. For example, if two countries are operating a service between themselves, and there is a country operating on a sixth or seventh freedom basis, this will affect the gains and costs of liberalization between the two countries. In particular, if the two countries are considering liberalizing the route, for example by allowing the home and foreign airlines more capacity, this will change the balance with third countries. It will mean that the home and foreign airlines will gain traffic at the expense of the country airlines, and therefore additional profits at their expense, as long as the home country airlines are profitable (which is likely since the home country would not be likely to agree to the change unless its airlines were so). Home country passengers would also gain through the third country airlines being forced by competition to lower their fares. All in all, liberalization will be more attractive to the home country than if the market were limited to the home and foreign countries.

On the other hand, liberalization which allows third countries to access the route will be less attractive to the home country. Allowing sixth or seventh freedom traffic will create benefits for home country passengers, along with tourism benefits which the country can gain from, but it will mean that the home country airlines will suffer a loss of market share and of profits. In this situation it is still possible for the home country to gain as a result of liberalization, since the gains to the passengers and tourism benefits may outweigh the costs to the countries airlines. A country may have a choice between allowing more home airlines on to the route (if they exist) and opening up to competition to third countries. In this case there may be a trade-off between greater airline profits if the route is served for home airlines and greater fare reductions and consumer and tourism benefits if the route is opened up. This was a choice faced by Australia when it considered allowing Singapore Airlines to enter the Australia–US route.

3.5 Climate Change Policies

Climate change polices have not yet made much of an impact, though they are poised to do so. Some countries are instituting polices which are ostensibly directed towards climate change, though they are primarily directed to raising revenue, such as the British Air Passenger Duty (APD) and its successors. However, serious climate change policies, and in particular the European Emissions Trading Scheme (ETS), and the New Zealand ETS which is already in operation and affecting airlines, will change this. The ETS will not have a big impact on aviation initially, but over time it will become much more significant. It will be necessary to factor in these impacts when assessing the case for liberalization.

Consider a situation in which one country imposes a climate change policy but the other does not. Both countries' airlines might be subject to the impost. This would be the case under arrangements for the European ETS, where foreign airlines flying to Europe, such as airlines from the US, are required to obtain permits (though this Scheme is currently suspended for non-EU carriers). In such a situation, both the airlines and their passengers will be affected, though which of these, and by how much, will depend on how the permits are allocated.

Suppose that the permits are sold to the airlines or auctioned. It is likely that the tax or auction price will be passed on (mostly) to the passengers, and that, at least in the long run, the airlines will not bear much of the cost. In this case, there will not be a large impact on the case for liberalization – if a country gains from liberalization without the policy, then it will gain when the policy is in place, unless there is a large imbalance in the flows of traffic.

The situation can change if permits are not sold or auctioned, but given away to airlines according to some rule, such as grandfathering. This is what the European scheme is planned to do for at least several years – while some permits will be sold, the bulk of them will be allocated according to a formula. This could give rise to changes in the balance of benefits from liberalization.

With limited permits available, these permits will become valuable – like airport slots. If airlines behave as profit-maximizers, they will price the value of the permits into their fares, and the fares will be the same as when they had to pay for the permits. Passengers will be unaffected by whether the airline pays for its permits or receives them free. The airline will gain when it gains free permits. This can result in changes to the balance of costs and benefits from liberalization. For example, a liberalization option might be unattractive to a country if airlines are required to pay for permits, because the country does not have a high share of airline profits. If permits are free, the countries airlines will gain in profits and the additional profits may tip the balance, and render the liberalization option positive for the foreign country. By giving away free emissions permits a country will be giving away valuable rights to profits, and foreign countries can gain from this.

It is also possible that the airlines might not behave in a profit-maximization way – for example, they may take advantage of the free permits and pass the gains on to their passengers, perhaps to gain sales revenue. In such a situation the airlines will not gain, but the passengers will be faced with a lower price increase than they would have (they would still have some price increase). This would lessen the impact of the ETS on both airline profits and passenger benefits.

What is clear is that the imposition of a climate change policies, such as an ETS, can change the balance of costs and benefits from a liberalization option. Interestingly, a country can actually gain a greater share of the gains from liberalization if another country imposes a policy such as an ETS. This will be something which needs to be taken account of when evaluating options.

3.6 Exchange Rates

Exchange rates are not usually factored in when assessing the costs and benefits from liberalization proposals. However, perhaps they should be. Most studies simply assume an exchange rate, often implicitly rather than explicitly, and analyse on this basis. If exchange rates remain unchanged for the period of the policy change, which can be a very long time, then there will be no problems. On the other hand, exchanges rates are quite variable, and this can affect the costs and benefits. The experience of the changes in the US$, the UK pound and the euro in the recent past shows how volatile exchange rates can be.

Exchange rate changes will systematically alter the costs and benefits of a liberalization option. If a countries exchange rate appreciates, its airlines will become less cost competitive (Forsyth and Dwyer, 2010). They will be paying some of the costs in the home currency, while all of the other competitors will be paying all of their costs in the foreign currency. This will mean that home country passengers will gain, but home countries' airlines will lose profits. Depending upon the shares of passengers and airline traffic, this can tip the balance of benefits and costs of a liberalization option. This suggests that it would be good practice when evaluating an option to test how it would be affected by changes in exchange rates.

3.7 Frequency and Agglomeration Effects

There are several models now which allow for the effects of frequency and for economies of density (e.g. Gregan and Johnson, 1999). These tend to handle the externality implicitly rather than explicitly – in other words they tend not to draw out the effect if higher output leading to higher frequency (leading to a consumer benefit) and lower costs (from use of higher-capacity aircraft). The gain from reaping economies of density will be relatively measureable, though it will not be likely to be very large – perhaps 5–10 per cent of total costs.

In recent years there has been a growing interest in the economies of agglomeration in surface transport, especially in road and rail transport (Graham, 2007; Venables, 2007). It is difficult to measure these economies, especially when done rigorously. However, those studies which have been done are suggesting that these economies could be quite significant – at around 10–30 per cent of total benefits. There may be some scope for applying these types of models to air transport – better transport links may have similar effects to those from surface transport. One needs to be careful however – one of the main benefits from further service links comes about from the effects of labour markets. This may not be so important with aviation markets which have less of a role in the role of carrying people to work. One should also be careful of studies which claim large benefits of airline liberalization based on input output models – such models do not factor the costs of creating the output, and thus they are inherently overestimates. However, there may be some effects of liberalization through agglomeration which have, to date, been ignored – this could be an interesting area for investigation.

4. Changes in Perspective

Granted that there are new challenges for evaluating the costs and benefits of proposals for liberalization, how much difference will they make? Will the changes be large, and will be changes be widespread?

Ownership changes are likely to be the most important – they are likely to be widespread and quantitatively significant. A large number of international airlines are partly or fully foreign owned, and when they are, this will have an effect on which country gains or loses from liberalization. For many airlines, perhaps half or more of the profits accrue to overseas interests. This will have a large effect on how a country fares from a liberalization proposal. Because airline profits will be negatively affected by liberalization, a country will be much more inclined to accept a proposal than before. Admittedly, producer interests will still lobby the government, and highlight how the nation gains from their existence, but the popular attitude towards airlines which only have a historical link to the home country will cool. Countries will be less defensive of the home airline and more prepared to support liberalization.

The impact of regional groups will be different. Most countries are not in regional groups, but for those that are, they could be quite significant. As outlined, the cost–benefit calculation for the home country will be changed if it is in part of a regional group. Regional groupings also pose a new problem – to what extent will countries in these groups identify with the region, or will they still pursue their own home country interests?

Tourism benefits are rather different in further ways. They are very widespread, though quantitatively quite modest. As noted, tourism flows stimulated by airline liberalization go in both directions, though most countries will have a net benefit from additional tourism. There will be some situations where countries gain a lot from additional tourism, especially developing countries or those which have unemployment. Some countries are recognizing that airline liberalization has an impact on tourism, though so far these impacts have not been measured rigorously. It is time to measure these effects systematically and determine what difference they make for the cost–benefit calculus.

Some but not all countries will be affected by the growth of sixth and seventh freedom routes – much will depend on a country's geographical position vis-à-vis its airline partners. Those that are will have a further complication when assessing how they are affected by liberalization options. The presence of sixth freedom carriers on a route can alter the calculus facing a country – it will make it more in its interest to liberalize than before. The extent to which this will make a difference can only be resolved on a case by case basis, however.

Not many airlines are yet affected by serious climate change policies. However, this will change – initially, airlines will be affected by these policies in a small way, though their impacts will grow, and in a decade or two, airlines may be finding that policies to reduce carbon will be a significant area of cost. Also, at least for a time, countries will be imposing very different policies, and this will affect the costs and benefits of liberalization proposals. In particular, some of the important proposals have interesting implications for addressing the climate change problem, such as the EU proposal, and will make a difference to the balance of costs and benefits from liberalization. While passengers will lose because they will have to pay for carbon, airlines can gain, if permits are free or partly free. Foreign airlines can actually gain from the EU scheme, and this will affect the balance of gains and losses faced by EU and foreign countries.

The remaining two sources of change are difficult to assess in terms of theory significance. Changes in exchange rates will impact on airline competitiveness, and thus they will affect the calculus of whether a country will be a gainer from liberalization. It might be good practice when evaluating a country's fares to see how much the calculation changes when exchange rates change. The final source of change is something for the future. The agglomeration effect is not something that has been given much attention in the evaluation of air services – however, given the interest in this effect in surface transport, it could be something which warrants more attention in the case of air transport.

5. Conclusions

The economic, or cost–benefit, approach to assessing whether a country gains from a proposal to liberalize international air services has been gaining in its influence, and many countries are recognizing the economic approach when determining their policies. The model is a quite straightforward one which pays particular attention to the benefits of travellers and airline profits though other aspects of benefits and costs can be important and can be incorporated. The basic approach has been used for a couple of decades and has not been subject to much revision.

However, during this time, there have been some large changes in airline markers. This poses the question of how does the model stand up to the changing environment? It stands up quite well up to a point, but there are some changes which need to be addressed. This chapter identifies a range of factors which need to be addressed if the model is not to become misleading or yield wrong evaluations. These factors can make a large difference – for example, foreign ownership can mean that that the home country has a much reduced stake on the profits of the airline – a country may be more willing to liberalize if it is less concerned to protect airline profits. Some of the factors which should be taken account of are quantitatively modest, they are widespread and can be significant in particular situations. While the model is robust, it does need to be adapted to the new market environment so that it gives an accurate evaluation of how a country will fare if it liberalizes its air services.

References

Air New Zealand Limited and Qantas Airways Limited (2002) *Submission to the Australian Competition and Consumer Commission in Support of the Application for Authorisation*, 9 December., Qantas Airways Ltd, Sydney.

Australian Competition and Consumer Commission (2003) *Draft Determination Applications for Authorisation, Qantas and Air New Zealand*, 10 April., ACCC Canberra.

Commerce Commission (New Zealand) (2003) *Final Determination: Qantas Air New Zealand Application*, 23 October. Commerce Commission Wellington.

Department of Transport and Communications (Australia) (1988) *Negotiating International Aviation Rights*, Consultants' Report, June., DTC Canberra.

Doganis, R. (2006) *The Airline Business*, 2nd edn. London and New York: Routledge.

Forsyth, P. (2006) Tourism benefits and aviation policy. *Journal of Air Transport Management*, 12, 3–13.

Forsyth, P. and Dwyer, L. (2010) Exchange rate changes and the cost competitiveness of international airlines: the Aviation Trade Weighted Index. *Research in Transportation Economics*, 26, 12––17.

Forsyth, P. and Ho, T. (2003) Air Transport Policy and the Measurement of Tourism Benefits. Paper presented at the Air Transport Research Society Conference, Toulouse, July.

Gillen, D, Hinsch, H., Mandel, B. and Wolf, H. (2001) *The Impact of Liberalizing International Aviation Bilaterals: The Case of the North German Region*. Aldershot: Ashgate.

Gillen, D., Harris, R. and Oum, T. (1996) *Assessing the Benefits and Costs of International Air Transport Liberalisation*. Ottawa: Transport Canada.

Graham, D. (2007) Agglomeration, productivity and transport investment. *Journal of Transport Economics and Policy*, September, 317–343.

Gregan, T. and Johnson, M. (1999) Impacts of Competition Enhancing Air Services Agreements: A Network Modelling Approach. Productivity Commission, Staff Research Paper, AusInfo, Canberra.

Morrison, S. and Winston, C. (1986) *The Economic Effects of Airline Deregulation*, Washington, DC: Brookings Institution.

Productivity Commission (1998) *International Air Services: Report No 2*. Canberra: Ausinfo.

Street, J., Smith, J.D. and Savage, S. (1994) *An Analysis of the Trade-offs in International Aviation Rights*. Australasian Transport Research Forum, vol. 19. Melbourne: Transport Research Centre, University of Melbourne.

Venables, A. (2007) Evaluating urban transport investments. *Journal of Transport Economics and Policy*, 41, 2, 173–188

Chapter 22

Multilateral Interlining in Deregulated Air Transport Markets

Frank Fichert

1. Introduction

The multilateral interline system organized by the International Air Transport Association (IATA) might be considered as one of the last relics from an era in which cooperation among independent airlines was much more common than competition between airlines and airline alliances. Since the 1950s, interlining has been an essential feature of international aviation. Based on several multilateral agreements, IATA has developed a complex interline system, enabling passengers to 'seamlessly' combine the services of two or more independent airlines. As the traditional IATA interline system included a comprehensive tariff consultation and coordination mechanism, it evoked a growing opposition of antitrust authorities throughout many countries, finally forcing IATA to reorganize the entire interline system. In this chapter, the traditional as well as the recently modified IATA interline system for passenger transport[1] will be analysed from an economic point of view, dealing with consumer benefits as well as with potential impediments on competition.

2. Multilateral Interlining – an Airline-specific Type of Cooperation

2.1 Interlining – Definitions, Features and Preconditions

In general, interlining allows an air transport user to combine services of two or more independent airlines by using one single ticket. This combination of services could be planned in advance (programmed interlining) or might be rather 'spontaneous' (flexibility interlining). Planned interlining occurs if a passenger purchases a single ticket which is valid for flights with several airlines. This type of interlining includes connecting traffic (e. g. travelling from C1 to C3 via C2, using airline A1 on the flight from C1 to C2 and airline A2 on the flight from C2 to C3) as well as return flights (e. g. travelling from C1 to C2 with airline A1 and back from C2 to C1 with airline A2).

'Spontaneous' interlining occurs if a passenger takes a flight with another airline than the one they originally intended to use without buying an additional ticket. For example, a passenger who has bought a ticket for a return flight with airline A1 might choose to take airline A2 on the way back (maybe because a meeting has finished earlier than expected or airline A1's flight is delayed). This example already indicates that flexibility interlining might be particularly valued by time-

---

1   Interlining is applied to passenger as well as cargo transport. This chapter concentrates on passenger transport. For a discussion of the peculiarities of cargo interlining see IATA (2004b: 14–18).

sensitive travellers. Empirical evidence shows that the share of interline passengers in premium classes (first or business) is much higher than in economy class.[2]

Passengers who have booked a fully flexible interline ticket within the IATA system do not only have the free choice of airline and flight; they are also allowed to add intermediate stops on direct flights or to change the intermediate airport. For example, a passenger who has booked a direct flight from C1 to C3 might add an intermediate stop at C2 – as long as the total mileage of the journey increases by no more than 20 per cent (routing flexibility).[3]

In general, the interline option makes travelling by plane more convenient and reduces passengers' transaction costs. Without 'planned' interlining a passenger would have to purchase several tickets (possibly in different currencies), if they intended to combine flights with more than one independent airline. Moreover, on a connecting flight the passenger would have to collect their luggage from airline A1 at the intermediate airport in order to check it in again for the second part of the journey with airline A2. This would not only be less convenient, but also more time-consuming than a 'check-through' which is offered by interlining airlines. Consequently, the additional baggage collecting and check-in process would increase connecting time and thereby the total time of the journey.[4]

If spontaneous interlining was not possible, a passenger would have to buy a new ticket if they wanted to fly with a different airline than the one they originally booked. As the purchase of a new ticket is – more or less – time-consuming, flexibility might be reduced. Furthermore, the passenger would have to bear additional transaction costs for returning the non-used ticket.[5]

In order to provide the quality-enhancing features mentioned above, interlining requires an intense cooperation among the participating airlines. First of all, airlines have to agree on the acceptance of tickets issued by another carrier, requiring the implementation of a revenue-sharing mechanism. Furthermore, airlines have to develop common procedures for the through-checking of baggage on connecting flights with interline passengers. Those agreements among airlines might be bilateral, for example within a strategic airline alliance, or multilateral, as offered within the interline system organized by IATA. It is obvious that an interlineable ticket is a joint product which requires cooperation and therefore cannot be produced by an individual airline.

2.2 The Traditional IATA Interline System

The traditional IATA interline system[6] was based on several pillars. In the recent past, some of these elements have been changed, whereas others have been transferred into the new system. Among the most important features of the traditional system are the tariff conferences and the prorating agreement.

Tariff conferences, in which every IATA member airline has the right to participate, are organized for different regions and cover only international traffic. At these meetings, fully flexible business class and economy class interline fares were fixed for every possible origin-and-destination market

---

2   See ACCC (2005: 69).

3   In case of an increase in mileage of more than 20 per cent, an additional charge will be levied.

4   Low-cost airlines generally do not offer interline services. Moreover, most low-cost airlines do not even provide connecting flights and a through-checking of luggage within their own network.

5   As an alternative, the passenger might buy several tickets in advance, which gives them maximum flexibility. Nevertheless, this is also less convenient than interlining, especially if more than two airlines serve this particular city pair market.

6   For a comprehensive description see European Commission (2001), Annex 1.

(O&D).[7] Furthermore, for some city pairs the conference agreement also covered discounted fares. All decisions on tariffs had to be taken unanimously. From a legal point of view, the fare which has been agreed on at the tariff conference only served as the basis for revenue-sharing among airlines. Therefore, airlines have not been obliged to sell their interlineable tickets at the respective IATA fare. Nevertheless, as fully flexible interline tickets are a homogenous product and serve as the base for revenue-sharing, airlines have no incentive to deviate from the tariff fixed within the IATA interline system.

The Multilateral Prorate Agreement, which is also open to non IATA members, determines that the revenues from actual interline traffic are divided among airlines according to the so-called prorate factor.[8] On connecting flights, the general rule says that revenue is split in proportion to the mileage flown by each airline ('straight rate proration'). Nevertheless, as airlines' costs differ among regions, the prorate factor is not simply the mileage-share, distance is multiplied by an area cost weighting factor.

On connecting flights which consist of short-haul and long-haul segments, the revenue share of the airline operating the short-haul leg might be very small if the revenue distribution is only based on the prorate factor. Therefore, the prorate agreement enables airlines to fix a minimum rate on short-distance flights, the so-called proviso. Nevertheless, a complicated mechanism blocks the application of the proviso rate if it should lead to an 'unreasonable' revenue distribution among airlines, i.e. too small revenues for the long-haul carrier.

The allocation of revenues generated from interline tickets among participating airlines is organized by the IATA clearing house.

2.3 Intra-alliance Code-sharing as an Imperfect Substitute to Multilateral Interlining

The IATA interline system was introduced long before the first strategic airline alliances were founded. One basic element of all strategic airline alliances is code-sharing,[9] which basically describes the sale of tickets for airline A1's flights by airline A2 under A2's code and flight number.[10] Similar to the different forms of interlining, parallel and complementary code-sharing can be distinguished, the latter is also referred to as interline code-sharing.

From a passenger's perspective, the effects of bilateral code-sharing on direct flights show some similarities to the features of multilateral interlining. If a city pair market is served by only two airlines and those two airlines have agreed on a comprehensive reciprocal code-sharing, a carrier-specific flexible ticket provides the passenger with almost the same advantages as an interline ticket. However, in most cases the addition of an intermediate stop might not be possible if this itinerary requires the service of a third airline which does not participate in the code-sharing agreement. If three or even more airlines offer direct flights on a city pair market and only two of them have agreed on code-sharing,[11] this bilateral cooperation might be seen as a rather limited substitute to multilateral interlining.

---

7 In order to facilitate the fare-setting process, so-called 'add-ons' were fixed for similar connecting flights at an identical level.

8 For a comprehensive description see IATA (2004a).

9 There are also many bilateral code-share agreements outside strategic alliances.

10 For a comprehensive description of the different forms of code-sharing see Steer Davies Gleave (2007).

11 Take as an example the LHR–FRA market, where LH and BD code-share and their competitor BA holds a significant market share.

On connecting flights, code-sharing provides the passenger with almost the same advantages as planned interlining.[12] Nevertheless, airlines which are participating in an alliance only offer connecting flights within the alliance network. If the most convenient connection requires the service of airlines which do not code-share with each other, the multilateral IATA interline still provides additional benefit.

For code-sharing agreements airlines can choose from a large variety of potential fare setting and revenue sharing models.[13] One option is the so-called freesale, where the marketing carrier has access to the booking system of the operating carrier with the latter deciding on the availability of a particular fare. Under a freesale regime, the marketing carrier often receives a commission for the sale of code-share tickets from the operating carrier. Another possibility for code-sharing is the so-called blocked-space agreement, where a given number of seats is reserved for the code-share partner, who pays a fixed amount of money and might sell those seats at its own fare, but also at its own risk.

For connecting flights, different rules of revenue allocation might apply, some of them based on the 'industry standard' as formulated by IATA in the Multilateral Prorate Agreement. As an alternative, the partner airlines might refer to individually negotiated Special Prorate Agreements (SPA). One important type is the 'net SPA', which specifies a fixed amount the marketing carrier has to pay for booking one passenger on a given flight, independent of the fare that has to be paid by the passenger for the entire transfer flight.

With the growing market share of strategic airline alliances, the importance of the multilateral IATA interline system has decreased. A large number of connecting flights might be booked with one single ticket issued by a member airline of one of the large strategic alliances. Nevertheless, the above discussion shows that code-share agreements within airline alliances are only an imperfect substitute for a comprehensive multilateral interline system. As the competitive effects of code-sharing and strategic airline alliances have to a large extent been analysed in the literature,[14] the remainder of this chapter concentrates on multilateral interlining within the IATA framework.

2.4 Interrelations Between a Multilateral Interline System and Airlines' Pricing Strategies

Especially since the deregulation of the industry, airlines have developed various ways of product differentiation which can be broadly classified according to two categories: 'flexibility' and 'quality'. Flexibility offers a convenient way of changing one's travel plans, whereas 'quality' stands as a synonym for several factors such as in-flight comfort, lounge access, and frequent-flyer advantages. If, for reasons of simplicity, only two distinctions apply to each category (full flexibility vs. reduced flexibility and high quality vs. low quality) the 'air transport-product' might be offered in four different versions (see Table 21.1). In the IATA wording, fares for tickets with full flexibility are called 'normal' fares, whereas fares with restrictions are called 'special fares'.[15]

It is obvious that a 'high-quality product' will always be more expensive than a 'low-quality product'. Consequently, full flexibility justifies a price premium when compared to a product with reduced flexibility. Therefore F1 will always be the highest fare and F4 will be the lowest.

---

12   These effects are described in detail in Section 3.4.
13   An extensive description can be found at Steer Davies Gleave (2007).
14   See for example Brueckner (2001), Gurrea (2006), Czerny (2009).
15   It should be kept in mind that the majority of tickets contain some restrictions, making the IATA 'special' fare the prevalent fare in air transport markets.

Nevertheless, deciding on the proportion between F2 and F3 is more complex and requires information on customers' preferences as well as on competitors' pricing policy.

From an airline's perspective, enabling passengers to buy interlineable tickets might be interpreted as part of a price and product differentiation strategy. The joint product 'interlineable ticket' is a supplement to the carrier-specific flexible tickets offered by each individual airline. As interlineable tickets are the superior product, there has to be a price difference between interlineable tickets and tickets that allow flexibility only within one carriers' network. The amount of this price span is likely to be dependent on the magnitude of consumers' benefits generated by the interlining option. Suppose that there are two competing airlines which offer an identical schedule on a certain city pair. An interlineable ticket would only be useful in the event of delays or overbooked planes. Therefore the willingness to pay a price premium for interlineable tickets on this city pair would probably be rather small.

Whereas all airlines are likely to charge the same price for interlineable tickets, prices for carrier-specific flexible tickets might differ among airlines. Consider again the hypothetical example of two airlines offering exactly the same schedule. Price differences between carrier-specific flexible tickets might only be justified by quality factors such as service, punctuality, safety, image or the attractiveness of the frequent flyer programme. Nevertheless, a schedule which fits passengers' preferences better than the one of the competitor might allow an airline to charge higher prices for carrier-specific flexible tickets.

Considering the interline option, the number of possible flexibility-quality-combinations increases up to six (see Table 22.2). Again, it is obvious that F1 will be the highest fare overall and F6 should be the cheapest fare available. Analogous to a situation without interlining, the decision on fares F2 and F3 in relation to F4 and F5 is not trivial.[16] Nevertheless, many airlines do not actually make use of all possible options.

Table 22.1   Options for airlines' product differentiation and pricing policy (without interlining)

	High quality	**Low quality**
Full flexibility	Flexible business-class ticket (fare F1)	Flexible economy-class ticket (fare F3)
Reduced flexibility	Restricted business-class ticket (fare F2)	Restricted economy-class ticket (fare F4)

Table 22.2   Options for airlines' product differentiation and pricing policy (with interlining)

	High quality	**Low quality**
Interline flexibility	Interlineable business-class ticket (fare F1)	Interlineable economy-class ticket (fare F4)
Carrier flexibility	Flexible business-class ticket (fare F2)	Flexible economy-class ticket (fare F5)
Reduced flexibility	Restricted business-class ticket (fare F3)	Restricted economy-class ticket (fare F6)

---

16   The following options might be valid: F2>F3>F4>F5; F2>F4>F3>F5; F2>F4>F5>F3; F4>F2>F5>F3 and F4>F2>F3>F5.

3. Pros and Cons of the Traditional Interline System

3.1 Criteria for an Economic Assessment of Interline Systems

As the IATA interline system, like almost all other IATA activities, covers air transport services worldwide, it has to be approved by several competition authorities, including the European Commission (Directorate General Competition) and the Australian Competition and Consumer Commission (ACCC).

Apart from several differences in wording and procedures, the legal framework in different jurisdictions shows some fundamental similarities. In general, agreements between undertakings are prohibited if they restrict competition. Nevertheless, if these agreements produce benefits for consumers which cannot be enabled by less restrictive agreements, an agreement might be exempted from the general prohibition of anti-competitive agreements.

In the 1980s and 1990s, when liberalization of air transport markets was just beginning, competition authorities tended to accept IATA's arguments in favour of the multilateral interline system. For example, an Authorisation of the IATA interline system was granted in Australia in 1985 (Authorisation A90435), and the European Commission granted a block exemption in 1993 (Regulation 1617/93). In the following sections of this chapter, the recent controversy about the IATA interline system is illustrated and the change in the perception of the pros and cons of the multilateral interline system will be explained. A distinction is made between interlining on direct flights and on connecting flights. Furthermore, markets for direct flights are differentiated according to market structure.

3.2 Parallel Interlining Within a Symmetrical Duopoly Market

3.2.1 Assessing consumers' benefits As already stated above, the benefits from an interline system for passengers who travel on city pairs with two or even more airlines offering direct flights result from the option to change flights between the different airlines at short notice (flexibility interlining). For hub-to-hub routes, the European Commission questions the benefits of the IATA interline system, because the high frequency offered by each individual airline might provide even time-sensitive passengers with a sufficient degree of flexibility.[17] Similar to this view, the ACCC sees a decline in the need for IATA flexibility interlining on city pair markets with a large number of flights.[18] Nevertheless, even on such 'trunk routes' a passenger who changes their original travel plans might save a significant amount of time, possibly including the avoidance of an overnight stay in a hotel, when owning an interlineable ticket instead of a non-interlineable ticket.[19]

From the passengers' perspective, buying an interlineable ticket instead of a non-interlineable ticket can be interpreted as an insurance against time losses.[20] For a risk-neutral customer, the maximum premium they are willing to pay for an interlineable ticket is given by the expected average time advantage of interlining (depending on the individual likelihood of having to change one's travel plans as well as on the probability that the booked flight is delayed or cancelled) multiplied with the passenger's individual value of time.[21]

---

17   See European Commission (2004), paragraph 60.
18   See ACCC (2005: 68).
19   See IATA (2005: 8). For an example also see Fichert (2007).
20   See IATA (2005: 9).
21   As businessmen normally travel on their company's expenses, a principal-agent-conflict might arise, especially if an increase in total travel time reduces the passenger's leisure time. These incentives might

In order to analyse the behavior of airline customers with respect to interlining, two stages have to be distinguished. First, a passenger has to decide whether to purchase an interlineable ticket or a non-interlineable ticket. If an airline offers all flexibility-quality-combinations described above (see Table 22.2), the purchase of an interlineable ticket would clearly show that the passengers' willingness to pay for the interline option is larger than the price premium the airline claims. Many airlines do not offer premium class tickets with a reduced flexibility. In these cases, a passenger who buys a premium class ticket opts for a bundle consisting of quality and flexibility, and therefore the willingness to pay for the interline option cannot be observed.

On the second stage, holders of interlineable tickets might indeed decide to use the services of different airlines. The publicly available data on passengers who are actually making use of their interline option is rather limited and should be interpreted with caution.[22] Whereas the European Commission and the ACCC focus on the rather low share of passengers who are actually interlining, IATA points out that the absolute number of passengers is not negligible and that these passengers show a significant willingness to pay for interline tickets.

Competition authorities view the low share of passengers who are actually interlining as an indication for a decline in the benefits provided by the IATA interline system, caused by increasing flight frequencies on trunk routes. Nevertheless, with respect to the insurance character of an interlineable ticket, the small percentage of actual interlining on trunk routes might also indicate a rather low number of business travellers who have to adjust their travel plans. As long as customers are free to choose between interlineable and carrier-specific flexible tickets, a small number of actual interline passengers does not indicate that this product is no longer relevant in the market.

3.2.2 Competitive effects of tariff consultation and tariff coordination One important source of competition authorities' distrust against the traditional IATA interlining system is the so-called 'coat-hanger effect'. If airlines meet at a tariff conference and agree on increasing the interline fare at a certain percentage, they subsequently might also raise other fares, especially the carrier-specific fully flexible fares. According to the coat-hanger argument, the interline fare in many cases serves as a focal point. A – jointly decided – rise of the IATA interline fare gives a signal to the airlines that increasing the carrier-specific fares will restore the previous fare structure and raise revenues for all airlines serving this particular market.

Analysing air transport markets without the traditional interline system might help to understand the possible anti-competitive effects of the IATA tariff consultation and coordination mechanism. If an airline raises its carrier-specific fully flexible fare, the competing airline's reaction is a priori unknown. It might, for example, raise its fare by the same amount or it might leave its fare unchanged in order to increase its market share. This uncertainty about competitor's behaviour, which is a fundamental feature of oligopoly markets, might be reduced if beforehand the competing airlines have agreed on raising the price for a joint product – the interline ticket – which is a close substitute to their carrier-specific tickets. As many trunk routes are characterized by significant barriers to entry (especially capacity restrictions at one or even both airports, consumer loyalty induced by frequent flyer programmes and the large number of daily flights which cannot be easily reproduced by a new entrant), coordinated fare increases for fully flexible tickets are likely to be profitable for the airlines serving a particular city pair market.

---

contribute to a rather price-inelastic demand for interline tickets.

22   For example, British Airways stated that between July 2003 and June 2004 8 per cent of its customers travelling within the EEA purchased a fully flexible ticket at the IATA fare: 15 per cent of these passengers actually made use of their option to interline (i.e. 1.2 per cent of all passengers). See BA (2004: 2). Overall data can be found at IATA (2004c).

The theoretical justification of the coat-hanger argument has been questioned in economic studies prepared for IATA.[23] Among other aspects, these studies refer to the multitude of factors influencing airlines' pricing decisions, and the complex interdependencies between prices and quantities of two partially substitutable products. Furthermore, the studies point out that an effective coordination of behaviour requires that airlines do not only coordinate fares but also capacity.[24] Nevertheless, a coordination of capacities might not be indispensable in markets which show a low price elasticity of demand combined with some degree of customers' airline loyalty, e.g. caused by frequent flyer programmes. Under these circumstances, airlines might simply assume that a coordinated increase in fares might leave market shares unchanged.

In order to support the coat-hanger argument, different market studies have been conducted. On many European markets the carrier-specific flexible fares (economy class) analysed by UK authorities matched exactly.[25] Examples include flights from Paris to Budapest, Madrid, Prague and Rome as well as from Paris to eight airports in Germany. As air transport on these city pairs is a relatively homogenous product[26] and market transparency is high (at least for the so-called published fares), identical fares do not necessarily reflect collusion, but might also be the outcome of an intense duopolistic competition. Nevertheless, the data suggests that many airlines set their carrier-specific flexible fares by multiplying the respective IATA interline fare by a fixed factor. For example, Air France's carrier-specific flexible fare (economy class) was 90 per cent of the IATA fare on flights from Paris to many destinations in Italy and Germany and was 85 per cent of the IATA fare on flights from Paris to many airports in Eastern Europe and Scandinavia. Moreover, it can be shown that after the IATA fare has been increased, for example, Lufthansa and Air France raised the prices of their carrier-specific flexible tickets at the same percentage, presumably in order to keep the carrier-specific fare at a constant proportion to the IATA fare.

Whereas there seemed to be rather stable relations between the IATA interline fares and the carrier-specific fully flexible fares for some airlines, other airlines showed different pricing behaviour. There are some examples where after an increase of the IATA interline fare an airline left its carrier-specific fully flexible fare unchanged or where the percentage of the fare increases differed.

The ACCC compared the development of the IATA interline fares and carrier-specific fares over time for several city pair markets to/from Australia. In the first class and in the business class segment of many city pairs similar movements of the IATA interline fare and carrier-specific fares could be observed. ACCC concluded that carrier-specific fares can be influenced by the fares set by the tariff conference.[27] Nevertheless this view has been challenged by IATA, using sophisticated statistical analysis and denying influences between the fares observed.[28]

Summing up, the empirical picture with respect to the coat-hanger effect is mixed. There seem to be linkages between the IATA interline fare and carrier-specific fares for some airlines and/or selected periods. So far no explanation has been given for the significant number of deviations from this pattern. From a theoretical perspective, they might be caused by carrier or route specifics, like fluctuations in demand, or market entry of low-cost carriers, just to name a few. A comprehensive empirical study, covering all these potential determinants of fare setting behaviour, is still missing.

---

23   See IATA (2004c: 26–30).
24   See also IATA (2004b), Annex IV.
25   See UK (2004), Annex.
26   The competing airlines offer a similar schedule and product quality.
27   See ACCC (2006).
28   See CRA (2006).

It is important to notice that the above discussion of airlines' pricing policy is entirely based on the so-called published fares. Large customers, e.g. multilateral firms, often negotiate company rebates with individual airlines. As most business-class tickets are purchased by business travellers, the share of rebated tickets is presumably rather high. Due to the fact that there is hardly any information available on company rebates in the airline industry, the picture on the competitive effects of the IATA tariff consultation and coordination mechanism is somewhat limited. Nevertheless, if rebates are negotiated as a percentage of published fares, an increase of published fares caused by the coat-hanger effect would also drive negotiated fares up.

3.3 Parallel Interlining on Markets Dominated by One Airline

On city pairs where the market share of the competing airlines differs significantly, an interline system may even show some pro-competitive effects. If airline A1 offers a much higher frequency than airline A2 and only carrier-specific tickets were available, time-sensitive passengers would predominantly choose A1. The option to interline enables A2 to effectively compete in this high yield market segment.

If A1 intends to limit the market opportunities of A2, several potential strategies exist. First, empirical evidence shows that incumbent carriers sometimes try to withhold the interline option from a newcomer or a smaller competitor. Examples include Lufthansa as well as SAS.[29] In some cases, competition authorities even had to order the incumbent to interline with its smaller competitor.[30] Second, as the interline ticket offers only a rather small benefit when compared to the carrier-specific fully flexible ticket of A1, the incumbent should be interested in keeping a considerable difference between the interline fare and its carrier-specific fully flexible fare. Within the traditional IATA tariff coordination mechanism, the principle of the unanimous decision enables A2 to prevent such fare increases.

3.4 Complementary Interlining

For connecting passengers, benefits of (planned) interlining include the through-checking of luggage which makes flying much more convenient and reduces minimum connecting time. Furthermore, an interlining ticket ensures that in the event of a delayed flight, the passenger will be rebooked to another connecting flight without additional costs. On city pairs with more than one airline in the market, flexibility interlining also provides additional benefit to time-sensitive passengers. Nevertheless, the relevance of the IATA interline system diminishes with the growing number of code-sharing arrangements and the extension of strategic airline alliances who offer 'seamless' connecting flights within the alliance network. Furthermore, many airlines have negotiated bilateral interline agreements on city pairs with a sufficient level of demand, allowing them to offer seamless connecting flights at fares below the IATA interline level.

On connecting flights with both airlines holding a monopoly position on one city pair, the benefits of the interline system can be described by the Cournot effect; i.e. interlining might be seen as a kind of vertical integration. Microeconomic theory shows that the profit-maximizing price for the joint product is smaller than the sum of the separate fares for the two flight segments. If a connecting flight consists of one monopoly market and one competitive market, the double

---

29   See Nordic Competition Authorities (2002: 98).

30   The obligation to interline with newcomers is also a common remedy in merger control, attempting to limit the anti-competitive effects of airline mergers.

marginalization problem does not occur. In the air transport industry, this situation might be relevant for O&D markets consisting of a monopoly feeder-traffic route and a competitive trunk route.

As an empirical snapshot, market observations by the ACCC show that the IATA interline fare on the few connecting markets not being served by an airline or an airline alliance is far above a joint fare which might be constructed by travel agents using carrier-specific fares of independent airlines.[31]

4. Flex Fares and E-tariffs as Key Elements of the New IATA Interline System

During the consultation process dealing with the revision of the EU block exemption, IATA and many of its member airlines argued fiercely in favour of the traditional interline system. However, the DG Competition finally suspended the block exemption which ended on 31 December 2006 for flights within Europe, on 30 June 2007 for flights from Europe to the USA and Australia, and on 31 October 2007 for all other flights between Europe and third countries (Regulation 1459/2006). Therefore, in order to maintain the possibility of multilateral interlining, a new system had to be developed, eliminating the tariff consultation and coordination mechanism which gave cause for serious concerns regarding its anti-competitive effects. Whereas several competition authorities suggested replacing the tariff consultation and coordination mechanism by a posted-price model, IATA dismissed this option as being not workable.[32]

In 2007, IATA has introduced a new interline system named 'Flex Fares'.[33] Within the Flex Fares system, IATA automatically calculates an average fare for every city pair market based on information on airlines' carrier-specific fully flexible fares. The IATA Flex Fare, which enables multilateral interlining, is calculated by adding a given percentage onto the calculated average fare. Before the implementation of the new system, the interline premium has been agreed on by the tariff conference member airlines.[34] Changes to the agreed Flex Fares model are possible within an also newly developed system named e-Tariff. E-Tariff is an Internet-based system managed by IATA. It allows IATA member airlines to anonymously make proposals for changes in the Flex Fare system and to vote on these proposals also in an anonymous way. Therefore, face-to-face-meetings during tariff conferences and joint discussions on the appropriate interline fares are no longer necessary. Furthermore, the sequence of fare-setting has been reversed. Whereas within the traditional system carrier-specific fares could have been set after the tariff conference had agreed on a new interline fare, the Flex Fares follow individual decisions on fares.

5. Conclusions

In principle, the multilateral interline system organized by IATA for more than 50 years makes flying more convenient and therefore provides benefits to consumers. Nevertheless, the extent of these benefits is declining due to an overall growth in air transport markets, which is increasing flexibility within one airlines' network, and the extension of strategic airline alliances, providing seamless travel for most connecting passengers.

---

31   See ACCC (2005: 77).
32   See IATA (n.d.). The pros and cons of a posted price model are discussed in Fichert (2007).
33   For a description of the Flex Fares system see IATA (2008).
34   Currently, the premium is between 6–10 per cent, depending on the traffic region.

It cannot be ruled out that the IATA tariff conferences simplified information-sharing and even collusion among competing airlines. Competition authorities' general 'unease' with the traditional interline system is therefore justified and finally forced IATA to react, leading to the introduction of the Flex Fares and e-Tariffs system.

The ACCC has granted its authorization for the new interline system for only a limited period of time, maintaining the possibility of reviewing whether the Flex Fares system has an influence on carrier-specific fares. Therefore, in its redesigned form the IATA multilateral interline system will remain in the focus of competition authorities' attention and also gives some room for controversial debates among aviation economists.

References

ACCC (2005) *Discussion Paper A90855/3, IATA Tariff Coordination: Passengers*, Document published on ACCC website.

ACCC (2006) *Revised Fare Analysis, Attachment*.

BA (2004) *British Airways Comments in Response to DG Competition Consultation Paper*. 24 September. London, Document published on DG COMP website.

Brueckner, J. (2001) The economics of international code sharing: an analysis of airline alliances. *International Journal of Industrial Organization*, 19, 1475–1498.

CRA (2006) *Response to ACCC Revised Fare Analysis*, prepared for IATA, Document published on ACCC website.

Czerny, A. (2009) Code-sharing, price discrimination and welfare losses. *Journal of Transport Economics and Policy*, 43, 193–212.

European Commission (2001) *DG Competition Consultation Paper, IATA Passenger Tariff Conferences*. Brussels: European Commission.

European Commission (2004) *DG Competition Consultation Paper Concerning the Revision and Possible Prorogation of Commission Regulation 1617/93 on the Application of Article 81(3) to Certain Categories of Agreements and concerted Practices Concerning Consultations on Passenger Tariffs on Scheduled Air Services and Slot Allocation at Airports*. Brussels: European Commission.

Fichert, F. (2007) Interlining and IATA tariff co-ordination – do consumer benefits justify potential restrictions of competition? In F. Fichert, J. Haucap and K. Rommel (eds) *Competition Policy in Network Industries*. Berlin: LIT Verlag, 135–156.

Gurrea, S.D. (2006) International airline code sharing and entry deterrence. In D. Lee (ed.) *Advances in Airline Economics*. Cambridge: Emerald Group Publishing Limited, 109–140.

IATA (2004a) *Annex to Discussion Paper on Posted Prices. Overview of IATA Proration Mechanism*. Geneva: IATA.

IATA (2004b) *Comments on DG-Competition Consultation Paper Concerning Commission Regulation 1617/93*, non-confidential version, 6 September. Geneva: IATA.

IATA (2004c) *DG-Competition Consultation on Regulation 1617/93: IATA Observations on Third-party Comments*, non-confidential version, 22 December. Geneva: IATA.

IATA (2005) *Comments on DG Competition March 2005 Discussion Paper Concerning Commission Regulation 1617/93*, 4 April. Geneva: IATA.

IATA (2008) *IATA Passenger Tariff Coordination for Multilateral Passenger Interlining, Application for Authorisation by the ACCC*. Document published on IATA website.

IATA (n.d.) *Discussion Paper on 'Posted Prices'*. Document published on IATA website.

Nordic Competition Authorities (2002) *Competitive Airlines. Towards a more Rigorous Competition Policy in Relation to the Air Travel Market.* Copenhagen, Helsinki, Oslo, Stockholm: Self published.

Steer Davies Gleave (2007) *Competition Impact of Airline Code-share Agreements.* Document published on DG COMP website.

UK (2004) *UK response to the DG Competition consultation paper on regulation 1617/93 (EC).* Document published on DG COMP website.

Chapter 23

US Bilateral Air Transport Policy

Martin Dresner

Introduction

After the failure of the Chicago Conference in 1944 to arrive at a multilateral system for regulating international air transport, international air transport has been mainly governed by a web of country-to-country bilateral agreements. These air transport bilaterals specify the international routes that airlines of each country may fly, the method for determining airfares on the routes, the number of carriers that may fly on the routes, methods for settling disputes between the signatories of the agreement, and a myriad of 'doing business' rules concerning, for example, the provision of ground services at airports in each country.

The United States, as the world's largest economic power, the home of the biggest air transport market and the headquarters of many of the world's largest airlines, has, historically, been a leader in setting standards for air transport bilaterals. From the time of its precedent-setting 1946 Bermuda I agreement with the United Kingdom, to the 1990s and 2000s open skies bilaterals with over 90 partner countries, the US has favoured market-based liberal air transport agreements. Whereas other countries have pushed for anti-competitive provisions in bilateral air transport agreements, the US has generally been a proponent of competitive, not cooperative, forces determining market outcomes. However, in recent years, this liberal reputation has faded as aviation partners, most notably the European Union (EU), have argued for the elimination of nationalistic ownership restrictions on US-based air carriers, and for the opening of the US domestic market to cabotage operations by foreign-owned carriers. In addition, the recent willingness of the US government to grant antitrust exemptions to anti-competitive actions by airline alliances has called into question the US's commitment to a liberalized international air transport market.

In this chapter, we examine US air transport bilateral policy over the past 60-plus years. In particular, we consider the reasons behind the US market-based approach to air transport bilaterals, from Bermuda 1 to open skies. We also examine the less liberal policies the US has employed, including antitrust exemptions for alliances, the prohibition of cabotage and restrictions of foreign ownership of US carriers. Finally, we draw conclusions as to future US bilateral policies.

The Bermuda I Regime

The underlying rationale for international air transportation regulatory system predates the Chicago Conference of 1944 and the Bermuda I agreement of 1946. It stems from the recognition that air transport is distinct from ocean transport. Whereas the principle of 'freedom of the seas' underlies the operations of ocean carriers, a similar principle of 'freedom of the skies' is not suited to international aviation. Due to national defence considerations, governments find unregulated over-flight by foreign carriers to be unacceptable. As a result, the principle of national sovereignty over air space trumped freedom of the skies, as confirmed at the Paris Convention of 1919.

The national sovereignty principle implies, most importantly, that a country's airlines cannot operate internationally without the consent of foreign governments. Therefore, even a powerful country such as the United States, must seek the permission of other governments for the international operations of its air carriers. Recognizing this principle, US President Franklin D. Roosevelt convened an air transport conference in Chicago in 1944 (now known as the Chicago Conference) to facilitate the regulatory procedures for international air transportation in the post-Second World War era. Given recent technological developments in aviation, it was evident that the industry would experience rapid growth in the years following the war, and that a formalized regulatory structure would be useful. O'Connor (1971: 19) lists key aims of the Chicago Conference as follows:

- the founding of a permanent international organization for civil aviation;
- the regulation of air safety; and,
- the economic regulation of international air transportation.

Although the conference was successful in reaching agreement on the establishment of a permanent international organization for civil aviation, the International Civil Aviation Organization (ICAO), and agreed on procedures for regulating air safety, there was no agreement on the economic regulation of international air transportation. The major obstacle to an agreement stemmed from the US desire for a market-based approach to the air transport regime, and the British wish for a system with greater regulatory oversight. As Straszheim (1969: 17) outlined in his classic book on the international airline industry:

> Various nations differ in their attitudes with regard to international air transport objectives; this can be explained in part by fundamental differences in social and economic institutions and ideologies. Objectives of the United States are generally consistent with its historical advocacy of free world trade and unrestricted capital markets. Similarly, American reliance on private ownership without government regulation, and the American dislike for pooling arrangements and other non-market procedures for the allocation of resources, are important in the formulation of U.S. objectives in the industry. At the same time, many other countries have very different inclinations. European nations, for example, appear more likely to permit restrictions in their markets, and European firms seem more anxious to form pools and divide the existing market than to enter into competition, which might expand the market for all.

In particular, the US favoured a broad exchange of route rights in bilateral agreements, including fifth freedom rights (i.e., the right for an airline of Country A to transport passengers between Countries B and C on routes originating or ending in Country A). With respect to tariffs, the US was opposed to an international regulatory authority that would set or approve tariffs, preferring to leave rate-making to the airlines (Haanappel, 1984; O'Connor, 1971).[1] Although this market-based position was in keeping with the general American support for open markets, the US position also favoured the US airline industry. The United States was emerging from the Second World War in reasonably strong financial condition, and had developed a fleet of long-range bomber aircraft that could be converted to civilian use. US airlines had both the financial resources and the physical resources to readily compete against foreign rivals. Thus, a market-based system favoured US carriers.

---

1   Although not its preferred alternative, the US was willing to cede rate-making to an airline conference, which could operate in a manner similar to the ocean carrier conferences.

On the other hand, the British supported the creation of an international regulatory authority that could determine capacity levels, frequencies, and airfares on international routes.[2] Weakened by the Second World War, and with an air fleet not as suitable as the Americans' for civil aviation, the British argued for a regulatory authority that would allocate traffic on international air routes to airlines in general proportion to the share of traffic generated from a country.

Given the extensive strategically located overseas territorial holdings of the British at that time, the Americans were obliged to reach an accommodation with the UK. In the Bermuda I bilateral accord, the Americans agreed on anti-competitive clauses allowing airlines collectively through the International Air Transport Association (IATA) to set airfares, subject to governmental approval. On the other hand, the British yielded on capacities, permitting carriers on routes between the two countries (third and fourth freedoms) to set capacities, subject only to *ex post facto* review. Fifth freedom traffic was permitted as well, but this traffic was to be subsidiary to third and fourth freedom traffic. Finally, routes to be operated by the airlines of the two countries were specifically outlined in the agreement, with the multiple designation of carriers on each route allowed.

The Bermuda I agreement was important not only because it represented a compromise between the two most important aviation nations of the time, but also because it served as a precedent-setting agreement for the United States, and for many other countries as well, for the next 30 years. Richards (2001) analyses the reasons for the longevity of the Bermuda regime. First, the emergence of IATA as a forum for joint fare-setting created the cartel necessary to generate rents for the industry. Second, sufficient provisions were included in the Bermuda agreements (e.g., restrictions on fifth freedom operations, the division of route authorities between airlines of different countries) to ensure a reasonably 'fair' distribution of rents among carriers. Third, the IATA system required the unanimous approval of all carriers operating in a broadly defined market (e.g., the North Atlantic) to agree on airfares. As a result, even the weakest carrier could, theoretically, veto the IATA airfares if they were too low, in order to ensure profitability for all carriers operating in the market. Finally, the US was willing to tolerate the Bermuda regime, despite its anti-competitive aspects, because the cooperation of other governments was required for the international operations of its own carriers.

Bermuda II

In the 30 years following the signing of Bermuda I, the United States stuck fairly religiously to the Bermuda I principles. However, as with most cartels, the international air transport system was not without problems. There were difficulties reaching agreement on airfares at the IATA meetings, with the more efficient carriers pushing for lower fares and the less efficient carriers claiming that higher fares were required. In addition, carriers sought to gain market share by competing on service; for example, through the introduction of in-flight movies and the offering of free alcohol and elaborate meals, thereby eroding the profitability of international air services. Finally, a number of non-IATA 'charter carriers' began operating in international markets.[3] At first, charter operations were limited to 'affinity' groups, with the requirement that all passengers on a charter flight be members of the same affinity group or organization. However, in 1966, the United States authorized 'split charters', allowing two or more organizations to jointly charter an aircraft.

---

2   The routes themselves would be set in the bilateral agreements (Chuang, 1972).
3   Provisions for charter operations were generally not included in Bermuda agreements.

Soon, the affinity rules became unenforceable, with charter groups formed solely for the purpose of booking seats on air flights (Haanappel, 1978).

Although the United States remained fairly true to the Bermuda principles, other countries acted in a more deliberate manner to reduce competition on international air routes and protect their carriers' market shares. In particular, many other countries substituted the relatively liberal capacity clauses in the Bermuda I-type agreements with 'predetermination of capacity' clauses. These clauses required carriers to jointly agree on frequencies and capacities prior to operating services.

By the mid-1970s, the United States too changed its position and began promoting capacity sharing agreements as a means of protecting its flag carriers. The early 1970s had been a difficult time for the US carriers. They had invested heavily in wide-bodied aircraft, but expectations of huge increases in passenger traffic had not been realized, in part due to the oil crisis and recession of that period. In order to improve the position of its major international carriers, the US authorized Pan American and TWA to discuss capacity agreements with their British counterparts, leading to a reduction in the number of flights between Britain and the US (Dempsey, 1978). In addition, the US began intergovernmental negotiations to alter key bilateral agreements in order to improve the opportunities for US carriers to increase their traffic (Lowenfeld, 1975; Haanappel, 1976).

The culmination of the US retreat from its free-market position was the signing, with the UK, of the Bermuda II agreement in 1977, replacing Bermuda I. Although US carriers had been performing poorly on many North Atlantic markets, they had been doing quite well on routes between the US and the UK. It was the British, dissatisfied with the market shares of their carriers, who demanded that Bermuda I be renegotiated (Bridges, 1977). In particular, the British demands included the following (Larsen, 1977):

- An equal division of the US–UK market between British and American carriers;
- The designation of only one carrier per country on each route;
- A continuation of IATA price-setting, and governmental cooperation to ensure that IATA fares were enforced; and,
- A severe reduction in fifth freedom routes allocated to US carriers.

Although the British were not able to achieve all of their aims, the resultant Bermuda II agreement did contain, most importantly, a predetermination of capacity clause requiring US and British carriers to submit schedules for governmental approval prior to operations taking place. Either government could disapprove the schedules. In addition, the designation of carriers was restricted to one per country on all routes but two, severely restricting access to Heathrow airport by most US carriers. Finally, some of the fifth freedom routes previously allocated to US carriers were withdrawn.

The Liberal Bilateral Period

Unlike Bermuda I, Bermuda II did not serve as a precedent-setting agreement for the US. In fact, almost immediately following the signing of the agreement, the US began to move in a diametrically opposite direction, towards bilateral agreements that supported competitive market outcomes. A number of studies by economists had demonstrated the negative effects of regulated air transport markets (notably high prices, low load factors, and excess service competition) (e.g., Jordan, 1972; Douglas and Miller, 1974), and in 1978, the US Congress passed legislation to deregulate the US domestic air transport system. Alfred Kahn, the chair of the Civil Aeronautics Board (CAB), saw no reason why US international routes should not be likewise 'deregulated'. Under his leadership, the US sought to liberalize its international air markets in five ways (Dresner, 1989):

- By promoting low-cost international scheduled services, especially the services of the pioneering low-cost carrier, Laker Airways, to compete with established carriers;
- Through the liberalization of charter rules;
- By ordering airlines and other concerned parties to 'show-cause' why IATA tariff coordination should continue to be granted antitrust immunity;
- By passing pro-competitive legislation governing international air transportation; and, perhaps most importantly,
- By signing 'liberal' bilateral agreements with willing parties.

Until the US entered into negotiations over liberal air transport bilaterals, the negotiating process for bilateral agreements was generally viewed as a means for balancing benefits between the airlines of the two negotiating parties. As the most important air market in the world, the United States restricted access to US cities by foreign carriers, since other countries could not provide equal benefits to US carriers. Airlines of small countries often faced the most severe restrictions, since it was impossible for their governments to offer equal benefits to US carriers.[4]

The US negotiating philosophy was completely transformed in the liberal bilateral era. Instead of seeking to balance benefits among airlines, the US aim changed to producing a pro-competitive market-based outcome, regardless of the size or significance of the negotiating party. The first liberal agreement was reached with The Netherlands in 1978, a country that could in no way balance route rights with the US. However, The Netherlands did have an active flag carrier (i.e., KLM) that could use its Amsterdam hub to provide services throughout Europe. Thus the US sought to promote competition throughout Europe with its liberal agreement with The Netherlands.

Liberal agreements differed from Bermuda I and Bermuda II agreements in a number of important ways. In particular, they included the following features (Haanappel, 1984; Dresner, 1989):

- Country-of-origin or double disapproval price-setting clauses. Whereas Bermuda I and II agreements allowed either government to disapprove an airline's fare offering, liberal agreements allowed only the government where the airline was located to reject a fare offering (country-of-origin), or required both governments to jointly agree that a fare offering should be rejected (double disapproval).
- Multiple designation of air carriers. A government could designate any number of air carriers to operate on an approved route.
- Increased number of allowable routes. More routes between more cities were allowed, including fifth freedom routes.
- Inclusion of charter flights. Charter flights were allowed as long as they met the regulations of the country where the flights originated.
- A fair and competitive practices clause. Each carrier was allowed a 'fair and equal opportunity' to compete on a route.

---

4 For example the Dutch carrier, KLM, may wish access to several US cities, but it is doubtful that US carriers would wish access to The Netherlands, beyond Amsterdam.

Empirical studies of the liberal bilateral agreements indicate that they had the desired effect of producing more competitive outcomes. Dresner and Tretheway (1992) found that discount prices on long-distance (over 4,000 kilometres) international routes covered by liberal agreements were about 35 per cent lower than discount prices on long-distance international routes covered by Bermuda I and II-type agreements. They estimated that the liberal agreements contributed to welfare gains for North Atlantic passengers of $325 million in 1981 alone. Dresner and Windle (1992) estimated the impact of liberal agreements on passenger traffic on US international air routes. They found that over their period of estimation (1975–1989) that the presence of a liberal agreement resulted in a passenger growth rate 11 per cent higher than would otherwise be expected. In addition, the level of passenger traffic on a route covered by a liberal agreement was 46 per cent higher than would be expected on a route covered by a Bermuda I or II agreement. Although the propensity to sign liberal bilateral agreements waned during the Reagan years of the 1980s, the agreements already signed remained in place, thus contributing to better market outcomes for travellers on US international air routes.

Open Skies Agreements

In the 1990s, the US resumed its liberal international air transport initiative. Most importantly, it signed a series of open skies agreements, with 94 such agreements listed by February, 2010 (U.S. State Department, 2010).[5] Button (2009) provides a comparison of the US liberal agreements of the 1970s and 1980s to the open skies agreements of the 1990s and 2000s.[6] Most importantly, the open skies agreements expanded market access, allowing foreign carriers access to any US city, and US carriers access to any city in the foreign partner's country. Under these agreements, airlines of both countries are also allowed unlimited fifth freedom rights. These expanded route rights (third, fourth and fifth freedom) are especially valuable, because under open skies they can be operated on a code-share basis.

Two in-depth studies of the impact of open skies agreements have been conducted by the US Government Accountability Office (GAO) (U.S. Government Accountability Office, 2004) and the consulting firm, InterVISTAS-ga[2] (2006). The GAO (2004) looked specifically at the impact of open skies agreements on US–European markets. The conclusion was that these agreements benefited both consumers and airlines; airlines benefited from being able to integrate their route networks with allied partners, while consumers benefited through access to a greater number of 'online' code-share flights.[7] The InterVISTAS-ga[2] (2006) report quantified the impact of open skies agreements (and liberalization of air transport markets in general), finding positive and significant benefits in terms of passenger traffic and economic development. Both studies make a strong case for further liberalization of air transport markets. Finally, Micco and Serebrisky (2006) looked specifically at the impact of open skies agreements on air cargo markets. They found that these agreements contributed to a 9 per cent reduction in cargo air transport costs, and to an increase in

---

5   Includes all of the European countries that were party to the US–EU multilateral agreement that entered into force in 2008.

6   A pro-forma model agreement is maintained by the US State Department (2008).

7   Online services are associated with shorter connecting times and easier (same terminal) connections, compared to interline services.

the share of imports arriving into the US by air.[8] Overall, the authors calculated that open skies agreements increased trade by about 12 per cent between the US and partner countries.[9]

The US–EU Multilateral Open Skies Agreement

On 30 March 2008, Stage 1 of a multilateral US–EU open skies agreement came into effect, superseding the existing bilateral agreements between the US and EU countries. Although this was not the first multilateral air transport agreement signed by the US,[10] it was by far the most significant, given the size of the US–EU air transportation market. The initiative for this agreement came not from the US but from the Europeans. As Abeyratne (2003) describes, the basis for the agreement dates to the formation of the single European air transport market in the 1990s. The single market created a 'level playing field' for all EU carriers. In practice, this meant that carriers of all EU countries have the right (known as the 'right of establishment') to operate in any market within the community, including cabotage and seventh freedom markets.[11] The EU Commission took the view that open skies bilateral agreements disadvantage carriers from countries not party to these accords; thus a level playing field was not being achieved.[12] A series of rulings by the EU Court of Justice in 2002 confirmed the view of the EU Commission.

As a result of these rulings, the European Union requested discussions with the United States on a new US–EU multilateral air transportation agreement. As Bryerly (2004) writes, the major negotiating objectives of the United States included the following:

- The extension of open skies provisions to all EU countries.
- Improved US airline access to European airports, most notably London Heathrow.
- A reduction in night-time curfews at EU airports to facilitate air cargo operations.
- An assurance that airlines from EU countries with low labour costs would not be used as 'flags of convenience' to disadvantage US carriers.

The Europeans took a more radical position, envisioning a North Atlantic Open Aviation Area that would encompass both the EU and the United States (Calleja, 2004). Within this area, all carriers would be treated equally, regardless of where they were headquartered. In essence, under this proposal, the EU right of establishment for air carriers would be extended to US carriers, allowing them to operate on par with EU carriers. Reciprocal privileges would be afforded to EU carriers,

---

8   The size of the increase varied by country.

9   Yamaguchi (2008) drew similar conclusions, finding that open skies agreements are associated with lower air cargo costs. However, Yamaguchi (2008) also found that cargo air routes covered by open skies agreements have higher levels of market concentration. Since higher concentration levels are associated with higher transportation costs, the direct cost reductions from open skies agreements may be offset due to cost increases from the higher concentration levels.

10   The US entered into a multilateral air transport agreement with Brunei, Chile, New Zealand and Singapore in 2001. The agreement and a related protocol allow (among other provisions) for seventh freedom cargo operations between the signatories. For a summary of the provisions, see New Zealand (2001).

11   A seventh freedom route for an airline established in Country A would be between cities in two other countries, say B and C. Unlike fifth freedom routes, seventh freedom routes do not originate or terminate in the country where an airline is established.

12   In particular, only carriers established (i.e., owned and headquartered) in the EU country that signed an open skies agreement with the US had operating rights under that agreement.

allowing them to operate US cabotage routes. Finally, ownership rules would be liberalized, permitting US majority control of EU carriers and vice versa.

The initial outcome of the negotiations, known as Stage 1, was much closer to the US view. Devall (2008) summarizes key Stage 1 provisions:

- All US and EU airlines have the right to compete on all routes between the US and the EU, as well as on all fifth freedom routes. EU carriers no longer are restricted to routes originating or terminating in the particular country in which they are based, but may operate to the US from any EU country.
- The right for cargo airlines to operate seventh freedom routes, including intra-European routes (between EU countries) for US cargo carriers.
- No frequency or capacity restrictions for airlines on approved routes.
- Fares set by the airlines with no governmental approval required.
- Code-sharing and other commercial agreements are permitted.
- The right for EU carriers to compete for certain US governmental traffic previously restricted to US airlines (US Department of Defense traffic excluded).

A major gain for the US was the superseding of the Bermuda II agreement by the multilateral accord, thus effectively removing restrictions on the number of US carriers allowed to serve London Heathrow. Shortly after the implementation of the agreement, additional US carriers did start serving Heathrow with newly purchased slots (Devall, 2008). There were no comparable gains for EU carriers. In particular, they remain barred from US cabotage routes, and continue to be precluded from assuming control over US carriers. The agreement does require additional negotiations to take place, leaving open the possibility that the EU could achieve some wins in a Stage 2 agreement. Finally, either side may give notice for the termination of the agreement if they deem satisfactory progress is not being made in the Stage 2 negotiations. If the agreement is terminated, the regulatory structure would revert back to the bilaterals in place prior to March, 2008.

Impediments to Further Liberalization

Since the Chicago Conference, the US has generally held itself out as the leader in promoting a competitive environment for international aviation. With few exceptions (Bermuda II being the most notable), the US has led the movement towards a more liberalized international air transportation system. At the Chicago Conference, the US fought the formation of an international regulatory agency to determine capacities, frequencies and airfares on international routes. The US insisted, with Bermuda I, that airlines have the right to freely determine capacities and frequencies on approved routes, and only reluctantly agreed to allow the airlines to collectively set prices through IATA. In the 1960s and 1970s, the US promoted competition by relaxing air charter rules. In the 1970s and 1980s, the US abandoned the concept of strictly trading benefits for airlines in bilateral negotiations, and concluded liberal agreements designed to increase competition. In the 1990s and 2000s, the US continued these efforts with open skies agreements. Yet recently, with the EU negotiations, the US finds itself opposing major liberal reforms. In addition, the US policy towards airline alliances may be viewed as anti-competitive. In this section, we examine the US rationales behind these positions and the prospects change.

The US restricts foreign control to no more than 25 per cent of US carriers, and prohibits foreign-based carriers from operating US cabotage routes.[13] As noted above, the EU has been unable to convince the US to remove these restrictions.[14] Dresner (2008) discusses the reasons behind these US policies. First, there are defence considerations. US carriers participate in the Civil Reserve Air Fleet (CRAF) programme. In exchange for governmental incentives, participating airlines agree to make a certain percentage of their fleets available for defence purposes at the request of the US Government. Proponents of maintaining restrictions on US airline ownership are concerned that if US-based carriers were foreign controlled, they may be reluctant to participate in CRAF, thus reducing US defence capabilities. Second, US labour groups oppose ownership and cabotage changes. The fear is that US labour could be displaced by foreign workers if foreign carriers were allowed to operate US domestic routes, or US carriers were controlled by foreign interests. Finally, US carriers have historically been split over the removal of foreign ownership restrictions.[15]

It is not clear whether progress can be made on removing cabotage and ownership restrictions. Certainly, both defence and labour interests enjoy strong support among members of Congress. Removing either of these restrictions would require considerable will on the part of Congress, and this may be difficult to achieve.

A second US Governmental policy that may be viewed as anticompetitive is the granting of antitrust immunity to allied carriers for the purposes of coordinating fares and capacity, and the pooling of revenue.[16] Although the US only immunizes carriers operating under open skies agreements, and does place limitations on coordination efforts,[17] it is clear that allowing airlines to cooperate in fare and capacity-setting is anti-competitive. Restraint on competition is most probable with 'parallel alliances', where (potentially) competing carriers are permitted to coordinate fares.[18] In effect, the alliances have replaced IATA as joint fare-setting forums, and have the additional authority to cooperatively determine capacities and pool revenues.

The US Department of Transportation (DOT) justifies antitrust immunity for airline alliances by claiming that coordination benefits outweigh anti-competitive costs. For example, in granting American Airlines, British Airways, and their oneworld alliance partners antitrust immunity, the US DOT (2010) stated that the immunized alliance would provide 'lower fares on more routes, increased services, better schedules and reduced travel and connection times'. In addition, oneworld carriers would be better able to compete against carriers in the other two main alliances.[19]

---

13 Cabotage rights are specifically prohibited in the US model open skies agreement (U.S. State Department, 2008, Article 2.4).

14 Canada attempted to get the United States to yield on cabotage as well. See Dresner (1992).

15 Among US carriers most favourably inclined to removing foreign ownership restrictions are United Airlines, which conceivably would like access to foreign capital, and FedEx, which may want to operate a European cargo subsidiary (Hofer and Dresner, 2007).

16 See, U.S. Department of Transportation (2009) for a list of immunized airline agreements.

17 See Brueckner and Proost (2009).

18 Parallel alliances are commonly found on operations between international gateway cities (e.g., Frankfurt–Washington, DC) where allied carriers (in this case, Star Alliance carriers, Lufthansa and United) have hubs at both end points.

19 Richard Branson, head of Virgin Atlantic Airways, was less positive about the antitrust exemption, claiming that the immunized oneworld alliance would provide a 'kick in the teeth' for consumers. See Dobson (2010).

A number of researchers have examined the welfare implications from alliances.[20] Studies have generally found positive benefits, in terms of fare reductions, for complementary alliance routes.[21] The evidence for parallel alliances is mixed, with findings of price increases, price decreases, and little or no price effects (Brueckner and Whalen, 2000; Bilotkach, 2007; Wan et al., 2009). Since most alliances contain both complementary and parallel aspects, on net, the alliances may, in fact, provide positive net benefits to consumers, and the DOT may be justified in providing these alliances antitrust immunity.

Conclusions

The United States has taken a reasonably consistent open-market approach to its air transport bilateral policies since the 1940s. Although there have been illiberal lapses, most notably Bermuda II, the US has been the leader in support of market-based bilateral agreements ever since Chicago and Bermuda I. In particular, no other country with a major origin/destination market has consistently supported an open-market approach to bilateral negotiations over a balance of benefits approach. However, the US policy has also been pragmatic, favouring competitive outcomes that support its interests (e.g., opening access to Heathrow; multiple designation of carriers), and opposing those that face domestic opposition (e.g., the removal of cabotage and ownership restrictions). Given the political reality of the US system, this open-market, but pragmatic approach, is likely to continue into the future.

References

Abeyratne, R. (2003) The decision of the European Court of Justices on open skies: how we can take liberalization to the next level. *Journal of Air Law and Commerce*, 68, summer, 485–518.
Bilotkach, V. (2007) Price effects of airline consolidation: evidence from a sample of transatlantic markets. *Empirical Economics*, 33, 427–448.
Bridges, Lord T.E. (1977) Bermuda II and after. *Air Law*, 3, 11–17.
Brueckner, J.K. (2003a) International airfares in the age of alliances: the effects of codesharing and antitrust immunity. *The Review of Economics and Statistics*, 85, 1, 105–118.
Brueckner, J.K. (2003b) The benefits of codesharing and antitrust immunity for international passengers, with an application to the Star Alliance. *Journal of Air Transport Management*, 9, 83–89.
Brueckner, J.K. and Proost, S. (2009) Carve-outs under airline antitrust immunity. Unpublished working paper.
Brueckner, J.K. and Whalen, W.T. (2000) The price effects of international airline alliances. *Journal of Law and Economics*, 43, 2, 503–545.

---

20 See Dresner (2010) for a summary of these studies.
21 See for example, Brueckner and Whalen (2000); Brueckner (2003a, 2003b); Bilotkach (2007); Whalen (2007). A complementary alliance is when two or more carriers operate complementary services. For example, a passenger wishing to fly from Duluth, Minnesota to Warsaw, Poland, can fly on United Airlines from Duluth to Chicago and Chicago to Frankfurt, and then on a United code-share flight with Lufthansa to Warsaw. Since neither United nor Lufthansa offer complete service from Duluth to Warsaw, their allied services are deemed complementary. In general, 'behind gateway' services offered by alliances are complementary.

Bryerly, J.R. (2004) U.S.–EU aviation relations – charting the course for success. Speech to the International Aviation Club of Washington, DC, http://www.iacwashington.org/speeches/Byerly071304.pdf, accessed 19 March 2010.

Button, K. (2009) The impact of US–EU 'open skies' agreement on airline market structures and airline networks. *Journal of Air Transport Management*, 15, 2, 59–71.

Calleja, D. (2004) Speech by Daniel Calleja to the International Aviation Club, Washington DC, 16 November 2004, http://www.iacwashington.org/speeches/Nov16_04_Callegja_IAC_Speech.pdf, accessed 19 March 2010.

Chuang, R.Y. (1972) *The International Air Transport Association*. Leiden: A.W. Sijthoff.

Dempsey, P.S. (1978) The international rate and route revolution in north Atlantic passenger transportation. *Columbia Journal of Transnational Law*, 17, 393–449.

Devall, J.L. (2008) The U.S.–EU agreement – a path to a global aviation agreement. In B.F. Havel (ed.), *CCH Issues in Aviation Law and Policy*. Chicago, IL: CCH Incorporated, 13,295–13,316.

Dobson, C. (2010) British Airways and American Airlines get antitrust immunity. *Epoch Times*, http://www.theepochtimes.com/n2/content/view/29833/, accessed 19 March 2010.

Douglas, G.W. and Miller, J.C. (1974). *Economic Deregulation of Domestic Air Transport: Theory and Policy*. Washington, DC: The Brookings Institution.

Dresner, M.E. (1989). *The International Regulation of Air Transport: Changing Regimes and Price Effects*. Unpublished Ph.D. dissertation, University of British Columbia.

Dresner, M.E. (1992) The regulation of U.S.–Canada air transportation: past, present and future. *Canadian–American Public Policy*, 9, 1–35.

Dresner, M.E. (2008) An analysis of U.S. international air transport agreements: from liberal bilaterals to the U.S.–EU multilateral accord. *Journal of Transport Research*, 15, 115–127.

Dresner, M.E. (2010) The Economics of Airline Alliances. Unpublished working paper, University of Maryland.

Dresner, M.E. and Tretheway, M.W. (1992) Modeling and testing the effect of market structure on price: the case of international air transport. *Journal of Transport Economics and Policy*, 26, 2, 171–184.

Dresner, M.E. and Windle, R.J. (1992) The liberalization of U.S. international air policy: impact on U.S. markets and carriers. *Journal of the Transportation Research Forum*, 32, 2, 273–285.

Haanappel, P.P.C. (1976) Background of the Dutch–American aviation conflict. *Annals of Air and Space Law*, 1, 63–81.

Haanappel, P.P.C. (1978) The International Air Transport Association (IATA) and the international charter airlines. *Annals of Air and Space Law*, 3, 143–153.

Haanappel, P.P.C. (1984) *Pricing and Capacity Determination in International Air Transport: A Legal Analysis*. Deventer: Kluwer Law and Taxation Publishers.

Hofer, C. and Dresner, M.E. (2007) United States–European Union open aviation area: the American perspective. *Journal of the Transportation Research Forum*, 46, 1, 129–143.

InterVistas-ga² (2006) *The Economic Impact of Air Service Liberalization*. http://www.intervistas.com/4/reports/2006-06-07_EconomicImpactOfAirServiceLiberalization_FinalReport.pdf, accessed 19 March 2010.

Jordan, W.A. (1972) Producer protection, prior market structure and the effects of government regulation. *Journal of Law and Economics*, 15, 151–176.

Larsen, P.B. (1977) Status report on the renegotiation of the U.S.–U.K. Bilateral Air Transport Agreement (Bermuda Agreement). *Air Law*, 3, 82–89.

Lowenfeld, A.F. (1975) CAB vs. KLM: Bermuda at bay. *Air Law*, 1, 2–19.

Micco, A. and Serebrisky, T. (2006) Competition regimes and air transport costs: the effects of open skies agreements. *Journal of International Economics*, 70, 1, 25–51.

New Zealand (2001) *Multilateral Agreement on the Liberalization of Air Transportation*. Summary at http://www.maliat.govt.nz/, accessed 19 March 2010.

O'Connor, W.E. (1971) *Economic Regulation of the World's Airlines*. New York: Praeger Publishers.

Richards, J.E. (2001) Institutions for flying: how states built a market in international aviation services. *Industrial Organization*, 55, 4, 993–1017.

Straszheim, M.R. (1969) *The International Airline Industry*. Washington, DC: The Brookings Institution.

U.S. Department of Transportation (2009) *Airline Alliances Operating with Antitrust Immunity*, http://ostpxweb.dot.gov/aviation/X-50%20Role_files/All%20Immunized%20Alliances.pdf, accessed 19 March 2010.

U.S. Department of Transportation (2010) Cited in Dobson, C., British Airways and American Airlines Get Antitrust Immunity. *Epoch Times*, http://www.theepochtimes.com/n2/content/view/29833/, accessed 19 March 2010.

U.S. Government Accountability Office (2004) *Transatlantic Aviation: Effects of Easing Restrictions on U.S.–European Markets*. Report No. GAO-04-835, http://www.gao.gov/new.items/d04835.pdf, accessed 19 March 2010.

U.S. State Department (2008) *Air Transport Agreement Between The Government of The United States of America and The Government of [country]*. http://www.state.gov/documents/organization/114970.pdf, accessed 18 March 2010.

U.S. State Department (2010) *Countries With Bilateral Open Skies Agreements*, http://ostpxweb.dot.gov/aviation/X-40%20Role_Files/bilatosagreement.htm, accessed 1 February 2010.

Wan, X., Zou, L., and Dresner, M. (2009) Assessing the Price Effects of Airline Alliances on Parallel Routes. *Transportation Research E*, 45, 4, 627–641.

Whalen, W.T. (2007) A panel data analysis of code-sharing, antitrust immunity, and open skies treaties in international aviation markets. *Review of Industrial Organization*, 30, 39–61.

Yamaguchi, K. (2008) International trade and air cargo: an analysis of US export and air transport policy. *Transportation Research Part E*, 44, 4, 653–666.

Chapter 24

Canadian International Aviation: Policy and Challenges

David Gillen[1]

1. Introduction

In 2008 world air traffic grew by 1.6 per cent, air cargo fell by near 4.7 per cent year over year, but December figures give pause; passenger traffic down 4.6 per cent and air cargo a stunning 22.6 per cent. In 2009 both passenger and cargo traffic were down considerably as, in both cases, yields were down 14 per cent. However, 2010 has exhibited a dramatic about face as passengers, passenger kilometres and freight have all grown significantly; total freight was up 9 per cent and passenger growth up 3 per cent. This resulted in strong financial performance across most all carriers. Yet the underlying consequences of both the financial crises and bailouts are having a lingering effect. The US economy is slow to recover and is carrying an enormous amount of debt; debt held in 2011 is approximately 70 per cent of GDP. Monetary authorities are still engaged in quantitative easing. Europe is facing sovereign debt issues with Greece and Ireland already bailed out and Spain, Portugal and possibly the UK on the brink of needed assistance to deal with their high debt loads. Germany on the other hand is carrying the EU in terms of economic performance. South East Asia, South America, Africa and the Middle East are all showing positive signs of both economic and aviation market growth.

There is an interesting juxtaposition within the US and between the US and Canada in terms of general protectionism and international aviation policy/strategy. In the US in 2008 the economy shed jobs in numbers in the thousands and this across the entire economic spectrum from Caterpillar to Macys. Time to circle the wagons as the US builds the protectionist walls? Such moves have been quickly damned by the business elite in Davos and in the halls of parliament in Ottawa that such an outcome will result in the US losing its 'moral authority' to stem global protectionism, it will undo years of negotiations under the World Trade Organization (WTO) that has led to such gains in overall economic welfare. So the picture as we see it is the US leaning toward protectionism and Canada, as well as others, arguing such a move would lead to long-term economic recession and undo years of welfare-improving negotiations. However, when we examine international aviation policy, Canada and the US are in exactly opposite camps.

As of 2011 the US had signed over 101 open skies agreements touching and including every continent, except Antarctica.[2] The US pursues a 'single' open skies policy with every country with the 'open skies' being as liberal as possible; unrestricted first through sixth freedoms with optional cargo sevenths, market-based pricing freedoms, extensive doing business protections and strong safety and security articles contained in the agreements. In effect the US seems to have a one size fits all approach. As John Byerly, the Chief US Air Negotiator recently stated:

---

1 I am indebted to Adam Robertson and Kevin Huang for excellent research assistance.

2 The US has been pursuing open skies agreements since the mid-1990s. Some key markets, however, still do not have open skies agreements with the US including China, Hong Kong, Russia, Mexico and South Africa

the alternatives to a consistent Open Skies policy – whether labeled a case-by-case approach, a holistic view, or a philosophy of progressive liberalization – are often too focused on the bottom line of the national flag carrier and frequently represent a smokescreen for unjustified protectionism.[3]

Like the US, Australia, New Zealand and the EU have been aggressive in pursuing liberal air agreements; albeit Australia has been protective of its former national carrier in some instances. Canada claims to have signed 11 open skies agreements (Ireland, Iceland, New Zealand, Barbados, the Dominican Republic, Costa Rica, South Korea, El Salvador, Switzerland, Trinidad and Tobago and Jamaica) including the recent agreement with the EU.[4] Canada also claims to have signed agreements with 50 countries since the 'Blue Sky' policy was introduced in 2006, included in this are the 27 member states in the EU. Canada has signed many bilateral agreements with numerous provisions for restrictions, so secret the public is not privy to them; all the restrictive provisions are contained in the annexes, which are considered confidential. Interestingly, Canada's recently signed agreement with the EU, which was in negotiation for a year before the US had finally signed an agreement with the EU, and was finalized a year after the EU–US agreement was signed, is more restrictive than the EU–US agreement. Table 24.2 is a list of agreements that Canada has signed (InterVISTAS, 2008). Also noted in this table is the size of the market measured in international passengers and the total value of trade Canada does with the 'other' country in the bilateral. In most cases these are small markets by both measures. Note the open skies agreements are with small to very small markets. An agreement with a country that is dominated by a Star Alliance member is a hollow agreement because Star Alliance controls the market before and after the agreement, nothing really happens as a consequence of the negotiated bilateral.

This chapter is organized in the following way. The next section looks at the history of the nature and process of air service agreements. Many of the institutional features as well as roadblocks are a result of history. Section three examines Canada's recent 'open skies' agreement with the EU and details as much as we can know. Section 4 looks at Canada's record with open skies agreements and Air Service Agreements (ASAs) in general. Following this is a discussion of whether air liberalization is better for economic welfare. This section contains the results of some statistical modelling to assess Canada's record. Section 6 contains a summary and a listing of next steps.

2. History of Bilateral Agreements

The international air transport sector has grown under a complex regime of regulations since the conclusion of the Chicago Conference of 1944. Lack of agreement at that time on how the market for air services should be regulated led to the growth of bilateral agreements between countries. The US wanted open skies with no control on tariffs or capacity and a maximum exchange of rights, including fifth freedoms. The UK and other European countries were more protectionist.[5] The two divergent views could not be reconciled and no multilateral agreement on traffic rights, tariff control and capacity was reached. The most important outcome of the Chicago Convention

---

3   See Byerly (2008) 2008 ACI-NA International Aviation Issues Seminar, December 4, 2008.

4   These numbers are taken from the Department of International Affairs website. See http://www. international.gc.ca/trade-agreements-accords-commerciaux/agr-acc/facts-air-eclair.aspx. It is not clear they would all fit under the true définition of open skies.

5   The US wanted a free and open market while the UK wanted more restrictions; the fact that the US aviation sector was in excellent shape after the Second World War and the UK was in a shambles had a good deal to do with each country's perspective and position.

was the agreement and signing of the Convention on International Aviation, known as the Chicago Convention. This provided a framework for the orderly development of international air transport. The Chicago Convention also agreed on the first and second freedoms. The key institutions that emerged from Chicago Convention were ASAs for the exchange of traffic rights, the ASAs were matters for negotiation between states not carriers, second, the tariff-fixing machinery of IATA and third, the control of capacity and frequencies by inter-airline agreement.[6] All agreements that emerged were highly protectionist or 'predetermined'. The ASAs are trade agreements between governments, not airlines, and contain administrative (soft) and economic (hard) provisions. The 'soft' provisions cover taxation, exemption from duties on imported aircraft parts, airport charges, transfers of funds from ticket sales from abroad and so on. The 'hard' provisions cover pricing and capacity limits. What we see even today in more restrictive regimes such as Canada are a direct outgrowth of Chicago; negotiations by international affairs not operation departments like Transport Canada (thus little concern of or for efficiency), the implied property rights of traffic to airlines, the protection of scheduled carriers (producer protection) and the complexity (and secrecy) of bilateral agreements.[7] It also may explain in part why the international aviation 'policy' is directly at odds with the underlying philosophy of the Canada Transportation Act.

In 1946 the UK and US negotiated an air services agreement for travel between the US and UK. It became known as the Bermuda Agreement and was more liberal that agreements emerging from the Chicago Convention. The two 'liberal' features of these agreements were that fifth freedoms were more widely available and there were no controls on capacities or frequencies on the route.8

The Bermuda II Agreement was signed in 1977, also between the US and UK. This was a renegotiation of the 1946 Bermuda Agreement: it allowed four airlines to operate direct flights from London's Heathrow airport to the United States, and barred any other carriers from operating such flights. The designated airlines were British Airways, Virgin Atlantic (added in 1991), American Airlines (replaced Pan American World Airways in 1991), United Airlines (replaced Trans World Airlines in 1991). Other airports in Britain, including Gatwick, are fair game for other airlines. Understandably, those airlines that were excluded were not happy with this arrangement.

Over time although there were attempts at negotiating Bermuda-type agreements most were generally restrictive and they controlled market entry, fares and service levels. Such a system probably did little to impede the growth of international air transport in the early years, but as technology has evolved and markets have developed, the limitations of such bilateral air service agreements have become apparent.

Cracks in the international air agreements began to emerge in the early 1970s when nearly 30 per cent of transatlantic traffic was flying on charter carriers, a segment that had developed as a result of the high fares and capacity restrictions inherent in the international bilateral agreement arrangements. The rapid deregulation of the US air transport market from 1978 on and the domestic market deregulation in numerous other countries soon after gave an impetus for international reform of both cargo and passenger air services. Considerable progress has been made since that time in liberalizing international air transport. Some of the changes have come through renegotiation of bilateral agreements to remove many barriers to competition. The open skies policy of the US reflected a new approach to international markets. They were successful in their divide and

---

6   A convention in Geneva in 1947 did not lead to any changes despite some attempts.

7   It is perplexing to see that Canada's trade negotiators, who have for many years successfully negotiated multilateral and open trade deals, are now negotiating restrictive bilateral and limited numbers of open skies agreements. One wonders where the protectionist sentiment comes from.

8   Despite their liberal appearance the Bermuda-type agreements had review provisions that allowed airlines to have restrictions imposed if they felt they were being adversely affected.

conquer strategy, particularly in Europe where individual countries still negotiated ASAs. From the early 1990s, it allowed the US and many trading partners to sign a liberal template bilateral accord, which has led to a common framework of agreements. The US open skies policy is a conspicuous example of bilateral liberalization, with 101 agreements having been signed to date.

There have been a number of liberal regional 'air trade agreements' which have open skies features. Canada signed its first open skies agreement with the US in 1995 and this agreement was re-negotiated and broadened, made even more open, in 2005. Australia and New Zealand have also a liberal accord, particularly across the Tasman. The EU has taken additional steps, which focus on liberalization within the European Economic Area, although individual Member States and the EU have also concluded aviation agreements with countries outside the EU. The emergence of an internal European Community air transport market represented a major achievement in creating a liberal regional market for air services. The three packages of reform introduced over a decade from the mid-1980s gradually removed impediments to the free provision of transport services within the EU. An airline substantially owned and effectively controlled by citizens of a country within the European Economic Area (EEA) can now establish itself anywhere within the EEA and can offer services, including cabotage, within the area. There are no tariff controls (except in exceptional circumstances) and there is a gradual movement to liberalize and introduce effective competition in ancillary services. Currently the EU has moved to signing multilateral agreements where the agreement covers all member states. However, Member States may negotiate bilateral agreements with third countries but bilateral air service agreements between an individual Member State and a non-EU country have to include an 'EU designation clause' recognizing that the terms apply equally to all EU airlines, and not just the airlines of that Member State.

In 2008 the EU and US signed an open skies (first stage) agreement which provided significant liberalization for air services and included the entire EEA. In this first stage both the commercial agreement and the legal framework for cooperation had to be negotiated. In their second stage the details become stickier and legal issues thornier; night flight bans in the EU, symmetric traffic rights, foreign ownership and control, US homeland security, EU-style slot coordination and so on. Rising marginal costs and declining incremental benefits are likely going to be the outcome. (Button, 2008)

There are also other more recent harbingers of freer trade areas in air services, such as the MALIAT agreement which was signed in 2001 and includes the US, Chile, Singapore, New Zealand, Brunei, Samoa and Tonga.[9] This development is less extensive than the EU Single Market in air services, but it represents movement forward. The Yamoussoukro Decision reached in July 2000 at the Organization of African Unity meeting in Togo and the 2004 Association of Southeast Asian Nations (ASEAN) roadmap to permit unlimited services between all ten member countries by target dates are also encouraging initial moves towards liberalizing air transport.

---

9   The key features of the Multilateral Agreement are: an open route schedule; open traffic rights including seventh freedom cargo services; open capacity; airline investment provisions which focus on effective control and principal place of business, but protect against flag of convenience carriers; multiple airline designation; third-country code-sharing; and a minimal tariff filing regime.

3. Canada's Open Skies Agreement with the EU

On 9 December 2008 Canada and the European Union successfully concluded negotiations on a Comprehensive Air Transport Agreement. The negotiations had commenced in November 2007 and parts of the Agreement will come into effect in the first half of 2009.

This Agreement is the latest agreement pursued as part of Canada's Blue Sky international air policy. The purpose of the Blue Sky policy, as stated, is to negotiate increasingly liberalized international air transport agreements. Canada currently has bilateral agreements with 19 of the 27 EU Member States. A single regime will now govern Canada's air transport relations with every member of the EU.

The Canada–EU Agreement is more far-reaching and open than any similar pact that the EU or Canada has with other countries. Canada and the EU have agreed to remove restrictions on direct flights between Canada and EU Member States and ultimately to remove restrictions on foreign ownership of airlines. The Agreement will provide for increased traffic rights, allowing for unrestricted direct services (on an airline's own aircraft or that of another carrier) between Canada and the EU, without any limitations on the number of flights operated, the routes, or the fares to be offered. All-cargo airlines will also be permitted to operate to or from third countries on flights involving Canada or the EU.

The Agreement provides for phased market opening linked to the granting of greater investment freedoms by both sides:

- Phase I takes effect when the Agreement is signed, expected to be in the first half of 2009. Airlines will have unlimited freedom to operate direct services between any point in the EU and any point in Canada. There will be no restrictions on the number of airlines flying between the EU and Canada or on the number of services operated by any airline. Cargo airlines will have the right to fly onward to third countries.
- Phase II anticipates that Canada will amend its legislation to enable European investors to own up to 49 per cent of a Canadian carrier's voting equity, an increase from the current 25 per cent. At that time, further traffic rights will be granted, including the right for cargo carriers to operate services to third countries from the other party to third countries without connection to their point of origin.
- In Phase III, both sides will allow investors to establish and control new airlines in each other's markets. At that point, passenger airlines will be able to fly onward to third countries.
- In Phase IV, EU and Canadian carriers will be granted full rights to operate between, within and beyond both markets, including between points in the territory of the other party (known as cabotage). These rights will be granted once both sides complete the necessary steps to allow the full ownership and control of their carriers by the other's nationals.

If Canada and the EU have indeed made binding commitments with respect to Phases two through four, it would represent a fundamental change in Canada's regulatory framework for aviation and would present significant opportunities for carriers in both jurisdictions. If these commitments are realized, the Agreement would likely lead to consolidation and integration between air carriers in the two jurisdictions. Given Canada's record to date this seems highly unlikely unless a real crisis emerged. Given the current financial climate, it just may.

4. Canada's Record with Open Skies Agreements: Evaluating the Blue Sky Policy

Historically, Transport Canada approached the issue of bilateral air service negotiations on an ad hoc basis that featured incremental negotiations. In order to facilitate a proactive approach to liberalizing Canada's bilateral air transportation agreements, Transport Canada announced Blue Sky, Canada's new international air policy, in 2006. Broadly speaking, Blue Sky claims that Canada will seek to 'negotiate "Open-Skies"-type agreements when deemed in the country's overall interest'.

The Blue Sky policy has the following five objectives:[10]

1. Provide a framework that encourages competition and the development of new and expanded international air services to benefit travellers, shippers and the tourism and business sectors.
2. Provide opportunities for Canadian airlines to grow and compete successfully in a more liberalized global environment.
3. Enable airports to market themselves in a manner that is unhindered by bilateral constraints to the greatest extent possible.
4. Support and facilitate Canada's international trade objectives.
5. Support a safe, secure, efficient, economically healthy and viable Canadian air transportation industry.

Objectives 1–3 are the primary objectives of Blue Sky and are the aspects of Canada's air transportation industry that can be most directly influenced by the policy. Objectives 4–5 are secondary, here Blue Sky has a supporting role. These five objectives are the intended consequences of new and/or expanded bilateral agreements. In pursuing these objectives, the negotiating process is guided by the following four principles that guide the approach represented by Blue Sky:

• Recognize that air transportation is a direct contributor to a dynamic economy and is a leading trade and tourism facilitator;
• Market forces should determine the price, quality, frequency and range of air services options;
• Canadian carriers should have the opportunity to compete in international markets on a reasonably level playing field; and
• Air liberalization initiatives will continue to be guided by safety and security considerations.

The primary objective of Canada's international air policy is to seek to negotiate reciprocal Open Skies-type agreements, similar to the one negotiated with the US in November 2005, where it is deemed to be in Canada's overall interest. Open Skies-type agreements cover the following elements for scheduled passenger and all-cargo services:

• Open bilateral markets/access (third and fourth freedom rights);
• No limit on the number of airlines permitted to operate;
• No limits on the permitted frequency of service or aircraft type;
• Market-based tariff/pricing regime for bilateral and third-country services;
• Open and flexible regime for the operation of code-sharing services;

---

10   The discussion in this section is based on the official Blue Sky policy document; see http://www.tc.gc.ca/pol/en/ace/consultations/blueSky.pdf

- Unrestricted services to and from third countries (fifth and sixth freedom rights); and
- Rights for stand-alone all-cargo operations (seventh freedom rights).

The Blue Sky document states that in determining Canada's negotiating priorities, several issues will be taken into consideration in consultation with both airlines and airports:

- Canadian airline and airport priorities and interests;
- Likelihood and extent of new Canadian and foreign carrier services, giving preference where early start-up of air services is planned;
- Size and maturity of the air transportation markets and potential for future growth;
- Foreign government requests;
- Canada's international trade objectives;
- Safety and security issues;
- Foreign relations; and
- Bilateral irritants and disputes.

So how would one judge the Blue Skies policy? There are a number of metrics including the number of treaties, the type of treaties, who the treaties are with, the impact on passengers, cargo and the economy; generally these can be divided into inputs and outputs of the policy implementation process.

If the Blue Skies policy is to enhance the number and liberalization of air agreements the first thing one would expect is an increase in the number of negotiating teams. This has *not* happened; the institutional framework and process (and perhaps even the players) are still the same as before the new policy. One has to wonder how the increase in productivity was going to occur.[11] Another metric is; is the Blue Sky policy resulting in an increase in the number of new bilateral agreements signed?

Other metrics would look at the number of bilaterals signed. Figure 24.1 shows the number of ASAs signed in each year. Prior to Blue Skies, between 1949 and 2004, 50 ASAs were signed (over a period of 56 years). Since 2005, 32 ASAs have been signed, a rate four times that prior to 2005. By this measure Blue Skies has been a huge success. Therefore, one would want to look at who the ASAs have been signed with and perhaps the contents of the agreements. Figure 24.1 provides a list of the countries and their rank in market size (based on 2007 figures). In 2005 three ASAs were signed, including a renewed open skies treaty with the US (signed in 2007). The changes were not minor but were not major either. The open skies treaty existed prior to 2005 so not much of a success. The other two were with Guyana, market rank 105, and Algeria, market rank 102, hardly to be considered great coups. In 2007 there were eight ASAs signed, a record number for Canada. Glancing at who they were signed with, one is struck by the paltry size of the markets. Mexico which ranks sixth in importance for Canada is not an open skies type of agreement. The open skies agreements with New Zealand and Singapore, while appearing as successes, are countries

---

11   The US process and team composition is available for everyone to see. However, International Affairs website states, 'in collaboration with Transport Canada, the Chief Air Negotiator at Foreign Affairs and International Trade Canada leads the negotiation of air transport agreements with foreign countries, enabling and enhancing international air transportation for Canadian passengers and businesses. Transport Canada develops and implements Canada's international air transport policy while the Canadian Transportation Agency is in charge of managing Canada's air agreements. Canada currently has bilateral air agreements with more than 75 countries.' See http://www.international.gc.ca/trade-agreements-accords-commerciaux/agr-acc/facts-air-eclair.aspx?view=d

also dominated by domestic carriers which are members of the Star Alliance as is Air Canada; one suspects alliance agreements will trump ASAs.

In 2008 three ASAs were signed, most significantly the open skies agreement with the EU. The other two again are with quite minor markets. The ASA with the EU has been described in detail earlier. On the face of it, it appears as a giant leap forward, however the 'giant leap' depends on phasing in and the trigger values or even variables are not known, nor will they be. If they were designed to promote the objectives of the Blue Sky policy one would have thought they would be made public: after all, the title is 'open skies'. The secrecy of the annexes that contain the detail means in fact there is little change with the ASA between Canada and the EU. The agreement with China in 2009 is not an open skies agreement.

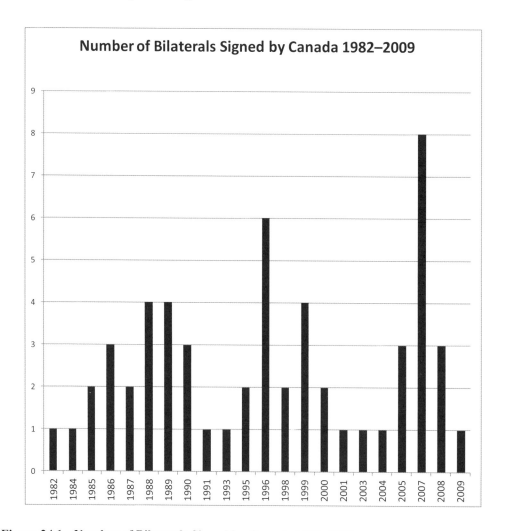

Figure 24.1   Number of Bilaterals Signed by Canada 1982–2009

	Country	Rank in Market Size*	Rank by Int'l Pax	Star Alliance	Open Sky
2005	USA	1	1	yes	yes
	Guyana	79	>50		no
2006	Algeria	12	>50		no
	Croatia	109	>50		no
2007	Ireland	21	24		yes
	New Zealand	47	32	yes	yes
	Jordan	103	>50		no
	Iceland	89	>50		yes
	Kuwait	93	>50		no
	Mexico	5	6		no
	Serbia	128	>50		no
	Singapore	28	29	yes	no
2008	EU	3	2	yes	eventually
	Phillipines	41	21		no
	Barbados	106	39		yes
	Panama	94	>50		no
	Dominican Republic	65	10		yes
	China	2	5		no
2009	South Africa	32	36	yes	no
	Republic of Korea	8	>50	yes	yes
	Japan	4	7		no
	Turkey	40	>50	yes	no
	Costa Rica	59	28		yes
2010	Egypt	55	40	yes	no
	Jamaica	51	20		yes
	Trindad & Tobago	50	35		yes
	Switzerland	17	17	yes	yes
	El Salvador	96	>50		yes
	Tunisia	83	>50		no
	Ethiopia	130	>50		no
	Morocco	58	44		no
	Cuba	36	9		no
2011	Qatar	97	>50		no

* rank by total Imports & Exports with Canada

Figure 24.2   List of bilateral agreements signed from 2005 through 2011 between Canada and other countries

Figure 24.3 provides a list of passenger flows between Canada and its top 30 markets. It is telling that prior to the signing of the Canada–EU open skies, Canada had open skies agreements with only two (indicated in bold) of its top 30 markets (based on 2007 data); the first and twenty-fourth largest markets.[12]

_____

12   This is the most recent data available. Canada refuses to release even aggregate data on air passenger flows between Canada and foreign countries.

Country	Pax (000)	Rank by Int'l Pax
US	31150	1
UK	1820	2
France	1413	3
Italy	725	4
China	678	5
Mexico	600	6
Japan	574	7
Germany	564	8
Cuba	533	9
Dom. Republic	521	10
Hong Kong	412	11
Australia	343	12
S. Korea	310	13
India	257	14
Netherlands	249	15
Spain	235	16
Switzerland	185	17
Thailand	158	18
Brazil	154	19
Jamaica	143	20
Philippines	143	21
Taiwan	139	22
Israel	130	23
Ireland	128	24
Port	127	25
Austria	116	26
Greece	113	27
Costa Rica	104	28
Sing	104	29
Belgium	95	30

Figure 24.3   Air passengers to and from Canada (2007)

What about some other metrics such as (a) How successful is the Blue Sky policy in leading to the initiation of the negotiating process? (b) How successful is the Blue Sky policy in facilitating the negotiation process? That is, of planned negotiations, how many are successful? (c) How has the Blue Sky policy affected the negotiation process in terms of process timelines? Of course the answers to these questions are 'protected', we do not know and if history is any indicator, I doubt we ever will.

In judging the success of the Blue Sky policy one can also look at outcomes. These metrics would include:

- To what extent is the new policy leading to new international air services?
- How is the new policy affecting the level of service provision of international air services?
- To what extent has the new policy liberalized air travel between Canada and other countries?
- How has the new policy affected the price of international air travel, the degree of

competition on Canadian routes, the level of service provided by Canadian airlines, the operating efficiency of Canadian airlines, the volume of traffic at Canadian airports, the route network of Canadian airports, the number of airlines serving Canadian airports, the connectivity of Canadian airports, the financial performance of Canadian airports and the total value of international air freight in Canada?

How successful is the Blue Sky policy in achieving open skies-type agreements? Based on the number of open skies policies signed to 2011, it would appear to be a success. But this view should be tempered by two factors; Canada still continues to negotiate ASAs that are not in keeping with the Blue Sky policy. There is a lack of consistency in ASA content and focus. Where open sky agreements have been signed they have been incremental to previous agreements or held so secret one could hardly judge.

4.1 Is Liberalization Better for Economic Welfare?

In a number of papers there has been an attempt to assess the extent to which air travel is to be affected by current economic conditions. Oum et al. (2008) for example estimate a model in which they include GDP growth, fuel prices and some dummy variables to reflect events such as SARS, 9/11 and Asian financial crises. They use aggregate data from 1980 to 2008 to examine how these factors listed affected total air travel – domestic plus international. They find the elasticity of air travel with respect to GDP is 1.58 but argue this value is inflated because it captures influences which were not included in the model such as increased services and new routes, and the changes in air fares which would have been very important for domestic air traffic.

The model estimated below uses a data panel from 1996–2008 to look at international traffic between eight regions; Africa, Asia, Europe, Middle East, Latin America, North America, South America and the south-west Pacific region. The dependent variable is revenue passenger kilometres. The explanatory variables include GDP growth, foreign direct investment into the region, total trade in merchandise and services, price of jet fuel, dummy variables to capture the influences of events such as SARS and 9/11 and a connectivity variable. The connectivity information was contributed by IATA who construct the index using information on flight frequency, seat per flight, number of destinations and a weighting factor which is designed to measure the importance of the airport. The 'connectivity index' is designed to measure how well a country, or region, is connected to the international air network. It is a measure of the number and economic importance of destinations served, the frequency of service to each destination and the number of onward connections available from each destination. Connectivity increases as the range of destinations and/or frequency of service increases. The index also reveals how connectivity changes over time. This index provides a measure of service improvements, route extensions and increased frequency. Most importantly the index is highly correlated with liberalized ASAs. The results are reported in Table 24.1.

The results differ considerably from the model of Oum et al. (2008), but this model was estimated on only international air passengers whereas their model was estimated on total world air traffic. The model was composed of a panel data set with 8 cross sections (regions) and 12 years for each region. The variables are in logs so the coefficients can be interpreted as elasticities. Note the GDP elasticity is quite low, a mere 0.06, which is sensible in that the amount of international travel will be influenced by domestic growth but only in a small way. Also having trade, foreign investment and connectivity in the equation takes a good deal away from the magnitude of the coefficient. If one estimates essentially the same model as Oum et al. (2008) the estimated elasticity is only 0.31,

Table 24.1   **Factors influencing the amount of interregional international air travel 1998–2008**

Panel Fixed Effects Model		
8 cross section		
12 years; 1996–2007		
Variable (in logs)	Coefficient	T-Statistic
Constant	-0.2849	-1.34
GDP	0.0652	2.10
Trade	0.8382	3.34
Connectivity	0.2201	2.37
Fuel Price	-0.2785	-3.34
Foreign Direct Investment	0.1306	2.28
Time	0.0884	1.80
9/11 Dummy	-0.1144	1.26
Adjust R-sq	0.96	
Log Likelihood	168.96	

considerably less than the 1.58 of their model. What really matters for international travel is the amount of trade in merchandise and services; the elasticity is 0.83. Thus a drop in trade of 10 per cent leads to a drop in international air travel of 8.3 per cent. The next most important variable is connectivity, in which an increase in connectivity of 1 per cent leads to a 0.2 per cent increase in international air traffic.

Over the most recent three years in the data the connectivity index has risen on average by 8 per cent across the world. This has been due to both growth in existing markets and increased liberalization in a number of international markets, particularly with the US signing increasing numbers of open skies agreements, thus boosting traffic growth by 1.6 per cent on average. As connectivity declines through route abandonment, industry consolidation and capacity reduction one can expect traffic to shrink accordingly.

The increase in jet fuel prices has a sizeable impact on international air traffic; the elasticity is –0.3, so a 10 per cent increase in fuel prices leads to a 3 per cent decrease in traffic. Estimates show the elasticity of fuel prices with respect to increase in world oil prices is about 0.26 for auto fuel; because of differences in taxes this elasticity in aviation would be higher at 0.4 (see Gillen et al., 2006)

Another important factor not previously considered is the magnitude of foreign direct investment (FDI) inbound; that is, foreign investment from outside the region. This is a rough measure of the degree of globalization and as more investment takes place air traffic increases. The elasticity of international air traffic with respect to FDI is 0.13. A time trend variable was inserted to pick up temporal trend effects and it shows a positive gradual increase in international air traffic

What do these estimates indicate regarding future international air traffic growth? This model indicates it is not GDP growth we should be looking at but rather trade in goods and services, changes in connectivity and changes in FDI. Fuel price increases and the application of fuel surcharges can also have an impact. It is unlikely that fuel prices will reach the levels they did in summer 2008, but oil is trending upward over the longer term. The Energy Research Institute forecasts fairly steady prices for jet fuel in the next few years following 2008. The IMF however forecasts a decline in GDP growth by 1.4 per cent and an increase in 2010–11 of 2.5 per cent. The IMF also forecasts FDI will fall by near 30 per cent to 2010 and trade in goods and services will decline by 11 per cent in 2009 and increase in 2010 by only 0.6 per cent. These numbers suggest that international air traffic will fall in the near term and be weak in the foreseeable future.

While useful in identifying the importance of the supply side in facilitating international air traffic movements, connectivity is an indirect measure. Improvements in connectivity, to some degree by liberalized air traffic agreements, will improve international air traffic and this may be interpreted as improving Canada's economic well-being. There is the basic question of what do all the metrics identified above measure or what should they measure? Different players in the industry – airlines, airports, shippers, passengers, governments – will all have their own views, but what is the purpose of any government economic policy? It is to improve real economic welfare, to improve real incomes.

An important part of this assessment is to address the question of who has the property rights to allowing access to markets. Earlier the evolution of the bilateral process was described, its roots and evolution. It seems clear that the property rights were by default given to nations and they in turn transferred them to their 'national airlines'. This has remained the norm in most all countries but is changing in the US, EU, New Zealand and Australia.

If one examines the Canada Transportation Act (CTA), section 5, the objectives of transportation policy and the means by which these objectives can be achieved are set out. The CTA is also clear in stating the objectives of Canadian Transportation Policy: serving the needs of users and advancing the well-being of Canadians are achieved through market forces. In other words the purpose of transport policy is to improve the economic welfare of Canadians and Blue Sky is part of transport policy. The achievement of these ends through market forces begs the question whether increased competition in aviation leads to the outcomes envisaged by the Canada Transportation Act (CTS); increased efficiency, prices close to costs and greater output.

In a recent paper Gillen and Hazledine (2011) explored the impact of market structure on the level of fares as well as the structure of fares in the North American aviation market. Domestic Canadian markets and transborder markets were included in the analysis. Among other results they found that there is extensive intertemporal price discrimination based on date of purchase of ticket and other factors; that average prices paid are nevertheless still significantly determined by the number and size distribution of airlines supplying a route; and that established 'legacy' carriers can still charge a substantial price premium over LCCs (low-cost carriers) They also find that routes with one carrier offering more than 70 per cent of seats facing competition from one or more much smaller airlines have *lower* prices, not higher as would be predicted by dominant-firm models. This suggests that a little competition can go a long way in terms of disciplining large firm pricing in this industry. More competition and open skies is in keeping with the objectives of the CTA and there is evidence it works.

In a recent paper Piermartini and Rousova (2008) examined the impact of liberalizing air transport services on air passenger flows in a sample of 184 countries. They find robust evidence of a positive and significant relationship between the volumes of traffic and the degree of liberalization of the aviation market. An increase in the degree of liberalization from the 25th percentile to the 75th percentile increases traffic volumes between countries linked by a direct air service by approximately 30 per cent. In particular, the removal of restrictions on the determination of prices and capacity and the possibility for airlines other than the flag carrier of the foreign country to operate a service is found to be the most traffic-enhancing provision of air service agreements. The results are robust to the use of different measures of the degree of liberalization as well as the use of different estimation techniques. This is strong evidence that in Canada's case having more than one carrier, and certainly more than one alliance, is important in achieving the objectives of the CTA and the aims of the Blue Sky policy.

To test the impact of ASAs and the new aviation policy for Canada, a model illustrated below was estimated on a data panel covering the top 50 international passenger destinations for Canada based on statistics for 2003–2007. The model uses a conventional gravity model form with dummy variables added for open sky ASA – the variable took the value 1 if the country had an open sky ASA, otherwise zero. Also included are two additional dummy variables, one to capture the difference between a liberal and restrictive bilateral (measured by whether the ASA had fifth freedoms) and also a dummy variable for when the Blue Skies policy was introduced, 2005. The model was estimated with random fixed effects. A significant problem with this specification is the lack of information on price or yield; however, lower prices and more capacity should be positively correlated with greater liberalization.[13]

$$\ln passengers = \alpha + \beta_1 \ln distance + \beta_2 \ln GDP + \beta_3 \, OpenSky + \beta_4 \, Fifths + \beta_5 \, BlueSky + \epsilon$$

The results are presented in Table 24.1 together with calculated elasticities. Without going into too much detail, we can see distance has a negative effect on the total number of passengers as expected with an elasticity of –0.67; a 10 per cent increase in distance reduces the number of annual passengers by nearly 7 per cent.[14] Larger economies will have higher passenger flows; the elasticity of passenger flows with respect to GDP is 0.45.

The more interesting results are those which capture the impact of the degree of liberalization. Countries that we have an open sky ASA with have significantly more passenger flows and when our ASA is liberal, measured by the presence of fifth freedoms, we also have higher passenger flows. The impact of open sky ASA is nearly four times larger than a liberal ASA. Finally the Blue Sky policy introduced in 2005 has had no statistically significant impact on total passenger flows between Canada and its top 50 international passenger destinations, most likely there are too few observations to obtain a reasonable test of significance.

6. Conclusions

The character of bilateral agreements and the process by which they are created emerged from an institutional setting that provided the basis for secrecy, protectionism and complexity. These agreements were treated as private contracts between countries negotiated by their departments of international affairs on behalf of their 'national' carriers. The property right for access to markets was transferred to the airlines because of the outcome of the Chicago Convention and the fact each country has their own national or flag carrier, except in the US.

---

13   In fact with data on price the systems of equations would have to reflect that price is endogenous being a function of liberal ASAs.

14   I expect this high value is because of the US data effect.

Table 24.2   Regression results – panel 2003–2007 top 50 markets

Dependent Variable: LOGPAX				
Sample: 2003 2007				
Periods included: 5				
Cross-sections included: 50				
Total panel (balanced) observations: 250				
	Coefficient	Std. Error	t-Statistic	Elasticity
C	3.509	0.277	12.65	
LOGDIST	-0.674	0.078	-8.65	-0.67
LOGGDP	0.447	0.026	17.39	0.45
OPENSKY	0.504	0.131	3.86	0.66
FIFTHS	0.141	0.042	3.35	0.15
BLUESKY	0.023	0.038	0.62	na
R-squared	0.719			
Adjusted R-squared	0.713			
Log likelihood	-41.904			
F-statistic	124.724			

In most jurisdictions, including Canada, highly protectionist approaches and policy continued both domestically and internationally until the late 1970s when the US deregulated its domestic aviation market and immediately sought to liberalize, if not deregulate, international aviation markets, focusing first on the transatlantic market. As more countries followed the US lead over the 1980s and 90s and undertook domestic market deregulation, there was increased support for greater international aviation market liberalization by many countries. This view was also in keeping with the general increase in trade liberalization and new trade rules under the WTO. A number of countries have signed highly liberalized regional accords; Australia–New Zealand, MALIAT and the Yamoussoukro Decision, for example.

Examining the Canada–EU accord one is struck by the initial openness with unrestricted direct access but it is not until one gets to phase four that it appears that fifth or sixth freedom rights will be granted. The phases are to be introduced at certain points when trigger values for some parameters occur. Which variables and what value of trigger is secret, contained in the annexes.

It is quite clear, certainly from the success of the first Canada–US open sky agreement in 1995 (and re-established with greater openness in 2007), that such agreements result in significant traffic growth of passengers and cargo. They open markets for Canadian exports of goods and services, grow investment and facilitate trade and connectivity. In essence they do what government policy is designed to do, make Canadians better off by improving their economic welfare.

The Blue Sky policy was stated to be a shift to a more liberalized regime in establishing air service agreements, specifically it was to encourage open skies agreements similar to that which we have with the US. The only 'real' open skies ASA signed thus far is with Ireland and the US. The ASA signed with Korea, Singapore and all the other countries listed in Figure 24.1 have not been open skies. Amazingly the ASA signed with Panama provided unlimited access between Canada and Panama except for Panama City, the only real commercial airport in the country. There was restricted access to some cities in Canada as well. This treaty seems to have hardly been worth the effort.

How successful is the Blue Sky policy in achieving open skies-type agreements? Based on the analysis thus far, not that good. The number of open skies policies is small and they are with countries with relatively inconsequential passenger and trade markets. Canada still continues to negotiate ASAs that are not in keeping with the Blue Sky policy. There is a lack of consistency in ASA content and focus. Where open sky agreements have been signed they have been incremental to previous agreements or held so secret one could hardly judge. The statistical analysis, albeit meager due to lack of full information, points to the success of liberal policies and that open skies policies generate a four times larger impact, while for Blue Skies it is not statistically significant. The US has an open skies policy. Australia, similar in many respects to Canada, has been much more liberal; there are 84 weekly flights by Emirates to five cities in Australia, Canada has three weekly flights to one city.

The Blue Sky policy has in effect reintroduced the public convenience and necessity criterion into decision making, something that was removed when Canada deregulated in the mid-1980s. It is time to move away from this nineteenth-century 'public convenience and necessity criterion' idea to a twenty-first century fit willing and able for allowing entry into the Canadian market; which is what we have for the domestic market and for the Canada–US opens skies agreement. There is virtually no other industry in this country that makes decisions on who can enter on the basis laid out in the Blue Sky Policy.

References

Button, K. (2008) The impact of US–EU 'Open Skies' agreement on airline market structures and airline networks. *Journal of Air Transport Management*, 1, 1–13.

Byerly, John (2008) 2008 ACI-NA International Aviation Issues Seminar, December 4, 2008.

Gillen, D. and Hazledine, T. (2011) The New Pricing in North American Air Travel Markets: Implications for Competition and Antitrust in James Peoples (ed.) *Pricing Behaviour and Non-Price Characteristics in the Airline Industry: Advances in Airline Economics, Volume 3 (Emerald Publishers)* 55–83

InterVISTAS (2008) *Compilation of U.S. Open Skies Agreements with Canadian Blue Skies Agreements*, http://www.intervistas.com/default.asp.

Oum, T., Fu, X. and Zhang, A. (2008) Air Transport Liberalization and its Impacts on Airline Competition and Air Passenger Traffic. Working paper OECD, Task Force Session 2009, presented in Sydney, Australia, 13 January 2009.

Piermartini, R. and Rousuva, L. (2008) Liberalization of Air Transport Services and Passenger Traffic. WTO Working Paper ERSD 2008–06.

Transport Canada, Blue Sky Policy, http://www.tc.gc.ca/pol/en/ace/consultations/blueSky.pdf

Liberalization of Air Transport: Some Key References

1. Deregulation of US Industry

Borenstein, Severine (1992). The Evolution of US Airline Competition, *Journal of Economic Perspectives*, 6(2), 45–73.

Borenstein, S. and Rose, N. (2007). How Airline Markets Work ... Or Do They? Regulatory Reform in the Airline Industry, NBER Working Paper 13452, Cambridge.

Brueckner, J., Lee, D. and Singer, E. (2011). Airline Competition and Domestic U.S. Airfares: A Comprehensive Reappraisal, Working Paper, Irvine.

Kahn, A.E. (May 1988). Surprises of Airline Deregulation, *American Economic Review*, Papers and Proceedings 78, 316–22.

Levine, M.E. (1987). Airline Competition in Deregulated Markets: Theory, Firm Strategy, and Public Policy, *Yale Journal on Regulation*, 4(2), 393–494.

Levine, M.E. (1965). Is Regulation Necessary? California Air Transportation and National Regulatory Policy, *Yale Law Journal,* 741416.

Morrison, S.A. and Winston, C. (1986). *The Economic Effects of Airline Deregulation*. Brookings.

Morrison, S.A. and Winston, C. (1995). *The Evolution of the Airline Industry*. Brookings Institution, Washington DC.

Winston, C. (1993). Economic Deregulation: Days of Reckoning for Microeconomists, *Journal of Economic Literature*, 1263–1289.

2. EU-Deregulation

Abbott, K. and Thomson, D. (1991). De-regulating European Aviation: The Impact of Bilateral Liberalization, *International Journal of Industrial Organization*, 9(1), 125–140.

Arndt, A. (2004). *Die Liberalisierung des grenzüberschreitenden Luftverkehrs in der EU*. Frankfurt a.M., Lang Publishers.

Button, K.J. (2004). *Wings Across Europe: Towards an Efficient European Air Transport System*. Aldershot, Ashgate.

Button, K.J. (1998). *Flying into the Future: Air Transport Policy in the European Union*. Cheltenham, Elgar.

CAA UK (1998). *The Single European Aviation Market: The First Five Years*, CAP 685. London, Civil Aviation Authority.

Doganis, R. (1994). The Impact of Liberalization on European Airline Strategies and Operations. *Journal of Air Transport Management*, 1(1), 15–25.

Ehmer, H. (2001). Liberalization in German Air Transport – Analysis and Competition Policy Recommendations Summary of a German Study, *Journal of Air Transport Management*, 7(1), 51–55.

Gillen, D., Hinsch, H., Mandel, B. and Wolf, H. (2000). *The Impact of Liberalizing International Aviation Bilaterals on the Northern German Region*. Aldershot, Ashgate.

Good, D. H., Röller, L. and Sickles, R. C. (1993). US Airline Deregulation: Implications for European Transport, *The Economic Journal*, 103(419), 1028–1041.

Graham, B. (1998). Liberalization, Regional Economic Development and the Geography of Demand for Air Transport in the European Union, *Journal of Transport Geography*, 6(2), 87–104.

3. Deregulation in other Parts of the World

Abeyratne, R. (1998). The Future of African Civil Aviation, *Journal of Air Transport Worldwide*, 3(2), 30–48.

Abeyratne, R. (2003). Implications of the Yamoussoukro Decision on African Aviation, Air & Space Law, 28(6), 280–293.

Adler, N. and Hashai, N. (2005). Effect of Open Skies in the Middle East Region, *Transportation Research Part A: Policy and Practice*, 39(10), 878–894.

Centre for Asia Pacific Aviation (CAPA) (2007). Liberalisation of Air Services in the APEC Region, 1995–2005, APEC Transportation Working Group and the Australian Department of Transport and Regional Services.

Gillen, D. (1989). Privatization of Air Canada; Why it is Necessary in a Deregulated Environment, *Canadian Public Policy*, 15, 285–299.

InterVISTAS (2009). The Impact of International Air Service Liberalization on Chile, prepared by InterVISTAS-EU Consulting Inc., July 2009.

Oum, T.H., and Yu, C. (1999). *Shaping Air Transport in Asia Pacific*. Aldershot, Ashgate.

Schlumberger, C.E. (2010). *Open Skies for Africa: Implementing the Yamoussoukro Decision*. World Bank, Washington DC.

4. Nature of Airline Competition: Contestability, Network, and Structure

Borenstein, S. and Rose, N. (1994). Competition and Price Dispersion in the U.S. Airline Industry, *Journal of Political Economy*, 103, 653–683.

Bowen, J. (2002). Network Change, Deregulation, and Access in the Global Airline Industry, *Economic Geography*, 78(4), 425–439.

Brueckner, J.K and Pels, E. (2005): European Airline Mergers, Alliance Consolidation and Consumer Welfare, *Journal of Air Transport Management* ,11, 27–41.

Burghouwta, G. and Hakfoort, J. (2001). The Evolution of the European Aviation Network, 1990–1998, *Journal of Air Transport Management*, 7(5), 311–318.

Brueckner, J.K. and Spiller, P.T. (1991). Competition and Mergers in Airline Networks, *International Journal of Industrial Organization*, 9, 323–342.

Caves, D.W., Christensen, W. and Tretheway, W.M. (1984). Economies of Density versus Economies of Scale: Why Trunk and Local Service Costs Differ, *RAND Journal of Economics* 15, 471–489.

Dempsey, P. (1990). Airline Deregulation and Laissez-Faire Mythology: Economic Theory in Turbulence, *Journal of Air Law and Commerce*, 56, 305–412.

Hurdle, G., Johnson, R., Joskow, A., Werden, G. and Williams, M. (1989). Concentration and Potential Entry in the Airline Industry, *Journal of Industrial Economics,* 38, 119–139.

Levine, M.E. (2002). Price Discrimination Without Market Power, *Yale Journal on Regulation*, 19, 1–36.

Morrison, S.A. (2001). Actual, Adjacent and Potential Competition: Estimating the Full Effect of Southwest Airlines, *Journal of Transport Economics and Policy*, 35, 239–256.

Morrison, S. and Winston, C. (2000). The remaining Role for Government Policy in the Deregulated Airline Industry, in Peltzman, S. and Winston, C. (eds), *Deregulation of Network Industries: What's Next,* AEI-Brookings Joint Centre for Regulatory Studies, Washington, DC.

Oum, T., Park, J. and Zhang, A. (2000). *Globalization and Strategic Alliances: The Case of the Airline Industry*, UK, Elsevier.

Park, J., Zhang, A. and Zhang, Y. (2001). Analytical Models of International Alliances in the Airline Industry, *Transportation Research Part B: Methodological*, Vol. 35, No. 9, 865–886.

Transportation Research Board (1999). Entry and Competition in the U.S. Airline Industry: Issues and Opportunities, TRB Special Report 255, Washington D.C.

Werden, G., Joskow, A.S. and Johnson, R.L. (1991). The Effects of Mergers on Price and Output: Two Case Studies from the Airline Industry, *Managerial and Decision Economics*, 12, 341–352.

5. International Liberalization

Australia Productivity Commission (1998). International Air Services, Inquiry Report No. 2, Aussinfo, Canberra.

Forsyth, Peter, Ken Button and Peter Nijkamp (eds) (2002). *Air Transport*. Edward Elgar Publishers

Gillen, D., Harris, R. and Oum, T. (2002). Measuring the Economic Effects of Bilateral Liberalization on Air Transport, *Transportation Research*, 28E.

Kasper, D.M. (1988). *Deregulation and Globalization: Liberalizing International Trade in Air Services*. Cambridge: Ballinger.

OECD (1997). *International Air Transport: The Challenges Ahead*. Paris

OECD (1997). *The Future of International Air Transport Policy – Responding to Global Change*. Paris.

OECD (1999). *Regulatory Reform in International Air Cargo*. Paris.

OECD (2002). *Liberalisation of Air Cargo Transport*. Paris.

Piermartini, R., and Rousova, L. (2008). Liberalisation of Air Transport Services and Passenger Traffic, Staff Working Paper ERSD-2008-06, World Trade Organisation.

Index